Tolley's Estate Planning 2002–03

by

Simon McKie MA(Oxon), FCA, FTII, ASFA, TEP
of Lincoln's Inn, Barrister-at-Law

and

Sharon Anstey, LLB(Hons), ATII, IAC
Solicitor
both of McKie & Co (Advisory Service) LLP

Members of the LexisNexis Group worldwide

United Kingdom	LexisNexis Butterworths Tolley, a Division of Reed Elsevier (UK) Ltd, 2 Addiscombe Road, CROYDON CR9 5AF
Argentina	LexisNexis Argentina, BUENOS AIRES
Australia	LexisNexis Butterworths, CHATSWOOD, New South Wales
Austria	LexisNexis Verlag ARD Orac GmbH & Co KG, VIENNA
Canada	LexisNexis Butterworths, MARKHAM, Ontario
Chile	LexisNexis Chile Ltda, SANTIAGO DE CHILE
Czech Republic	Nakladatelství Orac sro, PRAGUE
France	Editions du Juris-Classeur SA, PARIS
Hong Kong	LexisNexis Butterworths, HONG KONG
Hungary	HVG-Orac, BUDAPEST
India	LexisNexis Butterworths, NEW DELHI
Ireland	Butterworths (Ireland) Ltd, DUBLIN
Italy	Giuffrè Editore, MILAN
Malaysia	Malayan Law Journal Sdn Bhd, KUALA LUMPUR
New Zealand	LexisNexis Butterworths, WELLINGTON
Poland	Wydawnictwo Prawnicze LexisNexis, WARSAW
Singapore	LexisNexis Butterworths, SINGAPORE
South Africa	Butterworths SA, DURBAN
Switzerland	Stämpfli Verlag AG, BERNE
USA	LexisNexis, DAYTON, Ohio

© Reed Elsevier (UK) Ltd 2002

All rights reserved. No part of this publication may be reproduced in any material form (including photocopying or storing it in any medium by electronic means and whether or not transiently or incidentally to some other use of this publication) without the written permission of the copyright owner except in accordance with the provisions of the Copyright, Designs and Patents Act 1988 or under the terms of a licence issued by the Copyright Licensing Agency Ltd, 90 Tottenham Court Road, London, England W1T 4LP. Applications for the copyright owner's written permission to reproduce any part of this publication should be addressed to the publisher.

Warning: The doing of an unauthorised act in relation to a copyright work may result in both a civil claim for damages and criminal prosecution.

Crown copyright material is reproduced with the permission of the Controller of HMSO and the Queen's Printer for Scotland. Any European material in this work which has been reproduced from EUR-lex, the official European Communities legislation website, is European Communities copyright.

A CIP Catalogue record for this book is available from the British Library.

ISBN 0 7545 1682 2

Typeset by Kerrypress Ltd, Luton Beds
Printed and bound in Great Britain by William Clowes Limited, Beccles and London

Visit Butterworths LexisNexis *direct* **at www.butterworths.com**

Preface

In producing this our sixth edition of Tolley's Estate Planning we have been very conscious of the high standards set by our predecessors. We have endeavoured to build upon their excellent work.

We are grateful to the enormous help we have received from Ken Chapman on the chapters on *Insurance* and *Pensions* and from Michael Conlon of the Bower Cotton Partnership on the chapter on *Matrimonial Breakdown*.

Our thanks are also due to the editorial staff at LexisNexis Butterworths Tolley for entrusting us with this task and for their help and encouragement in bringing it to fruition.

Simon McKie
Sharon Anstey

July 2002

Contents

		Paragraph
1	**What is Estate Planning?**	
	How is it done?	1.1
2	**Lifetime Planning**	
	Introduction	2.1
	The mitigation of inheritance tax	2.2
	Asset reduction	2.3
	Asset conversion	2.28
	Asset freezing	2.29
	Conversion of capital assets	2.34
	The organisation of an estate	2.35
3	**Introduction to Trust Law**	
	Introduction	3.1
	What is a trust?	3.2
	Settlors	3.3
	Trustees	3.4
	Beneficiaries	3.5
	Making a trust	3.6
	No illegality	3.7
	Divorce	3.8
	Inheritance laws	3.9
	Trustees' powers and duties	3.10
	Beneficiaries' rights	3.20
	Focus on: power of maintenance	3.21
	Focus on: power of advancement	3.25
	Focus on: protective trusts	3.31
4	**Creating Settlements**	
	Introduction	4.1
	Why not an outright gift?	4.2
	What is a settlement? — general principles of tax law	4.3
	Preliminary considerations	4.12
	Accumulation and maintenenance settlements	4.23
	Interest in possession settlements	4.32
	Trusts for the disabled	4.38
	Discretionary settlements	4.39
	Creating an offshore settlement	4.51
5	**Existing Settlements**	
	Introduction	5.1
	What steps may be taken to deal with the settled property?	5.2
	Dealing with the interests of the beneficiaries	5.6

	Accumulation and maintenance settlements	5.17
	Life interest settlements	5.21
	Discretionary settlements	5.51

6 Offshore Trusts

Introduction	6.1
Export charges	6.3
Taxing the settlor	6.9
Supplementary charge	6.18

7 Insurance

Introduction	7.1
Nature and type of insurance	7.4
Life policy taxation	7.16
Planning in early years	7.24
Planning in middle years	7.35
Planning in later years	7.48

8 Pensions

Introduction	8.1
Pensionable employment	8.2
Non-pensionable employment and self-employment	8.13
Pensions and divorce	8.14
Lump sum death benefits under retirement annuity contracts or personal pension arrangements	8.15
Pensions and bankruptcy	8.16

9 The Family Home

Introduction	9.1
Ownership of property	9.2
Purchasing a family home	9.3
Making provision in a will	9.4
Lifetime planning	9.5

10 The Family Business

Introduction	10.1
Inheritance tax	10.2
Capital gain tax	10.4
Incorporation	10.5
The sole proprietor	10.6
Partnerships	10.7
Limited liability partnerships	10.23
The family company	10.24
Enterprise Investment Scheme	10.34
Venture capital trusts	10.38

11 The Family Farm

Introduction	11.1

Contents

Inheritance tax	11.2
Capital gains tax	11.10
Structure of the business	11.11
Milk quotas	11.15
Foot and mouth disease	11.18
Some strategies for the farmer	11.19

12 Woodlands

Introduction	12.1
Income tax	12.2
Capital gains tax	12.3
Inheritance tax	12.4
Making sensible use of the tax treatment of woodlands	12.7

13 Gifts to Charities, Etc.

Introduction	13.1
Capital gifts	13.2
Gifts out of income	13.8
Other way of benefiting charity	13.12
General rules for charitable gifts	13.15
Creating your own charitable trust	13.16
Drafting gifts to charity	13.17
Temporary charitable trusts	13.18
Community Amateur Sports Clubs	13.21
Gifts for national purposes	13.22
Gifts for public benefit	13.23
Gifts to political parties	13.24

14 National Heritage Property

Introduction	14.1
Inheritance tax	14.2
Claiming conditional exemption from inheritance tax	14.7
Capital gains tax	14.12
Maintenance funds	14.13
Settled heritage property	14.18
Strategy	14.24

15 Matrimonial Breakdown

Overview	15.1
Establishing dates	15.2
Maintenance	15.4
Income tax effects of maintenance payments	15.8
Inheritance tax implications of paying and receiving maintenance	15.9
The matrimonial home	15.10
Pension rights	15.14
Transfers of other property	15.15
Use of trusts	15.16
Overseas aspects	15.17

Contents

Stamp duty	15.18
Council tax	15.19
The effect of separation and divorce on wills and intestacy	15.20
Conclusion	15.21

16 Planning for Death

Wills	16.1
Use of exemptions and reliefs	16.2
Dividing the estate between the family	16.11
Types of gifts and legacies	16.23
Safe keeping and review of wills: personal assets log	16.30
Variation of the will after death	16.31
Death in service benefits and pension schemes	16.32
Death-bed planning	16.33
Funding the inheritance tax payable on death	16.34
Methods of avoiding probate	16.39
Lloyd's underwriting interests	16.47

17 Post-Death Estate Planning

Introduction	17.1
Inheritance tax	17.2
Capital gains tax on variations	17.14
Income tax on variations	17.15
Discretionary wills	17.16
Precatory trusts	17.17
Intestacy—redemption of surviving spouse's life interest	17.18
Changes in value after death	17.19
Payment by instalments	17.20
Interest on unpaid tax	17.21
Capital gains tax exemption and rates of tax	17.22
Death benefit under insurance policies and pension schemes	17.23

18 Investing Abroad

Introduction	18.1
Direct ownership	18.2
Ownership by a nominee and other possibilities	18.3
Ownership by a company	18.4
Exchange control	18.5
Offshore settlements	18.6

19 Immigration and Emigration

Introduction	19.1
Domicile, residence and ordinary residence	19.2
Overseas law	19.9
The long-term immigrant	19.10
The short-term visitor	19.25
The long-term emigrant	19.26
The short-term emigrant	19.27

Contents

20 The Foreign Client

Introduction	20.1
Tax considerations	20.2
Other considerations	20.8
Benefiting persons resident in the United Kingdom	20.12
Conclusions	20.15

21 Lifetime Planning—A Case Study

Planning when single
On getting married
Becoming a parent
Gaining a daughter-in-law
Losing a parent
Becoming a grandparent
Entering the final years
Summary—when to consider estate planning

Table of Cases
Table of Statutes
Index

1 What is Estate Planning?

How is it done?

1.1 This is a work on taxation but estate planning is not merely a sub-division of tax planning. Estate planning is planning to preserve, protect and devolve family wealth. If taxation did not exist, estate planning would still not be simple. An individual would still be faced with hard choices in protecting their wealth against investment risk and political interference and in balancing their children's need to gain experience in the management of wealth against the dangers of youthful improvidence.

In writing about taxation for estate planning, therefore, one needs to keep always in mind a variety of non-taxation considerations which define the problems to be solved as well as constraining the solutions.

One should take account of the client's wishes, expectations, opinions and prejudices and the nature of their relationships with their spouse, children, grandchildren and wider family. One needs to make informed guesses about the future; as to how their family relationships will develop, what will happen to their major assets, how they will want to live and how the political and economic environment will change.

Dealing with such subjective and uncertain matters, estate planning can never be either uniform or absolute. It is a bespoke service and not a retail product. It should also be a continuing service and not a once and for all event. The future becomes the present and then the past in ways which are never completely predictable. Our predictions about the new future which replaces it are similarly provisional. Estate plans must be continually revised.

Perhaps it is only the saints who are indifferent to protecting their wealth. The rest of mankind needs some form of estate planning. For most people the irreducible minimum is to make a will, to take some life assurance cover to protect one's dependants from the consequences of one's death and to write those insurance policies in trust so that the proceeds will be available to one's personal representatives before probate is granted. In addition, joint owners of property need to consider whether that property should be held as joint tenants or as tenants in common and members of pension schemes should ensure that the scheme trustees have been informed of their wishes for the application of death benefits.

Readers of this book are likely to have, or to advise clients who have, more complex estates demanding tax planning which is similarly more complex than this bare minimum.

1.1 What is Estate Planning?

The basic principles of all estate planning, however, are simple.

First, one must determine the client's objectives. In order to do so one needs to explore the nature of their wealth, their relationships with their family, their expectations for the future and their attitudes towards financial risk and the devolution of wealth.

Secondly, as most estate planning involves making gifts of some sort, one should determine whether they currently have, or expect to have, a surplus of wealth over required expenditure. We deliberately express it in that way because one of the greatest barriers to estate planning is often an over-emphasis by clients on the need to preserve capital and to spend only income. A man of eighty with an annual expenditure of only £40,000 may yet have a portfolio of £1 million. Whatever view one takes of his life expectancy he does not need to hold on to all of his capital in order to be quite secure that he will be able to continue to maintain his expenditure for the rest of his life. Holding on to wealth too long is far commoner than giving away too much too early.

Thirdly, in making gifts one must determine the appropriate assets to be given away. For example, it may be useful to give assets which have the prospect of substantial future capital gain to younger family members. One must also determine the appropriate form of the gift; should it be absolute or in trust? In coming to these decisions one must consider the effect of the gift on the recipient and avoid creating unnecessary administrative difficulties. For example, it is usually unwise to give absolute control of a family company to a child who is just eighteen.

Fourthly, although most estate planning will be directed towards avoiding particular tax charges, it is important to keep an eye on the whole range of taxes which can apply to family wealth.

Fifthly, one should aim for the greatest possible flexibility so that one can adapt the chosen strategy to changes in circumstances and expectations; hence the ever-increasing popularity of wide discretionary trusts and of discretionary wills.

Finally, whatever plan is adopted, one needs to review it formally at regular intervals to determine changes in the client's intentions and expectations for the future and to adapt the plan to those changes.

2 Lifetime Planning

Introduction

2.1 The purpose of this chapter is to give a general outline of the basic principles involved in lifetime estate planning. It will outline a number of matters which receive more detailed treatment in other chapters.

So: 'what is the primary purpose of lifetime planning?'. The traditional response will be the mitigation of inheritance tax payable on a person's death'. However, in today's world, consideration will also be given to the mitigation of capital gains tax and, in some cases, income tax. Tax saving is not the only purpose of estate planning. Whilst the deceased's heirs will usually regard the inheritance tax payable on death as being most instrumental in reducing their share of the estate, the legal and other costs of winding up the estate, which these days can be considerable, have the same effect. Therefore, one aspect of lifetime planning should be to organise your estate into a form which minimises the costs of administration after death.

Whilst one motive a client may have for passing assets on to his children may be to take a proportion of his estate out of the inheritance tax charge on his death, there are other motives for passing on assets. These include the desire to give children a 'start in life', by helping them, for example, to buy a flat or a car or to buy a partnership in a profession; or the desire to help with the cost of educating their grandchildren. The client will therefore be seeking advice on the most tax efficient ways of making such gifts; in particular, ways which give rise to minimum inheritance tax or capital gains tax liabilities.

These three aspects of lifetime planning — the general mitigation of the inheritance tax charge on death, tax efficient ways of giving and the general organisation of an estate — are the subject matter of this chapter. There is a clear overlap between the first and second of these because one of the most obvious ways of mitigating inheritance tax on death is by immediate lifetime gifts. Thus, whilst a client may have differing motives for making a gift during his lifetime, the general principles involved will be the same and accordingly the second of these three aspects will be dealt with as part of the first.

The mitigation of inheritance tax

2.2 Broadly, inheritance tax may be mitigated in one of the following four ways.

2.3 Lifetime Planning

(a) Reducing the estate through immediate lifetime gifts, the intention being to take assets out of the inheritance tax charge on death. This is known as 'asset reduction'.

(b) Converting assets of the estate which do not qualify for any form of inheritance tax relief into assets which do (for example, agricultural property or business assets), the intention being to reduce the value of the assets when calculating the inheritance tax charge on death. This is known as 'asset conversion'.

(c) Freezing the value of assets in the estate so that any future growth in value will pass to the next generation, the intention being to take the 'growth element' out of the inheritance tax charge altogether. This is known as 'asset freezing'.

(d) Converting capital assets of the estate into high income producing assets. This is known as 'conversion of capital assets'.

Each of these headings will be dealt with in turn.

Asset reduction

2.3 Inheritance tax is a tax both on lifetime gifts and on the ultimate gift a person is deemed to make on his death. The 2002/03 death rates are:

£0–£250,000	0%
Above £250,000	40%

The rate of inheritance tax on chargeable lifetime gifts is one half of that applicable on death, i.e. 20% (IHTA 1984, s 7(2)). Where a person dies within three years of a chargeable gift, then the tax payable is recomputed either at the death rates in force at the date of the gift or, if the rates have been reduced, at the rates applicable at the date of death, and the additional tax, if any, becomes payable (IHTA 1984, s 7(1)(4), Sch 2). Similarly, where a person dies more than three years after the chargeable gift, taper relief is available. The tax is recomputed at the tapering percentages of either the death rates in force at the date of the gift or, if the rates are lower, the death rates in force at the date of death. Again, any additional tax becomes payable (IHTA 1984, s 7(4), Sch 2). There will usually only therefore be an additional tax charge if the deceased dies within five years of a chargeable gift, but it is important to remember that this will not necessarily always be the case.

Where the subject matter of the gift:

(a) is still in the hands of the donee or his spouse at the date of death and has a lower value at that date than at the date of the gift; or

(b) has been sold on the open market before the death at a lower value,

then the additional tax payable on death is calculated by reference to the lower value (IHTA 1984, s 131). For this to apply, however, the gift must not comprise tangible movable property which are wasting assets (IHTA 1984, s 132).

Lifetime Planning **2.5**

Inheritance tax is a 'cumulative' tax in the sense that all chargeable gifts made within a specific period are aggregated in order to determine the rates of tax applicable to the latest chargeable gift. This period is currently seven years (IHTA 1984, s 7(1)).

Exemptions and quasi-exemptions

2.4 Because inheritance tax is charged by reference to the reduction in value of a person's estate (IHTA 1984, s 3(1)), any gift will *prima facie* give rise to a tax charge. There are, however, a number of important exemptions and, what could be termed, 'quasi-exemptions' which enable a person to reduce his estate without giving rise to an immediate tax charge.

These exemptions and quasi-exemptions will now each be considered in turn.

Potentially exempt transfers

2.5 Potentially exempt transfers enable an individual to make specified gifts of unlimited value which will escape tax completely if he survives for a period of seven years following the gift (IHTA 1984, s 3A). The gift must be made either to:

(*a*)   another individual; or

(*b*)   the trustees of a trust in which an individual has an interest in possession; or

(*c*)   the trustees of an accumulation and maintenance trust within IHTA 1984, s 71; or

(*d*)   the trustees of a disabled person's trust within IHTA 1984, s 89.

The types of trust in (*b*) to (*d*) above are discussed in more detail in chapter 4 *Creating Settlements*. Where the donor dies within three years of the gift, inheritance tax at the full death rates is charged unless those rates have increased in which case the rates at the time of the transfer are used. Where the gift is made more than three years before the death, the rates are 'tapered' as follows.

Years between transfer and death	*Percentage of full tax rate*
More than 3 but not more than 4	80%
More than 4 but not more than 5	60%
More than 5 but not more than 6	40%
More than 6 but not more than 7	20%

In addition, when calculating the inheritance tax payable on the donor's estate, any potentially exempt transfers and chargeable transfers will be aggregated with the value of his estate. This may increase the amount of tax payable on death.

The potentially exempt transfer is very important in estate planning. It is possible to make gifts without any charge to inheritance tax at all provided the donor survives for the necessary period. The risk of the donor dying within this period may be insured against at rates which, depending upon the age and

2.6 Lifetime Planning

state of health of the donor, are often only a small percentage of the potential tax liability. This is considered in more detail in chapter 7 *Insurance*.

How long the present inheritance tax legislation, and in particular the potentially exempt transfer, will continue is an open question. The best advice to clients who have the ability to make potentially exempt transfers may be to act now, subject to capital gains tax and other tax considerations.

The annual exemption

2.6 A person may make gifts of up to £3,000 each year completely free of inheritance tax (IHTA 1984, s 19). Unlike the potentially exempt transfer, this exemption applies regardless of the nature of the recipient of the gift. In addition, there is no requirement for survival by the donor. If this exemption is wholly or partly unused in any year, it or the balance may be carried forward to the next year. However, if it is not used in that year it will be lost.

> *Example*
>
> A donor who makes a gift in year 1 of only £1,000 may make gifts within the annual exemption of up to £5,000 in year 2. If he only makes gifts of £3,000 in year 2, the £2,000 shortfall in year 1 will be lost forever.

It will be apparent that in the case of outright gifts either to an individual, an interest in possession trust or an accumulation and maintenance trust there is an overlap between this exemption and the potentially exempt transfer. Thus, a donor who reasonably expects to survive for the next seven years need not limit himself to annual gifts of only £3,000. He could give away significantly more each year. The existence of the annual exemption will only become material if the donor dies within seven years of one of these gifts.

> *Example*
>
> A father could give his son £38,714 in each of years 1 to 7. If the father then dies at the end of year 7, all the previous gifts will become chargeable but only as to £35,714 of each, because the annual exemption will be available to exempt the first £3,000 of each gift. As the chargeable gifts amount to £249,998, which is within the current nil rate tax band, the lifetime gifts will not give rise to any tax charge. They will, however, be aggregated with the value of the deceased's free estate in order to calculate the inheritance tax due on the death.

Even with the existence of the potentially exempt transfer, the annual exemption is of importance.

The 'normal expenditure out of income' exemption

2.7 This exemption applies to a gift if, or to the extent that, it is shown that:

(*a*) the gift is made as part of the normal expenditure of the donor;

(*b*) taking one year with another, the gift is made out of his income; and

Lifetime Planning **2.7**

(c) after allowing for all other gifts or dispositions forming part of his normal expenditure, the donor is left with sufficient income to maintain his usual standard of living.

(IHTA 1984, s 21).This exemption must be claimed and will not apply automatically.

Whether a gift will qualify for this exemption will be a question of fact in each case. According to the CTO Advanced Instruction Manual, 'normal' is considered to mean 'typical or habitual' but typical of the transferor and conforming with his or her habits and pattern of expenditure, not those of the average or reasonable man (CTO Advanced Instruction Manual M.110). So what may be 'normal expenditure' for a person with a net income of £150,000 is unlikely to be so for a person earning £30,000. On the other hand, a person who does earn £30,000 net, with no mortgage, wife, or children and a simple lifestyle may be able to make gifts, for example, to nieces and nephews, which qualify for this exemption to an extent which a person with a much higher income but with a wife and children and a high standard of living cannot.

To be normal, the gift does not necessarily have to be one of a series of regular payments but if not, it must be the type of payment which by its nature is likely to recur (as in the case of the examples given below). As it is essential that the gifts are made out of income, it is advisable that they are payments of cash.

The scope of IHTA 1984, s 21 has been considered in the case of *Bennett and Others v CIR, Ch D 1994, [1995] STC 54*. A useful summary of the case and its implications can be found in the CTO Advanced Instruction Manual M.111. The *Bennett* decision answered a number of key questions concerning the operation of the exemption. The term 'normal expenditure out of income' simply means expenditure which at the time it takes place accords with the settled pattern of expenditure adopted by the transferor. This pattern may be established in one of two ways, by reference to a sequence of payments by the transferor in the past, or by proof of some prior commitment or resolution adopted by him as regards future expenditure, and which he complied with thereafter.

The High Court affirmed that there is no fixed minimum period during which the expenditure must have been incurred. All that is necessary is for there to be evidence of a pattern of actual or intended regular payments, and that the payment in question falls within that category. This means that a single payment might qualify, provided sufficient resolution or commitment for future payments also exists. However, what is important is the prospect that the pattern of such gifts continues for more than simply a *de minimis* period of time, barring unforeseen circumstances. This effectively precludes death bed schemes (CTO Advanced Instruction Manual M.116). The Revenue consider that a reasonable period would normally be three to four years. However, the amount of the expenditure does not have to be fixed, nor does the identity of the recipient have to be the same on each occasion (CTO Advanced Instruction Manual M.116). However, if the details provided over that period do not illustrate normality, an individual may be asked to provide particulars over a longer period. This means that gifts to a discernible class, such as

2.7 Lifetime Planning

members of the same family could qualify. In the case of *Nadin v CIR, Sp C [1997] SSCD 107 (Sp C 112)* the Special Commissioners held that irregular payments to close relatives did not constitute normal expenditure.

Normal expenditure out of income is an important exemption, which can be used in the following ways.

(a) A deed of covenant from a grandparent to a grandchild or parent to a child. As long as the payments are made by the covenantor out of taxed income and do not affect his usual standard of living, the payments should be exempt from inheritance tax. However, such covenants no longer have any income tax advantages for the donor and donee as the former cannot claim any deduction for the covenanted payments and the latter is precluded from reclaiming any tax from the Inland Revenue.

(b) Deeds of covenant by individuals who are non-resident for tax purposes but domiciled in the UK.

Such individuals with large net incomes can make regular and substantial gifts out of that income free of inheritance tax to members of their families or to family trusts. It is advisable that the recipients are non-UK resident as otherwise the covenanted payments will be subject to income tax and, in effect, non-taxable income will be converted into taxable income.

(c) A parent takes out a ten-year endowment policy on his life and declares himself a trustee of the policy for the benefit of his children. He pays all the premiums under the policy out of his income. On the maturity of the policy the beneficiaries under the trust benefit from the proceeds. If the premiums are paid direct to the life assurance company, such payments will not be potentially exempt if the amount of the premium is not fully reflected in the increased value of the policy. However, provided the parent pays the premiums out of his income and is able to maintain his usual standard of living, such payments should fall within the normal expenditure out of income exemption. If an alternative investment vehicle is required, there seems no reason why the same arrangement could not be set up by means of a regular monthly savings contract with a unit trust or an investment company, the units and shares themselves being held in trust for the next generation. The disadvantage of this alternative is that it will be necessary for the trustees to make annual returns of trust income.

(d) Premiums on a life policy written in trust to fund all or part of any potential inheritance tax liability on lifetime transfers or on death.

(e) Annuities paid gratuitously by partners out of their trading profits to a retired partner or the spouse of a deceased partner.

Regular gifts out of income may also be made to help the donee of an earlier chargeable gift pay the inheritance tax due where there is a facility to pay the tax by annual instalments — see 2.26 below

The above examples show how this exemption can be used to pass assets down to the next generation on a regular basis whilst still preserving the £3,000 annual exemption for other gifts. Ideally, both exemptions should be used in tandem.

Small gifts

2.8 Gifts of up to £250 can be made to any one person in any one year free of inheritance tax (IHTA 1984, s 20). This exemption cannot be used in conjunction with another exemption, e.g. the annual exemption. It will be lost if the total annual gifts to any one person exceed £250. The gifts must be outright and therefore cannot be made to trustees. In an estate planning context the exemption is '*de minimis*'.

Gifts in consideration of marriage

2.9 Parents may each give outright gifts in consideration of marriage of up to £5,000 to the parties to the marriage completely free of inheritance tax. Grandparents and great grandparents may similarly make outright gifts of up to £2,500. Other persons may make such gifts of up to £1,000 (IHTA 1984, s 22).

The exemption applies not only to outright gifts but also to gifts into a settlement. The beneficiaries of such a settlement must, however, be limited to those persons specified in IHTA 1984, s 22(4) to which special reference should be made by anyone wishing to create such a settlement.

To ensure that the gifts are made 'in consideration of the marriage', they must be made either before or at the date of the marriage. The gifts should also be accompanied by a suitable letter evidencing the fact that the gift is conditional on the marriage taking place.

Gifts between spouses

2.10 Gifts between spouses are completely exempt from inheritance tax except where the donor spouse is domiciled in the UK for inheritance tax purposes but the donee spouse is not, in which case the exemption is limited to a cumulative total of £55,000 (IHTA 1984, s 18). This does not, however, preclude the treatment of such gifts as potentially exempt transfers in appropriate cases.

This exemption has two very important uses in estate planning. Its first use is in equalising estates. Instead of spouses leaving all their respective estates to the other on death, which will result in their joint estates being taxed on the second death, it is advantageous for inheritance tax purposes if the first to die leaves a proportion of his or her estate directly to their children on death so as to use up his or her nil rate band.

> *Example*
>
> Spouses with a joint estate of £600,000 will, if the first to die leaves his or her estate to the survivor, incur on the second death an inheritance tax liability of £140,000 (at current rates). If, however, the first to die were to

2.10 *Lifetime Planning*

leave, say, £275,000 to the next generation, inheritance tax of £10,000 would be immediately payable but the tax payable on the second death would come down to £30,000, making a total tax liability of £40,000.

Since there is only one rate of tax payable above the nil rate, there is no overall tax saving to the extent that property passing on the first death exceeds the nil rate band. In fact there is a cash flow advantage in deferring any charge to tax until the second death, although this must be balanced against the possibility that the rates of tax may increase before the second death occurs or even that inheritance tax might be superseded by a more onerous form of death duty.

It is, however, quite common for there to be a concentration of assets in the hands of just one of the spouses, thus making it critical as to the order in which they die. It is therefore advisable for spouses to distribute their joint estates between themselves so that whoever dies first has assets of a value which will at least be covered by the nil rate band.

Example

A wife owns assets of £50,000. Her husband owns assets of £450,000. If the wife dies first, then if she leaves her estate to her children, £200,000 of her nil rate band will be unused and therefore the chance of saving £80,000 (£200,000 × 40%) inheritance tax will be lost. The husband should therefore consider transferring at least £200,000 to the wife.

The equalisation of estates should be seen not only as an element of planning for death but also as part of an overall lifetime strategy designed to enable both spouses to have sufficient assets which they can each use to make potentially exempt transfers and gifts within the annual exemption. Spouses should consider the equalisation of their estates both when acquiring new assets and when deciding out of which estate an intended gift should be made. Where one spouse has a significantly greater life expectancy than the other, then apart from ensuring that the other spouse has sufficient assets to use up his or her nil rate band on death, there is much to be said for keeping the bulk of their assets in the estate of the first spouse to allow potentially exempt transfers to be made. On the other hand, any assets showing large unrealised gains should perhaps be kept in the estate of the other spouse to get the benefit of the capital gains tax free base uplift on his or her death.

In addition, an equal distribution of assets between the spouses may also result in income tax and capital gains tax savings. An outright gift of assets between spouses will not be regarded as a 'settlement' for the purposes of the income tax settlement provisions so that any income arising from property given to the spouse will not be taxable in the hands of the donor (ICTA 1988, s 660A(6)).

The second use of the spouse exemption is to enable assets to be given by one spouse to the other so that the other spouse may then give away the assets and thereby use his or her annual exemption or make a potentially exempt transfer (on the basis that he or she may be the more likely of the two to survive for the necessary seven-year period). The danger of this type of 'channelling' exercise is that the Inland Revenue may apply the 'associated operations' provisions contained in IHTA 1984, s 268 and tax the gift as if it had been

Lifetime Planning **2.12**

made directly to the ultimate donee by the first spouse. The Inland Revenue have indicated, however, that they would not regard the provisions as applicable unless in such circumstances it was a condition that the second gift was made (Inland Revenue Press Release dated 8 April 1975). The Inland Revenue still adopt this practice (CTO Advanced Instruction Manual C.114), although care should be taken over the timing of the gifts and the evidencing of them.

Gifts for maintenance of family

2.11 There are complete exemptions from inheritance tax for gifts made:

(*a*) by one party to a marriage in favour of the other party for his or her maintenance;

(*b*) by one party to a marriage in favour of a child of either party for the maintenance, education or training of the child and made up to the later of the year in which the child attains 18 or ceases full-time education or training;

(*c*) in favour of a child who is not in the care of his parent for his maintenance, education or training and made up to the later of the year in which the child attains 18 or ceases full-time education or training. Gifts made to such a child who is over 18 are only exempt if they are made by a person in whose care the child has been for substantial periods prior to attaining 18;

(*d*) in favour of an illegitimate child of the donor for his maintenance, education or training and made up to the later of the year in which he attains 18 or ceases full-time education or training; and

(*e*) in favour of a 'dependent relative' which constitute reasonable provision for his or her care or maintenance. A 'dependent relative' is defined as any relative of the donor or of his spouse who is incapacitated by old age or infirmity from maintaining himself; or a person's mother or mother-in-law, if widowed, or living apart from her husband or single as a result of a divorce or annulment of marriage. By concession, a gift made by a child to his or her unmarried mother is also treated as an exempt transfer, whether or not the mother is incapacitated, provided she is genuinely financially dependent on the child (Inland Revenue Extra-statutory Concession F12).

(IHTA 1984, s 11). Where a gift is made on the occasion of a divorce or annulment, 'marriage' includes a former marriage. Thus in the context of a divorce, this exemption covers gifts to a former spouse.

These provisions are important in that they exempt all expenditure by a parent on the education of his children.

Gifts within the nil rate tax band

2.12 No tax is payable until the cumulative total of all gifts made within any seven-year period exceeds £250,000.

2.13 Lifetime Planning

Although unlimited tax-free gifts can be made by way of potentially exempt transfers, in some circumstances it may be preferable to make gifts within the nil rate band to a discretionary trust. This would apply, for example, to individuals who prefer to have the flexibility of placing assets in a discretionary trust under which they are excluded as beneficiaries or to individuals who as yet have no children. This will allow further gifts to be made to the trust, or to another trust, seven years after the initial gift.

Gifts to discretionary trusts have a significant advantage over outright gifts and gifts to other types of settlement. An election to hold-over any chargeable gains which would otherwise arise on the gift may be made (TCGA 1992, s 260), whereas in relation to the other types of gifts hold-over relief is restricted to certain types of business asset (see 2.17 below). It is possible that in the future this form of relief may be limited to those cases where inheritance tax is payable on the occasion of the gift to the trustees.

Gifts of 'excluded property'

2.13 For the purposes of inheritance tax no account is taken of 'excluded property' which ceases to form part of a person's estate (IHTA 1984, s 3(2)). Thus, gifts of excluded property may be made completely free of inheritance tax.

Excluded property appears in two main situations. The first is in connection with property owned by, or settled in trust by, a person who is neither domiciled in the UK nor treated as being so domiciled for inheritance tax purposes. This aspect is considered further in chapter 19 *Immigration and Emigration* and chapter 20 *The Foreign Client*.

The other situation is in that of settlements and settled property. Broadly, any future interest under a settlement, called a 'reversionary interest' (IHTA 1984, s 47) is excluded property unless it has been acquired for a consideration in money or money's worth or is one to which the settlor of the settlement or his spouse is or has been beneficially entitled (IHTA 1984, s 48(1)). Therefore, a remainderman under a settlement may, during the lifetime of the life tenant, assign or re-settle his interest in remainder on trust for the benefit of his children without incurring any inheritance tax charge. This is considered in more detail in chapter 5 *Existing Settlements*.

The type of settlement under which there is a life tenant with one or more remaindermen often arises under wills drawn up in estate duty days when an exemption applied on the death of a surviving spouse, where that spouse had been left a life interest in the estate of the deceased. In the case of property settled in this way by a person dying before 13 November 1974, the exemption continues to apply on the death of the surviving spouse or on any prior termination of the life interest (IHTA 1984, Sch 6 para 2).

This type of settlement can also arise from the intestacy rules where the deceased dies intestate leaving a spouse and children: the spouse will take absolutely the deceased's personal chattels and the first £125,000 and a life interest in one half of the residue of the deceased's estate with the children taking the interests in remainder on the statutory trusts (Administration of Estates Act 1925, s 46).

Lifetime Planning **2.15**

Gifts to charities

2.14 The making of gifts to charities may perhaps not be regarded as an aspect of estate planning by some, although such gifts will clearly reduce the amount of inheritance tax payable on a person's death. As many wealthy individuals feel a moral obligation to pass some of the benefit of their good fortune or hard work to those less fortunate than themselves, the subject is properly within the scope of this book. Immediate, unconditional and indefeasible gifts to charities are completely free of inheritance tax (IHTA 1984, s 23). Regular gifts made under deeds of covenant which are capable of lasting for more than three years and most one-off payments have the added advantage of being deductible in computing an individual's total income for income tax purposes. Income tax relief is also available for single gifts made by individuals to charities. As charities may realise chargeable gains free of tax (TCGA 1992, s 256), a donor proposing to give a capital sum to a charity should consider transferring over investments or property which show large unrealised gains rather than cash. The gift of the investments or the property will not give rise to a charge to capital gains tax (TCGA 1992, s 257). The value of listed shares, securities, certain collective investments and qualifying interests in land given to charities will be deductible from the donor's income for income tax purposes (ICTA 1988, s 587B).

These reliefs, with some further restrictions, also apply to gifts to Community Amateur Sports Clubs.

Charities generally and community Amateur Sports Clubs are dealt with in more detail in chapter 13 *Gifts to Charities, Etc.*

Gifts with reservation

2.15 Having looked at the most important exemptions and quasi-exemptions from inheritance tax, and before dealing with some of the practical aspects of giving, consideration must first be given to the provisions contained in FA 1986, ss 102–102C and Sch 20. The legislation provides that a gift of property subject to a reservation is treated, so far as the donor is concerned, as a partial nullity for inheritance tax purposes. This is achieved by deeming the relevant property still to form part of the donor's estate on death. The rules apply where either:

(*a*) possession and enjoyment of the property is not *bona fide* assumed by the donee at least seven years before the donor's death; or

(*b*) the property is not enjoyed to the entire exclusion, or virtually to the entire exclusion, of the donor and of any benefit to him by contract or otherwise (or by virtue of any associated operations within the meaning of IHTA 1984, s 268) at any time within seven years of the donor's death.

In essence, this means that a gift of property may fall foul of these provisions if the donor receives, or is capable of receiving, any direct or indirect benefit whatsoever which is in some way referable to the gift. The benefit does not have to be provided out of the donated

2.15 Lifetime Planning

property (*Attorney-General v Worrall, QB [1895] 1 QB 99*), nor does it have to be provided by the donee. The benefit may be financial, such as an annuity (*Attorney-General v Worrall, QB [1895] 1 QB 99*), a rent charge (*Grey (Earl) v Attorney-General, KB [1900] AC 124; [1900-1903] All ER 268*) or a right to remuneration (*Oakes v Commissioners of Stamp Duties of New South Wales, PC [1954] AC 57*). Equally, it may well be the use or occupation (even as a bare licensee) of, or the ability to use or occupy, the donated property (*Chick & Chick v Commissioners of Stamp Duties of New South Wales, PC [1958] AC 435; [1958] All ER 623*).

There is a wealth of complicated and contradictory case law on the meaning of the original provisions contained in the estate duty legislation. As the current provisions are closely based on earlier estate duty sections, the principles that can be extracted from the cases are relevant to the current provisions. However, it should be remembered that inheritance tax is fundamentally different from estate duty so that old cases should be considered with a degree of circumspection. In the case of *Melville and Others v CIR, Ch D [2000] STC 628* Lightman J in the High Court said at page 636

'. . . I do not think that authorities on the estate duty legislation are helpful on the quite different legislation which replaced it.'

Although that may be true of the relationship of estate duty and inheritance tax generally, it does not indicate that one cannot refer to estate duty cases on reservation of benefit where the old and new legislation have substantially similar wording.

It is beyond the scope of this book to provide a detailed analysis of the complexities of the current provisions and of the old case law, but the following comments are offered as a guide to what is at present, at least in the context of inheritance tax, a relatively uncharted area.

1. In determining whether there has been any reservation of benefit, it is of crucial importance first to identify the property which has been given away (see, for example, *Munro v Commissioners of Stamp Duties of New South Wales, PC [1934] AC 61* and *St Aubyn v Attorney-General (No 2), HL 1951, [1952] AC 15; [1951] 2 All ER 473*). The creation by the donor of a settlement under which he reserves an interest for himself and an interest in the remainder for his children will not amount to a reservation of benefit and will be treated as a partial gift. However, the inclusion of the settlor as a beneficiary under a discretionary trust or as the object of a power of appointment is unlikely to amount to the creation of an interest sufficient to enable a severance of the beneficial interests under the trust into a donated part and a retained part (see *CIR v Eversden and another (executors of Greenstock, deceased), Ch D [2002] STC 1109*).

2. This concept of first carving a separate proprietary interest out of an asset to be given away and then giving away the remaining interest (often called 'shearing') was accepted practice in estate duty days and the Inland Revenue appeared to accept its efficacy under the

inheritance tax regime, subject to certain important qualifications — see the exchange of letters on pages 3728 and 3729 of the Law Society's Gazette for 10 December 1986 and the Inland Revenue letter of 18 May 1987 published in the Law Society's Gazette for 1 June 1988 on page 50. Reference should also be made to *Nichols v CIR, CA [1975] STC 278* as an object lesson in how not to go about this exercise.

The lease carve out scheme was a tax planning scheme, commonly used by estate planners, which was a particular application of the shearing principle. The House of Lords considered the scheme and found in favour of the taxpayer in *Ingram & Palmer-Tomkinson (Lady Ingram's Executors) v CIR, HL 1998, [1999] STC 37*. That case led to the introduction of the anti-avoidance provisions contained in FA 1986, ss 102A-102C. These provisions extend the reservation of benefit provisions to certain gifts of interests in land where the donor continues to occupy, or enjoy some right in, the land after the gift. They are examined in more detail in chapter 9 *The Family Home* at paragraph 9.9.

3. Gifts which qualify for certain inheritance tax exemptions — in particular, the spouse exemption and the exemption for gifts in consideration of marriage — cannot constitute a gift with reservation (FA 1986, s 102(5)). For example, a gift by one spouse to the other of an interest in the matrimonial home in which both continue to reside (in order to equalise estates) will not fall foul of these provisions. Gifts to charities are also outside their scope but this is not surprising as the charity exemption already contains its own reservation of benefit provisions in IHTA 1984, s 23(4). Potentially exempt transfers and gifts within the annual exemption or normal expenditure out of income can, however, be caught by the provisions.

4. There are two other specific exemptions from the gifts with reservation provisions contained in FA 1986, Sch 20 para 6. First, if the donor gives full consideration, the retention or assumption by him of the actual occupation or enjoyment of land, or of a right over land, or the actual possession of a chattel, is to be disregarded in determining whether the property is enjoyed to his exclusion or virtual exclusion and of any benefit to him by contract or otherwise. The Inland Revenue's interpretation of full consideration in this context is given in the Revenue Interpretation 55. This is set out in greater detail below. Secondly, there is an exemption of limited application which, broadly speaking, will cover the case where a donor gives a house to a relative whose circumstances have changed since the original gift and who has become unable to maintain himself for reasons of old age or infirmity.

5. The provisions only catch benefits reserved to the donor and not those reserved to his or her spouse whereas the estate duty provisions caught both. Whilst this does give some scope for flexibility in estate planning — for example, the donor's spouse could be a discretionary beneficiary of a trust while the donor may not be — great care must

2.15 *Lifetime Planning*

be taken to ensure that any benefit reserved to a spouse cannot be treated as a benefit to the donor including a benefit obtained by virtue of any associated operations (FA 1986, Sch 20 para 6(1)(c)). Thus, for example, a wife who receives a distribution of capital from a discretionary trust of which her husband was the settlor should not pay the money into a joint bank account or one on which her husband has drawing facilities. Nor should she use the money to maintain him or to discharge any liabilities which would normally be regarded as his responsibility. It should be borne in mind that the inclusion of the settlor's spouse as a beneficiary under a trust can have adverse income tax and capital gains tax consequences for the settlor.

6. It is unwise to assume, relying on the authority of *Attorney-General v Seccombe, KB [1911] 2 KB 688*, that the words 'by contract or otherwise' in FA 1986, s 102 will be construed in accordance with the 'ejusdem generis' rule. It was categorically stated by the government spokesman in the Standing Committee G debates on the 1986 Finance Bill that the non-enforceable enjoyment or benefit of property is, in the Revenue view, sufficient to bring the gifts with reservation provisions into play. Only those who are able and willing to fight the matter right up to the House of Lords should ignore this warning.

7. The gifts with reservation provisions also do not apply where the donor and donee occupy the land and the donor does not receive any benefit, other than a negligible one, which is provided by or at the expense of the donee for some reason connected with the gift (FA 1986, s 102B(4)). The donee must not pay more than his or her share of the outgoings. There is not, however, a requirement for the proportionate sharing of expenses. It would cover the situation where elderly parents make unconditional gifts of a share in their house to their children and the property is occupied by the parents and their children each bearing his or her pro rata share of the running costs. This is not a gift with reservation because the children have taken up occupation and the parents' occupation is referable to their joint ownership and not the gift. (CTO Advanced Instruction Manual D.41). The scope for this type of arrangement is fairly limited and problems may arise if one or more of the children leave home but retain their interest.

8. FA 1986, Sch 20 contains various provisions enabling the property subject to the reservation to be 'traced' into other property. These provisions are necessary in order to ascertain the value and nature of the property which is to be treated as forming part of the donor's estate immediately before his death. However, where the original gift is one of cash (and the gift is not to a settlement), it is arguable that the tracing provisions do not apply. This will effectively freeze the value of the property subject to the reservation, but in addition it raises the interesting argument that if, by the time of the death of the donor, the cash has ceased to exist there will be nothing on which FA 1986, s 102 can bite. Thus, for example, if a donor gives his son a cash gift and the son subsequently uses the money to buy a property which the donor occupies until his death, it might be thought that

there is a reservation of benefit by associated operations to the donor (by virtue of his occupation of the property provided by his son) (CTO Advanced Instruction Manual D.61). However, one argument is that as the cash ceases to exist as from the date of the purchase of the property, and because there are no provisions tracing the cash into the property, it is difficult to see how there can be any property subject to a reservation at the donor's death. The contrary argument is that by being expended the cash does not cease to exist but merely becomes the property of another (and so on *ad infinitum*) so that the property subject to the reservation continues to exist (although not in the hands of the donee) until the donor's death.

9. A director or employee of a company who wishes to give away some or all of his shares in the company should beware of reserving any benefits. The continuation of reasonable commercial arrangements in the form of remuneration or other benefits for the donor's services in the company entered into prior to the gift will not be considered by the Revenue to be a reservation of benefit provided the benefits were in no way linked to or affected by the gift (CTO Advanced Instruction Manual D.48). What is reasonable will depend upon all the facts. Generally speaking, it will be determined by what might be reasonably expected under arm's length arrangements between unconnected persons. However, if the donor attempts to entrench his position and benefits, e.g. by way of a fixed term service contract, or if following the gift he receives remuneration or other benefits in excess of normal commercial rates, he will be running the risk of reserving a benefit.

10. If the donor is the sole trustee, or one of the trustees, of the donated property, his interest as trustee will not amount to a reservation of a benefit. This was the position under the estate duty legislation (*Commissioners of Stamp Duties of New South Wales v Perpetual Trustee Co Ltd, PC [1943] AC 425*). The Revenue have confirmed that the donor or his spouse being a trustee of a settlement does not of itself give rise to a reservation of benefit (CTO Advanced Instruction Manual D.75). This position is the same even if the donor and spouse are entitled to payment for their services as trustees provided the remuneration is not excessive. This is despite the decision in the *Oakes* case.

11. Simply because a settlor is a trustee of a settlement established in favour of his or her minor children should not itself cause a reservation to arise. Yet where such settled funds are subsequently applied to meet a contractual liability of the parent which was incurred to maintain his children, a reservation would then arise.

12. The position is more complex in the case of a settlor who acts as trustee of shares in a company of which he or she is a director. Specific relieving provisions are generally required in the trust instrument if the trustee is to retain the remuneration received from that company, unless a timely application is made to the court for relief (*Keeler's Settlement Trust (Re), [1981] 1 Ch 156; [1981] 1 All*

2.15 Lifetime Planning

ER 888). In this type of situation, the Capital Taxes Office has adopted a pragmatic approach, apparently accepting that the continuation of reasonably commercial arrangements governing remuneration and benefits entered into prior to the gift would not, by itself, amount to a reservation (see CTO Advanced Instruction Manual D.76). This assumes that the remuneration package was not linked to, or affected by, the gift. However, it has been suggested that the donor should enter into a legally binding long-term service agreement prior to settling the shares, whilst having due regard to company law considerations. The idea is for the donor to 'carve out' rights in his favour, excluding those from the property gifted. Doubts have been expressed concerning this interpretation. The argument being that the associated operations provisions contained in FA 1986, Sch 20 para 6(1)(c) might be applied to link the contractual arrangements with the subsequent gift of shares.

As a result it may be generally prudent to dissuade an executive director from being a trustee when settling shares in his or her private company. As such settlors are often reluctant to relinquish control in this way it will be necessary to arrange matters within the published parameters. A further safety precaution might be for the donor to enter into a suitable long-term service agreement prior to giving the shares away, albeit that doubts may exist over the degree of protection this may afford in some cases.

In view of the complex issues outlined above, the Revenue have published their interpretation of the *de minimis* rule (see Revenue Interpretation 55 and CTO Advanced Instruction Manual D.44–46). The CTO accepts that the word 'virtually' in FA 1986, s 102(1)(b) is not defined but according to them means 'to all intents' or 'as good as'. The Inland Revenue interprets 'virtually to the entire exclusion' as covering 'cases in which the benefit to the donor is insignificant in relation to the gifted property'. Whilst acknowledging that each case will turn on its own facts, the Inland Revenue accepts that they will not apply FA 1986, s 102(1)(b) in such a way that donors are unreasonably prevented from having limited access to property they have given away and a measure of flexibility will be adopted in applying the test.

The interpretation issued by the Inland Revenue also considers a number of situations where limited benefit could arise to a donor without causing the reservation of benefit rules coming into play. These are set out below.

(a) A house which becomes the donee's residence but where the donor subsequently stays, in the absence of the donee, for not more than two weeks each year, or stays with the donee for less than one month a year.

(b) Social visits, excluding overnight stays made by a donor as a guest of the donee, to a house which he had given away. The extent of the social visits should be no greater than the visits which the donor might be expected to make to the donee's house in the absence of any gifts by the donor.

(c) A temporary stay for some short term purpose in a house the donor had previously given away, for example, while the donor convalesces

Lifetime Planning **2.15**

after medical treatment or looks after a donee convalescing after medical treatment or while the donor's own home is being redecorated.

(*d*) Visits to a house for domestic reasons, for example, baby-sitting by the donor for the donee's children.

(*e*) A house together with a library of books which the donor visits less than five times in any year to consult or borrow a book.

(*f*) A motor car which the donee uses to give occasional (i.e. less than three times a month) lifts to the donor.

(*g*) Land which the donor uses to walk his dogs or for horse riding provided this does not restrict the donee's use of the land.

The following were suggested in the interpretation as representing cases where the reservation rules were more likely to apply.

(i) A house in which the donor stays most weekends, or for a month or more each year.

(ii) A second home or holiday home which both the donor and the donee use on an occasional basis.

(iii) A house with a library in which the donor continues to keep his own books, or which the donor uses on a regular basis, for example, because it is necessary for his work.

(iv) A motor car which the donee uses every day to take the donor to work.

The Inland Revenue Interpretation also provides a useful insight into the potential application of FA 1986, Sch 20 para 6(1)(a). The underlying principle is that the reservation rules will not bite where an interest in land is given away and the donor pays full consideration for the future use of the property. What constitutes full consideration has always been of concern for those involved in estate planning because, taken literally, the failure to satisfy this requirement by however small a margin would be fatal. However, the Inland Revenue Interpretation in this respect is reassuring, and represents a welcome pragmatic approach.

> 'While we take the view that such full consideration is required throughout the relevant period — and therefore consider that the rent paid should be reviewed at appropriate intervals to reflect market changes — we do recognise that there is no single value at which consideration can be fixed as "full". Rather we accept that what constitutes full consideration in any case lies within a range of values, reflecting normal valuation tolerances, and that any amount within that range, can be accepted as satisfying the para 6(1)(a) test.'

The Inland Revenue state that it is unlikely that any arrangement could be overturned if the parties can demonstrate that it resulted from a bargain negotiated at arms' length by parties who were independently advised and which followed the normal commercial criteria in force at the time it was negotiated (CTO Advanced Instruction Manual D.52). With regard to chattels, the procedure in the Bills of Sale Acts should be followed.

2.16 *Lifetime Planning*

The effects of the gift with reservation provisions are far reaching. In the event of these provisions being of relevance when advising a client, one should consider whether the client is making a gift of the right property. One has to consider the wasted time and costs of not only implementing the transaction but any subsequent correspondence with the Inland Revenue together with the uncertainty for the client of whether or not he has a potential inheritance tax charge. If the reservation of benefit provisions are found to apply, the donor will have to pay the inheritance tax on his death as if he still owned the property but will not benefit from any capital gains tax uplift.

Other taxes

2.16 So far, we have concentrated on the inheritance tax implications of gifts. Capital gains tax and stamp duty also need to be considered.

Capital gains tax

2.17 Under TCGA 1992, s 165 and TCGA 1992, s 260, when making a gift it is possible to elect to hold-over certain chargeable gains which would otherwise arise to the donor. The donee in effect acquires the gifted property at the donor's acquisition cost, thus deferring the payment of tax until such time as the donee disposes of the property in circumstances where it is either not possible to make, or the donee chooses not to make, a further hold-over election.

TCGA 1992, s 165 applies to gifts by individuals of the following types of assets.

(a) An asset, or an interest in an asset, used for the purposes of a trade, profession or vocation carried on by

  (i) the donor; or

  (ii) his personal company (as defined in TCGA 1992, Sch 6 para 1); or

  (iii) a company which is a member of a trading group of companies (as defined in TCGA 1992, Sch 6 para 1) of which the holding company is the donor's personal company.

(b) Shares or securities of a trading company (as defined in TCGA 1992, Sch 6 para 1) or of the holding company of a trading group where

  (i) the shares or securities are neither quoted on a recognised stock exchange nor dealt in on the Alternative Investment Market; or

  (ii) the trading company or holding company is the donor's personal company.

  Hold-over relief will not apply to a transfer of shares or securities to a company.

(c) Agricultural property, or an interest in agricultural property, within the meaning of IHTA 1984, Part V, Chapter II which is not used for the purposes of a trade carried on as mentioned in (a) above.

Lifetime Planning **2.17**

TCGA 1992, s 260 applies to gifts by individuals and trustees to individuals and trustees which are either

(a) chargeable transfers within the meaning of IHTA 1984 (and transfers which would be chargeable transfers but for IHTA 1984, s 19 (the annual exemption)) and which are not potentially exempt transfers; or

(b) exempt transfers within IHTA 1984, s 24 (transfers to political parties), IHTA 1984, s 26 (transfers for public benefit), IHTA 1984, s 27 (transfers to maintenance funds for historic buildings) and IHTA 1984, s 30 (transfers of designated property).

Relief under TCGA 1992, s 260 is used mainly on gifts to discretionary trusts, whether or not its value falls within the 'nil rate' band, and on gifts covered by the annual exemption.

The rationale behind the existing statutory rules seems reasonably clear. Where the gift is a potentially exempt transfer and comprises readily realisable assets (e.g. stock exchange investments) capital gains tax is chargeable on the gift. In the case of most types of illiquid assets (e.g. land, unquoted shares) either hold-over relief will apply or the tax arising may be paid by equal instalments over ten years — TCGA 1992, s 281. The instalment option applies to the following assets:

(a) land or an estate or interest in land;

(b) shares or securities giving control of a company;

(c) unquoted shares or securities.

Interest on the unpaid tax will run from the due date under TCGA 1992, s 7 and not from the date on which each instalment is due. This detracts from the attraction of the facility.

Where, on the other hand, the gift is subject to inheritance tax or eats into the donor's 'nil rate' band (which will affect subsequent chargeable transfers), the relief under TCGA 1992, s 260 will be available to avoid any double charge to tax. Potentially exempt transfers do not fall within the ambit of this relief.

In cases where both reliefs might otherwise be applicable, TCGA 1992, s 260 relief takes priority (TCGA 1992, s 165(3)(d)).

Both reliefs operate to defer any chargeable gain arising on the gift until the donee sells the donated property or otherwise disposes of it in circumstances where it is not possible to make a further hold-over election. Any chargeable gain which would otherwise arise on the gift (called the 'held-over gain') is reduced to zero whilst the donee's acquisition cost of the donated property is reduced by a like amount so that in effect the donee takes over the donor's acquisition cost (TCGA 1992, s 165(4) and TCGA 1992, s 260(3)).

In calculating the amount of the held-over gain, the donor's acquisition cost will be indexed up to 5 April 1998 to take account of inflation (TCGA 1992, ss 53–55). On the transfer of assets after 6 April 1998 taper relief is lost when a hold-over election is made. With the relevant period of ownership only being two years for business assets disposed of after 5 April 2002, the loss of taper

2.17 Lifetime Planning

relief will be significant. As a result of which the inheritance tax benefits need to be weighed against the capital gains tax disadvantages.

Where the donor acquired the asset on or before 31 March 1982, his acquisition cost for the purposes of calculating the held-over gain will be the asset's value on 31 March 1982 (TCGA 1992, s 35(2)) except in the circumstances specified in sub-section 35(3), unless an election is made under sub-section 35(5).

Where the disposal of an asset giving rise to a potential capital gains tax charge also gives rise to an inheritance tax charge (either immediately or as a result of the death of the donor within seven years) and a claim for hold-over relief is made under either section, the inheritance tax paid may be deducted from the chargeable gain when calculating the capital gains tax due on a subsequent disposal of the asset by the donee (TCGA 1992, s 165(10) and TCGA 1992, s 260(7)). Alternatively, IHTA 1984, s 165 allows the capital gains tax arising on the gift, provided it is paid by the donee, to be deducted when calculating the value transferred for inheritance tax purposes.

Example

A transfers her shares in X Ltd to her son B. The value of the shareholding is £750,000. It has a base cost of £125,000 and 75% business taper relief is available. A has already used her nil rate band. B sells the shares shortly after the gift. Less than a year after the gift A dies. Should A's executors claim hold-over relief allowing B to deduct the inheritance tax chargeable on the gift on his subsequent disposal of the shares or should they bear the capital gains tax on the gift so that it will be deductible in calculating the inheritance tax on the gift?

Claim for hold-over relief

	£'000		£'000
IHT on gift (£750,000 @ 40%)			300
CGT on subsequent disposal			
Proceeds	750		
Base cost	(125)		
IHT	(300)		
	325		
Taper relief	Nil		
	325	@ 40%	130
			£430

No claim for hold-over relief

Proceeds	750		
Base cost	(125)		
	625		
Taper relief at 75%	(469)		
	156	@ 40%	62
Value of shares on gift	750		
Less CGT	(62)		
	688	@ 40%	275
			£337

Where an election is made for hold-over relief under TCGA 1992, s 165 or TCGA 1992, s 260 (or has been made prior to 14 March 1989 under FA 1980, s 79), the held-over gain can in certain circumstances be assessed on the donor (but in the name of, and at the rates applicable to, the donee) if the donee becomes neither resident nor ordinarily resident in the UK within six years after the end of the year of assessment in which the relevant disposal took place. The length of this period results from the combined effects of TCGA 1992, s 7 and TCGA 1992, s 168(7)(8).

Methods of protecting the donor against the contingent liability include:

(a) the retention by him of an amount of the donated property equal to the held-over gain as bare trustee for the donee for the six year period; and

(b) the taking of indemnities from relatives of the donee who are not likely to go abroad,

although these both may represent 'reserved benefits' thereby possibly tainting the gift for inheritance tax purposes.

The inability to claim hold-over relief on gifts to non-residents (TCGA 1992, s 166 and TCGA 1992, s 261) makes gifts of chargeable assets to non-resident trusts unattractive, although there can be circumstances where the immediate capital gains tax charge is an acceptable price to pay for the ability to defer payment of any future capital gains tax on a subsequent disposal of the assets by the trustees, especially where the capital gains tax can be paid by instalments.

Capital gains tax is an essential element of lifetime estate planning. Both the nature of assets to be given away and the identity of the donee need to be carefully considered, as will the funding of any tax charge arising. The following points should be borne in mind when considering any planning strategy.

(1) Where a gift is being made solely to save inheritance tax at 40%, an immediate charge to capital gains tax at 40% (after taper relief) on the gift may be too high a price to pay for the potential saving. There is an obvious cash flow advantage in deferring any tax charges for as long as possible (i.e. until death when there will also be the benefit of the capital gains tax free base uplift or holding the asset for either a two or a ten-year period, depending on the nature of the asset, to take advantage of taper relief), although the risk in such a strategy is that the rates of inheritance tax may change for the worse or a less favourable form of taxation may come into force. Another relevant factor is the extent to which the current value of the asset reflects chargeable gain — the charge to capital gains tax is only on the amount of the gain whereas the charge to inheritance tax will be on the asset's full value, including any increase in the value of the asset as time goes on. Where an asset is expected to increase significantly in value, an immediate gift of it (even if subject to an immediate capital gains tax charge) will save inheritance tax both on its present value and on the 'growth' element.

(2) Gifts of non-chargeable assets (e.g. cash, gilts, qualifying corporate bonds, life policies and chattels under £6,000 in value) do not give rise to any capital gains tax considerations.

2.17 Lifetime Planning

(3) Chargeable assets showing the lowest gain should be identified and given away. The rebasing of gains to their 31 March 1982 value may assist here.

(4) The capital gains tax arising on a gift may be reduced if the donor also realises capital losses (e.g. by sales or by gifts to the same donee) in the same tax year.

(5) Gifts falling within the donor's 'nil rate' band can currently be made to a discretionary trust which may be then converted into an interest in possession or accumulation and maintenance trust or the assets distributed outright to one or more beneficiaries possibly before the first ten-year anniversary. There may be a risk here of an attack under the *Ramsay* principle. After the decision in the case of *MacNiven v Westmoreland Investments Ltd, HL [2001] STC 237* the exact scope of the *Ramsay* principle is uncertain. It would appear that the principle will now only apply where the Courts consider that the statutory provisions are framed in a wide commercial usage rather than a narrow legal one. Where the principle applies, the Courts may recharacterise a series of individual transactions as a composite whole. It should be noted that any outright distribution from the discretionary trust will be another disposal for capital gains tax purposes (under TCGA 1992, s 71) which may give rise to a chargeable gain, although it should be possible to hold it over under TCGA 1992, s 260. Timing, however, is vital. Section 260 applies only where a chargeable transfer occurs. This will exclude a transfer in a quarter beginning either with the date of the settlement or the date of a ten-year anniversary charge. The analysis of the operation of section 260 was confirmed in the case of *Frankland v CIR, CA [1997] STC 1450* and *Harding and Leigh (Loveday's Executors) v CIR, Sp C [1997] SSCD 321 (Sp C 140)*.

(6) Where the gift is a potentially exempt transfer and a chargeable gain arises which cannot be held-over, the tax should be paid by the donee so that, if the donor dies within seven years of the gift, the tax paid will reduce the value transferred by the chargeable transfer (IHTA 1984, s 165). There is a slight possibility that any agreement between the donor and the donee that the donee will be responsible for the capital gains tax might create a 'gift with reservation' for inheritance tax purposes. On the donee paying the tax, the benefit would then come to an end and the donor would be deemed by FA 1986, s 102(4) to have made a further disposition of the property by way of a potentially exempt transfer. This will, in effect, start an additional seven-year period running which the donor must survive to avoid an inheritance tax charge. The authors have never known the CTO to raise this argument

(7) Where possible, advantage should be taken of the option to pay the capital gains tax by instalments.

(8) Gifts of chargeable assets should be made by whichever spouse has the lower capital gains tax rate or has available capital losses. To allow this to be done, it may be necessary for one spouse to first give

Lifetime Planning **2.19**

the asset to the other. This is, of course, subject to a possible challenge under the *Ramsay* principle.

(9) Because moving assets around a family may create a capital gains tax charge, it is very important that chargeable assets are acquired by the right person (whether an individual or a family trust) at the outset, having regard to each person's present and likely future tax rates.

(10) Taper relief reducing capital gains is given according to the type of asset concerned and the length of time that it has been owned by the disponer. In choosing assets to be given away or retained one needs to consider the likely incidence of taper relief on the gift and on future disposals.

Stamp duty

2.18 Stamp duty is not chargeable on an instrument giving effect to a gift provided that it can be certified in writing as falling within Category L in the Schedule to the Stamp Duty (Exempt Instruments) Regulations 1987 (SI 1987 No 516). Where the instrument effecting the transfer of property is a declaration of trust it will be subject to a fixed charge of £5 under the heading 'Declaration of any use or trust' in FA 1999, Sch 13 para 17 where the assets settled include cash or exempt assets (e.g. Government stock) or there is provision in the trust for further assets to be transferred to the trust fund.

Which assets to give away?

2.19 Given that there are a number of ways in which an individual may make immediate gifts without incurring an immediate charge to inheritance tax or capital gains tax, the next aspect to consider is whether in fact he has any assets which he can afford to give away. This can be a very difficult matter. On the one hand, the individual may be concerned about the amount of tax that will be payable on his death, or on the death of his wife, but on the other hand he may be very reluctant to jeopardise his or his wife's present and future standard of living and financial security. He should only be encouraged to give away those assets which are clearly surplus to his present and estimated future living requirements. In theory, the more wealthy a person is, the more surplus assets he will have. In practice, however, it is often the case that the more wealthy a person is, the more he will want to retain to cushion and secure his, usually high, standard of living. The inheritance tax 'gifts with reservation' provisions, as we have seen, can make it extremely difficult for a person to give away an asset whilst retaining the ability to get it back in times of hardship. There are various insurance products currently being marketed which allow individuals to make large capital investments whilst retaining a right to 'income' during their lifetime. These products have been designed to avoid the reservation of benefit rules. For a more detailed consideration see chapter 7 *Insurance*. However, most effective estate planning has to be conducted on the basis that once an asset is given away, it is gone for good. Whilst every

2.20 *Lifetime Planning*

case is different and must be judged on its own merit, the following are the types of assets which are usually the most suitable subjects of gifts.

Non- or low-income-producing assets

2.20 Many people tend to live off their income (whether earned or unearned), regarding their capital primarily as a source of income and secondly as a reserve which can be called upon in times of hardship. Any assets which produce little or no income may be suitable for giving away, although it is important not to forget the psychological importance of the mere existence of the reserve.

Unfortunately, in many cases, the major non-income producing asset — indeed the major asset itself — will be the principal residence and the gifts with reservation provisions have rendered most methods of giving away the entire home whilst retaining the ability to live there either ineffective or, at least, of uncertain effect. There may be more scope for estate planning with regard to a second home, but again the possible implications of these provisions must be fully explored. These aspects are dealt with in greater detail in chapter 9 *The Family Home*.

On the other hand, valuable paintings, books or similar chattels are clearly suitable candidates, provided that both ownership and (to avoid any reservation of benefit) possession are ceded. Woodlands, another non-income-producing asset, is a possible candidate.

Assets likely to grow in value or suffering a temporary reduction in value

2.21 These types of assets, such as shares in private companies or let property, are obvious candidates because of the advantage in taking the future growth out of the donor's estate.

In making gifts of assets which are pregnant with gain or in respect of which significant gains are anticipated, it is important to bear in mind that whilst the asset will on the donor's death escape the charge to inheritance tax, the ability of the donor's heirs to acquire the asset at its market value at the death of the donor under TCGA 1992, s 62(1), thereby wiping out any chargeable gain then latent in the value of the asset, will be lost. This may be a significant factor if it is anticipated that the assets will one day be sold by the donee.

Although the rate of inheritance tax on death is now the same as the top rate of capital gains tax subject to taper relief, property which is capable of qualifying for inheritance tax business property relief or agricultural property relief can pass on death at either half of that rate or entirely free of inheritance tax. Thus, if property qualifying for relief is both pregnant with gain and likely to be sold by the intended donee it may, for tax purposes, be beneficial to allow the property to pass to the intended donee on the donor's death, in order to take advantage of the capital gains tax-free uplift to base cost, rather than to remove the property from the donor's estate only to permit the donee then to suffer a 40% capital gains tax charge on any tapered gain arising on the sale. Obviously, much will depend on how much of the value of the asset reflects a potentially chargeable gain and the level of inheritance tax relief available.

Lifetime Planning **2.22**

The other factor which now has to be considered is whether, on the gift, any capital gain already latent in the value of the asset can be 'held-over' to the donee. This will depend upon the nature of the asset and the type of gift — see 2.17 above. In the case of shares in private companies, hold-over relief is likely to be available; but in relation to other assets where the relief is not available, an immediate charge to capital gains tax may be a small price to pay to take the expected increase in value out of the donor's estate.

Creating surplus assets

2.22 It is sometimes possible to create surplus assets where none appear to exist. For example, an investment portfolio worth £100,000 and yielding (say) 3%, could be split into two. One half is then invested in higher yielding fixed interest investments to produce (say) a 6% yield and the other half is then free to be given away. This releases assets for a gift whilst maintaining the current income. Two points should, however, be borne in mind. First, the re-investment may create a significant capital gains tax charge. Secondly, the investment in fixed interest securities is likely to destroy the potential for future capital growth.

Encouraging an individual to live off capital itself rather than the income produced by that capital is another way of creating a surplus. For example, an elderly person who expects to live for another ten years and who has an investment portfolio worth £100,000 which produces an annual income of £5,000 could retain £60,000, giving away the balance. The individual could then fund a part of their annual expenditure from capital.

Another method which is sometimes suggested for freeing assets, otherwise required to produce income, is for an individual to borrow (usually on the security of his home) in order to buy an annuity, the income of which is intended (after tax) to cover the mortgage payments and provide a suitable level of maintenance. However, the annuity rates are unlikely to be attractive (they are usually below the life office's normal rates) and the net return after the interest payments have been made is often poor. The loss caused if the individual dies prematurely can wipe out the benefit of any saving in inheritance tax as the individual is exposed to the risk of fluctuating property prices and interest rates.

Where it is necessary for the individual to continue to occupy the property, a method of creating a surplus in relation to farmland is for him to grant to a family company or partnership, a lease of the land. This then frees the freehold reversion for a gift. This principle has already been mentioned in connection with reservation of benefit and does not appear to have been nullified by IHTA 1984, s 102A. This is examined in more detail in chapter 9 *The Family Home* and chapter 11 *The Family Farm*.

The grant of a tenancy can also be used to reduce the value of land to facilitate a gift of the land. The grant of any tenancy which confers statutory security of tenure on the tenant, or which confers a significant term of years on the tenant, will effect an immediate reduction in the value of the property over which the tenancy is granted. In the case of a rack rent agricultural tenancy this can be by as much as 60%. The grant may have inheritance tax,

2.23 *Lifetime Planning*

capital gains tax and income tax implications all of which will need to be considered. The main use in estate planning of the granting of a tenancy specifically to reduce value is to enable a subsequent transfer of the freehold reversion to be made to the tenant at a significantly lower value than if the unencumbered freehold had been transferred. Again, this technique is subject to the application of IHTA 1984, s 102A. It is also considered in more detail in chapter 11 *The Family Farm*.

Cash gifts

2.23 Gifts of cash and investments are both equally effective for inheritance tax purposes. There are, however, two points worth considering.

1. If an individual is contemplating giving his son a cash sum in order for him to buy, say, a car, it is in theory better for the individual to buy the car himself and then give it to his son. The second-hand value of the car is likely to be less than the amount of the cash gift. Clearly, this device will only work in relation to assets which depreciate on resale (unlike land) and, in practice, is only worth doing in respect of assets which are of substantial value and exempt from capital gains tax. Furthermore, the purchase and the gift are so clearly associated operations within IHTA 1984, s 268 that the Inland Revenue may well seek to tax the donor on the total loss to his estate resulting from the purchase and the gift.

2. Gifts of investments may give rise to a capital gains tax charge where these are chargeable assets which cannot be 'held over' under either TCGA 1992, s 165 or TCGA 1992, s 260.

The donee

2.24 An individual who has decided that he wants to give assets away and has identified those assets which are surplus to his requirements must also consider the recipient of the gift and the manner in which the gift should be made.

Where the individual is considering a gift to his children, and there are also grandchildren in existence, some thought should be given to skipping the first generation and passing the assets over to the second. This is a course which usually only commends itself to children who consider themselves already adequately provided for, but any property passed to the second generation may, if held in trust, be used to maintain the grandchildren and to meet the cost of their education in an income tax efficient manner (see below). Such an approach can thus indirectly benefit their parents as well.

A gift may be in the form of an outright gift to an individual or may be a gift into trust. The most common types of trust encountered in estate planning are as follows.

(*a*) A bare trust for the benefit of a minor.

(*b*) An accumulation and maintenance trust for children and/or grandchildren.

Lifetime Planning **2.25**

(*c*) A discretionary trust.

(*d*) An interest in possession (life interest) trust.

Each type of trust has its own uses and limitations and these are dealt with in more detail in chapter 4 *Creating Settlements*. The advantages and disadvantages of a gift to an offshore trust are also briefly discussed in the same chapter. A more detailed analysis is contained in chapter 6 *Offshore Trusts*.

Outright gifts to an individual, together with gifts within (*a*), (*b*) and (*d*) above, can be potentially exempt transfers, whereas gifts to a discretionary trust cannot. Discretionary trusts are now most likely to be used as vehicles to receive regular gifts within the inheritance tax annual or 'normal expenditure out of income' exemptions or gifts within a person's nil rate tax band.

An outright gift to a minor child of the donor does not provide income tax advantages, as any income arising on the property given away is taxed as part of the donor's total income under ICTA 1988, s 660B whilst the child is unmarried and under 18 years of age, subject to the £100 limit for small amounts of income. It used to be possible to obtain an income tax advantage by settling income-producing assets on bare trusts for a minor child. This advantage was nullified by FA 1999, s 64 which amended ICTA 1988, s 660B(1) bringing income of bare trusts within section 660B. Such settlements may remain useful, however, because the capital gains of the trustees are treated as arising to the minor beneficiary who is thus able to use his annual exemption and the lower rates of tax.

An outright gift to an individual donee of an asset which is subsequently sold realising a chargeable gain will result in the gain potentially being taxed at either 20% or 40%. However, if the asset had been transferred to a trust under which the individual donee had an interest in possession with the trustees having power to advance capital to him, any gains realised by the trustees would be taxable at a maximum rate of 34% (TCGA 1992, s 4(1)). A transfer into trust can therefore offer a capital gains tax advantage. Unfortunately, it cannot be used to benefit a settlor because of the anti-avoidance provisions contained in TCGA 1992, ss 77–79, which operate to tax gains made by the trustees of a trust in which the settlor or his spouse are interested at the rate applicable to the settlor. What is more, if unrealised gains have already accrued at the time of transfer, it will be necessary to hold over the gain if an immediate capital gains tax liability is to be avoided. In that case, taper relief lost on the transfer may outweigh the reduction in the capital gains tax rate.

Timing of gifts

2.25 A gift of property may be effected in two ways, namely by the appropriate transfer of ownership or by a declaration of trust by the owner. A gift by way of declaration of trust will take effect on the date of the declaration. A gift by transfer of ownership will take effect on the date of the transfer.

In the case of gifts to trustees there are further requirements; there must be an effective transfer of property on trusts that are certain and are administratively workable. In reality, there should be little difficulty in establishing that the

2.25 Lifetime Planning

trust property has been given in a manner complying with the appropriate legal formalities, and some of these rules are set out below. In practice, if difficulties are going to arise it is far more likely that this will be because the gift has not been perfected. As a general rule, if the donor does not complete all the formalities associated with the gift, then it will fail (*Fry (Re), [1946] 2 All ER 106*); if the donor (including his agents) has accomplished all that can reasonably be undertaken, but an independent third party delays the legal formalities, the gift is valid (*Rose (Re), [1952] Ch 499*). (See also the recent decision in *Rennington v Crompton (the Times, 1 April 2002)*.

Transfers of some types of property (e.g. registered stocks and shares, land, life insurance policies) can only be effected by an instrument of transfer.

If a transfer of chattels is made by deed, except in the case of a marriage settlement, the chattels must be delivered within seven days of the date of the deed. If this is not the case, the deed will be treated as a bill of sale and must be registered under the Bills of Sale Act 1878 if it is not to become void as against the donor's trustee in bankruptcy and creditors. Delivery is effected by change of possession. Where the chattel is in the possession of a third party, the donor must in some way indicate to the third party that he is to look to the donee as the owner of the chattel. Where the chattel is already in the possession of the donee, the transfer may be effected simply by words (oral or written) indicating an intention to transfer ownership (*Stoneham (Re), [1919] 1 Ch 149*). Gifts of money in the form of bank notes or an irrevocable banker's draft are made by delivery. Gifts by way of cheque are not effective until the donee's account is credited (*Owen Dec'd (Re), Ch D, [1949] 1 All ER 901*).

When making a number of gifts, one of which is a gift to a discretionary settlement, the order of the gifts has been thought to be important. The discretionary trust should always be made a day before, or if the other gifts do not involve the creation of a settlement, on the same day as, the other gifts, in order to avoid the gifts being taken into account when calculating any inheritance tax charges in respect of the discretionary trust. Where one or more other gifts involve the creation of a settlement, then the gift to the discretionary trust must be on an earlier day in order to avoid the settlements being 'related settlements' within IHTA 1984, s 62.

Where a number of gifts are to be made, none of which include the making of a discretionary trust, there is some merit in making them all on the same day so that any inheritance tax payable as a result of the gifts (whether immediately payable or payable as a result of the donor's death within seven years) is charged on each gift pro rata. This is the effect of IHTA 1984, s 266(2) and avoids the later gifts bearing the tax charge due to the earlier gifts using up the nil rate band and any exemptions.

Where, however, the proposed gifts include both chargeable transfers and potentially exempt transfers the overall inheritance tax charge can depend on the precise order of events. Sometimes the most favourable result is achieved if the potentially exempt transfers are made before (and on separate days from) the chargeable transfers, but this is not always the case. Where the donor survives the potentially exempt transfer by seven years, then the order is immaterial. It is also usually immaterial if the donor dies within three years of

Lifetime Planning 2.25

the gifts because then they will all be chargeable at death rates. However, the order does become material if the donor survives the gifts by three years but dies within seven years of them.

The most important point is that, where tax is paid on a lifetime chargeable transfer, it is impossible to obtain a refund of any of the tax paid in the event of the tax recomputed on death producing a lower liability as a result of taper relief. Of course, in the converse position, additional tax would indeed be due. This means that the order of making gifts can be very important where potentially exempt transfers and chargeable transfers together exceed the donor's nil rate band. The following example, ignoring annual exemptions, illustrates the point.

Example

		Tax £
Day 1: Potentially exempt transfer of £250,000		Nil
Day 2: Chargeable transfer of £320,000		
Donee pays tax (320,000 − 250,000) @ 40% × 50%		14,000
Donor dies six years later.		
Further tax due:		
Tax on potentially exempt transfer		
(250,000 − 250,000) @ 40% × 20%		Nil
Tax on chargeable transfer:		
320,000 @ 40% × 20%	25,600	
Tax previously paid	(14,000)	11,600
Total tax		£25,600

If, however, the chargeable transfer precedes the potentially exempt transfer

		£
Day 1: Chargeable transfer of £320,000		
Donee pays tax (320,000 − 250,000) @ 40% × 50%		14,000
Day 2: Potentially exempt transfer of £250,000		Nil
Donor dies six years later.		
Further tax due:		
Tax on chargeable transfer:		
(320,000 − 250,000) @ 40% × 20%	5,600	
Tax paid	(14,000)	Nil
Tax paid on potentially exempt transfer:		
250,000 @ 40% × 20%		20,000
		£34,000

It is important to bear in mind that for the purposes of the annual exemption and the small gifts exemption the year runs from 6 April to 5 April, whereas the inheritance tax rate bands although subject to indexation on a tax year basis, have in some years been altered as from Budget Day and in other years as from the beginning of the tax year. If a donor is contemplating a gift early in the year, it can sometimes be advantageous to wait until Budget Day or the start of the next tax year for the rate bands to change. However, he should accept the risk that in some cases, no change will be made.

2.26 *Lifetime Planning*

Who should pay the inheritance tax?

2.26 It is always important for the donor to decide whether he or the donee should pay the inheritance tax on a gift.

There are two distinct advantages in ensuring that the burden of the tax falls on the donee.

1. In the case of a chargeable transfer, there will be no 'grossing-up' (i.e. when calculating the inheritance tax payable no account will be taken of the tax itself in determining the reduction in the donor's estate).

2. Where the donated property is business property or land which qualifies for agricultural property relief there may, where applicable, be the option of paying any inheritance tax by ten equal annual interest-free instalments. The payment of the tax may then be funded by the donor by his making further gifts to the donee within his annual exemption or regular gifts within the 'normal expenditure out of income' exemption. In the case of the inheritance tax payable in respect of a potentially exempt transfer, the interest-free instalment option (if available) may depend on the donee retaining the donated property until the death of the donor or until his own death if he predeceases the donor.

For potentially exempt transfers, inheritance tax will only be due if the donor fails to survive for the necessary seven-year period. If he fails to do so and tax becomes payable, there is no question of grossing-up as the donor himself has no liability to pay the tax so that the provisions which allow the liabilities to be taken into account in determining the value of a transferor's estate immediately after the transfer do not apply (IHTA 1984, s 5(4)).

The tax liability on a potentially exempt transfer which becomes chargeable falls primarily on the donee. If, however, the tax is not paid within twelve months after the end of the month in which the donor died, the donor's personal representatives also become liable. To avoid any question as between the donee and the donor's personal representatives as to who should pay the tax, the matter should be settled at the outset. If the donee is to pay the tax — and in many cases this is the preferable course especially if the interest-free instalment option is likely to be available — the donee should enter into a binding commitment to do so. It is difficult to see that such a commitment could amount to a 'reserved benefit' for the donor as it does no more than reflect where the primary statutory liability for the tax falls. The Inland Revenue are understood to take the same view. If, however, the donor wishes the tax to be borne by his estate, then a specific provision to this effect should be put in his will. This would amount to a legacy in favour of the donee for inheritance tax purposes, and if the will includes gifts of residue which in whole or in part qualify for exemption, then the legacy may have to be grossed-up when calculating the inheritance tax payable on the donor's death (IHTA 1984, s 38).

Regardless of whether the inheritance tax is to be borne by the donee or by the donor's personal representatives, consideration should be given to term assurance being effected on the life of the donor. The term should be for seven years but the policy should ideally have an option to extend the term to cater

Lifetime Planning **2.28**

for any legislative changes. Where the liability to tax is to be borne by the donee, the policy may be taken out either by the donee, as he has an insurable interest in the life of the donor, or by the donor himself and then assigned to the donee. Where the liability is to be borne by the donor's personal representatives, the donor should take out the policy and ensure that the policy proceeds do not form part of his estate on death by holding the policy on separate trusts, either similar in terms to those in his will concerning his residuary estate or (where appropriate) wide discretionary trusts for the benefit of his family. The premia on the policy may continue to be paid by the donor and if met out of income may be exempt from inheritance tax within the 'normal expenditure out of income' exemption. Otherwise, the premia may be covered by the annual exemption. In the case of a policy taken out by or for the donee, decreasing term assurance may be appropriate as the tax charge decreases as time elapses. In the case of a policy taken out by the donor, however, decreasing term assurance may well be inappropriate since although the tax payable on the potentially exempt transfer will decrease, the amount of the potentially exempt transfer will be aggregated with the donor's estate on death and may therefore operate to increase the overall rate at which his estate is taxed. Indeed, it may be worth considering additional insurance cover to meet this potential increased liability.

Who should pay the capital gains tax?

2.27 If the gift gives rise to a chargeable gain which cannot be held-over, then the primary liability to the tax falls on the donor. However, under TCGA 1992, s 282, if the tax is not paid by the donor within 12 months from the date when it becomes payable, the donee may be assessed and charged (in the name of the donor) to the tax.

The advantage of the donee bearing the burden of the tax is that if the gift is, or becomes (by reason of the death of the donor), a chargeable transfer for inheritance tax purposes, the amount of capital gains tax borne by the donee is treated as reducing the value transferred by the chargeable transfer (IHTA 1984, s 165).

It is possible that any agreement between the donor and the donee that the donee should be responsible for the capital gains tax might amount to a 'gift with reservation' for inheritance tax purposes. However, even if this were to be the case, the reservation of benefit should cease on the tax being paid by the donee, with the result that a second potentially exempt transfer would be made by the donor at that time (FA 1986, s 102(4)).

The option of paying capital gains tax by instalments conferred in certain circumstances by TCGA 1992, s 281 applies whether the tax is paid by the donor or the donee.

Asset conversion

2.28 The second basic way in which the inheritance tax payable on a person's death may be mitigated is by asset conversion. An estate comprising a portfolio of gilts and securities quoted on the Stock Exchange

2.28 Lifetime Planning

and a house worth in total (say) £400,000 will (at current rates) suffer on death an inheritance tax charge of £60,000. If, however, that estate had solely comprised property which qualified for 50% agricultural property relief, the value of the estate for inheritance tax purposes would reduce to £200,000 and no tax would be chargeable.

This is an extreme example, but it illustrates the basic principle that in inheritance tax terms it is better for a wealthy client with surplus assets which he is not prepared to give away to invest those assets in commercially sound property which qualifies for some form of relief. The types of property most suitable for this exercise include the following.

(*a*) Agricultural property, tenanted or untenanted.

(*b*) *Woodlands.* Provided the statutory rules are met, full 100% business property relief should apply. Woodlands also have certain capital gains tax advantages for their owner. For a more detailed analysis, see chapter 12 *Woodlands.*

(*c*) *Lloyd's underwriting assets.* A Name at Lloyd's may qualify for business property relief on his Lloyd's deposit, his special reserve fund, his general (or personal) reserve, his share of the profits of open years and any assets which secure a guarantee or letter of credit issued by a bank to satisfy his means test up to the amount of the guaranteed sum. The Revenue have confirmed that the amount of business property relief will no longer be restricted by reference to the nature of the underlying asset or assets against which the guarantee is secured (Lloyds Market Bulletin dated 23 April 2002). It should be noted, however, that the Revenue will treat the value of underlying assets as reduced by the amount of the guarantee for the purposes of giving any other reliefs or exemptions. Therefore, guarantees should not be secured against assets that would qualify for either business property relief or agricultural property relief. Against the potential inheritance tax saving the prospective Name should be sure to weigh his potential liability and the very real possibility of his making substantial underwriting losses as so many have in past years. For a more detailed consideration, see chapter 16 *Planning for Death.* Where a shareholder in an underwriting company at Lloyds provides collateral to secure a bank guarantee, the CTO no longer regards the assets forming the collateral as qualifying for business property relief (Lloyd's Market Bulletin dated 3 July 2002).

(*d*) *Shares or securities in a company which is not quoted on The Stock Exchange.* These include shares or securities dealt in on the 'over the counter' market or under Rule 4.2 of the Stock Exchange and those dealt with on the Alternative Investment Market, which allows smaller companies to raise capital by issuing securities to the public, yet avoiding the stringent regulations and higher costs applicable to a full listing.

(*e*) *Sleeping partner in unincorporated business.* An individual not wishing to take an active role in a business may consider becoming a sleeping partner of an unincorporated business or a member of a limited liability partnership. Business property relief of 100% will be available.

It must be remembered that in order to qualify for business property relief, agricultural property relief or woodlands relief, the deceased must have satisfied various conditions, relating, for example, to the period of ownership of the assets in question.

For the client with a surplus which he prefers not to realise and invest — either because he likes the existing investment or because to do so would give rise to a large chargeable gain — an alternative way of proceeding would be for him to borrow on the security of the non-qualifying assets (thereby reducing their value for inheritance tax purposes) and to invest the borrowings in assets which do qualify for relief. The interest on the borrowings can be a deterrent to this exercise, but in some cases — for example, where the asset purchased is shares in certain close companies or agricultural property which is subsequently let — loan interest may be deducted from his total income for income tax purposes.

One other device for converting assets not qualifying for relief into assets that do, although one which is extremely rare in practice, concerns shareholdings in publicly quoted companies. A controlling shareholding in a quoted company qualifies for 100% business property relief (IHTA 1984, s 105(1)(b)). A non-controlling holding does not qualify for any relief. If two or more individuals own shareholdings which together (but not separately) give control of a public trading company, they could transfer their shares to a newly formed unlisted holding company in return for shares in that company. The shares in the holding company would then qualify for 100% or 50% business property relief depending upon the size of the holding. Section 105(3) provides that business property relief will not apply to shares in companies whose only or main business is, *inter alia*, making or holding investments. However, under section 105(4)(b) the relief will still apply to the holding company of one or more trading subsidiaries.

It will be appreciated that the scope for the 'asset conversion' type of inheritance tax mitigation will be fairly limited. It is also a device to be used with care.

Asset freezing

2.29 The third way of mitigating inheritance tax is by asset freezing.

Loans

2.30 The simplest example of an asset freezing measure is a loan. This freezes the value of the monies lent in the lender's estate and, the borrower having invested the monies, allows any capital growth to accrue outside it. To ensure making the loan does not itself give rise to an inheritance tax charge, the loan is usually expressed to be interest free and repayable on demand, so that there is no immediate reduction in the value of the lender's estate.

2.30 Lifetime Planning

Where the borrower uses the proceeds of the loan to purchase an asset which is not readily realisable, or which is only immediately realisable for a lower figure than its cost, and has no other liquid assets available to repay the loan and (for whatever reason) is not in a position to borrow funds commercially to do so, then it is conceivable that the Inland Revenue may try to argue that although the loan is expressed to be repayable on demand there may be a possibility that it will not be repaid and therefore there is an immediate reduction in the lender's estate.

It is also possible that the Inland Revenue may attempt to argue that the failure to charge interest represents a waiver of interest and may seek to treat this as a succession of gifts made over the duration of the loan. Such an attempt would be entirely misconceived.

It is sometimes suggested that any income arising from the benefit of the loan in the borrower's hands will form part of the total income of the lender under the income tax settlement rules. This is, however, a difficult argument to sustain because, even if a straightforward loan can be regarded as a 'settlement' for the purposes of ICTA 1988, Part XV, it is necessary first to identify the settled property and then to show that income arises from that property. As the lender is merely exchanging the property lent for a chose in action (namely his rights against the borrower), the settled property can only be either the chose in action, which does not give rise to any income, or the proceeds of the loan in the hands of the borrower in which the lender would seem to have no interest. Nevertheless, the risk of some form of attack from the Inland Revenue clearly exists (as witness the case of *CIR v Levy, Ch D 1982, 56 TC 68; [1982] STC 442*). The Inland Revenue may attempt to argue that the loan constitutes part of a wider 'arrangement' that the interest would not be paid. In such circumstances, they may seek to argue that any income earned from the capital lent constitutes assessable income in the hands of the lender. In practice it is unlikely that the Revenue will take such an approach.

Another possible problem is the gifts with reservation provisions, but again it is difficult to see how a straightforward loan (even interest-free) could be regarded as a gift for the purposes of FA 1986, s 102. The Inland Revenue's view on this appears to be that the grant of an interest-free loan repayable on demand is not a transfer of value but it is a gift because there is a clear intention to confer bounty; the property disposed of being the interest foregone (see CTO Advanced Instruction Manual D.31). That view is clearly incorrect. The lender cannot be said to have disposed of property which is the interest arising on the loan because that 'property' has never existed. Nor can the lender be said to have disposed of the income arising on the investment of the money lent because that income has never belonged to the lender.

The loan may be made either to an individual or to a trust, such as an accumulation and maintenance trust or a discretionary trust. However, great care is required where a loan is made by a settlor and the trustees invest in income-producing assets. Any repayment of the loan to the lender may give rise to a higher rate income tax liability under ICTA 1988, s 677. This is broadly to the extent of the amount repaid if the trustees then, or in the future, have any undistributed income.

Lifetime Planning **2.32**

Where there is a trust with a life tenant and one or more remaindermen, an on-demand loan by the trustees to the remaindermen of assets in the trust fund will effectively freeze the value of those assets in the estate of the life tenant. It may be advisable to charge a modest level of interest on the loan as a means of countering the argument that there has been a partial termination of the life tenant's interest in possession.

A loan is a very effective and much used estate planning device. It is particularly attractive to moderately wealthy parents with some free capital who wish to help out their children but are reluctant to part completely with a part of their estate. The lender can always write off the loan over a period of time using his annual £3,000 exemption and may write it off completely by way of a potentially exempt transfer, if he later finds that he can do without the capital. (Whilst the loan and the subsequent release will undoubtedly amount to associated operations within IHTA 1984, s 268(1), section 268(3) will operate to prevent there being an overall chargeable transfer.)

Where no consideration is given for the release of a loan, the release can only be effected by deed. For a deed to be validly executed, the intention that the instrument is a deed must be made clear in the document. The instrument must either be signed by the person making it in the presence of a witness or be signed at the direction of the person making it in the presence of two witnesses.

Sales of assets

2.31 A sale is another, but less obvious, type of asset freezing measure. If a father sells his cottage in the country to his son at full market value, any future growth in value will accrue for the benefit of the son. If the father goes on to spend the sale proceeds over a period of time, rather than to retain and invest them, then so much the better as he is reducing his own estate as well. Should the father wish to continue to occupy the property, then the gifts with reservation provisions will not be a problem as the disposal of the cottage will have been by way of a sale rather than by way of a gift. The disadvantage of the sale is that it could give rise to a capital gains tax charge for the father and also to a stamp duty liability for the son.

Grants of option to purchase

2.32 Another example is the grant of an option to purchase property at its market value at the date of the grant. On the exercise of the option any increase in value in the property will flow through to the grantee free of inheritance tax. The grant of the option must be made for full consideration, otherwise the existence of the option will not be fully taken into account when valuing the property in the grantor's estate on his death or on an exercise of the option (IHTA 1984, s 163).

The grant of an option for consideration will be treated as a disposal of a chargeable asset (with a nil base cost) for capital gains tax purposes and may give rise to a chargeable gain (TCGA 1992, s 144(1)). A gain may arise on the exercise by reference to the unencumbered value of the asset where the parties are connected (TCGA 1992, s 18(7)). It should be borne in mind that options

2.33 Lifetime Planning

over land are only valid for a period of 21 years (Perpetuities and Accumulations Act 1964, s 9(2)).

The grant should not be a gift with reservation for inheritance tax purposes because no benefit is received by the donor from the subject matter of the gift (the option) nor does he receive any collateral benefit referable to the gift.

If an option is allowed to lapse without being exercised, this may result in a transfer of value for inheritance tax purposes (IHTA 1984, s 3(3)) which is not capable of constituting a potentially exempt transfer (IHTA 1984, s 3A(6)).

Other arrangements

2.33 There are other more sophisticated types of asset freezing arrangement. Those involving companies and partnerships are dealt with in more detail in chapter 10 *The Family Business*. One such arrangement for a company (now usually an investment company) involves the creation of two classes of shares, one of which receives the present value of the company on a winding-up, which is retained by the original shareholders, and the other of which carries the excess value, which is given away. There is a similar arrangement involving the issue of deferred shares which is also dealt with in more detail in that chapter.

So far as partnerships are concerned, it is often the case that the entitlement of a retiring or deceased partner will be limited to the balance on his capital account plus his pro rata share of accrued profits. The effect of this is that any underlying growth in value in the partnership assets accrue for the benefit of the continuing partners, who will often be members of the next generation in a family.

Various insurance companies offer products designed to freeze the value of an estate at a given time. These products involve an individual making a capital investment which is treated as a potentially exempt transfer. The capital is invested in a single premium bond which consists of a capital fund and an income fund. The income fund provides an income from an endowment policy which if it is 5% or less will be free from higher rate income tax. For a more detailed explanation see chapter 7 *Insurance*.

Conversion of capital assets

2.34 The fourth basic method by which the inheritance tax payable on death may be mitigated is by the conversion of capital assets into income producing assets.

Where an individual has capital which he no longer requires or needs he may consider purchasing assets which produce income only for a given period of time. For example, income shares of a split capital investment trust which confer rights to receive dividends but not to assets on a winding up. As the predetermined winding-up date approaches the market value of the income share decreases. Thus, the investor receives a stream of large income payments

Lifetime Planning **2.35**

(which he uses for his living expenses) matched by a decrease in the capital value of his investments which reduces the inheritance tax liability on his estate.

The organisation of an estate

2.35 The last topic to consider is the best way of organising an estate with a view to facilitating an easy and cost-effective administration after death. This aspect of estate planning should be kept in mind throughout the individual's lifetime and the following is a list of relevant points all of which are further considered in chapter 16 *Planning for Death*.

(*a*)   *Joint names*. If spouses acquire assets in joint names as joint tenants, the assets will pass to the survivor automatically on the first death without the delay and expense of the personal representatives of the deceased having to transfer them to the survivor. (Where the spouses die in circumstances rendering it uncertain which of them survive the other, they will be deemed to die in order of seniority (Law of Property Act 1925, s 184).) There may, however, be a number of good reasons for vesting assets in the sole name of one of the spouses, for example, where the other is a sole trader or partner in a trading partnership.

(*b*)   *Foreign assets*. It is a costly procedure to register a UK grant, or to take out a fresh grant, in a foreign jurisdiction in order to obtain title to foreign stocks and shares. Small holdings should therefore be liquidated if possible before death. If an individual makes investments abroad, either they should be registered in the name of a UK nominee company, which will avoid the need for a foreign grant, or he should be encouraged to consider indirect investment through a UK unit trust or investment company. The same problems will be encountered with a foreign holiday home and can again be avoided by holding the property in the name of a nominee (which could be a UK incorporated unlimited company specially set up by the client for the purpose). See also chapter 18 *Investing Abroad* for more on this aspect.

(*c*)   *Life policies*. These should be inspected to see whether the proceeds are payable to the insured's estate or are held in trust. If the former, then unless the insured leaves the proceeds to his spouse and the spouse survives the insured, they will give rise to an inheritance tax charge on his death. Where the proceeds are intended for the spouse and/or children, the benefit of the policy should be put in trust for them during the insured's lifetime. New policies should similarly be settled on trust from the outset. The additional advantage of the trust is that the policy proceeds may be paid out immediately following the death (on production of the death certificate) without the need to wait for a grant. See also chapter 7 *Insurance* for more on this aspect.

(*d*)   *Pensions*. Where the individual has a right of nomination over a lump sum death benefit payable under a pension scheme, he should be sure

2.35 Lifetime Planning

to exercise the right to avoid the benefit falling into his estate on death and possibly being charged to inheritance tax. The exercise of the right of nomination could in theory itself give rise to an inheritance tax charge, but provided the client is in good health at the date of the nomination (which will be presumed if he survives for two years) it is understood that the Inland Revenue treat the value transferred as being negligible. Where the benefit is payable under a discretionary trust, then he should make sure that the trustees are aware of his wishes as to their ultimate destination.

These lump sum death benefits can provide useful estate planning opportunities in that by directing the lump sums to his children and leaving his wife to inherit his free estate, an individual may leave all members of his family well provided for on his death without incurring any inheritance tax charge. Reference should also be made to chapter 8 *Pensions* for more on this aspect.

(e) *Accident/death in service policies.* Similar considerations apply here. Where the individual has a right of nomination over the proceeds or may express wishes to trustees as to their destination, he should be sure to do so.

(f) *The will.* No client should ever die intestate. Not only is it usually more costly and more time consuming to obtain a grant of letters of administration rather than a grant of probate but also the trusts which can arise under the intestacy rules can be very costly to administer and they are unlikely to reflect the client's true wishes regarding the devolution of his estate.

3 Introduction to Trust Law

Introduction

3.1 It is common to create trusts as an integral part of estate planning strategies. For those who do not have a legal background (and even sometimes for those more experienced in this area), trust law can prove to be particularly problematic. The aim of this chapter is to outline some of the key concepts involved and highlight potential problem areas. In addition, at the end of the chapter there is a more detailed examination of three areas: power of maintenance, power of advancement and protective trusts.

The Trustee Act 2000 has substantially widened trustees' powers in several important administrative areas. These include the powers of investment, purchasing property, delegating investment management and other decision-making functions, and the power to employ nominees and custodians.

What is a trust?

3.2 Probably one of the most useful definitions was provided by Sir Arthur Underhill, who described a trust as:

> 'An equitable obligation binding a person (who is called a trustee) to deal with property over which he has control (which is called trust property) for the benefit of persons (who are called beneficiaries or *cestuis que trust*) of whom he may himself be one and any one of whom may enforce the obligation.'

This definition highlights three important areas: first, the legal rules which bind trustees are equitable in nature. Secondly, the trustees do not personally own the property; they hold it for the benefit of the beneficiaries who own the equitable interest in the property subject to the terms of the trust. The trustees own the legal interest. Thirdly, the equitable rules binding the trustees can be enforced in the courts, primarily by the beneficiaries themselves.

Settlors

3.3 As a general rule if a person can give property away, he has sufficient legal capacity to settle the property. In addition, the settlor requires sufficient mental capacity to settle the property. He must fully understand the nature of his actions. However, simply because a settlor subsequently becomes incapacitated does not automatically invalidate any prior settlement he may have made.

It is important to appreciate that a settlor can establish a trust under which he is the principal beneficiary whilst also being the sole trustee. Legally he is regarded as acting in a number of different capacities. However, if the demarcation lines are not observed, the court may determine that the settlement was a sham and that no settlement was created.

Trustees

3.4 Trustees are a continuing body of persons who hold the property in a fiduciary capacity on behalf of beneficiaries. Any person can be a trustee provided he or she possesses sufficient legal capacity. There is no requirement for trustees to be individuals and therefore companies can also act as trustees.

Legally there are few restrictions on the number of persons who may be trustees, although practically there should always be two, and rarely more than four. There is a limited number of cases where statute imposes a restriction on the number of trustees who can or should hold trust property. For example, there has to be a minimum of two trustees to give a valid receipt for capital received on the sale of land, unless the trustee is a trust corporation.

Beneficiaries

3.5 A beneficiary does not have to be legally competent to benefit under a trust. However, any lack of legal capacity may have other ramifications. For example, where a beneficiary is a patient of the Court of Protection, because he cannot manage his affairs, it does not mean that the trustees cannot exercise their discretion in his favour. It means that they cannot give him the money or property direct, as he is unable to give a valid receipt. Accordingly, the trustees would have to transfer the trust property to his Receiver, appointed by the Court, who could then apply the property received for his benefit.

Making a trust

3.6 In order for a valid trust to be created there must be an effective transfer of property by means of a complete gift on trusts, which are certain and not illegal. It is essential that not only the correct legal procedures are observed but that the donor completes the gift so that the gift is effective. Where the donor is entirely responsible for the delay, the gift will fail. However, as a general rule, if the donor has done all that he can in order to complete the gift but the delay is as a result of the inaction of a third party, the gift will be valid following *Rose (Re), [1952] Ch 499* and *Pennington v Crompton (The Times, 1 April 2002)*.

Whilst no particular form of wording is required to establish a trust, its terms must be certain. In *Knight v Knight, [1840] 3 Beav. 148* Lord Longdale identified three certainties that had to be present before a valid trust could exist namely, certainty of words, subject matter and persons or objects intended to benefit under the terms of the deed.

No illegality

3.7 Over the centuries, case law has evolved indicating that in certain circumstances trusts may be held to be invalid where the object of the trust is clearly illegal, or where recognising their full effect would not be in the public interest.

(a) *Perpetuities.* Under English law, property must vest in a beneficiary within the perpetuity period. Under the terms of the Perpetuities and Accumulations Act 1964 the maximum duration of a trust established after 1964 may be specified as 80 years (in place of the old common law rule of lives in being at the date of settlement plus 21 years). It is comparatively rare for trusts established by modern trust deeds to fall foul of the perpetuity rules. The effect of the 1964 Act has been to mitigate the harshness of the old perpetuity rules by introducing a 'wait and see' rule.

Charitable trusts have no perpetuity period limitations.

(b) *Accumulations.* The rule on accumulations of income was introduced to avoid the excessive build-up of wealth in trusts. The permitted accumulation periods are as follows.

(i) the life of the settlor in relation to lifetime settlements where no other period is specified;

(ii) 21 years from the date of death of the settlor or the testator (in the case of will trusts this period will apply where no other period is specified);

(iii) the minority or minorities of any person benefiting under the terms of the trust who was alive at the date of death of the settlor or testator;

(iv) the minority or minorities of any person who would be entitled under the terms of the settlement if of full age;

(v) 21 years from the date of making the disposition;

(vi) the minority or minorities of any person alive at the date of creation of the settlement where a lifetime gift is involved.

Where there is a direction to accumulate for a period in excess of the statutory periods specified above, the entire gift is void if that period is also longer than the perpetuity period. However, where the accumulation period does not exceed the perpetuity period, the direction to accumulate is only invalid as to the excess over the statutory period.

(c) *Bankruptcy.* Any gift, transaction in consideration of marriage, or sale at an undervalue where the price paid is significantly less than the

3.8 *Introduction to Trust Law*

value of the assets sold in money or monies worth will amount to a transaction at an undervalue within the terms of the Insolvency Act 1986. There are four possible situations where the court can set aside such transactions:

(i) Where a petition leading to adjudication in bankruptcy is presented within two years. It is not necessary to prove that the transaction was intended to prejudice creditors or to establish the financial status of the donor at the time of the transaction (IA 1986, s 341).

(ii) Where it pre-dates the presentation of the bankruptcy petition by more than two but less than five years. The donor must either have been insolvent at the time that the transaction was undertaken or have become insolvent as a result of the transaction. For these purposes a donor is deemed to be insolvent if he cannot pay his debts as they fall due or if the value of his liabilities exceed the value of his assets after taking into account cash flow factors. Where the transaction is with an associate of the donor the burden of proof is on the donor (IA 1986, s 341(2)). The trustee of a family trust will be an associate of the donor where the trust beneficiaries include, or the terms of the trust confer a power that may be exercised for the benefit of, the donor or his associate (IA 1986, s 435(5)).

(iii) Where it can be proved to the court's satisfaction that the transaction at an undervalue was undertaken by the donor in order to put his assets beyond the reach of his existing or future creditors (IA 1986, s 423). In the case of *Hashmi & Hashmi, CA 3 May 2002 unreported* the issue arose as to whether it was necessary for an applicant under section 423(3) to show that the statutory purpose had been the dominant purpose behind the transaction, or whether it was sufficient that the statutory purpose was the substantial purpose. The Court of Appeal held that the statutory purpose did not have to be the sole or predominant purpose.

(iv) Where the donor becomes bankrupt as a result of a crime the property can be recovered without any regard to a time limitation.

The result of the transactions being set aside is that they will be void *ab initio* — that is, they will be treated as not having taken place.

Divorce

3.8 On a divorce a trust will not, by itself, avoid a division of property between the parties.

First, the court will have jurisdiction under Matrimonial Causes Act 1973, s 21 to make a property adjustment order in relation to the marriage under section

24(1) of the Act. The court has the power to make one or more property adjustment orders as it thinks fit.

Secondly, it might be tempting for a spouse to give away family wealth so as to exclude the current spouse from benefiting on divorce. Under section 37, a disposition may be set aside if it is made with the intention of preventing financial relief being granted to a party to the marriage. Where an application is made to the court within three years of the settlement there is a rebuttable presumption that the settlement was made with the intention to defeat a claim for financial relief (MCA 1973, s 37(5), see *Whittingham v Whittingham, [1978] 3 All ER 805*).

The court can also have regard to the availability of other trust funds, not falling within any of the above categories, to be taken into account in dividing the family assets on divorce. In *Browne v Browne, (Times Law Reports, 25 November 1988)*, the Court of Appeal held that assets held outside the jurisdiction on discretionary trusts in favour of one spouse were financial resources to be taken into account in considering the other spouse's application in matrimonial proceedings for financial relief. Where a spouse has an interest in a settlement, the Court will ask what the beneficiary may reasonably expect to receive from the settlement, see *J v J, [1989] 1 All ER 1121*.

Inheritance laws

3.9 Unlike most civil law jurisdictions, English law does not impose forced heirship or reserved property rights. For example, a Frenchman is required under the Code Napoleon to leave a very substantial portion of his estate to his surviving lineal descendants where he is survived by his issue. The minimum proportion of property that must devolve to such issue varies from one half where there is one child to three quarters where there are three or more children. A surviving spouse has a right to one quarter of the estate absolutely, and if there is no surviving issue, the spouse has a right to three quarters of the whole of the estate.

By way of contrast, under English common law a testator's spouse and children have no legal right to inherit a fixed proportion of his estate. However, when a person dies domiciled in England and Wales, the court has power after death to make provisions out of the deceased's net estate for the following.

(i)   The deceased's spouse.

(ii) A former spouse of the deceased who has not remarried or any person who, for the whole period of two years ending immediately prior to the date of death, was living in the same household as the deceased and as the husband or wife of the deceased. This is designed to deal with co-habitees.

(iii) A child of the deceased.

(iv) A person treated by the deceased as a child of the family in relation to any marriage of the deceased.

3.10 *Introduction to Trust Law*

(v) A dependant of the deceased.

This applies irrespective of whether the deceased left a will or died intestate (Inheritance (Provision for Family and Dependants) Act 1975).

Applications under the Act must be made within six months of the date on which a grant of probate or letters of administration of the deceased's estate were first taken out. The court has an unfettered discretion to extend this time limit in appropriate cases. Where gifts predate the date of death by at least six years, they fall outside the ambit of the court's review. It would be unwise to rely on this, however, as it is at least arguable that such a transfer could be challenged under the law concerning fraudulent transfers and bankruptcy.

Trustees' powers and duties

3.10 Over the centuries a considerable body of case law has evolved clarifying trustees' powers and duties. In addition, there is legislation including the Trustee Act 1925, Trustee Investments Act 1961, the Trusts of Land and Appointment of Trustees Act 1996 and the Trustee Act 2000. These are discussed in outline in this chapter. Where lay trustees are involved, the court judges the actions of the trustees by reference to the standard of behaviour that would be expected of an ordinary and sensible businessman. However, far higher standards of care and skill are expected from professional trustees.

When accepting the position of trustee, there are three key areas which require immediate action. First, the trustee should ensure that he understands the trusts involved. In the event of any ambiguity the trustee is under an obligation to clarify matters as soon as possible. It is also essential for the trustee physically to examine the trust instrument. For example, this may reveal a notice of assignment by a beneficiary of a beneficial interest. If the trustee was unaware of this he might distribute trust property to the wrong claimant.

Secondly, all property should be placed in the joint names of the trustees or in proper custodial care. Where a new trustee is appointed to a continuing trust, or where he replaces an existing trustee, certain categories of trust property will automatically vest in the trustees as a result of Trustee Act 1925, s 40 where the appointments are by deed. The category of assets where automatic vesting occurs is restricted but includes freehold land and bank accounts. It does not extend, for example, to land conveyed by way of mortgage for securing money subject to the trust, certain leases of land, life assurance policies or stocks and shares.

Thirdly, where the trustee appointed succeeds another he may, in the absence of unduly suspicious circumstances, safely assume that the previous trustees have acted properly in discharging their duties. However, where there are suspicious circumstances suggesting earlier previous breaches of trust, he is under a duty to investigate these matters.

Investments

3.11 Trustees are under a duty to invest trust funds, maintaining an even balance between beneficiaries where they have differing interests in relation

Introduction to Trust Law 3.11

to income and capital. Lord Lindley, Master of the Rolls, stated in *Whiteley (Re), [1910] 1 Ch 600* that the duty of care expected of a trustee is:

'to take such care as an ordinary prudent man would take if he were minded to make an investment for the benefit of other people for whom he felt morally bound to provide'.

'Invest' *prima facie* means to apply money in the purchase of some property from which interest or profit is expected and which property is purchased in order to be held for the sake of income which it will yield (*Re Wragg, Wragg v Palmer, [1919] 2 Ch 58*). The purchase of freehold land for some purpose other than the receipt of income is not an investment (*Re Power, Public Trustee v Hastings, [1947] Ch 572*).

The trustees may only invest trust funds in investments authorised by the trust instrument or permitted by legislation. The powers of trustees of land are governed by the Trusts of Land and Appointment of Trustees Act 1996 (TLATA). 'Trusts of land' are trusts that include land whether or not there are also other assets subject to the trust (TLATA, s 1(1)(a)). Trustees of land have all the powers of an absolute owner and are given an express power to purchase land for investment (TLATA, s 6). The trustees must exercise these powers according to the statutory duty of care under the Trustee Act 2000 (see below).

With regard to other investments, trustees of trusts with narrowly drawn investment clauses were until recently governed by the Trustee Investments Act 1961 which permitted trustees to invest up to 75% of the trust fund in wider range investments. The statutory framework was often therefore considered to be unduly restrictive. The Trustee Act 2000 has replaced the previous system with one which gives the trustees a 'general power' of investment. This general power permits a trustee to make any kind of investment he could make if he were absolutely entitled to the assets of the trust (Trustee Act 2000, s 3(1)). This general power does not, however, permit a trustee to make an investment in land other than loans secured on land (Trustee Act 2000, s 3(3)). However, Trustee Act 2000, s 8 (see below) gives a specific power in relation to land.

In exercising any power of investment, a trustee must have regard to the standard investment criteria which are:

(*a*) the suitability to the trust of investments of the same kind as any particular investment proposed to be made or retained and of that particular investment as an investment of that kind; and

(*b*) the need for diversification of investments of the trust in so far as is appropriate to the circumstances of the trust (Trustee Act 2000, s 4).

The trustee is also required to review the investments of the trust from time to time and consider whether, having regard to the standard investment criteria, they should be varied (Trustee Act 2000, s 4(2)).

The general power of investment is in addition to powers otherwise conferred on trustees but is subject to any restriction or exclusion imposed by the trust deed.

3.11 Introduction to Trust Law

'Suitability' includes consideration as to the size and risk of the investment and the need to produce an appropriate balance between income and capital growth to meet the needs of the trust. It also includes any relevant ethical considerations as to the kind of investment which it is appropriate for the trust to make.

Before exercising any power of investment, a trustee must obtain and consider proper advice about the way in which, having regard to the standard investment criteria, the power should be exercised. However, a trustee need not obtain such advice if he reasonably concludes that in all the circumstances it is unnecessary or inappropriate to do so (Trustee Act 2000, s 5(1)(3)).

The Trustee Act 2000, s 8 details the specific trustee powers in relation to land. A trustee may acquire freehold or leasehold land in the UK for investment, for occupation by a beneficiary or for any other reason. This power is subject to any restriction or exclusion imposed by the trust deed. These provisions apply to all trustees and not just to trustees of land. However, the provisions do not apply to a trust which consists of, or includes, settled land.

The provisions of the Trustee Act 2000 apply to a trust whether or not it was created before, or on or after, 1 February 2001. It is unclear whether the Act applies to trusts which are not in writing (such as constructive or resulting trusts) or to bare trusts. The better view appears to be that it does. Rather surprisingly, the Act does not widen the definition of investment derived from case law. Many assets popularly regarded as investments, such as life insurance policies and financial futures contracts are not investments within this definition.

The leading case on trustees' investment duties is *Cowan v Scargill, [1984] 2 All ER 750*. Arthur Scargill, as trustee of the Mineworkers' Pension Scheme, brought proceedings against the union trustees, seeking directions whether they were in breach of their fiduciary duties by investing funds outside the UK and in oil and gas interests which competed with coal. The challenge failed. The Vice-Chancellor Sir Robert Megarry's comments summarise the position of trustees as regards investment duties in general:

> '[The] trustees [have] to exercise their powers in the best interests of the present and future beneficiaries of the trust, holding the scales impartially between different classes of beneficiaries . . . When the purpose of the trust is to provide financial benefits for the beneficiaries, as is usually the case, the best interests of the beneficiaries are normally their best financial interests. In the case of a power of investment . . . the power must be exercised so as to yield the best return for the beneficiaries, judged in relation to the risks of the investment in question; and the prospects of the yield of income and capital appreciation both have to be considered in judging the return from investment . . . .'

Case law also imposes on the trustees a duty to keep investments under review to the same extent as would a reasonably prudent businessman in respect of his own affairs. This principle has now been given statutory expression by the Trustee Act 2000. Although a trustees' general duty of investment is now founded in statute, older case law will continue to give valuable guidance on the application of general principles to various situations.

Accounts

3.12 Trustees are under a duty to maintain accounts, and produce them to the beneficiaries on request. Whilst the trustees are not obliged to provide beneficiaries with free copies of the accounts, this has evolved into normal practice. Beneficiaries with interests in the capital of the trust are entitled to see capital accounts, whereas income beneficiaries may see full accounts.

Under Trustee Act 1925, s 22 trustees may arrange for their accounts to be audited once every three years, unless good cause exists to increase the regularity. The audit fees will be payable by the trust. It is unusual for trust deeds to require trusts to be audited. Audit investigations can be instigated by either trustees or beneficiaries, by agreement or by the Public Trustee under the terms of the Public Trustee Rules 1912.

Distributing trust assets

3.13 Although it may appear self-evident, trustees are under a positive duty to distribute trust assets to the correct beneficiaries. Where there is an overpayment of income or capital is payable in instalments, adjustments can usually be made to later payments. The trustees can recover trust property where the payment is made to the wrong person, due to a mistake arising from an issue of fact rather than one of law. An aggrieved beneficiary, as well as having recourse against the trustees, can seek to trace the property given to the wrong person by the beneficiaries. This right extends to the proceeds of sale of the property concerned. However, it does not extend to the property itself where a *bona fide* purchaser for value has acquired it, without notice of the breach of trust.

Where trustees have acted honestly and responsibly, they may claim relief against liability for breach of trust in distributing property incorrectly under Trustee Act 1925, s 61. In any event it is good practice for the trustees to seek an indemnity from beneficiaries upon the trustees presenting their final accounts on termination of a trust. However, the trustees do not have an absolute right to such an indemnity or other discharge.

Duty not to profit

3.14 Owing to the strict fiduciary nature of trusteeship, there is no entitlement to fees or remuneration other than those authorised in the trust deed itself, by a court or by statute. Trustees must not place themselves in a position of conflict as regards their fiduciary duties. They cannot purchase trust property, or derive any benefit from it, unless expressly permitted by the trust instrument.

However, the Trustee Act 2000, s 28 gives a power to receive reasonable remuneration to any trustee which is a trust corporation or a professional person where no contrary intention is expressed. It is also made expressly clear that remuneration does not constitute a gift which would otherwise cause problems if the spouse of an executor and trustee under a will is witness to its execution.

3.15 Introduction to Trust Law

Where there are no existing charging provisions in the trust, professional trustees and trust corporations other than charities can now receive reasonable remuneration for services provided to or on behalf of the trust if the other trustees so agree (Trustee Act 2000, s 29).

Trustees' decisions

3.15 Trustees can only exercise powers which are available to them either under the terms of the general law including any statutory provisions, or the express wording of the trust deed itself. Even where sufficient powers do exist, an effective decision will only be made where the trustees have directed their minds to the issues. Trustees have to consider all the circumstances of the case, and especially the legal consequences of any proposed course of action.

Trustees must make their own decisions, unless they are authorised to delegate them. A failure to make their own decisions will result in a purported disposition of trust property being a nullity, as seen in *Turner v Turner, [1983] 2 All ER 745*. The Trusts of Land and Appointment of Trustees Act 1996, s 9 allows trustees of a trust of land to delegate 'any of their functions as trustees which relate to the land' to a life tenant.

The Trustee Act 2000 provides that trustees may authorise any person to exercise any or all of their delegable functions as their agent. A distinction is made between charitable and non-charitable trusts. This chapter will deal only with non-charitable trusts.

The trustees' delegable functions consist of any function other than

(a) any function relating to whether or in what way any assets of the trust should be distributed;

(b) any power to decide whether any fees or other payment due to be made out of the trust funds should be made out of income or capital;

(c) any power to appoint a person to be a trustee of the trust; or

(d) any power conferred by any other enactment or the trust instrument which permits the trustees to delegate any of their functions or to appoint a person to act as a nominee or custodian.

The persons whom the trustees may authorise to exercise functions as their agent include one or more of their number, and a person who is also appointed to act as their nominee or custodian. A beneficiary cannot be authorised by the trustees to exercise any function as their agent, even if the beneficiary is also a trustee. In addition, two or more persons can only be authorised to exercise the same function if they are to exercise the function jointly.

The statutory duty of care is limited to trustees only. It does not apply to an agent in the performance of his agency, although he will owe a separate duty of care to the trust under the general law of agency. Where a person is authorised under these provisions to exercise a function, whatever the terms of the agency, he is subject to any specific duties or restrictions attached to the function. A person who is authorised to exercise a power subject to a requirement to obtain advice is not subject to that requirement if he is the kind of person from whom it would have been proper for the trustees, in compliance with the requirement, to obtain advice, for example, a reputable independent financial adviser.

Where the trustees have a duty to consult beneficiaries and to give effect to their wishes, the trustees may not authorise a person to exercise any of their functions on terms that prevent them from complying with that duty. The duty is not delegable.

The trustees are able to authorise a person as their agent on such terms as to remuneration and other matters as they may determine. The trustees may not authorise a person to exercise functions as their agent on the following terms unless it is reasonably necessary for them to do so.

(i) A term permitting the agent to appoint a substitute.

(ii) A term restricting the liability of the agent or his substitute to the trustees or any beneficiary.

(iii) A term permitting the agent to act in circumstances capable of giving rise to a conflict of interest.

Where asset management functions are delegated by the trustees, a person may not be authorised by the trustees to exercise any of their asset management functions as their agent except by an agreement which is in writing or evidenced in writing. In addition, the trustees must first prepare a policy statement which gives guidance as to how the functions should be exercised in the best interests of the trust. This must be in, or evidenced in, writing. The agreement under which the agent is to act must include a term to the effect that the agent will secure compliance with the policy statement or, if the policy statement is revised or replaced, the revised or replacement policy statement.

In addition, trustees may appoint a person to act as their nominee in relation to such of the assets of the trust as they determine (other than settled land), and may take the necessary steps to secure that those assets are vested in a person so appointed. Similarly, trustees may appoint a person to act as a custodian in relation to certain assets of the trust. In both cases, the appointment must be in writing or evidenced in writing. These provisions do not apply to any trust having a custodian trustee.

The appointment of a nominee or custodian is subject to certain restrictions. A person may not be appointed as a nominee or custodian unless one of the following conditions is satisfied.

1. The person carries on a business which consists of or includes acting as a nominee or custodian.

2. The person is a body corporate which is controlled by the trustees.

3. The person is a body corporate recognised under the Administration of Justice Act 1985.

The trustees may appoint as a nominee or custodian one of their number, if a trust corporation, or two or more of their number, if they are to act as joint nominees or joint custodians. The person appointed as nominee or custodian

3.15 *Introduction to Trust Law*

may also be appointed as custodian or nominee, as the case may be, or be authorised to exercise functions as the trustees' agent.

Generally, the trustees may determine the terms on which a person is appointed to act as a nominee or custodian as they so wish. They may not, however, appoint a person to act as a nominee or custodian on any of the following terms unless it is reasonably necessary for them to do so.

(i) A term permitting the nominee or custodian to appoint a substitute

(ii) A term restricting the liability of the nominee or custodian or his substitute to the trustees or any beneficiary

(iii) A term permitting the nominee or custodian to act in circumstances capable of giving rise to a conflict of interest.

There are statutory provisions relating to the review of, and liability for, agents, nominees and custodians. These apply whether they were authorised or appointed under the Trustee Act, or under the trust instrument or by any enactment or any provision of subordinate legislation.

Whilst the agent, nominee or custodian continues to act for the trust

(*a*) the trustees must keep under review the arrangements under which the agent, nominee or custodian acts, and how those arrangements are being put into effect;

(*b*) if circumstances make it appropriate to do so, the trustees must consider whether there is a need to exercise any power of intervention that they have; and

(*c*) if the trustees consider that there is a need to exercise such a power, they must do so.

An agent authorised to exercise asset management functions has a duty of review which includes, in particular

(i) a duty to consider whether there is any need to revise or replace the policy statement;

(ii) if the trustees consider that there is a need to revise or replace the policy statement, a duty to do so; and

(iii) a duty to assess whether the policy statement (as it has effect for the time being) is being complied with.

A trustee is not liable for any act or default of an agent, nominee or custodian unless he has failed to comply with the duty of care applicable to him either when entering into the arrangements under which the person acts as agent, nominee or custodian or when carrying out his duty of review.

Where a trustee has agreed a term under which the agent, nominee or custodian is permitted to appoint a substitute, the trustee is not liable for any act or default of the substitute unless he has failed to comply with the duty of care applicable to him when agreeing that term or when carrying out his duty of review insofar as it relates to the use of the substitute.

Introduction to Trust Law **3.16**

There are wider obligations placed upon trustees of land to consult beneficiaries and give effect to their wishes so far as is consistent with the general interest of the trust (Trusts of Land and Appointment of Trustees Act 1996, s 11).

It is important to identify those powers which have to be exercised, and those where an element of discretion is present. In simple terms, the former are known as trust powers and the latter as mere powers. There are also a class of intermediate powers which are somewhere 'betwixt and between' these two categories.

(*a*) *Trust powers*. These are obligatory, in that there is a direct legal requirement for the trustees to exercise them. This obligation arises from the intention of the settlor, and the courts will enforce these powers if the trustees do not exercise them.

(*b*) *Mere powers*. These impose an obligation on the trustees to consider whether the power should be exercised, but they are under no obligation to exercise it. They only need consider exercising the power where it would be appropriate to do so.

In the case of a trust power, the trustees have to make a decision within a reasonable length of time. However, in the case of a mere power the trustees simply have to consider periodically whether or not to exercise the power, and, if they think it is proper, to exercise it within a reasonable period of time.

The length of time the trustees can delay in taking a decision is unclear. In the case of a mere power, they will lose the ability to exercise it after a reasonable period of time unless there are special circumstances. By way of contrast, in the case of a trust power, this continues to be exercisable albeit only in favour of those beneficiaries who would have been eligible to benefit had the power been exercised promptly. Where the trustees fail to execute a trust power, a court itself will, if necessary, exercise it or procure its execution. In a case of a mere power a court is extremely reluctant to interfere unless it is clear that the trustees are acting improperly, or simply not addressing their minds to the issue.

The Hastings- Bass principle

3.16   In the case of *Hastings- Bass (deceased), [1975] Ch 25* it was held that the court would interfere with an exercise of a trustee's power where it was clear that the trustees would have acted differently had they fully appreciated the consequences of their actions. In the case of *Re Mettoy, [1990] 1 WLR 1587* the principle was better stated as

> 'Where a trustee acts under a discretion given to him by the terms of the trust, the court will interfere with his action if it is clear that he would not have acted as he did had he not failed to take into account considerations which he ought to have taken into account.'

This principle has been used in a number of cases to avoid disastrous unforeseen consequences such as in *Abacus Trust Company (Isle of Man) Ltd v NSPCC, [2001] STC 1344* where a deed of appointment made by the trustees was void *ab initio* on the grounds that they had failed to take into

3.17 *Introduction to Trust Law*

account the tax consequences of making the appointment as advised by leading counsel. The principle does, however, have its limits. In *Breadner v Granville-Grossman [2001] Ch 523*, Park J refused to set aside a power of appointment exercised by trustees one day after the time limit for its exercise had expired. On the evidence, they would have exercised the power to appoint particular trusts had they properly appreciated the time limit. It was held that the setting aside the exercise of the power would in this case have been an unwarranted extension of the principle. It would not be declaring a decision of the trustees to be void, but rather declaring they should be treated as having exercised it at some other time. Park J said that

> 'It cannot be right that whenever trustees do something which they later regret and think that they ought not to have done, they can say that they never did it in the first place.'

In the recently reported case of *Green and others v Cobham and others, Ch D 2000, [2002] STC 820* the principle was successfully applied. The High Court held that there was no room to doubt that had the then trustees of the will trust under consideration had regard to the possible capital gains tax consequences of an appointment which they had made, they would not have gone ahead with it. It followed that this was a clear case for the application of the principle in *Re Hastings-Bass* which required the court to interfere, by declaring the 1990 deed to be an invalid exercise of a trustee's power of appointment and consequently void in its entirety.

Whilst this principle can in certain circumstances be helpful to avoid disastrous consequences resulting from the trustees exercise of a power, it is clear that there are limitations as to when the courts will accept its use and cannot always be relied upon to unravel a trust.

Unanimity

3.17 The general rule is that trustees must make collective decisions. There is no 'majority rule' and all decisions must be unanimous. Where a difference of opinion arises, a trustee can quite validly endorse the views of the other trustees where he is relying on their greater experience or simply to avoid deadlock. The general rule will be overridden where the trust deed itself provides for majority decisions. Often in such cases the minority will have the right to record the fact that they dissented.

Common powers over income

3.18 Trustees may have powers to apply income in favour of beneficiaries and there are three main areas to consider.

(i) *Fixed entitlements*. Under many trusts, beneficiaries will have a definable and fixed interest in the trust's income. For example, X might be entitled to receive the income from the trust for his life with the remainder going to Y absolutely thereafter. Accordingly, the trustees have no discretion over the beneficiary's current entitlement, although they might have other powers under the trust deed permitting them to redirect the flow of income. This may be achieved

Introduction to Trust Law **3.19**

in the above example by establishing fresh trusts, so that Z thereafter becomes entitled for life instead of X.

(ii) *Powers of appointment.* In cases not within (i) above, principally involving discretionary trusts, trustees will have a power of appointment in respect of income. This will often enable them to allocate trust income amongst a wide class of potential beneficiaries, completely at their discretion. Usually the balance of any income retained is accumulated provided the accumulation period has not expired. This has the effect of transforming 'income' into trust capital. Where the accumulation period has expired, trustees cannot retain income and it has to be distributed amongst the income beneficiaries. However, trustees will usually retain an element of discretion as to who receives the income within this class.

(iii) *Powers of maintenance.* In the case of infant beneficiaries, it is quite common for express or implied trust powers to enable the trustees to apply income in their favour. Express drafting is less common in view of the statutory rules introduced by Trustee Act 1925, s 31. These statutory rules enabling trustees to maintain infant beneficiaries can be expressly or impliedly excluded, so great care is required in examining a trust deed in order to establish the trustees' powers. This aspect is considered in more detail below.

Common powers over capital

3.19 There are four common types of powers that trustees may exercise over capital in favour of beneficiaries.

(i) *Powers of appointment.* These are usually exercisable in favour of a limited class of persons or objects. Limitations created following their exercise are treated as written into the original trust instrument which created them; they do not normally create a new trust. Lord Romer explained in *Muir and Williams v Muir, (1943) AC 468* it 'is as though the settlor had left a blank in the settlement which [the donee of the special power of appointment]. . . fills up for him if and when the power . . . is exercised'. In some cases a special power of appointment can expressly or by necessary implication authorise trustees to remove assets from the original settlement, by making them subject to the trusts of a separate settlement.

(ii) *Transfers between settlements.* It is common practice to include wide powers of appointment or expressly authorise transfers between settlements. Some older trust deeds contain narrow powers of appointment which will not enable trust assets to be transferred to another settlement.

(iii) *Powers of allocation.* Such powers enable trustees to 'shuffle' assets amongst various beneficiaries within the overall framework of the existing trusts without enabling the trustees to establish fresh or overriding trusts.

(iv) *Powers of advancement.* Advances, whether under an express power or statutory rules, are not solely limited to outright payments or transfers to beneficiaries. They can include settled advances, altering or varying the trusts created by the settlement from which it was derived. This aspect is considered in more detail below.

Beneficiaries' rights

3.20 Beneficiaries do not have an automatic right to interfere with the administration of a trust the affairs of which are being properly run. However, where the trust administration is not being carried out correctly, the beneficiary can take steps to ensure proper administration and preserve his interests under the trust. This will almost invariably involve the assistance of the court. When a beneficiary considers that a trust is not being properly administered he can apply to the court either as regards specific issues, or generally. Similarly, a beneficiary can apply to the court where the trustees fail to take steps to preserve the trust assets. The right of application to the court has been considerably widened in respect of beneficiaries with an interest in property subject to a trust of land (Trusts of Land and Appointment of Trustees Act 1996, s 14). A beneficiary also has the right to see trust documents and records and this is a proprietary right which exists independently of whether a court action has been commenced. Minutes recording the reasons for trustees exercising their discretion are generally private to the trustees.

The courts will not support attempts by the beneficiaries to limit or fetter the exercise of the trustees' discretion. In *Brockbank (Re), Ch D [1948] 1 All ER 287* the beneficiaries were ascertainable and legally competent. Due to a disagreement with the existing trustee they wanted to appoint a new trustee. The court held that the power of appointing a new trustee was exercisable by the existing trustees, and that the beneficiaries could not usurp this discretion. However, where all the beneficiaries were known and of full age and capacity, they could bring a trust to an end or alter it. In the event that some of the beneficiaries have insufficient legal capacity, or where there is a prospect of as yet unascertained or unknown beneficiaries benefiting under the trust, the necessary consent for terminating or varying the trust will have to be given by the court. As a result of Trusts of Land and Appointment of Trustees Act 1996, s 19 beneficiaries under a trust who are of full age and capacity and together absolutely entitled to the trust property, in the absence of any person nominated to appoint new trustees in the trust deed may give a written direction that a trustee retire from the trust or that a specified person be appointed as a new trustee.

Focus on: power of maintenance

3.21 The Trustee Act 1925, s 31(1) provides trustees with an implied statutory power of maintenance where trust property is held for an infant beneficiary. This enables the trustees to pay trust income to the child's parents or guardian or otherwise apply it for their education, maintenance

Introduction to Trust Law **3.23**

or benefit. In exercising their discretion the trustees have to consider the availability of any other fund which could be used, together with the legal obligations of any other person to maintain or educate the child. Any income which is not paid or applied in this manner has to be accumulated 'in the way of compound interest' by investing it, and any resulting income, in authorised investments (section 31(2)). However, the trustees are able to apply such accumulations, or any part of them, as if they were income arising in the current year. This power is particularly interesting as it must represent one of the limited number of ways of converting capital into income for tax purposes, following *Stevenson v Wishart and Others (Levy's Trustees), CA [1987] STC 266; [1987] 2 All ER 428.*

Income at majority

3.22 Another key feature of the statutory power of maintenance for minors is that Trustee Act 1925, s 31(1)(ii) provides that where a beneficiary has not already attained a vested interest in the trust income by the age of 18, the trustees must immediately pay to him the income of that property and any accumulations until either he attains a vested interest in income, he dies or his interest fails. This is particularly important in the context of accumulation and maintenance settlements within IHTA 1984, s 71.

Excluding Trustee Act 1925, s 31

3.23 It is important to appreciate that Trustee Act 1925, s 31 cannot apply in any event where the trust predates 1926, and more importantly that it can be expressly or impliedly excluded by the trust instrument itself (*Turner's Will Trust (Re), [1937] Ch 15; [1936] 2 All ER 1435*). This last attribute can make the provision extremely hard to 'pin down' and establish whether or not it does apply to a particular trust with any degree of certainty. In *Delamere's Settlement Trusts (Re), CA 1983, [1984] 1 WLR 813; [1984] 1 All ER 584*, Lord Justice Slade said:

> 'The present case well illustrates that the existence of section 31 . . . for all its obvious advantages and uses, could in one sense, be said to present a potential trap . . . In many cases the draftsmen may well be advised out of caution either expressly to provide that the section is to apply with or without stated modifications, or expressly to exclude its application altogether.'

This power cannot apply where another beneficiary has a prior entitlement to receive the trust income; similarly an express direction to accumulate the whole of the trust's income would have the effect of excluding the statutory power. In addition, the provision has no application where income is distributable amongst a discretionary class of beneficiaries.

Unlike the statutory power of advancement considered below, the statutory power of maintenance will apply irrespective of the type of assets held by the trust. However, like the statutory power of advancement it is quite common for the draftsman to 'tinker' with the terms of the statutory power of maintenance in the instrument itself, usually extending the trustees' discretion

3.24 *Introduction to Trust Law*

so that they can apply income whilst disregarding other sources of income which might be available for these purposes.

The statutory power also has a curious side effect of apparently converting what appear to be vested income interests into contingent interests.

> *Example 1*
>
> Unless otherwise expressly or impliedly excluded under the terms of the trust, Trustee Act 1925, s 31 will apply in the circumstances listed below. As a result of the provision, all the beneficiaries can only benefit from the trust income at the discretion of the trustees whilst they are under the age of 18. The balance of any income will be accumulated.
>
> (a)   Income to Anne for life.
>
> (b)   Income to Brian for life if he attains twenty-five.
>
> (c)   Trust funds to Claudia absolutely if she attains eighteen.
>
> (d)   Trust funds to Donald absolutely if he attains twenty-five.

Entitlement to accumulations

3.24 A beneficiary's entitlement to income accumulations will be primarily governed by the trust instrument. Where there is no such direction, a beneficiary with a vested income entitlement will become entitled to the accumulations on attaining 18 or marrying under that age. Similarly he or she will become entitled to the accumulations on attaining 18, or marrying under that age, if as a result he or she thereby becomes entitled to the trust's capital.

> *Example 2*
>
> Continuing *Example 1*, each beneficiary's entitlement to income accumulations is as follows.
>
> (a)   Anne has a vested income entitlement and will be entitled to income accumulations on attaining 18. If she dies under that age, accumulations will be added to capital.
>
> (b)   Brian has an interest contingent on attaining 25. Accordingly, irrespective of whether Brian attains 18 or not, accumulations will be added to capital.
>
> (c)   Claudia has an interest contingent on attaining eighteen, at which time she will be absolutely entitled to the trust capital. As a result she will also receive the income accumulations at that time. If she dies under that age, the accumulations are added to trust capital.
>
> (d)   Donald's position is the same as Brian's in (b) above.

Focus on: power of advancement

3.25 The implied statutory power of advancement contained in Trustee Act 1925, s 32 represents an invaluable planning tool to those concerned with estate planning for the private client. The power enables trustees to pay or apply trust capital to or for the benefit of those entitled to the trust capital. In this context it does not matter whether the right to participate in trust capital is to some or all of the property or that the interest itself is absolute or simply contingent upon some occurrence. Although the power has a number of important limitations, its great value is its flexibility — particularly in the case of settled advances.

Advancement and benefit have special meanings.

Advancement

3.26 Viscount Radcliffe in *Pilkington's Will Trust (Re), 41 ATC 285; [1962] 3 All ER 622* perhaps best summarised the meaning.

> '[the] word "advancement" itself meant in this context the establishment in life of the beneficiary who was the object of the power, or at any rate some step that would contribute to the furtherance of his establishment.'

He cited typical instances of such expenditure in the nineteenth century as being 'an apprenticeship or the purchase of a commission in the army or an interest in business. In the case of a girl, there could be an advancement on marriage'. However, the word does also have a slightly restrictive inference. Viscount Radcliffe commented that advancement had to some extent a limited range of meaning since it was thought to convey the idea of some step in life of permanent significance. There was a suggestion in another case that advancement would only really be appropriate where the recipient was starting to make his way in life (*Kershaw's Trust (Re), 1868 LR 6 Eq 322*). In reality, it is not clear how relevant these cases might be in the modern context, and in any event the question is largely redundant because of the width given to the meaning of the word 'benefit'.

Benefit

3.27 The actual scope of the term 'benefit' is immense being 'the widest possible word one could have' (*Moxon's Will Trust (Re), [1958] 1 All ER 386; [1958] 1 WLR 165*). It includes outright applications to the beneficiary direct as well as trustees settling funds on new trusts for a beneficiary (*Pilkington's Will Trust (Re), 41 ATC 285; [1962] 3 All ER 622*) even where the objective is to save tax (*Re Moxon's Will Trust* above). Also, in order to mitigate the charge to tax, an advancement can still be for the benefit of a beneficiary despite his not taking any direct financial interest in the property advanced (*Clore's Settlement Trust (Re), [1966] 1 WLR 955; [1966] 2 All ER 272*). Indeed, 'benefit' need not meet a 'need'. As a result, an advance of funds to establish a new trust for a beneficiary is perfectly proper irrespective of whether the beneficiary actually requires access to those funds.

When does Trustee Act 1925, s 32 apply?

3.28 The provision of Trustee Act 1925, s 32 can be expressly or impliedly excluded by the provisions of the trust instrument. For example, an express power of advancement contained in the trust deed which does

3.29 Introduction to Trust Law

not refer to 'benefit' has been held to exclude the wider statutory provision (*Evan's Settlement (Re), [1967] 1 WLR 1294; [1967] 3 All ER 343*) whilst in *CIR v Bernstein, CA 1960, 39 TC 391; [1960]1 All ER 320*, a provision for accumulation was held to have the same effect.

The scope of the statutory power is also quite narrow. It only applies to trusts created or effective after the enactment of the Trustee Act 1925. It will not apply to capital money arising under the Settled Land Act 1925. However, it will apply to trusts of land. In a well-drafted trust deed it is quite common for the statutory power to be widened. Usually this relates to the requirement for consent by a beneficiary with a prior interest, and to enable the trustees to advance up to the entire expectant interest concerned. Both these aspects are considered below.

Statutory limits

3.29 Trustee Act 1925, s 32 cannot be exercised without the prior written consent of a beneficiary who is of full age and legal capacity and who would be prejudiced by the advancement. Following the case of *Forster's Settlement (Re), [1942] 1 All ER 180* a power will be improperly exercised where there has been a failure to obtain the consent of a beneficiary who is incapable of being contacted, the court having no jurisdiction to provide the consent required.

The statutory power can only be validly exercised if no more than half of a beneficiary's vested or presumptive share is advanced. The value of the trust fund taken into account is the value at the time of the actual advance itself. As a result, if the value of the fund subsequently increases but a beneficiary has already received his maximum entitlement under the statutory power, no more can be advanced. Similarly, if the value of the trust assets decreases after a beneficiary has received his maximum entitlement — so that retrospectively it appears that he or she has received far too much — the other beneficiaries would not be able to challenge the prior advancement solely on these grounds.

Another limiting factor is the requirement that any advance must be brought into account as part of the share. However, if a beneficiary never becomes absolutely entitled, for example, because his interest ultimately fails, there is no liability to repay the amount advanced or bring it into account.

Settled advances

3.30 Trustees are able to advance funds on new trusts for the benefit of an individual beneficiary. There are, however, two limitations that have to be considered, namely the range of the powers possessed by the new trustees and the perpetuity period.

The trustees must take into account all the terms of the new trusts — and in so doing they must look not only at those under which the new trustees are likely to act in practice but all the provisions. Viscount Radcliffe outlined the starting point in *Pilkington's Will Trust (Re), 41 ATC 285; [1962] 3 All ER 622*:

'The law is not that trustees cannot delegate: it is that trustees cannot delegate unless they have authority to do so. If the power of advancement which they possess is so read as to allow them to raise money for the purpose of having it settled, then they do have the necessary authority to let the money pass out of the old settlement into the new trusts.'

It is therefore necessary to look at the power being used to determine if trust assets can be passed to new trustees who also possess particularly wide dispositive powers. In the context of the section 32 power, it may be unlikely that an advance could be made to a purely discretionary trust.

As regards the perpetuity period, a power of advancement is treated in very much the same way as a special power of appointment. The perpetuity period for the property settled by the advance must be tested by reference to the provisions of the original trust instrument. However, the 'wait and see' test under the Perpetuities and Accumulations Act 1964 will only apply where the original settlement itself was constituted after 15 July 1964.

Focus on: protective trusts

3.31 The Trustee Act 1925, s 33 provides the statutory mechanism for creating protective trusts. By simply referring to the term 'protective trusts' a draftsman can incorporate the trust provisions set out in section 33. The effect of the Insolvency Act 1986 must, however, be considered.

Protective or spendthrift trusts are particularly useful where a settlor has real concerns over the financial stability or maturity of a beneficiary. Since the problems experienced in the Lloyd's insurance market, these have become more popular.

The statutory provisions state that where income (including an annuity) is held on protective trusts for the benefit of a person (called 'the principal beneficiary') for a period of his life or a lesser period of time ('the trust period') then the income will be held on the following trusts.

(*a*) Upon trust for the principal beneficiary during the trust period or until some event occurs whereby that beneficiary would lose the right to receive the income concerned. (This would extend, for example, to situations where the principal beneficiary purported to sell his interest or where he becomes bankrupt.)

(*b*) If the trust fails or determines during the trust period, then the income is to be held on trust for the remaining period for the maintenance and support of

   (i)   the principal beneficiary and his or her immediate family; or

   (ii) the principal beneficiary and the persons who would be entitled to the trust property and income if he were dead, provided that the principal beneficiary is not married and has no issue in existence.

The statutory wording can be modified by the trust instrument, and can only apply to trust instruments that post-date the Trustee Act 1925. In practice, a

3.31 *Introduction to Trust Law*

great deal of care has to be taken when dealing with such trusts not to inadvertently trigger the protective discretionary element. For example, in *Dennis's Settlement Trusts (Re) [1942] 1 All ER 520* the execution by a principal beneficiary of a deed varying the terms of a protective trust caused the protective discretionary trusts to come into play. However, section 33(1)(i) expressly provides that advances under any express or statutory power will not bring the discretionary trusts to come into operation.

4 Creating Settlements

Introduction

4.1 Settling assets on accumulation and maintenance or interest in possession settlements is often used as a means of passing assets to succeeding generations free of inheritance tax. Such transfers will only become chargeable to inheritance tax if the settlor dies within seven years of making them. Therefore, until this condition is fulfilled they remain potentially exempt transfers.

Transfers to discretionary settlements are immediately chargeable and are not potentially exempt transfers.

The 'reservation of benefits' rules, however, make it imperative that assets which are given away are surplus to the donor's immediate and future requirements either as a source of income or as capital. Any arrangement permitting the donor to benefit from, or have recourse to, assets given away may cause those assets still to be treated as forming part of his estate when he dies.

Why not an outright gift?

4.2 An outright gift to an individual is the most straightforward method of making a potentially exempt transfer (IHTA 1984, s 3A(1)(c)). Administratively this form of gift is the least burdensome; the asset is dealt with by the donee as he thinks fit and any income arising from the asset belongs to him and will be taxed as such (unless, under the provisions of ICTA 1988, s 660B the income is treated as the donor's because the donee is his own child who is unmarried and under 18).

However, an individual may not wish to make an outright gift relinquishing all control over the future application of the property given away. The donees may be too young to manage their financial affairs or indeed to hold property or they may be irresponsible in financial matters. Assets given outright will subsequently pass under the will or intestacy of the donee and the devolution of property in this way may not accord with a donor's intentions. The donor may wish to retain some influence over the property to be given away (particularly, for example, shares in a family company or land adjacent to his retained property) by remaining a trustee of a settlement to which the property is transferred. He may wish to postpone the time when a donee becomes entitled as of right to income, providing in the meantime for its accumulation,

4.2 Creating Settlements

or he may wish capital to be preserved until a beneficiary has established himself in a career, or marries, or wishes to purchase a property. In these circumstances an accumulation and maintenance settlement or an interest in possession settlement may be the appropriate vehicle to enable the donor to give assets away.

The donor may anticipate the birth of further intended beneficiaries and may, as yet, be uncertain as to the proportions in which he would wish the intended beneficiaries to benefit. These considerations may suggest that an accumulation and maintenance settlement or a discretionary settlement would best achieve the donor's wishes.

The creation of a settlement may therefore enable a person to give earlier than he might otherwise have thought fit to do if the making of an outright gift were the only means of giving. It may also enable him to arrange the acquisition and ownership of assets within the family in the most efficient manner even though those for whom the assets are held should not (as yet) or could not hold those assets for themselves absolutely.

The unification of the rates of income tax and capital gains tax in 1998/99 tipped the balance further in favour of gifts into settlements rather than outright to individuals. Since 1998/99 there has been a uniform rate of capital gains tax at 34% on trustees of settled property (the chargeable gain being progressively reduced by taper relief depending on the length of ownership after 5 April 1998 and the reduction being more generous for business assets as opposed to non-business assets). Since 6 April 1999, tax credits attached to dividend income cannot be included in the 'tax pool' of discretionary trusts. The net result is that where a discretionary trust fully distributes its dividend income to a beneficiary paying higher rate tax, the total tax suffered on the gross income will be 46%, a significant tax penalty on discretionary trusts.

One other factor to be considered before establishing a settlement is the capital gains tax position on a transfer of assets to the settlement. Gifts of any types of assets to a discretionary settlement will qualify for hold-over relief (TCGA 1992, s 260(2)(a)), whereas gifts to other forms of settlement and outright gifts to individuals will only qualify if the assets are essentially 'business assets' within TCGA 1992, s 165. This is examined in more detail under 4.21 below.

This chapter considers principally the creation of settlements having trustees resident in the UK by a settlor who is domiciled and resident in this country and whose beneficiaries are likewise domiciled and resident and will remain so. Chapter 6 *Offshore Trusts* considers the creation of offshore settlements. Other aspects of settlements are dealt with in chapter 5 *Existing Settlements*, chapter 18 *Investing Abroad*, chapter 19 *Immigration and Emigration* and chapter 20 *The Foreign Client*.

Provisions were introduced in the Finance Act 1998 to prevent the use of trusts for tax avoidance. It is important to appreciate that estate planning is a long term programme. Anyone considering setting up a settlement should therefore consider not only its tax effect in the short term but also its likely tax effects over the coming years.

Creating Settlements **4.5**

What is a settlement? — general principles of tax law

Definitions

4.3 A settlement is defined for inheritance tax purposes as any disposition of property which is:

(a) held in trust for persons in succession or for any person subject to a contingency; or

(b) held upon trust to accumulate the whole or part of the income of the property. The accumulation of income may be obligatory or only possible by the exercise of a power to accumulate income surplus to that paid out by the trustees for the benefit of any persons; or

(c) charged with the payment of an annuity or similar payment for any period

(IHTA 1984, s 43).

A lease granted for life or lives or for a period ascertainable only by reference to a death will also be treated as a settlement unless full consideration is paid.

For capital gains tax purposes settled property is any property held on trust other than property held for any person absolutely entitled as against the trustee or held for any person who would be so entitled but for being a minor or under a disability (TCGA 1992, ss 60, 68).

Bare trusts

4.4 Property held on bare trusts (i.e. property held by a trustee as nominee for another where all the beneficiaries have absolute interests) does not fall within the definition of settled property for either inheritance tax or capital gains tax purposes. The use of bare trusts should not, however, be overlooked — see chapter 2 *Lifetime Planning* under paragraph 2.24.

Fixed interest trusts and discretionary settlements

4.5 The terms upon which trustees hold assets for the benefit of individual beneficiaries fall broadly into two categories.

(a) Those under which a beneficiary is entitled to the income from the whole or a fixed share of the trust fund irrespective of whether or not he will become entitled to a fixed share of the capital of the fund, e.g. on attaining a specified age or on the happening of some event (commonly known as fixed interest trusts).

(b) Those under which the distribution of capital and income between a class of beneficiaries is determined (in whole or part) at the discretion of the trustees (known as discretionary settlements).

Settlements may, of course, change from one category to another during their existence.

4.6 Creating Settlements

Inheritance tax

4.6 The inheritance tax treatment of settlements draws similar distinctions. The beneficiary under a fixed interest trust who is entitled to the income as it arises from the whole or part of the trust fund is treated as owning the capital to the income of which he is entitled. In the words of the inheritance tax legislation, he has an 'interest in possession' (IHTA 1984, s 49), irrespective of whether or not he has any prospective entitlement to that capital.

There is an important distinction between a 'fixed interest' (a term which does not appear in the taxation legislation) and an 'interest in possession' (which does but is not defined). The decision in *Pearson & Others v CIR, HL [1980] STC 318; 2 All ER 479* established that only a beneficiary who has an immediate entitlement to income as it arises, net only of proper income-related trust expenses, has an interest in possession. Any dispositive powers of the trustees which may be exercised to withhold income from a beneficiary or direct it to another will prevent the beneficiary from having such an interest. Thus, the trustees' power to accumulate the income of the beneficiary's share of the trust fund prevented the beneficiary from having an interest in possession for the purposes of (then) capital transfer tax in *Pearson v IRC*. The beneficiary could not demand that the income as it arose from her share was paid to her. Nevertheless the beneficiary had a 'fixed interest' in the settlement.

Property held on trusts

(*a*) under which no beneficiary is entitled to an interest in possession, and

(*b*) in respect of which no favoured treatment is available,

is called 'relevant property' (IHTA 1984, s 58). Such trusts can include therefore not only discretionary trusts but also some fixed interest trusts. Relevant property is subject to inheritance tax charges. These are a ten-yearly charge at three tenths of one half of the rates of inheritance tax applicable to chargeable transfers on death and intermediate charges on property leaving the settlement in the interim.

Within these two broad classes of settlement there are further sub-categories for inheritance tax purposes.

Accumulation and maintenance settlements

4.7 An accumulation and maintenance settlement receives favoured treatment. No ten-yearly charges to inheritance tax are imposed provided the beneficiaries become entitled to their share of capital, or to an interest in possession in it, on or before attaining 25. This is considered in more detail at 4.23 below.

Settlements for disabled persons

4.8 Settlements for disabled persons within IHTA 1984, s 89 are treated as settlements in which the disabled person has an interest in possession, even if the property is in fact held upon trusts which would fall

Creating Settlements **4.10**

within the 'relevant property' regime or (as it is commonly called) the 'discretionary trust' regime during the life of the disabled person. There is a condition, however, that at least half of the settled property distributed during the lifetime of the disabled person is applied for his benefit. These types of settlement are considered in more detail below.

Protective trusts

4.9 A protective trust is a trust of a type within or similar to those described in Trustee Act 1925, s 33 which provides that a life tenant's interest in income will divest if he attempts to charge or assign his interest or is declared bankrupt. If any of these events happen, the income will be held on discretionary trusts for the benefit of the life tenant, his or her spouse and his or her children and remoter issue. If a life tenant of property held on protective trusts for his benefit attempts to alienate his interest, IHTA 1984, s 88 prevents the discretionary trust regime from applying to the discretionary trusts which then arise. Instead, the protected life tenant is treated as continuing to have an interest in possession.

Capital gains tax

4.10 The capital gains tax rules relating to settlements similarly distinguish between

(*a*) those settlements under which a beneficiary is entitled to a life interest i.e. the income from, or use of, the trust property (whether for his own life, that of another or any other period); and

(*b*) those under which no beneficiary is so entitled (TCGA 1992, s 72).

A life interest does not include any right contingent on the exercise of a discretion by the trustees or some other person, nor an annuity charged on settled property (unless a fund is appropriated by the trustees as a fund out of which the annuity is payable and there is no right of recourse to settled property, other than that fund, for payment of the annuity).

This distinction is drawn to permit the same capital gains tax uplift on death in the base cost of assets held in a settlement in which a life interest subsists as would be available if the beneficiary had owned the assets absolutely. By virtue of TCGA 1992, ss 72, 73 this washing of unrealised gains accruing until the death of the beneficiary is permitted in the following circumstances when (subject to the provisions of section 74 of that Act, see 4.35 below) the life interest terminates, another beneficiary becomes absolutely entitled to the settled property or the property remains settled for the benefit of other beneficiaries.

Under TCGA 1992, ss 4, 5 a disposal by the trustees of assets held in the settlement is charged to capital gains tax regardless of whether they are actual sales of assets or deemed disposals by the trustees. Such deemed disposals arise when a beneficiary becomes absolutely entitled to the trust property as against the trustees and thereby being entitled to call for the transfer of those assets so that the property ceases to be settled property within the capital gains tax definition of that term; and when one set of trustees becomes absolutely

4.11 *Creating Settlements*

entitled to the trust property as against the original trustees, as where assets are advanced from one settlement into another.

If the settlor and his spouse cannot benefit from the settlement, the rate of capital gains tax payable by the trustees in respect of gains realised by them will be 34%, regardless of the type of settlement. If the settlor or his spouse has an interest or can benefit from a settlement, gains realised by the trustees will be taxed as the settlor's at his marginal rate.

In order to determine whether the capital gains tax liability is that of the trustees or of the settlor, it is important to consider the nature of the interests of the various beneficiaries of the settlement. The capital gains tax treatment of settlements corresponds fairly closely with their treatment for income tax purposes, as the capital gains tax provisions in part emulate the income tax 'settlement' provisions in ICTA 1988, Part XV.

A change in the interests of beneficiaries under a settlement (as, for example, where a beneficiary of an accumulation and maintenance settlement attains an interest in possession) is not a chargeable occasion for capital gains tax purposes.

Income tax

4.11 In general, as a result of the creation of a settlement, income arising from the assets settled will be taxed in the hands of the trustees only at the basic rate (currently 22%). However, the legislation distinguishes between settlements under which beneficiaries are entitled to the income from the trust property and those where it may be accumulated. ICTA 1988, s 686 subjects income which may be accumulated or paid out at the discretion of the trustees to the rate applicable to trusts (34%). The provisions of ICTA 1988, Part XV may operate to deem the trustees' income to belong to the settlor and these provisions should be carefully considered when a settlement is created.

In addition, the rates of income tax will differ depending upon the source of the income.

Preliminary considerations

Reservation of benefit

4.12 On the creation of a settlement, one must consider the inheritance tax 'reservation of benefit' rules in FA 1986, s 102. For trusts created after 17 March 1986, unless the settlor is excluded from benefit, he will be treated for inheritance tax purposes on death as beneficially entitled to the trust property. If the settlor's spouse is a beneficiary this will not in itself bring the reservation of benefit provisions into effect (FA 1986, s 102(5)(2)). However, property distributed from the trust and used for the benefit of both the settlor and his spouse will not be property enjoyed to the settlor's entire exclusion. The value of the gift is not even frozen at the date on which it is made. The current value of the property in which the benefit was reserved will be taken into account in calculating the inheritance tax charge. This charge may arise on death or, if the settlor is subsequently excluded from benefit but dies within seven years of the exclusion, on a potentially exempt transfer which as a result of his death becomes chargeable (subject to the provisions relating to double charges in such circumstances under The Inheritance Tax (Double Charges Relief) Regulations 1987). The provisions of FA 1986, Sch 20 para 5 ensure that the value of any property representing or deriving from the original property will be taken into account in order to calculate the charge to inheritance tax in such circumstances.

To ensure that the trust property is enjoyed to the exclusion of any benefit to the settlor the terms of the settlement require careful scrutiny. A settlor as trustee of his settlement may be remunerated for his service without giving rise to a reservation of benefit provided the remuneration is not excessive.

Further, the possibility of a benefit being reserved to the settlor as a result of the nature of the property given away must not be forgotten. For example, a service contract with unusually favourable terms as to remuneration or duration entered into between the settlor and his family company may, in the light of the gift, fall foul of the requirement that the property must be enjoyed to the entire exclusion of the donor and of any benefit to him by contract or otherwise (see CTO Advanced Instruction Manual D 48). Similarly, land given away which continues to be farmed by a partnership in which the donor is a partner may not be enjoyed to the exclusion of the donor unless a full rent is paid.

It will be important to analyse the subject matter of the gift carefully to determine whether a benefit has been reserved from property given away or whether the gift was of a lesser interest in that property. This is considered in more detail in chapter 2 *Lifetime Planning* under paragraph 2.15.

Part XV of the Income and Corporation Taxes Act 1988

4.13 The considerations which arise from the complex provisions in ICTA 1988, Part XV are closely related to the reservation of benefit rules although in some respects are more severe. These provisions must also be carefully considered in conjunction with the terms of the proposed settlement to ensure that the settlor *and his spouse* are excluded from all possible enjoyment and benefit, whether, for example, by loan of the trust property or because the property settled will revert to the settlor if all the trusts of the settlement fail (other than in the circumstances set out in ICTA 1988, s 660A(4)). If the settlor and his spouse are not excluded in this way, the settlor will be taxable on all the income arising to the trustees.

Sections 77–79 of the Taxation of Chargeable Gains Act 1992

4.14 The capital gains tax provisions relating to settlements in which the settlor has retained an interest must also be taken into account when selecting the type of settlement to be created. Generally, the effect of these provisions will be avoided provided care is taken to draft a settlement in such a way that neither the inheritance tax reservation of benefit provisions

4.15 *Creating Settlements*

nor the income tax provisions in ICTA 1988, Part XV will apply. If the intention is that the gains of the trustees should not be taxed as those of the settlor, care should be taken to ensure that neither the settlor nor his spouse have any rights to or prospect of benefiting — and indeed do not in practice benefit — from the income of the settlement or directly or indirectly from any property comprised in the settlement.

Duties of trustees and the terms of the settlement

4.15 An individual should understand that by creating a settlement he is giving assets to trustees to be held upon stated terms for the benefit of chosen beneficiaries. Although the donor (or his spouse) may be a trustee of a settlement, thereby retaining a measure of control over the assets given away, their actions must be governed by the terms of the settlement and their powers must be exercised and their duties carried out solely for the benefit of the beneficiaries. The donor must consider situations in which possible conflicts may arise between his interests and those of the beneficiaries. While a settlement of quoted shares is unlikely to give rise to such problems, settlements of unquoted shares frequently do.

The introduction of new shareholders to a family company may make its management more tiresome, particularly if one or more of the beneficiaries for whom those shares are held (and who may become the outright owners of those shares) are not, and have no intention of becoming, active participants in the family business. In these circumstances the settlor, if a trustee, must, unless the settlement otherwise provides, have regard to his duties as a trustee in exercising the powers and discretions conferred by the settlement rather than letting outside considerations (perhaps those which he has as 'founder' of the business) influence his decisions. The trustees, if truly independent of the settlor, cannot merely act upon his instructions.

If the settlor wishes to retain a power to exclude those beneficiaries who show no interest in the business from benefit and to concentrate the shares of the company into the hands of those who are active participants, it may be advisable for him not to act as a trustee of the settlement. He may then exercise this power, conferred upon him other than in a fiduciary capacity, without regard to any duty to the beneficiaries which he would have as a trustee.

Whilst it may be possible to 'unwind' a settlement which does not achieve the settlor's aims, the terms upon which the trust property is held may make the undoing complex and expensive because of taxation and professional fees. The unscrambling may place property in the hands of the 'wrong' beneficiary. Further, any provision enabling the settlement to be undone in favour of the donor may, as a result of the reservation of benefit rules, negate the intended estate planning benefits. The settlor must, therefore, be sure that the terms of the trust achieve his aims and that they are (within the limits imposed by taxation rules) as flexible as possible in order to enable the trust to be adapted as circumstances require.

Creating Settlements **4.19**

Inheritance tax consequences of creating a settlement

4.16 An individual who has determined that he has assets and/or income surplus to his needs (both present and future) which he wishes to pass to succeeding generations in the most efficient manner must identify those beneficiaries he wishes to benefit and those assets most suitable to give away.

Accumulation and maintenance settlements

4.17 Where the intended beneficiary or beneficiaries are aged under 25, the donor should consider creating an accumulation and maintenance settlement unless he wishes to either make outright gifts or to transfer property to be held on bare trusts for beneficiaries aged under 18. The donor can make potentially exempt transfers to such settlements which may be extremely flexible, permitting accumulation of income and alteration of the shares of the beneficiaries, subject to the restrictions discussed under 4.23 *et seq.* below. The settlement will ultimately enable the beneficiaries to become entitled to capital or, alternatively, to an interest in possession, free of inheritance tax.

Interest in possession settlements

4.18 If none of the intended beneficiaries are of an age suitable for the creation of an accumulation and maintenance settlement, an interest in possession settlement may be the appropriate means of making the gift. Again, property may be transferred to such settlements by potentially exempt transfers.

It is no longer of importance to consider whether or not an interest in possession settlement or an accumulation and maintenance settlement should be created because there are uniform rates of capital gains tax. However, the settlor must still consider whether or not the trust deed should enable the trustees either to accumulate the income for the benefit of the beneficiaries or oblige the trustees to pay that income to or for the benefit of those beneficiaries. To some extent the risk of paying income to young beneficiaries can be mitigated by using a 'bare trust', whereby the trustees are unable to distribute the income to a beneficiary until he attains 18, after which time the beneficiary can give a valid receipt. The income retained, however, would vest absolutely in the beneficiary on his reaching the age of 18.

Discretionary settlements

4.19 Where the donor is uncertain as to the beneficiaries he wishes, ultimately, to benefit *or* uncertain as to the shares in which he would wish identified beneficiaries to benefit *or* if his intended beneficiaries (for example, future grandchildren) are not yet born, consideration must be given to the creation of a discretionary settlement. Potentially exempt transfers may not be made to such a settlement, so alternative means of transferring assets free of inheritance tax to such settlements must be considered.

4.20 *Creating Settlements*

1. The regular use of the annual exemption of £3,000 to transfer money or assets will enable a donor, over a number of years, to build up a fund for his intended beneficiaries.

2. Additional sums may be added to an existing settlement or a new settlement upon the marriage of a beneficiary using the marriage exemption provided the beneficiaries fall within the categories specified in IHTA 1984, s 22(4).

3. The donor may have sufficient income to make regular transfers to a settlement within the normal expenditure out of income exemption. This may be particularly appropriate for a high earning donor who is no longer supporting and educating children but who has few or illiquid assets or who does not wish to give away those assets he has.

4. The donor may not have used his nil rate band and so may be able to create a discretionary settlement of at least £250,000 free from inheritance tax. Spouses with sufficient assets should consider equalising the assets in their estates so that each may create settlements and make use of their available nil rate band. This is subject to the usual warning about the associated operations rules being applied by the Inland Revenue. In practice, the Inland Revenue is unlikely to attempt to apply these rules; however, care is still required.

Business property and agricultural property

4.20 Careful consideration should be given to whether property eligible for business property relief or agricultural property relief should be transferred to a lifetime settlement. The issue becomes most acute where inheritance tax relief at 100% will be available. Capital gains tax considerations will be a vital factor, because if the assets are held until death any inherent gain will be 'washed out' as a result of TCGA 1992, s 62. Giving away the assets during the settlor's lifetime will cause a charge to capital gains tax to arise, albeit that hold-over relief under TCGA 1992, s 165 will usually be available. However, the position becomes more complex where the assets are likely to be sold prior to death, or where inheritance tax relief at only 50% is available.

In transferring business property or agricultural property to a settlement the donor should be aware that, if his transfer is potentially exempt, the trustees must continue to own the property, or replacement property, for seven years and it must continue to be eligible for relief if that relief is to be available in the event of the potentially exempt transfer becoming chargeable. Nor will a lifetime chargeable transfer of business or agricultural property which, by virtue of the settlor's death, becomes chargeable at the higher rate benefit from relief if the property has not been retained.

Further, there will be a time lapse (of two years for business property relief and two or seven years in relation to agricultural property relief) before the trustees satisfy the length of ownership qualifications and are themselves able to obtain relief on such property held by them on any occasion giving rise to a charge to inheritance tax.

Creating Settlements **4.21**

The ownership qualifications should be borne in mind on two other occasions even where the property settled has been held by the trustees for more than two years. The following illustrates the general principle — but it is not solely an issue restricted to accumulation and maintenance trusts.

(*a*) Where property qualifying for business or agricultural property relief is transferred by way of potentially exempt transfer to an accumulation and maintenance settlement it (or any replacement property) must continue to be owned by the transferee if that relief is to be available on a potentially exempt transfer becoming chargeable (IHTA 1984, s 113A and IHTA 1984, s 124A). If within seven years of the potentially exempt transfer one or more of the beneficiaries of the settlement attain an interest in possession in their respective shares of the trust fund, they will then become the 'owners' of the trust property for the purposes of these provisions because they are treated as beneficially owning the capital underlying their interests in possession (IHTA 1984, s 49). Therefore, the requirement that the property given should continue to be owned by the transferee throughout the seven years following the potentially exempt transfer will not be satisfied and if the transferor dies after the beneficiary has attained an interest in possession but within the seven-year period business property relief or agricultural property relief will not be available.

(*b*) As a further consequence of the change of 'ownership' which occurs when a beneficiary attains an interest in possession under an accumulation and maintenance settlement it should be borne in mind that for the two years following the attainment of the interest in possession by the beneficiary (or, if his interest is an absolute interest, for the two years after the attainment of that interest) the ownership qualifications will not be satisfied and business property relief and agricultural property relief will not be available if the beneficiary dies, surrenders or assigns his interest during this time.

Where there is likely to be such a change of ownership, consideration should be given to creating an interest in possession settlement rather than an accumulation and maintenance settlement.

Other tax consequences of creating a settlement

Capital gains tax

4.21 The gift to a settlement, of whatever type, may give rise to a charge to capital gains tax for the settlor. Retirement relief may be available if the settlor is disposing of shares in a personal company or an interest in a business, although after 2002/03 the relief will not be available. Alternatively, a claim for hold-over relief under either TCGA 1992, s 165 (gifts of business assets) or TCGA 1992, s 260 (gifts chargeable to inheritance tax etc.) may be made to postpone the charge, in which case the trustees will acquire the settled assets at the base cost of the settlor and indexation (if any). On any subsequent disposal of those assets the trustees

4.21 Creating Settlements

will suffer capital gains tax not only on the gain accruing during their period of ownership but also on that accruing during the ownership of the settlor. The effect of making a hold-over claim is that the benefit for taper relief purposes of any qualifying period of ownership before the transfer will be lost.

Section 165 applies to most forms of business assets: broadly, assets used for the purposes of a trade, profession or vocation carried on by the settlor or his personal company, unquoted shares or securities of a trading company, quoted shares or securities of a trading company which is the settlor's personal company and agricultural property which qualifies for the inheritance tax agricultural property relief. On the other hand, section 260 applies to all forms of property but only in relation to gifts which are chargeable transfers (or would be but for the annual exemption), and not potentially exempt transfers, for inheritance tax purposes. Therefore, gifts to interest in possession settlements, accumulation and maintenance settlements and trusts for disabled persons cannot qualify for hold-over relief under section 260, but gifts to discretionary trusts under current rules may, even if they fall within the nil rate band.

Settlors wishing to transfer assets which will not qualify for hold-over relief under section 165 should now consider transferring the assets to a discretionary trust especially if their value falls within the nil rate band. After a suitable interval, it should then be possible, subject to any attack under the *Ramsay* Principle, for the discretionary trust to be converted into an interest in possession trust, an accumulation and maintenance trust or a trust for a disabled person.

Section 260 applies only where a chargeable transfer occurs, albeit currently chargeable at a nil rate of tax. Accordingly, this will exclude a transfer in a quarter beginning either with the date of the settlement or the date of a ten-year anniversary charge. This analysis of the operation of section 260 was confirmed in *Frankland v CIR, CA [1997] STC 1450*. It is also important to assess the inheritance tax position. If the initial value of the trust property, when aggregated with the settlor's cumulative total immediately prior to the transfer to the settlement, falls within the nil rate band and the conversion is made before the first ten-year anniversary, there will be no resulting charge to inheritance tax. However, it is important to take into account any potentially exempt transfers that have already been made or assess the consequences for the trust should those earlier transfers become chargeable.

Disposals of assets to beneficiaries by the trustees of a discretionary settlement may also be held over under section 260, regardless of whether the disposal gives rise to an inheritance tax liability. However, this is subject to the constraints outlined above. This is not the case in relation to interest in possession settlements or trusts for disabled persons, but the relief *is* available, in very limited circumstances, when a beneficiary of an accumulation and maintenance settlement becomes absolutely entitled to the trust property on or before 25. The condition is that the beneficiary must not have a pre-existing interest in possession in the assets concerned. This latter aspect is considered in more detail under 4.30 below.

Assuming one or other of the hold-over reliefs is available, the decision as to whether or not to elect to hold over a gain realised on a settlor's disposal of assets to the settlement may be influenced by the respective rates of capital gains tax suffered by the settlor and the trustees and the availability of taper relief. Frequently, the settlor will be liable to capital gains tax at 40% and therefore a decision to hold over the gain on his disposal will be made if the held-over gain will only suffer capital gains tax in the trustees' hands at 34%. In the event that the settlor has substantial capital losses and is chargeable only to capital gains tax at 20% he may decide not to hold over his gain.

Because taper relief is given by deduction from the aggregate gains for the year, gains held over under TCGA 1992, ss 165 and 260 are not reduced by taper relief. Claiming relief on a transfer will therefore result in a permanent loss of any taper relief which would otherwise be available on the transfer. With the introduction of more generous rates of taper relief for business assets, an effective rate of either 5% (if a lower rate taxpayer) or 10% (for higher rate taxpayers) after two years will mean that individuals will not necessarily be prohibited from claiming hold-over relief on the transfer of business assets in order to pass business assets down to future generations at the appropriate time.

The transfer to a settlement may also result in a loss of taper relief in two other circumstances.

(*a*) Where the settlor satisfies the conditions for determining whether the asset which is subject to the disposal is a business asset but the trustees do not satisfy the test for settled property.

(*b*) Where the asset is not a business asset with the result that the transfer restarts the initial three-year ownership period during which no taper relief is given.

Stamp duty

4.22   There is no *ad valorem* stamp duty on lifetime transfers.

A voluntary disposition of property for nil consideration to a trust is exempt from stamp duty under the Stamp Duty (Exempt Instruments) Regulations 1987 provided the appropriate certification is given. However, a £5 fixed charge still remains in respect of some documents not covered by the exemption. These include declarations of trust and a 'surrender of any kind whatsoever not chargeable with duty as a conveyance on sale'. A declaration of trust over a policy of life assurance, however, is exempt.

Accumulation and maintenance settlements

Inheritance tax

4.23   Due to the inheritance tax treatment of gifts to, and property comprised in, accumulation and maintenance settlements and the flexibility of dealing with the trust property that may be achieved by the terms of such

4.24 *Creating Settlements*

settlements, accumulation and maintenance settlements will almost undoubtedly best achieve the aims of parents and grandparents wishing to make provision for children or individuals aged under 25.

To ensure that the transfer of property to such a settlement is a potentially exempt transfer it must become settled property (IHTA 1984, s 3A(3)). This would not be the case where, for example, a premium was paid by a donor on a life policy already held on accumulation and maintenance trusts (although such transfers may be exempt as normal expenditure out of income or fall within the annual exemption of the donor).

Whilst an outright gift or a gift to an interest in possession settlement for a beneficiary will also qualify as a potentially exempt transfer, the property given will become, or be treated as becoming, part of the estate of the recipient and, if he dies, that property may be subject to an inheritance tax charge. Property settled on accumulation and maintenance trusts does not form part of a beneficiary's estate until he becomes absolutely entitled either to the capital or, if earlier, to the income from the trust fund or his share of it.

In its simplest form, therefore, an accumulation and maintenance settlement for one beneficiary provides the safety net that if the beneficiary dies before attaining an interest in possession and the property becomes held for another there will be no charge to inheritance tax on the beneficiary's death. In a more complex form, an accumulation and maintenance settlement for a class of beneficiaries can secure complete flexibility in altering their prospective shares before they attain interests in possession.

Moreover an outright gift cannot be made to a beneficiary as yet unborn. By creating an accumulation and maintenance settlement a settlor may divest himself now of property for a class of beneficiaries including those yet unborn (provided at least one beneficiary is in existence) and in shares yet to be determined. Such settlements facilitate earlier and larger gifts; a donor can afford to give twice as much to an accumulation and maintenance settlement of which there is currently only one beneficiary, but may soon be two, than he might otherwise have given outright to the existing beneficiary because of the need to hold property in reserve for subsequently born beneficiaries.

Qualifying conditions

4.24 The flexibility that may be achieved by the creation of an accumulation and maintenance settlement stems from the relevant inheritance tax rules. It is even more important than ever that these rules are satisfied, otherwise not only may the settlement be taxed as a discretionary trust but also the gift to the settlement will not be a potentially exempt transfer. The requirements in IHTA 1984, s 71 are as follows.

(*a*) One or more beneficiaries will, on or before attaining a specified age not exceeding 25, become beneficially entitled to the trust property or to an interest in possession in it.

(*b*) No interest in possession subsists in the trust property and the income from the trust property which is not applied for the maintenance, education or benefit of a beneficiary is to be accumulated.

Creating Settlements **4.24**

(*c*) Either

    (i) less than 25 years have elapsed since the time at which the trust property becomes held upon accumulation and maintenance trusts; or

    (ii) all the persons who are or have been beneficiaries are *either* grandchildren of a common grandparent *or* children, widows or widowers of such grandchildren who were themselves beneficiaries but died before the time when, had they survived, they would have attained an interest in possession.

A settlement created primarily for one person's children or grandchildren may, therefore, continue for longer than those created primarily for children of different families or children from different generations. (Although step-children may not actually have a common grandparent — for instance if both parties to a marriage have children by a previous marriage — they count as their parents' children and therefore the test is satisfied (section 71(8)).)

At least one of the class of beneficiaries must become entitled to the income from the trust property on or before attaining the age of 25. No powers incorporated into the settlement, such as the power to vary the beneficiaries' prospective shares and to accumulate income, must be exercisable so as to prevent this happening. It is not sufficient that such powers are not exercised; their terms must be restricted so that they cannot in any event be exercised to prevent at least one beneficiary becoming so entitled. It is now common practice for well-drafted trust instruments to include a 'catch all' provision designed to ensure that the mere existence of a dispositive power will not cause an accumulation and maintenance settlement to fail from its inception.

The general flexibility of an accumulation and maintenance settlement arises from the requirement in (*b*) above that until such time as a beneficiary does become entitled to an interest in possession in, or to the capital of, the trust property as required by (*a*) above, no interest in possession must subsist in the trust property to which a beneficiary is prospectively entitled and the income from the trust property which is not applied for the maintenance, education or benefit of a beneficiary must be accumulated. Since to qualify as an accumulation and maintenance settlement no beneficiary can have an interest in possession in the settlement, any alteration in his prospective interest in the settled property prior to his attaining an interest in possession or an absolute interest as required by the section will not give rise to an inheritance tax charge. This applies regardless of whether the alteration results from the birth of a further beneficiary into the class of beneficiaries, from a power of variation being exercised to reduce his share or from his death prior to attaining an interest in possession.

Maximum flexibility in dealing with the trust fund without giving rise to any potential inheritance tax charges can be achieved only by postponing for as long as possible (but not beyond 25) the age at which a beneficiary becomes entitled to the income of the fund (whether or not he then becomes entitled to the capital). The entitlement to capital may be postponed beyond 25, or the

4.25 *Creating Settlements*

beneficiary may never be entitled to capital, whereas his entitlement to income (his interest in possession) must vest on or before his 25th birthday.

Accumulation period

4.25 To achieve the postponement of the time at which a beneficiary becomes entitled to the income from his prospective share of the trust fund, reliance may be placed upon Trustee Act 1925, s 31. At one stage it was doubted whether as a result of section 31(2) the vesting of a beneficiary's interest in possession on his attaining his majority satisfied the requirement that a beneficiary's interest in possession must vest at a 'specified age'. This fear was removed by Inland Revenue Extra-Statutory Concession F8. However, the statutory trust to accumulate income in section 31 ceases when a beneficiary attains 18. To postpone the vesting of income beyond this age it is necessary to have an express power of accumulation capable of lasting for one of the accumulation periods permitted under the Law of Property Act 1925 and the Perpetuities and Accumulations Act 1964 assuming that the trust is governed by an English 'proper' law.

An older settlor will normally be best advised to select an accumulation period of 21 years from the date of the settlement. The income from the share of any beneficiary who has attained the age of four or more at the date of the settlement may be accumulated until he attains 25 since the accumulation period will not expire until after he attains that age. A beneficiary aged under four or born within three years after the making of the settlement will become entitled to the income from his share at an age between 18 and 25. Any beneficiary born thereafter will become entitled to the income of his share at 18 since the power of accumulation will lapse before his 18th birthday. However, unless excluded, the Trustee Act 1925, s 31 will permit the trust to accumulate income until age 18 and so satisfy the requirements in IHTA 1984, s 71.

A different accumulation period may be appropriate for a settlement created by an elderly settlor for very young beneficiaries. If the potential beneficiaries are, at the time of creation of the settlement, unlikely to attain 18 before the settlor's death then section 31 may be relied upon initially for the trust to accumulate and thereafter an express power to accumulate for a period of 21 years from the settlor's death may operate. If, however, a beneficiary becomes entitled to income at 18 and the settlor's death subsequently enables the trustees to accumulate income from his share, his interest in possession will cease for inheritance tax purposes and a charge to inheritance tax may arise. For this reason provisions should be incorporated in the settlement to ensure that the settlor's death does not destroy an existing interest in possession.

A younger settlor may select his lifetime as the accumulation period. Although to some extent uncertain, this may be longer than the period of 21 years from creation of the settlement. The ages of the children may govern whether the settlor's lifetime or a fixed 21 years is more appropriate.

Death of all beneficiaries before the age of 25

4.26 If the entire class of beneficiaries die before attaining the age of 25, income may be accumulated for so long as the accumulation period

Creating Settlements **4.28**

continues in the hope that another beneficiary will be born to take an interest. If no child is born before the accumulation period expires and some other person then attains an interest in the settled property, a charge to inheritance tax will arise. The termination of the accumulation and maintenance trust will not have resulted from the death of a beneficiary under IHTA 1984, s 71(4)(b) but from the termination of the accumulation period.

Again, if, during the lifetime of the settlor, all beneficiaries have died before attaining 25 and Trustee Act 1925, s 31 was to have been relied upon until an accumulation period linked to the death of the settlor commenced, unless other provision has been made, the income will revert back to the settlor under a 'resulting trust', until either new beneficiaries are born or the birth of new beneficiaries ceases to be a possibility. No charge to inheritance tax will arise, however, as the death of the last beneficiary will have been the occasion on which the trust property ceased to be held on accumulation and maintenance trusts and this will not be an occasion of charge (IHTA 1984, s 71(4)). The subsequent birth of a beneficiary will determine the settlor's (or other default beneficiary's) interest in possession and there will be a chargeable occasion for inheritance tax purposes. Whilst the class of beneficiaries has not closed, the commencement of the accumulation period (on the death of the settlor) will cause the trust property to fall into the discretionary trust regime until a beneficiary is born or the accumulation period ends. Clearly, a power to close the class of beneficiaries early will be invaluable in these unusual circumstances.

Accumulated income

4.27 Care should be taken to ensure that accumulated income cannot be added to the shares of those beneficiaries who have attained the specified age, although there is no need for the income applied for the benefit of a beneficiary under the specified age to be only the income from his or her prospective share and in this respect the trust may be truly discretionary in nature.

'Borrowed beneficiaries'

4.28 A parent or grandparent wishing to make a gift mainly to benefit children or grandchildren not yet born may 'borrow' a beneficiary (as yet aged under 25 and preferably very young) from another branch of the family (or even a total stranger) around whom the settlement is constructed until such time as the true intended beneficiaries are born. At that time the share of the 'borrowed' beneficiary may be reduced or withdrawn. This carries the risk that if no intended beneficiaries are born the borrowed beneficiary benefits from the entire fund. It is safer, therefore, for the borrowed beneficiary, on attaining the specified age, to become entitled to an interest in possession (which can then be terminated by being appointed away from him) rather than to receive the capital outright. Such an arrangement provides the power to divest the 'borrowed' beneficiary, who may never have been intended to take any benefit under the trust, of the trust property in favour of others who, although too old to be capable of

4.29 *Creating Settlements*

being beneficiaries of the accumulation and maintenance trust when created, the settlor would prefer to benefit if none of his intended beneficiaries are born.

Provided that the appointed funds become held on accumulation and maintenance trusts for the intended beneficiaries or pass absolutely to, or on to interest in possession trusts for, other individuals, the 'borrowed' beneficiary will be treated as having made a potentially exempt transfer. If the borrowed beneficiary survives the appointment by seven years no charge to inheritance tax will arise.

When the intended beneficiaries are born, if they will be first cousins of the 'borrowed' beneficiary (i.e. children of brothers or sisters of either parent of the borrowed beneficiary), the trust will satisfy the conditions of IHTA 1984, s 71(2)(b) since all the beneficiaries will be grandchildren of a common grandparent. Difficulties may emerge, however, if no suitably related beneficiaries of the same generation as the intended beneficiaries are available for 'borrowing'. In this instance, an unrelated individual of suitable age, or a related beneficiary of a different generation, may be chosen as the original beneficiary. The Inland Revenue have confirmed that the mere existence, as opposed to its actual exercise, of a power to appoint in favour of beneficiaries who are not grandchildren of a common grandparent does not take a trust outside the common grandparent category (Tax Bulletin Issue 55, October 2001 p 892). However, as the intended beneficiaries and the 'borrowed' beneficiary will not all be grandchildren of a common grandparent, the time period over which the settlement may continue before the beneficiaries attain their interests in possession must be limited to 25 years (IHTA 1984, s 71(2)(a)). This may result in some intended beneficiaries being excluded (if not born within the 25-year period) and others becoming entitled to income or capital at a younger age than had been hoped.

The power to appoint the trust property away from a 'borrowed' beneficiary should be vested in someone other than the trustees if it is to be used to cut out that beneficiary altogether. If this is done, the power, conferred upon the outsider other than in a fiduciary capacity, may be exercised without regard to any duties towards the beneficiary whose interest is to be reduced. Such a power conferred upon trustees could not be exercised with such freedom unless specific provision were made in the settlement to this effect. If the power is conferred upon the settlor, its terms should clearly provide that the settlor may not confer a benefit upon himself. This is in order to ensure that the existence of the power does not amount to a benefit reserved by the settlor over the trust property.

A mechanism in the settlement for the automatic exclusion from benefit or divesting of the 'borrowed' beneficiary's interest on the birth of an intended beneficiary is an alternative means of ensuring that the trustees are never placed in a position of conflict between their duties to their beneficiaries and the intentions of the settlor when he created the settlement.

Varying shares of beneficiaries

4.29 It has already been said that the terms of an accumulation and maintenance settlement may be very flexible. The power to vary shares of

Creating Settlements **4.30**

beneficiaries may be used to exclude them altogether, provided that as a result a beneficiary aged over the specified age does not benefit. Once a beneficiary has attained an interest in possession, any further births into the class of beneficiaries will reduce his share (assuming them to be eligible to benefit and the class not to have closed when the first beneficiary reaches the specified age). No charge to inheritance tax will arise if the beneficiary survives the event by seven years since he will be treated as having made a potentially exempt transfer of that part of his share of which he has been divested. Whilst this will not necessarily be desirable, and a power for the trustees to exclude beneficiaries born after a certain date may be useful, the reduction of a beneficiary's share, whether by the birth of further beneficiaries or by the exercise of a power of appointment once he has attained an interest in possession, does not prevent IHTA 1984, s 71 applying whilst the beneficiary is under the specified age. Further, any inheritance tax charge arising after the beneficiary has attained an interest in possession (whether on his death or a reduction of his share which he does not survive by seven years) will be calculated by reference to the beneficiary's cumulative total and estate.

An intending settlor, wishing to benefit his unborn grandchildren and whose children (or at least one of them) have not yet attained 25, may create an accumulation and maintenance settlement for those grandchildren. Once the children have attained their interests in possession, the trustees may appoint each child's share upon accumulation and maintenance trusts for the grandchildren who are then living or are subsequently born. Each child whose interest has been divested will be treated as having made a potentially exempt transfer of the share of the trust fund to the income of which he was entitled. However, even if the beneficiary does not survive the termination of his interest by seven years, if the child's nil rate band is unused at that time, the charge to inheritance tax may be small. In any event it may be possible to take out insurance at reasonable rates to cover the liability.

This power to appoint away from beneficiaries must be limited so that it is exercisable only once a beneficiary has attained an interest in possession and over that share of the trust fund in which he has attained his interest. Otherwise, it would be doubtful whether any beneficiary would, on or before attaining a specified age, become entitled to an interest in possession in the trust property and the provisions of IHTA 1984, s 71 will not be satisfied. If such a power is desired in addition to a similar power exercisable before a beneficiary attains an interest in possession, it will be necessary to provide two such powers. The first power would be exercisable only before a beneficiary attains an interest in possession and only in favour of other beneficiaries of the same settlement who have not yet attained an interest in possession. The second power would arise only after the beneficiary has attained an interest in possession and, since the constraints of section 71 need no longer be satisfied at that stage, this power may be exercisable in favour of a wider class of beneficiaries.

Capital gains tax

4.30 It may be possible if the assets are 'business assets' to elect to hold over the capital gains tax charge that might otherwise arise on the transfer

4.31 *Creating Settlements*

of assets to an accumulation and maintenance settlement under TCGA 1992, s 165. However, one should consider the loss of taper relief on such a disposal. Alternatively, it may be possible to pay any tax due by instalments under TCGA 1992, s 281.

The trustees will suffer capital gains tax at 34% on their actual and deemed disposals of property during the continuance of the trust. The tax rates are uniform for both accumulation and maintenance and interest in possession settlements.

On a beneficiary becoming absolutely entitled to the whole or part of the trust property, the trustees will be deemed to dispose of and reacquire the trust property at its market value as the beneficiary's nominee or bare trustee. Any gains arising may either be held over at the election of the trustees and the beneficiary under TCGA 1992, s 165 (if arising in respect of 'business assets') or under TCGA 1992, s 260(2)(d) if the beneficiary has not already become entitled to an interest in possession in the settled property (which will often be the case by reason of the operation of Trustee Act 1925, s 31).

The fact that section 260(2)(d) will only operate on a disposal to a beneficiary who has not already become entitled to an interest in possession means that the terms of accumulation and maintenance settlements ought to be drafted in such a way as to postpone the conferring of an interest in possession for as long as is possible under an appropriate accumulation period (e.g. the life of the settlor or 21 years from the creation of the settlement). Allowing the Trustee Act 1925, s 31 to apply will automatically confer an interest in possession on the beneficiary at age 18, which will mean that if he or she subsequently becomes entitled to the capital (e.g. on attaining the age of 25) a hold-over election under section 260 cannot be made at that stage. Therefore, consideration ought to be given to allowing the beneficiary to become entitled outright to the trust property at age 18, although there may be other non-tax reasons why this is not desirable. Alternatively, the trustees could transfer the trust assets to a new trust under which the beneficiary receives an immediate interest in possession. The feasibility of this approach very much depends on the availability of suitable trust powers. In order to avoid such problems, it is preferable that the drafting of all accumulation and maintenance trusts should be as flexible as possible. The deed should therefore ensure that a beneficiary becomes entitled to an interest in possession on or before attaining 25 but never becomes entitled to the capital outright: this should be left at the discretion of the trustees pursuant to an express power of advancement. This will at least give the trustees the ability to vest the trust assets in the beneficiary outright at a time which is most favourable from the capital gains tax point of view, rather than having the terms of the settlement create an automatic disposal at a specified age.

Income tax

4.31 The income tax consequences for a parental settlor of creating an accumulation and maintenance settlement must be carefully considered. To the extent that capital or income is applied for the benefit of an unmarried child aged under 18 or would otherwise be treated as the income of such a child, the income of the settlement will be treated as the settlor's income

Creating Settlements **4.31**

(ICTA 1988, s 660B(1)). If, however, the income is accumulated and no payments of capital are made under an irrevocable settlement, no income tax charge will fall upon the parental settlor (ICTA 1988, s 660B(2)). A parental settlor will, therefore, normally wish all income to be accumulated until the beneficiaries have attained 18. However, there are exceptions, for example, if the settlor has large farming losses, he may not be paying tax. Aggregation with his income may save tax and it will be appropriate to pay the income out to his children. Generally, however, income will be accumulated and will be chargeable to income tax in the hands of the trustees at the rate applicable to trusts under ICTA 1988, s 686.

On a distribution of income from an accumulation and maintenance settlement the recipient beneficiary will be treated as receiving a net amount from which income tax at the rate applicable to trusts has been deducted (ICTA 1988, s 687). The amount of tax which is treated as having been deducted may (in whole or part) be reclaimed if the beneficiary's personal rates of income tax are lower than 34% (the income tax rate applicable to trusts). Once again (see 4.2 above), it should be noted that because tax credits on dividends are no longer repayable, the total tax charged on dividends which arise to trustees and which are distributed may be higher than it would have been had the dividends arisen directly to the recipient beneficiary.

Where income has been accumulated in a settlement created by a parent for his children whilst those children are aged under 18 (and unmarried) and provided that provision is made in the settlement to enable the trustees to apply accumulated income as income of the current year and the beneficiary has not yet become entitled to income, it may be possible to recover some of the tax paid by the trustees by distributing accumulated income to beneficiaries once they have attained 18. Following the line of cases culminating in *Stevenson v Wishart and Others (Levy's Trustees), CA [1987] STC 266; [1987] 2 All ER 428*, this may have the effect of converting capital (accumulated income) back into taxable income. Even in cases where an express power does not exist, such a power may be implied in any event by reason of Trustee Act 1925, s 31. Accordingly, by taking advantage of a power to apply capital (past accumulations) as current income, it should prove possible to enable beneficiaries to reclaim tax treated as deducted from income payments received by them (ICTA 1988, s 687) if their own personal liability to income tax is at a lower rate than that of the trustees.

Grandparent settlors (and parents whose children are aged over 18) do not suffer such problems. Income tax at the rate applicable to trusts is charged on the income in the trustees' hands and, if distributed to beneficiaries, the income will again be treated as being a net receipt from which income tax at 34% has been deducted. Tax will be paid or reclaimed by them according to their personal circumstances. In this way settlements by grandparent settlors enable the use of grandchildren's personal allowances (which might otherwise be unused). Such settlements may, therefore, be particularly efficient if regular payments out of the settlement are to be made, for example, to meet school fees.

4.32 *Creating Settlements*

Interest in possession settlements

Inheritance tax

4.32 For those who wish to retain control over assets given away or do not wish the intended beneficiary to acquire full control following the gift, at least until a later date, the interest in possession settlement may provide a solution. The transfer of property to the settlement may be a potentially exempt transfer for inheritance tax purposes (IHTA 1984, s 3A(1)(2)). The beneficiary or beneficiaries must be entitled to the income from the trust fund, however, the vesting of capital may either be postponed to a later age or retained for the succeeding generation. Powers for the trustees to pay over capital to the beneficiary may be included. The beneficiary may, by the exercise of a power of appointment, be given freedom to determine the distribution of remaining capital (either between a defined class of beneficiaries or without limitation) following his death. Alternatively, a similar power to appoint the fund in favour of other beneficiaries at any time may be vested in the trustees or the settlor (provided the settlor cannot benefit in order to ensure that the 'reservation of benefit' provisions do not apply).

There is no reason why, following the creation of an interest in possession settlement, more severe charges to inheritance tax should be suffered than would arise if the beneficiary had been given the capital outright. This is particularly so as a premature termination of a beneficiary's interest by surrender or assignment in favour of others may be a potentially exempt transfer.

Since the beneficiary entitled to an interest in possession is only *treated* as being, and is not in fact, beneficially entitled to the settled property in which his interest subsists, any termination of his interest (or part of it) during his lifetime will be treated as though it were a transfer of value of the settled property (or part of it). Where the termination results from the surrender or assignment of the interest, IHTA 1984, s 51 provides that the disposal is not a transfer of value but shall be treated as the coming to an end of the interest under section 52. It is that coming to an end which constitutes the transfer of value. The termination of a life interest will generally be a potentially exempt transfer. Where the termination is a result of the terms of the settlement, the life tenant is deemed to have made a disposal (IHTA 1984, s 52(1)) and his interest will be deemed to come to an end. Providing the life tenant survives for seven years following the termination, no inheritance tax will be chargeable.

It is important to note that the value on which inheritance tax is charged on a lifetime termination of an interest in possession is the value of the settled property in which the interest subsisted prior to the termination. The charge is not by reference to the diminution of the beneficiary's estate as a result of the termination of his interest. This may provide advantages when transferring holdings of private company shares. A transfer of shares which thereby reduces the transferor's holding below 50% will cause a greater diminution in the value of his estate than the value of the shares received by the donee. If

84

Creating Settlements **4.32**

the donor's interest in possession in a similar holding is terminated; only the appropriate percentage of the total value of the shares held subject to the donor's interest in possession prior to the termination, and not the diminution of the estate, will be taken into account in charging inheritance tax on the termination if the potentially exempt transfer becomes chargeable. This is of less importance now that such deemed transfers may be potentially exempt transfers but may still provide favourable planning opportunities to an older transferor, or where he or she suffers from ill health. The application of this principle would permit a settlor with a 60% holding of shares in a private investment company to create three settlements each holding 20% of the shares and in which he had an initial interest in possession. No transfer of value would occur on the creation of the settlements since he will be treated as remaining beneficially entitled to the settled property (IHTA 1984, s 49) and the definition of a person's estate in IHTA 1984, s 5 includes all property to which he is beneficially entitled. His transfer will not, therefore, be a transfer of value within IHTA 1984, s 3. The trustees might then exercise a power to defeat the settlor's interests in the settlements. His entire shareholding would have passed out of his estate at a potentially lower inheritance tax cost because the interests so released were in three minority holdings whereas an outright gift by the settlor of a 60% holding would have reduced the value of his estate by the value of a majority holding.

The Capital Taxes Office has accepted the above interpretation, subject to a number of important caveats. They agree that the settled property in which the interest subsisted should be valued in isolation, without reference to any similar property. As indicated in the published letter to the Law Society dated 9 May 1990, see Tolley's Yellow Tax Handbook 2002/03, the Inland Revenue reserves the right to apply in appropriate circumstances the *Ramsay* principle or the inheritance tax associated operations provisions. Despite these comments, using a number of interest in possession trusts is likely to prove particularly useful, especially where there is a gift of investment company shares or where 100% business property relief is unlikely to be fully available as a sale of the shares is likely prior to the expiry of the seven year period.

Such trusts could be established during a settlor's lifetime or on his death. This latter approach could be especially useful where the testator is in poor health, and is likely to be survived by a spouse who might be the beneficiary with the interest in possession under a number of settlements established under the terms of the will. Having a number of trusts could be entirely reasonable, as each ultimately could be earmarked for separate children or other beneficiaries.

In addition, the terms of each separate trust established by the will would differ. This should avoid any argument that the trusts together constitute a single settlement. Not only would the value transferred by any future potentially exempt transfers be minimised, but also any capital gains tax liability would have been washed out on the testator's death. This would have been achieved without inheritance tax being payable on the testator's death, owing to the availability of the spouse exemption.

On any *inter vivos* termination of his interest in possession the beneficiary's annual exemption (or part of it) or the gift in consideration of marriage

4.32 *Creating Settlements*

exemption is available (IHTA 1984, s 57) and these may then be taken into account for the purposes of calculating the inheritance tax charge should the deemed transfer made on that occasion become chargeable. The beneficiary must give notice to the trustees of the availability of the exemption and the relief must be claimed (IHTA 1984, s 57(2)). This notice must be given within six months of the event.

Special anti-avoidance provisions exist to limit the inheritance tax planning opportunities of routing property destined for a discretionary trust through an intermediate interest in possession trust. IHTA 1984, ss 54A, 54B impose a special charge when the following conditions are satisfied:

(i) an interest in possession comes to an end during the lifetime of the person beneficially entitled to it, or upon his death;

(ii) the interest in possession ceases and a discretionary trust arises within seven years of the potentially exempt transfer having been made;

(iii) the settlor is alive at the time the interest in possession comes to an end.

The inheritance tax charge is taken to be the higher of two alternative calculations. In the first instance, the tax due is calculated in the normal way on the termination of the interest in possession. The rates will either be half rates (where there is an *inter vivos* termination) or full death rates where termination occurs as a result of the life tenant's death.

The second calculation imputes the settlor's cumulative total of transfers at the time the settlement was established to the beneficiary whose interest ceases. In this calculation half rates are used. The rules can be extremely complex in their operation.

There is a further condition to be satisfied before the special rate can apply. The net effect of IHTA 1984, s 54A(2)(d) is that no charge will arise if within six months of the interest in possession ceasing, the trust property becomes either:

(*a*) held on an interest in possession or an accumulation and maintenance trust; or

(*b*) owned outright by individual beneficiaries.

It is necessary to bear the above rules in mind where an interest in possession trust holds assets which do not qualify for hold-over relief under TCGA 1992, s 165 (business assets), and there is a pressing need to relocate the assets concerned out of that trust. One possibility might be to route the assets through a discretionary trust, taking advantage of a hold-over claim under TCGA 1992, s 260, albeit that a charge to inheritance tax might arise on the deemed transfer. However, the trustees would have to bear in mind that to avoid the special charge they had only a further six months to rearrange the trust's affairs.

The death of an individual who has an interest in possession will give rise to a charge to inheritance tax on the trustees of the settlement since the trust property in which his interest subsists is treated as forming part of his estate (IHTA 1984, s 5 and IHTA 1984, s 49). The individual will be treated as having made a transfer of value. The result would have been the same if he had owned the capital outright. Unless it reverts to the settlor or his spouse or his widow, if the settlor has died less than two years previously, (IHTA 1984, s 53), the trust property will be aggregated with the property to which the individual is absolutely entitled at death for the purposes of calculating the applicable rate of inheritance tax. If the deceased individual's spouse succeeds to his interest in possession the transfer of value will, however, be exempt since the settled property will be treated as becoming comprised in the estate of his spouse (IHTA 1984, s 18 and IHTA 1984, s 49).

If a beneficiary's interest in possession in settled property comes to an end as a result of his becoming absolutely entitled to the property or part of it there will be no charge to inheritance tax (IHTA 1984, s 53(2)). This is in keeping with the treatment of a beneficiary who has an interest in possession in settled property as the beneficial owner of that settled property in which his interest subsists. Thus, advances of capital to the beneficiary will not give rise to an inheritance tax charge, nor will inheritance tax be charged when a beneficiary satisfies a contingency and becomes entitled to the underlying capital, albeit that there may be capital gains tax implications to consider.

Capital gains tax

4.33 The capital gains tax position on transfers of chargeable assets to the settlement is the same as for accumulation and maintenance settlements.

Whilst the life interest continues, the trustees will be chargeable to capital gains tax on gains made on the disposal of assets held in the settlement at a rate of 34%, subject to taper relief. As explained under 4.18 above, this rate is the same as the rate applicable to accumulation and maintenance settlements.

Termination of life interest other than on death

4.34 When on such a termination some person becomes absolutely entitled to the trust assets the trustees will, under TCGA 1992, s 71, be deemed to dispose of the assets forming part of the settled property to which the person becomes absolutely entitled and to reacquire that property as nominee for the person so entitled within TCGA 1992, s 60. Such an occasion will arise, for example,

(a) when a beneficiary satisfies a contingency and becomes absolutely entitled to the settled property;

(b) by an arrangement between the life tenant and the remainderman whereby the life interest is surrendered in favour of the remainderman or the remainderman disposes of his interest to the life tenant;

(c) or where the trustees (if they have the requisite power) advance assets to the life tenant (or the remainderman) free of the trusts.

All these occasions give rise to a capital gains tax charge for the trustees on the difference between their acquisition cost of the assets held (subject to indexation, if any, and taper relief) and the market value of those assets at the time of the deemed disposal.

4.35 *Creating Settlements*

Where the assets concerned are 'business assets' within TCGA 1992, s 165, an election may be made by the trustees and the person who becomes absolutely entitled to hold over any gain arising so that that person acquires them at the trustees' base cost. The transfer of the assets to the beneficiary may not occur at that stage but, since the trustees now hold as nominee for the beneficiary, in the future capital gains tax will be charged as though the trust property was owned by the beneficiary absolutely. The election for hold-over relief is available even on a deemed disposal. With a capital gains tax liability at 34%, it may be beneficial not to elect to hold over gains realised by the trustees on the occasion of their deemed disposal. Instead, it may be preferable for them to pay this liability rather than holding over their realised gains to the beneficiary if he will suffer capital gains tax on them at the higher rate (i.e. 40%). Where business asset taper relief is available and the overall rate of capital gains tax has been reduced significantly, it may be advisable not to elect to hold-over the gain.

If a life interest terminates, other than on the death of the person entitled to it, there will not be a deemed disposal by the trustees if there is no person to become absolutely entitled to the settled property. So, if the settled property continues to be held by the same settlement for capital gains tax purposes no tax charge will arise. This would be the case, for example, where a life tenant surrendered his life interest prematurely and a succeeding life tenant's interest fell into possession.

Termination of life interest on death

4.35 As has already been mentioned, on the death of the life tenant (whether the interest in the settled property terminates at that time or not) the assets held in the settlement will be deemed to have been disposed of by the trustees (TCGA 1992, s 72). If the assets remain settled property they are deemed to have been immediately reacquired by the trustees at their market value at the date of death. No chargeable gain, however, will accrue on the disposal. If the assets do not remain settled property but, following the termination of a life interest by the death of the life tenant, are held for someone absolutely or free of the trusts of the settlement, the trustees are deemed to dispose of those assets and reacquire them as a nominee for a consideration equal to their market value (TCGA 1992, s 71). Again, by virtue of TCGA 1992, s 73, no charge to capital gains tax will arise.

One important distinction should be drawn between the capital gains tax free uplift on death which applies where a person is absolutely entitled to the assets (TCGA 1992, s 62) and the uplift available on the death of the life tenant which arises from the provisions of TCGA 1992, s 74. On the death of a person absolutely entitled to assets which, at the time of the gift, were the subject of an election for hold-over relief, all unrealised gains (accruing both during the ownership of the donor and the donee) will not be subject to capital gains tax since the deceased donee makes no disposal. The donee's personal representatives acquire those assets at their market value at the date of his death, thereby washed of unrealised gains. Section 74, however, prevents assets in a settlement, which were the subject of a hold-over election under either FA 1980, s 79, TCGA 1992, s 165 or TCGA 1992, s 260 when transferred to the settlement, being washed of the gains so held over on the death of the life tenant. Relief under TCGA 1992, s 260(2)(a) to defer the charge to tax will not always be available, because the relief will not apply where an exempt transfer arises after the life interest ceases. For example, section 260(2)(a) would not be applicable where a surviving spouse held the succeeding interest and full relief under IHTA 1984, s 18 was available. The position would be similar where the succeeding interest was held by a UK charity, so that exemption would be available under IHTA 1984, s 23. Where hold-over relief is available both on gifts into and distributions by the trustees out of settlements, consideration should be given, if within the trustees' powers, to the distribution of assets incorporating large gains to a life tenant. Those assets then form part of his estate on death and are completely washed of gains at his death. The inheritance tax consequences of the assets forming part of the life tenant's estate on death may not be a disadvantage if inheritance tax would in any case otherwise be charged on the settled property as though it was owned by the life tenant and he had made a transfer of it immediately before his death, or if the property qualified for business property relief.

Termination of other interests in possession on death

4.36 TCGA 1992, ss 72, 73 also apply to interests which are in possession but which are not life interests, e.g. an interest in possession which will come to an end when the income beneficiary attains a certain age.

Income tax

4.37 A beneficiary entitled to the income from settled property will be charged to income tax on that income at the rates applicable when the income from the settlement is aggregated with his own income. The income may be mandated directly to him (in which case it may be unnecessary for the trustees to submit returns as regards the income concerned) or may be received by the trustees and subsequently paid over to him. The trustees will account for tax on the whole of the trust fund (with no deduction for expenses). After deduction for expenses, the income paid over to the life tenant will be treated as being a net amount from which income tax has been deducted.

Trusts for disabled persons

4.38 Potentially exempt transfers may be made to settlements which qualify as trusts for disabled persons. Disabled persons are defined as individuals who are incapable, by reason of mental disorder within the meaning of the Mental Health Act 1983, of administering their property or managing their affairs or individuals who are in receipt of an attendance allowance or a disability living allowance under Social Security Contributions and Benefits Act 1992 (IHTA 1984, s 89(4)). Such a trust may be

4.38 *Creating Settlements*

appropriate where a donor wishes to provide for a disabled person and to ensure that property surplus to the requirements of a disabled person may be accumulated or used for the benefit of others.

Trusts within this provision, although often discretionary in nature, will suffer no inheritance tax charge under the discretionary trust regime but will be taxed as though the disabled person has an interest in possession in the settled property. This is so even though others may also benefit from the income and capital of the settled property.

The provisions of IHTA 1984, s 89 and those in TCGA 1992, Sch 1 (relating to the capital gains tax exemption available to trustees of a trust for a disabled person) do not lie easily together and may, at first, appear to be mutually exclusive.

Schedule 1 also provides that the capital gains tax annual exemption (which is restricted to half for trustees of other settlements) will be available in full to trustees of a settlement for a disabled person in the following circumstances:

(*a*) the settled property is held on trusts which provide that, during the lifetime of a mentally disabled person or a person in receipt of an attendance allowance or disability living allowance, not less than half of the property which is applied is applied for the benefit of that person; and

(*b*) either that person is entitled to not less than half of the income arising from the property or no such income may be applied for the benefit of any other person.

The provisions of section 89 require, however, that no interest in possession exists in the settled property and that the provisions of the settlement secure that not less than half of the settled property which is applied during his life may be applied for the benefit of the disabled person. One solution is to give the disabled person a life interest in the income of the settlement but to make it subject to a power for the trustees to accumulate income and to provide that any income so accumulated cannot thereafter be applied for the benefit of any other person during the disabled person's lifetime. The disabled person will not, therefore, have an interest in possession for inheritance tax purposes under general principles but (*b*) above will be satisfied. Once the accumulation period expires, where an English proper law trust is being used, the disabled person (if still alive) must become entitled to at least one half of the income of the trust fund if the full annual exemption is to be available to the trustees, although the remainder of the income may, at the discretion of the trustees, continue to be applied either for the disabled person or for other beneficiaries. One half of the settled property would therefore cease to satisfy the requirements of section 89 (because an interest in possession would then subsist in it) but although the disabled beneficiary has become entitled to an interest in possession in one half of the settled property there would be no charge on this occasion as a result of IHTA 1984, s 53(2). The remaining half of the settled property would still be treated as being within section 89 provided no interest in possession subsisted in that property at that time. This will be the case whether or not the objects of the trustees' discretion over income include the disabled person.

Creating Settlements **4.39**

During the accumulation period, the income of the settlement will be taxed at 34% and this also applies following the expiry of the accumulation period, unless the disabled person then becomes entitled to an interest in possession in the whole of the trust fund in which case his personal income tax rate will apply.

As has been stated above the inheritance tax and capital gains tax provisions require that the terms of the settlement should not permit more than half of the settled property applied during the lifetime of the disabled person to be applied for persons other than him. This requirement may be satisfied either by

(i) excluding altogether any power to pay out capital during his lifetime (apart from Trustee Act 1925, s 32 — IHTA 1984, s 89(3); TCGA 1992, Sch 1); or

(ii) by providing that capital may only be applied for his benefit during his lifetime; or

(iii) by permitting capital to be applied for the benefit of all beneficiaries with a proviso that the trustees may not apply capital for the benefit of beneficiaries other than the disabled person unless they have already applied an equal amount for the benefit of that person.

An interest in possession settlement would have the same inheritance tax effect as a settlement within IHTA 1984, s 89 even if the trustees were given power to apply capital for the benefit of others during the lifetime of the disabled person with the interest in possession. The main advantages, however, of creating a settlement which satisfies section 89 and TCGA 1992, Sch 1, as opposed to creating an interest in possession settlement for the disabled beneficiary, will be to allow surplus income to be accumulated without creating a discretionary trust for inheritance tax purposes. However, in practice, the same net effect may be achieved in the case of an interest in possession settlement through the use of offshore funds without distributor status.

A discretionary trust which includes the disabled person in its class of income beneficiaries but restricts the application of capital as required by both the inheritance tax and capital gains tax provisions would satisfy the requirements of IHTA 1984, s 89 but not those of TCGA 1992, Sch 1 para 5. It would also not have the benefit of the capital gains tax free base uplift on the death of the disabled person.

The gains realised by the settlement will suffer capital gains tax at 34%.

Transfers of chargeable assets to a settlement for a disabled person may be held over under TCGA 1992, s 165 if the assets are 'business assets' within that section, but not under TCGA 1992, s 260.

Discretionary settlements

Inheritance tax

4.39 The donor who wishes to give assets away now rather than retain them in his estate (perhaps because they are likely to increase significantly

4.40 *Creating Settlements*

in value in the near future) but is uncertain as to his intended beneficiaries and the proportions in which he would wish them to benefit (or is certain of his intentions but as yet the beneficiaries do not exist) should consider creating a discretionary settlement. As potentially exempt transfers may not be made to such settlements they may increasingly become a 'last resort'.

A discretionary settlement may be particularly appropriate, as an alternative to 'borrowing' a beneficiary (see 4.28 above), for a settlor who anticipates that grandchildren whom he would wish to benefit may be born within a short period of time. In these circumstances, his children and future grandchildren would form the class of beneficiaries. On the birth of grandchildren, the whole or part of the trust fund could be 'converted' into a settlement for the benefit of his existing and future born grandchildren by the appointment of funds on accumulation and maintenance trusts.

Although the maximum rate at which any distribution from a discretionary settlement can be charged to inheritance tax is three tenths of one half of the rates of tax applicable on death (i.e. 6%), such a settlement should particularly be considered where a settlor has not used his nil rate band (currently £250,000). He can then create a settlement from which distributions may, in many circumstances, be made prior to the first ten-year anniversary without incurring any inheritance tax charge even though the property in the settlement has increased in value beyond that nil rate band. If the settlor survives for seven years, the amount of the gift will then fall out of aggregation with his later transfers and he will start with a new nil rate band.

To understand the possible uses of discretionary settlements, it is necessary to consider the way in which inheritance tax will be levied on the funds of a discretionary settlement created now. (The rules are modified in relation to discretionary settlements created before 1974.)

There are two occasions of charge. As has already been stated, capital in a discretionary settlement is subject to inheritance tax at each ten-year anniversary of the creation of the settlement. There is an additional charge whenever distributions are made from the settled property.

Related settlements

4.40 Other settlements made on the same day by the same settlor will be 'related settlements' unless the property is held for charitable purposes only (IHTA 1984, s 62). Whether or not they are discretionary settlements, the property comprised in them immediately after they commence will be taken into account when calculating the inheritance tax on any ten-year anniversary or distribution from the discretionary settlement. Thus, a settlor should not create a discretionary settlement on the same day as any other.

It should be noted that this does not apply where property is added to a number of discretionary settlements on the same day. That was the principle of which the taxpayers in the case of *Rysaffe Trustee Co (Channel Islands) Ltd v CIR, Ch D [2002] STC 872* were trying to take advantage (see below).

Ten-yearly charge

4.41 At each ten-year anniversary of a discretionary settlement an inheritance tax charge arises which is calculated as though a transfer of value of the property in the settlement, together with the value of property in any related settlement immediately after it commenced, had been made at that date by an individual who had a cumulative total equal to

(*a*) the value of chargeable transfers made by the settlor in the seven years prior to the creation of the settlement; plus

(*b*) the amounts upon which inheritance tax has been charged on distributions from the settlement made by the trustees in the preceding ten years.

The Inland Revenue accept that undistributed income retained by the trustees but not as yet accumulated does not fall within the charge (Statement of Practice SP 8/86).

If, therefore, the settlor's cumulative total was nil immediately before the creation of the settlement and there have been no distributions from the settlement in the ten years preceding the anniversary in question, no charge will be levied provided the value of property in the settlement does not exceed the current nil rate band of inheritance tax (although this is not always the case where the property falls within the nil rate band only because of the availability of agricultural or business property relief). It is for this reason that a settlor, with property currently worth less than £250,000 which will increase substantially in value over the next ten to twenty years, who has made no previous chargeable transfers and does not anticipate distributions being made from a settlement for some considerable length of time, may be best advised to create several discretionary settlements on separate days. He should divide the assets to be transferred between these settlements in the hope that a charge to inheritance tax may be avoided, at least on the first ten-year anniversary (and consequently on distributions between the first and second ten-year anniversaries, see below), because the property comprised in each separate settlement has not, by the time of the first ten-year anniversary, risen to a value greater than the nil rate band after deducting the settlor's cumulative transfers at the time immediately before each settlement is made. The settlor may, thereby, buy himself more time in determining which beneficiaries are to benefit and permit further beneficiaries to be born into the class, the cost being the professional fees of creating and administering on a continuing basis several such settlements.

Any arrangement whereby a string of 'unrelated' settlements are created may be open to attack under the *Ramsay* principle. Such an attack is likely to be unsuccessful, particularly if it can be shown that separate settlements were created for good reason. This could be because the class of beneficiaries varies between settlements; because the trustees of each settlement are not the same and, for example, voting control of private company shares forming the trust fund is thereby not held by one group of trustees; or because the trusts and powers differ between settlements. Any purely artificial differences, however, are likely to be ignored by the court. It is interesting that in the case of *Rysaffe*

4.42 *Creating Settlements*

Trustee Co (Channel Islands) Ltd v CIR, Ch D [2002] STC 872 the Revenue did not advance an argument based on the *Ramsay* principle.

Charges on distributions

4.42 Distributions from a discretionary settlement are charged at a proportion of the effective rate charged at the first ten-year anniversary or, if the distribution is made prior to the first ten-year anniversary, on the rate fixed at the inception of the settlement. The proportion is one-fortieth for each complete quarter from the last ten-year anniversary (or creation of the settlement) and the date of distribution (IHTA 1984, s 69).

On any distribution prior to the first ten-year anniversary, the rate of tax is calculated as though an individual with the cumulative total of the settlor immediately prior to the creation of the settlement had made a transfer of value equal to the total of

(*a*) the value of the property in the settlement immediately after it commenced; plus

(*b*) the value of any additional property at the date of addition; plus

(*c*) the value of any property in a related settlement (see above) immediately after its commencement.

The rate of charge is multiplied by a fraction of which the numerator is the number of complete successive quarters that has elapsed from the creation of the settlement to the date of the section 65 charge and the divisor is forty. Thus the earlier the distribution the lower the rate.

The effective rate of inheritance tax so determined is applied to any distribution made from the settlement prior to the first ten-year anniversary.

The value of the distribution is calculated by reference to the fall in value of the fund. If the tax is to be paid out of property remaining in the settlement, the reduction in value includes the amount of inheritance tax so payable.

As a result of this method of charging inheritance tax, where the settlor, immediately prior to the creation of the discretionary settlement, had made no chargeable transfers in the previous seven years and the value of property comprised in the settlement immediately after it commenced, together with the value of later additions, did not exceed the maximum amount that can (at the time of distribution) be transferred without incurring a charge to inheritance tax (currently £250,000) distributions from a discretionary settlement may be made free of inheritance tax before the first ten-year anniversary. This is because the rate of tax for distributions before that date is under those circumstances fixed at nil. However, where the property settled qualifies for agricultural or business property relief, no such relief is taken into account when determining the applicable rate under IHTA 1984, s 65 (see 4.45 below). It is necessary to ensure that the economic value of the property settled falls below the nil rate band unless appointments of property which qualify for 100% agricultural or business property relief are to be made before the first ten-year anniversary.

Creating Settlements **4.44**

Additional property

4.43 Care must be taken if at any time property is to be added to an existing discretionary settlement. If the settlor has made any chargeable transfers since creating the settlement, his cumulative total prior to the date of any addition, if greater, may be substituted for his pre-settlement cumulative total for the purposes of calculating the rate of inheritance tax on the subsequent ten-year anniversary (IHTA 1984, s 67). It should be noticed, however, that this only applies where a settlor makes an addition to a settlement by way of chargeable transfer; his annual exemption may, for example, be used to top up discretionary settlements without adverse effect as might transfers falling within the normal expenditure out of income rules outlined earlier. Further, the substitution will not occur if the only chargeable transfers made by the settlor between the creation of the settlement and the date of the addition were transfers to the settlement. Additions may therefore be made before the first ten-year anniversary without affecting the rate at that time if the nil rate band (including any uplift since creation of the settlement) has not been fully utilised.

Creation of several discretionary settlements

4.44 Where substantial wealth is actually or prospectively involved it should be possible to take advantage of the rules relating to nil rate band trusts (described above) by adopting either a 'cascade' of discretionary trusts, or by using the 'added property route'.

(*a*) *The 'cascade' effect*

Under this approach a series of pilot discretionary trusts are established at intervals over a period of time by a settlor with no history of chargeable transfers (and ideally no potentially exempt transfers) made within the last seven years. For example, the establishment of ten successive settlements of £25,000 would have the result that the first settlement of £25,000 would itself have to reach £250,000 in value at its ten-year anniversary before paying any inheritance tax. However, the 'clock' of each subsequent settlement would take into account the earlier settled gifts, with the scope for future inheritance tax-free growth in the later trusts being reduced accordingly. It may be prudent in implementing such an arrangement in order to avoid the application of the *Ramsay* principle that the trusts differ as much as possible as to beneficiaries and accumulation and perpetuity periods. Differing governing law should also help. A practical disadvantage of this approach is that the number of trusts involved may be unwieldy and might be difficult to co-ordinate.

Example

Discretionary Trust No	Initial value £	Available 'margin' for future growth £
1	25,000	225,000
2	25,000	200,000
3	25,000	175,000

4.44 *Creating Settlements*

4	25,000	150,000
5	25,000	125,000
6	25,000	100,000
7	25,000	75,000
8	25,000	50,000
9	25,000	25,000
10	25,000	Nil
	£250,000	£1,125,000

(b) *The 'added property route'*

As outlined earlier, chargeable additions should rarely be made to existing settlements, due to IHTA 1984, s 67. Where such additions have occurred the settlor's prior transfers to be taken into account under IHTA 1984, s 66(5) will be the greater of

(i) the cumulative total of the settlor's chargeable transfers made during the period of seven years, ending with the commencement of the settlement, but disregarding transfers made on that day; and

(ii) the aggregate of his chargeable transfers in the seven years preceding the addition, whilst similarly disregarding transfers made on that day. In addition, no account is to be taken of the value of transfers to the trust to the extent that these have been taken into account under IHTA 1984, ss 65 and 66.

Although complex, these rules can be used to a settlor's advantage.

Example

An individual who has made no inheritance tax transfers establishes five discretionary trusts A, B, C, D and E at three-monthly intervals, each with initial cash gifts of £3,000. He then makes further cash additions of £40,000 to each trust all on the same day. Ignoring the availability of his annual exemptions, the margin for growth of each trust is as follows.

	A	B	C	D	E
Initial value	3,000	3,000	3,000	3,000	3,000
Added property	40,000	40,000	40,000	40,000	40,000
Trusts' 'clock'	–	3,000	6,000	9,000	12,000
	43,000	46,000	49,000	52,000	55,000
Margin for growth	207,000	204,000	201,000	198,000	195,000
Nil rate band	£250,000	£250,000	£250,000	£250,000	£250,000

At the ten-year anniversary of the discretionary trusts, the effect of IHTA 1984, s 67(3)(b)(i) is that trust A is looked at in isolation, ignoring the others. Unless the value of the property contained in each trust exceeds the current nil rate band, these trusts should never be subject to inheritance tax either in respect of an 'exit' charge under section 65 or a ten-year anniversary charge.

The total scope for future growth taking all of the trusts together is £1,005,000.

The idea is not to mitigate inheritance tax upon establishing the settlements but to enable a number of settlements to qualify as nil rate band trusts. In practice, it is advisable that each trust is established with sufficient value to preclude any argument that it commenced as a result of an addition although

Creating Settlements **4.44**

such an argument is unlikely to be successful given the wording of IHTA 1984, s 60. Upon a narrow construction the trusts would have commenced when they were established, even if purely nominal consideration was used. In practice, it is advisable to avoid this issue by ensuring that each trust is established with a realistic amount of property. Ideally, the terms of each settlement should differ, for example, by varying the class of eligible beneficiaries, the trustees, perpetuity and accumulation periods and the relevant governing law. This should avoid any argument under the general law that the trusts together constitute one settlement. As with the 'cascade' approach, it is the implementation aspect of this arrangement which is just as important as the technical strategy if difficulties are not to be encountered under the *Ramsay* principle.

Techniques such as these, in which settlements are created on successive days, were regarded by the Inland Revenue as creating single settlements by associated operations at the time that the final settlement was made.

In the recent case of *Rysaffe Trustee Co (Channel Islands) Ltd v CIR, Ch D [2002] STC 872* two brothers each made five discretionary settlements by separate trust instruments. Each settlement was in exactly the same form, except for the date which was inserted by the settlors' solicitors after the execution of the deeds. The trust fund of each settlement was £10 paid by each settlor. When the settlements were made, the settlors intended to issue bonus deferred shares in a private company (of which they were shareholders and directors) and to transfer these to the trustee, one fifth of the total for each settlement. Those transfers subsequently took place, but the issue of the bonus deferred shares was later found to be invalid and some of the existing ordinary shares were therefore redesignated as deferred shares and transferred to the trustee.

A 'settlement' is defined in IHTA 1984 s 43(2) as 'any disposition or dispositions of property' and IHTA 1984 s 272 provides that a 'disposition' includes a disposition effected by associated operations. 'Associated operations' is defined as any two operations of which one was effected with reference to the other, or with a view to enabling the other to be effected or facilitating its being effected, and any further operation having a like relation to any of those two (IHTA 1984, s 268(1)(b)). The Revenue considered that, in respect of each settlor, the creation of the five settlements and the transfer of the shares to the trustee were all associated operations. Therefore, there was a single settlement within the meaning of IHTA 1984 s 43 and, for the purposes of the ten-year anniversary charge, tax should be charged under IHTA 1984 s 64 at the rate applicable to the total value in all five settlements. In the alternative they considered that the five settlements were five 'dispositions of property' within the meaning of IHTA 1984 s 43 which resulted in one settlement.

The Special Commissioner rejected the trustee's appeal deciding that the creation of each settlement, and the subsequent transfer of the deferred shares, were associated operations.

The High Court held that it was not relevant that the five settlements were identical. There were separate documents with separate dates and the settlor had intended to create five different settlements. Merely because their terms

4.45 *Creating Settlements*

were similar, the five settlements could not be artificially amalgamated. The associated operations rule in IHTA 1984 s 268 was not a 'catch-all' anti-avoidance provision which could be invoked to nullify the tax advantages of any scheme. The section came into effect only insofar as the expression 'associated operations' was used elsewhere. In the *Rysaffe* case the making of the five settlements was a disposition for IHT purposes and there was therefore no reason to consider the associated operations rule. That rule was designed to identify a disposition made by several transactions and here there was a disposition by the single making of each settlement. The associated operations provisions did not apply and it was not appropriate to regard the five settlements as created by associated operations. It is understood that the Revenue have lodged a notice of appeal.

Business and agricultural property relief

4.45 On any distribution of property from a discretionary settlement prior to the first ten-year anniversary, the rate of charge is calculated by reference to the value of property comprised in the settlement immediately after it became so comprised. No account is taken of the fact that the property (when it became comprised in the settlement) may have been of a type eligible for business or agricultural property relief. This is because one of the steps in calculating the inheritance tax on such a distribution involves calculating the tax that would be due on a hypothetical transfer of property. Business property relief and agricultural property relief apply only to reduce the value of property transferred by an actual or deemed transfer of value or a chargeable event under the discretionary trust regime. The calculation of tax which would be chargeable if a hypothetical transfer were made is not one of these occasions. Thus, it may be advantageous to postpone a distribution until immediately after the ten-year anniversary, except where the property transferred qualifies for either 100% agricultural or business property relief (see later). The charge at that time will take account of any business or agricultural property relief (as it is made by reference to the value of the property then in the settlement which will be reduced by these reliefs) as will, therefore, the charge on any distributions following that anniversary. If a distribution is made within three months of the ten-year anniversary, no additional inheritance tax is payable (IHTA 1984, s 65(4)).

More importantly, a settlor who wishes to create a nil rate band discretionary trust which will suffer no inheritance tax on distributions made prior to the first ten-year anniversary and wishes to transfer property eligible for agricultural or business property relief should consider the following. The value of the property comprised in the settlement immediately after its commencement will *not* be reduced by agricultural or business property relief and if held in one settlement would cause that settlement to exceed its nil rate band. In certain circumstances a charge can arise where assets are subsequently appointed out of the trust before the first ten-year charge. Paradoxically, no inheritance tax charge should arise where assets qualifying for the full 100% relief have been appointed before the first ten-year charge provided that the assets have been held by the trustees for a minimum of two years.

Creating Settlements **4.45**

Although a rate of inheritance tax may be applicable on the assets so appointed, their tax value is nil so that no charge to tax should in fact arise.

Where the assets will not qualify for business property relief on leaving a discretionary trust because, for example, the property has been replaced by property which does not qualify, the tax charge may be reduced by forward planning.

Example

Mr A intends to settle property qualifying for 100% business property relief on discretionary trusts. He has made no prior transfers and anticipates that the property will be sold for cash within one year. In five years' time it is likely that the trustees will decide to distribute the trust property to the beneficiaries.

If Mr A makes a single settlement the consequences would be as follows:

There would be no charge on making the settlement because the property would be wholly relieved by business property relief. On the distribution to the beneficiaries the tax charge would be calculated by reference to a deemed transfer when the settlement was created which did not take into account BPR as follows:

	£
Amount transferred	500,000
Nil rate band	250,000
Subject to tax	£250,000

Tax charged on hypothetical transfer

£250,000 × 20% = £50,000

Effective rate = $\frac{£50,000}{500,000} \times 100 = 10\%$

Appropriate fraction = $10\% \times 30\% \times \frac{5}{10} = 1.5\%$

Inheritance tax charged on distribution:

1.5% × £500,000 = £7,500

Instead, Mr A considers two alternative strategies.

Strategy A

Mr A makes two similar discretionary settlements on successive days, settling £1 in each. A few days later he adds £249,999 to each settlement on the same day. These two settlements are not related settlements because they were not made on the same day even though the additions to the settlements were (IHTA 1984, s 62). Because Mr A made additions to the settlement, the calculation of the appropriate proportion of the effective rate is based on a hypothetical transfer by a transferor with the same cumulative transfers as Mr A had on the day before the addition (IHTA 1984, s 67). Therefore, neither settlement had to take into account the addition made to the other.

There is no inheritance tax charge on the making of the settlements or the additions because the property is wholly relieved by business property relief. The inheritance tax on the distributions is calculated as follows:

4.46 *Creating Settlements*

	Settlement A £	Settlement B £
Settlor's cumulative transfers on day before additions	1	1
Value of property in settlement immediately after the additions	249,999	249,999
Value of property in related settlements	Nil	Nil
	250,000	250,000
Nil rate band	(250,000)	(250,000)
	Nil	Nil
Tax chargeable on hypothetical transfer	Nil	Nil
Effective rate	$\frac{\text{Nil}}{249,999} \times 100 = \text{Nil}\%$	$\frac{\text{Nil}}{249,000} \times 100 = \text{Nil}\%$

Strategy B

Mr A makes two discretionary settlements on succeeding days settling £250,000 on each. Again there is no inheritance tax on making the settlements because Mr A's transfers of value are wholly relieved by business property relief. On the distribution from the settlement Mr A's cumulative transfers which are taken into account in calculating the appropriate proportion of the effective rate on the second settlement include his transfer to the first settlement the value of which will have been reduced by business property relief to nil.

	Settlement A £	Settlement B £
Mr A's previous chargeable transfers	Nil	Nil
		(250,000 – 250,000)
Value of property in settlement immediately after it commenced	250,000	250,000
Value of property in settlements	Nil	Nil
	250,000	250,000
Nil rate band	(250,000)	(250,000)
	Nil	Nil
Tax chargeable on hypothetical transfer	Nil	Nil
Effective rate	$\frac{\text{Nil}}{250,000} \times 100 = \text{Nil}\%$	$\frac{\text{Nil}}{250,000} \times 100 = \text{Nil}\%$

Of course, in deciding upon these strategies one must take into account the application of the associated operation provisions and of the *Ramsay* principle.

Anti-avoidance provisions

4.46 Those who have used their nil rate band but wish to make a transfer ultimately to a discretionary settlement without suffering material inheritance tax charges should be aware of the pitfall presented by one particular provision. A solution might appear to be to confer an interest in possession upon a beneficiary who has not used his nil rate band by a potentially exempt transfer and, after a limited interval, to exercise a power

Creating Settlements **4.48**

of appointment to determine that beneficiary's interest in possession and create discretionary trusts. However, the net effect of the anti-avoidance provisions in IHTA 1984, s 54A and IHTA 1984, s 54B is that in calculating the inheritance tax on the determination of the beneficiary's interest, the settlor's cumulative total in the seven years prior to the date of termination may be substituted for that of the beneficiary, if a greater charge to inheritance tax is thereby incurred.

Transfers between spouses

4.47 Where, however, a settlor creates an interest in possession settlement for his spouse which is subsequently terminated and the settled property then becomes held on discretionary trusts the anti-avoidance provisions referred to above will not apply, since the settlor's transfer for the benefit of his spouse was not a potentially exempt transfer but rather an exempt transfer (IHTA 1984, s 18). The provisions of IHTA 1984, s 80 will treat the date on which the spouse's interest in possession ceases and the settled property becomes held on discretionary trusts as being the date of commencement of a separate settlement. The spouse's cumulative total immediately prior to that time (rather than that of the settlor before the creation of the interest in possession settlement for his spouse or at the time that the property then becomes held on discretionary trusts) will be taken into account for the purposes of calculating the inheritance tax charges on the property held on discretionary trusts.

Therefore, 'estate equalisation' can be achieved between spouses, if one wishes to create discretionary settlements using both his and his spouse's nil rate bands, without the settlor giving property outright to his spouse and relying on her, of her own free will, to create discretionary settlements with that property.

This device has also been suggested as a means of establishing a discretionary trust with the settlor as a beneficiary, something which would normally be inadvisable in the light of the 'reservation of benefit' provisions. These provisions will not apply to the initial gift into the interest in possession settlement because FA 1986, s 102(3) disapplies section 102(1) where the gift is an exempt transfer between spouses. Provided the interest in possession of the spouse comes to an end under the terms of the settlement, there will be no further 'gift' to which section 102(1) can apply. There is a risk that there will be an attack under the *Ramsay* principle.

The case of *CIR v Eversden and another (executors of Greenstock deceased), Ch D [2002] STC 1109* confirmed that the spouse exemption prevented the application of the reservation of benefit rules in those circumstances. The application of the *Ramsay* principle, however, was not argued in the case and therefore the case does not provide authority to suggest that the *Ramsay* principle does not apply to arrangements planned to take advantage of the exemption in FA 1986 s 102(3).

Conclusions

4.48 Although the rules relating to the inheritance tax charge on discretionary settlements are complex and there are pitfalls, these settle-

4.49 *Creating Settlements*

ments are extremely flexible. A settlement in this form, on which inheritance tax is never charged at full death rates, may be preferable to a settlor retaining assets in his estate which will on his death be charged at the full rates on the value at the date of death, albeit that the base cost of the assets held in the free estate will benefit from a step up in value for capital gains tax purposes (TCGA 1992, s 62). Further, the inheritance tax charge on the settlement will be unaffected by the fortunes of the beneficiaries themselves; the death of a beneficiary will have no inheritance tax consequences for the settlement. A discretionary settlement may, therefore, in some circumstances be preferable to a settlement giving successive life interests if the life expectancy of one of the intended beneficiaries is short.

Caution should be exercised when creating a discretionary settlement if other gifts are to be made at or about the same time. A potentially exempt transfer made before a chargeable transfer to a discretionary settlement, which subsequently becomes chargeable, will affect not only the amount of charge on the transfer to the discretionary settlement but also the ten-yearly charge, and charges on distributions from that settlement for so long as the settlement continues. This is particularly relevant where it is proposed that the trustees make a transfer of some or all of the trust property prior to the seventh anniversary of the creation of the discretionary trust. In establishing the applicable rate of inheritance tax to be levied on property ceasing to be held in discretionary trusts, IHTA 1984, s 68(4)(b) requires that the settlor's cumulative history of chargeable transfers is taken into account. Where potentially exempt transfers have been made prior to the establishment of the discretionary trust, which would have the effect of using up some or all of the settlor's available nil rate band, his or her history of cumulative chargeable transfers will be unquantifiable. As a result the applicable rate of tax on value leaving the discretionary trust will not be known. No doubt in most cases it will be possible for the trustees to retain sufficient assets as a reserve to guard against this risk. However, the problem is most acute where prior to the expiry of the seven-year period it is proposed that a discretionary trust should appoint all its assets to an interest in possession trust subject to a hold-over election in order to mitigate capital gains tax on a future disposal. Whilst some sort of indemnity arrangement might be possible, it is generally preferable to avoid this type of issue. Accordingly, as far as possible it may be prudent to ensure that transfers to such discretionary trusts pre-date any potentially exempt transfers.

Capital gains tax

4.49 For capital gains tax purposes the creation of a discretionary settlement will be a disposal and a charge to capital gains tax may arise on the gains arising on the assets settled. However, an election for hold-over relief under TCGA 1992, s 260 may be made regardless of the nature of the assets transferred. It is possible for hold-over relief to apply where transfers are made within the settlor's nil rate band.

A charge to capital gains tax will subsequently arise on any distribution, appointment or other occasion, such as the end of the settlement period, on

Creating Settlements **4.50**

which one or more beneficiaries become absolutely entitled to the whole or part of the trust property. At that time the trustees will be deemed to have disposed of the assets to which a beneficiary has become so entitled and to reacquire them as nominees or bare trustees for that beneficiary. Here again an election for hold-over relief under TCGA 1992, s 260 will usually be available.

Whilst the settlement continues, the trustees will be liable to capital gains tax on realised gains at 34%, subject to taper relief and their annual exemption. The trustees' annual exemption is half of the amount available to an individual, or a smaller proportion if the settlor has created more than one settlement, subject to a minimum of one-tenth of the individual's exemption if the settlor has created ten or more settlements.

Income tax

4.50 Trustees (subject to the provisions of ICTA 1988, Part XV) will be liable to income tax at the rate applicable to trusts since, even if they have no power to accumulate, they will have a discretion as to the distribution of income amongst the beneficiaries. The beneficiaries to whom the trustees decide to distribute income will receive a net amount from which income tax at the rate applicable to trusts has been deducted. They may recover this tax in whole or in part if their personal rates of income tax are less than 34%.

Where trustees do have the power to accumulate, it is advisable that they should also have power to distribute accumulated income as though it were income of the year in which it is so distributed. In this way the ability to utilise the credit for the tax paid by the trustees will not be lost. Accumulated funds may subsequently be distributed as income rather than capital if consideration of the beneficiary's rates of income tax and the rate of inheritance tax charged if a capital payment is made suggest that this would be advantageous.

Payments received by a beneficiary from trustees of a discretionary settlement which form part of his income do not suffer an inheritance tax charge on distribution to him (IHTA 1984, s 65(5)(b)). This power to convert capital back to income may be valuable if

(*a*) the tax paid by the trustees may thereby be recovered; or

(*b*) it is used to distribute accumulated income from a discretionary trust prior to a ten-year anniversary without incurring an inheritance tax charge, thereby reducing the property in the settlement for the purposes of that ten-yearly charge.

If the trustees have power to retain undistributed income, it should not be necessary to distribute that income prior to a ten-year anniversary. Any *undistributed* or *unaccumulated* income will not suffer a charge to inheritance tax at that time although *accumulated* income will (Statement of Practice SP 8/86).

Conversely, of course, the beneficiaries' personal rates of income tax may suggest that income should be capitalised and paid out as such. Provided

4.51 *Creating Settlements*

regular payments are not made, the beneficiaries should not suffer an income tax charge.

Creating an offshore settlement

4.51 An individual may wish when creating a settlement to do so offshore, i.e. by establishing a settlement with all or a majority of the trustees resident outside the UK. He may wish to do this for a number of reasons.

(a) He may wish to establish a fund outside the UK whilst no exchange control provisions are in force which prevent him from doing so, in anticipation that such controls might in future be reintroduced and restrict his ability to invest worldwide. By creating a settlement outside the UK to hold funds he should secure the ability to continue to invest worldwide in the highly unlikely event that exchange controls are re-introduced in this country. Settlements established for exchange control reasons were frequently ones which conferred a life interest on the settlor and gave the trustees power to distribute capital to him. The tax consequences of creating this type of settlement are considered in chapter 18 *Investing Abroad*.

(b) If the settlement is established under a foreign law it may be possible under that law (such as the law of Jersey, Guernsey or Liechtenstein) to ensure that income may be accumulated for longer than the permitted periods under English law. This may be advantageous if the settlor does not wish very young or unborn beneficiaries to become entitled to income from their shares of the trust fund until they attain 25 or if the settlement to be created is discretionary and the settlor anticipates that income will be accumulated in the settlement.

The Lord Chancellor's Department have published a consultation paper (CP10/02) proposing to implement the Law Commission's recommendation to abolish the restrictions on accumulations. It is proposed that the changes should take effect some time in 2003.

The tax consequences

4.52 The creation of an offshore, rather than an onshore, settlement by a UK resident and domiciled settlor does not result in any difference in the inheritance tax treatment of the settlement. Inheritance tax will be chargeable on the settlor's gift to the settlement, during the life of the settlement and on distributions from it in the same way as described above according to the nature of the settlement. So far as capital gains tax is concerned, hold-over relief cannot be claimed in respect of the transfer of assets direct to the trustees of an offshore settlement (TCGA 1992, s 166 and TCGA 1992, s 261), so the creation of the settlement may give rise to an immediate capital gains tax charge.

The tax consequences for the settlor and beneficiaries of a non-resident settlement are considered in detail in chapter 6 *Offshore Trusts*. As will be

Creating Settlements **4.52**

seen, the capital gains tax benefits of creating an offshore settlement have been greatly reduced as any chargeable gains realised by non-resident trustees (calculated as if they were resident in the UK) are attributed to the settlor, if either

(*a*)   the settlor or his spouse,

(*b*)   any child of the settlor or his spouse,

(*c*)   the spouse of any such child,

(*d*)   any grandchild of the settlor or his spouse,

(*e*)   the spouse of any such grandchild,

(*f*)   any company controlled by any of the persons in (*a*)–(*e*) above, or

(*g*)   any company associated with such a controlled company

benefit, or are capable of benefiting from, the capital or income of the settlement.

In addition, TCGA 1992, s 87 imposes a capital payments charge on beneficiaries who receive capital payments from a non-resident settlement regardless of whether the settlor was domiciled or not in the UK. There is also a supplementary capital gains tax charge in addition to the primary charge on beneficiaries who receive capital payments from the settlement. The result of these provisions is that there are limited advantages in creating an offshore settlement purely for capital gains tax reasons where the beneficiaries include the settlor or his immediate family unless a particular tax strategy is being followed.

The creation of a settlement with non-resident trustees by a person who is domiciled in the UK gives rise to a duty on any person concerned with the making of the settlement in the course of his trade or profession (other than a barrister) to report to the Inland Revenue within three months of the making of the settlement the names and addresses of the settlor and the trustees (IHTA 1984, s 218).

5 Existing Settlements

Introduction

5.1 Although a settlement may achieve the settlor's aims when it is created, one cannot anticipate all events and changes in taxation which may make it appropriate to alter the interests of the beneficiaries in the future or to terminate the settlement earlier than originally planned.

The creation of a settlement is not a concluded chapter in the settlor's affairs. A settlement, like the individual's estate, should be kept under review to determine whether any steps should be taken in relation to the settled property or the terms upon which it is held; and the settlement should not be considered in isolation from the beneficiaries and their circumstances.

Any reorganisation may be prompted by an overall consideration of the assets of the settlement and the interests and personal circumstances of the beneficiaries. However, more frequently, it is precipitated by a request from one or more of the beneficiaries for capital or the prospect of an occasion on which the interests of the beneficiaries will alter, such as the death of a life tenant or the attainment by a beneficiary under an accumulation and maintenance settlement of an interest in possession.

This chapter considers steps that may be taken in relation to existing settlements. It considers

(*a*) the extent to which the familiar techniques of estate planning may be applied to settlements;

(*b*) means of dealing with the interests of beneficiaries under settlements and the advantages in leaving some older settlements untouched; and

(*c*) the export of existing settlements.

Except where otherwise indicated it is assumed that all beneficiaries of the types of settlement considered are resident and domiciled in the UK and that the settlors are all UK resident domiciliaries.

What steps may be taken to deal with the settled property?

General principles

5.2 The basic principles of estate planning are equally applicable when considering whether any steps should be taken in relation to settled

5.3 Existing Settlements

property. This is particularly so when considering the interest of a life tenant who, whilst not owning the capital of the trust, will, to the extent that he is indefeasibly entitled to income from the trust property, be treated as owning that property in which he has an interest in possession (IHTA 1984, s 49). The steps that may be taken to minimise the inheritance tax charge that will arise on the life tenant's death are similar to those that may be taken by an individual in relation to his own estate. He could, for example, surrender his interest in possession in the settled property in a series of tranches over a number of years in order to make use of his annual exemption of £3,000 per annum. Alternatively, the life tenant may assign or surrender his interest in possession by way of a potentially exempt transfer. Provided that, as a result of the transfer, the estate of another individual is increased or property becomes held upon particular types of trust and he survives his deemed transfer of value on the assignment or surrender by seven years no inheritance tax will be chargeable.

The principles discussed in chapter 2 *Lifetime Planning* of making gifts in order to reduce exposure to inheritance tax at a later date, and implementing a policy of doing so at an early stage, have less application in relation to settlements in which no qualifying interest in possession subsists (commonly called discretionary settlements). Provided the settlor has not reserved a benefit in the property settled under FA 1986, s 102, no individual will at any time be treated, for inheritance tax purposes, as being beneficially entitled to the trust property. Unless the settled property is held upon trusts of a nature favoured with special inheritance tax treatment in IHTA 1984, Part III Chapter III and thus excluded from the 'relevant property' regime, the settlement may suffer an inheritance tax charge on each ten-year anniversary of its creation and at the time of any distribution being made. Nevertheless, the approach of a ten-year anniversary and the rates of inheritance tax applicable to distributions before and after the anniversary may suggest that any distributions proposed should be made sooner rather than later. Each of the main categories of settlement (for inheritance tax purposes) and the possible steps that should be considered in relation to them during their lives are examined below but these points are raised to emphasise that planning does not stop once a settlement has been created.

Asset conversion

5.3 Other estate planning steps of a type discussed in chapter 2 *Lifetime Planning* may be advantageously taken by the trustees or beneficiaries of a settlement.

Inheritance tax on property in a settlement may be mitigated if the assets held are converted from ones which do not qualify for any form of inheritance tax relief to those which do, such as agricultural property or relevant business property. This will reduce the value on which inheritance tax will be charged on the death of a life tenant or a ten-year anniversary of a discretionary settlement. However, any sale of property in order to release funds to acquire property qualifying for relief is likely to give rise to a capital gains tax charge for trustees resident in the UK which may outweigh the inheritance tax

Existing Settlements **5.4**

benefits. For this reason the most obvious occasions for converting assets may arise in relation to settlements with non-resident trustees which are outside the provisions of TCGA 1992, s 86 and TCGA 1992, Sch 5 (see chapter 6 *Offshore Trusts*). These settlements will be outside the charge to capital gains tax and any disposal of assets made in order to re-invest the trust fund in other assets will not trigger a capital gains tax charge for the trustees (although beneficiaries resident in the UK will suffer a capital gains tax charge in respect of the gains realised by the trustees if they receive a distribution or other benefit from the settlement). An important exception to this general rule is where such trustees own assets used in connection with a trade, profession or vocation undertaken in the UK through a branch or agency. The fact that trustees are non-resident will not prevent a liability arising on a disposal of the assets or in some cases where the activity undertaken ceases (TCGA 1992, ss 10, 25).

In the case of a non-resident interest in possession settlement which was created by a settlor domiciled in the UK and which remains liable to inheritance tax even though the life tenant is now domiciled and resident abroad, it may be worth disposing of at least part of the property held and re-investing the proceeds in exempt gilts, subject to the duties that a trustee has in relation to investments. Whilst the life tenant remains domiciled and resident outside the UK no inheritance tax will be chargeable on his death or on a lifetime surrender or assignment by him of his interest in respect of that part of the trust fund invested in exempt gilts (IHTA 1984, s 48(4)). In addition, no capital gains tax will be suffered as a result of the change of investments provided the settlement is outside the provisions of TCGA 1992, s 86 and TCGA 1992, Sch 5.

Similarly, where a settlement with non-resident trustees was created by a settlor domiciled outside the UK for inheritance tax purposes but holds property situated in the UK, that property will not be excluded property within IHTA 1984, s 48 and inheritance tax will be chargeable upon the value of that property. In the case of an interest in possession settlement, by selling the UK situated property to a company incorporated outside the UK the property held by the trustees becomes the foreign situated shares in the foreign company and is therefore excluded property and outside the charge to inheritance tax. The conversion of trust property to excluded property in the manner set out above should not give rise to an inheritance tax charge, although a stamp duty charge may arise. The rules relating to discretionary trusts are different, as an inheritance tax charge will arise where 'relevant property' (IHTA 1984, s 58(1)(f) ceases to be held. For these purposes excluded property is not relevant property. It would be arguable that, where the trustees dispose of relevant property and acquire excluded property, an exit charge under IHTA 1984, s 65 could arise. There is, therefore, a specific exemption preventing a tax charge arising when relevant property ceases to be situated in the UK, thereby becoming excluded property (IHTA 1984, s 65(7)).

Value freezing

5.4 Techniques of estate planning involving freezing the value of assets held in a settlement are useful in relation to settled property as they

5.4 Existing Settlements

are in relation to an individual's free estate. However, legislative provisions and the terms upon which settled property is held may restrict the opportunities available to the trustees to deal with their trust assets more efficiently and their general duty to consider the interests of all beneficiaries and their specific duties in relation to the exercise of investment powers may mean that the steps they may take are more limited.

Value shifting exercises may be less appropriate for settlements since trustees should not, as a matter of trust law, participate in the reduction or freezing of the value of their trust property. However, such exercises may be valid if the persons benefited by them hold the interests, the values of which are frozen. It may, therefore, be appropriate to create a 'parallel' settlement with similar beneficiaries and to arrange for assets with a frozen or gradually depreciating value to remain in one settlement with increasingly valuable assets being held in the 'parallel' settlement.

One possible route is for an interest in possession settlement holding shares in a family company to create a new class of shares in the company with little value at the time of their creation but which will participate in the future growth in value of the company or at a future date become of greater value. The original shares would remain in the settlement in which the interest in possession subsists and, provided that the trustees have power to do so, the new (deferred) shares could be advanced to a new settlement for the benefit only of the remaindermen of the original settlement. Provided the new shares advanced are of little or no value at the time of the advance, no inheritance tax should become chargeable as a result of the advance. On the death of the life tenant it would be hoped that the original shares would have lost a substantial part of their value or at the very least would not have increased in value from the date at which the new class was created and that this value or the growth in value since that date would have accrued to the new settlement for the benefit of the remaindermen of the original settlement. (Clearly a sufficiently large holding of shares carrying the necessary degree of control must be held in the first settlement or the other shareholders must agree to the issue for such an arrangement to be implemented.) If the mechanism by which this is achieved is for the deferred shares subsequently to rank equally, or become merged with, shares of another class, in the Inland Revenue's view IHTA 1984, s 98(1)(b) applies because there will be an alteration of rights (Law Society Gazette, 11 September 1991).

In private trading companies, the necessity to carry out such value freezing exercises has been reduced because of the availability of 100% business property relief.

Another estate planning opportunity to consider is for the trustees of an interest in possession settlement to make a loan at a low rate of interest, with the life tenant's consent, to a new settlement for the benefit of the remaindermen of the original settlement. The difference between the return obtained (in the form of both income and capital appreciation) by the trustees of the new settlement from the use of the money and the interest being paid to the original settlement would accumulate in the new settlement. The capital value of the loan in the original settlement would have been frozen. Since interest on the loan would be charged it should not be possible for the Inland

Existing Settlements **5.5**

Revenue to argue that the life tenant's interest in possession had terminated in favour of the beneficiaries of the second settlement; a dubious argument in any case. However, where those beneficiaries are the minor or unmarried children of the life tenant, care should be taken to ensure that the income of the new settlement cannot be taxed as the income of the life tenant under ICTA 1988, s 660B since the life tenant's consent to the arrangement would almost undoubtedly make him a 'settlor' within those provisions.

These arrangements, which may be subject to attack under the associated operations provisions in IHTA 1984, s 268, are likely to be less useful as the termination of an interest in possession in settled property may be a potentially exempt transfer, provided that the estate of another individual is increased by the transfer or that property becomes held on the appropriate type of trust (IHTA 1984, s 3A). The professional fees will be less and the administration more simple if the life tenant merely assigns or surrenders his interest or part of it. The trustees can insure against the inheritance tax which would become payable if the life tenant were to die within seven years of the assignment or surrender. Nevertheless, other means of transferring value may be preferable if the life tenant has only a short life expectancy and his life is only insurable at substantial cost.

Creation of 'surplus assets'

5.5 One estate planning measure discussed in chapter 2 *Lifetime Planning* which should also be considered in relation to settlements is that of creating 'surplus assets'.

Surplus assets may be created by investing the trust fund in higher income yielding assets. The life tenant may consider assigning or surrendering part of his interest in possession or giving away income-producing assets from his free estate in the knowledge that his income will be undiminished by doing so. For inheritance tax purposes this assignment or surrender will be a potentially exempt transfer provided that the relevant conditions are fulfilled. An element of 'value freezing' will also be achieved since high income yielding investments are unlikely also to grow substantially in capital value. The value of the fund to which the life tenant will be treated as being beneficially entitled by virtue of his income entitlement will not therefore increase as substantially as it might otherwise have done. Therefore, the potential charge to inheritance tax on his death will have been reduced both by this and by his having given away his interest in part of the fund.

Where an interest in possession was conferred upon a surviving spouse under the will or intestacy of an individual who died before 13 November 1974, the value of the capital to which the surviving spouse is treated as being beneficially entitled will be left out of account in calculating the inheritance tax payable on his or her death (IHTA 1984, s 273 and IHTA 1984, Sch 6 para 2). By increasing the amount of income arising to the surviving spouse from such a trust it may be possible to place him or her in a position to give away assets which do not benefit from this exemption during their lifetime by way of potentially exempt transfers, thereby enabling the bulk of his estate to pass free of tax. The capital gains tax implications of restructuring the investment

5.6 Existing Settlements

portfolio, as well as that relating to any gift, must always be taken into account.

Dealing with the interests of the beneficiaries

5.6 The circumstances in which a reorganisation of interests under a settlement or the distribution of capital from a settlement may be appropriate and the most efficient methods of achieving the desired result (together with other means of dealing with settled property to achieve similar ends) are considered later in this chapter in relation to accumulation and maintenance settlements, life interest settlements and discretionary settlements. First, it is necessary to consider, briefly, the means by which the interests of beneficiaries may be altered either by the exercise of powers incorporated in a settlement or otherwise and some of the advantages of allowing existing settlements to continue.

How can the interests of beneficiaries be altered?

5.7 Frequently the terms of older settlements are more rigid than those of more recently drafted settlements. More recent settlements may include wide and flexible powers of appointment exercisable in favour of a wide class of beneficiaries or powers to revoke the existing trusts and declare completely new trusts which may be exercised (by the settlor, the trustees or others) to rearrange the interests of the beneficiaries, whereas older settlements may only incorporate powers to pay over capital to beneficiaries.

It may still be possible to vary older settlements (and will trusts) without such internal powers to alter beneficial interests. Where all of the beneficiaries are of full age and capacity, the rule in *Saunders v Vautier, (1841) 4 Beav 115* allows them to require the trustees to advance the settled property to them absolutely. However, the beneficiaries can only modify the existing trusts with the consent of the trustees (*Brockbank (Re), Ch D [1948] 1 All ER 287*). In most circumstances, however, this will result in the creation of a new settlement rather than the variation of an existing one. In any event, where there are minor, unborn or unascertained beneficiaries, an application to the court to sanction a variation under the Variation of Trusts Act 1958 will be necessary. Occasionally, an alteration of interests may arise from a compromise following a dispute between beneficiaries as to their rights and interests under a settlement and where minor or unborn beneficiaries are interested the court has power to sanction the compromise on their behalf. However, the court will not exercise its jurisdiction to sanction a compromise where it believes that there is no real dispute or point of uncertainty as to the interests of the beneficiaries (*Chapman v Chapman, [1954] AC 429; [1954] 1 All ER 978*). In such circumstances an application under the Variation of Trusts Act 1958 is appropriate; it was as a direct result of the decision in *Chapman v Chapman* that this statute was enacted.

Alternatively, one beneficiary of an interest in possession settlement may 'sell' his interest to another or he may surrender or assign his interest to another by

Existing Settlements **5.7**

way of gift. However, the surrender of an interest by the life tenant will not be sufficient to place capital in the hands of the remaindermen if the interests in remainder are held for a class of beneficiaries living at the death of the life tenant and, therefore, as yet undefined. If the interests of the remaindermen are contingent upon their surviving the life tenant and their interests do not expressly carry the intermediate income, undesirable inheritance tax consequences may follow if as a result of the surrender the income of the trust fund becomes held upon resulting trust for the settlor. When a beneficiary wishes to sell his interest he must consider the capital gains tax implications of doing so. A capital gains tax charge will arise in certain circumstances where a beneficiary of a trust sells his or her interest in it to someone else. Generally, this will affect UK settlements in which the settlor has an interest or where any of the trust property is derived from a trust which was a settlor-interested trust at any time in the previous two tax years. The effect of the provisions is to treat the underlying assets to which the interest relates as though they are disposed of by the trustees and immediately reacquired by them at market value (TCGA 1992, Sch 4A).

It may be possible to exercise statutory or other powers of advancement to place some or all of the trust fund in the hands of one or more of the beneficiaries, although in some older settlements there may be no express powers to advance capital to a life tenant and the statutory power of advancement (Trustee Act 1925, s 32) may not be extended (as is now common) to include the whole of the beneficiaries' presumptive shares.

Similarly, if property is held on protective trusts, any attempt by the life tenant to assign or surrender his interest will trigger the discretionary trusts which follow the protected life interest. It will be impossible to vary such trusts, whether before or after a forfeiture, without the consent of the court since minor and unborn beneficiaries (and future spouses) will be included in the class of beneficiaries who would or may benefit in the event of the life interest divesting from the protected life tenant. However, under the terms of the statutory protective trusts set out in Trustee Act 1925, s 33, the life tenant may consent to the statutory power of advancement, or an express power of advancement may be exercisable without giving rise to a forfeiture, and similar provisions may have been incorporated in express protective trusts; such powers may therefore be used to achieve some alteration of the interests.

Strict settlements within the Settled Land Act 1925 provide fewer opportunities for variation without the approval of the court since the statutory power of advancement is not applicable and so no rearrangement may be achieved unless specific powers are incorporated in the settlement. However, the life tenant may still assign or surrender his interest (unless it is a protected life interest in which case the planning steps that may be taken without an application to court under the Variation of Trusts Act 1958 will be very limited). Such settlements are now a dying breed since the enactment of the Trusts of Land and Appointment of Trustees Act 1996.

Discretionary trusts, being by their nature more flexible, do not, generally, give rise to these problems. The capital and income may be appointed to beneficiaries absolutely or upon new trusts which, for example, may qualify as accumulation and maintenance trusts.

5.8 Existing Settlements

Not only may the beneficial trust provisions of older settlements be less flexible than those of their modern counterparts but other dispositive powers, not strictly part of the beneficial trusts, may be more limited. Dispositive powers, incorporated in a settlement, such as that to permit beneficiaries to occupy properties owned by the trust or to lend trust money free of interest to the beneficiaries, may be exercised to confer benefits on individual beneficiaries other than by the outright appointment of capital to them or for their benefit.

When should existing settlements be left alone?

5.8 Existing settlements are not always burdensome. If no assets incorporating held-over gains are held at the death of the life tenant there will be an uplift in the base value of all the settled property to its market value at the date of his death free of capital gains tax. If, instead, the settlement had been broken before the life tenant's death and assets passed absolutely to the remaindermen (e.g. by way of potentially exempt transfer in the hope of avoiding an inheritance tax charge on the trust assets on the death of the life tenant) any gains inherent in the value of any assets which had been held-over into the hands of the remaindermen would still be potentially chargeable to capital gains tax.

If assets incorporating gains have been transferred to a life interest settlement and a hold-over election under either TCGA 1992, s 165 or (assuming the settlement was not initially a life interest one) TCGA 1992, s 260 has been made, the death of the life tenant will trigger a claw-back charge on the gains held over if the assets subject to the election are still held in the settlement at the life tenant's death (TCGA 1992, s 74). It may be possible to make a further election for hold-over relief at the life tenant's death to avoid this charge but as noted earlier this will not be possible where a surviving spouse or a UK registered charity have the succeeding interest as the provisions of TCGA 1992, s 260(2)(a) would not be satisfied. In such cases it may be more advantageous to advance the assets to the life tenant absolutely and elect to hold over the gain realised provided the terms of the settlement permit this and the relevant assets still fall within the scope of TCGA 1992, s 165. If the assets fall within his estate at death they will benefit from the tax-free uplift to their market value at the date of the life tenant's death. No claw-back provisions operate in relation to held-over gains crystallising on the death of an outright owner of assets. This technique will operate most successfully where the life tenant is likely to be survived by his UK-domiciled spouse, so that no inheritance tax charge will arise on the beneficiary's death where the spouse inherits the property concerned. Obviously, the trustees should not be solely motivated by the tax considerations.

Accordingly, careful consideration will be required in each case to determine whether the capital gains tax advantages of leaving assets in a settlement until the death of the life tenant outweigh the inheritance tax and other advantages of breaking or altering the settlement before it has run its course (whether by advance to the life tenant or by some other means). Much will depend on whether the assets are ever likely to be sold. The decision as to whether or not to break a life interest settlement and if so, in whose favour, may be finely

Existing Settlements 5.8

balanced. The maximum rates of capital gains tax and inheritance tax are now 40% and where, for example, 100% business property relief is available on the settled assets and no hold-over relief was claimed in respect of gains arising on the transfer of the assets to the settlement, there may be advantages in leaving the assets settled until the death of the life tenant. This will clearly be the case if a substantial part of the value of the assets represents unrealised gain (potentially chargeable at 40%) which will fall out of charge to capital gains tax on the life tenant's death, whilst the availability of 100% business property relief may relieve the property from all inheritance tax on death provided the settled assets remain unsold.

Some settlements still exist which benefit from the surviving spouse exemption of estate duty days which, by virtue of IHTA 1984, Sch 6 para 2 continues where the surviving spouse is still living. This exemption provides that property subject to this provision is not taken into account in calculating for inheritance tax purposes the value of the surviving spouse's estate on death, although the property can be taken into account for certain valuation purposes. Such settlements should, ideally, be left untouched to ensure that this protection remains on the death of the surviving spouse. Although the termination of the surviving spouse's interest in possession in such a trust, whether by a lifetime surrender or assignment or on death, would not give rise to a charge to inheritance tax, it is preferable for her not to make a lifetime gift of her interest but to retain the benefit of the complete inheritance tax exemption for the funds in which her interest subsists until her death and to give away by means of potentially exempt transfers other assets which fall within the inheritance tax charge. Unless there is need for income, the assets of such a settlement should ideally be invested for capital growth since the gains will pass free of inheritance tax.

Discretionary settlements created before 18 March 1986 and under which the settlor is included as a beneficiary do not fall within the gifts with reservation provisions since FA 1986, s 102 requires a gift to have been made after 17 March 1986. Such settlements are, therefore, likely to be best left alone. No property should now be added by any interested beneficiary (including the settlor) since the provisions of section 102 would apply to treat the donor beneficiary as beneficially entitled to that property (and property deriving from it) which is held in the settlement at his death. This would necessitate keeping the property separate from the other property in the settlement for identification purposes which from an administrative point of view could be inconvenient. If the settlor at some time during his lifetime is excluded from benefit he would be treated as having made a disposition of the property given (and property deriving from it) at that time by way of a potentially exempt transfer (FA 1986, s 102(4)). Any gains realised by the trustees will be taxed in the hands of the settlor under TCGA 1992, ss 77–79 whilst either he or his wife remain interested under the settlement, within the terms of the statutory rules. Equally, as a result of the income tax settlement rules, the settlor will be assessed on the income received by the trustees. For both capital gains tax and income tax purposes, the settlor should have a statutory right of recovery against the trustees for any tax so assessed on him.

Previously there was a considerable capital gains tax advantage in extending life interests rather than allowing beneficiaries to become absolutely entitled to

5.9 Existing Settlements

trust assets. The uniform rate of 34% on the capital gains of settlements has lessened that advantage. Gains realised by the trustees of settlements will be charged to capital gains tax at 34%, provided that neither the settlor nor his spouse have an interest under the settlement. If the life tenant or the remaindermen, in whose favour the settlement might be broken, will suffer capital gains tax at 40% on assets which they own absolutely, it may still be beneficial to retain those assets in the settlement. It may also be that advancing assets to a beneficiary will result in a loss of taper relief.

A reversionary interest which is defined to include any future interest under a settlement whether vested or contingent (IHTA 1984, s 47) is excluded property for inheritance tax purposes. The assignment of a reversionary interest will not usually give rise to a charge to inheritance tax and this is one of the least painful ways in which individuals may pass assets to others. Not only is there no inheritance tax charge arising on the gift but also the donor does not have to survive for seven years after the gift to achieve this. Further even if the assignment could not be a potentially exempt transfer (because made to a discretionary settlement) no inheritance tax will be payable and the donor's cumulative total will be unaffected. Since a reversionary interest is necessarily a future interest in settled property the donor is less likely to count on receipt of any benefit from the interest or to include it in his present assets when considering the resources available to him. He may be more prepared to give away something which he has not yet considered to be his (or at least part of it). For this reason it may be preferable to leave an existing settlement unbroken and for estate planning steps to be taken instead in relation to the reversionary interests existing under it.

Business and agricultural property relief

5.9 If business property relief or agricultural property relief is available on settled assets should a chargeable occasion arise, care should be taken to ensure when rearranging the interests of beneficiaries under a settlement that this is not lost.

Where an interest in possession subsists in a settlement the life tenant will be treated as owning the settled property for the purposes of determining whether the period of ownership qualifications are satisfied. If the life tenant's interest terminates (by whatever means) the succeeding 'owners' will have to own the settled assets (whether by being absolutely entitled to them, by having an interest in possession in them or by holding them on trusts within IHTA 1984, Part III Chapter III) for the relevant period before that relief will be available. Careless reorganisations may cause business property relief or agricultural property relief to be unavailable at the crucial moment.

Further, if a life tenant's interest in settled property qualifying for business property relief or agricultural property relief is terminated in favour of others and the termination, because of the nature of the interests which follow, is a potentially exempt transfer, the requirement that the transferees must continue to 'own' that property, or its qualifying replacement, if the relief is to be available should the potentially exempt transfer become chargeable should not be forgotten. Thus where, for example, accumulation and maintenance trusts follow the interest of the life tenant, if any of the beneficiaries of those trusts

Existing Settlements **5.10**

attain an interest in possession within seven years from the termination of the life tenant's interest, they would become the 'owner' of the share of the settled property in which their interest subsists and the original transferees (the trustees of the accumulation and maintenance settlement) would cease to 'own' the property; as a consequence the relief, if required, would not be available.

Capital gains tax issues

5.10 It is of increasing importance to ensure that new trusts are sufficiently flexible to permit their internal reorganisation without first precipitating a capital gains tax charge especially where hold-over relief would not be available.

When reorganising older, perhaps less flexible, settlements, it is vitally important to ensure that any steps taken do not themselves cause a new settlement to arise for capital gains tax purposes. In such an instance there would be a deemed disposal and reacquisition of the property held giving rise to a charge under TCGA 1992, s 71. The fact that the same individual trustees continue to act will not prevent a charge to tax arising, where they are seen to be acting in different capacities.

Provided such reorganisations are structured correctly they can be used to exclude TCGA 1992, s 77 (the onshore settlor charge) in respect of subsequent years of assessment. Alternatively, they can be effectively used to make gifts to members of a family by enhancing their interests under a settlement, again without incurring any immediate capital gains tax liability.

Another possibility is for trustees to exercise their powers in such a way as to preserve the tax advantages enjoyed by the settlement. In spite of the introduction of the uniform rate of capital gains tax on settlements, it is still often beneficial for interest in possession settlements to continue as long as possible, subject to the perpetuity rules and general legal considerations.

> *Example*
>
> Trustees of an accumulation and maintenance settlement hold shares in an investment company for two beneficiaries aged 23 and 24, contingent upon each attaining 25.
>
> Assuming that the Trustee Act 1925, s 31 has not been expressly or impliedly excluded, the beneficiaries will have already attained an interest in possession upon reaching 18. This is because under section 31(1)(ii) the trustees are required to pay to any beneficiary with a contingent interest in the trust capital, the entire net income arising from his share once he has attained 18. This obligation continues until the contingency is satisfied, or the interest fails.
>
> Hold-over relief under TCGA 1992, s 165 will not be available because the property held does not fall within the categories of qualifying business assets; TCGA 1992, s 260 will not apply because the provision of IHTA 1984, s 71(4) has already been satisfied.
>
> In order to defer the capital gains tax charge on the beneficiaries receiving the shares outright on reaching 25, the trustees might exercise powers under the

5.11 *Existing Settlements*

trust deed altering the date when the beneficiaries become entitled to the shares outright. Depending on the circumstances, it might be possible to postpone capital vesting until they were (say) 35.

However, such an internal reorganisation can only take place if the requisite powers are contained in the trust or, in other circumstances, conferred by statute.

Key considerations

5.11 If an internal trust reorganisation is to work, it is essential to consider the types of powers which enable trusts to be reorganised and how best to avoid the capital gains tax pitfalls, with which such trust reorganisations can be fraught. In particular, if steps are to be taken to alter the status of a trust, whether for capital gains tax or inheritance tax mitigation purposes, it is vitally important to identify those situations where a deemed disposal and reacquisition might arise. In particular, it is suggested that there are three key considerations to bear in mind:

(a) the nature of the power effecting the reorganisation;

(b) the extent to which such power is being used;

(c) in cases of doubt, the nature of the external evidence that exists indicating that a new settlement has been created.

Under the terms of the trust instrument, the trustees will be subject to a number of binding obligations which regulate the manner in which they hold the settled property on behalf of the beneficiaries. They will also usually benefit from a whole range of powers thereunder. Broadly, these will divide into those of a purely administrative nature, and those of a dispositive nature enabling the trustees to apply the trust property in the beneficiaries' favour.

In order to achieve a trust reorganisation, the trustees will be relying primarily upon powers in the latter category. Such powers come in a variety of forms, each having its own distinct characteristics. Some are more powerful tools than others. Accordingly, the basic approach adopted by the courts has been to identify the type of power the trustees are exercising in order to establish whether a new settlement has arisen. There are four leading cases in this area.

(i) In *Roome and Another v Edwards, HL 1981, 54 TC 359; [1981] STC 96; [1981] 1 All ER 736*, a settlement was established in 1944. In 1955 further deeds were executed with the net effect of appointing some of the assets to be held primarily for two beneficiaries absolutely, contingent upon their attaining the age of 25 (the appointed fund). After this date the 1944 settlement (the parent trust), and the appointed fund were administered separately, but there continued to be common trustees of both funds. In 1972 non-resident trustees were appointed in respect of the parent trust, whilst the appointed fund continued to have UK resident trustees. The non-resident trustees realised a significant capital gain and the Inland Revenue sought to assess the UK trustees of the appointed fund. They argued that both trusts together constituted one settlement for capital gains tax purposes, with the result that the resident trustees of the

Existing Settlements **5.11**

appointed fund were liable in respect of the capital gains made by the non-resident trustees. The House of Lords found in favour of the Revenue, and their reasoning is of key importance in determining whether an internal trust reorganisation will trigger a charge under TCGA 1992, s 71.

In essence, the leading judgment given by Lord Wilberforce suggested that the existence of separate trusts, separate trustees and separate and defined trust property would not necessarily be decisive. He suggested that a practical and commonsense approach should be adopted, in deciding whether a new trust had been created, after taking into account established legal doctrine. He also sought to distinguish between situations where different types of powers had been exercised by the trustees.

The illustrative comments he made were in the particular context of special powers of appointment (*[1981] STC at e-f p100*), and these should be read in the light of the later gloss added by Vinelott J in *Ewart v Taylor* (post). Taking this into account, where a special power of appointment is exercised it would not be correct to say that 'a separate settlement had been created . . . if it were found that provisions of the original settlement continued to apply to the appointed fund, or that the appointed fund were liable in certain events, to fall back into the rest of the settled property'.

Lord Wilberforce contrasted such an exercise with a power to appoint and appropriate a part or portion of the trust property to beneficiaries and to settle it for their benefit:

> 'If such a power is exercised, the natural conclusion might be that a separate settlement was created, all the more so if a complete new set of trusts were declared as to the appropriated property, and if it could be said that the trusts of the original settlement ceased to apply to it. There can be many variations on these cases each of which will have to be judged on its facts.'

(ii) The facts in *Ewart v Taylor, Ch D [1983] STC 721* were complex, but a subsidiary issue depended on whether a separate settlement (Angela's fund) had been created for a beneficiary following the exercise by the trustees of a power of appointment. Following Lord Wilberforce's observations in *Roome and Another v Edwards*, the fact that a power of appointment, albeit of a wide nature, had been used suggested that no new settlement had arisen. Against this, the appointment was exhaustive in that it represented a complete severance from the beneficiaries' interest under the main trust, it had its own key management powers and new trustees could be appointed without reference to the original trust provisions.

The intention of the parties in separating Angela's interests from the rest of the original trust and how the trustees' accountants had treated the reorganisation resulted in the court holding that a new trust had been established. They had prepared separate accounts, and the notes to these clearly suggested that they considered that a separate settlement had arisen.

5.11 Existing Settlements

(iii) In *Bond v Pickford, CA [1983] STC 517* property was transferred to trustees on discretionary trusts for the benefit of a settlor's child and grandchildren in 1961. In 1972, the trustees executed two deeds allocating part of the settled property to the settlor's grandchildren absolutely, contingent upon their attaining 22. The provisions in the 1961 settlement dealing with investments, execution of trusts and powers, appointment and remuneration of trustees still applied to the allocated property and the 1961 settlement trustees continued to act. However, the new trusts exhausted the beneficial interests. The Inland Revenue, relying on this, argued that a new settlement had been created. This, they argued, was supported by the wording of the power of allocation which suggested that the allocated funds were to be governed by their own separate administrative powers. The trustees contended that as the allocated property continued to be held by the same trustees and subject to the same administrative powers as the remainder of the settled property, no separate settlement had arisen. The Court of Appeal found in favour of the trustees.

Here the most influential judgment was given by Lord Justice Slade. He considered that:

> 'there is . . . a crucial distinction to be drawn between (*a*) powers to alter the presently operative trusts of a settlement which expressly or by necessary implication authorise the trustees to remove assets altogether from the original settlement (without rendering any person absolutely beneficially entitled to them); and (*b*) powers of this nature which do not confer on the trustees such authority.'

He felt that the former represented 'powers in the wider form' and the latter 'powers in the narrower form'.

(iv) In *Swires v Renton, Ch D 1991, 64 TC 315; [1991] STC 490* the trustees of a settlement executed a deed of appointment by which the trust fund was divided into two parts. One part was appointed to Isabelle, the settlor's daughter, absolutely. The second was placed on trust, and the income paid to Isabelle for life. It was agreed that the absolute appointment gave rise to a charge to capital gains tax under TCGA 1992, s 71(1). However, the Inland Revenue argued that a deemed disposal and reacquisition also took place in connection with the second appointment on the basis that a new and separate settlement had been created.

Here a widely drawn special power of appointment was exercised, albeit that the trustees of the original settlement continued to act in connection with the newly appointed settled fund. The new trusts affecting the settled fund were exhaustive in that no part of the original trusts were still subsisting, and there was no possibility of them reviving to govern the future disposition of the trust assets. However, the administrative powers and provisions were still to govern the trust assets, under the terms of the deed of appointment, which was expressed to be supplemental to the original trust deed.

Despite the fact that the power exercised was found to be in the 'wider form', Hoffmann J found that no new settlement had been

Existing Settlements **5.13**

created using the approach set down by Lord Wilberforce in *Roome and Another v Edwards* (supra). Accordingly, the case is a useful authority demonstrating that simply because the power exercised by trustees in establishing a settled fund is itself in the wider form, its exercise need not necessarily create a new settlement. Rather, it is necessary to establish the intent behind the exercise of the power itself. Hoffmann J also observed that where a power in the wider form is exercised which expressly purports to vary the beneficial trusts in some relatively minor way, it would be somewhat artificial for this to be 'construed as the creation of a new settlement to be read with all the provisions of the old one together with the variation' (*at p 500, g*).

The position of three commonly encountered powers is discussed below.

Special powers of appointment

5.12 Special powers are generally exercisable by the trustees under the terms of the trust instrument. They are exercisable in favour of a limited class of persons or objects. The person who exercises the power is seen as fulfilling the original intention of the settlor. Generally, the limitations which arise as a result of such powers being exercised are treated as if they had been written into the original trust instrument which created them. As such they do not usually create a new trust, for example, if a special power of appointment is exercised to alter the vesting age of a beneficiary who has to satisfy some contingency, it is unlikely that any deemed disposal will arise under TCGA 1992, s 71. This is provided that the balance of the trust provisions remains otherwise unaltered.

However, this does not mean that special powers of appointment cannot be exercised either expressly or impliedly to authorise trustees to remove assets from the original settlement, and make them subject to trusts of a new settlement. In such circumstances a chargeable disposal and reacquisition of the trust assets would arise for capital gains tax purposes within TCGA 1992, s 71. For an example of a case where the court held that the exercise of a power of appointment did not operate to resettle an appointed fund and precipitate a capital gains tax disposal, see *Swires v Renton, Ch D 1991, 64 TC 315; [1991] STC 490*.

Powers of advancement

5.13 Traditionally, advancement was thought to be something similar to setting up a beneficiary for life. Irrespective of whether such advances are made under an express provision in the trust deed or under the statutory power of advancement in Trustee Act 1925, s 32 there is no reason why they should be limited solely to straightforward payments or transfers of assets to beneficiaries. They can include settled advances which effectively alter or vary the trusts created by the settlement from which it was derived. As a result, powers of advancement are generally within the wider category of powers capable of removing assets from one settlement and subjecting

5.14 Existing Settlements

them to the provisions of another. However, not every exercise of a power of advancement will necessarily create a new settlement.

Power of allocation

5.14 In simple terms a power of allocation represents the ability of trustees to 'shuffle' assets amongst various beneficiaries within the overall umbrella of a trust but without empowering the trustees to create fresh or overriding trusts. This type of power was considered in *Bond v Pickford, CA [1983] STC 517*. Accordingly, this type of power falls within the 'narrower form' and no charge under TCGA 1992, s 71 should arise as a result of its exercise. This should prove to be the case even if certain administrative provisions that had previously applied under the original trust instrument cease to be applicable as a result of the exercise of the power of allocation.

Inland Revenue guidelines

5.15 Following the Court of Appeal's decision in *Bond v Pickford, CA [1983] STC 517*, the Inland Revenue issued a Statement of Practice (SP7/84) which states:

'... the Board considers that a deemed disposal will not arise when ... [powers in the wider form, which may be powers of advancement or certain powers of appointment, are] ... exercised and trusts are declared in circumstances such that:

(a) the appointment is revocable, or

(b) the trusts declared of the advanced or appointed funds are not exhaustive so that there exists a possibility at the time when the advancement or appointment is made that the funds covered by it will on the occasion of some event cease to be held upon such trusts and once again come to be held upon the original trusts of the settlement.

Further, when such a power is exercised the Board considers it unlikely that a deemed disposal will arise when trusts are declared if duties in regard to the appointed assets still fall to the trustees of the original settlement in their capacity as trustees of that settlement ... Finally, the Board accept that a power of appointment or advancement can be exercised over only part of the settled property and that the above consequences would apply to that part.'

This statement is very helpful, as it sets out a 'shopping list' of features that should be taken into account in devising any internal reorganisation.

Conclusions

5.16 Provided both the guidelines established by the case law outlined above and the Statement of Practice are observed, it should be possible to internally reorganise a trust without incurring an immediate capital gains tax charge.

Accumulation and maintenance settlements

5.17 Due to their favourable treatment accumulation and maintenance settlements have become increasingly important. Since many of these settlements are more recent than other settlements their terms are frequently more flexible. However, the potential flexibility that may be incorporated into such settlements only became fully apparent with time. Generally, any alteration of the interests of beneficiaries under these settlements (if desired at all) will be through the exercise of the powers conferred by the settlement itself although it may be appropriate for steps to be taken by the beneficiaries themselves to deal with their interests.

Settlements which are accumulation and maintenance settlements within IHTA 1984, s 71 will, necessarily, if incorporating powers to vary shares of beneficiaries, also incorporate restrictions on the exercise of those powers. A power to vary the share of a beneficiary who has not yet attained 25 must not be exercisable to increase the share of one who has, since otherwise it could not be said without doubt that a beneficiary will on or before attaining a specified age no greater than 25 attain an absolute interest in capital or an interest in possession in the settled property as required by IHTA 1984, s 71. Provided the requirements of section 71 are satisfied (and the terms of the settlement allow), the share of any beneficiary who has not attained an interest in possession may be reduced in favour of any beneficiary who has not attained 25 (even if he has already become entitled to an interest in possession). No charge to inheritance tax will arise from the reduction of the beneficiary's share.

The provisions of IHTA 1984, s 71 only apply to prevent a reduction of a beneficiary's share from being a chargeable occasion for inheritance tax purposes whilst the beneficiary has not attained an absolute interest or an interest in possession in the settled property. Once he does so the condition in section 71(1)(b) will no longer be satisfied and his share of the settled property will cease to be held upon accumulation and maintenance trusts. Any alteration of a beneficiary's interest in possession once it has arisen (whether as a result of his having attained a specified age no greater than 25 or because an accumulation period has expired) will have the consequences discussed under 5.21 below.

To avoid a charge to inheritance tax a beneficiary's prospective share under an accumulation and maintenance settlement should be altered before he has attained an interest in possession. However, in any event the surrender or assignment in favour of an individual or for the benefit of children will be a potentially exempt transfer. Therefore, providing the beneficiary survives for seven years, no inheritance tax charge will arise.

There will be no capital gains tax consequences on the exercise of a power of appointment or variation to reduce (and correspondingly increase) the shares of beneficiaries of an accumulation and maintenance settlement who have no absolute interests in the capital of their prospective shares, even if the beneficiary whose share is increased has attained an interest in possession. Provided that the property remains settled and no-one becomes absolutely entitled to the settled property as a result of the exercise of these powers no occasion of charge will arise under TCGA 1992, s 71.

5.17 Existing Settlements

Such powers of variation and selection can only be exercised in favour of other beneficiaries of the accumulation and maintenance settlement who will, usually, be the beneficiary's siblings whose share is being reduced. If a beneficiary, who has not yet attained an interest in possession or an absolute interest in capital, has children of his own he may wish, if he has other resources available to him, to arrange his affairs so that the whole or part of his prospective share under the existing settlement passes to a settlement for his children. Provided that he has attained 18 it may be possible, with the co-operation of the trustees, to pass part of his interest into a new accumulation and maintenance settlement for his children without incurring any charge to inheritance tax.

Generally, where a beneficiary under an accumulation and maintenance settlement becomes entitled outright to some or all of the trust assets, the gains arising on the disposal can only be held over if they are 'business assets' within TCGA 1992, s 165 unless the beneficiary becomes absolutely entitled to the assets *before* attaining an interest in possession in them, in which case hold-over relief under TCGA 1992, s 260 will be available regardless of the nature of the assets (TCGA 1992, s 260(2)(d)). In practice, this relief is likely to be of limited application because the beneficiary will often have already become entitled to an interest in possession under the Trustee Act 1925, s 31 (unless expressly or impliedly excluded) which automatically confers an interest in possession at 18. Section 260(2)(d) only applies where the disposal to the beneficiary does not constitute an occasion of charge to inheritance tax under IHTA 1984, s 71(4). That sub-section will only apply where the beneficiary has not already become entitled to an interest in possession. Where the beneficiary has already become so entitled, IHTA 1984, s 53(2) prevents an inheritance tax charge arising when the interest in possession is enlarged to outright ownership.

Where there is an existing settlement under which a beneficiary will become entitled outright to the trust assets but only after first attaining an interest in possession, various steps can be taken to avoid a charge to capital gains tax.

First, the outright vesting of all or part of the assets could be accelerated to occur on or before the date on which the beneficiary attains his interest in possession. This could be done by exercising either an express power of advancement or the statutory power of advancement (Trustee Act 1925, s 32).

Secondly, the provisions of the settlement could be amended to defer the vesting of the interest in possession until the date on which the beneficiary becomes entitled outright. However, this may only be done without an application to the court under the Variation of Trusts Act 1958 if the settlement contains an internal power of variation and the accumulation period applying to the settlement is long enough to permit such a deferment of the vesting of the interest in possession. Provided the beneficiary still becomes entitled either to the capital outright or to an interest in possession at an age not exceeding 25, then such a variation should not have any inheritance tax consequences.

A third possibility is to convert the beneficiary's absolute interest in capital into a life interest in income with the capital passing on his death to his children or to other beneficiaries. The life interest could be coupled with a power for the trustees to advance capital to the life tenant. This will defer any

Existing Settlements **5.18**

capital gains tax disposal until such time (if any) as the trustees exercise the power of advancement. The alteration in the trusts may be effected by exercising either an express power in the settlement (if wide enough in scope) or the statutory power of advancement (Trustee Act 1925, s 32). If, however, the statutory power has not been extended to permit the advancement of the *whole* (and not just one half) of the beneficiary's presumptive share of the trust fund this course will only be partially effective. Care must be taken when exercising the power *not* to create a separate settlement for capital gains tax purposes since this will simply give rise to the disposal which the whole exercise is designed to avoid. The Inland Revenue Statement of Practice SP 7/84 provides guidance as to when in the Inland Revenue's view a separate settlement will be created.

Resettlement of part of a beneficiary's share before he attains an interest in possession

Use of an 'advanced fund'

5.18 The trustees may exercise powers of advancement (if conferred upon them by the terms of the settlement or by statute) to advance a fund to new trusts for the benefit of the beneficiary. These trusts must provide for all income arising from the 'advanced fund' to be accumulated and for the capital of the fund to be held for the benefit of the beneficiary contingently upon him surviving for a period which must expire before he attains 25 (or before an accumulation period expires if this would be earlier). Provision should be included for the advanced fund to revert back into the original settlement if the beneficiary does not survive for the specified period. At this stage this advanced fund continues to qualify as a fund held upon accumulation and maintenance trusts within IHTA 1984, s 71. Even though the advanced fund is now held upon separate trusts from those of the original accumulation and maintenance settlement no inheritance tax charge will arise (IHTA 1984, s 81). Section 81 provides that where property ceases to be held in one settlement and becomes held in another without any person becoming entitled in the meantime to an absolute interest in that property then the property will be treated, for the purposes of IHTA 1984, Part III Chapter III, as remaining in the first settlement.

The beneficiary may then assign his contingent interest in the capital of the advanced fund to a completely new accumulation and maintenance settlement for the benefit of his children. As a result of IHTA 1984, s 81 the property held in the 'new' settlement will still be treated as remaining in the original settlement. Accordingly, the accumulation and maintenance trusts in this new settlement should be capable of lasting only until 25 years after the date of the creation of the original settlement in order to ensure that they satisfy the condition in IHTA 1984, s 71(2)(b)(ii). The children of the beneficiary (who will benefit under the new settlement) will not have the same grandparent as the beneficiaries of the original settlement nor will they have become beneficiaries as a result of their parent's death, but rather because of his

5.18 Existing Settlements

assignment of part of his interest to the new settlement for their benefit, and so will not satisfy the 'common grandparent' test in section 71(2)(b)(i).

The beneficiary's assignment of his interest under the advanced fund will not give rise to any inheritance tax charge for two reasons. First, at the time of his assignment his interest in capital is a future interest and is, therefore, excluded property (IHTA 1984, ss 47, 48). He, therefore, does not have to survive for seven years after the gift to avoid a charge to inheritance tax. Second, the property passing into the new settlement will under IHTA 1984, s 81 be treated as remaining in the first settlement. There will be no inheritance tax charge on the property passing out of the first settlement as at no stage has any person become absolutely entitled.

To ensure that the beneficiary's assignment of his interest has no inheritance tax consequences it is essential that, during the period of transition of the advanced fund from the first settlement to the second, the income of the advanced fund is held upon trusts which accumulate all income. If this is not the case and income of the advanced fund may be applied for the benefit of the beneficiary or is payable to him under the trusts on which the advanced fund is held his assignment will not (for the reasons given in the next paragraphs) escape a possible inheritance tax charge. It is for this reason that it is essential for an advanced fund to be created, his contingent capital interest in which the beneficiary can then assign to the new settlement, rather than the beneficiary assigning the whole or part of his future interest in the original settlement to the new settlement.

The trusts of the original settlement are unlikely to provide for the accumulation of all the income arising from the beneficiary's share of the trust fund even if they confer a contingent interest in the capital of his share upon the beneficiary which he may assign. If the income of the fund in which the beneficiary has assigned his interest can still be applied in any way for the benefit of the beneficiary he may be treated as having reserved a benefit in that fund within FA 1986, s 102. Thus, when he satisfies the contingency and the advanced fund becomes held on the trusts of the second settlement he would be treated, under section 102(4), as having made a potentially exempt transfer at that time. To avoid inheritance tax being chargeable he would need to survive for seven years.

Similarly, if the beneficiary were entitled to the income of the advanced fund he would have an interest in possession in the fund and be treated as beneficially entitled to the fund. The assignment or the assigned contingent capital interest vesting in the second settlement will constitute a potentially exempt transfer. No charge to inheritance tax will result if he survives for seven years.

The capital gains tax consequences of the arrangement also need to be considered, since depending upon the nature of the trust assets and the extent to which their value reflects unrealised gains, a charge to tax may result which cannot be held over.

The creation of the advanced fund itself should have no capital gains tax consequences provided the fund will fall back onto the trusts of the original settlement in the event that the beneficiary fails to satisfy the contingency.

Existing Settlements **5.19**

This is because a separate settlement should not have been created for capital gains tax purposes and the trustees will not have become absolutely entitled to the advanced fund as against themselves as trustees of the original settlement (TCGA 1992, s 71).

However, the movement of the settled property from the original settlement to the settlement for the beneficiary's children will be an occasion upon which a capital gains tax charge would arise under TCGA 1992, s 71 since the trustees of the second (separate) settlement would become absolutely entitled to the settled property as against the trustees of the first. Depending on the nature of the trust assets involved, it may be possible to make a hold-over election under TCGA 1992, s 165 or it may be possible to pay the tax due by instalments. Where neither hold-over relief nor the instalment option are available, the potential capital gains tax charge may be sufficient to outweigh the inheritance tax advantages of the arrangement.

Resettlement of funds

5.19 An alternative means of achieving a similar end may be available to the trustees of an accumulation and maintenance settlement where a beneficiary who has children of his own has not yet attained a vested interest in the capital of the settled property. The trustees may, in certain circumstances, exercise powers of advancement (if available to them) to advance funds, held in a beneficiary's prospective share, direct into a new accumulation and maintenance settlement for his children. Walton J in *Buckinghamshire (Earl of) Settlement Trusts, Cole and Another v Hope-Morley and Another (In re), TLR 29 March 1977*, held that the exercise of the power of advancement in this way was a proper exercise of that power because it was for the benefit of the primary beneficiary as the trustees were applying capital of the trust property by resettling it on his children (present and future) for whom he would otherwise feel a considerable duty to make provision. However, in coming to this conclusion Walton J did express the view that the exercise of a power of advancement in this manner would not always be for the benefit of the beneficiary and, therefore, proper. Each case will depend on its own facts.

If a power of advancement were exercised in this manner to resettle funds on the children of a beneficiary who has not yet attained an interest in possession in the trust property (or a share of it) the advance would not give rise to a charge to inheritance tax because the property advanced into the new settlement would be treated as remaining in the first settlement (IHTA 1984, s 81). However, it would be necessary to restrict the period for which the trust property would continue to be held on accumulation and maintenance trusts to that of 25 years from the date of creation of the original settlement in accordance with IHTA 1984, s 71(2)(b) so as to secure the favourable inheritance tax treatment. If the primary beneficiary had attained an interest in possession, but not a vested interest in capital, there would be a termination of his interest in possession but no inheritance tax would arise provided he survived for seven years.

The capital gains tax consequences of the resettlement need to be considered as a charge to capital gains tax may arise when the trustees of the new

5.20   *Existing Settlements*

settlement become absolutely entitled to the funds advanced to them as against the trustees of the first settlement (TCGA 1992, s 71).

Comparison of the alternatives

5.20   Where it is not clear that an exercise of a power of advancement under an accumulation and maintenance settlement to resettle funds upon the children of a beneficiary of that settlement is for the benefit of the beneficiary, it may be preferable to use the former course discussed above to achieve the resettlement. Provided that the advance or appointment of an advanced fund for the benefit of the beneficiary contingently on his surviving for a specified period is not specified as conditional on his assigning part of his contingent interest to a new settlement for his children, the exercise by the trustees of their powers may be less open to question by other beneficiaries or potential beneficiaries of the original settlement. If the beneficiary for whose benefit the advanced fund is originally held determines that he wishes to assign his interest in the whole or part of that fund to a settlement for his children, the decision is his and the trustees have only to determine whether it is for his benefit to create the advanced fund which, unless assigned, will be held for the beneficiary absolutely if he survives for the requisite period.

It may be preferable to resettle funds in the manner discussed formerly rather than by a direct advance to a new settlement when the beneficiary in relation to whose prospective interest these steps are being considered has, as yet, no children of his own, but anticipates that he will have in the (near) future. In these circumstances it would be possible for him to assign the whole or part of his interest in an advanced fund to an accumulation and maintenance settlement, the class of beneficiaries of which is constructed around a 'borrowed beneficiary' (e.g. a brother or sister of the beneficiary who is considerably younger than he or nephews or nieces of his). The concept of 'borrowing' a beneficiary for the purposes of creating an accumulation and maintenance settlement is discussed in detail in chapter 4 *Creating Settlements* but, in outline, is used where the intended beneficiaries of a proposed settlement do not yet exist but the proposed settlor wishes to make provision for them in advance of their birth. A settlement may be created for the benefit of an unconnected individual who is alive but aged under 25 with provision for the intended beneficiaries to become members of the class of beneficiaries upon birth. It is doubtful whether trustees of an accumulation and maintenance settlement could justify as being for the benefit of a beneficiary a direct advance from a settlement under which he is prospectively entitled to an interest in possession or an absolute interest to a settlement under which it is only a possibility that his children will benefit because they are not yet born.

The advantage of a resettlement of a beneficiary's prospective entitlement, or part of it, by means of a direct advance by trustees is that the beneficiary whose children are to benefit under the new settlement should not be a settlor in relation to that settlement within ICTA 1988, s 660B. Accordingly, the income arising in that settlement should not be treated as his even if paid to or for the benefit of his children.

Existing Settlements **5.23**

Such complicated arrangements are only likely to be worthwhile where the funds held in the original accumulation and maintenance settlement are substantial and the costs are less than the cost of premiums to insure against the beneficiary's death within seven years. Alternatively, it might be simpler to await the time at which he attains an interest in possession or an absolute interest and make a gift to a settlement for his children by means of a potentially exempt transfer. Nevertheless, in limited circumstances where the sums involved are substantial the exercise may be of benefit.

Life interest settlements

5.21 The treatment for inheritance tax, capital gains tax and income tax purposes of interest in possession settlements is discussed in detail in chapter 4 *Creating Settlements*.

The following paragraphs recap briefly on the distinctions between a 'life interest' in trust terms and an 'interest in possession' for inheritance tax purposes and consider the basic inheritance tax and capital gains tax rules relating to the termination of such interests.

A life interest for trust purposes

5.22 A life interest is an interest conferred upon an individual, the life tenant, by the terms of a settlement. The life tenant will generally have a right to receive the income arising from the trust property (or a fixed part of it) during his life. Powers may be vested in the trustees of the settlement (such as a power of accumulation) to divert income away from the life tenant or to terminate the interest early. Although a life tenant may not have an entitlement to capital, the trustees may have power to pay capital to him if they think fit or he may become entitled to capital if he either survives to a certain age or to the end of a specified period. Unless he is prospectively entitled to capital at some future time, the statutory power of advancement (Trustee Act 1925, s 32) will not be exercisable by the trustees in favour of the life tenant.

An interest in possession for inheritance tax purposes and the consequences of termination

5.23 Generally, an interest in possession for inheritance tax purposes corresponds with a life interest in trust terms but there are exceptions. An interest under a settlement can only be an interest in possession for inheritance tax purposes if it confers upon the life tenant an immediate entitlement to income as it arises net only of proper income related expenses (*Pearson & Others v CIR, HL [1980] STC 318; 2 All ER 479*). In principle, any powers conferred upon the trustees (or any other person) to deprive the life tenant of income after it has arisen will prevent his interest from being an interest in possession even though it is a life interest.

The crucial distinction in this instance is between 'dispositive' and 'administrative' powers. For example, a power of accumulation, or the power to

5.23 Existing Settlements

distribute income amongst a class, is a dispositive power. The fact that such powers may divert income away from a beneficiary after it has arisen, will prevent an interest in possession arising for inheritance tax purposes. It is the simple existence of such powers, rather than their exercise which will cause an interest in possession not to arise. However, where a dispositive power, such as the exercise of a power of appointment, can only affect the right to future income, its mere existence will not in itself preclude an interest in possession from arising.

Administrative powers are far less problematic; for example, a power to apply income in payment of insurance premiums for trust property should not preclude an interest in possession coming into existence, even where this is expressed to be in priority to the entitlement of the life tenant to the trust income. However, there will be cases where it is difficult to distinguish between administrative and dispositive powers, see *Miller & Others v CIR, CS 1986 [1987] STC 108.*

For the purposes of the discussion below it has been assumed that the expressions 'life interest' and 'interest in possession' are synonymous, i.e. that the terms of the settlements considered confer on the life tenant an interest in possession during his life.

For inheritance tax purposes where a life tenant is entitled to an interest in possession in settled property he is treated as being beneficially entitled to the trust property in which his interest subsists, i.e. to the income of which he is entitled (IHTA 1984, s 49). Any termination of the life tenant's interest in possession will be treated as though it were a transfer of value made by the life tenant (IHTA 1984, ss 51, 52). This treatment applies whether the termination results from his own act (e.g. assignment or surrender of his interest) or from the terms of the settlement (e.g. the ending of his interest on his death or on the birth of another beneficiary or the exercise by the trustees of powers conferred upon them to determine his interest). IHTA 1984, s 51 provides that where he disposes of the interest there is no transfer of value; instead the disposition is treated as the coming to an end of his interest within section 52 so inheritance tax is charged as if the life tenant had then made a transfer of value. Where the life tenant has not himself made a disposition IHTA 1984, s 52 provides that inheritance tax is to be charged on the 'coming to an end' of his interest in possession as if he had then made a transfer of value.

The fact that the termination of the life tenant's interest is not an actual transfer of value but is merely treated as being such has some important inheritance tax consequences which must be considered on the termination of a life tenant's interest in possession.

(a) *Life tenant becoming absolutely entitled to the settled property.* If, as a result of a deemed transfer of value, the life tenant becomes absolutely entitled to the property in which his interest has terminated, no inheritance tax will be chargeable (IHTA 1984, s 53(2)).

(b) *Potentially exempt transfers.* If, as a result of the termination (in whole or part) of a life tenant's interest in possession, the property in which his interest subsisted becomes

Existing Settlements **5.23**

(i) comprised in the estate of another (whether absolutely or only because that individual takes an interest in possession in the property), or

(ii) held upon accumulation and maintenance trusts satisfying the conditions in IHTA 1984, s 71 or a disabled trust within IHTA 1984, s 89,

the life tenant will be treated as having made a potentially exempt transfer. Provided he survives for a period of seven years after this, it will not become chargeable (IHTA 1984, s 3A and IHTA 1984, ss 51, 52).

(c) *Other exemptions.* Although IHTA 1984, s 3(4) provides that references in the Act to a transfer of value made by any person include references to events on the happening of which tax is chargeable 'as if' a transfer of value had been made by that person and that 'transferor' is to be construed accordingly, the operation of this sub-section is specifically excluded by IHTA 1984, ss 19–22 which relate to annual exemptions, the small gifts exemptions, the normal expenditure out of income exemption and the gifts in consideration of marriage exemption respectively.

However, IHTA 1984, s 57 provides that a life tenant may give notice to the trustees that the whole or part of his annual exemption or his exemption for gifts in consideration of marriage is unused. This can be set against the deemed transfer of value made on the termination of his interest. Even where the deemed transfer of value is not chargeable but is potentially exempt at the time it is made the life tenant should, if appropriate, give notice to the trustees of the availability of these exemptions under section 57. Otherwise, if he dies within seven years of the deemed transfer of value, the exemptions will not be available to the trustees to set against the potentially exempt transfer which has now become chargeable. A claim must be made within six months of the termination on the prescribed form of notice (Form 222). However, the Revenue will not disallow the exemption solely for the reason it was out of time (CTO Advanced Instruction Manual M.60).

(d) *Reliefs for certain dispositions.* Since there is no actual transfer of value on the termination of a life interest, the reliefs relating to dispositions which would be transfers of value (i.e. dispositions not intended to confer gratuitous benefit (IHTA 1984, s 10), dispositions for family maintenance (IHTA 1984, s 11) and dispositions allowable for income tax (IHTA 1984, s 12)) do not apply. However, IHTA 1984, s 51(2) provides that if the assignment or surrender by the life tenant satisfies the conditions in IHTA 1984, s 11, the assignment or surrender will not be treated as the coming to an end of his interest and, accordingly, no inheritance tax will be chargeable on this occasion.

5.24 *Existing Settlements*

The value on which inheritance tax is charged

5.24 There is a further difference between the charge to inheritance tax made when an interest in possession is terminated during the life of the life tenant and that made if he gives away part of his free estate. IHTA 1984, s 52(1) provides that on the termination of an interest in possession by whatever means, the life tenant will be treated as having made a transfer of value equal to the value of the property in which his interest subsisted. This value must be distinguished from the value which he would be treated as having transferred if, instead, he had made a lifetime gift of the same property from his free estate. In this case inheritance tax would be chargeable on the value by which his estate was diminished as a result of the transfer. This may be greater, for example, where a majority shareholding in a private company is held in an interest in possession settlement. If the life tenant surrenders or assigns his interest in a part of the fund representing a minority shareholding in the company and, after the assignment, has an interest in possession only in a minority shareholding, the charge to inheritance tax will be calculated on the value of the minority holding in which he has released his interest. Had the majority holding of shares initially been part of his own free estate, the charge to inheritance tax under similar circumstances would have been calculated, not by reference to the value of the minority holding given away, but by reference to the loss in value of his estate, i.e. the difference between the value of a majority shareholding and the value of the minority shareholding he retained. As discussed earlier, the Inland Revenue have now accepted that this approach is in principle correct (CTO Advanced Instruction Manual E.100).

A life interest for capital gains tax purposes and the consequences of termination

5.25 The capital gains tax legislation includes provisions relating to 'life interests'. A non-exhaustive definition is given in TCGA 1992, s 72 for the purposes of extending the meaning ascribed by trust law. The reason for making reference to life interests in the capital gains tax legislation relates largely to how the provisions operate on the death of the life tenant. Since this chapter considers only variations of interests under settlements made during the lifetime of a life tenant, detailed consideration will not be given to the capital gains tax position on the death of the life tenant. Briefly, the death of a life tenant will cause a revaluation to market value at the date of his death of the assets in which his interest subsisted without giving rise to any capital gains tax charge except where hold-over relief has been claimed on the transfer of assets to a settlement. As mentioned in 5.8 above there may be good reason not to terminate the life tenant's interest prior to his death if the assets in which his interest subsists represent substantial gains (and no held-over gains) which will fall out of charge to capital gains tax on his death.

However, where settled property includes assets in respect of which there are held-over gains which will suffer a claw-back charge on the death of the life tenant if they remain settled (TCGA 1992, s 74) it may be advantageous to

Existing Settlements **5.25**

advance those assets to the life tenant provided the settlement terms allow and section 165 hold-over relief is available. The trustees and the life tenant will have to make an election for hold-over relief. On the life tenant's death the held-over gains will fall out of the charge to capital gains tax. These considerations will only be relevant if assets which were the subject of a hold-over election when transferred to a settlement have not been, and are not to be, disposed of prior to the life tenant's death since the actual sale of these assets would in any event trigger the capital gains tax charge on held-over gains.

If assets acquired before 31 March 1982 were transferred to trustees prior to 6 April 1988 (but after 5 April 1981 when hold-over relief was extended to gifts from individuals to trustees) and a hold-over election was made under FA 1980, s 79 for gains accruing on that disposal, the held-over gain brought into charge on a future disposal of those assets (or on an event crystallising a capital gains tax charge on the held-over gains) will in most cases be reduced by one-half. Unfortunately, an omission from the provisions of TCGA 1992, Sch 4 means that this will not be the case where assets incorporating gains were transferred to a life interest settlement in the above circumstances and remain settled until the death of the life tenant. The provisions of TCGA 1992, Sch 4 para 4 overlook the postponed charge on held-over gains imposed by TCGA 1992, s 74. Therefore, on the death of the life tenant the full amount of any such gains held over will, at least in theory, be clawed back into charge to capital gains tax (Capital Gain Manual CG17063). In view of this statement in the Manual it cannot now be assumed that the Revenue will continue their previous practice of ignoring this charge on the death of a life tenant (see Taxation, 7 September 1989 at p 688).

In accordance with the general policy of the capital gains tax legislation in relation to settlements, the lifetime termination of a life interest will not give rise to a charge to capital gains tax unless as a result some person becomes absolutely entitled to the settled property. No occasion of charge will arise on the change of interests provided that the property remains settled after the termination of the interest. The sale of assets by the trustees will be the trigger for a charge to capital gains tax. Where a person does become absolutely entitled to the trust property (either the life tenant who has had the settled property transferred to him or a beneficiary with a succeeding interest who, as a result of the termination of the life tenant's interest, becomes absolutely entitled to the trust property) the trustees will be treated as having disposed of the trust property at market value at the date of termination of the life interest and as having reacquired it at that date as nominees for the individual who has become absolutely entitled (TCGA 1992, s 71). A capital gains tax charge will arise if the market value of the assets at the date of termination is greater than their indexed acquisition cost. Depending upon the nature of the trust assets, it may be possible to hold over the gain under TCGA 1992, s 165 by the trustees and the individual who has become absolutely entitled to the trust property making an election. However, one has to consider the impact of any taper relief lost on a hold-over claim being made.

In making any decision as to whether to terminate a life interest settlement in favour of the life tenant or the remaindermen or whether to accelerate the interests of the remaindermen or assign the life tenant's interest to others

5.26 *Existing Settlements*

(outright or into some other form of settlement) the capital gains tax rules will be a significant factor. The differing rates of capital gains tax payable by trustees and outright owners which may vary between nil (if losses are available to offset gains) and 40% should always be taken into account in a review of whether or not any steps should be taken, together with any taper relief considerations.

Motives for breaking a life interest settlement

5.26 The reasons for breaking a life interest settlement may be many. It may simply be that the settlement is thought to be too expensive to continue, the administration charges being disproportionately high in comparison to the value of the trust fund. The life tenant or the remaindermen may decide to assign or surrender their interests to each other and thus terminate the settlement or they may partition the fund, each taking part of the capital.

Alternatively, when income tax rates are high, the life tenant may be receiving little benefit from his entitlement to the income of the trust property and he might prefer to assign that interest to his grandchildren if they are taxable at the lower rates of income tax. If the remaindermen are his unmarried minor children, the income arising may be treated as being the assignors (ICTA 1988, s 686). If the remaindermen are his grandchildren, he may determine to surrender his interest in their favour. Alternatively, the life tenant may propose a partition of the trust property. The capital he receives may then be applied in the acquisition of capital growth assets instead of income-yielding assets. He will also be free to give away that capital as and when and to whom he chooses. Another option is for the life tenant to apply capital received on the partition of the trust property in acquiring an annuity the capital element of which would not suffer income tax in his hands. Since the annuity will have no value at his death, his estate will have been reduced because there will no longer be capital owned by him nor settled property to which he will be treated as being entitled by virtue of his interest in possession.

Whilst the capital of a trust remains settled, it may be tied up and not available to either the life tenant or the remaindermen for use. The property in which the interest in possession subsists will be aggregated with the life tenant's estate for the purposes of calculating the rates of inheritance tax applicable to the settled property on his death. Both the life tenant and the remaindermen may wish to mitigate this potential charge. This can be achieved either by the life tenant surrendering his interest to the remaindermen, by the partition of the trust property between the life tenant and the remaindermen or by the purchase by the remaindermen of the life tenant's interest. However, one must consider the capital gains tax charge that may arise on the trustees under TCGA 1992, Sch 4A. In accordance with the general principle that capital should be passed on down the generations in order to mitigate inheritance tax, the most sensible course for the life tenant to adopt (if he has sufficient other assets available for his needs) would be to surrender his interest in favour of the remaindermen. However, if they are not the people he would wish to benefit, a partition of the fund or the sale by the life tenant or the remaindermen of their interests should be considered. The life tenant would then secure some free capital with which he would be able to make gifts (by potentially exempt transfer) to those he would wish to benefit.

The remaindermen, as yet receiving no benefit from the trust property, may need capital to start a business or to invest with complete freedom and may, therefore, prefer to receive capital now rather than to await the death of the life tenant and to suffer an inheritance tax charge on that occasion. They may prefer to take immediate estate planning steps of their own with any capital they receive rather than to risk receiving it when efficient measures may no longer be taken. For this reason they may propose a partition of the trust property, a purchase of the life tenant's interest or a sale to the life tenant of their interests.

Where, on a trust reorganisation, one or more of the beneficiaries becomes absolutely entitled to some of the trust assets, any capital gains arising may be held over if the trust assets are business assets within TCGA 1992, s 165. Even if this relief is not available, it may be possible to pay any capital gains tax due by ten equal annual instalments (TCGA 1992, s 281) although the outstanding balance will bear interest. A charge to capital gains tax at rates of up to 40% may be considered too high a price to pay for the perceived advantages (whether a saving in inheritance tax or some other benefit) of the reorganisation. Each case will have to be considered on its own facts and this will entail considering not only the nature of the assets of the trust but also the extent to which their value reflects unrealised gains.

Means of dealing with the interests under a life interest trust

5.27 The trusts upon which property will be held following a termination of the life tenant's interest may dictate what steps, if any, a life tenant and the remaindermen and/or the trustees may wish to take in relation to the beneficiaries' interests.

There are two basic methods available to a life tenant of dealing with his interest in possession: assignment or surrender of the interest. In practice, similar results may be achieved by the exercise of powers conferred upon the trustees (such as powers of appointment or revocation). However, the essential difference between an assignment and a surrender is considered here together with other means of dealing with the interests of the beneficiaries in order that further consideration can then be given to particular situations.

Assignment of a life interest

5.28 An assignment by the life tenant of his interest is effected by a written document of assignment (in order to comply with the requirements of Law of Property Act 1925, s 53(1)(c)). The assignment may be made by the life tenant in favour of others who are beneficiaries of the settlement or to complete strangers to the settlement. In either case the assignee or assignees step into the life tenant's shoes and become entitled to the income arising from the trust property in which his interest subsists during his lifetime. The life tenant may assign his life interest either outright to one or more individuals or to trustees of a new settlement. In the former case the

5.29 *Existing Settlements*

assignee may deal with the income to which he is now entitled as he chooses and in the latter case the trustees must deal with the income which they are entitled to receive in accordance with the provisions of the trusts imposed upon them.

It is possible that a similar result may be achieved by the exercise of powers conferred upon the trustees of the settlement under which the life tenant's interest exists. For example, the trustees may have power to revoke the life interest and to declare that in future the income will be paid to some other beneficiary of the settlement during his life. In this case there will not have been the assignment of an asset; the first life tenant's asset (his life interest) will have ceased to exist and his interest under the settlement will have been replaced by another. Where the trustees exercise their powers in this way they may (provided the terms of the settlement permit them to do so) confer a capital interest upon the beneficiary for whose benefit they create the new interest. They may, for example, declare that in future they will pay the income of the trust property to X during his life or until he attains 35 at which time they may specify that they will transfer the capital to him. (Provision will also be made for the eventuality that X dies before attaining 35.)

The life tenant himself will have no power to declare such new interests in the trust property unless the power is expressly reserved to him by the terms of the settlement. So unless the trustees can and are willing to exercise their powers to achieve the same result he can only assign or surrender his interest. It will be necessary for a life tenant to assign his interest in income where the individuals upon whom the life tenant wishes to confer a benefit are not beneficiaries of the settlement or are not within a class in whose favour the trustees may exercise their powers. In this case the life tenant has no alternative but to assign his interest to those he wishes to benefit if he is intent on dealing with his interest under the settlement in this way. Those to whom he assigns his interest will become entitled to his income interest and can have no greater entitlement to capital than he had. If, under the terms of the settlement the life tenant will become entitled to capital if he attains for example 35, he may assign this contingent interest to those he wishes to benefit in addition to assigning his income interest. Provided he does not die before his 35th birthday, his assignees will take his share of capital. However, if, under the terms of the settlement, the life tenant is entitled to income only, he can only confer this benefit on others by assignment.

Surrender of a life interest

5.29 The alternative means by which a life tenant may deal with his interest is to surrender it in favour of those whose interests succeed his. They may either take capital absolutely as a result of his surrender or if their interests are only life interests following that of a life tenant these may be accelerated. The interests under the settlement following the life interest then fall into possession. There may be a temporary gap in the beneficial interests giving rise to a resulting trust for the settlor where there are no interests ready to fall into possession. A surrender by a life tenant may therefore not, in the circumstances discussed in 5.34 below, operate to vest capital in the hands of succeeding beneficiaries and, indeed, their income

Existing Settlements **5.29**

interests may not even be accelerated. In these circumstances it may be advisable for the life tenant to assign his interest to them rather than to surrender it.

A similar effect to the surrender of the life tenant's interest may be achieved instead by the exercise of express or statutory powers vested in the trustees or others to appoint interests in favour of those whose interests follow the life interest, to extinguish the life interest or to advance assets to remaindermen. Such powers are particularly useful where a surrender by the life tenant will not accelerate the interests of the remaindermen or where the life interest is a protective life interest and an attempted surrender by the life tenant would give rise to a forfeiture. It is suitable to mention here that there may be income tax, capital gains tax and inheritance tax advantages if the trustees can exercise powers to achieve an end which, otherwise, the life tenant would achieve by assigning or surrendering his interest. If those who would benefit from the life tenant's assignment or surrender are his minor, unmarried children then for income tax purposes he would be treated as having made a settlement for the benefit of his children. He would be treated as continuing to be entitled to that income unless it is accumulated for so long as his children remain under 18 and unmarried (ICTA 1988, s 660B).

Similarly, if the life tenant (or his spouse) is capable of benefiting from the interest he assigns (for example, by being a beneficiary of a settlement to which he has assigned his interest), the income may continue to be taxed as his, under the provisions of ICTA 1988, Part XV regardless of whether or not he receives it, subject to limited exceptions.

It is occasionally argued that an assignment or surrender by a life tenant of his interest will be treated as the direct provision by him of property or income to a settlement (unless the assignment or surrender is in favour of one or more individuals outright) and he will be treated for the purposes of TCGA 1992, ss 77–79 as a 'settlor' of the settlement. Sections 77–79 will (with limited exceptions) operate to cause gains realised by the trustees to be charged to capital gains tax as being gains realised by him if he or his spouse retains an interest under that settlement (whether in capital or income). This argument has no merit.

The revocation of a life tenant's interest by the trustees or an appointment away from him is not a gift made by him within the gifts with reservation provisions in FA 1986, s 102 despite being treated as a transfer of value by the life tenant. If the life tenant continues to enjoy a benefit in some way from the property in which his interest has been lost by the exercise of the trustees' powers, he cannot be treated as having reserved a benefit and the property in which his interest has ceased will not be treated as being part of his estate on death.

As indicated, on a surrender by the life tenant, or an exercise of the trustees' powers to achieve the same result, the life tenant's interest ceases and the interests of the remaindermen may be accelerated. It will be appreciated that a total surrender will only be appropriate where a life tenant wishes to benefit those whose interests follow his. He cannot confer any benefit on strangers to the settlement by surrendering his interest.

5.30 Existing Settlements

Assignment by the remaindermen of their interests

5.30 For inheritance tax purposes an interest in remainder being a future interest under a settlement is a 'reversionary interest'. As reversionary interests are generally excluded property for inheritance tax purposes (IHTA 1984, s 48(1)) interests in remainder may be dealt with by way of gift either to other beneficiaries of the settlement under which it exists or to strangers to the settlement without giving rise to any inheritance tax consequences.

It is for this reason that assignments to their children, or to trusts for the benefit of their children, by remaindermen of their interests are particularly efficient for inheritance tax purposes.

Normally, the gift will not give rise to any inheritance tax charges and as a result does not require the assignor to survive seven years; nor can his cumulative total be in any way affected by the gift. Yet when the prior interests terminate, the children or the trust for their benefit will receive the whole benefit of the fund or that part of it in respect of which the reversionary interest was assigned. Although a charge to inheritance tax is likely to arise on the cessation of the prior interests this charge would have arisen even if the assignor had retained his interest. The potential inheritance tax charge avoided is that which might have arisen (either on the death of the assignor or on his making a gift of the assets in which his reversionary interest subsisted) after the reversionary interest had fallen in.

If the remaindermen are all ascertained and of full age and between them will take the entire trust fund on the death of the life tenant, they may assign their interests to the life tenant and he will as a result of the merger of the interests in his hands become entitled to the capital of the trust fund, although as a result a capital gains tax charge under TCGA 1992, s 71 might arise. Although the assignments by the remaindermen of their interests will not have any inheritance tax consequences and for this reason this course of action may be looked upon favourably, it is likely that the life tenant will be older than the remaindermen and it will therefore generally be unwise to place the capital in his hands where it will be chargeable to inheritance tax as part of his estate on his death. Ordinarily, it would be preferable for the life tenant to assign or surrender his interest to the remaindermen thereby passing capital on to future generations in accordance with the policy of giving and doing so early.

If the life tenant is not old and intends to deal with the capital to which he becomes entitled, by making gifts of that capital, for example, by way of potentially exempt transfers, the assignment by the remaindermen of their interests to the life tenant may present advantages. However, more frequently, it will be advantageous for inheritance tax purposes for remaindermen to assign their interests, which may be vested (in that they may be 'kept out' of their interests only by the prior entitlement of the life tenant) or contingent (i.e. dependent upon a particular event happening, for example, their surviving the life tenant), to younger generations.

Sale of the interests of life tenant or remaindermen

5.31 Any assignment or surrender by the life tenant or remainderman of their interests may be made by way of sale.

Existing Settlements 5.32

In general trustees do not exercise their powers to alter interests under settlements for consideration (although in certain commercial situations they may do so).

The life tenant or the remaindermen may each be prepared, and have the resources available, to buy the interests of the other to become entitled to the capital of the trust fund. If the sale is an arm's length transaction between unrelated parties it is expected that the cash price paid will relate to the value of the interest to be acquired, assessed by an independent actuary.

If the parties are related and the sale price does not reflect the value of the interest acquired, because it is too high, the inheritance tax consequences may be severe.

Whether undertaken strictly on an arm's length basis or not, the benefits arising from a sale of interests for each party will be that each takes a sum of money or assets absolutely with which they can deal as they please.

If neither remaindermen nor life tenant have sufficient resources to acquire the interests of the other, either may sell his interest to a third party. The life tenant would thereby obtain a capital sum in place of his income interest and the remaindermen would replace their future interests with capital sums in hand.

As will be seen, sales of interests present both inheritance tax and capital gains tax pitfalls and are for these reasons generally to be avoided, at least where estate planning considerations are the main driving force.

Partition of the trust fund

5.32 One of the most usual forms of reorganisation of interests under a settlement is that where a life tenant surrenders his life interest in part of the trust fund to the remaindermen (who following the termination of his interest will become absolutely entitled to the capital of that part of the fund in which the life tenant has surrendered his interest). In return the remaindermen assign their interests in remainder in the balance of the fund to the life tenant. In each part of the fund the interests of the life tenant and remaindermen merge. The life tenant takes the capital of that part of the fund in which he has not surrendered his interest and the remaindermen take the capital of the rest. This arrangement places capital in the hands of each which they may then spend, invest or take estate planning steps with as they independently determine. Neither has to find a capital sum in order to acquire the interest of the other and this route may, therefore, be preferable to the sale of interests discussed above.

A partition of the trust property as described in the preceding paragraph will frequently be undertaken on an arm's length basis. An actuarial valuation of the life tenant's interest having regard to the prospective lifespan remaining to the life tenant will be obtained. The funds to which each of the life tenant and the remaindermen become absolutely entitled as a result of the partition will be determined according to the values placed upon each of the respective interests.

5.33 Existing Settlements

The transaction is sometimes analysed as one under which each is taking what he is entitled to from the trust fund, assessed according to the value of his interest. The better view is that each of the life tenant and the remaindermen surrenders their interest in part of the fund in order to acquire the other's interest in the remainder so the partition is therefore akin to a sale by each of them of part of their interests.

Such a partition might also be appropriate where one or more of the life tenant and the remaindermen wish to confer a gratuitous benefit on the other or others of them in part of the fund and the amounts of capital to pass to each may be determined by estate planning motives and without regard to the actuarial values of their respective interests.

Exercise of a power of appointment in favour of the life tenant

5.33 As a means of placing capital in the hands of the life tenant which he can then give to others, the exercise of such a power of appointment is not now as popular because the life tenant may assign or surrender his interest by way of potentially exempt transfer. It is doubtful whether trustees should exercise their power of appointment to confer a capital benefit on a life tenant whom they know intends to use that capital for the benefit of persons who are not beneficiaries under the settlement. This would be the main instance in which consideration may be given to the exercise of a power of appointment to place a life tenant in funds to make potentially exempt transfers. Where, however, this is the only means by which capital can be passed to remaindermen under the terms of a settlement, there may be less risk of a claim for breach of trust if they exercise their power of appointment to enable the life tenant to make gifts of capital to the remaindermen.

The taxation consequences

Assignment or surrender by the life tenant by way of gift or sale

(i) Inheritance tax

5.34 The life tenant's assignment or surrender by way of gift will be a deemed transfer of value which may be potentially exempt if the relevant conditions are fulfilled.

The surrender by a life tenant of his interest may not be sufficient to vest capital outright in the remaindermen if they comprise a class of beneficiaries which has not closed. In this case, the remaindermen then living will become entitled to interests in possession in the settled property. Although this will not enable them to deal with the underlying capital the deemed transfer by the life tenant will still be a potentially exempt transfer. When the class closes the remaindermen then living would become entitled to the capital of the fund. No inheritance tax will be chargeable as a result of their becoming so entitled as IHTA 1984, s 53(2) provides that where a person has an interest in possession and that interest ends, no tax shall be chargeable on the transfer of value

Existing Settlements **5.34**

deemed (by virtue of sections 51 and 52) to have taken place. This is subject to the person whose interest ends becoming on the same occasion beneficially entitled to the property or to another interest in the property. New beneficiaries born into the class prior to the closing will result in partial terminations of the existing remaindermen's interests in possession but these should also be potentially exempt transfers.

In some cases, a surrender by the life tenant may not accelerate the interests of the remaindermen: for example, where their interests are contingent upon their surviving the life tenant. In such a case, the attempted surrender might cause a gap in the beneficial interest and a resulting trust of the income to the settlor (or his estate) may arise. This is unlikely to have been the parties' intention and may have future inheritance tax consequences when the life tenant dies and the contingent interests of the remaindermen vest. At this stage the settlor's interest will cease and he (if living) will make a transfer of value which may be potentially exempt. The surrender by the life tenant will also be a potentially exempt transfer to the settlor. There will be no exception under section 53(3) as this only excepts from a charge to tax a deemed transfer on the termination of an interest in possession if the *property* in which that interest subsisted reverts to the settlor. It is not sufficient that the settlor becomes entitled to an interest in possession. If the settlor has died the position may become better or worse.

(*a*) If his estate has passed to his widow, no charge would arise, provided that two years had not elapsed since the settlor's death, even if the life tenant did not survive the termination of his interest for seven years. IHTA 1984, s 53(4) provides an exception which only requires the settlor's widow to become beneficially entitled to the settled property and not to become entitled to the property itself.

(*b*) If the settlor's estate has passed outright to individuals or is held on accumulation and maintenance trusts, the termination of the life tenant's interest will be a potentially exempt transfer.

(*c*) If, however, the settlor's estate is now held on discretionary trusts there could be most unfortunate results. The life tenant's deemed transfer would not be a potentially exempt transfer. Inheritance tax would be chargeable on this deemed transfer and also might be chargeable (depending on the rates applicable to the discretionary trusts created by the settlor's will) when the life tenant died at which point the interests of the remaindermen would vest.

In these circumstances, the life tenant should assign his interest in possession to the trustees of the settlement to be held for the benefit of the remaindermen on the same trusts as would apply to the trust fund if the life tenant were dead. Although the vesting of the remaindermen's interests in capital would be postponed until the life tenant's death, there will be no gap in the beneficial interest and the remaindermen will take immediate interests in possession and, as a result, the life tenant's deemed transfer of value will be a potentially exempt transfer. If one of the remaindermen died before the life tenant there would be a possible occasion of charge to inheritance tax since his interest in possession would then terminate in favour of either the surviving remaindermen or others depending on the terms of the settlement. However, on the

5.35 Existing Settlements

death of the life tenant no inheritance tax charge will arise, assuming that the proportions of the interests of the remaindermen under the assignment and as capital beneficiaries on the death of the life tenant are identical, each remainderman will then become entitled to the proportion of the capital to the income of which he is already entitled (IHTA 1984, s 53(2)).

If the life tenant sells his interest for a consideration equal to the market value of the interest, to whomsoever, either by assigning it or by surrendering it, inheritance tax will be chargeable as if the value transferred (i.e. the value of the property in which his interest subsisted) was reduced by the amount of the consideration (IHTA 1984, s 52(2)). It is important to note that for the reasons explained under 5.23 above, even if the life tenant sells his interest to a complete stranger on a negotiated basis for the full value of the life interest (which will, of course, be less than the value of the underlying capital), the provisions of IHTA 1984, s 10 (dispositions not intended to confer gratuitous benefit) cannot apply. Even though the sale by the life tenant of his interest was made on arm's length terms between unconnected persons, and was not intended to confer a gratuitous benefit the transfer of value which he is deemed to make on the termination of his interest (i.e. the differences between the consideration received and the value of the underlying property) will be a potentially exempt transfer if the relevant conditions are satisfied.

The purchaser of the life tenant's interest may also make a transfer of value of part of the amount of the consideration. This is determined by reference to the actual value of the life interest sold without regard to the fact that the life tenant is treated for inheritance tax purposes as owning the capital of the fund to the income of which he is entitled (IHTA 1984, s 49(2)). Thus, if a purchaser pays to the life tenant an amount in excess of the capitalised value of the life tenant's interest that excess will be a transfer of value by the purchaser (since his estate will have been reduced by that excess) unless it is a disposition not intended to confer gratuitous benefit under IHTA 1984, s 10. Any transfer of value made by a purchaser of a life interest may, however, be a potentially exempt transfer.

(ii) Capital gains tax

5.35 The assignment by the life tenant of his interest (whether to the remaindermen or to strangers to the settlement) or the surrender by him of his interest will only have capital gains tax consequences for the trustees or the life tenant if

(*a*) as a result one or more people become absolutely entitled to the trust property. The trustees will be deemed to have disposed of the trust property in which the life tenant's interest ceased (TCGA 1992, s 71) and to have reacquired it at market value as nominees for those who become absolutely entitled. Depending upon the nature of the trust assets, the trustees and the beneficiaries may be able to elect under TCGA 1992, s 165 to hold over some or all of the gain arising to the beneficiaries who become absolutely entitled and thereby avoid an immediate charge to capital gains tax;

Existing Settlements **5.37**

(*b*) the life tenant acquired his interest for a consideration in money or money's worth or the settlement has been at any time resident outside the UK. A capital gains tax charge will arise to the life tenant on the difference (reduced by taper relief) between the market value of his interest at the date of his disposal (assuming no consideration for his assignment or surrender) or the actual sale price (if made to an 'unconnected' person) and his indexed acquisition cost taking into account the wasting asset rules in TCGA 1992, s 44 and TCGA 1992, s 46; or

(*c*) the beneficiary sells his interest to another. The underlying assets to which the interest relates are deemed to be disposed of by the trustees and immediately reacquired by them.

If as a result of the surrender or partial surrender any of the remaindermen become absolutely entitled to some or all of the trust property, then any gains realised in respect of that property following the surrender will no longer be taxable in the hands of the trustees but in the hands of the remaindermen, but the rate of charge in that case can be as high as 40%.

(iii) Income tax

5.36 Subject to the points made below, if the life tenant has assigned or surrendered his interest but the property remains settled, the income arising to the assignee or those whose interests are accelerated by the surrender will be chargeable at his or their personal rates of income tax. Where one or more persons have become entitled to the income, basic rate income tax will be collected by assessment upon the trustees and an assessment will be made on the assignee or remaindermen for any higher rate income tax due unless the trustees have authorised the income of the trust assets to be paid direct to the assignee or remaindermen in which case all income tax in respect of that income will be assessed on him or them (TMA 1970, s 76).

However, where a life tenant has assigned his interest to an accumulation and maintenance trust or, following a surrender of his interest, the settled property becomes subject to such trusts, the trustees (of the new settlement in the case of an assignment) will be liable to the rate applicable to trusts (ICTA 1988, s 686). Where the income is applied to or for the benefit of the beneficiaries it will be treated as having been received by them net of the rate applicable to trusts and the sum of tax which is treated as having been deducted from the distribution received will be treated as income tax paid by the recipient beneficiary (ICTA 1988, s 687).

Exceptionally, where the minor and unmarried children of the life tenant are the outright assignees or receive absolute interests following the surrender or if the income or capital is distributed to them from the continuing settlements, the life tenant will suffer income tax on the income now due to his children (ICTA 1988, s 660B).

(iv) Stamp duty

5.37 An assignment or surrender by way of sale will suffer *ad valorem* stamp duty at 1% if the consideration is between £60,001 and £250,000;

5.38 *Existing Settlements*

3% if the consideration is between £250,001 and £500,000; and 4% if the consideration is more than £500,000. No *ad valorem* stamp duty will be chargeable on an assignment or surrender by a life tenant of his interest by way of gift. Nor will the assignment or surrender attract even a nominal £5 stamp as being a 'conveyance or transfer of any other kind' or need to be adjudicated if certified as exempt from stamp duty under Category L in the Schedule to the Stamp Duty (Exempt Instruments) Regulations 1987.

Revocation of the life tenant's interest by the trustees or the exercise of a power of appointment by them to terminate the life tenant's interest and confer benefits on others

5.38 The taxation consequences of the termination of a life tenant's interest by these means are very similar to those discussed in relation to the assignment or surrender by way of gift by a life tenant of his interest. However, there are a number of differences. The first of these is the possible avoidance of the charge to income tax under ICTA 1988, Part XV where the trustees exercise their powers to terminate the life tenant's interest rather than the life tenant surrendering or assigning his interest to achieve the same result. The second is the avoidance of the inheritance tax gifts with reservation provisions if the termination of the life tenant's interest results from the action of the trustees and not of the life tenant. The third is the avoidance of the capital gains tax provisions in TCGA 1992, ss 77–79, 86 and 87–98A even if the life tenant can benefit from the settled property or its income following the revocation of his interest or the appointment away from him. To be certain that the life tenant cannot be treated as being a 'settlor' within the provisions of ICTA 1988, Part XV or TCGA 1992, ss 77–79 or as having made a gift with reservation, it may be prudent to ensure that the life tenant is not a trustee at the time of exercise by the trustees of their power of revocation or appointment. Otherwise it may be argued that he has become a settlor or made a gift within the above mentioned provisions by virtue of his having participated in the exercise by the trustees of their powers. This is a tenuous argument, unlikely to find favour in a court of law.

As explained earlier, it is of less importance to consider the effect of the capital gains tax rate on gains realised by the trustees because of the uniform rate of capital gains tax on settlements of 34%.

Assignment of interests in remainder by way of gift or sale

(i) Inheritance tax

5.39 An interest in remainder, being a reversionary interest, is usually excluded property for inheritance tax purposes. The principal exceptions are where the interest was acquired for a consideration in money or money's worth or is one to which the settlor or his spouse is (or has been) beneficially entitled. Any disposition of the interest, if excluded property, cannot be a transfer of value under IHTA 1984, s 3(2).

A sale of a reversionary interest will not give rise to any potential inheritance tax charge for the assignor and assignee. This is unless a sale is made to the life tenant or between connected persons and is not a bargain at arm's length. If the sale is to the life tenant of the fund in which the reversionary interest subsists the consideration paid by the life tenant will be treated as being a transfer of value since his estate will be reduced by payment of the consideration but will not be increased by the value of the reversionary interest (IHTA 1984, s 55). Moreover, the payment will not qualify as a transaction not intended to confer gratuitous benefit as the operation of IHTA 1984, s 10 is excluded for transactions to which IHTA 1984, s 55(1) applies.

In response to the decision in *CIR v Melville and others, CA [2001] STC 1271*, IHTA 1984 s 272 was amended to provide that a settlement power is not property for the purposes of inheritance tax. A settlement power for this is '... any power over or exerciseable (whether directly or indirectly) in relation to settled property or a settlement'.

Because of this charge, IHTA 1984, s 55A was inserted to make similar provisions in relation to settlement powers to those applying to reversionary interests under IHTA 1984,s 48. Where a person makes a disposition by which he acquires a settlement power for consideration in money or money's worth

(a) the exemption for dispositions not intended to acquire a gratuitous benefit does not apply;

(b) the person is treated as making a transfer of value;

(c) the value transferred is determined without taking account of any value acquired by the disposition; and

(d) the exemptions for transfers to spouses, charities, political parties, housing associations, maintenance funds for historic buildings, etc. and for national purposes do not apply to the transfer.

(ii) Capital gains tax

5.40 Where the reversionary interest is sold for actual consideration, the trustees will be treated as having disposed of the underlying trust assets to which the interest relates and immediately reacquired them at market value (TCGA 1992, s 76A and Sch 4A). Any gain will not be eligible for hold-over relief under TCGA 1992, s 165 as there is no gift of business assets. If the reversionary interest was acquired for a consideration in money or money's worth or if the trustees of the settlement have been at any time resident outside the UK, a charge to capital gains tax will arise on any gain realised on the disposal of the reversionary interest (TCGA 1992, s 76 and TCGA 1992, s 85). If as a result of the assignment someone becomes absolutely entitled to the settled property, the trustees will be treated, under TCGA 1992, s 71, as disposing of the settled property to which that person has become absolutely entitled and reacquiring it at market value as the nominee of that individual. Depending upon the nature of the trust assets it may be possible for some or all of the gain arising to be held over under TCGA 1992, s 165 by the trustees.

5.41 *Existing Settlements*

The sale of a trust power which is not an interest in a settlement, or which was acquired for consideration, or which subsists in a settlement the trustees of which have been at anytime resident outside the UK, will be a disposal chargeable to capital gains tax.

(iii) Income tax

5.41 There will be no income tax consequences as the reversionary interest is a future interest which produces no income. However, if the interest is assigned to the minor children of the remainderman who are unmarried, or to trusts for their benefit, and falls in whilst those children remain unmarried minors, the income arising may be treated as the income of the assignor (ICTA 1988, s 660B).

(iv) Stamp duty

5.42 No charge to stamp duty will arise on the assignment unless made by way of sale (see 5.37 above).

Partition of a life interest settlement between life tenant and remaindermen

(i) Inheritance tax

5.43 Under a partition between life tenant and remaindermen the life tenant who surrenders part of his interest to the remaindermen will be treated as having made a transfer of value under IHTA 1984, s 52 equal to the value of the capital in which his interest has ceased. This transfer of value should be treated as being potentially exempt. However, if it becomes chargeable, no account will be taken, in calculating the inheritance tax payable, of the value of the reversionary interest assigned to him by the remainderman in the part of the fund which the life tenant takes absolutely (IHTA 1984, s 52(2)). The provisions of IHTA 1984, s 10 will not prevent the life tenant's surrender from being treated as a transfer of value.

The remainderman will not make a transfer of value by assigning his reversionary interest in that part of the fund to the life tenant since his interest is excluded property (IHTA 1984, s 3(2) and IHTA 1984, s 48(1)).

(ii) Capital gains tax

5.44 Neither life tenant nor remainderman will suffer a charge to capital gains tax as a result of the disposal by each of part of his interest provided that neither acquired their interests for a consideration in money or money's worth (TCGA 1992, s 76(1)) and the trustees have always been resident in the UK or that no actual consideration is given for the disposal of any trust interest.

However, under TCGA 1992, s 71 the trustees will be treated as having disposed of the entire settled property to which the life tenant and the remainderman become absolutely entitled as a result of the partition and having reacquired it at market value as nominees for the life tenant and the remainderman. They may, therefore, realise a gain although in some cases an election for hold-over relief under TCGA 1992, s 165 may be made.

(iii) Income tax

5.45 The life tenant and each of the remaindermen will become absolutely entitled to part of the trust fund and will subsequently suffer income tax at their own personal rates in respect of future income. It is less likely in these circumstances that there may be income tax consequences under ICTA 1988, Part XV for the life tenant. Unless the partition of the trust fund is undertaken with court approval, a partition will not be possible where the remaindermen are not of full age and capacity. Accordingly, it is less likely that the remaindermen will be the unmarried minor children of the life tenant, income applied for whose benefit may be treated as being the income of the life tenant under the provisions of ICTA 1988, s 660B.

(iv) Stamp duty

5.46 An instrument effecting a partition is charged with a fixed duty of £5 under the heading 'Partition' in Stamp Act 1891, Sch 1 (but see 5.37 above for comments on the general stamp duty position).

Exercise of a power of appointment in favour of life tenant

(i) Inheritance tax

5.47 This will not give rise to an inheritance tax charge by virtue of IHTA 1984, s 53(2).

(ii) Capital gains tax

5.48 The life tenant will become absolutely entitled to the settled property and as a result gains may be chargeable on the trustees under TCGA 1992, s 71 subject to the possible availability of hold-over relief under TCGA 1992, s 165.

Future gains may be taxable in the hands of the life tenant at a higher rate (i.e. 40%) than that applicable to the trustees (i.e. 34%).

(iii) Income tax

5.49 There will be no change in the income tax position.

(iv) Stamp duty

5.50 The instrument effecting the exercise of the power will not be stampable. Any instrument transferring legal title to the settled property to the life tenant will be exempt from stamp duty provided it is certified as falling within Category F in the Schedule to the Stamp Duty (Exempt

5.51 Existing Settlements

Instruments) Regulations 1987 (but see 5.37 above for the general stamp duty position).

Discretionary settlements

5.51 Since discretionary settlements generally incorporate wide powers which may be exercised to alter the trusts upon which the trust property is held, little needs to be said about the precise mechanics of any changes in the beneficial interests under such settlements. However, the inheritance tax charge that may arise on funds leaving such a settlement or ceasing to be held on discretionary trusts should be considered carefully in the light of the proposed timing of any distribution.

Inheritance tax

5.52 As the rates of inheritance tax on distributions from post-1974 discretionary trusts are calculated by reference to the value of the trust fund at the preceding ten-year anniversary or, if a ten-year anniversary has not passed, at the time of commencement of the settlement, there is much to be said for making distributions prior to a ten-year anniversary.

> *Example*
>
> A discretionary settlement is created by a settlor who had made no previous transfers of value and whose cumulative total at the time of creation of the settlement is, therefore, nil. The property was then worth £50,000 but is now worth £500,000. This property can be distributed prior to the first ten-year anniversary without incurring any charge to inheritance tax. But on the ten-year anniversary inheritance tax will be charged on the present value of the fund and future charges will be made at rates calculated by reference to the value of the fund at that date.

In two particular circumstances consideration should be given to postponing a distribution from a discretionary settlement (whether outright to beneficiaries or on to interest in possession or accumulation and maintenance trusts for their benefit) beyond a ten-year anniversary namely:

(*a*) If the business property or agricultural property relief available is less than 100% in respect of the trust fund or part of it, it may be worth postponing distributions from the settlement until after the first ten-year anniversary of creation of the settlement. However, this is only relevant where the settlement does not qualify as a nil rate band discretionary trust, as in such circumstances there would be no inheritance charge on a distribution prior to the first ten-year anniversary. This is because on any distribution prior to the first ten-year anniversary the rate of tax applicable will be calculated by reference to the value of the property in the settlement immediately after it commenced. This value is not reduced by business or agricultural property relief as the trustees would not have then owned the property gifted for the requisite period of time. Accordingly, the value of the trust assets, unrelieved by business or agricultural property relief, has to be taken into account in calculating the rate of

Existing Settlements **5.52**

tax to be applied on any exit charge prior to the first ten-year anniversary. That does not mean that business property relief or agricultural property relief is to be ignored. Such relief would reduce the value of the trust property (the subject of the exit charge) provided that the trustees had then held the assets concerned for the requisite period of time. By way of contrast, on the first ten-year anniversary (and subsequent ones) inheritance tax is charged on the trust fund as if there had been a transfer of value of the trust fund at that time. Accordingly, business property relief and agricultural property relief may operate to reduce the value of the trust property and will set the applicable rate of tax for the next ten years until the next ten-year anniversary charge. As a result, the operation of the rules can make it very difficult to decide whether relieved assets should be appointed from a discretionary trust before, or after, the first ten-year anniversary. A great deal will depend on the growth in value of the property concerned, as well as the level of the nil rate band at the relevant time. Of course, in the case of assets which fully qualify for 100% business property relief or agricultural property relief, these particular considerations are not present and it may well be worthwhile retaining the assets within the trust in any event.

(*b*) Where a distribution (whether outright or on to new trusts) is being considered a few years prior to the occasion of a ten-year anniversary charge to inheritance tax, it may be worth postponing the distribution beyond that anniversary if in the intervening time it is likely that the amount of the nil rate band will increase more substantially than the value of the trust property. However, there is always the risk that the nil rate band will remain static as it did between March 1992 and April 1995. This aspect will have to be taken into account.

Example

The ten-year anniversary of a settlement falls in the tax year 2002/03. A distribution of property from the settlement had been under consideration in the tax year 2001/02. The settled property had a value, when the settlement commenced, in excess of the nil rate band at that time and the settlor had made no chargeable transfers in the seven years prior to the creation of the settlement.

The postponement of the distribution until after the ten-year anniversary would remove the settled property from charge to inheritance tax on distributions during the ten years following the ten-year anniversary if the settled property is at that ten-year anniversary worth less than the applicable nil rate band. If the value of the property is currently less than £250,000 there is a good chance that this will be so, provided the trust assets do not out-perform the rate of inflation.

As has been mentioned, discretionary settlements created prior to 18 March 1986 and under which the settlor is a discretionary beneficiary should, if possible, be left alone. The settlor will not be treated as having reserved a benefit in such settlements since FA 1986, s 102 only operates in relation to gifts made after that time. The settlor, therefore, remains able to benefit from such a settlement but the property in it remains entirely outside his estate.

5.53 *Existing Settlements*

Certainly the settlor should not now add any further funds to this type of settlement (other than possibly by will) since to do so would cause the gifts with reservation provisions to apply.

Generally, the decision whether or not to break a discretionary settlement depends to a large extent on the prevailing rates of inheritance tax applicable to distributions and to the charge on each ten-year anniversary. Where these rates are low (as at present — the maximum rate being 6%), there is every incentive to keep the settlement intact if the flexibility it provides is still considered important. The tax charges can often be serviced out of accumulated income. On the other hand, discretionary settlements are very much pawns in the political tax game and may be subject to more penal tax regimes in the future (as they have been in the past). The trustees should always keep this political factor in mind.

Capital gains tax

5.53 When a beneficiary becomes absolutely entitled to an asset as against the trustees (on the occasion of a distribution to him) they will be deemed to dispose of the asset and reacquire it at that time as the nominees of the beneficiary. It will usually be possible to hold over to the beneficiary under TCGA 1992, s 260 any chargeable gain arising, unless the distribution does not constitute a 'chargeable transfer' for inheritance tax purposes. This will be the case where, for example, a distribution is made within three months of the commencement of the settlement or within the three months following a ten-year anniversary of the commencement.

Any other form of reorganisation of the interests under a discretionary settlement (for example, its conversion into an accumulation and maintenance settlement) will not give rise to any charges to capital gains tax provided that no beneficiary becomes absolutely entitled to any of the trust property as a result.

Income tax

5.54 If on a reorganisation of interests under a discretionary settlement any person becomes entitled to receive the income from a part or the whole of the settled property the trustees will suffer income tax at the basic rate on such income but will cease to suffer the rate applicable to trusts. Instead, the beneficiary entitled to the income will suffer income tax at his marginal rates on the income to which he is entitled but will receive a credit for the tax suffered thereon by the trustees.

6 Offshore Trusts

Introduction

6.1 The aim of this chapter is briefly to examine the main issues arising from the offshore trust rules, together with some of the tax planning strategies which are still available despite the introduction of those rules. A comprehensive review of the subject is outside the scope of this book.

This chapter is only concerned with non-UK resident trusts established by UK resident domiciliaries. The position of UK resident but non-UK domiciled settlors is considered in chapter 19 *Immigration and Emigration*.

Background

6.2 Tax legislation contains a number of measures to discourage individuals who are both resident and domiciled in the UK from seeking to avoid or defer their capital gains tax liabilities through the use of offshore trusts. This is done in three ways. First, a capital gains tax charge is introduced on the trustees at the time they become non-resident, calculated on the basis that they dispose of all the settled property at the time they change their residence and immediately reacquire it at market value ('the emigration charge') (TCGA 1992, s 80). Secondly, the gains of a non-resident settlement are attributed to its settlor if he is domiciled and either resident or ordinarily resident in the UK and (broadly) the settlor or his spouse, or any of their children and their spouses or any companies controlled by any of them, are capable of benefiting from the income or capital of the settlement ('the offshore settlor charge') (TCGA 1992, s 86 and TCGA 1992, Sch 5). Thirdly, an additional charge to capital gains tax arises which is calculated as if it were an interest charge, on any beneficiary who receives capital distributions or benefits from a non-resident settlement which are taxable under TCGA 1992, s 87 ('the supplementary charge') (TCGA 1992, ss 91–97). The list of persons by reference to whose interest a settlement is brought within the offshore settlor charge was extended by the Finance Act 1998 so as to include grandchildren, their spouses and their controlled companies. The Finance Act 1998 also amended the provisions relating to the charge on capital payments. Provisions were introduced by the Finance Act 2000 to create a capital gains tax charge which arises in certain circumstances where trustees make a transfer of value to another person and the transfer is treated as linked with trustee borrowing.

6.3 Offshore Trusts

Export charges

6.3 Under TCGA 1992, s 80 where a UK resident trust becomes resident outside the UK, the trustees will be deemed to have disposed of the 'defined' assets and immediately reacquired them at their current market value, and will be assessed to tax on the amount due. 'Defined assets' are all trust assets, other than those which would in any event remain within the UK tax charge because they are used for the purposes of a trade carried on in the UK by the trustees (TCGA 1992, s 80(4)). Anti-avoidance rules have been introduced dealing with UK trusts which fall to be treated as non-resident under the terms of an applicable double taxation agreement (TCGA 1992, s 83). A number of ancillary provisions restrict rollover relief, and prevent a double charge to tax arising by reference to disposals of interests under trusts. Further provisions limit the charge to tax where there is an inadvertent change in residence resulting from the death of a trustee, and the former residence status is resumed within six months. Finally, there are provisions governing the liability for tax of past trustees, where a UK trust becomes non-resident and an export charge remains unpaid.

> *Example*
>
> In 1985, Mr Arnold, a UK resident domiciliary settled his 25% stake in Widget Enterprises, a UK trading company, on a UK resident interest in possession trust in his favour. The shares were then valued at £30,000 on a minority basis and had an original base cost on purchase in 1984 of £10,000. The gain was held over. In July 2000, the trust was exported immediately prior to the sale of the shares for £2 million as part of a takeover. Ignoring indexation and taper relief, the capital gains tax position would be as follows.
>
> (i) There would be no clawback of the held-over gain, as such charges no longer apply in the case of exported trusts.
>
> (ii) The 'export charge' would be £796,000 [(£2,000,000 – £10,000) × 40%].
>
> (iii) The gain would be chargeable on Mr Arnold, as a result of his retained interest under the trust.
>
> (TCGA 1992, s 77).

The net effect of these provisions in practice normally confines the export of settlements to cases where

(*a*) either the settlement is holding non-chargeable assets, such as cash, or the gain which will arise on the export of the trust is considered to be a price worth paying for the ability to defer the capital gains tax charge on gains realised by the trustees once non-resident; *and*

(*b*) either the beneficiaries of the settlement do not include the settlor or members of his immediate family or the settlor is dead; and

(*c*) there is likely to be a significant gap between the making of the gain and the distribution of its proceeds to any beneficiaries.

Prior to the changes introduced by the Finance Act 1998, there were considerable capital gains tax benefits if the settlor was non-UK domiciled when he created the settlement, and he did not after that time become

Offshore Trusts **6.4**

domiciled in the UK. By appointing non-resident trustees, the settlement could be taken completely outside the scope of capital gains tax, subject only to the tax charged on the export itself. As is explained below, such settlements continue to offer considerable advantages because, although they are now brought within the capital payments and supplementary charges provisions, they are still outside the scope of the offshore settlor charge.

The overall tax position on exportation of a trust is set out below.

(i) Capital gains tax

6.4 There are several points to consider where an export of a settlement is proposed.

(*a*)   Most importantly, where the settlement is one in which the settlor has an interest (as defined in TCGA 1992, Sch 5 para 2). This broadly is where either the settlor or his spouse, any of their children and their spouses, any grandchild of the settlor or his spouse and the spouse of any grandchild, or any companies controlled by any of them (or any companies associated with any companies so controlled) benefit or are capable of benefiting from the income or capital of the settlement. The settlor will be taxable on any gains realised by the trustees, unless he is

   (i)   domiciled outside the UK in the relevant tax year; or

   (ii) neither resident nor ordinarily resident in the UK during any part of the year; or

   (iii) dead.

   This offshore settlor charge arises in the year following the exportation of the settlement. However, TCGA 1992, s 77 imposes a similar charge ('the onshore settlor charge') in the years up to and including the year of the export of the settlement.

   In a family context, therefore, the scope for deferring the payment of capital gains tax by the export of a settlement the settlor of which is domiciled and either resident or ordinarily resident in the UK will only arise where the beneficiaries of the settlement are the great-grandchildren or remoter issue of the settlor, unless a specific tax strategy is being followed.

(*b*)   On the trustees of the settlement becoming neither resident nor ordinarily resident in the UK, the trustees will be deemed to have disposed of the settled property and to have immediately reacquired it at its market value. Any chargeable gain arising as a result will be taxable in the hands of the retiring trustees. However, if it is not paid by them within six months from the time when it becomes payable, the Inland Revenue can recover the tax from any other person who was a trustee of the settlement within twelve months of the date of export unless he retired before the end of the twelve month period and can show that when he retired there was no proposal that the settlement might be exported.

6.4 Offshore Trusts

For some settlements this potential capital gains tax charge may outweigh the advantages of the settlement becoming non-resident. However, there may be cases where the prospect of deferring capital gains tax following an expected growth in the value of an asset will outweigh the disadvantage of triggering an immediate charge to capital gains tax.

Where the settlement is outside the scope of the onshore settlor charge because neither the settlor nor his spouse can benefit from the settled property or its income, it should be noted that the export charge is taxable at the rate applicable to the trustees. Accordingly, where a person wishes to settle property for the benefit of (say) his grandchildren and wishes that property to be held offshore, capital gains tax may be reduced if he transfers the property to a settlement with trustees resident in the UK (assuming that he is able to hold over the gain under either TCGA 1992, s 165 or TCGA 1992, s 260). The trustees can then retire in favour of non-resident trustees, giving rise to a capital gains tax charge at the trustees' rate of 34%, instead of him transferring the assets immediately to trustees resident outside the UK, when there will be a capital gains tax charge at the settlor's own rate. One must consider the implications of taper relief before adopting such a strategy.

(c) If the trustees are *at any time* resident in the UK they will be treated as being resident there throughout that tax year. No concession is available to allow the tax year to be split. Therefore, the trustees will not be outside the UK capital gains tax net until the start of the tax year immediately following that in which the settlement is exported. The retiring trustees should also be aware that they will remain liable to capital gains tax in respect of gains realised on disposals of trust assets made by the new non-resident trustees until the end of the tax year in which the new appointment is effected. It is preferable for UK resident trustees to retire towards the end of a tax year in order to minimise their exposure to charges which they will have no assets to meet. Funds should not be retained to cover such possible liabilities or indeed those that have arisen prior to their retirement since this might give rise to arguments that the administration of the settlement has not been transferred abroad. Indemnities from reputable non-resident trustees for such liabilities are the safest course for the retiring trustees and do not risk prejudicing the effectiveness of the export of the settlement for capital gains tax purposes.

(d) Non-resident trustees will not usually themselves have any capital gains tax liability in respect of gains realised by them, even in the case of settlements in TCGA 1992, s 86 and TCGA 1992, Sch 5. A further charge ('the capital payments charge') exists, however, to visit those gains upon beneficiaries resident and domiciled in the UK who receive 'capital payments' from the settlement in which those gains were realised. The following is a brief discussion of the position under those rules.

Offshore Trusts 6.4

TCGA 1992, s 87 applies where, in any tax year, the trustees of a settlement are throughout the year resident outside the UK, and a beneficiary receives a capital payment from that settlement. A beneficiary will only be chargeable when he is both resident and domiciled in the UK when the gain is deemed to accrue to him. Gains realised (on actual and deemed disposals) by the non-resident trustees which had the trustees been UK resident would have been chargeable to capital gains tax will be apportioned to the beneficiary to the extent that they do not exceed the value of his capital payment. Where the gains realised by the non-resident trustees exceed the value of the capital payment received by the beneficiary the excess may be apportioned, to any beneficiary who receives a capital payment in subsequent years. Where a beneficiary receives a capital payment from non-resident trustees in a year before any trust gains have arisen, gains realised by the trustees in subsequent tax years may be apportioned to the beneficiary. Due to the unified rates of income tax and capital gains tax, the capital payments charge is a significant factor in deciding whether a trust should be exported. The beneficiaries may suffer capital gains tax of between 40% and 64% in respect of gains realised by the non-resident trustees (depending upon the length of time that gains have been 'stockpiled') whereas a lower rate (34%) might have been applicable had the settlement not been exported. In addition, taper relief may be available to reduce the overall capital gains tax rate.

The capital payments charge can operate in an advantageous manner because, until a capital payment is received by a UK resident and domiciled beneficiary, no capital gains tax will be payable as a result of any disposal by the trustees. If the beneficiaries do not need the sale proceeds, they can be reinvested by the trustees and funds that would have been used to pay capital gains tax can earn profits for the benefit of the beneficiaries. This 'deferral' aspect of section 87 has now been partially blocked by the supplementary charge. (This aspect has been touched on above and is considered in greater detail later in this chapter.)

What is a 'capital payment'? This phrase is defined, by TCGA 1992, s 97 to mean any payment which is not chargeable to income tax on the beneficiary or, if the beneficiary is not resident or ordinarily resident in the UK, any payment received otherwise than as income, any transfer of assets or the conferring of any benefit. Where a capital payment is made by way of a loan to a beneficiary the value of the capital payment is taken to be equal to the value of the benefit conferred by the loan (TCGA 1992, s 97(4)).

Most informed opinion considered that capital payments would accrue over time where trustees allowed a life tenant the use of a trust asset on favourable terms, subject to the trustee's right to require the return of the asset at will. An example of this would be where trustees permitted a life tenant to occupy a property without charge but subject to a condition that he must quit the property on being given notice by the trustees. In *Cooper v Billingham; Fisher v Edwards*, CA

6.4 Offshore Trusts

2001 [2001] STC 1177 the Court of Appeal held that where the trustees of a non-resident settlement lent trust moneys interest-free and repayable on demand to a life tenant, a capital payment arose.

The capital payments charge applies to any settlement irrespective of the domicile of the settlor.

A non-resident may be deemed to realise capital gains under TCGA 1992, s 87 and yet be outside the charge to capital gains tax by reason of his non-residence. Therefore, an export will be particularly advantageous if all beneficiaries are resident outside the UK or if it is anticipated that the beneficiaries who will receive capital payments will become non-resident so that capital payments may be made to beneficiaries who are not within the charge to capital gains tax. Even where some beneficiaries are resident in the UK and it is intended that they will receive capital payments, by careful organisation it may be possible to make payments to non-resident beneficiaries in an earlier tax year than that in which payments are to be made to UK resident beneficiaries. This will ensure that the gains realised by the non-resident trustees are matched first with the payments to the non-resident beneficiaries who will suffer no capital gains tax in respect of them.

The charge on temporary non-residents under TCGA 1992, s 10A provides that gains allocated to non-residents whose period of non-residence is less than five years will become chargeable when they resume UK residence.

A beneficiary will not suffer a charge to capital gains tax in respect of a capital payment received from an offshore trust unless he is domiciled in the UK at some time during that year (TCGA 1992, s 87(7)).

As already mentioned, where a capital payment to a beneficiary precedes the realisation of gains by non-resident trustees, the capital payments charge operates to attribute the trustees' subsequent gains to the beneficiary if they were resident outside the UK when he received his capital payment. A capital payment made to a beneficiary prior to the export of a settlement may also cause gains realised by the trustees once they have become non-resident to be attributed to him. However, TCGA 1992, s 89 gives protection from the capital payments charge if the capital payment received by the beneficiary was not made in anticipation of a disposal made by the trustees in a non-resident period.

(e) Difficulties may also arise where funds held on separate trusts derive from one settlement. TCGA 1992, s 69 provides that trustees are to be treated as a single and continuing body of persons being resident in the UK unless the administration of the settlement is carried on outside the UK and a majority of the trustees are resident outside the UK. The exportation of one fund of a settlement leaving another with trustees resident in the UK may leave the trustees of the UK fund bearing the capital gains tax liability for gains made by the offshore

Offshore Trusts **6.6**

trustees of the fund exported as happened in *Roome and Another v Edwards, HL 1981, 54 TC 359; [1981] STC 96; [1981] 1 All ER 736* and *Bond v Pickford, CA [1983] STC 517*. It may be difficult to determine on the face of the trust documents whether the funds are separate funds of the same settlement or two different settlements relating to those funds (and by which they were created). However, the Inland Revenue practice set out in Statement of Practice SP 7/84 may be of assistance. In practice it will be helpful to know whether any charge to capital gains tax was incurred or held over under FA 1980, s 79 (pre-14 March 1989), TCGA 1992, s 165 or TCGA 1992, s 260 when the two funds separated (as it should have been if separate settlements were created since the trustees of the newly created settlement would then have become absolutely entitled to the settled property over which the power of appointment was exercised) and whether each fund claims its own share of the annual exemption available to trustees. If there is any doubt as to whether or not separate settlements exist, for safety's sake both should be exported.

(ii) Inheritance tax

6.5 The export of an existing settlement by the appointment of non-resident trustees will have no inheritance tax consequences. If, at the time of creating the settlement, the settlor was domiciled in the UK (whether as a matter of general law or under the deemed domicile provisions in IHTA 1984, s 267) the settlement will remain subject to UK inheritance tax even if the trustees become non-UK resident and whether or not the settlor and all beneficiaries are now domiciled and resident outside the UK.

(iii) Income tax

6.6 For income tax purposes, the residence of the trustees of a settlement is determined under FA 1989, s 110. Where the settlor of the settlement was at the time of the making of the settlement, or at the time of any further provision of funds, either resident, ordinarily resident or domiciled in the UK, for income tax purposes the trustees will be regarded as resident in the UK if any of the trustees are resident in the UK, even if a majority are non-resident. In any other case, the trustees will not be regarded as resident in the UK provided there is at least one trustee who is *not* resident there, even if a majority of the trustees *are* resident in the UK. It should be remembered, however, that in this latter case the trustees will not be regarded as resident outside the UK for capital gains tax purposes.

Trustees resident outside the UK for income tax purposes are not liable to UK income tax except on income arising here.

Tax on income arising in the UK is usually deducted at source and so UK income tax will generally be of little concern to non-resident trustees since they will receive their income net of basic rate tax and will have no further income tax liability subject to one exception. Non-resident trustees of settlements under which income may be accumulated or paid out at the

6.6 Offshore Trusts

discretion of the trustees are liable to the income tax rate applicable to trusts under ICTA 1988, s 686. Whilst the Inland Revenue may have some difficulty collecting this tax from the non-resident trustees, they may be able to do so should circumstances change. For example, if the trust is repatriated to the UK, the new UK trustees will have to deal with any arrears of tax. Encouragement is given to the trustees to discharge their liability by Inland Revenue Extra-Statutory Concession B18 which is discussed below, albeit that the tax can be avoided in a relatively straightforward manner where UK source income is involved through the use of a foreign incorporated company to hold the assets previously held by the trustees directly. However, the other tax implications of this must be considered. The application of additional rate tax to foreign trustees is less common now because of FA 1995, s 128.

If a life tenant resident and domiciled in the UK is entitled to the income of the trust fund, that income, whether arising to the non-resident trustees from a UK source or not, will remain taxable in his hands at his personal rates of income tax. Beneficiaries who receive distributions of income from a non-resident discretionary settlement will not be entitled to the tax credits or double tax reliefs to which they might have been entitled had they received the income direct from its original source. Nor will that income be within ICTA 1988, s 687 and, therefore, treated as being a net payment from which income tax at the rate applicable to trusts has been deducted. If income is to be distributed on a regular basis to beneficiaries, it may be advantageous for the non-resident trustees to submit tax returns to the Inland Revenue and pay any tax due on UK source income since under the provisions of Inland Revenue Extra-Statutory Concession B18, the Inland Revenue will then allow the beneficiaries to claim relief for any foreign and UK tax paid by, or withheld from, the trustees.

The same income tax treatment is given to an accumulation and maintenance settlement but if income or capital is distributed to minor unmarried children of the settlor the income of the settlement will be treated as being that of the settlor (ICTA 1988, s 660B).

If the settlor (and his spouse) are not entirely excluded from benefit under the settlement, the settlor may be charged to income tax on income arising to the trustees whilst he remains resident and domiciled in the UK even though he does not actually receive that income (ICTA 1988, Part XV). Even if he is excluded from benefit but is able to direct how income from the settlement is distributed or has in some other way 'power to enjoy' that income within ICTA 1988, s 739 the settlor would be deemed to receive the income as it arose to the trustees and he would be charged to income tax on that income under Schedule D, Case VI. Section 739 has effect not only where the settlor has power to enjoy *income* but also where he may receive *capital* from the settlement.

If income is accumulated in an accumulation and maintenance settlement for the benefit of the settlor's children and no capital sums are paid out to or for their benefit until they attain 18, subsequently each child may suffer a charge to income tax under ICTA 1988, s 740 on the income which arose to the trustees (before or after they attained 18) and was accumulated and which could, when it arose, have been (directly or indirectly) used to provide a

Offshore Trusts **6.8**

benefit for them. This charge will arise to the extent that they subsequently do receive a benefit from the trustees if, when they receive that benefit, they are resident and domiciled in the UK. Benefit is widely defined and does not merely include benefits of an income nature.

ICTA 1988, s 740 will also operate to impose an income tax liability on a beneficiary (other than the settlor) of a discretionary settlement who receives benefits (from the settlement) to the extent that income has arisen or, in the future arises, to the trustees and has been or is accumulated but which may be used to provide a benefit for him.

It will be seen that provided the settlor and his spouse are excluded from benefit and cannot direct how the income of the settlement should be applied, a measure of income tax deferral may be achieved by the creation of an offshore discretionary or accumulation and maintenance settlement since income will only be charged to UK income tax when beneficiaries resident here receive income or benefits from the settlement. For so long as the income is rolled up offshore no charge will arise.

Actual tax cost of export

6.7 One of the results of the export charge is that many old settlor retained interest trusts will remain UK resident for the indefinite future.

However, there may still be UK resident trusts which were established by settlors who are now dead, or for individuals outside the settlor's immediate family circle. It may be still advantageous for these to be exported, especially where the value of the property settled is low under current market conditions.

Legal issues

6.8 Before a trust can be exported, the following legal issues are relevant, in addition to the tax implications of the export.

(i) When may non-resident trustees be appointed?

It is sometimes suggested that it is not possible to exercise the statutory power conferred by the Trustee Act 1925, s 36 to appoint non-resident trustees or, at least, that it is improper to do so. This is based on the following argument.

It is argued that as section 36(1) enables new trustees to be appointed where a trustee 'remains out of the UK for more than 12 months' this necessarily implies that a non-resident person cannot be appointed as a trustee.

This argument was rejected by Sir John Pennycuick VC in *Whitehead's Will Trusts (Re), [1971] 1 WLR 833; [1971] 2 All ER 1334* but *obiter dicta* in that case suggested that in most circumstances such an appointment would be improper.

> 'On the other hand, apart from exceptional circumstances, it is not proper to make such an appointment, that is to say, the court would not, apart from exceptional circumstances, make such an appointment; nor would it be right for donees of the power to make such an appointment out of court.'

6.8 Offshore Trusts

The court has been asked to assent to variations of trust involving the appointment of non-resident trustees under Variation of Trusts Act 1958, s 1. In *Seale's Marriage Settlement (Re), [1961] Ch 574; [1961] 3 All ER 136* and *Windeatt's Will Trusts (Re), [1969] 1 WLR 692; [1969[2 All ER 324* the court approved a variation in cases where the beneficiaries were long-term residents of the foreign jurisdiction. In *Weston's Settlements (Re), [1969] 1 Ch 223; [1968] 1 All ER 720, 3 All ER 388* a variation was refused where a family had taken up residence in Jersey for tax avoidance purposes in circumstances where the court suspected the change of residence might be temporary.

It is therefore argued on the basis of Sir John Pennycuick's *dicta* in *re Whitehead* and by analogy to the principles applied in *re Weston* that the appointment of non-resident trustees would normally be 'improper.'

Few now find this argument compelling. In the unreported case, *Richard v Mackay (1990) 1 OTPR 1* which was followed by Vinelott J in another unreported case, *Beatty's Will Trusts (No 2)(Re), (unreported)* Millett J said:

'. . . I doubt that the language of Sir John Pennycuick is really in tune with the times. In my judgment where the trustees retain their discretion . . . the court should need to be satisfied only that the proposed transaction is not so inappropriate that no reasonable trustee could entertain it'.

So the appointment of non-resident trustees under an express or statutory power is unlikely of itself to be 'improper'. It is true that, in *Richard v Mackay*, Millet J commented as *obiter* that the Court was unlikely to appoint non-resident trustees 'where the scheme is nothing more than a scheme to avoid tax and has no advantages of any kind'. He drew a distinction, however, between the Court's approach when it exercised a discretion of its own from its approach when asked to authorise the trustees' exercise of their own discretion.

'Where the Court is invited to exercise an original discretion of its own . . . the Court will require to be satisfied that the discretion should be exercised in the manner proposed . . . Where, however, the transaction is to be proposed to be carried out by the trustees in exercise of their own discretion, entirely out of court, . . . then in my judgment the question the Court asks itself is quite different. It is concerned to ensure that the proposed exercise of the trustees' power is lawful and within the power and that it does not infringe the trustees' duty to act as ordinary, reasonable and prudent trustees might act, but it requires only to be satisfied that the trustees can properly form the view that the proposed transaction is for the benefit of the beneficiaries or the trust estate.'

If the appointment is 'improper', however, what is the effect of that?

It appears from *re Whitehead* that this is unlikely to mean that the exercise of the power is invalid. If it is invalid then the original trustee will not have been validly discharged from the trusts. If that were the case, the result could be that the settlement concerned will have remained resident in the UK after the purported change of trustees and it will, therefore, have remained within the charge to capital gains tax.

It is more likely, however, that the retirements and appointments would be valid though improper at the time they were made and therefore the court

Offshore Trusts **6.8**

would be called upon to exercise its jurisdiction to avoid the retirements and appointments on an application of the beneficiaries under, for example, the Trustee Act 1925, s 41. The result of such a decision is that the appointments and retirements would be reversed from the time that the court's judgment was made.

As has been said, in all but the most exceptional circumstances, it is unlikely that the court would interfere with the appointment of non-resident trustees under the statutory, or an express, power of appointment. This must particularly be so where the trust deed expressly authorises the appointment of non-resident trustees.

It is common practice, however, for trustees to protect themselves against whatever residual risk there may be by seeking the agreement of, and an indemnity from, the adult beneficiaries of the settlement.

(ii) Other trust points to be watched

There are two particular provisions of the Trustee Act 1925 which must be considered with care when a settlement is to be exported.

1. Trustee Act 1925, s 37(1)(c) provides that a trustee shall not be discharged from his trust unless there will be either a trust corporation or at least two persons to act as trustees to perform the trust. The exception to this is where a sole trustee was originally appointed and a sole trustee will be able to give a good receipt for all capital money because the settlement only permits the trustees to hold property which is personalty. It is not clear that section 37(1)(c) can be expressly excluded under the terms of the settlement.

    If the settlement provides powers for the trustees to buy and sell land, as most will, a sole trustee (other than a trust corporation) should not be appointed even if only one trustee was originally appointed. Since a foreign incorporated company cannot be a trust corporation (Trustee Act 1925, s 68(18) and rules made under Public Trustee Act 1906, s 4) such a company should not be appointed as a sole trustee on the export of a settlement. Where a foreign incorporated company is appointed to be the trustee of a settlement which is to be exported, two additional individuals should be appointed to be trustees to ensure that the retiring trustee or trustees are discharged from their trusts. If the UK resident retiring trustees are not properly discharged as required by section 37(1)(c) they will remain trustees. The Inland Revenue have been known to argue in particular cases that the result has been that there has not been a majority of the trustees of the settlement who are resident outside the UK and that, accordingly, the UK resident trustees remained liable to capital gains tax in respect of gains realised on disposals of the settled property.

2. Trustee Act 1925, s 40 provides that, on the appointment by deed of a new trustee, the settled property will, save in circumstances mentioned below, vest automatically in the new trustee or trustees whether or not that deed contains an express declaration that it should do so. However, certain types of assets are expressly excluded from vesting

6.8 Offshore Trusts

automatically (section 40(4)). Therefore, on the appointment of a new trustee or trustees the transfer into the names of the new trustees must be effected by the usual means for transferring such assets. These assets include land conveyed by way of mortgage, land held under a lease and any shares or securities or property which are only transferable in books kept by a company or in a manner directed by Act of Parliament.

The appointment of non-resident trustees will only remove the trustees from the capital gains tax net if a majority of them are resident outside the UK and the administration of the settlement is transferred outside the UK. Accordingly, all assets held in the settlement should be transferred to the new trustees before the beginning of the tax year for which it is desired to ensure that the trustees are non-resident. Care should be taken to ensure that all stock transfer forms have been signed by the retiring trustees and that, so far as possible all formalities have been completed. Although it should be sufficient if all that remains is for the non-resident trustees to arrange the registration of themselves as shareholders in the various companies.

Doubts have been raised as to whether section 40 is effective to transfer from retiring trustees to new trustees equitable interests (such as reversionary interests) held by trustees or whether, as a result of the provisions of Law of Property Act 1925, s 53(1)(c), these fall within one of the exceptions in sub-section 40(4) as being property the transfer of which must be carried out as prescribed by Act of Parliament. The safest course is to ensure that any equitable interest which is to pass to the new trustees is assigned in writing (this can be incorporated into the deed of appointment of new trustees). Again this avoids any argument that the administration of the settlement has not been transferred outside the UK.

One situation which frequently concerns non-resident trustees and their beneficiaries in relation to the question of whether the administration of a settlement has been transferred abroad is where UK investment managers manage the investment portfolio of the settlement. In these circumstances, if the management is carried out on a fully discretionary basis it may be arguable that the non-resident trustees have not fully assumed the administration of the settlement. However, if the argument is to succeed that the administration of the settlement is carried on outside the UK, it is advisable for the trustees to establish an investment policy to be pursued by the managers, to review their performance on a regular basis, to be notified of all sales and purchases made and to review regularly whether or not to continue the management agreement which should be terminable by them on reasonable notice. Most of these procedures will, in any event, be required under the Trustee Act 2000 if the trust s governed by English law. Ideally, investment management should not be carried out by UK investment managers nor should substantial investment advisory services be received from UK investment managers. The meaning of 'the place of effective management' was considered in the case of *Wensleydale's Settlement Trustees v CIR, Sp C, [1996] SSCD 241 (Sp C 73)* where it was held to mean where the shots were called, to use a vivid transatlantic colloquialism. It was held that it was not sufficient just to operate a bank account in the name of the trustees.

Finally, since most civil law jurisdictions do not have any concept of the nature of a trust and do not recognise the division of ownership of assets into legal and equitable ownership, it is preferable, when exporting a settlement, to appoint trustees resident in a common law jurisdiction where the courts will enforce the duties and responsibilities of the trustees. Usually, trustees resident in a tax haven are appointed in order to ensure that the jurisdiction in which the new trustees are resident will not impose charges on realised gains similar to the UK capital gains tax they seek to avoid.

Taxing the settlor

6.9 Under the offshore settlor charge (TCGA 1992, s 86) gains realised by non-UK resident trustees are attributed to a UK resident and domiciled settlor where a retained interest exists. The settlor is entitled to recover the tax so paid from the trustees. Gains arising during a period of less than five complete fiscal years during which the settlor is non-resident will be assessable either in the settlor's year of departure or return under the charge on gains of temporary non-residents (TCGA 1992, s 10A and TCGA 1992, s 86A).

This charge applies irrespective of the time the settlement was made. Before 6 April 1999 only settlements made on or after 19 March 1991 and certain 'tainted' settlements were within the charge.

In general terms, a settlor has an interest in a settlement for the purposes of the offshore settlor charge where he or his immediate family can benefit under the settlement, unless the benefit can only arise as a result of certain specified events outside the settlor's control. The charging provisions do not apply if the settlor dies in the relevant year, or if the beneficiary, by virtue of whom the settlor has an interest, dies.

The five linking factors

6.10 The substantive provisions are contained in TCGA 1992, Sch 5. There have to be five linking factors present before the rules can apply in any year of assessment.

(*a*) There must be a qualifying settlement.

(*b*) The trustees must be non-UK resident, or dually resident.

(*c*) A settlor must be domiciled and resident or ordinarily resident in the UK (subject to TCGA 1992, s 86A).

(*d*) The settlor must have a retained interest.

(*e*) Applying the fiction that the trust was UK resident during the year of assessment, there must be a gain arising in respect of a disposal of settled property originating from the settlor.

6.11 Offshore Trusts

Qualifying settlements

6.11 Since 6 April 1999 all settlements are qualifying settlements. Until that date qualifying settlements were settlements created on or after 19 March 1991 and other settlements which had become 'tainted'. A trust became tainted where, following 19 March 1991, property or income was added to the 'old' trust, or the trust became non-resident, or the settlor or his immediate family benefited for the first time in an unforseeable and unexpected manner. The final category of tainting normally involved a breach of trust.

Non-resident trusts and settlors

6.12 The trusts caught under these provisions are those which are either non-UK resident or ordinarily resident for any part of a year of assessment, or become non-UK resident for any part of a year by operation of any applicable double taxation arrangement.

For a settlor to be caught he must be UK domiciled, and resident or ordinarily resident during any part of the year of assessment. A person is treated as a settlor where the settlement concerned contains property treated as originating from him (TCGA 1992, Sch 5 para 7). This will largely occur where he provided the property himself or the property in certain circumstances itself represents assets which he originally provided (TCGA 1992, Sch 5 para 8). The rules also catch property added by companies, treating shareholders as settlors (TCGA 1992, Sch 5 para 8(4)). Property added as a result of reciprocal arrangements with others is also caught. Property is to be taken as being added if it is provided directly or indirectly by a person.

Retained interests caught

6.13 In broad terms a settlor is treated as having an interest under a settlement if income or property originating from him can or does become available for the benefit of any one or more of the following ('defined') persons, namely

(*a*) the settlor;

(*b*) the settlor's spouse;

(*c*) any child of the settlor or of the settlor's spouse;

(*d*) the spouse of any such child;

(*e*) any grandchild of the settlor or of the settlor's spouse;

(*f*) any spouse of any such grandchild;

(*g*) a company controlled by any of the above; or

(*h*) a company associated with a controlled company.

There are a number of limited exclusions which reduce the possibility of a person inadvertently being treated as a settlor as a result of circumstances beyond his control.

Offshore Trusts **6.17**

A chargeable gain must arise

6.14 The final condition is that, as a result of the disposal of any settled property originating from the settlor (which has a wide definition), there is an amount on which the trustees would be chargeable to tax if they were to be UK resident, disregarding the terms of any applicable double taxation treaty.

In quantifying the chargeable gains involved, no account is to be taken of the annual exemption. However, taper relief should be taken into account. Similarly the effect of the UK domestic settlor retained interest rules for capital gains tax is to be ignored. However, in principle, full deduction is available for past and current losses made by the trustees in quantifying the amount of gain. In the past the Revenue have taken the view that losses arising at a time before the new rules applied to the settlement could not be set against gains arising at a time when the rules did apply. The Revenue now accept that the set-off is possible. The trust gains taxable on the settlor can be increased where the trustees hold shares in a non-UK resident company and, had the trust been UK resident, gains would have been apportioned to it under TCGA 1992, s 13. Special provisions apply where a trust holds double taxation treaty protected assets.

Provided all linking factors are present and apply, an amount of chargeable gains equal to the aggregate gains of the trustees is treated as arising to the settlor in the year of assessment in which the trustees' gains arose. The apportioned gains are treated as forming the highest slice of the settlor's chargeable gains for that year.

Exceptions to charge

6.15 The charging provisions do not apply where the settlor dies during the year of assessment (TCGA 1992, Sch 5 para 3). Similarly, if the only reason the settlor is caught is because someone other than the settlor has or may benefit under the trust, the settlor's liability will cease when that person dies during that year of assessment (TCGA 1992, Sch 5 para 4). Where the settlor is excluded from benefit, but is caught because two or more persons have or may benefit under the trust, the rules provide that their deaths during the year of assessment will cause his liability to cease (TCGA 1992, Sch 5 para 5).

The link with TCGA 1992, s 87

6.16 Where a gain is charged on a settlor under the offshore settlor charge, it should be set against and cancel the amount of any trust gains for the purposes of the capital payments charge (TCGA 1992, s 87(3)). However, this will not occur in every situation.

Losses

6.17 In the past there was a disadvantage in holding one's assets in an offshore trust because personal losses could not be set against gains allocated to an individual under the capital payments and offshore settlor

6.18 Offshore Trusts

charges. The Finance Act 2002 provides that a settlor will be able to set personal losses first against personal gains and then against gains attributed under the onshore and offshore settlor charges. This will not, however, apply in certain cases where amounts are attributed to a settlor who has been temporarily non-resident and returns to the UK. The new provisions will apply in respect of gains treated as accruing to any person in 2003/04 and later years of assessment. Settlors will be able to elect for the new provisions to apply in respect of gains arising in the tax years 2000/01, 2001/02 or 2002/03. If an election means that trustees would have to reimburse the settlor a greater amount in respect of 2000/01, 2001/02 and 2002/03 taken together than under the current rules, then the election must be made jointly by the settlor and the trustees of the settlement. The time limit for an election in respect of any of these tax years will be 31 January 2005.

Supplementary charge

6.18 The supplementary charge applies where beneficiaries receive capital payments which are subject to the capital payments charge. It is important to appreciate that the offshore settlor charge considered earlier, and the supplementary charges rules are not mutually exclusive. In some circumstances it is possible for both sets of provisions to operate in respect of the same settlement.

The idea behind the supplementary charge is to discourage the long term retention of gains within an offshore trust. In essence, the longer trust gains remain undistributed, the greater the potential tax charge when the beneficiary receives a capital payment.

The supplementary charge is calculated by applying a notional rate of interest (currently 10% a year for a maximum of six years) to the amount of tax payable under the capital payments charge where the beneficiary receives a capital payment (TCGA 1992, s 97). The amount of the capital payment is allocated to past gains previously made by the trustees, and operates to increase the amount of tax due on the capital payments received by the beneficiary. Hence, if the beneficiary receives a capital payment of, say, £100,000 on which he has to pay capital gains tax of £40,000, he could be faced with an additional tax liability of as much as £24,000 (i.e. £40,000 × 60%) if the maximum supplementary charge were to apply.

Three additional points are worth noting.

(*a*) The supplementary charge cannot operate unless a capital payment is made after 5 April 1992. This may still be relevant where a later trust gain is being matched with an earlier capital payment.

(*b*) The supplementary charge applies regardless of when the trust was established.

(*c*) The supplementary charge can only apply where the capital payment charge applies.

Offshore Trusts **6.19**

Operation of the rules

6.19 A supplementary charge will be imposed where there is at least one tax year between the tax year in which the gain is realised and the tax year in which the capital payment is made. Although the overall effect of these provisions is reasonably straightforward, they are in themselves extremely complicated. Broadly, they operate by matching capital payments made after 5 April 1991 with the gains accruing to the trustees in each tax year. The capital payments are matched with the gains of each year (called 'qualifying amounts') on a 'first in, first out' basis (TCGA 1992, s 92(3)-(6)). Where a number of capital payments are made in the same tax year, they are only matched to the extent that the capital payment results in a trust gain accruing to a beneficiary under TCGA 1992, s 87(4).

Where a capital payment made after 5 April 1992 is matched with a qualifying amount for a particular tax year and there is a gap of at least one tax year between the tax year in which the capital payment is made and the tax year of the qualifying amount, the capital gains tax paid by the beneficiary under section 87 as a result of the capital payment is increased by a deemed interest charge of 10% per annum. This is limited to a six year period and therefore the time covered by the charge begins on the later of:

(*a*) 31 January in the tax year following the year in which the disposal occurred; and

(*b*) 31 January six years before 31 January in the year of assessment following that in which the capital payment was made

(TCGA 1992, s 91).

This is in fact a very modest charge which will be immaterial if there are several decades between a trust gain being realised and the making of the capital payment with which it is matched.

Where only part of a capital payment is matched with a particular qualifying amount, or where a capital payment is matched with more than one qualifying amount, then the capital gains tax charge to which the capital payment gave rise has to be apportioned, to enable the interest charge to be calculated on the appropriate proportion of the capital gains tax and by reference to the appropriate number of years (TCGA 1992, s 93).

An example may help to show how the provisions work in practice.

> A settlement realises trust gains of £100 in the tax year 1996/97 and trust gains of £300 after taper relief in the tax year 1998/99. A capital payment of £300 is then made in the tax year 2002/03 to a beneficiary resident and domiciled in the UK. This gives rise to a capital gains tax charge of £120 (i.e. 300 × 40%). The capital payment will be matched as to £100 with the 1996/97 trust gains and as to £200 with the 1998/99 trust gains. The interest charge on the capital gains tax will be £56, calculated as follows.
>
> *On 1996/97 trust gains*
>
> £120 × $\dfrac{100}{300}$ × 10% × 6 years (i.e. 31.1.98 – 30.1.04) =   24

6.20 Offshore Trusts

On 1998/99 trust gains   b/f 24

£120 × $\frac{200}{300}$ × 10% × 4 years (i.e. 31.1.00 − 30.1.04) = $\underline{32}$
                                                                                          $\underline{£56}$

In the light of the provisions of TCGA 1992, s 87 and TCGA 1992, ss 91–97 it is prudent to assume that, where all involved are resident and domiciled in the UK, gains realised by the trustees will eventually give rise to capital gains tax charges equal to (or possibly greater than) those that would have been suffered had a UK trust been established. Thus, if it is anticipated that on the disposal of an asset incorporating large gains the proceeds will be distributed almost immediately to UK resident and domiciled beneficiaries, the appointment of non-resident trustees will not achieve any postponement of the capital gains tax liability and the costs of the exercise will be wasted.

Even where the interval between the realisation of the gain and any distribution from the settlement is likely to be less than six years (the maximum period over which the interest charge may be calculated), the appointment of non-resident trustees will only really be advantageous if the funds which would otherwise have been paid over to the Inland Revenue in capital gains tax can earn profits for the beneficiaries in excess of 10% per annum. Where, however, the gap between the disposal and the distribution is likely to exceed six years, then there is still likely to be merit in appointing offshore trustees.

Minimising the charge to tax

6.20 As the supplementary charge is based upon the amount of capital gains tax levied on a capital payment, any planning should focus on minimising the tax due on a capital payment as far as possible. There are a number of techniques which, if properly implemented, should avoid or minimise any capital gains tax charge arising on providing a benefit to the beneficiaries. These include:

(*a*) the offshore trustees providing free use of assets to a beneficiary rather than providing him or her with the funds to acquire the property concerned; and

(*b*) the offshore trustees investing for income rather than capital gains in cases outside ICTA 1988, s 739 and the income tax rules relating to settlor retained interest settlements. The supplementary charge will only apply in respect of capital gains and not income 'gains', although it will be important to consider the position under ICTA 1988, s 740.

7 Insurance

Introduction

7.1 Effecting of life assurance is unlikely to be the only facet of an estate planning strategy adopted by a client but it is nonetheless an extremely important part of what is sometimes referred to as the machinery of succession. It can:

(a) divide capital from income;

(b) encourage the smooth passage of an asset from one generation to another, unhindered by tax liabilities en route;

(c) make provision for the payment of a lump sum at a given date or on the happening of a particular event, whether or not as part of a savings scheme; and

(d) provide for the payment of income (or what, in effect, amounts to income), whether on retirement or earlier by virtue of an immediately payable annuity or under a single premium bond.

Reform of policyholder taxation

7.2 The Inland Revenue announced in October 1997 that the Government would no longer be proceeding with the package of proposals for the reform of policyholder taxation which were set out in the consultation document published on 27 November 1996. However, the Finance Act 1998 contained provisions that closed the widely known 'dead settlor' loophole and also reduced the attractiveness of Personal Portfolio Bonds (PPBs). Furthermore, in May 1999 agreement was reached between the Inland Revenue and the Association of International Life Offices on the issue of reporting requirements for chargeable events on offshore policies.

The Sandler Review into Medium and Long-term Retail Savings in the UK, published in July 2002, proposes the abolition of the 5% withdrawal rule for new life policies (see 7.20 below). At present, it is unknown when any abolition would take place.

Further details on policy taxation are given under 7.16 *et seq.* below.

The Financial Services Act 1986

7.3 Professional advisers should also be aware of the provisions of the Financial Services Act 1986 generally, but particularly in relation to the

7.4 *Insurance*

giving of investment advice which can constitute investment business. Since 29 April 1988, it has been a criminal offence to carry on investment business without appropriate authorisation, and all agreements entered into in breach of this prohibition are unenforceable at the election of the other party (FSA 1986, s 3).

Nature and types of insurance

7.4 Before considering in detail the uses that can be made of insurance in the context of estate planning — and this will be done in relation to an individual's 'early years', 'middle years' and 'later years' — it is important to understand in general terms the nature and types of insurance available and also the bases on which insurance policies may be held.

The basic contract

7.5 In general terms, insurance involves a contract (evidenced by the policy) by virtue of which an insurance company (the insurer) undertakes in return for the agreed consideration (the premium) to pay to another person (the insured) a sum of money on the occurrence of a particular and specified event, the happening of which is uncertain. In life assurance, this uncertain event will be the death of a named person (the life insured).

Uses

Protection

7.6 Life assurance was originally designed and developed to provide protection and financial stability for dependants from adverse financial consequences in the event of a person's premature death. This function has continued and perhaps grown in importance. In many cases, protection is the main reason for effecting appropriate cover. Life assurance has become important in business, with the advent of 'Keyman' life policies which are specifically designed to protect businesses against the loss of key executives and to provide appropriate financial compensation. Also, in the context of partnerships, each partner in a firm may effect a policy on his own life, written in trust for the benefit of his surviving partners, or effect policies on a life of another basis on each other, and include where appropriate 'cross-option' agreements.

Home ownership

7.7 Life assurance is also important in the area of home ownership. Although it is becoming less common, lending institutions may well insist on life assurance to ensure that a repayment mortgage is discharged on the premature death of the borrower. This will be a form of term assurance and will either secure a decreasing capital sum, in line with a repayment mortgage, or a fixed capital sum, in line with an interest only mortgage. Endowment mortgages were very common in practice and are also insurance based. The proceeds of a related endowment policy (which is charged to the lender as additional security) are used to repay the loan, with the policy maturing at the end of the mortgage term or earlier on the death of the life assured. Some insurance companies now attach critical illness cover to endowment policies so that the mortgage is paid off on diagnosis of one of a number of pre-defined diseases.

Funding tax liabilities

7.8 Life assurance has grown in importance in the context of funding tax liabilities arising on the death of an individual. As inheritance tax and the potentially exempt transfer stand at present, seven-year (decreasing) term assurance on the life of a donor is common to cover the potential inheritance tax liability should the donor die within seven years of making such a transfer. Also, appropriate insurance (if written in trust) can provide the family and dependants of the life insured with funds shortly after death to settle any inheritance tax due, without the need to wait for the administration of his estate to be completed. To this end, insurance companies will provide model trust-wordings. Independent advice should be taken to ensure the applicability of the model wordings to an individual's circumstances.

Investment

7.9 In recent years, assurance-based savings schemes have become a popular mode of investment. These provide for a capital sum to be paid on maturity which, in normal circumstances, can be received free of higher rate tax in the hands of the policyholder.

Types of policy

7.10 Many different types and variations of policy have been produced by insurance companies and life offices over the years to meet the needs of the public. In general, however, they can be divided into the following basic types, namely term policies, endowment policies, single premium investment bonds and whole life policies.

Term policies

7.11 These provide for a capital sum to be paid in the event of death within a specified period or before a specified age. No payment will be made, however, if the insured survives to the end of the period or attains the specified age, hence these are one of the cheapest forms of life assurance available.

Basic term policies lack flexibility. Due to this most life offices market a convertible term assurance where, at the end of the term, there is a right to convert the policy (sometimes without further medical evidence) to an endowment or whole life policy (or, sometimes, to renew the existing policy for another term). The value of this right is that it preserves insurability in cases where the policyholder in question becomes uninsurable or insurable

7.11 Insurance

only at a higher than normal premium, perhaps because of a health problem which has arisen.

Term policies are not investment vehicles as they do not usually acquire a surrender value. Their main use in estate planning, apart from preserving insurability, has been as a comparatively inexpensive way of providing 'disaster' cover. For example, a young newly-married man may have few resources which could help to maintain his young family if he died. He might therefore take out life cover by term assurance as a temporary measure which would be cheaper than the cost in premiums per annum of maintaining whole life cover for a similar amount. (Whole life cover is dealt with in 7.13 below.)

An important use for term assurance is to cover the potential inheritance tax liability of donees (including trustees) should a donor die within seven years of making a potentially exempt transfer. This is commonly known as a gift inter vivos policy which is in effect a decreasing term assurance which ensures that life cover reduces with the level of tapering relief.

Potentially exempt transfers give rise to no immediate inheritance tax liability and no tax liability at all provided the donor survives for seven years from making or effecting the transfer of value. If, however, a donor fails to survive the seven-year period, the potentially exempt transfer becomes a chargeable transfer (as of the date when it actually took place) but the primary liability for any inheritance tax due will be that of the donee (IHTA 1984, s 199). It is therefore prudent for term assurance to be effected to cover this potential liability.

The insurance industry has responded to the increased market for term policies. Some insurance companies offer policies which enable cover to be increased or decreased if circumstances change or if the period of cover needs to be extended.

The policy can be taken out by the donor on his own life and then assigned to, or into trust for the benefit of, the donee. Alternatively, the donee could take out the life cover for his own benefit but on the life of the donor, since he will have a sufficient insurable interest in the donor. The question of insurable interest is also dealt with later in the chapter. In either case, the donor may require the donee to enter into a legally binding commitment with the donor to be responsible for the inheritance tax liability in exoneration of the donor's personal representatives (who have a secondary liability to pay the tax if the donee fails to pay within twelve months of the end of the month in which the donor died (IHTA 1984, s 199(2) and IHTA 1984, s 204(8)).

Although the inheritance tax liability if the donor dies within the seven-year period will be determined by using the death rates prevailing at the time of the death where they have altered for the better (IHTA 1984, Sch 2 para 1A), the level of cover will usually be fixed by reference to the rates in force at the time of the gift. Decreasing term assurance will also usually be appropriate because the rate at which inheritance tax is charged will be tapered where the donor dies more than three years after making the gift. However, to provide adequate protection for the donee, it will be necessary to insure for the full amount of inheritance tax potentially payable for the first three years after the gift was made by the donor.

Insurance **7.11**

In assessing the likely tax liability (and therefore in effecting the appropriate level of term cover), other factors may need to be taken into account. For example, where a potentially exempt transfer may prove to be a chargeable transfer, and thus become subject to inheritance tax, and business property or agricultural property relief may then be in point, additional requirements relating to the donee must be satisfied. That is to say, in the case of relevant business property (for example), if such relief is to be available in full, the original property given must have been retained in the ownership of the donee from the date of the gift until the death of the donor or the earlier death of the donee or the conditions relating to replacement property must be satisfied (see IHTA 1984, ss 113A, 113B). Any term assurance effected should therefore take account of the possibility that the relief in question may not be available. In other words, when planning for inheritance tax one may wish to consider the 'worst possible case' to prevent an unwelcome shortfall in the insurance cover which is to meet the tax liability. This aspect has become more important with the introduction of 100% relief in respect of certain property. Such property may be entirely free of inheritance tax at the time of the transfer but failure to satisfy the necessary conditions on the death of the donor will result in a full 40% tax charge arising.

Term cover may also be considered where a donor makes an actual chargeable transfer as death within the seven-year period following the transfer will result in death rates (subject to tapering relief) rather than lifetime rates being applicable. The position may be further worsened where the chargeable transfer is made after a potentially exempt transfer. The death of a donor, who has made both potentially exempt transfers and subsequent chargeable transfers in the seven years before his death, will necessitate the re-calculation of the inheritance tax payable on the chargeable transfers. The inheritance tax on the chargeable transfers will originally have been calculated on the basis that the potentially exempt transfers were exempt. This has to be corrected since the potentially exempt transfers will come into cumulation as prior chargeable transfers if made within the previous seven years. The personal representatives will also need to calculate the liability to inheritance tax in respect of the potentially exempt transfers themselves and the amount of tax will also be determined by reference to the cumulative total of chargeable transfers (if any) in the previous seven years prior to the date of the potentially exempt transfers in question.

The existence of chargeable transfers in the seven years prior to the donor's death (whether original chargeable transfers or potentially exempt transfers which have been brought into charge by reason of the death) may also affect the amount of tax payable on the donor's estate because the earlier transfers will be brought into cumulation. Therefore, consideration should be given to taking out seven-year *level* term assurance to cover the increased amount of tax payable by the personal representatives and putting the policy in trust for the donor's residuary beneficiaries under his will who can then use the proceeds to help fund the tax. As there is currently a single rate of inheritance tax above the nil rate, the increase is effectively limited to 40% of the value of the nil rate band (currently £242,000).

Another use for term policies is as a means of providing the funds to pay inheritance tax where an individual emigrates from the UK. Under IHTA

7.12 Insurance

1984, s 267 a person cannot shed his UK domicile for inheritance tax purposes until he has ceased to be resident in the UK for at least three complete tax years. For inheritance tax purposes, an individual is deemed to be domiciled in the UK if he has been resident in the UK for 17 out of the last 20 years. The risk of the emigrant dying within this period and incurring an inheritance tax charge in respect of his world-wide estate can be insured against, with the policy proceeds being settled outside his estate.

Term assurance, when used in inheritance tax planning, is normally limited to seven years. However, longer terms, extending well beyond the likely date of the life assured's death, might be used as a way of funding for an eventual liability, similar to a whole of life contract (see 7.13 below).

Endowment policies

7.12 Pure endowment insurance provides for a specified capital sum to be paid not on the death of the insured, but at the end of a specified period if the insured is still alive at that time. The contingency in the case of pure endowment insurance is thus the survival of the life insured until a specified date, rather than the event of death. Although a pure endowment policy may provide that, in the event of death before the specified date, a proportion of the specified sum will be payable or a return (in whole or in part) of premiums may be made, these policies are rare in practice.

More usually there will be a combination of pure endowment and term assurance in the same policy, commonly called simply an endowment policy, so that the sum assured will be payable either at the end of the specified period or on earlier death. Alternatively, a pure endowment policy may be effected in conjunction with a matching term policy, with the same effect with regard to when the specified sum will be payable.

Endowment insurance was very common in the context of home ownership with, typically, a 25-year mortgage endowment policy combining insurance and investment. This provides a capital sum to redeem the mortgage should the policy holder(s) die before the policy matures, or a capital sum on maturity which should facilitate complete repayment of the mortgage. Regular projections should be obtained to ensure the endowment is 'on target' as more and more homebuyers are finding their maturing endowment insufficient to repay their mortgage.

As the major part of the premium will be used for investment, the extent to which the policy increases in value will depend upon the investment performance and charges of the insurance company issuing the policy. In recent years endowment policies have been the subject of much criticism. High commission payments to intermediaries or life company salespersons have often eaten into the investment growth over the first five to ten years, forcing policyholders to increase premiums or face being unable to pay off their mortgage. This is known as front end loading and is a very good reason for not terminating a policy. At the outset one should always check the reduction in yield figures on the illustration provided as there can be substantial variations between the costs of different life offices. Rather than terminate the policy one should consider loans against the value of the policy, having the policy paid up or even selling the policy to a third party in the traded endowments market. Low-cost/low-start endowments have been the subject of particular criticism.

There are basically two types of endowment policy. First, the traditional with-profits contract where there is a guaranteed sum assured which is increased each year with the addition of annual (reversionary) and terminal bonuses. Traditional with-profits policies have become far less popular and are now only offered by one or two life offices. They have been largely replaced by unit-linked policies. The unit-linked endowment policy provides no guaranteed sum assured on maturity and so repayment of the mortgage depends entirely on investment performance.

In addition to providing a mortgage repayment vehicle, endowment policies may be used to fund school and university fees. The main attraction of the endowment in this context is the regimented savings approach that it forces upon individuals. However, more tax-efficient savings plans that use the individual's annual capital gains tax exemption are often overlooked.

The market in traded endowment policies (TEPs) has developed considerably in recent years. 'With profits' policies are sold to a market maker and can then be purchased from the market for a capital sum. They are either purchased on a 'paid up' basis or subject to an agreement to pay all future premiums. If the original policyholder dies during the term, the new policy owner receives a pay-out representing the guaranteed sum assured plus bonuses. Similarly, on maturity of the policy, the policy owner receives the final maturity value. For taxation purposes, qualifying second-hand policies are subject to capital gains tax (see under 7.18 below). Non-qualifying second-hand policies are subject firstly to income tax and secondly capital gains tax.

Whole life policies

7.13 Whole life policies provide for a capital sum to be paid only on the death of the insured, whenever it occurs.

A combination of a 'with-profits' whole life policy and a decreasing term assurance policy is often marketed as a 'low cost' whole life policy. The basic cover required is made up of the initial sums assured under both the whole life policy and the term policy. The cover under the whole life policy increases with the bonuses declared annually on the policy and the sum assured under the term policy decreases at the rate at which bonuses are expected to accrue to the whole life policy. Eventually the sum assured under the term policy reduces to zero by which time the cover under the whole life policy should (if bonuses are declared at the projected rate) have reached the amount of the original cover under both policies. This type of arrangement is usually cheaper than a traditional with-profits whole life policy for the full sum assured.

Whole life policies are often employed to fund the likely inheritance tax payable on death, in respect of an individual's estate, regardless of when the death occurs. Where one is advising a married couple, the basic question to be decided is which of the two lives should be insured:

(*a*)   the first to die (whether husband or wife), or

7.14 *Insurance*

(*b*) the survivor.

The answer will depend on when the main (or only) inheritance tax charge will fall. Whole life policies can be applicable in either situation. The appropriate policy under (*b*) is a joint life and survivor policy.

Whole life cover is the best way of establishing a fund which will grow over the years and will be available to fund the anticipated inheritance tax charge on death, but the provision of such cover (particularly full cover) is usually expensive, except for young individuals. Also, whilst the level of cover is likely to be fixed by reference to the inheritance tax payable should the life assured die immediately after the policy is taken out, regard should be had to the likely increases in the assured's estate through income accumulation, capital growth and inflation and augmentation by gifts or legacies. A level of cover which seemed originally appropriate may, after a number of years, become inadequate (even with the addition of bonuses). The amount of cover should always be kept under review.

Long-term nursing care insurance

7.14 This type of insurance falls into two categories.

(1) Pure insurance contracts which provide for the payment of nursing home fees up to a certain level if the life assured fails two or three 'Activity of Daily Living' tests. If there is no claim during the insured's lifetime the policy terminates and there is no return to the estate.

(2) Insurance and investment contracts which work on a unit-linked basis, with a certain number of units cancelled each month to provide the insurance cover. If there is no claim during the insured's lifetime the remaining investment fund can be returned to the estate and is subject to inheritance tax. Some companies, however, provide standard trust documentation so that the policy may be held outside the policyholder's estate. One life company offers a contract combining long-term care and inheritance tax planning.

The profit element

7.15 Life policies may be arranged on one of the following bases (some of which have already been referred to above).

(*a*) *Without-profits.* The capital sum payable under the policy will be a guaranteed amount, fixed at the time the contract is made. Term policies are almost invariably without profits.

(*b*) *With-profits.* A minimum or fixed capital sum will be specified, but it will be increased by bonuses related to the profits of the insurance company issuing the policy. In effect, a policy written on this basis carries an entitlement for the policyholder to participate in the profits made by the company on the investment of the funds provided by policyholders. Consequently, the premium for a given minimum sum will be higher than it would be under a without profits policy.

'Reversionary bonuses' are usually added to the value of the policy each year and, once declared, they cannot be withdrawn. In addition, on reaching maturity a final 'terminal' bonus is usually added to the maturing value of the policy.

(c) *Unit-linked.* The policy will be notionally linked to a unitised fund (operating in a similar way to a unit trust) with a capital sum payable which will reflect the value of the notional units in the fund at the relevant date, which itself will be dictated by the value of the underlying assets in the fund. Many different types of fund exist, specialising in different types of investment and many policies allow investors to switch between funds. In effect, each premium paid in respect of such a policy buys a number of notional units in the fund so that the overall level of cover under the policy is therefore the value of those units from time to time (which can of course go down in value as well as up). Some unit-linked policies provide for a minimum guaranteed level of cover, in which case not all of each premium paid will be used to acquire 'units'. Some of the premium will be allocated to 'buy in' underlying cover and units in the fund are cancelled to pay for this cover.

Life policy taxation

Qualifying policies

7.16 The proceeds of qualifying policies are not normally subject to income tax in the hands of the policyholder unless the policy is surrendered or otherwise realised prematurely. Although it is not appropriate to set out in detail here the precise basis on which policies are thereby classified, a general understanding of the rules and their taxation consequences is important.

A policy issued after 31 March 1976 has to be certified by the Inland Revenue in order to be classified as a qualifying policy, or has to conform to a standard form of policy which has already been so certified. The conditions for such classification are contained in ICTA 1988, Sch 15. Generally speaking, most policies issued by UK companies (apart from single premium policies) will be qualifying policies.

Conditions

7.17 The following is a summary of the more important conditions applying to the main types of assurance policy described above if they are to be qualifying policies.

(a) Where *term assurance* is taken out for ten years or less, the only qualifying condition is that the surrender value (if any) must not exceed the total premiums paid. A term assurance policy for less than one year however cannot be a qualifying policy.

7.18 *Insurance*

(*b*) The premiums payable in respect of *whole life assurance* must be payable at yearly or shorter intervals until the death of the life assured or for a minimum period of ten years. The sum assured on death must not be less than 75% of the total premiums that would have been paid if death occurred at the age of 75. Where, however, two lives are insured by means of a single policy, for the purposes of calculating the minimum sum assured, the relevant age is assumed to be that of the older life if the sum assured is payable on the first death or that of the younger life if the sum assured is payable on the second death.

(*c*) The term of an *endowment assurance* policy must not be less than ten years and premiums must be payable at yearly or shorter intervals for a minimum of ten years. The sum assured on death must not be less than 75% of the total premiums payable, if the age of the policyholder when the policy is taken out is under 55. If, however, the age of the policyholder when the policy is taken out exceeds 55, the 75% figure is reduced by 2% for each year of the excess over 55. Where an endowment policy is for more than ten years, premiums must be payable at yearly or shorter intervals until the death of the life assured or for a minimum period of ten years or three-quarters of the policy term (whichever is the shorter period).

One important result of these conditions is that a *single premium* whole life or endowment policy cannot be a qualifying policy.

Consequences

7.18 There are two main consequences of a policy being qualifying rather than non-qualifying.

The first is that, generally speaking, premiums paid on a qualifying policy of life assurance effected before 14 March 1984 are eligible for life assurance premium relief (ICTA 1988, s 266). Such relief is not, however, available in respect of premiums paid on policies effected after 13 March 1984. There are also rules which result in the withdrawal of tax relief if the terms of pre-14 March 1984 policies are varied, either making them non-qualifying or extending the term or increasing the benefits thereby capable of being provided.

In most cases the relief available is given at source. That is to say, the policyholder pays the premiums to the insurance company net of the available relief which is presently fixed at 12.5%. The insurance company then reclaims the difference between the gross and net premiums from the Inland Revenue.

A policy must be a qualifying policy if its proceeds are to be received free of further tax in the hands of the policyholder (ICTA 1988, ss 539–552). Generally speaking, if a policy has been maintained for a minimum period before realisation, the proceeds on realisation will be free of income tax although the investments within the insurance companies' funds will already have suffered corporation tax at approximately 20% on income and 22% on gains. The minimum periods in question are ten years from the making of the policy or, if sooner, three-quarters of the term of the policy. A realisation in the context of a life assurance policy is likely to be either its total or partial

Insurance **7.18**

surrender in return for a capital sum or its maturity (i.e. when it reaches the date on which it is set to mature) or the death of the life assured.

If a qualifying policy is surrendered (and sometimes when there is a partial surrender, such as a withdrawal of capital) or assigned for value before the expiry of ten years from the making of the policy or, if sooner, three-quarters of the term of the policy, a higher rate income tax charge will be made on any gain arising on such a chargeable event. A charge may also arise on any gain arising on a surrender, on an assignment for value, on the death of the insured or on the maturity of a policy if the policy has been converted into a paid-up policy within the same period (ICTA 1988, s 540 and ICTA 1988, s 542). (A policy is made 'paid up' when the policyholder agrees with the life office to stop paying premiums under the policy but not to surrender the policy, so that it still continues in being. In such a case the life office may reduce the sum assured payable under the policy.) Thus, neither the death of the insured nor the maturity of a qualifying policy will give rise to an income tax charge unless the policy has been paid up within the specified period.

The amount to be treated as the gain in respect of a policy depends on the chargeable event in question. If the event is an assignment for value, the amount will be the excess of the amount of the consideration received over the total premiums previously paid under the policy. If the event is the maturity of the policy, the surrender of rights under it or the death of the insured, the amount is the excess of the value of the sums then payable over the total premiums previously paid under the policy (ICTA 1988, s 541 and ICTA 1988, s 543).

Such a gain will be treated as part of the total income of the individual policyholder for the year of assessment in which the event occurs, but the tax charged will be the excess of the higher rate of income tax over the basic rate (40% and 22% respectively for the current year of assessment). Where immediately before the chargeable event giving rise to the charge to income tax, the policy in question is held on trusts created by an individual or is held as security for a debt owed by him, the tax liability in respect of the gain will fall on that individual (ICTA 1988, s 547(1)(a)).

An individual who is chargeable to tax in respect of amounts being included in his total income for a year of assessment (by virtue of ICTA 1988, s 547(1)(a)) may claim a form of 'top slicing' relief (ICTA 1988, s 550). The effect is that the whole gain will (subject to certain rules) be effectively charged to income tax at the rate which would be applicable if only an 'appropriate fraction' (broadly, the gain divided by the number of years for which the policy ran) was included in his total income. The detailed rules for calculating the relief are set out in section 550.

There will usually be no capital gains tax liability on the realisation of a life policy provided it is effected by the original beneficial owner. In the case of qualifying traded endowment policies (TEPs) the new policy owner will be subject to capital gains tax on any subsequent surrender, sale or on maturity. The price paid for the policy in the second-hand market, future premiums paid, indexation and taper relief are set against the proceeds to determine the gain.

7.19 Insurance

In the case of non-qualifying TEPs, a chargeable gain arises if the maturity value exceeds the total premiums paid over the entire life of the contract. The gain is charged to income tax. Capital gains tax can also be due on non-qualifying TEPs, although the chargeable gain will be computed subject to TCGA 1992, ss 37 and 39. Capital gains tax is only likely to be due when the premiums paid and the value exceed the amount paid for the policy by the purchaser who surrenders it.

Non-qualifying policies

Disadvantages

7.19 The main disadvantage of a non-qualifying policy is that any gain arising under or realised in respect of such a policy (whether arising on death, maturity, surrender — but see 7.20 below in relation to partial surrenders — or assignment for value) will be subject to the higher rate of income tax but not the basic rate in the same way as the gain on a qualifying policy surrendered within the minimum periods. As before, if the policy is owned beneficially by an individual, the gain will be deemed to form part of his total income in the year of assessment in which the chargeable event in question occurs (ICTA 1988, s 547(1)(a)). If, however, the policy has been transferred into trust and the individual who assigned the policy is still alive or his death gave rise to the gain, or if the policy is held as security for a debt owed by an individual, it will be deemed to form part of that individual's total income for the year of assessment in which the chargeable event in question occurred (also ICTA 1988, s 547(1)(a)). Again, top slicing relief may be available to the individual on making a claim to the Inland Revenue (ICTA 1988, s 550).

Partial surrenders

7.20 A partial surrender of a non-qualifying policy of an amount not exceeding 5% of the premiums paid is permitted each year without giving rise to a tax liability at that time (ICTA 1988, s 540(1)(a)(v) and ICTA 1988, s 546). Any unused part of the 5% may be carried forward to subsequent years. Thus, such surrenders can be used to provide the policyholder with a regular (annual) supply of money (often marketed as 'income') which can be utilised as the policyholder thinks fit. Indeed regular 5% annual withdrawals can be made for up to 20 years without a tax charge. However, when the policy is finally surrendered or matures, the gain subjected to higher rate income tax at that stage is the surrender or maturity value together with the amount or value of any previous partial surrenders, less the original premiums paid (ICTA 1988, s 541(1)(b)).

Onshore and offshore policies

7.21 Life policies may be issued onshore (i.e. by companies resident in the UK) or offshore (i.e. by companies not so resident).

Offshore policies cannot be qualifying policies unless issued by either:

Insurance **7.21**

(*a*) a company resident outside the UK which is lawfully carrying on life assurance business in the UK through a branch and the policy premiums are payable to that branch and form part of the company's business receipts arising from that branch, or

(*b*) a company resident outside the UK a portion of the income from whose life fund is subject to corporation tax under ICTA 1988, s 445 (ICTA 1988, Sch 15 para 24).

Offshore single premium bonds allow for gross roll-up of investment income and capital gains subject to withholding tax and imputed tax deducted in the country of origin. Over time this tax deferral can present the investor with a substantial benefit. Furthermore, a UK or overseas based portfolio can be held within an offshore insurance bond and still provide gross roll-up of income and exemption from capital gains tax on any sales made within the bond.

Where a bond is of a highly personalised nature, the Inland Revenue have in the past applied ICTA 1988, s 739 to assess all investment income on the policyholder, but section 739 does not apply to capital gains tax. In the case of *CIR v Willoughby & Another, HL [1997] STC 995; [1997] 4 All ER 65*, the House of Lords held that this distinction between bonds linked to the issuer's funds and bonds linked to an individual portfolio has no basis.

ICTA 1988, s 553C confers a wide power on the Treasury to make regulations to tax personal portfolio bonds (PPBs). In March 1999, the Inland Revenue laid new regulations relating to PPBs before Parliament. A PPB is defined as a policy which allows the policyholder to choose the investments that determine the benefits under the policy. Personalised investments include stocks and shares quoted on recognised stock exchanges including the AIM, family company shares, fine wines, vintage cars, paintings and racehorses.

However, there is still a wide range of permissible investments including unit trusts, hedge funds and other collective investment funds. Indeed, a number of international life offices offer an extensive range of both onshore and offshore collectives enabling the individual policyholder to put together a portfolio tailored to suit his own preferences.

For bonds that are personalised, a taxable gain arises each year from 6 April 2000. This is calculated as 15% of the sum of the total amount of premiums paid under the bond and the aggregate total of similarly calculated 15% amounts for earlier years since the bond was first taken out. Tax is charged at the individual's marginal rate on the gains each year.

PPBs taken out before 17 March 1998 can also continue to hold stocks, shares, warrants and options listed on a recognised stock exchange, AIM and the Unlisted Securities Market. Pre-17 March 1998 PPBs must, however, not be enhanced.

In computing a gain in respect of an offshore policy, a reduction may be made to take account of periods of residence which the policyholder may have spent outside the UK (ICTA 1988, s 553(3)). Generally, though, no reduction will be made if the policy is or was held by trustees resident outside the UK (ICTA 1988, s 553(5)).

7.22 Insurance

If the policyholder is resident but not domiciled in the UK, a qualifying offshore policy (or any policy issued under seal and held abroad) might be attractive as it would fall outside the ambit of inheritance tax (if any) payable on his death, being property situated outside the UK and thus excluded property for inheritance tax purposes (IHTA 1984, s 6(1)).

It should be noted that the level of investor protection for offshore policies can differ to the UK and varies between the different offshore jurisdictions.

The Insurance Companies Act 1982, which provides a regulatory framework for companies carrying on insurance business in the UK does not necessarily apply to a company issuing an offshore policy; nor is the Policyholders Protection Act 1975 generally applicable to offshore policies. The latter established the Policyholders Protection Board which has the power to make grants to the policyholders of an insurer which falls into financial difficulties. Under the Insurance Companies (Third Insurance Directive) Regulations 1994 an insurer may operate in the UK without approval under the Insurance Companies Act 1982 providing it has its head office in an EU state. The state which authorises the EU insurer also has the responsibility for supervising the insurer. A policyholder will only be eligible for assistance or protection from the Board in respect of policies which are issued by an authorised insurer or an EU insurer lawfully doing business in the UK. The Policyholders Protection Act does not cover policies issued by non-EU and unauthorised UK insurers. Not all non-resident companies will carry on insurance business in the UK.

Dead settlor

7.22 ICTA 1988, s 547 charges tax on trustees and beneficiaries where the creator has died and his estate would otherwise escape income tax.

Gains arising on bonds held within a trust can be taxed on the creator, the trustees or even the beneficiaries. Furthermore, bonds can be assigned out of the trust without creating an immediate tax charge, hence transferring the liability to the recipients of the bonds.

These rules, therefore, provide much scope for tax planning with a variety of different tax rates to select from. For example, if a bond is surrendered within a trust while the creator of the trust is still alive, then the tax charge will fall on the creator at his marginal rate. If the bond is surrendered after the creator's death, then the trustees will be liable to tax at 34% with an allowance for basic rate tax in the case of a UK policy. If the trustees assign the bond to beneficiaries who then surrender it, the beneficiaries will pay tax at their marginal rates.

Insurable interest

7.23 Life Assurance Act 1774, s 1 requires that a person taking out life insurance must have an insurable interest in the life insured and any policy effected in contravention of this provision is void. The insurable interest must exist when the insurance policy is taken out (*Dalby v London Life*

Assurance Co, (1854) 15 CB 365), but it is not required at the time of loss (for example, on the death of the life assured).

Thus, it is necessary to establish exactly what constitutes an insurable interest in a life. Section 3 of the Act provides that, when an insured has an insurable interest, he may recover under the policy in question no more than the amount of the value of his interest. On this basis, the person taking out the policy must have a pecuniary interest in the life of the life assured and case law has established that this will be measured by the amount or value of the pecuniary loss which the person for whose benefit the insurance is effected is likely to sustain by reason of the death of the life assured.

An individual may take out a policy on his own life, or on the life of his spouse for his own benefit. He is presumed to have an insurable interest of an unlimited extent in the policy regardless of the amount insured. In all other circumstances there must be a pecuniary interest which means that the insured must show that he would suffer financially by the loss of a legal right on the death of the life insured. Apart from the case of a spouse (and the special case of industrial life assurance), an insurable interest cannot be presumed merely from a family relationship. In the family context, therefore, a relative must have a claim for support enforceable by law, or some other pecuniary interest enforceable by law. Thus, generally speaking, parents will not have an insurable interest in the lives of their children. On the other hand, a child who is a minor would probably have an insurable interest in the lives of his parents who will usually have a legally enforceable duty to support the child who would clearly suffer financially by the loss of a legal right on their death. On the other hand, it might be argued that a liability of support only crystallises when a maintenance order is made by the court. Certainly, an adult child would be unlikely to have an insurable interest in his parent.

In practice, insurance companies are often prepared to take a relaxed view as to the presence or not of an insurable interest. To do otherwise in respect of a policy on which premiums had been duly paid and received would create bad publicity. In theory, however, if a policy is void, any premiums paid to the insurance company should be returned to the payer or to his or her personal representatives and, thus, are capable of falling back into the estate of that person.

The requirement for an insurable interest does not exist in many offshore jurisdictions. It is therefore possible to insure multiple lives, for example, parents and children.

Planning in early years

7.24 Most people over the age of 18 (the age of majority for the purposes of UK law) own some property the future devolution of which at least may concern them and so may have a need for estate planning.

There are practical limits to estate planning for persons who have not yet attained the age of majority. These arise mainly from the fact that persons under the age of 18 are unlikely, in normal circumstances, to own much property; and any interests they may have under trusts are likely to be

7.25 *Insurance*

contingent. The scope for utilising insurance in respect of persons falling within this category is therefore relatively limited.

The child's policy

7.25 Some life offices have devised a 'child's policy' which, in its basic form, is a good example of the way that insurance can be used in estate planning. Such a policy will usually be a regular premium endowment policy (either with-profits or unit-linked) on the life of a parent with a maturity date prior to (for example) the 18th or 21st birthday of the child. The policy will normally be effected by the child's parent for his own benefit and then subsequently written in trust for the benefit of the child. The mechanism for putting the benefit of a policy in trust will be dealt with later. The reason for doing so is to ensure that the parent retains no beneficial interest in the proceeds of the policy, so that they will fall outside his estate on death before the relevant maturity date.

Such policies can be a useful way of providing a means of support or maintenance for a child, in the event of the premature death of a parent. Alternatively, the proceeds of the policy could be used to fund the education of the child, depending on the maturity date provided for, or simply to provide the child with funds at a key stage in his or her later life.

By the careful use of the appropriate exemptions from inheritance tax when paying premiums on the policy, a parent can provide funds for the use or benefit of his child (on the policy maturing or on the earlier death of the parent) in a way which will have no inheritance tax consequences, whether during the life or on the death of that parent. Inheritance tax exemptions which are likely to be applicable in relation to the payment of premiums in these circumstances include the annual exemption from inheritance tax and the exemption for normal expenditure out of income. The inheritance tax implications of paying premiums are considered under 7.45 below.

Single premium bonds

7.26 Another arrangement involves a parent (or perhaps a grandparent) taking out a single premium whole life policy (either with-profits or unit-linked) on the life of a child or grandchild. The policy will normally be effected by the parent (as trustee) on trust for the benefit of the child on reaching a specified age (e.g. 18 or 21), with default trusts to take effect if the child fails to reach that age.

If the child dies before reaching the specified age, the policy will become payable in accordance with the terms of the trust. If, however, the child survives to the specified age, beneficial ownership of the policy will pass to the child who may then deal with it as he wishes. The policy could be surrendered in return for the payment of a lump sum or could, alternatively, be left in place to continue to grow in value. If the policy is surrendered when it is in trust, the settlor will be assessed on the gain if he is still alive and if he is not the gain will be assessed on the trustees. If the policy is surrendered after ownership is transferred to the beneficiary, the gains will be assessed on the beneficiary.

Insurance **7.29**

One particular advantage of life policies in the context of minor children is that they are non-income producing assets and so until their realisation there will be no income which can be taxed in the hands of a parental settlor or donor under ICTA 1988, s 660B. This is especially important now with the extension of this income tax charge on settlors to income arising under bare trusts.

School fees

7.27 Insurance-based means of planning ahead for the payment of school fees and the costs of further education for children have been devised using income or capital or a combination of both. The options available will depend on various factors such as when the fees will need to be met; who will be making the necessary provision and the extent to which resources are available.

If there is no time available for planning (i.e. the fees are required immediately), it may be possible for the parents (or grandparents) to meet the fees out of their current after-tax income or from accumulated capital, but there is little (if any) scope for insurance-based planning. If, however, there is time available for planning ahead, then there is scope for insurance-based planning, whether income or capital is to be used to make provision for the fees.

Traded endowment policies can provide an excellent way of planning for school fees. There are such a variety of policies available that a ladder of maturities can easily be arranged.

Endowment insurance

7.28 A series of regular premium with-profits or unit-linked endowment policies might be appropriate where school fees are not required for at least ten years as the tax charge on the income and gains of the policy is not at full rates. Each policy would be designed to mature in successive years. Although life assurance premium relief would not be available, the policies in question would be qualifying policies and the proceeds in normal circumstances received tax free by the policyholder. They need not, of course, necessarily be applied to pay school fees.

The payment of premiums under the policy should in most circumstances fall within the available inheritance tax exemptions.

Other income-based planning devices

7.29 There are various unit trust or investment trust savings schemes (usually requiring regular monthly contributions) which may be appropriate as a way of building up a capital fund to use for school fees. A series of individual savings accounts (ISAs) could also be taken out. These provide a very tax efficient method of saving since income arising and capital gains realised are free of tax for as long as the plan is kept intact. As far as dividends are concerned, the repayable tax credit is now limited to 10% and will be abolished entirely from 6 April 2004. Whether such schemes are a

7.30 *Insurance*

better savings medium than an endowment policy will be determined not only by the tax treatment of the schemes but also by their investment performance.

Since 6 April 1999 it is not possible to make contributions to PEPs although existing PEPs are able to continue in their current form. From 6 April 1999 investors have been able to save via ISAs which continue the theme of tax efficient savings started by PEPs and TESSAs, although the maximum levels of contributions to the new accounts have been reduced. TESSAs commenced before 5 April 1999 will be allowed to continue during their five-year term.

All the above schemes are basically income-based. There are also a number of schemes available for the investment of surplus capital.

Composition fee schemes

7.30 Some schools offer a discount to parents who can afford to cover future fees with a lump sum. These are commonly known as composition fee schemes and, where parents have a preferred school in mind for the child, a composition fee scheme may be appropriate. Many schools run such schemes, either on their own or in conjunction with life offices. What happens in most schemes of this sort is that the composition fee, consisting of a single lump sum payment, is paid to the school by the parent in lieu of stated amounts of fees which would otherwise be payable. The bursar of the school then purchases a deferred annuity contract with a life office, the contract being taken out on the child's life. The contract chosen will be written on the basis that guaranteed sums of money will be paid to the school on predetermined dates in the future. The moneys received tax free by the school will then be used to fund school fees payable at that time and, by these means, it is possible to secure a larger reduction in school fees than the initial composition fee paid by the parent. The level of the discount will depend on the terms of the annuity contract purchased by the school. Such contracts are likely to vary with the scheme in question. The initial transfer of capital by the parent should not, however, be a transfer of value for the purposes of inheritance tax, being a disposition for the education of the child, provided that there is a subsisting marriage (IHTA 1984, s 11(1)(b)).

There are, however, disadvantages to composition fee schemes. They will only be appropriate where parents are certain to educate their child at the chosen school as there may be problems if for some reason the child does not go to that school. Composition fee schemes may therefore be quite restrictive although many schools have arrangements to make transfers to other schools if the child does not go to (or leaves) the school with which the arrangements were originally made.

Educational trusts

7.31 The use of educational trusts used to be a popular way of planning for future school fees. However, in April 1996, the Charity Commissioners decided to withdraw charitable status from educational trusts run by insurance companies.

Deferred annuity

7.32 This involves the parent purchasing a deferred annuity on his child's life with a capital sum. The annuity commences when the fees are first required but clearly the longer the period between the date of investment and the date the annuity commences, the greater the annual return will be. Other schemes involve regular premium payments which are normally payable up to and during the education of the child in question. Annuities generally and their tax treatment are dealt with under 7.49 below.

Other capital-based planning devices

7.33 There are many other capital-based ways of providing for the payment of school fees, involving the investment of capital in a combination of zero dividend preference shares issued by split capital investment trusts, unit trusts, gilt-edged securities, PEPs and TESSAs. As mentioned earlier the latter two investments have been replaced from April 1999 by ISAs, although existing PEPs and TESSAs can remain in force. Each will have its own tax implications and may in investment terms be more advantageous than an insurance-based scheme.

Conclusions

7.34 In school fees planning particularly it is important that any scheme that is selected is flexible (as family circumstances and aspirations do change). It is also preferable not to be tied in to the scheme offered by a particular school as it may be that a child has to be educated elsewhere. The ideal arrangement would incorporate no penalties for early discontinuance and would enable the moneys produced to be used for purposes other than education if this became necessary, while also providing overall a good investment return.

Planning in middle years

7.35 From the age of 18 onwards many people start to acquire and own significant amounts of property. The acquisition of property is a continuing process and thus it is from this point in a person's life that estate planning becomes increasingly relevant; the more so the larger the estate in question.

The main uses of life insurance have already been outlined. The most important and basic use is that of protection. On the death of the life assured, a capital sum will be payable which may provide for dependants of the deceased. Here term and whole life policies are relevant. Another use of life insurance is to provide funds to meet the inheritance tax payable on the death of the life assured. Again, term (and particularly seven-year term) and whole life policies are relevant.

As has been seen in the context of planning for children, insurance policies can also provide a vehicle for making gifts out of income or capital for the benefit of the next generation; and they can be used simply as investment vehicles to produce a return on maturity.

7.36 *Insurance*

Basic estate planning

7.36 If an individual who has taken out a policy remains beneficially entitled to it (and, thus, to its proceeds) when he dies, those proceeds will form part of his estate for the purposes of calculating any inheritance tax payable on his death (IHTA 1984, s 4(1) and IHTA 1984, s 5(1)) and will devolve in accordance with his will or under the applicable intestacy rules. This may of course be exactly what the individual wants since he will retain complete control over the policy during his lifetime and the devolution of the proceeds on his death. Policies taken out as a form of savings contract or to fund school fees and policies linked to a mortgage fall into this category. However, if an individual divests himself of any beneficial entitlement to the policy or its proceeds, whether at the outset or subsequently, it need not fall into his estate. It is therefore important to consider whether and if so, when, an individual can and should divest himself of an insurance policy, wherever the proceeds of that policy are going to be significant.

Creation of trusts

7.37 The usual way of achieving this result is for the policy to be held in trust. Depending on the terms of the trust, this can allow the person taking out the policy a greater degree of control over the destination of the proceeds than an outright assignment of the policy so that he can ensure the proceeds are applied for the purpose he intends.

Mechanism

7.38 Procedures for creating an effective trust from the outset vary from life office to life office, but the usual way of doing this is for the individual concerned (as proposer) to complete a trust form declaring that the policy is to be held under trust and requesting that the office issue it to him as sole trustee. This should ensure that the trust is completely constituted and thus enforceable from the moment the life office goes on risk. Most life offices will have standard forms available to effect such a trust which can be completed by the individual before payment of the first premium. The policy itself will be effective once the proposal has been accepted by the life office which will usually go on risk once the first premium has been paid.

The sole trustee should always appoint additional trustees of the policy to act jointly with him, so that on his death when the policy proceeds become payable (assuming of course that the proposer is also the life assured, which will often be the case) they can be paid immediately to the continuing trustees on production of the deceased's death certificate without any need to obtain a grant of representation to the deceased's estate.

The creation of such a trust should only have inheritance tax consequences for the individual in relation to the payment of the first premium which will prima facie be a transfer of value but may fall within the individual's annual exemption or normal expenditure out of income exemption. Subsequent premium payments may also have inheritance tax implications (considered

Insurance **7.40**

under 7.45 below). Assuming that the declaration of trust is effective, beneficial ownership of the policy will have vested immediately in the named beneficiaries.

The main taxation benefit of the overall arrangement is that the policy (and thus its proceeds) will fall outside the estate of the individual for the purposes of inheritance tax on his or her death.

Married Women's Property Act 1882 policies

7.39 It will not, however, be necessary to create an express trust where a policy falls within the ambit of the Married Women's Property Act 1882. The effect of section 11 of that Act is to create in the appropriate circumstances a trust of a life policy where no express declaration of trust is made. When a policy is effected by a man on his own life and expressed to be for the benefit of his wife and/or children or, alternatively, effected by a woman on her life and expressed to be for the benefit of her husband and/or children, section 11 will then create a trust in favour of the beneficiaries named in the policy. There is no need to use words expressly declaring a trust or even to refer to the Act in the policy (although it is preferable to do the latter so as to ensure there is no doubt that the policy is intended to create a trust under the Act).

The Act only applies where policies are effected for the benefit of a spouse or children. An express trust remains necessary where a policy is effected for the benefit of remoter issue (such as grandchildren) or other relatives. The Act applies to all forms of life policies but only to those with a single life assured. It does not extend to policies on joint lives. A joint life policy for the benefit of a spouse or children needs therefore to be written in trust expressly.

Notwithstanding the ease with which the Act enables a trust of an appropriate policy to arise, it is wiser to specify the precise terms of the trust expressly so as to tailor the trust to the circumstances of the beneficiaries. Under Married Women's Property Act 1882, s 11 a policy for the benefit of a named spouse or child will give that person a vested interest in the whole policy. So far as children are concerned, it may be desirable to make their interests contingent perhaps on reaching a specified age or on surviving the life assured.

A trustee (or trustees) of the policy can be appointed by the assured in the policy itself or by any memorandum under his hand and legal title to the policy will vest in the trustees so appointed without there being an express assignment of the policy into their names. If he makes no appointment (or until he does so), he himself will be the sole trustee and, if he dies, his personal representatives will become the trustees.

There will be no liability to stamp duty under the heading in Stamp Act 1891, Sch 1 covering declarations of trust in respect of a policy issued pursuant to the Married Women's Property Act 1882 unless there is an express declaration of trust.

Existing policies

7.40 Where a policy is already in existence, its removal from the beneficial ownership of the insured will normally involve the insured

7.41 *Insurance*

assigning the policy either outright to another person or to trustees (who may include the insured) to be held by them for specified beneficiaries. If such an assignment is effective, the policy (and its proceeds) should no longer form part of the assignor's estate for inheritance tax purposes. It is therefore important to ensure that the assignment is effective.

Assignments

7.41 An assignment of a life policy must comply with the Policies of Assurance Act 1867. The Act provides for the legal assignment of life policies, giving an assignee the right to sue an insurer in his own name, if three conditions are satisfied.

(*a*) There must be an effective equitable assignment of the policy, indicating that its object is to transfer the benefit of the policy to the transferee (section 1). The assignment must be sufficient to transfer the property in the policy itself (i.e. beneficial ownership).

(*b*) The assignment must be in writing, either by endorsement on the policy itself or by a separate instrument, in the words or to the effect set out in the Act. It is also necessary for the instrument to bear the appropriate stamp duty (section 5) but such an assignment into trust will usually be exempt from 'Conveyance or Transfer' duty, falling within Category L in the Stamp Duty (Exempt Instruments) Regulations 1987, and should be certified as such in accordance with those Regulations. (As from a day to be appointed by the Treasury, assignments of life policies will be exempt from stamp duty (FA 1991, s 110). The appointed day was originally to coincide with the start of trading in uncertificated securities under The Stock Exchange's TAURUS system. Since the announcement in March 1993 that this system was not to be implemented, the stamp duty position has remained the same. As stamp duty is undergoing a process of modernisation, it may be that duty will no longer be payable under the new regime expected to be introduced by the Finance Act 2003.)

(*c*) Written notice of the date and purport of the assignment must be given to the insurers before the assignee can sue on the policy.

The initial transfer

7.42 The assignment itself may or may not have immediate inheritance tax consequences. If the policy is transferred by way of outright gift to an individual or into a bare trust for one or more persons, absolutely entitled, it will constitute a potentially exempt transfer for the purposes of inheritance tax. It will therefore occasion no immediate charge to tax, and no charge at all provided the transferor survives the required seven-year risk period. A transfer into an accumulation and maintenance or an interest in possession settlement or a trust for a mentally disabled person will also be a potentially exempt transfer. The donor must not be capable of benefiting under the trust or the gift will be rendered ineffective by the gifts with reservation provisions introduced by the Finance Act 1986 the application of which is examined in greater detail below.

Insurance **7.43**

A transfer into a discretionary settlement cannot be a potentially exempt transfer and thus remains capable of constituting a chargeable transfer. Such a transfer may therefore occasion an immediate liability to inheritance tax, depending on the value of the policy transferred. The value transferred will be the price that policy might reasonably be expected to fetch if sold on the open market at the time of transfer, subject (except in the case of most forms of term policy) to a minimum value equal to the total cost incurred in providing the policy (i.e. the premiums or other consideration paid) at that time less any sum which has been paid under the policy or contract in question (IHTA 1984, s 167).

A transferor in these circumstances, however, should be able to take advantage of his nil rate band and any other relevant exemptions (such as the annual exemption) to restrict his liability to inheritance tax on the initial transfer into settlement. The tax liability (if any) will also be affected by the type of policy to be transferred. Most types of life policy will have a low initial surrender value if they have one at all. For example, a term assurance policy will, on the basis mentioned above, have little if any value, having no surrender value in any circumstances, and (depending on the basis on which the policy is written and also on premiums paid to date) its transfer into settlement should not therefore occasion a transfer of value.

The assignment into trust will not give rise to any charge to capital gains tax (TCGA 1992, s 210).

The receiving trust

7.43 As to which form of trust should be used, much will depend again on the circumstances of the case (in particular, the type of policy involved) and on the basic tax treatment afforded the trust in question. For example, if a policy is transferred to an accumulation and maintenance trust, there will be no ten-year anniversary charge and no exit charge when the policy proceeds are distributed (IHTA 1984, s 71). An alternative, particularly where term insurance is taken out, would be to use a discretionary trust. As mentioned above, the transfer of the policy itself to the trust should occasion only a minimal charge to inheritance tax. Provided that the initial value of the policy when first settled and when aggregated with any chargeable transfers made by the settlor in the seven years preceding the creation of the trust do not exceed the inheritance tax nil rate band, there should be no exit charge (IHTA 1984, s 65) provided the proceeds are distributed before the first ten-year anniversary of the creation of the trust. It would, however, be necessary to check the settlor's history of chargeable transfers of value at the time the settlement is to be created before transferring the policy. Also, account would have to be taken at that time of any property likely to be added to the settlement by chargeable transfer as this will affect the computation of any exit charge.

It may also be unwise for the settlor to pay any premiums on the policy after it has been settled if such payments would be chargeable transfers, as the Inland Revenue would then have an alternative seven-year history of the settlor's chargeable transfers (i.e. those within seven years of the payment of the premium in question) for determining the rate of an exit charge (IHTA

7.44 *Insurance*

1984, s 67). The settlor should always, however, consider whether any of the inheritance tax exemptions would be applicable, as these could enable premiums to be paid without being chargeable transfers. In particular, the annual exemption and the exemption for normal expenditure out of income could be applicable.

Types of policy

7.44 The most appropriate type of trust to hold the policy will depend upon the purpose for which the policy was entered into.

If, for example, a whole life policy taken out to fund inheritance tax on death is to be held on trust, in most cases the trust should mirror the interests of the residuary beneficiaries under the insured's will, who can then use the proceeds to fund the tax.

It is of course always possible that the beneficiaries under the will may be changed. It may therefore be necessary to ensure that the trust employed is sufficiently flexible to cater for this and that some form of discretionary (or power of appointment) trust would be appropriate. However, such a trust is unlikely to be appropriate where the policy in question may continue in existence for ten years or more, as it might by then have acquired a surrender value which would be subject to inheritance tax on the first ten-year anniversary charge affecting the trust (IHTA 1984, s 64 and IHTA 1984, s 66). A discretionary trust may though be appropriate for term assurance which is unlikely to acquire a significant surrender value.

If a seven-year term assurance is taken out to cover a potential liability to inheritance tax and the policy is effected by the donor, it should undoubtedly be held on trust for, or assigned to, the donee of the gift in question so as not to be payable to the donor's estate on his death and be available to the donee to pay the tax.

Where some form of insurance-based savings scheme is entered into to provide a lump sum (when the policy matures) during the lifetime of the person taking out the policy, the capital sum in question can be accumulated outside the estate of that person by ensuring the policy is held on trust. For example, an individual could take out an endowment policy on his own life, but held on trust for the benefit of his children (say under an accumulation and maintenance settlement). When the policy matures, the proceeds will pass to the trust and then to his children free of any inheritance tax liability falling on him. If, however, the individual himself wishes to benefit from the policy, then a trust will be inappropriate.

Payment of premiums

7.45 Once the basic estate planning structure has been established and the policy in question has become held on trust, the question of who then should continue to pay the premiums under the policy must be decided. The settlor will probably have paid the first premium to ensure the life office assumes risk. If the settlor is to continue to pay them, they are clearly capable of being transfers of value for inheritance tax purposes. However, if the policy in question is beneficially owned by an individual or held in an accumulation and maintenance or interest in possession settlement or a trust for a mentally disabled person, there is no reason why the payment of premiums by an individual should not be structured so as to constitute potentially exempt transfers. The individual could make gifts of cash to the individual donee or trustees in question who could then use the cash to fund payment of the premiums. However, there are two occasions where it may be more appropriate for the settlor to pay the premium direct to the life office. These are where:

(a) the settlor wants to continue to obtain life assurance premium relief; or

(b) the policy was issued before 18 March 1986 and is held on trusts under which the settlor is capable of benefiting — in which case the inheritance tax gifts with reservation provisions will only not apply to the premium payments if they are paid by the settlor 'under the terms of' the policy and arguably this means direct to the life office (see under 7.46 below).

If, however, the settlor does pay the premiums direct to the life office, the payments will only constitute potentially exempt transfers if the policy is beneficially owned by another individual or is held on an interest in possession settlement and only then to the extent that an individual's estate is increased in value (IHTA 1984, s 3A(2)(b)). Thus, to the extent that the amount of the premium is not fully reflected in the increased value of the policy (which would usually *not* be the case), the payment will not be potentially exempt. This problem is most likely to arise where policies are held in an accumulation and maintenance settlement where it will generally be beneficial for the individual to make cash gifts to the settlement and for the trustees to use the cash to fund payment of the premiums.

If the payment of premiums can only be made as transfers of value, there are certain inheritance tax exemptions which may be applicable, such as the annual exemption and, if the premiums are funded from income, the normal expenditure out of income exemption. To qualify under this latter exemption, however, there is a need for regularity in the payments made for them to qualify them as part of the normal expenditure of the person making the payments and to apply, the exemption must be claimed (IHTA 1984, s 21(1)).

Reservation of benefit

7.46   The gifts with reservation provisions contained in the Finance Act 1986 (FA 1986, s 102 and FA 1986, Sch 20) can apply to any gifts of property made after 17 March 1986 including any gifts of property (e.g. the payment of premiums) made under the terms of policies issued in respect of an insurance made after 17 March 1986. They will not, however, apply to premiums paid under policies issued before that date even if held on trusts under which the donor is capable of benefiting unless the policy in question is varied after that date so as to increase the benefits secured or to extend the term of the insurance. For these purposes, any change in the terms of

7.47 *Insurance*

the policy made pursuant to an option conferred by the policy will be deemed to be a variation of that policy (FA 1986, s 102(6)).

Generally, if a donor simply takes out a policy and assigns it to trustees or makes a declaration of trust in respect of the policy, there should be no problems provided he is not capable of benefiting under the trust. For this reason, the so-called 'reverter to settlor' trust wording is no longer now an effective vehicle for a life policy. The presence of the settlor as one of the objects of the power of appointment would bring the gifts with reservation provisions into effect. Whilst the settlor should therefore be excluded from the trust, there is no reason why the settlor's spouse should not continue to be included, although it must be emphasised that if any appointment is made in favour of the spouse it will be vital to ensure that he or she does not deal with any property appointed in such a way as to benefit (directly or indirectly) the settlor, in case this brings the provisions back into effect. For this reason, it might be thought prudent not to include the spouse in the class of objects of the power of appointment as well, albeit that it might often be sensible to ensure that the settlor's widow or widower might be eligible to benefit.

Also, to ensure that the gifts with reservation provisions do not apply, the donor should receive no consideration from the trustees in respect of any assignment of a policy into trust. For example, if the donor pays the first premium in respect of the policy assigned (which, as mentioned above, is quite likely), there should be no agreement that he is to be reimbursed by the trustees.

The effect of the application of these provisions in respect of a policy (and, in particular, their continued application until the assignor's death) is that the policy will be treated as property to which the assignor was beneficially entitled immediately before his death (FA 1986, s 102(3)). The basic estate planning objective of transferring a policy into trust, and thereby removing it and its proceeds from the donor's estate, would thus not be achieved.

Inheritance trusts

7.47 The 'inheritance trust' is an insurance-based capital tax saving scheme once marketed by a number of insurance companies, the effectiveness of which was much impaired by the Finance Act 1986. In essence, the inheritance trust attempted to minimise capital transfer tax on the death of an individual by seeking to freeze the value of his estate at a particular point in time by the use of a loan coupled with the purchase of a life policy written in trust for the benefit of one or more beneficiaries. The basic scheme was said to appeal to those taxpayers whose estates were substantial, but not large enough to warrant the use of lifetime transfers up to the nil rate band or even more complex schemes for capital tax avoidance. On maturity, the proceeds of the policy would accrue outside the estate of the individual. In addition, the outstanding loan would be repaid by equal annual instalments paid over 20 years, with the lender being encouraged to use (and therefore dissipate) the repayments as if current income.

Insurance **7.47**

Several types of the basic scheme were marketed usually involving the establishment of a standard 'reverter to settlor' trust under which the default beneficiaries would usually be the children of the settlor.

The settlor would fund the trust by way of an outright gift of a nominal sum coupled with an interest free loan of a more substantial amount repayable on demand. These sums would be used by the trustees to purchase a single premium insurance bond on the settlor's life. The advantage of such an investment was that no income would be generated which could thereby be attributed to the settlor pursuant to ICTA 1970, s 448 (subsequently ICTA 1988, s 674, now replaced by ICTA 1988, s 660B). Also, the trustees were able to cash-in each year up to 5% of the original premium paid, by means of a partial surrender, without incurring any immediate charge to income tax.

Each year, therefore, for up to 20 years, the trustees would make a partial surrender and would effectively withdraw up to 5% of the capital originally invested in the bond. They would then pay this money to the settlor by way of repayment of the loan without occasioning any immediate liability to income tax by doing so, whether for the settlor or themselves. Over the 20-year period the loan would be repaid and the balance of the fund would build up in the bond outside the estate of the settlor, on trust for the default beneficiaries.

If the bond was eventually encashed by the trustees, or on the maturity of the bond on the settlor's death, there would be a charge to income tax in the hands of the settlor. In calculating the profit subject to such tax (i.e. the surrender value less the premium paid), the previous partial surrenders (or 'withdrawals') were taken as increasing the surrender value, thereby increasing the amount subject to tax and ensuring that the full amount of the 'gain' would be subject to tax. The proceeds of the policy would accrue for the benefit of the beneficiaries under the trust.

Inheritance trusts and their variants were however badly hit by the gifts with reservation provisions of the Finance Act 1986.

If the settlor is included in the class of persons who may benefit under the trust of the policy, then the Inland Revenue clearly will be in a position to contend that there has been a reservation of benefit. Not only will the initial amount settled by way of outright gift and the property deriving therefrom be caught but also any property deriving from the loan by the settlor (FA 1986, Sch 20 para 5(4)). Thus, where property is given as well as lent to the trustees of a settlement by the settlor, the settled property in its entirety is capable of being property subject to a reservation of benefit. This will be the case even if the settlor is not a beneficiary under the settlement because any repayment of the loan will result in the settled property not being enjoyed to the entire exclusion of the settlor thereby bringing the gifts with reservation provisions into play.

There are, however, two possible ways round the problem. First, the trust could be established by way of a nominal gift from a person other than the intended lender, so as to take the trust outside FA 1986, Sch 20 para 5(4). Alternatively, the trust could confer absolute beneficial interests only, so as to take it outside the definition of 'settlement' for inheritance tax purposes. This will also result in paragraph 5(4) not being applicable. Both alternatives

7.48 *Insurance*

depend, however, on a loan on favourable terms (i.e. interest free albeit repayable on demand) not itself constituting a disposal of property 'by way of gift' for the purposes of FA 1986, s 102. Given that a loan will always be given in return for consideration in the form of the covenant to repay, it is considered unlikely that a loan even if free of interest could be a gift for these purposes. Unfortunately this does not appear to be a view shared by the Inland Revenue. If the Inland Revenue's view is correct, then to avoid any application of the gifts with reservation provisions it will also be essential that the lender is not a beneficiary under the trust.

Some life offices are currently marketing variants of the original inheritance trust along these lines. As a way of enabling a person to make a gift for the benefit of his heirs whilst retaining an 'income' from the property (albeit strictly repayments of capital), this type of arrangement may be one of the few effective ones left following the introduction of the gifts with reservation provisions. Some of the schemes on offer provide an immediate discounted potentially exempt transfer calculated as the value of the potentially exempt transfer less the number of annually maturing bonds the life assured could expect to receive during his lifetime. When the bonds mature they fall back into the estate once more but if the life assured does not survive as long as expected, a useful discount will have been obtained.

Other schemes provide for a bond to mature annually which the life assured can either take and spend, or defer, in which case the value is reinvested into the original bond.

Both types of scheme rely heavily on the life assured only becoming entitled to the bond at maturity; there can be no prior claim, otherwise there would be a gift with reservation.

More recently schemes have been launched which split a capital amount into a gifted portion and a retained portion. The amount in the gifted portion is treated as a potentially exempt transfer and the retained portion remains in the estate. Importantly, the income, which falls within the 5% tax-free annual allowance, is calculated as 5% of the entire capital amount, not just 5% of the retained portion.

Many life offices still offer a loan trust plan. Here a trust is established with a small gift, often £3,000. The settlor then makes a loan to the trust of a more substantial sum which is then repayable at 5% per annum to utilise the annual tax-free withdrawal allowance. The entire loan is repayable on demand which reassures settlors that they can reclaim their capital if it is required. These loan schemes are often called 'freezer trusts' with the amount remaining in the life assured's estate frozen at the amount of the loan.

Planning in later years

7.48 This final section considers the position of property owners who have reached or are on the point of reaching retirement. They may by this stage have discharged any mortgage on their main residence and also have organised their property and affairs so as to minimise the inheritance tax payable on their deaths. They will also be finding out whether any pension

Insurance **7.49**

arrangements they have effected over the last 20 or 30 years are sufficient for them to live comfortably without having to realise any of their capital assets.

Life insurance for the elderly is often prohibitively expensive (if obtainable at all), although seven-year decreasing term policies (as a cover for potentially exempt transfers) can often be obtained at a low price. There is, however, one particular aspect of insurance-based estate planning which has not yet been fully discussed and is of particular application in relation to the elderly.

Annuities

7.49 The purchase of an annuity involves the payment of a capital sum to an insurance company in return for an income usually for life. As the annuity will normally come to an end on the death of the purchaser, his estate will be left with no corresponding asset and therefore without anything on which inheritance tax will be payable. In effect, a capital sum potentially chargeable to tax is converted into a stream of income ceasing on death. Whether or not this proves to be a good investment will depend on whether or not the annuitant survives longer than his actuarial life expectancy. Thus, an annuity may prove to have been a very good or a very bad investment depending on when the annuitant dies.

In times of falling interest rates, an annuity provides a measure of security since the level of return is fixed at the outset. In most cases, the only people to whom an annuity will be attractive will be those aged 70 or over; although deferred annuities (see below) are used in connection with school fees planning, and also as investment vehicles in their own right, the annuities in the latter case being encashed for a capital sum shortly before the income flow commences.

Purchased annuities may be immediate or deferred. A deferred annuity will commence at some predetermined time in the future, whilst an immediate annuity starts, unsurprisingly, immediately. An annuity may be for a fixed period (a temporary or fixed annuity) or for the life of the purchaser (a lifetime annuity). Annuities can also be for a guaranteed period, and will therefore continue to be paid until the end of a fixed term, notwithstanding the death of the annuitant. Some annuities provide for a cash sum equal to the original capital investment to be paid on death.

The returns from purchased life annuities are treated as containing a capital element and, to that extent, are exempt from income tax (by virtue of ICTA 1988, s 656(1)). The other element (which is income in nature) is, however, chargeable to income tax as an annual payment and will be treated as unearned income in the year of assessment in which it is received. Accordingly, it will normally be paid under deduction of basic rate income tax. This treatment, however, only applies to purchased life annuities which are life annuities granted for consideration (in money or money's worth) in the ordinary course of a business of granting annuities on human life. It does not apply to the various forms of annuity (such as retirement annuity contracts or any annuity payable under approved personal pension arrangements) listed in ICTA 1988, s 657(2).

7.49 *Insurance*

Generally speaking, an annuity will cease on death and ought therefore to have no inheritance tax consequences for the annuitant. If, however, a lump sum is payable on death there may be a charge to income tax if the amount payable exceeds the total amount paid in premiums (reduced by the capital element of any annuity payments already made). In these circumstances, the lump sum will also be included in the estate of the annuitant for the purposes of inheritance tax. Also, in the case of a guaranteed annuity, the actuarial value of any outstanding instalments of income will form part of the estate for inheritance tax purposes.

Where an elderly person has a low income and no real savings but owns a house with no mortgage, then if he is at least 65 years of age (although in practice 70 is often the minimum age allowed), he could use his house to produce additional income. He could borrow a proportion of the value of the house from an insurance company, securing the loan on the house, and use the money thereby obtained to purchase a life annuity. Part of the annuity payments subsequently received by him would be used to pay interest on the loan, and the rest would provide the income for him. The loan would then be repaid out of the proceeds of sale of the house on death. In the meantime, provided the conditions set out in ICTA 1988, s 365 are satisfied, interest relief at the basic rate on the loan, thus employed, up to £30,000 will be available (ICTA 1988, s 353). The interest would, however, have to be paid by the annuitant (if he was not the person to whom the loan was made), for the interest relief to be available (ICTA 1988, s 365(2)). This interest relief ceased for new loans taken out on or after 9 March 1999, unless agreement to the advance had been made by the lender before that date. Borrowers who already qualified for relief continue to receive relief, even beyond the abolition of MIRAS on 6 April 2000. A number of life companies operate this type of scheme. The interest under the loan may be payable either at a floating rate or a fixed rate depending upon the particular scheme. As the annuity payments themselves will remain static, the latter type of arrangement is the more secure as one can ensure that the annuity payments will always be sufficient to cover the loan interest, although specialist advice may be appropriate before finally deciding on such arrangements. In times of falling property values particular care may be required especially where a floating rate is selected. Indeed, many schemes arranged in the late 1980s left elderly people in financial hardship as a result of falling property prices, rising interest rates and decreasing investment return. As a result of this, the Safe Home Income Plan organisation (SHIP) developed.

This type of arrangement may be worth considering, as a last resort, so as to free other income-producing assets for potentially exempt transfers to the next generation (assuming the donor's life expectancy is at least three years). A person's home is usually not transferred in his lifetime — mainly because of the gifts with reservation provisions — and thus it can at least be partially converted into an income-producing asset.

An elderly taxpayer may wish to increase his net spendable income through a back-to-back insurance and annuity arrangement. First, he would purchase an annuity for the duration of his life. After having done so, in order to replace in his estate the capital he has used to purchase the annuity, he may then consider effecting a whole life policy on his own life, which he will put in

Insurance **7.49**

trust for his heirs, under which the original capital sum (plus bonuses) will be payable on his death. He has thereby provided himself with a source of income and also effectively removed the capital cost of the annuity from his estate.

Regard must be had to IHTA 1984, s 263 in relation to this type of arrangement. The section applies where the taking out of two policies are associated operations (as that expression is defined in IHTA 1984, s 268(1)(b)) and the taxpayer is deemed to have made a transfer of value at the time the life policy became held in trust equal to the lower of the total consideration paid for the annuity and the life policy and the value of the greatest benefit capable of being conferred by the life policy. In practice, however, policies and annuities taken out in such circumstances will not be regarded by the Inland Revenue as associated operations (and thus section 263 will not be applied) provided the life policy was issued on full medical evidence of the assured's health and would have been issued on the same terms if the annuity had not been purchased at the same time (see Inland Revenue Statement of Practice SP E4).

8 Pensions

Introduction

8.1 Whether employed or self-employed, everyone should consider making provision for their retirement at as early a stage in their career as possible. The last twenty years have seen many changes to the laws relating to pensions. There are now three tiers of pension provision; namely the State provision via the Basic State and State Earnings Related Pension Schemes ('SERPS'), occupational schemes and personal pension schemes.

Personal pension schemes were introduced by the Social Security Act 1986 and are operated under the regime set out in Chapter IV of Part XIV of the Income and Corporation Taxes Act 1988. They operate in addition to and, to some extent, in place of the arrangements for the employed and self-employed which previously co-existed for some years. Unlike SERPS and occupational pension schemes, they are capable of applying to all individuals whether employed or self-employed.

Further changes to all three regimes have been brought into force by the Pensions Act 1995.

In December 1998, a Green Paper on pensions was issued. This proposed that SERPS be replaced by a State Second Pension (SSP) from 2002 at the earliest. The SSP might then be replaced by a new flat-rate second tier State pension from 2006.

The basic State pension is to continue as a flat, non-means tested benefit. SSP should provide improved benefits for most employees earning less than £18,500 p.a. compared with the benefits under the present system.

The December 1998 Green Paper also contained proposals for stakeholder pensions. Stakeholder pensions came into effect on 6 April 2001 and permit contributions of up to £300 per month. Stakeholder pensions have a simple charging structure and do not have penalties for stopping or restarting contributions. They are designed to be a more cost-efficient alternative to personal pensions with a ceiling on charges set at 1% per annum.

Although pension arrangements will mainly be effected to provide income during retirement (which is, after all, the normal understanding of the term 'pension'), they are usually wider in effect. They can provide valuable death-in-service benefits, whether by way of a pension payable to a surviving spouse or dependant or simply by means of a lump sum payable on death before retirement. In fact, pension funds are quite justifiably regarded as a form of savings medium. This is particularly the case in the light of the tax

8.2 Pensions

advantages available to pension funds and pension contributions and, more particularly, because tax-free lump sum benefits may be available both on retirement (albeit with a corresponding reduction in the pension payable during retirement) and on death.

Pension funds are unable to reclaim tax credits on dividends paid by UK companies.

Pensionable employment

8.2 At present, if an individual is in employment, his or her pension on retirement will usually be provided by a combination of benefits from the State scheme and from any occupational pension scheme of which the employee in question has been a member.

The State scheme

8.3 An individual in employment can pay full national insurance contributions and receive a pension from the State on retirement. Any individual who has retired on reaching the appropriate age for retirement under the State scheme, and who has paid national insurance contributions for at least nine-tenths of his working life, will be entitled to the full basic State pension, payable weekly. State pension age is presently 65 for men and 60 for women but will be fully equalised at 65 by the year 2020 (by virtue of the Pensions Act 1995). He or she will also be entitled to an additional earnings-related pension from SERPS, also payable weekly. From 2002 SERPS will be replaced by a new State Second Pension which should provide better benefit levels for those earning up to £22,000 p.a. than under SERPs.

Occupational pension schemes

8.4 An individual may also receive pension benefits from a private scheme established by an employer for his employees (an 'occupational pension scheme'). An employee's entitlement to participate will depend on his or her contract of employment, subject to the relevant terms of the scheme (as to age and also length of service etc.) dealing with participation. The scheme may simply provide additional benefits to those provided by the State; but it may also provide the benefits that would otherwise be provided by the earnings-related part of the State scheme, in which case the scheme is said to be 'contracted-out' of SERPS and participating employees are said to be in contracted-out employment. In such a case the Class 1 National Insurance contributions of employees (which are automatically deducted from their salaries) and of employers will be less than if the employer had not contracted-out. As an incentive to occupational pension schemes becoming contracted-out for the first time between 1 January 1986 and 5 April 1993, the Secretary of State made an additional payment to the scheme in respect of each member (Social Security Act 1986, s 7). This 'incentive' payment amounted to 2% of that part of their earnings affected by National Insurance contributions or £1 (whichever is greater). From 6

Pensions **8.5**

April 1993 this was reduced to 1%, and confined to personal pension schemes (see below) where the employee was aged 30 or over (Pension Schemes Act 1993, s 45(2)). This incentive ceased from 5 April 1997 after which a full age-related basis is introduced.

In passing, it is also worth mentioning that it is possible for employers to enjoy the advantages of contracting-out of the State scheme without providing their employees with salary-related benefits (i.e. defined benefits pursuant to an occupational pension scheme). Employers may promise to pay a minimum level of contributions to a money purchase scheme (where pension benefits will not be defined but will depend on investment performance), so long as that scheme satisfies certain rules and thus qualifies as a money purchase contracted-out occupational pension scheme or 'COMP' (Pension Schemes Act 1993, s 9). Any such contributions must secure benefits for the members of the scheme calculated by reference to the employer's payments together with such other payments as may be made to the scheme by or on behalf of the employee. The regulations that such a scheme must comply with to qualify as a COMP are contained in the Money Purchase Contracted-Out Schemes Regulations 1987. From 6 April 1997 under the terms of the Pensions Act 1995, the minimum level of contributions is age-related.

The State Second Pension will be launched from April 2002 at the earliest. It will be possible to contract out of SSP using either a personal pension or a stakeholder pension. Occupational schemes are also expected to be able to offer a contracting-out facility.

Before taking up employment, a potential employee should investigate what pension arrangements (if any) have been established by his or her potential employer. There will be some scope for negotiation of the provision of retirement benefits, as part of the overall remuneration package. This will, however, depend on the circumstances of the case and, more probably, on the seniority (and thus the bargaining position) of the potential employee.

If an occupational pension scheme does exist, in most cases it will be an exempt approved scheme (as defined by ICTA 1988, s 592(1)) for the purposes of Chapter I of Part XIV of the Income and Corporation Taxes Act 1988. In such circumstances, the pension scheme will enjoy certain tax privileges. In particular, the employer's contributions will not represent taxable benefits as regards the employee and the fund's income and capital gains will be exempt from tax. Tax credits on UK dividends can no longer be reclaimed.

Contributions and additional voluntary contributions

8.5 Contributions to occupational pension schemes are made by the employer, this being one condition for Inland Revenue approval of the scheme (ICTA 1988, s 590(2)(d)), and may also be required from employees, up to a maximum of 15% of so much of their remuneration for the year of assessment in question as does not exceed the 'permitted maximum' (ICTA 1988, s 592(7)(8)(8B)). For 2002/03 the permitted maximum has been increased to £97,200 (from £95,400 for 2001/02). Any contribution so paid by an employee is deductible as an expense incurred in the year of assessment in which the contribution is paid, for the purposes of

8.5 Pensions

assessing income tax under Schedule E for that year. This cap on remuneration does not apply to the members of a scheme set up before 14 March 1989 who joined the scheme before 1 June 1989.

The rules of the scheme must also permit a member to make additional voluntary contributions ('AVCs') to the scheme in question, within the same 15% limit mentioned above and with the same effect. If an employee has surplus funds, it is therefore advisable for him to investigate the possibility of increasing his contributions to the maximum permissible under the scheme. Contributions made by any person will not be transfers of value for inheritance tax purposes if made to an exempt approved retirement benefits scheme (IHTA 1984, s 12).

Employees can boost their retirement prospects by buying free-standing additional voluntary contribution contracts (so-called 'FSAVCs'). In effect, such contracts are intended to be a form of exempt approved pension scheme to which only members of occupational pension schemes may contribute but which is separate from the occupational pension schemes provided by employers. Employers are not to be contributors (ICTA 1988, s 591(2)(h)).

The rationale behind the introduction of these provisions was that members of occupational pension schemes were to have the option of making additional contributions to a separate scheme of their own choice without being tied to their employer's scheme. However, any such contributions are still subject to the overall 15% limit applying to an employee's contributions to all approved pension schemes (ICTA 1988, s 592(7)(8)(8B) and ICTA 1988, s 593). Also, contributions must not be such as would be likely to take the aggregate of FSAVC benefits and occupational scheme benefits above the limits imposed by the Inland Revenue. On making any such contributions for which relief is available, the employee in question may deduct and retain an amount equal to the basic rate of income tax on the amount of the contribution.

These provisions give employees flexibility over the kind of AVC scheme they may join and the extent to which they can make additional contributions to provide for their retirement. They are no longer restricted to their employer's AVC scheme. Moneys paid into new AVC contracts cannot be taken in the form of a lump sum benefit.

The employee's contributions are deductible from earned income as an expense incurred in the year of assessment in which they are paid, subject again to the 15% limit.

However, care must be taken by employees to ensure that making additional voluntary contributions does not cause their total pension rights to exceed the allowable limits. The pension that he or she finally earns on retirement must not exceed a maximum of two-thirds of so much of the employee's final remuneration as does not exceed the 'permitted maximum' for the relevant year (ICTA 1988, s 590(3)(a) and ICTA 1988, s 590C). For 2002/03, the permitted maximum is £97,200. If this limit is exceeded, the employee can recover his excess contributions but subject to an income tax charge. This cap on final remuneration does not apply to the members of a scheme set up before 14 March 1989 who joined the scheme before 1 June 1989.

Pensions **8.6**

Salary sacrifice arrangements are also a popular way of improving pension entitlement. The employee waives the right to a bonus or part of a bonus before the bonus is declared. The employer then pays an equivalent amount into an executive pension plan on behalf of the employee. Maximum funding checks still apply but there is no cap on pre-1989 pension scheme members. Furthermore, this route leads to a valuable saving in employers national insurance contributions.

Lump sum benefits

8.6 An employee may also be entitled to a lump sum retirement benefit of up to one and a half times his final salary (ICTA 1988, s 590(3)(d)), usually with a corresponding reduction in the pension available. The pension payable will be taxed under Schedule E as earned income in the year of receipt. However, any lump sum benefit taken will be free of tax. Depending on when the employee joined the scheme and when the scheme itself was set up, the lump sum may be subject to certain financial limits.

The scheme may also provide for the payment of a pension to a widow or dependant of a deceased member (usually not exceeding two-thirds of the amount the member could have received if he had survived to normal retirement) and/or a lump sum on death before retirement. Such a sum, of up to four times the employee's final remuneration, as at the date of death, may be paid in addition to a return of the member's own contributions together with reasonable interest (ICTA 1988, s 591(2)(c)).

Whether or not inheritance tax will be payable on the member's death in respect of a lump sum death benefit will depend on the mechanism adopted for its payment. Such a benefit will be subject to inheritance tax on the death of the member if it forms part of his freely disposable estate on his death (that is to say, if his personal representatives have a legally enforceable claim to the benefit). It will also be subject to tax if the member had the right (immediately before his death) to nominate or appoint the benefit in favour of anyone he pleased and he failed to exercise the right irrevocably by the time of his death. However, if the benefit is payable only at the discretion of the trustees of the scheme, it will not be subject to inheritance tax Most schemes are set up in this way.

Where the death benefit is payable only to the deceased member's personal representatives, then to avoid a charge to inheritance tax on his death, he should leave the benefit to his wife under his will and rely on her to pass the benefit to the children (if any) by way of potentially exempt transfers made by her during her lifetime.

The fact that a charge to inheritance tax can be avoided if the death benefit is payable only at the discretion of the trustees of the scheme is generally recognised by employers nowadays when schemes are established. Accordingly, trustees of pension schemes are nearly always given wide powers to pay a lump sum death benefit to a wide class of potential beneficiaries centred around the member's family. The member in question will usually be able to indicate whom he wishes to receive the benefit (by means of a letter of wishes

8.7 Pensions

delivered to the trustees), but any such indication is, of course, not binding on the trustees. A member of a pension scheme should be sure to indicate to the trustees whom he would like to receive the death-in-service benefit and ideally this should tie in with his overall estate planning strategy.

If a scheme provides for an adequate widow's pension, a lump sum death benefit could in this way be paid or applied for the benefit of a member's children. This could be a useful and inheritance tax-free way for a member to provide for his dependants. Furthermore, by leaving to his wife the bulk of his free estate the member could so arrange his affairs that very little (if any) inheritance tax will be payable on his death, while at the same time he will have made adequate provision (within his means) for his dependants.

An extension to this approach might involve the use of a separate settlement to receive the death benefit. For example, the member could indicate that he wished the benefit to be paid to the trustees of a discretionary settlement (to be created, for example, by his will) the beneficiaries of that settlement including his wife and children. His wife could receive the income deriving from the lump sum, at the discretion of the trustees of the settlement, without the lump sum itself forming part of her estate on her death. The lump sum could then be used to meet some (if not all) of the eventual inheritance tax liability on her death (depending, of course, on the terms of the trust) or it could be distributed to the next generation.

The disadvantage, however, of such a discretionary trust would be that the lump sum would be subject to the inheritance tax regime applicable to such trusts. Generally speaking, inheritance tax would be charged on the value of property comprised in the settlement on each ten-year anniversary of the commencement of the settlement. Additionally, there could be a charge to inheritance tax on property leaving the settlement. By virtue of IHTA 1984, s 81, the property in the separate discretionary trust will be treated for inheritance tax purposes as remaining in the pension scheme discretionary trust with the result that any charge to tax will necessitate identifying both the settlor of that trust and its commencement date. It is understood that the Inland Revenue regard the settlor as being the individual employee whose death had triggered the benefit payment and the commencement date as being the date on which the employee transferred the death benefit into trust. This date will depend on the particular rules of the scheme in question but it is possible that a ten year charge could arise fairly soon after death and trustees of such separate discretionary trusts should be aware of this possibility. It is likely, however, that the tax saving on the death of the surviving spouse will far outweigh any such charge which might arise. At current rates, the maximum ten year charge can only be at 6% whilst the saving in tax on the death of the surviving spouse by using a separate discretionary trust of which she is a beneficiary rather than paying the benefit to her, may well be 40% of the lump sum benefit.

Unapproved schemes

8.7 Very few unapproved occupational pension schemes existed before rule changes were made by the Finance Act 1989, facilitating their creation and set up in the new flexible pensions environment. Previously a major

Pensions 8.7

obstacle had been the denial or withdrawal of approved status to other schemes when an unapproved scheme was created. However, the co-existence of approved and unapproved schemes has been allowed since 27 July 1989.

An unapproved scheme can either be funded or unfunded. A funded unapproved retirement benefit scheme ('FURBS') is normally financed by payments to a separate trust fund and offers a number of attractions, the principal one being that the whole of the benefits can be taken as a tax free lump sum. In general terms, provided the FURBS is not offshore (as discussed later), this will be the case if the employee has been assessed to tax under ICTA 1988, s 595(1) on all employer contributions to the FURBS. In an unfunded scheme the employer undertakes to provide retirement benefits at some future date and both pension and lump sum benefits are charged to tax on the employee. This section will concentrate on FURBS.

Benefits payable under approved schemes are subject to certain restrictions. Lump sums payable on death before retirement are limited to four times the final remuneration and on retirement to one and a half times final remuneration. Pensions are restricted to two-thirds of final remuneration and, under schemes established after 13 March 1989 and for any member joining a scheme after 31 May 1989, final remuneration will be further restricted by the 'permitted maximum' or earnings cap. This is £97,200 for 2002/03. There is a corresponding reduction in the amount of pension payable to a widow or dependant. For a highly paid employee, particularly if he is nearing retirement, a FURBS can now be considered as part of the overall remuneration package either as an alternative to an approved scheme or most probably as a top up facility with no restrictions applying as to the amount which can be taken as either pension or lump sum.

Contributions made by an employer under a FURBS are taxable on the employee as a Schedule E benefit in kind (ICTA 1988, s 595(1)) and are returned on form P11D. Where contributions cover more than one employee these are apportioned. Payment of the tax will be at the normal date under the self-assessment system, 31 January following the tax year. Large payments could necessitate payments on account becoming due for the next tax year. As an alternative, and providing the tax return is submitted by 30 September following the year end, the tax could be collected through PAYE coding. In any case, regular contributions could be taken into account through negative 'K' coding. Such contributions increase the pensionable remuneration for the purposes of determining benefits under an approved pension scheme. However, relief from the Schedule E charge can be claimed subject to a time limit if no payment of benefits has been made and some event has occurred so that no payment can be made (ICTA 1988, s 596(3)). An exception to the Schedule E charge is made where the employee is in receipt of 'foreign emoluments' and the pension scheme is accepted as having corresponding status (ICTA 1988, s 596(2)).

Tax relief will be obtained by the employer to the extent that contributions are actually paid and taxed on the employee (FA 1989, s 76). The potential tax relief appears to be unlimited, subject to satisfying the usual rules of deductibility of expenses set out in ICTA 1988, s 74. Until 5 April 1998, so

8.7 Pensions

long as the DSS regard the scheme as a genuine pension arrangement, neither the employer's contribution nor the benefits payable were treated as earnings of the employee for national insurance contributions purposes.

However, national insurance contributions are levied on the employer's contribution to a FURBS.

'Relevant benefits' (ICTA 1988, s 612(1)) can be paid as a pension, lump sum or benefit in kind on or in anticipation of retirement or on death, and this extends to the provision of benefits payable to the employee's wife, widow, dependants or personal representatives (ICTA 1988, s 595(5)). No stipulation is made as to the age of retirement although this cannot be beyond age 75.

Benefits taken as a pension are taxable under normal Schedule E rules. In effect this results in a double tax charge, to the extent that the employee will suffer tax on the contributions made by the employer, and also on the pension he eventually receives. There are provisions to tax lump sum benefits where the income and gains accruing to the scheme are not brought into charge to tax (ICTA 1988, s 596A as amended by FA 1994, s 108): they will affect mainly FURBS established offshore. Subject to this, all of the benefits can be taken in the form of a tax free lump sum provided that the employee has already been taxed on the employer's contributions (ICTA 1988, s 189(b)).

On receipt the lump sum can be invested taking into account current tax planning strategies and the needs of family members. For example, if an annuity is purchased then only the income element will be subject to tax not the return of capital.

In general terms, investments held by trustees of a FURBS are only subject to income tax at the savings rate and not subject to additional rate tax if the sole purpose is the provision of relevant retirement benefits (ICTA 1988, s 686(2)(c) and TCGA 1992, s 6(1)). For 2002/03, most investment income is subject to an effective tax rate of 10% on dividends and 20% on other savings income.

Whereas capital gains were previously taxed at the basic rate, they are now taxed at 34% in line with other trusts. However, FURBS also benefit from their own annual exemption which is £3,850 for 2002/03. This figure is split between the number of trusts operated by the employer, subject to a minimum of £770, i.e. 10% of £7,700.

The inheritance tax position of a FURBS can be fairly complex, and the following comments are necessarily of a general nature. Guidance is given in notes issued by the Capital Taxes Office in 1988 entitled 'IHT on benefits under superannuation schemes'. Most schemes are likely to be 'sponsored superannuation schemes' (ICTA 1988, s 624). This would appear to be the case where at least part of the costs of establishing and administering the fund are kept separate and identifiable. The net effect of this is that only part of the costs of the employer's payment is taxable on the employees for Schedule E purposes. However, an important consequence of this is that a FURBS established under trust, which also qualifies as a sponsored superannuation scheme, should also fall within IHTA 1984, s 151. As a result, the usual inheritance tax charges on settled property should not apply. However, death benefit payments may be subject to an inheritance tax charge. This will be the case where such payments are expressed to be payable only to the deceased's estate. No charge to inheritance tax should arise where the estate cannot benefit in this way. There may also be adverse implications under the gift with reservation of benefit provisions (FA 1986, s 102) in situations where the deceased's estate has not been excluded from benefit. Thus, as with approved schemes, care should be taken to ensure that the lump sum death benefit is payable only at the discretion of the trustees of the scheme with the employee having indicated whom he would wish to receive the benefit and, in addition, the deceased's estate should be excluded as a potential recipient from the trustees. This should be considered in conjunction with other estate planning arrangements.

Small self-administered schemes

8.8 A small self-administered scheme (SSAS) is advantageous to the sponsoring company, enabling it to develop a pension fund which can buy assets used in its trade.

SSASs are normally established for controlling directors and although up to twelve members are permitted, in practice, there are unlikely to be more than four. The SSAS has to be established for the purpose of providing benefits on retirement or death, although it can provide substantial investment flexibility.

The trustees of the SSAS are permitted to advance loans to the company for business purposes only at a commercial rate of interest and over a pre-defined term. The maximum loan in the first two years is 25% of the fund value, rising to 50% after two years which can include a transfer value from a previous scheme.

SSASs are also permitted to invest in commercial but not residential property. A commercial property may include within it a private residence which is occupied by an individual unconnected with the company; for example, a caretaker's flat. A SSAS cannot purchase assets from a member, e.g. a director of the company, and if a property owned by the company was previously owned by such a director the SSAS cannot acquire it until the company itself has owned the property for at least three years. Often, most of the property held within a SSAS is purchased from the sponsoring company. In these circumstances it is possible to establish a tax efficient structure whereby the company obtains a tax deduction for rent paid to the trustees of the pension fund who in turn receive the rent free of tax. Furthermore, all capital growth in the underlying property, once inside the SSAS, is free of tax.

The trustees are also allowed to borrow to purchase commercial property. However, the borrowing is limited to 45% of the value of the fund, together with three times the members' annual contributions and three times the employer's ordinary annual contribution. Strict rules apply regarding notification to the PSO of borrowing by scheme trustees or indeed loans made by the trustees to the sponsoring company.

SSASs can pay pensions to members who are aged between 50 and 75, yet defer purchasing an annuity until that individual attains the age of 75. With SSAS drawdown, income paid must be broadly in line with current annuity rates. There are obvious similarities between this facility and the pension fund

8.9 *Pensions*

drawdown facility available on personal pensions, although it is fair to say that personal pension drawdown offers greater flexibility.

The funding limits on SSASs often make them more attractive than personal pensions or group personal pensions. It is usually possible to fund for a maximum 2/3 pension in just 20 years. For individuals with little in the way of past pension provision (retained benefits) contributions at 40 can often be in excess of 50% of salary rising to over 100% of salary at the age of 50. If the wide-ranging self-investment capabilities of a SSAS are not required, then an executive pension plan can offer similarly attractive funding limits.

Personal pension arrangements

8.9 As mentioned above, instead of joining (or remaining in) his employer's occupational pension scheme, an employee may make his own pension arrangements by taking out personal pensions of his own. He may also use them to contract out of SERPS whilst remaining a member of a 'contracted-in' scheme. Personal pensions are therefore an alternative to the pension arrangements available to employees mentioned above. The tax legislation relating to these schemes is set out in ICTA 1988, ss 630–655. Many changes were introduced from 6 April 2001 (see 8.11 below).

The main advantage of a personal pension is its flexibility. It is an independent arrangement which will be made by the employee in question with the institution of his or her choice which runs a personal pension scheme. The institution must be one of the bodies mentioned in the list set out in ICTA 1988, s 632(1), basically an insurance company, friendly society, building society, unit trust or bank. There is no need for an employer to contribute to such an arrangement although the employer may choose to do so. A personal pension arrangement therefore will not be tied to a particular employment and thus will not be subject to any restrictions on transferability when an employee changes jobs.

It must, however, be recognised that employers are generally not willing to contribute to a personal pension arrangement. Thus, for an employee who will remain in service, the ultimate benefits from joining an occupational pension scheme are likely to be much higher than those which his own contributions would purchase in a personal pension scheme.

Personal pension schemes which are approved by the Inland Revenue will provide for the payment of an annuity which must not normally commence before the member reaches 50 or after he reaches 75 and must usually be payable for life (ICTA 1988, s 634(2)). In certain circumstances, though, where an individual becomes unable to work through illness or disability or where his occupation is one in which the normal retirement age is under 50 (e.g. football players, jockeys, etc.), an annuity may commence before an individual reaches the age of 50 (ICTA 1988, s 634(3)) but only in respect of earnings directly related to sporting activities, e.g. tournament earnings for golfers. Sponsorship and advertising revenues are excluded. The annuity may continue for a fixed period, not exceeding ten years, notwithstanding the member's death within that period (ICTA 1988, s 634(5)).

Pensions **8.9**

Schemes may also provide for a lump sum to be payable to the member (but only if the member so elects on or before the date on which the annuity is first payable to him), but this lump sum must not exceed one quarter of the difference between the total value (at the time when the lump sum is paid) of the benefits provided for the member by the scheme (including the value of any dependants' benefits) and (where the arrangement is being used to contract out of SERPS) the value of the fund providing the SERPS-equivalent benefits for the member and his widow (if any).

The Finance Act 1995 introduced a new facility (income drawdown) which enables the member to defer the actual purchase of an annuity, for any length of time until age 75 and instead make income withdrawals from his accumulated fund during the deferral period. Income withdrawals can be flexible subject to a maximum broadly equivalent to the level single life annuity which the fund could have provided at retirement and to a minimum of 35% of that maximum. Deferral may be an attractive option, particularly when annuity rates are unfavourable at retirement, although if drawdown is to be used, then the dangers should also be appreciated. An annuity is determined by two factors — long-term gilt yields and mortality subsidy. The latter represents the annuity provider's experience of paying annuities — a number of annuitants will die before receiving full value for the capital invested to acquire an annuity and these individuals effectively subsidise the others. Mortality subsidy is not present in a fund in drawdown. The mortality subsidy increases with the age of the annuitant.

For these reasons, drawdown is often used by individuals closer to age 50 who want to release their tax-free cash entitlement of 25%, possibly for a business venture or to pay off a mortgage. The balance of the fund is then left invested in a benign tax environment, to grow with minimum income withdrawn.

One of the most confused areas in income drawdown has been the position over death benefits and inheritance tax. The inheritance tax position on deaths during income drawdown is set out in a guidance note agreed between the ABI and the Capital Taxes Office. The two sections that may impact on death under drawdown are IHTA 1984, s 5(2) (as extended by IHTA 1984, s 151(4)) and IHTA 1984, s 3(3).

Section 3(3) treats an omission to exercise a right as a disposition and thus, possibly, a transfer of value if the omission decreases the taxpayer's estate and increases the value of the estate of another person or of settled property. It does not apply if the omission is not deliberate. Section 3(3) could apply where a PPP holder deliberately fails to take pension benefits but instead goes into income drawdown in order to financially advantage someone on his/her death. To counter such a claim by the CTO, it is important to be able to illustrate that the drawdown decision was driven by retirement planning when the individual was in good health. If an individual in drawdown deliberately reduces income after becoming terminally ill, then this could give rise to a potential inheritance tax charge.

Where a taxpayer has a general power to dispose of any property, that property is treated as forming part of the taxpayer's estate. Section 5(2) will apply, therefore, where a member has a general power to dispose of the death benefits. However, the section is unlikely to apply where the member has a

8.9 Pensions

power of nomination, in relation to a lump sum benefit, to select from a limited class of survivors.

Personal pension schemes may also provide for the payment of a lump sum on the death of a member before he reaches 75 or for the payment of an annuity at any time after death to the deceased member's spouse or dependants. Under personal pension legislation the value of the pension fund is normally paid out. However, some retirement annuities only provide for a repayment of premiums plus interest; for a fund invested over a number of years this can be a severe restriction. The provisions of the Finance Act 1995 enable the fund to be paid as a lump sum on death during the deferral period. The lump sum will be subject to an income tax charge of 35%. Where the residual fund is subject to the provisions of a discretionary trust, it is unlikely that it will be subject to inheritance tax.

Personal pension schemes may be:

(a) 'with profits' (where a minimum sum is guaranteed on retirement but will be increased over the term of the contract depending usually on the profits of the institution),

(b) 'managed fund' or 'unit-linked' (where the benefits are linked to the value of a fund of investments),

(c) 'self invested' (where the administration is handled by a professional pensions administrator and the investment by the pension holder or a fund manager of the pension holder's choice. Under a self invested pensions plan (SIPP) it is also possible to invest in property, including purchasing a new property from a non-connected person to use as business premises, although from 6 April 2001 any borrowing is limited to 75% of the interest being acquired or the estimated value of the property after refurbishment (The Personal Pension Schemes (Restriction on Discretion to Approve) (Permitted Investments) Regulations, SI 2001 No 117). This allows for tax planning with tax deductible rent payments made by the pension holder to the pension scheme trustees who receive the rent tax free).

Personal pension arrangements are an important medium for savings. Flexible arrangements may also be made for the payment of premiums either regularly (e.g. monthly, half-yearly or annually) or singly. It may also be possible for premiums to be waived in the event of sickness or injury to the individual. The effect this will have on the benefits provided will, of course, depend on the terms of the arrangement.

The immediate effect for an individual contributing to an approved personal pension arrangement is that such contributions may be deducted from or set off against any 'relevant earnings' of that individual for the year of assessment in which the payment is made (ICTA 1988, s 639). The maximum amount which may be deducted or set off in any year of assessment is a specified percentage of so much of the individual's 'net relevant earnings' for that year as do not exceed the 'allowable maximum' for the year (ICTA 1988, ss 640, 640A) and the scheme itself must provide, in general terms, that the aggregate amount of contributions that can be made in a year of assessment by the individual and his employer, together with the aggregate amounts of

Pensions 8.9

contributions to any other personal pension schemes, must not exceed the individual's permitted maximum (ICTA 1988, s 638(3)-(5)). The percentage is 17.5% for those under 36 increasing in a series of age bands to a maximum of 40% at age 61 or over (ICTA 1988, s 640(2)). The allowable maximum for 2002/03 is £97,200. 'Relevant earnings' are broadly income from an office or employment in respect of which the individual is not a participant in his employer's pension scheme and income chargeable under Schedule D derived from a trade, profession or vocation (for, as will be seen below, personal pension arrangements are also available to the self-employed) (ICTA 1988, s 644). 'Net relevant earnings' are relevant earnings less certain deductions which would be made therefrom in computing the individual's total income for income tax purposes (ICTA 1988, s 646).

Where an employer contributes under approved personal pension arrangements made by his employee, those contributions will not be regarded as emoluments of the employment chargeable to tax on the employee under Schedule E (ICTA 1988, s 643), but the maximum amount that may be deducted or set off by the employee will be reduced by the amount of any employer's contributions in the year in question (ICTA 1988, s 640(4)).

An individual can elect for a contribution paid under an approved personal pension arrangement in a year of assessment (whether or not a year for which he has relevant earnings) to be treated as paid in the immediately preceding year of assessment or, in the absence of net relevant earnings in that previous year, in the year of assessment before that (ICTA 1988, s 641(1)). This may be beneficial for the individual if there were more relevant earnings in respect of that earlier year or if the tax rates of the earlier year were higher. Prior to 6 April 2001, if the contributions paid in a particular year of assessment were less than the permitted maximum for that year, the unused amount could be carried forward and set against so much of any contributions paid by him in any of the next six years of assessment as exceed the maximum applying for that year (ICTA 1988, s 642). However, from 6 April 2001, it is no longer possible to carry forward unused relief from previous years in personal pension plans. Instead, a new system is in operation (see 8.11 below).

Under self-assessment, relief can be calculated as if the payment were carried back, but it will be granted when the payment is made. Therefore, relief on a payment made in, say, 2001/02 can still be claimed by reference to 2000/01 tax rates but it will not reduce the 2000/01 liability and hence the 2001/02 initial self-assessment.

Any contribution by a person under an approved personal pension arrangement will not be a transfer of value for inheritance tax purposes (IHTA 1984, s 12).

As already mentioned, members of a contracted-out occupational pension scheme and their employers pay less Class 1 National Insurance contributions than would be the case if the scheme was not contracted-out. Where an individual has entered into an approved personal pension arrangement and has opted to contract out of SERPS, his employer will pay full rate National Insurance contributions for himself and for the employee as if SERPS applied. However, the DSS will make certain minimum contributions to the personal pension scheme chosen by the employee (Pension Schemes Act 1993, ss 43,

8.10 Pensions

45). Generally speaking, these will be the rebate or difference between the full rate national insurance contribution due if the member were in SERPS and the lower rate payable if the employment were contracted-out, grossed up for basic rate tax relief on the member's share of the rebate. In most cases, until April 1997 the minimum contributions would also include an additional payment by the Secretary of State similar to the one described above intended to encourage contracting-out. From April 1997, the rebate remitted to a personal pension arrangement will become age-related and will be different from the rebates available under an occupational pension scheme.

An employee who is a member of his employer's contracted-in pension scheme may also use a personal pension arrangement to contract-out of SERPS and similarly the DSS will make the minimum contributions to the arrangement. However, in such a case neither the employer nor the employee may make any contributions themselves to the personal pension arrangement.

Income tax planning with PPPs

8.10 Most personal pensions are established in a number of segments — typically 1,000. This segmentation allows the pension holder to 'phase' their retirement by only encashing a small number of segments in one tranche. By using the tax-free cash element of the segments as income, it is possible to minimise income tax until, perhaps, the pension holder has moved into a lower overall tax rate band. Furthermore, by combining the added flexibility of income drawdown, it is possible to provide a client with some complex yet effective income tax mitigation strategies.

Personal pensions: revisions to rules from 6 April 2001

8.11 From 6 April 2001 the personal pension scheme rules have been extended and altered.

It is no longer possible to carry forward unused relief from previous years (except in the case of pre-1 July 1988 retirement annuity contracts). Any 'sweep up' payments had to be made before 31 January 2002 and carried back to the tax year 2000/01. From 6 April 2001, the maximum personal pension contribution is based on the net relevant earnings of a 'base' year, which will then support contributions for the next five years, even if earnings have fallen. Furthermore, it is possible to continue making contributions for five years after earnings have ceased. Individuals with no net relevant earnings can contribute up to £3,600 p.a. In the normal case where income rises from year to year, the 'base year' will be the current year.

The provisions for carry-back have also been simplified. From 6 April 2001 contributions paid on or before 31 January can, by irrevocable election, be treated as paid in the previous tax year. The election must be made at or before the time of payment.

The provisions for payment of life assurance premiums under personal pension rules and with tax relief become less attractive. Currently, premiums can be as high as 5% of net relevant earnings. From 6 April 2001 this drops to 10% of total contributions for new contracts.

Pensions **8.13**

It will also be possible to make contributions by transfer of shares held under SAYE share option schemes. The amount transferred will rank as a contribution net of 22% tax.

Finally, from 6 April 2001 all contributions are made net of basic rate tax. Currently only employees can take advantage of this facility.

Stakeholder pensions

8.12 It is too early to say whether stakeholders pensions will eventually replace personal pension plans. The stakeholder concept was introduced in the Green Paper on pensions published in December 1998 and came into effect from April 2001. The main points are as follows.

- There is a cap on annual costs of 1%.

- They offer total flexibility with no penalties for stopping or restarting contributions.

- There is tax relief on contributions and virtually tax-free growth.

- The maximum contribution is £3,600 per annum even if there are no net relevant earnings.

- Stakeholder members who cease to work can continue to contribute for up to five years.

- Employers are still be able to offer group personal pension plans providing the employer pays the excess costs over 1% p.a., contributes 3% p.a. of the employee's earnings and there are no transfer penalties.

- Stakeholder pensions are targeted at the five million people who are employed or self-employed and yet make no pension provision.

- Employers must offer to their employees access to a stakeholder plan unless they have fewer than five employees.

Stakeholder schemes offer interesting tax planning opportunities. It is possible for an individual to contribute up to £3,600 p.a. for schemes established for his/her spouse and any number of children. Basic rate tax relief is due on the contributions which are also effective for inheritance tax planning. Benefits cannot be drawn before age 50 and so for children such plans are to be considered very long term.

Non-pensionable employment and self-employment

8.13 An individual in work may be in non-pensionable employment (i.e. where he is not a member of his employer's pension scheme or where his employer does not have a scheme) or be self-employed. In these circumstances, he will need to make provision for his own retirement. Due to the tax advantages available, this is still an important investment for

8.14 *Pensions*

those who are not able, or do not wish, to participate in an occupational pension scheme.

Prior to 1 July 1988, the usual way for such individuals to make provision for their retirement was by means of retirement annuity or similar contracts approved by the Inland Revenue under ICTA 1970, s 226. Such contracts could be effected and maintained by individuals under the age of 75 who were chargeable to income tax in respect of relevant earnings (ICTA 1970, s 226(1)). Section 226A provided for two further types of contract to be approved. The first type was one whose main object was the provision of an annuity for a spouse or dependants (independent of the individual's own annuity under section 226). The other type provided simply for payment of a lump sum on the death of an individual before he reached the age of 75.

From 1 July 1988 the approved personal pension arrangement (see above) replaced the retirement annuity contract for individuals who are self-employed or in non-pensionable employment and who were previously capable of effecting such contracts whether pursuant to section 226 or section 226A. In fact, many of the provisions governing personal pensions are based on the old rules relating to retirement annuity contracts which they have replaced. Since 1 July 1988, it has not been possible to take out any new section 226 or section 226A retirement annuity contracts, although it is still possible to pay contributions to existing contracts if they are regular premium policies or if their terms permit the payment of additional single premiums.

The provisions governing retirement annuity contracts are now contained in ICTA 1988, ss 618–629. Tax relief remains available in respect of qualifying premiums paid under existing contracts which are for the time being approved by the Inland Revenue (ICTA 1988, ss 619, 620).

There are a number of differences between the retirement annuity contract and the approved personal pension arrangement. For example, employers may only contribute to the latter and only the latter may be used to contract out of SERPS. Annuities under personal pension arrangements may in all cases commence at age 50, but under retirement annuity contracts the age is 60. Perhaps the most significant difference is that for retirement annuity contracts, there is no limit on the amount of net relevant earnings used to calculate the permitted percentage of qualifying premiums, although the percentages (starting at 17.5% and rising to 27.5%) are less favourable than for personal pensions (compare ICTA 1988, s 626 with ICTA 1988, s 640). For high earners, existing retirement annuity contracts can still offer excellent potential for pension funding.

Pensions and divorce

8.14 Often, one of the most valuable assets that a married couple possess will be a pension. There are three main ways of dealing with pension rights on divorce.

(a) *Set-off.* This is often the simplest method. The pension rights are treated as an asset which can affect one of the party's claims to another asset. For example, one party to the marriage may take the matrimonial house and the other may take the pension rights. The set-off method can therefore facilitate a clean break, although the pension rights may need to be actuarially valued.

(b) *Earmarking.* This was introduced by the Pensions Act 1995 and has become a common way of handling pension rights. Part of the pension benefits, once they fall to be paid, are 'earmarked' to the ex-spouse. For practical purposes, 'earmarking' does not facilitate a clean break. The pension due to the ex-spouse will not come into payment until the pension-holding spouse actually draws a pension. Furthermore, if the pension-holding spouse dies, the payment to the ex-spouse will cease. It is possible for the court to order the pension holder to nominate the ex-spouse as the beneficiary of lump sum death benefits, although again the inheritance tax position will need to be considered.

(c) *Pension splitting.* For couples starting divorce proceedings on or after 1 December 2000, a new option is introduced, namely pension splitting. Where a pension is to be split, pension rights are divided in the same way as other matrimonial assets. Part of the pension is transferred to the ex-spouse who then becomes the actual owner of the benefits. It could then be possible for the ex-spouse to establish a personal pension plan with these benefits and draw an income from the age of 50, or alternatively take actual membership rights in the members scheme. The transferred amount still counts against the transferring spouse's fund for the purposes of the Inland Revenue maximum benefits. It is not possible, therefore, for the transferring spouse substantially to rebuild their pension fund after divorce.

Lump sum death benefits under retirement annuity contracts or personal pension arrangements

8.15 As mentioned above, a retirement annuity contract or personal pension arrangement may provide for the payment of a lump sum on the death of the individual before the age of 75.

If the death benefit is payable as of right to the personal representatives of the deceased, it may be liable to inheritance tax as part of the deceased's estate (by virtue of IHTA 1984, s 4(1) and IHTA 1984, s 5(1)). However, there is no requirement under the relevant legislation for the benefit to fall into the individual's estate on his death and the benefit may instead be written in trust in favour of beneficiaries chosen by the individual.

Whilst the death benefits under all retirement annuity contracts are freely assignable, the death benefits payable under most personal pension schemes are not, since some schemes give the scheme administrator the power to appoint the death benefit amongst a specified class of beneficiaries. The terms of each scheme should therefore be checked to find out the position. In particular the Inland Revenue's own model rules issued in 1991 for personal pensions are potentially flawed in that they oblige the scheme administrator to

8.15 *Pensions*

pay the lump sum benefits to the trustees of any valid trust which has been set up by a member.

Most life offices (or any of the other relevant financial institutions) have suitable trust declarations which could be completed at the same time as a proposal for the pension arrangement. A similar declaration of trust may also be effected with regard to existing contracts or arrangements.

Usually under the terms of the trust, the entirety of the contract or arrangement will become trust property but since under the relevant legislation all annuity benefits and the right to a lump sum on retirement must not be capable of assignment, these benefits must under the terms of the trust continue to be held for the persons who were originally entitled to them. Hence, it is only in respect of the lump sum death benefit that express trusts for the benefit of third parties may be declared.

The precise terms of the death benefit trusts will depend upon the facts of each particular case but there are considerable advantages in settling the benefit on wide discretionary trusts. Provided the discretionary trusts come to an end within two years after the death (either by way of outright distribution or by converting the trusts themselves into, for example, interest in possession or accumulation and maintenance trusts), the usual inheritance tax regime for such trusts will not be applicable either during their existence or on termination. Such property is not treated as 'relevant property' for the purposes of IHTA 1984, Part III Chapter III (which sets out the tax regime for discretionary trusts) so long as it remains part of, or is held for the purposes of, any fund or scheme mentioned in IHTA 1984, s 151(1). This includes a retirement annuity contract or an approved personal pension arrangement.

Although the settlor must be capable of benefiting under the trusts of the contract or arrangement (because of his remaining entitled to the annuity benefits and the lump sum on retirement), the Inland Revenue have stated that this will not bring the trust within the gifts with reservation provisions of FA 1986, s 102 (Inland Revenue Press Release dated 9 July 1986).

One practical advantage of the existence of such a trust (and the only real advantage where the recipient of a lump sum benefit is to be a surviving spouse and thus an exempt beneficiary for inheritance tax purposes) is that it will speed up payment of the benefit on death by the institution in question. Provided there are existing trustees, on the death of the individual the institution will not need to wait for his personal representatives to obtain a grant of probate. It will simply need to see appropriate evidence of death, such as an office copy of the death certificate.

Where a person has effected a number of retirement annuity contracts over the years (perhaps with different institutions), if each contract and, in particular, the relevant death benefit is written in trust separately, there will be multiple trusts in existence. However, each trust may well have similar objects. It is therefore possible (and, indeed, advisable) in these circumstances for a 'master' trust to be established (either for a particular individual with multiple policies or for a group of individuals, such as the partners in a professional firm, each with separate policies) to receive and administer all lump sum death benefits payable under the existing contracts which will be assigned to the trustees. The same structure can also be used for existing and future personal pension policies.

Pensions and bankruptcy

8.16 There is still uncertainty surrounding the area of pensions and bankruptcy.

Certainly occupational schemes are protected as they are established under a trust normally declared by the employer. Furthermore, the Inland Revenue require occupational schemes to contain provisions that prevent a member assigning his/her pension.

On personal pensions and retirement annuity contracts the position is less clear. In *Landau (a bankrupt) (Re), [1997] 3 All ER 322* a retirement annuity contract policyholder was declared bankrupt in 1990. On discharge in 1993, the trustee in bankruptcy claimed that the retirement annuity contract should vest in him and the court decided that the pension fell under the definition of 'property' for the purposes of the Insolvency Act 1986.

In order to stop the same decision applying to personal pension plans, many insurance companies are now including forfeiture clauses in their PPP rules. These rules stipulate that if a member is declared bankrupt, his pension rights are forfeited. However, there is considerable doubt as to whether these forfeiture clauses are effective.

The Welfare Reform and Pensions Act 1999 contained provisions to protect both occupational and personal pensions from a trustee in bankruptcy. This Act is now in force and should protect pensions from anyone who is declared bankrupt after 29 May 2000. The new legislation covers all approved pension schemes but not unapproved ones.

The trustee in bankruptcy can still apply for a recovery of excessive contributions and can apply to attach an income payments order in respect of moneys being received by a bankrupt in excess of those required to meet an individual's normal domestic needs.

9 The Family Home

Introduction

9.1 Over the past 100 years or so, there has been a dramatic increase in home ownership. In 1914 10% of the population owned their own homes, 70 years later the figure had risen to 60%; we are once again in a period of increasing house prices. As Lord Diplock observed in *Pettitt v Pettitt, [1970] AC 824*, we have witnessed 'the emergence of a property owning, particularly a real property mortgaged to a building society owning, democracy.' As the family home is now the principal asset of most people who seek estate planning advice, and often it is their only significant asset, the family home is considered to merit separate treatment in this book.

Although the opportunities for mitigating the charge to inheritance tax are limited, they are nonetheless the ones frequently of most concern to the average client. It is rare for an estate planner to have a client whose wealth (or whose spouse's wealth) does not include a home of some sort.

This chapter will not be exclusively concerned with the position of married couples and, where appropriate, will highlight estate planning considerations that are relevant to unmarried couples and others who buy a home jointly, or in their sole name. In addition, except where a planning suggestion depends on creating different interests in land, no distinction will be made between freehold and leasehold ownership.

Ownership of property

9.2 In order to set estate planning considerations in context, it is first necessary to outline the two forms of joint ownership recognised by English land law.

English law draws a distinction between legal and beneficial ownership of land. Where legal ownership is held by two or more individuals they will hold it as joint tenants. The legal joint tenants will hold the land on trust for the beneficial owners (who may be, and usually are, themselves) and on the death of one joint owner the legal title vests in the survivor or survivors.

The law recognises two forms of beneficial ownership, namely:

(*a*) joint tenancy; and

(*b*) tenancy in common.

9.2 The Family Home

While in both cases, each beneficial co-owner is as much entitled to possession of any part of the land as the other, i.e. no one joint owner can claim this or that piece of the land as his own, there are two essential differences, which are of fundamental importance for estate planning. First, in the case of a beneficial joint tenancy, each co-owner can only have an equal interest in the land, or in its net proceeds of sale if it is sold, whereas in the case of a tenancy in common, it is possible for one owner to have a greater or lesser share than the other co-owner(s). For this reason, when people contribute to the purchase price of land in unequal shares, they should insist on the beneficial ownership being in the form of a tenancy in common, unless they are content to accept the equality of interest created by a joint tenancy (which in itself will result in a gift by one of the co-owners to the other with possible inheritance tax consequences). Secondly, and more importantly, in the case of a beneficial joint tenancy, when a co-owner dies, his interest passes automatically (and irrespective of any will which he may leave) to the surviving co-owner; whereas, in the case of a tenancy in common, the share of a joint owner passes on death in accordance with his will or, if he leaves no will, the rules of intestacy. For these reasons, of the two forms of beneficial joint ownership, a tenancy in common is usually to be recommended as being the more useful and flexible form of joint ownership for estate planning purposes.

In the case of unmarried couples, if a property is held on a tenancy in common, each co-owner should make a will dealing with the property on their death. This will avoid any family members holding the property contrary to the deceased's intentions.

Married couples, however, are still frequently recommended to purchase property as beneficial joint tenants on the ground that this is the most convenient and cost effective method of holding property should one of them die. While it is true that, in the event of death, no probate or other formalities are required beyond the simple one of placing a certified copy of the death certificate with the title deeds, such advice overlooks the risk of marital breakdown and the lesser risk of both spouses dying at the same time, for example, in a road accident.

In the event of a break-up of the marriage, it is almost an inevitable first step that the couple will be advised by their respective lawyers to terminate the beneficial joint tenancy in order to ensure that, in the event of premature death before the financial settlement on divorce has been completed, their respective interests do not go to their spouse. Similarly, the risk of both dying at the same time should not be overlooked. The Law of Property Act 1925, s 184 provides that where two people die in circumstances where it is not possible to say which of them died first, the elder will be deemed to have died first. This rule is modified in the case of spouses where the elder dies intestate so that each spouse will be deemed to have pre-deceased the other (Administration of Estates Act 1925, s 46(3)). However, this modification to the terms of section 184 does not apply to beneficial joint tenancies, so that, irrespective of whether or not the elder spouse left a will, his or her interest will pass automatically to the other spouse and then in accordance with that spouse's will, or intestacy. This could result in unintended consequences, with the property, in the case of a young couple without children, passing to one set of

The Family Home 9.2

parents to the exclusion of the other. In the case of a tenancy in common, each spouse's interest in the property will pass on intestacy as if the other had predeceased and this may result in a fairer division of the property between each spouse's immediate family.

Whichever form of co-ownership is used, the legal ownership must operate through a trust of land (Law of Property Act 1925, ss 34–36). This means that the property is held by both parties for their benefit. Under the Trusts of Land and Appointment of Trustees Act 1996 (TLATA 1996) trustees are no longer under a duty to sell the property. Neither party can sell the property without the consent of the co-owner unless an application is made to the court.

Where co-owners cannot agree on a sale, either may apply to the court for an order of sale (TLATA 1996, s 14). As the Court has a discretionary jurisdiction, such an application will create uncertainty as well as expense. In considering whether or not to order a sale, the court, which has complete discretion in the matter, will take into account the intention(s) of the person who created the trust, the purpose for which the property subject to the trust is held and the welfare of any minor who occupies or might reasonably be expected to occupy any land subject to the trust as his home (TLATA 1996, ss 14, 15).

The legal joint tenants are under a statutory duty to consult beneficiaries and give effect to their wishes insofar as these are consistent with the general interests of the trust (TLATA 1996, s 5 and TLATA 1996, s 11). Naturally, that is usually only of importance where the legal interests are held by different persons or in different proportions to the beneficial interests.

For the estate planner, the principal advantage of a tenancy in common is that it permits each co-owner to deal with his or her interest during life, or on death, according to their wishes. When compared to this flexibility, the advantages of a beneficial joint tenancy are small in most circumstances although a joint tenancy can always be severed by a notice in writing to the other joint tenant (Law of Property Act 1925, s 36(2)). The property will then be held as tenants in common. In the case of *Grindal v Hooper (The Times 8 February 2000)* the High Court held that for a severance to be effective, notice had to be served. In that case, the conveyance to the parties specified that any notice of severance should be annexed to the conveyance. This notice whilst served was not attached to the conveyance until after the death of one of the owners. The Court held that annexation was not essential to the validity of the notice.

A beneficial joint tenancy has an appeal for married couples for whom there is peace of mind in the knowledge that when one of them dies the other automatically becomes entitled to the entire family home, without the need to go to the trouble and expense of obtaining probate. The surviving spouse will take the interest of the first to die subject to any subsisting mortgage debt unless the will provides that another part of the estate will have this burden (Administration of Estates Act 1925, s 35). However, this can be provided for by means of a mortgage protection policy or a low cost endowment policy. Apart from this, the surviving spouse is free to sell or mortgage the property without further formality, as the trust terminates on death and the survivor can give a good receipt for the sale proceeds. Where property is held as tenants in

9.3 The Family Home

common, the trust of land survives the death of the first co-owner (unless the survivor inherits the share of the deceased co-owner) and the survivor must appoint a co-trustee in order to sell or otherwise deal with the property.

For both inheritance tax and capital gains tax purposes, no distinction is drawn between a beneficial joint tenancy and a beneficial tenancy in common in equal shares. In either case each tenant will be treated as the absolute beneficial owner of his share in the property. In the case of the death of a beneficial joint tenant, this result comes about for inheritance tax purposes because the tax is calculated by reference to the value of the deceased's estate immediately before his death which will include his beneficial interest in the property. An act of severance will not give rise to either an inheritance tax or a capital gains tax charge; nor to any stamp duty liability.

When drafting a will purporting to dispose of a share in jointly owned property, the adviser is under a duty to ensure that the joint tenancy has been or is later severed (*Keckskemeti v Rubens Rabin & Co, TLR 31.12.1992*).

Purchasing the family home

9.3 The first concern of most married couples is to ensure that, in the event of one of them dying, there will be a secure roof over the head of the survivor. Therefore, the family home should be purchased in joint names so that, whoever provides the purchase price or pays the mortgage instalments, each spouse has a beneficial interest in the family home. Although a tenancy in common is generally to be preferred, if the total wealth of the couple does not, and is not likely in the foreseeable future, to exceed the inheritance tax nil rate band (£0–£250,000), then this will be a case where the convenience and cost effectiveness of a beneficial joint tenancy may well outweigh the advantages of a tenancy in common.

If the family home is purchased by a couple as tenants in common, then it is important that the spouses either make or review their wills at the same time as completing the purchase. This is of paramount importance if there are children, because in that event the surviving spouse may find that in the absence of a will her entitlement on intestacy may not be sufficient to give her the other half share in the family home.

The entitlement of a surviving spouse on intestacy is as follows (Administration of Estates Act 1925, s 46, as amended):

Surviving next of kin of the deceased	*Spouse's entitlement*
Spouse alone (i.e. no children, no parents, no siblings or their issue)	Whole of the estate
Spouse and other relatives (i.e. parents, brothers and sisters and their issue) but no children	(*a*) Personal chattels (*b*) Statutory legacy of £200,000 (*c*) Half interest in residue absolutely
Spouse and children	(*a*) Personal chattels (*b*) Statutory legacy of £125,000 (*c*) Life interest in half of the residue

The Family Home 9.3

The surviving spouse can elect to take the family home in whole or partial satisfaction of any absolute interest in the deceased's estate, including the capital value of any life interest (Intestates' Estates Act 1952, s 5, Sch 20). If, as is often the case, the family home consists of the larger part of the value of the estate, the spouse could find herself in the position where part of the family home is held in trust for the children. Moreover, the home is appropriated at its value when the spouse makes her election and not at its probate value, so that increasing property values can have the effect of reducing the value of the statutory legacy, unless an election is made promptly.

Although the rules of intestacy are intended to reflect the wishes of the average person, they should not be relied upon as a substitute for a will. The intestacy rules will not necessarily result in the most appropriate devolution of one's estate; indeed, they may have effects which are entirely out of accord with the deceased's wishes.

In the case of unmarried couples, security and provision for what is to happen on death is even more important than for married couples. Under the intestacy rules an unmarried partner has no right to any share of the deceased partner's estate. The Inheritance (Provision for Family and Dependants) Act 1975 provides a partial remedy in that if the survivor was immediately before the death of the other partner being maintained either wholly or partly by him, the survivor can apply to the court for reasonable maintenance out of the deceased partner's estate. This will provide the unmarried partner with provision in the nature of income. Although the court has power to capitalise the sum awarded, it has no power to make capital provision. It is therefore imperative that both partners make wills giving their respective interests in the property to their partner.

There will of course always be circumstances where the couple wish the house to be bought only in the name of one of them. For example, where one spouse is a partner in a business or a sole trader, it may be appropriate that the property is bought in the sole name of the other spouse in the hope of providing some protection against the possibility of the first spouse's bankruptcy.

Where property is occupied by an unmarried couple but has been purchased in the sole name of one of the parties, the entire value of the property is subject to inheritance tax on the death of the deceased cohabitee. The Inland Revenue have argued that even where the surviving cohabitee has made contributions to the cost of the property, this does not reduce the value of property on the death of the deceased cohabitee. The Inland Revenue take the view that the beneficial rights of the surviving cohabitee do not exist unless the relationship breaks down, become litigious and a court order is obtained. This view is clearly wrong as such arrangements create a beneficial tenancy in common either under a constructive trust or by proprietary estoppel which is then enforced by the court after litigation. Therefore, prior to the death of the deceased cohabitee, the surviving cohabitee is already a joint owner in equity of the property (Taxation, 22 May 1997). It is also arguable that the value of the deceased cohabitee's share should be discounted on the basis that a notional purchaser in the open market would have to share possession with the surviving cohabitee.

9.4 *The Family Home*

Making provision in a will

9.4 There are various ways in which a tenant in common can deal with his beneficial interest in a property by will. When provision for the surviving spouse is of overriding concern, the will of each spouse should contain an absolute gift of their respective interests in the home to the other. The terms of the gift should not be limited to the particular property they may own at the time, but should be phrased to apply to whatever property is owned at the date of death. This will avoid the need to amend the wills every time the couple move home.

It is also advisable to include in the gift the benefit of any mortgage protection or endowment policy in order to prevent any argument that the surviving spouse must account for the part of the policy which is used to repay the survivor's share of the mortgage debt. It is even more important to cover this point where the house and mortgage are in joint names but the policy is taken out on the life of the principal wage-earner alone. A specific gift of the policy will also mean that any surplus from the policy in excess of the sum needed to repay the loan will pass to the same legatee and will not pass under the gift of residue. If this is not desired, then the will should provide accordingly.

At the same time provision should be made for what should happen in the event that both spouses die at the same time; for example, in a road accident. While the gift to the surviving spouse will be free of inheritance tax, the gift in default may not be, and consideration should be given to whether or not the tax should be borne by the beneficiary who receives the interest in the family home or by the residuary estate. In the absence of express provision, the tax will be treated as a general testamentary expense and paid out of residue (IHTA 1984, s 211). An unmarried couple also need to consider who should bear the tax.

Where the family home is the principal family asset, the opportunity to pass part of the family wealth equal to the value of the inheritance tax nil rate band will be lost if the interest of the first spouse to die goes to the survivor (in default of undertaking a deed of family arrangement within the statutory provisions). This may not matter if the couple are childless, or if any children are minors, or adults living at home, since the parents may wish to continue the existing state of affairs rather than introduce an element of uncertainty about ownership and occupation. However, failure to utilise the nil rate band of the first spouse to die can result in the overall inheritance tax liability being increased by as much as £96,800 at current rates. One method of utilising the nil rate band is to leave a share of the property equal in value to the deceased's unused part of the nil rate band to the next generation either outright, if over 18, or in trust if under 18.

The risk for the widow of this type of arrangement is that, unless her occupation of the property is secured by some form of tenancy agreement, the other co-owners may seek to force a sale of the property in order to realise their interests in it by an application to the court under the Trusts of Land and Appointment of Trustees Act 1996, s 14 (see 9.2 above).

A further possibility is to include in the will a discretionary trust of the deceased's unused nil rate band to which a share of the property may be

The Family Home **9.4**

appropriated. The beneficiaries of the discretionary trust might be the surviving spouse (who might also be a trustee) and the next generation. The will trust would contain a power to enable the trustees to allow the surviving spouse to occupy the property. The main problem with this route is that if the surviving spouse is given an exclusive or joint right of residence, the Inland Revenue may argue that an interest in possession has been created (see Inland Revenue Statement of Practice SP10/79). In *CIR v Lloyds Private Banking Ltd, Ch D [1998] STC 559* the Court of Appeal held that a life interest was created where a will provided that a surviving tenant in common was to have the right of exclusive occupation of the property concerned for life. Similar decisions were reached in *Woodhall (Woodhall's Personal Representative) v CIR, Sp C [2000] SSCD 558 (Sp C 261)* and *Faulkner (trustee of Adams, dec'd) v CIR, Sp C [2001] SSCD 112 (Sp C 278)*. These decisions provide some support for the Revenue's views expressed in SP 10/79 but it should be noted that the cases did not concern the occupation of property at notice by a discretionary beneficiary. The impact of the *Lloyds Private Banking* case could be avoided if, on the death of the first spouse to die, his or her interest in the property is devised direct to one of the children of the marriage. The child could then settle the property on a life interest trust for the surviving parent; there should of course be no prior undertaking that this would be the course of action. The terms of the trust would be that on the death of the surviving parent, the property would revert to the child of the settlor. There would be no inheritance tax charge on the death of the surviving parent due to the provision of IHTA 1984, s 54(1).

If a discretionary trust is used, the surviving spouse should not be a beneficiary of the trust. He or she would then rely on the right given to him or her by virtue of being a co-owner under a tenancy in common in respect of the remainder of the property in order to occupy the property. Even so, the efficacy of this route may be in doubt after the decision in *CIR v Eversden and another (executors of Greenstock deceased), Ch D [2002] STC 1109*. As Lightman J pointed out in that case, since the enactment of TLATA 1996 a tenant in common no longer has an automatic right of occupation unless the conditions of section 12 of that Act are fulfilled. Furthermore, this strategy can bring other problems. First, the capital gains tax exemption for principal private residences will not be available in respect of the proportion of the property held in the discretionary trust (although, in practice, any liability on disposal may be small due to the uplift to market value that will have occurred on death, the availability of the indexation allowance to 6 April 1998 and taper relief thereafter). Secondly, there is a question as to whether the trustees are properly exercising their fiduciary obligations by retaining a proportion of a property which is not producing income and which is occupied by a non-beneficiary.

It is understood that the Inland Revenue are currently monitoring such situations which are already in existence and may seek to argue that an interest in possession exists at the time of the death of the surviving spouse (STEP Conference 8 October 1999).

Often the deceased will prefer to leave his share of the family home directly to the next generation or in trust. It may be felt that the decision as to whether

9.5 The Family Home

the property should be jointly owned is best left to the surviving spouse as the person directly involved and best placed to judge matters following the death.

The surviving spouse may decide to utilise the deceased spouse's nil rate band by varying the dispositions of property devolving under the will or passing by survivorship within two years of death (IHTA 1984, s 142). This may be done by the surviving spouse giving a share of the property equal in value to the deceased's unused part of the nil rate band to the next generation either outright if over 18 or in trust if under 18, by means of a deed of variation. Provided the necessary elections under IHTA 1984, s 142 are made the gift will be treated as if effected by the deceased. Even if the widow continues to occupy the property, there is no scope for the gift with reservation provisions contained in FA 1986, s 102 and FA 1986, Sch 20 to apply since, if a variation is made, the widow will be treated as not having made a gift within section 102(1). If the share is placed by the variation into trust, however, the same issues arise as to whether an interest in possession is created as are discussed above.

For unmarried couples, similar considerations apply to will drafting, but special care is needed when considering the payment of inheritance tax. As a spouse exemption is not available to unmarried couples, they must pay particular care as to how inheritance tax can be paid by the surviving partner. If cash or other assets are not available, life insurance is generally the cheapest solution. However, it is important that the policy proceeds are written in trust for the survivor so that they do not form part of the deceased's estate thereby increasing the inheritance tax payable.

There is also a trap for the unwary if the property is mortgaged and there is an endowment or mortgage protection policy. If such a policy is not written in trust the proceeds will form part of the deceased partner's estate for inheritance tax purposes. This may have two unexpected consequences. First more tax than would otherwise be the case may be payable so that the property may have to be sold in order to pay the tax. Secondly, the policy proceeds may fall into residue and pass to the wrong beneficiary either under the will or on intestacy.

Lifetime planning

9.5 Lifetime planning for the family home has always been an area of estate planning fraught with difficulties because of the inherent contradictions involved. On the one hand, an individual wishes to give away all or part of the value tied up in his home at a low or nil tax cost, and on the other to retain a roof over his head. Whilst potentially exempt transfers encourage lifetime planning as no immediate charge to tax arises, at the same time the gift with reservation provisions (FA 1986, s 102 and FA 1986, Sch 20) make it difficult for an individual to continue to live at the property and give away some of the wealth represented by his home.

Any gift by an individual, including a gift of his home or an interest in it, is capable of constituting a potentially exempt transfer. Where the following conditions apply, no inheritance tax will be chargeable unless the donor dies

The Family Home 9.6

within seven years of making the gift. In the event of a transfer between three and seven years before death tapering relief is available.

The conditions are that the gift is made

(a)   to another individual(s); or

(b)   into an accumulation and maintenance trust within IHTA 1984, s 71; or

(c)   into a disabled person's trust within IHTA 1984, s 89; or

(d)   into a settlement in which an individual has an interest in possession.

In practice, nearly all lifetime planning for the family home tends to concern a gift to another individual, and only in exceptional circumstances will an individual wish to make a gift that falls within (b), (c) or (d).

Gifts with reservation

9.6   Before considering the planning opportunities available, it is necessary to consider the gifts with reservation provisions in order to understand the restrictions they place on planning in this area.

Under FA 1986, s 102, where an individual makes a gift of property and either:

(a)   possession and enjoyment of the property is not bona fide assumed by the donee within seven years of the donor's death; or

(b)   at any time within the seven-year period the property is not enjoyed to the entire exclusion, or virtually to the entire exclusion, of the donor or of any benefit to the donor by contract or otherwise,

the property is said to be subject to a reservation, with the consequence that the property (or its traceable proceeds) will be brought into charge to tax when the donor dies as if he were still beneficially entitled to it at that time.

There are a number of exemptions to the application of this provision set out in section 102(5) but they are of limited relevance to an individual wishing to benefit anyone other than his spouse.

If the property ceases to be subject to a reservation, the donor is treated as making a potentially exempt transfer at the time of the cessation (FA 1986, s 102(4)).

FA 1986, Sch 20, and in particular FA 1986, Sch 20 para 6, provides two further exemptions of importance in the case of gifts of interests in land. First, the donor may retain or assume actual occupation of land in return for full consideration in money or money's worth. This is a valuable concession which will be considered later. Secondly, an exemption may apply where the donor has made a gift of a property to a relative, or to a relative of his spouse, in circumstances which did not give rise to a reservation of benefit, but subsequently comes to re-occupy it as a result of an unforeseen and unplanned change in circumstances. Provided that at the time the donor has become unable to maintain himself through old age, infirmity or any other reason and his occupation represents reasonable provision by the donee for his care and

9.7 The Family Home

maintenance, his re-occupation will not taint the original gift as a gift with reservation. For example, a father, on retiring to the country, gave a house in London to his son and subsequently became infirm through ill-health, which resulted in him no longer being able to look after himself. He could safely move back into the house in London and live with his son. Provided this represented reasonable provision by the son for the care of his father no gift with reservation would arise.

The self-evident problem of the gifts with reservation provisions is that they make it very difficult for a person to give away property but to continue to occupy it whether his occupation is long-term under some form of tenancy or other binding arrangement entered into by the donee or merely intermittent as the gratuitous licensee of the donee. Clearly, the use of the word 'virtually' in FA 1986, s 102(1)(b) is designed to prevent merely occasional visits by a donor to the donee from tainting the original gift (see CTO Advanced Instruction Manual, para D.49 for the Revenue's view on how the word 'virtually' is to be interpreted, discussed in detail in chapter 2 *Lifetime Planning* under paragraph 2.15) but beyond that there is a vast grey area. Four strategies have emerged which are of practical relevance to an individual whose wealth is tied up in his home and which attempt to enable him to unlock some of this wealth without sacrificing the roof over his head.

The four strategies are

(a)   co-ownership;

(b)   use of the 'full consideration' exemption;

(c)   'shearing'; and

(d)   trust of debt.

Co-ownership

9.7   This involves the donor making a gift of an undivided share in land so that, after the gift, the donor and the donee share ownership and occupation of the property. Normally the donees are the children of the donor. Beneficial interests may be conferred on the children by the original owners entering into a declaration of trust specifying in what proportions the beneficial interests are to be shared; and in the case of a sole owner (e.g. a surviving spouse) one or more other members of the family, or a professional adviser, should be appointed as co-trustee of the legal title to ensure there are at least two (Law of Property Act 1925, s 27(2)) but not more than four trustees of land (Trustee Act 1925, s 34(1)).

The gifts of the beneficial interest will constitute 'potentially exempt transfers' for inheritance tax purposes, but provided the beneficial owners actually occupy the property and meet their respective share of the costs of the property, the continued occupation of the donor(s) will not amount to a gift with reservation. FA 1986, s 102B(2) provides that all gifts by an individual of an undivided share of an interest in land are gifts with reservation, subject to two exceptions.

The Family Home **9.8**

One of these exceptions is found in FA 1986, s 102B(4) which provides that there is no gift with reservation of benefit where the donor and donee occupy the land and the donor does not receive any benefit other than a negligible one which is provided by or at the expense of the donee for some reason connected with the gift. Where there is some collateral arrangement (i.e. an agreement that the donee should pay all the running costs), this will amount to a benefit to the donor 'by contract or otherwise'.

A problem will arise if and when any one or more of the donees decides to move out of the property, because if the donor(s) continues to occupy the entire property the gifts to the donees who move out will become gifts with reservation and this will largely defeat their original purpose.

The second exception is found in FA 1986, s 102B(3) which provides that in the event that one of the joint owners does not occupy the property, there will not be a gift with reservation if the donor pays full consideration for his occupation (see 9.8 below). The examples given by the Revenue are on the basis that joint owners take the property in equal shares. In the event that the transferor takes less than an equal share, the case will be referred (see CTO Advanced Instruction Manual D.41.2).

Use of the 'full consideration' exemption

9.8 The above co-ownership arrangement is said to be effective because the donor(s)' continued occupation of the part of the property given away is for full consideration (namely, allowing the donee(s) to occupy the part retained) and hence the exemption conferred by FA 1986, Sch 20 para 6(1)(a) applies. There are, however, rather more overt examples of the application of this exemption.

An individual, whose income provides sufficient financial security, may give away his home entirely and enter into an arrangement with the donee which will allow him to continue living there. The arrangement may take the form of either a lease or a licence depending on the circumstances. What is important is that the occupation is for full consideration in money or money's worth (IHTA 1984, Sch 20 para 6(1)(a)). The Inland Revenue accept that if the terms are the result of a bargain negotiated at arm's length with the parties being independently advised and follow the normal commercial criteria in force at the time they are negotiated, the condition of IHTA 1984, Sch 20 para 6(1)(a) will be satisfied (CTO Advanced Instruction Manual, para D52). This gloss on the wording of paragraph 6(1)(a) is taken from the Inland Revenue Interpretation RI55 above. The provisions of FA 1986, s 102A explained in 9.9 below contain similar provisions to paragraph 6(1)(a) allowing a donor to occupy property for full consideration (FA 1986, s 102A(3)).

The terms of the agreement and the amount of any rent or licence fee would also be an important commercial consideration. 'Full consideration' implies, in the case of a tenancy, an open market rent. As full consideration is required throughout the period the rent paid must be periodically reviewed. However, the Inland Revenue do recognise that there is no single value at which consideration can be fixed as 'full'.

231

9.9   The Family Home

An alternative to charging an open market rent would be to grant a long lease, i.e. with a term of at least 21 years at a peppercorn rent but at a premium at a market rate. As the lease would normally be for less than 50 years, a part of the premium would attract an income tax charge at a rate of up to 40% depending on the donee's marginal rate of income tax. The lease would be within the terms of the Local Government and Housing Act 1989, Sch 10 which would give the donor, or if he had died in the meantime, his successor, the right to continue in occupation after the lease expired. In addition, the Leasehold Reform Act 1967 might give the donor the right to buy back the freehold on favourable terms.

The clear disadvantages of this type of arrangement from the donor's point of view are, first, the payment (out of net income or capital) of the rent or any premium and, secondly, that the lease itself may be a valuable asset in the donor's estate. Whether this is an acceptable price to pay for the ability to divest his estate of a capital asset free of inheritance tax will depend on individual circumstances.

'Shearing'

9.9   Apart from the addition of the words ' . . . or virtually to the entire exclusion' in FA 1986, s 102(1)(b), the gifts with reservation provisions are in identical terms to those applied under the estate duty regime. Both the Inland Revenue and commentators accept that the case law on the estate duty provisions and the principles that these cases establish are still relevant. The case of *Munro v Commissioners of Stamp Duties of New South Wales, PC [1934] AC 61* established the principle that there was no reservation of benefit where the donor retained a benefit referable to a prior right rather than to the property which is the subject of the gift. Thus, a strategy was developed under which an individual owning the freehold of his home would grant a lease to a nominee for himself, thereby creating a leasehold interest and a freehold reversion. He then gave away the reversion and continued to occupy the property by virtue of his leasehold interest without, it was hoped, falling foul of the gifts with reservation provisions. In the early days of inheritance tax replacing capital transfer tax the Inland Revenue stated that they would look carefully at any such arrangement to ensure that the creation of the lease and the subsequent gift of the reversion were 'independent transactions' — Inland Revenue letter of 18 May 1987 (see Butterworths Yellow Tax Handbook Part II 2001/02). It was never entirely clear what this meant but subsequently the scheme was considered by the House of Lords in *Ingram & Palmer-Tomkinson (Lady Ingram's Executors) v CIR, HL 1998, [1999] STC 37*. The following discussion sets out the theory of the scheme in detail and then discusses the *Ingram* decision and the insertion of FA 1986, ss 102A-102C which followed that decision.

The scheme involved a two-stage operation. First, the prospective donor granted a lease for a term equal to his life expectancy plus a margin of 5 or 10 years, as appropriate, to a nominee without reserving any rent. As the donor had to create the lease first, he had absolute control over the terms of the lease and, unlike the 'full consideration' exemption, there is no obligation to use

The Family Home 9.9

open market terms. However, to avoid an Inland Revenue claim that the lessor's covenants created a reserved benefit the covenants were not onerous, because when the reversion was given away, the donee took the benefit of the lessor's covenants.

Secondly, after a suitable interval, the donor gave the freehold reversion to the donee by way of a potentially exempt transfer.

If the lease still had some time to run at the donor's death, its remaining value would be subject to inheritance tax.

If the lease expired before the donor died, then the donor would have to either move out of the property or pay a rack rent to avoid being in receipt of a 'reserved benefit'.

If the donor did not own the freehold, it was possible to achieve the same result with a leasehold interest by creating a sub-lease, if the head lease permitted that. Unfortunately most modern leases do not.

To execute the scheme in reverse was fatal unless there was full consideration. By giving away the freehold first and accepting a lease back from the donee, the donor received a benefit out of the property given away and FA 1986, s 102(1)(b) was infringed.

The House of Lords found this scheme effective in *Ingram*.

Having lost in the House of Lords, the Inland Revenue announced that they would block the scheme by amending the legislation. In due course, the Finance Act 1999 inserted FA 1986, ss 102A to 102C.

Section 102A applies when an individual disposes of an interest in any land by way of gift after 8 March 1999. If the donor or his spouse enjoy a significant right or interest, or is a party to a significant arrangement in relation to the land, the interest disposed of will be property subject to a reservation. A right, interest or arrangement is 'significant' for these purposes if it entitles or enables a donor to occupy all or part of the land (or enjoy some other right), otherwise than for full consideration in money or money's worth. The right, etc. is not significant if it

(*a*) cannot prevent another person or persons enjoying the land virtually or entirely to the exclusion of the donor;

(*b*) does not enable the donor to occupy the land immediately after the disposal but would have done so were it not for the disposal; or

(*c*) was granted or acquired more than seven years before the gift.

Similar provisions also apply to gifts of undivided shares in land under section 102B.

For the purpose of these provisions, no account is taken of occupation in circumstances where it would be ignored under FA 1986, Sch 20 para 6(1)(b). This is, broadly, where the donor falls on hard times and the donee makes provision for the donor out of the gift.

The Ingram scheme clearly falls within these provisions. As is unfortunately becoming common where anti-avoidance provision are sponsored by the

9.9 The Family Home

Inland Revenue, so too will many other arrangements which are not their ostensible target. For example, the provisions will apply in relation to some family farming partnerships.

There was always, however, an alternative method of achieving the same economic effect whilst avoiding the difficulties of the lease carve out which, in many circumstances, will not be caught by sections 102A-102C. Instead of making a gift of the freehold subject to an immediate lease in the donor's favour, the donor could make a gift of a long lease the rights of which are deferred for a period. For example, one might grant a 999 year lease which is not to commence for twenty years. A lease may defer the right of possession which it confers for up to 21 years after its execution (Law of Property Act 1925, s 149(3)). As the deferred lease is of small value, the value of the potentially exempt transfer is only small. However, the longer the individual survives, the lower the value of the freehold as the period to the beginning of the lease shortens. In effect, the value of the property is transferred to the deferred lease which is outside the estate for inheritance tax purposes. The freehold on the death will therefore have a much reduced value. The Revenue have always indicated that in their view the associated operations provisions apply to this scheme. That seems entirely misconceived as, unless one regards death itself as an operation, the scheme consists of only one operation; the grant of the lease. The deferred lease version of the shearing scheme may circumvent section 102A if the freehold concerned was originally acquired by the donor more than seven years before the transfer. The CTO apparently consider that the grant of the deferred lease will be a 'significant arrangement' within FA 1986, s 102A(2) even if the grantor acquired the freehold of the land more than seven years before the grant. Now it is clearly true that the grant of the deferred lease is an 'arrangement' to which the donor is a party. The question is whether it is a significant arrangement. The provisions of section 102A(4) are obscure but appear to prevent such a grant from being a 'significant arrangement'. It has been acknowledged by the CTO Director that for reversionary interest lease schemes made before 9 March 1999, the schemes did work. At a STEP conference on 8 September 1999 he indicated that the CTO's view is that the strategy is ineffective in relation to reversionary leases executed on or after 9 March 1999, a view which he repeated in a College of Law video in the following year. That view is probably incorrect.

There are a number of disadvantages with this scheme, namely the base cost for capital gains tax purposes will be very low because, at the time of acquisition, the deferred lease is not very valuable. In addition, the holder of the deferred lease will not receive the principal private residence exemption (see above) and there will be only a small uplift on death. This scheme is only likely to be appropriate where the property is held until death and it is a family property which is not intended to be sold.

It may be possible for parents to sell their home for the full value to their children, thus ensuring that any future capital appreciation accrues to the children. The money may be raised by way of a qualifying loan to reduce the purchase price, with the parents paying full rent against which the children's interest liability could be set. This should avoid the gift with reservation of benefit problems because there is no disposal by way of gift. However, there

The Family Home 9.11

are problems with security of tenure and there may also be stamp duty on the sale by the parents to the children. In addition, the principal private residence exemption is unlikely to be available on the ultimate sale by the children.

Trust of debt strategy

9.10 The fourth strategy for reducing inheritance tax on the family home is the trust of debt strategy. Under this strategy, the owner of the home settles a small sum on trusts of which he is the life tenant. He then sells his home to the trustees of this trust for an amount which is to be payable upon his death and which is not to increase or bear interest in the meantime. He now has a debt due to him which he settles on trusts for those he wishes to benefit. He has reserved a benefit in the property which he transfers to the trustees but as he is treated by IHTA 1984, s 49(1) as the beneficial owner of that property, the fact that the property is subject to a reservation does not lead to an increase in inheritance tax charge (FA 1986, s 102(3)).

The donor has not reserved a benefit in the debt. Although the debt is not repayable until after his death and bears no interest, the property settled is the contractual debt itself including all of its terms. The net effect is that the donor will have taken the current value of the debt (which will normally be the market value of the property) out of his estate for inheritance tax purposes.

There should be no capital gains tax charge on the donor on the assumption that the house has been his principal private residence throughout the time that he has owned it. There will, however, be a stamp duty charge on this sale of the home to the life interest settlement trustees unless the sale of the house is allowed to rest in contract. When the debt is repaid, there will be a capital gain realised by the trustees holding the debt. Because they will not be the original creditor, the disposal will not be exempt from capital gains tax (TCGA 1992, s 251(1)). The trustees will be deemed to have acquired the debt at its market value at that time and, because the debt is not repayable until after the death of the donor, that value is likely to be less than the principal amount of the debt (TCGA 1992, s 17).

'*Eversden* Schemes'

9.11 The case of *CIR v Eversden and another (executors of Greenstock deceased), Ch D [2002] STC 1109* has also been widely seen as permitting a tax planning strategy. In that case a settlor settled her home ('Beechwood') as to 5% for herself absolutely and as to 95% on trusts giving her husband a life interest subject to a wide power of appointment in favour of a class of beneficiaries which included the settlor. The settlor and her husband occupied Beechwood together until the husband's death. Thereafter, the trustees sold Beechwood and brought another house ('Maitland') again as to 5% for the settlor absolutely and as to 95% subject to what was now a discretionary trust. The settlor continued to occupy Beechwood and then, after its purchase, Maitland until her death. The question for decision was whether the 95% interest held on discretionary trusts was property subject to a reservation in relation to the settlor.

9.12 *The Family Home*

The Court held that. by virtue of the settlor's occupation of the house. the trust fund was not enjoyed to the entire, or virtually to the entire, exclusion of benefit to the settlor. The settled property was not property subject to a reservation, however, because when the settlement was made it was an exempt inter-spouse transfer under IHTA 1984, s 18. FA 1986, s 102(5) disapplies the gifts with reservation provisions where the gift is exempt under various provisions which include section 18.

The general financial press has assumed that the facts in this case can be used as the basis of an *'Eversden* scheme'. Caution should, however, be exercised. The application of the *Ramsay* principle and of the associated operations provisions was not argued in the case. Nor was there a finding of fact that the settlement was deliberately designed to provide an inheritance tax advantage, whilst allowing the settlor uninterrupted occupation of the donated property. In a case concerning a pre-planned scheme, these issues may well be the subject of consideration by the Court.

Other considerations

9.12 Before embarking on any tax planning affecting the family home, the beneficial ownership of the property should be checked and also whether there is an outstanding mortgage. A transfer of the ownership of the property subject to a mortgage will require the consent of the mortgagee. The transfer of the equity can also trigger a stamp duty charge to the extent of the mortgaged debt.

Capital gains tax

9.13 The capital gains tax consequences of any gift of land (or of an interest in land) have to be carefully considered. In relation to the donor's only or main residence there is unlikely to be a problem because any gain arising on the gift is likely to be exempt under TCGA 1992, s 222. Where, however, the gift relates to a home where the principal private residence exemption is not, or not wholly, applicable, a chargeable gain will arise which can only be held over if the gift constitutes a chargeable transfer for inheritance tax purposes (TCGA 1992, s 260). Generally, this will only be where the gift is a gift to a discretionary trust (even if its value falls within the nil rate band).

If a charge to capital gains tax which cannot be held over does arise, then the tax may be paid by ten equal annual instalments (TCGA 1992, s 281), although interest on the tax will run from the date the tax is payable under TCGA 1992, s 7.

In relation to a second home, it may be possible to mitigate the capital gains tax charge by electing, under TCGA 1992, s 222(5)(a), for the second home to be treated as the donor's main residence for the two years immediately preceding the gift, although this may result in there being a charge on any later sale or gift of the donor's other property.

The Family Home **9.14**

Summary and other points

9.14 The deferred lease strategy achieves a significant inheritance tax advantage but it may be that this is obtained at the price of an equal capital gains tax disadvantage. The scheme is likely to be most appropriate when the donee intends to live in the property after the donor's death rather than to sell it. The trust of debt strategy normally comes closest to achieving the taxpayer's objective of taking a substantial amount of value out of the charge to inheritance tax whilst allowing the donor to continue to occupy the family home.

The other two approaches to saving inheritance tax mentioned above also suffer from the disadvantage that once the donor gives up his home or an interest in it, the benefit of the capital gains tax principal private residence exemption (TCGA 1992, s 222) on any subsequent sale will be lost. More important perhaps is the fact that he will lose the security that goes with being a home owner. By giving away his capital, he loses his financial freedom and, where a lease is used, his ability to move, unless the donee agrees to join in a sale and purchase an alternative property on similar terms.

CIR v Eversden and another (executors of Greenstock deceased), Ch D [2002] STC 1109 does not of itself permit settlements for spouses to solve the problem of making or effecting a gift of the family home.

In addition to the above arrangements, the following, rather more obvious but no less effective, options should always be considered.

(a) *Move to a smaller home.* Perhaps the most efficient step that can be taken is to sell the property, move to somewhere smaller and thereby realise some of the accumulated capital value. This creates two assets — the new home and a capital gains tax free cash sum that can be given away. This option is likely to be viable only where the children have all grown up and left home.

(b) *Reduce the value of the home by mortgage.* If a couple are reluctant to move, but still wish to give away during their lifetime some of the accumulated value of their home, they may be able to do so by borrowing against its value and giving away the proceeds. This is only feasible if there are sufficient funds available from other sources to service the borrowing and it should be borne in mind that the interest payments will not qualify for mortgage interest relief. On death the outstanding mortgage debt will be deductible for inheritance tax purposes, albeit that the debt itself will still have to be met by the estate.

Where the donors are prepared to give away a property, for example, a second home, without ever wishing to occupy it again, then the inheritance tax position is, by comparison, straightforward; but as we have seen the capital gains tax position may be more complicated.

As in all lifetime planning, but especially in the case of the family home, the primary concern will be for the financial and residential security of the owner or owners — tax saving should always take second place. For this reason,

9.14 *The Family Home*

lifetime estate planning for the family home is often very limited in scope and the individuals concerned may be better advised to use other assets.

10 The Family Business

Introduction

10.1 This chapter deals with estate planning for the person who carries on business either as a sole proprietor, as a partner in a family partnership, as a member of a limited liability partnership ('LLP') or as a shareholder in a family company. Planning for such persons is normally dealt with together under some general heading like 'business property' because of the connection between the financial affairs of the individuals and those of their businesses, stemming from the fact that interests in a business and shares in a trading company may all be capable of qualifying for inheritance tax business property relief and capital gains tax business asset taper relief. Although this chapter follows this practice, it should be borne in mind that the ideas presented here can apply to all types of 'business property' even if not technically capable of qualifying for the relief. Whilst the tax treatment of companies and partnerships can give rise to considerable complexities and, because of their legal nature, can require rather more sophisticated planning techniques, the basic estate planning principles set out in chapter 1 *What is Estate Planning?* and chapter 2 *Lifetime Planning* apply to shares and business interests in exactly the same way as they do to any other item of property.

Inheritance tax

Business property relief

10.2 The provisions relating to inheritance tax business property relief are contained in IHTA 1984, ss 103–114. The relief is capable of applying to the following types of property (referred to in those sections as 'relevant business property').

(*a*) Property consisting of a business or an interest in a business.

(*b*) Securities of an unquoted company which, either by themselves or together with other such securities owned by the transferor gave the transferor control of the company. 'Control' for these purposes means voting control on all matters affecting the company as a whole, other than questions as to the winding up of the company or the varying of class rights (IHTA 1984, s 269(1), (4)). The votes attaching to any shares owned by the transferor's spouse, or by a charity set up by the transferor or his spouse (IHTA 1984, s 269(2)), or by a trust in which

10.2 The Family Business

the transferor has a beneficial interest in possession (IHTA 1984, s 269(3)), will be taken into account in determining whether the transferor has control.

(c) Any unquoted shares (but not securities) in a company.

(d) Quoted shares which confer control.

(e) Land, building, machinery or plant used wholly or mainly for the purposes of a business carried on by a company controlled by the transferor or by a partnership of which he is a partner.

(f) Land, building, machinery or plant which is settled property in which the transferor has an interest in possession and which is used wholly or mainly for the purposes of a business carried on by him.

For the purposes of business property relief, shares or securities are 'quoted' if they are quoted on a recognised stock exchange (IHTA 1984, s 105(12A)). Shares dealt in on the Alternative Investment Market are regarded as unquoted.

It is provided that property to which an LLP is entitled, occupies or uses is treated as property to which its members are entitled or which they occupy or use as partners. (IHTA 1984, s 267A).

A business or an interest in a business which consists wholly or mainly of one or more of the following activities cannot be relevant business property, namely making or holding investments or dealing in securities, stocks, shares, land or buildings (other than as a market maker or a discount house); nor can shares and securities in a company whose business wholly or mainly consists of one or more of those activities unless the company is wholly or mainly the holding company of one or more trading companies whose businesses do not consist of one or more of those activities (IHTA 1984, s 105(3),(4)).

In determining of what a business consists one has to look at the whole question in the round, paying attention to the overall context of the business, the capital employed, the time spent by the proprietors and employees as well as at the turnover and profits (*Weston (Weston's Executor) v CIR, Ch D [2000] STC 1064*).

To qualify as relevant business property, property must have been owned by the transferor throughout the two years immediately preceding the relevant transfer (IHTA 1984, s 106). This requirement is modified where the property has been acquired to replace other relevant business property or has been acquired by a person on the death of his or her spouse (IHTA 1984, ss 107, 108).

Where part of the value of any relevant business property is attributable to an asset which is not used for the purposes of the business or is not required for future use in the business, the value of that asset will not be taken into account when determining the value of the relevant business property (IHTA 1984, s 112). An example of this would be where a company, shares in which qualify for business property relief, owns a house or a yacht which is used solely for the personal benefit of one of the shareholders. Where there is cash in a bank account which has not been used for a long period it may be

The Family Business 10.2

excluded from relief because it cannot be said to be 'required' for future use if it was not in fact used for a long period. See *Barclays Bank Trust Co Ltd v CIR, Sp C [1998] SSCD 125 (Sp C 158).*

The relief operates to reduce the value of any relevant business property transferred by an actual or deemed transfer of value by 100% in the case of property falling within paragraphs (*a*), (*b*) and (*c*) above. In all other cases, the reduction in value is 50%.

The relief applies to the value transferred by both transfers of value during a person's lifetime and on his death. The relief can also apply to a potentially exempt transfer which becomes chargeable, and to a lifetime chargeable transfer which becomes chargeable with additional inheritance tax, by reason of the transferor's death within seven years of the transfer. However, in the latter cases, for the relief to apply, certain additional conditions have to be met. Broadly speaking, the transferee must continue to own the property until the transferor's death, or until his own death if earlier, and on the assumption that a transfer of value of the property given were to take place on the transferor's death, or on the transferee's death if earlier, the property would then satisfy all the conditions necessary for the relief to apply other than the minimum period of ownership requirement i.e. it must continue to qualify as 'relevant business property' as defined in IHTA 1984, s 105 (IHTA 1984, s 113A). The transferee may dispose of the original property given to him provided, broadly, that he reinvests the proceeds in other 'relevant business property' within three years or such longer period as the Inland Revenue allow. (IHTA 1984, s 113B).

As much business property is wholly relieved from inheritance tax by business property relief it might be thought that the impact of inheritance tax can be ignored. It is, however, important to remember that, even if 100% business property relief is prima facie available in respect of a gift, that relief will be lost if the transferor dies within seven years of making the gift unless the necessary conditions are still satisfied at the time of the transferor's death.

The transferee should therefore be warned, for instance, of the consequences of a sale of the business property within the seven-year period. Less obvious perhaps is the impact of a quotation of shares on a recognised stock exchange within that seven-year period. For instance, where shares were previously unquoted, or dealt in on the Alternative Investment Market and the transferor, prior to the gift, did not have control of the company concerned, a quotation of shares on a recognised stock exchange would result in the complete loss of business property relief which would otherwise have been available at 100%.

Business property relief may apply to property owned both by individuals and by the trustees of a settlement whether the settlement is one with an interest in possession or not. Where the settlement is one with an interest in possession the beneficiary with that interest will be the 'transferor' for the purposes of the relief and he will also, by reason of his interest, be treated as the 'owner' of the property comprised in the settlement.

Any property which is subject to a binding contract for sale at the date of the transfer cannot be relevant business property, except where the property is either an unincorporated business, or an interest in one, and the sale is to a

10.3 The Family Business

company which will carry on that business in exchange for shares or securities of the company, or the sale relates to a reconstruction or amalgamation of shares or securities in a company (IHTA 1984, s 113). Section 113 can sometimes apply in unexpected situations. The Inland Revenue, for example, consider that it applies where under the terms of a partnership the personal representatives of a deceased partner are obliged to sell and the continuing partners are obliged to buy (either at valuation or in accordance with a stated formula) the deceased's share or interest in the partnership (Inland Revenue Statement of Practice SP 12/80). This view was reaffirmed in the Law Society Gazette 4 September 1996. This type of provision therefore should be avoided, although section 113 will not be infringed by a provision which either confers an option on the continuing partners to buy the share (or indeed cross options which can be exercised to compel such a sale). The problem might be overcome if the partner retains a small share of the partnership or the partnership agreement provides for the deceased partner's share to accrue automatically to the continuing partners, whether or not in return for a payment, because this will not constitute a binding contract for sale.

Interest-free instalment option

10.3 In addition to business property relief, certain types of business property may qualify for the option to pay inheritance tax by ten equal annual interest-free instalments. The relevant statutory provisions are to be found in IHTA 1984, ss 227-229 and IHTA 1984, s 234. This option applies to the following types of property.

(a) Property which consists of a business or an interest in a business.

(b) Quoted or unquoted shares or securities which confer control (as defined by IHTA 1984, s 269).

(c) Unquoted shares and securities where the charge arises on death and not less than 20% of the total tax charged at that time is attributable to the value of those shares or securities or to other property which qualifies for the instalment option.

(d) Unquoted shares or securities if the Inland Revenue are satisfied that the tax attributable to them cannot be paid in one sum without undue hardship. In considering whether undue hardship exists, the Inland Revenue look primarily to whether it is reasonable to expect the tax to be paid immediately in the light of available resources (Hansard Official Report, 22 June 1972, Standing Committee, Cols 1358–1359).

(e) Unquoted shares (but not securities) if the value transferred exceeds £20,000 and either the nominal value of the shares is not less than 10% of the nominal value of all shares of the company at the time of the transfer or the shares are ordinary shares and their nominal value is not less than 10% of the nominal value of all ordinary shares of the company at that time.

For the purposes of sections 227 and 228 'unquoted' in relation to any shares or securities means not listed on a recognised stock exchange.

The instalment option applies to chargeable transfers on death but only to lifetime chargeable transfers if the transferee bears the burden of the tax. The option only applies to the tax chargeable on a potentially exempt transfer which becomes chargeable, or to the additional tax payable on a lifetime chargeable transfer, because of the death of the transferor within seven years. The property must be either owned by the transferee until the death of the transferor (or until his own death if earlier) or, in calculating the tax payable on the death of the transferor, the property in question qualifies for business property relief on the death of the transferor. There is an additional condition in the case of unquoted shares or securities that they must remain unquoted until the death of the transferor or the earlier death of the transferee.

If the property qualifying for the instalment option, or part of it, is sold, then the option ceases to apply to the unpaid tax or, in the case of a sale of part, the relevant proportion of the unpaid tax. For these purposes the payment under a partnership agreement of a sum in satisfaction of the whole or part of a partnership interest will be treated as a sale of that interest.

The impact of the 100% rate of business property relief is significant when considering estate planning for sole traders, partners, members and shareholders.

Capital gains tax

10.4 Taper relief reduces the chargeable gains subject to capital gains tax. The amount of taper relief on a gain depends on whether the asset disposed of is a business or a non-business asset (TCGA 1992, s 2A(3)). The relief will apply to assets which have been held for a qualifying period of at least one year. The qualifying holding period is the period during which the asset has been held. This ends on the date of disposal and begins with the later of 6 April 1998 and the actual date of acquisition. Where non-business assets were acquired before 17 March 1998, the qualifying holding period is increased by one year. This also applied to disposals of business assets before 6 April 2000. The amount of taper is calculated by the percentage of the gain chargeable for the number of complete years in the qualifying holding period. Gains on business assets are written off more quickly than gains on non-business assets. After two complete years only 25% of the gain on business assets is chargeable to capital gains tax. Business assets are defined as follows.

(1) In determining whether an asset is a business asset for any period before 6 April 2000, the following assets are business assets.

   (*a*) Shares in a trading company or a holding company of a trading group where the taxpayer is an individual, the trustees of a settlement or personal representative and where at least 25% of voting rights in the company are exercisable by the taxpayer.

   (*b*) Shares in a trading company or holding company of a trading group which are owned by the taxpayer who is an individual or the trustees of a settlement and where at least 5% of the voting rights in the company are exercisable by the taxpayer and the

10.4 *The Family Business*

individual, or, as the case may be, an eligible beneficiary is a full-time working officer or employee of the company or of another company which has a relevant connection with it.

An eligible beneficiary is, loosely, a beneficiary with an interest in possession.

(c) Assets owned by an individual, the trustees of a settlement or personal representative which are used in a trade carried on by the owner or by a company whose shares qualify as business assets in relation to the owner.

(2) In determining whether an asset is a business asset for any period after 5 April 2000, the following assets are business assets. 'Shares' for this purposes include securities. The Finance Act 2002 provides that any debenture within TCGA 1992, s 251(6) will now be treated as a security for taper relief. The rules apply for disposals taking place after 5 April 2002.

(a) Shares in a company which is a qualifying company in relation to a shareholder.

A company is a qualifying company in relation to an individual shareholder if it is either a trading company or the holding company of a trading group (special rules have been introduced to allow companies taking part in joint ventures to satisfy this condition) *and*

(i) the company is unlisted; or

(ii) the individual was an officer or an employee of the company or a company in the same commercial association of companies; or

(iii) the voting rights in the company were exercisable as to not less than 5% by the individual.

For disposals and holding periods after 16 April 2002, the definitions of trading company and trading group have been amended. The definitions are now based on the activities of the company rather than its purposes. The definition of holding company has also been amended so that any company that has 51 per cent subsidiaries will be a holding company, irrespective of its other activities.

In relation to an individual who is an officer or employee of a company, the company will also be a qualifying company where it is a non-trading company provided that the individual does not have a material interest in the company or in a company which it controls. A material interest for this purpose is, loosely, a 10% interest.

Similar conditions apply in relation to trustees except that condition (ii) must be satisfied by an eligible beneficiary (loosely, a beneficiary with an interest in possession with the result that that condition cannot be satisfied in relation to

The Family Business **10.4**

discretionary trustees). Conditions (i) and (iii) but not (ii) may also be satisfied in relation to personal representatives.

(b) In relation to a disposal by an individual, an asset is used in a business if it is used for the purposes of:

(i) a trade carried on by that individual or by a partnership of which that individual is a member;

(ii) a trade carried on by a company which is a qualifying company in relation to that individual;

(iii) a trade carried on by a company which is a member of a trading group with a company within (ii); or

(iv) any office or employment held by that individual with a person carrying on a trade.

Similar rules apply for disposals of assets by trustees. An asset used in a trade carried on either by the trustees or by an eligible beneficiary qualifies as a business asset. This now includes trades carried on by trustees in partnership.

In relation to personal representatives, an asset is a business asset if it is *either* used in a trade which they carry on *or* used in a trade which is carried on by a company, which in relation to the personal representatives is a qualifying company or is part of a trading group, the holding company of which is such a company.

Two points should particularly be noted. First, it is possible to receive taper relief on assets used by a company with which the disponer has no other connection, even if the assets are leased or licensed to the company at a market value. Secondly, and absurdly, because different definitions of business assets apply according to the period for which an asset's status is to be determined, a disponor can be worse off if he has owned an asset since before 6 April 2000 than if he has acquired it on or after that date. This anomaly has forced many people to transfer their business assets into trust so as to maximise relief on a future sale.

An asset which is used partly for trade purposes and partly for other purposes is treated as two separate assets, and an apportionment must be made according to use. An apportionment will be made where an asset has been a business asset for part only of the relevant period of ownership. The company must carry on trading activities and its whole activities must not include to a substantial extent non-trading activities, but if that condition is satisfied there is no restriction relating to the company's assets. Thus, there is no chargeable business asset test and no asset-based exclusion, although in determining the activities of the company, the Inland Revenue will have regard to the nature of its assets. In addition, for acquisitions after 6 April 1998, the qualifying holding period runs from when the asset is first purchased. There is no restriction if the value of the asset is disproportionately enhanced by subsequent allowable expenditure. Thus, a taxpayer who buys a parcel of land

10.4 The Family Business

for £1,000 in year one and subsequently spends £100,000 in building on it will enjoy full taper relief if he sells the building during year eleven.

The implications of the hold-over relief provisions in TCGA 1992, s 165 and TCGA 1992, s 260 have been considered in chapter 2 *Lifetime Planning* at paragraph 2.17 and reference should be made to that coverage for a more detailed discussion of these provisions.

The hold-over relief conferred by section 165 will apply to most forms of 'business asset' dealt with in this chapter. The relief is capable of applying to disposals made by both individuals and the trustees of settlements. In the case of trustees owning assets used for the purposes of a trade, profession or vocation, the trade, etc. may be carried on either by the trustees or by a beneficiary with an interest in possession in the settled property (TCGA 1992, Sch 7 para 2(2)(a)). Where trustees own shares or securities of a trading company or of the holding company of a trading group, the shares or securities must either be unquoted (and for these purposes shares dealt in on the Alternative Investment Market are unquoted) or the trustees must hold at least 25% of the voting rights exercisable by the company's shareholders (TCGA 1992, Sch 7 para 2(2)(b)).

It is interesting to note that section 165 refers to assets 'used for the purposes of a trade, profession or vocation' but not to 'a business or an interest in a business' (compare, for example, retirement relief: TCGA 1992, s 163(2)(a)). At first sight this might seem to preclude any application of the relief to a gift of the whole or part of a business or an interest in a partnership; but since a business is usually made up of a collection of separate assets used for the purposes of the business (e.g. stocks, plant and equipment, goodwill, etc.), there appears to be nothing preventing section 165 applying to each separate asset and thus in effect to the whole business. Indeed, the Inland Revenue accept that section 165 applies to a transfer of an entire business to a company.

Since section 165 applies both to business assets and to 'an interest in' business assets, the same argument should admit the application of section 165 to gifts of interests in a partnership. The business in question must, of course, be a trade, profession or vocation.

If the asset has not been used by the transferor for the purposes of the trade, etc. throughout its period of ownership, the amount of the held-over gain will be correspondingly reduced (TCGA 1992, Sch 7 paras 5, 6). On the disposal of shares, if the assets of the relevant company, or where that company is a holding company, any of its subsidiaries, include chargeable assets which are *not* used in the company's trade, profession or vocation, then the held-over gain is reduced to reflect the proportion which the chargeable business assets bear to all the chargeable assets of the company or group (TCGA 1992, Sch 7 para 7).

When considering estate planning for the businessman, it is essential to bear in mind that for capital gains tax purposes all assets owned by a deceased person immediately prior to his death are deemed to be acquired by his personal representatives at their current market value (TCGA 1992, s 62). This provides a tax-free uplift on death. However, this will not arise where the asset has

The Family Business **10.5**

been given away during his lifetime so that any inheritance tax savings which may be achieved by lifetime planning must be considered in the light of the loss of this capital gains tax-free uplift.

The gains held over under section 165 are gains before reduction by taper relief. That is because taper relief is given by reducing the aggregate gains for the year under TCGA 1992, s 2(2) and not individual chargeable gains accruing under TCGA 1992, s 2(1) (TCGA 1992, s 2A).Therefore when a hold-over claim is made in respect of any gain the benefit of any taper relief is lost.

Since 9 November 1999, hold-over relief is not available on disposals of shares or securities to a company (TCGA 1992, s 165(3)(b)).

As inheritance tax and capital gains tax are payable at the same maximum rates (40%) and 100% business property relief may be available for inheritance tax purposes even where the businessman still owns the business property on his death, consideration of the capital gains tax implications of estate planning is extremely important and may be a significant deterrent to making lifetime gifts. This situation has, to some extent, been alleviated by the business asset rate of taper relief being 75% after two years of ownership. However, other factors may still prevail and it should always be remembered that business property relief may be changed or abolished in the future, so that there may be considerable merit in taking advantage of the generous rates of relief whilst they remain.

Incorporation

10.5 Before considering in detail estate planning in relation to each of the businesses of a sole proprietor, a partnership, a limited liability partnership ('LLP') and a company, a few general points will be made about the advantages and disadvantages of incorporating a business.

A business may be either incorporated or unincorporated. The decision whether or not to start a new business through a company or a LLP or to roll an existing business into a company or LLP will be governed by a number of factors, including the need for limited liability and the taxation consequences. Some of these factors are pertinent to estate planning although with 100% business property relief applying to small minority shareholdings in private trading companies, the major tax advantage previously associated with a partnership as opposed to a company or LLP (i.e. the availability of 100% relief of any partnership interest irrespective of its size) no longer applies.

There are, of course, far more formalities involved in setting up and running a company or LLP than a partnership. There are accounts to be made up and filed, annual returns to be made, annual meetings to be held. In a family context, this extra degree of administration is an important consideration. On the other hand, shares in a company are, subject to any restrictions or rights of pre-emption contained in the Articles of Association, generally more easily transferable around a family than interests in a partnership. The same point applies to a LLP. Whilst a partnership interest can be assigned without the assignee becoming a partner (Partnership Act 1890, s 31), more usually

10.5 The Family Business

partnership interests are transferred by inviting the intended donee to join the partnership. It is easier in practice to be a passive shareholder in a company or a passive member of a LLP than a passive partner in a partnership.

A further important tax consideration in comparing a partnership or LLP with a company arises if the vehicle is holding, or is likely to hold, chargeable assets on which a significant capital gain is likely to be realised. A common example is land. On any sale of such an asset by a partnership or LLP, there is only one disposal by the partners or members, which is charged to capital gains tax at up to 40% on the chargeable gain, subject to the availability of taper relief. The proceeds are then freely distributable to the partners or members without further tax cost. On the other hand, the same sale by a company would result in a corporation tax charge for the company at 30% (19% if the small companies rate applies) of the chargeable gain and a further capital gains tax charge for the shareholders, if the company is ever liquidated or the shares are sold, of up to 40% on the increase in value in their shares attributable to the gain in the value of the underlying asset. Thus, increases in the value of company assets are potentially subject to a double charge. What is more, whereas taper relief is available to individuals, it is not given to the chargeable gains of companies which continue to receive indexation relief up to the month of disposal.

The position, however, is somewhat alleviated by the reduced rates of tax which apply to dividend income and the non-repayable tax credit which attaches to them.

> *Example (at 2002/03 rates of tax)*
>
> A company sells some land with a base cost of £20,000 for £120,000 so that a chargeable gain of £100,000 arises.
>
> There will be a corporation tax liability (assuming the full rate applies to the whole gain) of £30,000. If a dividend of £70,000 is paid out of the sale proceeds, it will be accompanied by a non-repayable tax credit of £7,778. If the shareholders are basic or lower rate taxpayers, there will be no further tax charge. If they pay higher rate tax, they will have an additional liability of £17,500, giving rise to a charge at an overall rate of 47.5%.
>
> Had the asset been sold by a partnership or LLP then (ignoring the availability of any annual or other exemptions and assuming all the partners are higher rate taxpayers) chargeable gains after two year's taper relief would be £25,000 and would have suffered a capital gains tax charge on the tapered gain of £10,000 or 10% of the gross gain.

This system of reduced rates of tax on dividends coupled with non-repayable credits was introduced to replace the previous imputation system of advance corporation tax and repayable credits which was abolished with effect from 6 April 1999.

From the point of view of flexibility and simplicity there is much to commend the unincorporated business though, for many businesses, the limited liability conferred by incorporation will often be the deciding factor.

A sole proprietor, partners in a partnership or members of a LLP wishing to transfer their business to a limited company in exchange for shares in that company can do so without any inheritance tax or capital gains tax arising. For inheritance tax purposes, there will be no transfer of value (IHTA 1984, s 10) and for capital gains tax purposes either TCGA 1992, s 162 or TCGA 1992, s 165 will apply to 'roll-over' or hold-over any gain which would otherwise accrue on the disposal of the business into the shares issued in exchange. 100% business property relief is available on small minority holdings in private trading companies. In addition, the replacement property provisions (IHTA 1984, s 107) ensure that minority holdings received on incorporation will qualify for relief immediately.

It used to be the case that incorporating a business by making gifts within TCGA 1992, s 165 had the added advantage that only nominal stamp duty was payable. Unfortunately, in most incorporations a gift of land to a company will now be treated as a transfer on sale for a consideration equal to the market value of the property. It will therefore be stampable at rates of up to 4%.

Incorporation may also have income tax consequences (for example, there will be a cessation of the business) which will need to be carefully considered.

The sole proprietor

10.6 The sole proprietor of a business will usually depend on that business for his livelihood. He is therefore likely to retain it either until his death, when it will be brought into charge to inheritance tax (although 100% business property relief will be available provided the necessary conditions are satisfied) or at least until he retires, when the business may either be sold or passed on to other members of his family who are interested in taking it over. At this stage he may wish to give the business to, for example, his children and again it is possible that 100% business property relief will be available for inheritance tax purposes. Even if it is not because, for example, he does not satisfy the two year ownership rule, the gift may constitute a potentially exempt transfer (IHTA 1984, s 3A) which will escape the inheritance tax net completely provided he survives for a period of seven years after the gift. Any chargeable gains arising on the gift may be held-over under TCGA 1992, s 165.

In addition, retirement relief may be available (TCGA 1992, ss 163, 164 and TCGA 1992, Sch 6) to provide capital gains tax relief on chargeable gains realised on disposals of certain types of business property by persons who have attained 50 whether or not they have retired and individuals under 50 who retire early on grounds of ill-health. Retirement relief is to be abolished with effect from 6 April 2003.

The relief applies to disposals of the whole or part of a business, assets which have been used for the purposes of a business or shares or securities in certain companies. There are various conditions attaching to the relief, relating (for example) to the period of ownership of the property in question.

The amount of retirement relief is dependent upon the period of time that the relevant conditions have been satisfied. This period must be a continuous period of a minimum of one year prior to disposal and, to obtain full relief, the qualifying period must be ten years. If full relief is available for 2002/03,

10.6 The Family Business

the first £50,000 of gain is wholly exempt from capital gains tax and 50% of the gain between £50,000 and £200,000 is exempt. The appropriate percentage being determined according to the length of the qualifying period and being on a scale rising from 10%, where the qualifying period is one year, to 100% where the period is ten years. The qualifying period is broadly the length of time during which the relevant property has been owned by the transferor. This is the last year in which retirement relief will be available. The relief will be withdrawn after 5 April 2003.

The possible availability of this relief should always be considered where a disposal has been made or is to be made. Retirement relief is automatic in its application and has the obvious advantage over hold-over relief and rollover relief of reducing some or all of the gains completely, rather than simply carrying them forward. To the extent that any gain accruing on a disposal *is* wholly relieved by retirement relief then TCGA 1992, s 165 will not apply (TCGA 1992, s 165(2)(a)).

A gift of a business may involve the donee agreeing to indemnify the donor against his liabilities to unpaid creditors. Whilst the commercial reality behind such an agreement is clear and in effect simply means that the donee takes over the net assets of the business, the true legal analysis of the gift is that it involves the sale of the business for a consideration equal to the outstanding liabilities, which will have certain tax consequences. First, stamp duty will be payable on the consideration if it is in excess of £60,000. Secondly, the ability to hold-over any chargeable gains which would otherwise accrue to the donor on the gift under TCGA 1992, s 165 may be restricted if the consideration exceeds the donor's acquisition cost (TCGA 1992, s 165(6)). Thirdly, there may arguably be a gift with reservation for inheritance tax purposes under FA 1986, s 102, although this may not cause difficulty in practice. It is argued that, even assuming that a sale at an under-value can be a gift within section 102, as to which there must be some doubt, those provisions can only apply to the gift element of the transaction and provided no benefit is reserved to the donor which is referable to the gift element, there can be no reserved benefit. The indemnity from the donee does not, the argument goes on, relate to the gift element. To amount to a gift with reservation there must be a benefit additional to the indemnity. It is understood that the Inland Revenue accept this view.

The sole proprietor of the business may, however, wish to share the running of the business, and its profits, prior to his retirement with other members of his family. In practice, it is most likely that he will do this by bringing them into either a partnership or a LLP with him. For example, he may bring his wife into a partnership or LLP in order to share with her some of the profits of the business with a view to reducing their overall income tax burden. Provided that his wife takes an active role in the partnership or LLP and her share of the profit is commensurate with this there may be a resulting income tax saving. Alternatively, the proprietor may wish to bring one or more of his children or grandchildren into a partnership or LLP with him. The tax consequences of his doing this are both more complex and more far reaching and are dealt with in the next section.

Before turning to consider the creation of a partnership, however, two further points should be made. The first is in relation to borrowings. This general point is relevant to any property which is capable of qualifying as relevant business property for inheritance tax purposes. If the sole proprietor proposes to provide additional funds for his business by borrowing, he should ensure as far as possible that the borrowings are charged on assets owned by him which do not form part of the business. In this way the charge will be an incumbrance under IHTA 1984, s 162(4) and should, in principle, reduce the value of that property, which will not qualify for any relief on his death, rather than reduce the value of property which would in any event qualify for 100% business property relief. It should be noted, however, that the Inland Revenue may seek to argue that the value of the business for the purposes of the relief must still be calculated after deducting the liability (CTO Advanced Instruction Manual W.9). This is on the basis that IHTA 1984, s 110 provides that the value of a business for the purposes of the relief is its net value and that the net value is after deducting liabilities 'incurred for the purposes of the business'. It is not clear whether section 110 overrides section 162(4) or vice versa.

It is important to remember that in the context of a sole proprietor, inheritance tax business property relief only applies to a transfer of the whole business, or to a share in that business; it does not apply to a transfer of an asset used in the business unless that asset is so fundamental to the business that it effectively amounts to a part of the whole. This is a result of the application in an inheritance tax context of the principles applied in the case of *MacGregor v Adcock, Ch D [1977] STC 206; [1977] 3 All ER 65* where capital gains tax retirement relief was denied on the disposal of part of a farm on the grounds that the asset disposed of was not a part of the taxpayer's farming business.

In practice, however, provided some thought is given to the gift in advance, it should not be difficult to structure it in such a way that the disposal is of a share of the business, or alternatively of a separate business, rather than merely an asset used in that business.

Finally, one of the kinds of sole business proprietor frequently met in practice is the Lloyd's Underwriter or 'Name'. However, the nature of his business is such that there is no scope for lifetime estate planning in relation to the Name's underwriting interests other than making sure his will is properly drawn up and for this reason Lloyd's underwriting interests are dealt with in chapter 16 *Planning for Death* at paragraph 16.47.

Partnerships

10.7 Partnerships are extremely flexible vehicles but are subject to considerable complexities and uncertainties in their tax treatment. In particular, it is very difficult to apply the capital gains tax legislation to them largely because of the legal distinction which exists between (on the one hand) the notion of partnership property and (on the other) the share or interest of a partner in a partnership. The latter is a chose in action comprising a bundle of contractual rights which one partner has against the other partners and does not necessarily represent a specific quantifiable

10.7 *The Family Business*

interest in the underlying partnership assets, although each partner has an interest in those assets and they are jointly owned by the partners. For capital gains tax purposes, the chose in action is largely irrelevant and each partner is treated as owning a specific proportion (whatever that may be) of the underlying assets (see TCGA 1992, s 59).

As a result of the uncertainty which the complex legal nature of partnership rights creates, reliance is placed upon Statements of Practice SP D12, SP1/79 and SP1/89.

When creating a partnership many factors have to be considered, but foremost from an estate planning point of view are the following.

(a) The amount of cash or other property to be contributed to the partnership by each partner and the extent to which this is to be reflected in his or her capital account.

(b) The rights of each partner (or his personal representatives) to extract from the partnership his share of the partnership assets on his death or retirement.

(c) The proportions in which the partners are to share both the trading profits of the partnership and on a dissolution any surplus assets remaining after all creditors and all capital contributions of the partners have been repaid. (Surplus assets will be shared by the partners in the same proportions as they share in the trading profits, unless the partnership agreement states otherwise.)

An asset surplus on a dissolution will only usually arise as a result of an increase in value in the partnership assets above their original book values (i.e. ignoring any depreciation and any replacement of assets). Unless there is a revaluation of the partnership assets, with a corresponding increase or decrease in the partners' capital accounts, the original book value of the partnership assets will correspond to the amounts of capital contributed by the partners. Any increase in value therefore will represent a capital profit of the partnership which may be realised or unrealised by the time of dissolution. On a dissolution, the surplus will be distributed between the partners either in stated proportions or, if the partnership agreement is silent on the matter, in the proportions in which the trading profits of the partnership are shared. The partnership agreement may, on the other hand, state that all the capital profits (whether realised or unrealised) arising in respect of a particular asset shall belong to one or more particular partners, and the result of this is that on the dissolution the division of surplus assets will be modified accordingly.

For capital gains tax purposes, the disposal of a partnership asset is taxed in the hands of the partners in the proportions in which they share the surplus assets of the partnership, unless all profits in respect of one particular asset are expressed to belong to one or more particular partners, in which case the gains will be taxed only in his or their hands (Statement of Practice D12 paragraph 2). Where an automatic accruer or option provision applies on the death of a partner (see below), he may still be treated for capital gains tax purposes as owning a share in the assets of the partnership during his lifetime and taxed accordingly.

The Family Business **10.8**

The possible permutations on all the factors mentioned above are enormous and the following are examples of some of the more common types of partnership arrangement.

(1) A, B, and C agree to introduce capital equally and to share trading profits and any surplus assets on dissolution equally. On the death or retirement of any one of them, he (or his personal representatives) is entitled to take from the partnership the full value of his partnership interest, subject to the continuing partners having the option to buy it for its full market value. Alternatively, if A, B and C contribute capital in unequal shares, they may decide to share the trading profits and surplus assets in the same proportions rather than equally.

(2) As in (1), except that on the death or retirement of any partner, he (or his personal representatives) is entitled only to take the balance on his capital account and his share of accrued trading profits, with the rest of his partnership interest accruing automatically without payment to the continuing partners.

(3) A, B and C agree to introduce capital equally and to share trading profits equally, but agree that any surplus assets on a dissolution shall belong only to B and C equally. On the death or retirement of A, he (or his personal representatives) is entitled only to take the balance on his capital account and his share of accrued trading profits (with the rest of his share accruing automatically without payment to B and C); but on the death or retirement of B or C, they (or their respective personal representatives) are entitled to receive the full value of their partnership interests subject only to an option for the continuing partners to buy it at its full market value.

Each arrangement will have differing inheritance tax and capital gains tax consequences for the partners which are discussed in what follows.

The formation of a partnership

Inheritance tax

10.8 In the case of the sole proprietor of a business who wishes to bring his son into partnership, it is probable that 100% business property relief will be available so that no actual inheritance tax liability will arise. It is, however, useful to consider how the transaction will be analysed for inheritance tax purposes as there may be occasions where the relief is not fully available, or is subsequently lost because the proprietor dies within seven years of the gift and the necessary conditions are not met at that time (IHTA 1984, s 113A).

The proprietor and his son are connected persons under IHTA 1984, s 270. There will be no transfer of value on the formation of the partnership if the father did not intend to confer any gratuitous benefit on his son (or indeed on any other person) and that the terms of the son's entry into the partnership were such as might be expected to be made in a similar arrangement at arm's length between unconnected persons (IHTA 1984, s 10). In general, for this

10.8 The Family Business

condition to be satisfied it will be necessary for the son to provide such consideration as would have been required had the transaction been a normal commercial one, but in the context of a family partnership, it is often difficult to identify precisely what would amount to normal commercial terms. Some of the relevant factors are considered below.

If the formation of the partnership cannot be brought within IHTA 1984, s 10, there will be no transfer of value provided the formation does not result in any reduction in the value of the father's estate. For example, if the father has the business valued and then introduces it to the partnership with his capital account being credited with the full value of the business then, even if he and his son share the trading profits of the partnership equally, there should be no inheritance tax consequences for the father, provided he is able to determine the partnership and recover his capital contribution on demand or within a reasonably short period (say three months).

If the full value of the existing business is not credited to the father's capital account and, for example, the father and son share profits equally, then on the partnership being wound up and the business sold, unless otherwise agreed, the son will share the proceeds of sale equally with his father after the balances on capital account have been repaid. This is the effect of Partnership Act 1890, s 44, which provides that, in the absence of any express agreement, any surplus assets left after the payment of all debts, advances and capital contributions are shared between the partners in the proportions in which they shared the profits. Partners do not share surplus assets in proportion to their capital contributions unless this is expressly agreed. As a result, the father, on taking his son into partnership on such terms, will clearly have made a gift to him of part of the business unless the partnership agreement was such as might have been made between unconnected persons dealing at arm's length and the father had no gratuitous intent towards either his son or any other person.

One would generally expect that in a normal commercial arrangement the son would have to buy into the partnership and effectively purchase a share of the business from his father. Arguably, a capital contribution by the son which is credited to his own capital account would not be sufficient. There would have to be some consideration passing to the father — either outside the partnership or perhaps by way of credit to the father's capital account. The case of *Attorney-General v Boden, KB [1912] 1 KB 539* is often cited as authority for the proposition that consideration may be non-monetary. In that case, it was held that two sons had given full consideration (in the form of an agreement to devote as much time and attention to the business as it required as compared with their father being only required to devote as much time and attention to the business as he thought fit) for a provision that their father's share in the goodwill of the business would automatically accrue to them without payment on his death. It is, however, dangerous to rely on the principles of this case applying to circumstances other than ones very similar to its facts. It may be appropriate to regard a covenant to work full-time in a business as adequate consideration for the deferred acquisition of goodwill on the death of a partner — goodwill being an asset which depends to a great extent on the amount of time and energy put into a business — but it is quite another thing to regard such a covenant as adequate consideration for the acquisition of an immediate interest in a partnership and an interest extending beyond the goodwill to the other assets of the partnership. Undoubtedly, each case will turn on its own facts and there may be circumstances where a similar covenant could make up the difference between partial and full consideration.

Even if 100% business property relief is not fully available, any element of gift inherent in the formation of the partnership may constitute a potentially exempt transfer by the father to his son and will escape inheritance tax provided the father survives for the necessary seven-year period. One can insure against the risk of his death in this period.

Reservation of benefit

10.9 Will the formation of a partnership amount to a gift with reservation for inheritance tax purposes? The provisions of FA 1986, s 102 can apply to a gift where either possession and enjoyment of the property concerned is not *bona fide* assumed by the donee or the property is not enjoyed to the entire exclusion of the donor and of any benefit to him by contract or otherwise. In the context of a partnership, it is often quite difficult to decide whether or not the provisions have any application. Clearly, if the formation of the partnership is on full commercial terms, there is no gift and therefore no question of the provisions applying. Where, however, there is an element of gift, it is essential to first identify the subject matter of the gift. On the formation of the partnership, the subject matter of the gift will not be an interest in the partnership because prior to the gift the partnership will not exist. Instead, it is the granting of certain contractual rights against the donor in respect of the property which is to become the property of the partnership (the business) coupled with the acquisition of the legal title to and/or a beneficial interest in that property. In almost all cases, possession and enjoyment of the subject matter of the gift will be *bona fide* assumed by the donee; so it is important to establish whether or not the donor is excluded from any benefit from the property given away. One must also consider the anti-shearing provisions of FA 1986, ss 102A-102C (see chapter 9 *The Family Home* at paragraph 9.9).

A father who is already in partnership with one of his sons, may give his partnership share to another son and retire from the partnership but remain as a consultant or employee. Provided the employment is on commercial terms and the remuneration is not excessive, this would not be regarded as a gift with reservation (CTO Advanced Instruction Manual D.48). What is reasonable is to be tested by reference to what might reasonably be expected under an arm's length arrangement between unconnected parties.

If the father were to give his son an interest in a specific percentage of the capital assets of the partnership (e.g. by way of crediting his capital account), together with an interest in a corresponding percentage of the trading profits, it is unlikely that there will be a problem. However, there may be a problem where the son is given an interest in a particular share of the assets of the partnership but a lesser share of the profits so that the father takes a share of the profits greater than his retained share of the capital assets. This is because the father could be said to have reserved a benefit out of the property given to his son by reason of his receiving a share of the profits in excess of the capital

10.10 *The Family Business*

retained by him. If, therefore, the father wishes the son to take a greater share of the assets of the partnership but a lesser share of the profits, it is probably safer from the gifts with reservation viewpoint to defer the son's right to share in the assets by means of an automatic accruer or option provision to take effect on the father's death or retirement rather than by giving him an immediate interest (see below). However, as we shall see, the introduction of an automatic accruer or option provision gives rise to other inheritance tax problems.

A similar reservation of benefit problem could arise where the father reserves a right to receive the first slice of any profits of the partnership up to a specific amount.

Capital gains tax

10.10 If the business introduced by the father into the partnership includes any chargeable assets (e.g. goodwill, land or tangible movables worth more than £6,000 each), then there may be a 'disposal' of these assets for capital gains tax purposes giving rise to a capital gains tax charge. As the assets of a partnership are, for capital gains tax purposes treated as belonging to the partners in the proportions in which they share surplus assets (which in turn will be the proportions in which they share the profits of the partnership unless stated otherwise), for capital gains tax purposes there will be a disposal to the extent of the interest taken by the son. For example, if the father and son simply agree to share profits equally, then there will be a disposal of 50% of the chargeable assets. If the father was given full credit for the value of the business in his capital account, he will have received actual (and full) consideration for the disposal so he could not elect to hold over the gain under TCGA 1992, s 165.

There will, however, be no disposal if, under the terms of the partnership, all capital profits in relation to the business are expressed to belong to the father. If the partnership agreement is subsequently altered so that the son becomes entitled to a proportion of those profits, this alteration will be treated by the Inland Revenue as a part disposal for capital gains tax purposes of the father's partnership interest (see Statement of Practice SP D12 paragraph 7) but hold-over relief (under TCGA 1992, s 165) should then be available as no consideration would have been given for the disposal. Where there is a change in the ratios in which surpluses on assets are shared between *unconnected* partners, the Inland Revenue treat the disposal as taking place at book value (i.e. on a no gain/no loss basis), unless there is a direct payment of consideration outside the partnership or there is or has been a revaluation of the partnership assets and a corresponding increase in the partners' capital account (Statement of Practice SP D12 paragraph 4).

A similar capital gains tax problem arises if the father has first taken his wife into partnership with him. At that stage he may well not have had his business valued because of the availability of the spouse exemption (IHTA 1984, s 18) preventing any inheritance tax consequences. However, if their son is taken into partnership having first valued the business and having that value credited to their capital accounts, then on the son receiving a share in the assets of the

The Family Business **10.11**

partnership, the Inland Revenue would treat his parents as making a part disposal of the partnership assets (Statement of Practice SP D12).

Options and accruers

10.11 The terms of the partnership deed will also need to outline the position on the death or retirement of one of the partners. It is quite common for an agreement to contain a provision which allows the retiring partner or the personal representatives of the deceased partner to extract his capital contributions and his share of accrued trading profits with the remainder of his partnership interest accruing automatically to the surviving partners or, alternatively, granting the continuing partners an option to acquire the interest for a nominal consideration. In such a case, when valuing the interest of the deceased or retiring partner in the partnership, its value should be restricted to the sums due under the partnership agreement and no account should be taken of the then value of the underlying assets of the partnership business. Although the case of *Burdett-Coutts v CIR, [1960] 1 WLR 1027; [1960] 3 All ER 153* is sometimes cited as authority for the proposition that the value of the partnership interest of a deceased partner should be by reference to the underlying assets of the partnership, that case was in fact dealing with the position where the death caused the partnership to dissolve. That is not comparable to a situation which a partnership continues notwithstanding the death of one partner.

In the opinion of the Inland Revenue such an automatic accruer or option provision amounts to an exclusion or restriction on the right of the deceased or retiring partner to dispose of his share and it should only therefore be taken into account when valuing his interest to the extent that consideration was given for it (IHTA 1984, s 163). Whilst the Inland Revenue's argument may have some force if the automatic accruer or option provision is added as a term of a partnership *after* its formation, it is more difficult to sustain where the provision is a term of the partnership from the outset. This is because, on introducing any property to the partnership, the partner concerned will exchange his interest in that property for the 'chose in action', comprising his bundle of partnership rights in which the restriction on what he may extract from the partnership on his death or retirement is inherent from the outset. There is no question of the partnership agreement itself placing an exclusion or restriction on his right to dispose of any property which pre-existed the agreement.

If, however, the Inland Revenue's argument is correct — and, in practice, it is advisable to order one's affairs on the assumption that it is correct, unless one is prepared to go to considerable time and expense in arguing to the contrary — then on the death of the outgoing partner the existence of the automatic accruer or option provision will only be taken into account in valuing the interest if the continuing partners gave full consideration. This will be a question of fact in each case and will depend on all the circumstances surrounding either the formation of the partnership or, if later, the time when the provision was introduced as a term. In determining this the precise scope of the accruer or option will have to be taken into account: whether it relates to the entire partnership share, or just to the outgoing partner's interest in

10.11 *The Family Business*

surplus assets, or to his share of the goodwill of the partnership. Other factors include the respective amounts of capital contributions; the profit-sharing ratios and the surplus asset-sharing ratios; the time each partner is required to devote to partnership matters; the respective ages of the partners; the duration of the partnership; and the terms on which distributions will be made on the death or retirement of any of the partners. It is understood that if all the partners are of commensurate age, and each partner's share is subject to the same automatic accruer or option provision, then each gives full consideration for its existence because none of them know which of them is likely to die first. However, the same argument cannot be applied where there is a considerable divergence in the ages and therefore is of little help in a family partnership which includes members of different generations. Possibly, on the strength of *Attorney-General v Boden, KB [1912] 1 KB 539*, a covenant to work full-time in the partnership business by members of the younger generation could count as (or towards) full consideration, if no similar covenant is required of the older generation. In addition, an agreement by the younger partners to provide an annuity to any retiring partner or to the widow of a deceased partner could be taken into account as full or partial consideration, although in the Inland Revenue's view (see the ICAEW Memorandum of 19 September 1984 reproduced at 1994 STI p 651) an automatic accruer on death in return for a widow's annuity will result in a loss of business property relief.

Subject to what is said above, the existence of such an automatic accruer or option provision will not prevent the partnership interest of the deceased partner from qualifying for inheritance tax business property relief (see the Inland Revenue's Statement of Practice SP 12/80 dated 13 October 1980 and the table published in the Law Society's Gazette of 6 May 1981 at page 480). Although, once the deceased partner's estate has received all sums due from the partnership, the instalment option will cease and outstanding inheritance tax (if any) will be payable immediately.

Unless an automatic accruer or option provision has been incorporated for full consideration, it is unlikely to prevent an inheritance tax charge arising on the death of a partner in respect of the whole of his partnership share subject, of course, to the availability of business property relief. Subject to this, when bringing one or more children into partnership, the father should aim to give to them as large an interest in the partnership as he feels comfortable about giving away in the hope that he will survive the gift by seven years. Due to the impact of the gifts with reservation provisions, the share of trading profits retained by the father should not exceed his interest in the assets of the partnership. An automatic accruer or option provision could also be inserted in an attempt to limit the taxable part of the father's partnership interest to (say) just the balance on his capital account plus his share of any accrued trading profits, but as we have seen this may not be successful.

Alternatively, the partnership agreement could provide that any capital profits, whether realised or unrealised, of the partnership should belong to the next generation. As the passing of the growth element is immediate rather than deferred until death or retirement, IHTA 1984, s 163 should not apply. However, if there is any element of gift in the creation of the partnership the reservation of benefit rules may apply. Another problem with this type of

The Family Business **10.13**

provision is that to insert it in the partnership *ab initio* may well result in a disposal for capital gains tax purposes by the father of the entire business (to the extent it includes any chargeable assets) and (as we have seen) TCGA 1992, s 165 may not be available to hold-over the gains. However, such a provision could subsequently be inserted in a pre-existing partnership and in such circumstances the relief should be available.

Existing partnerships

10.12 Returning to the earlier example, let us assume that the father has now brought his son into partnership with him. The full value of the father's business has been credited to his capital account. The son has introduced a sum of £10,000 into the business which has been credited to his capital account. They share profits equally; but on the death or retirement of either, he, or his personal representatives, are only entitled to extract from the partnership the sum credited to his capital account and his share of accrued trading profits. The balance of the share in the partnership automatically accrues to the survivor without payment. The son has also covenanted to devote his full time to the business but there is no corresponding obligation on the father.

As we have seen, this type of arrangement is designed to freeze the value of the father's partnership interest so that any growth in value of the partnership assets will accrue automatically to the son. What further estate planning steps are now available to the father?

In considering the following paragraphs it should be remembered that, in most instances, 100% business property relief will be available whether further steps are taken during the father's lifetime (subject to potential loss of relief if he dies within seven years of the gift) or whether the son inherits under his father's will. In addition, there will be a capital gains tax-free uplift if the father still owns his share at the time of his death. However, the uplift will be lost if he makes lifetime gifts, although retirement relief may be available to reduce the amount of gains to be held-over under TCGA 1992, s 165.

Transfer of capital

10.13 The father may over a period of time make gifts to his son of his partnership capital, simply by debiting his capital account and crediting his son's. This process can use up the father's annual inheritance tax exemption of £3,000; alternatively, larger sums may be passed over as potentially exempt transfers. The Inland Revenue appear to accept that a partner's capital account amounts to an interest in a business, rather than just an asset used in the partnership business (CTO Advanced Instruction Manual L.15.1). Therefore, if the father were to die within seven years of making a potentially exempt transfer, 100% business property relief will be available (assuming all the other conditions are satisfied) to reduce the value of the gift to nil.

Where sums are left on capital account after a partner's retirement from the partnership, they will not represent an interest in a business and will not,

10.14 *The Family Business*

therefore, receive business property relief (*Beckman v CIR, Sp C [2000] STCD 59 (Sp C 226)*).

Is a gift of part of the capital account a gift with reservation for inheritance tax purposes? As the sum still remains part of the capital of the partnership, it is clearly arguable that the donor continues to benefit from it whilst he remains a partner. However, perhaps the better argument is that any such benefit is not referable to the gift itself, but arises from the pre-existing partnership agreement which binds, and continues to bind, the subject matter of the gift, so that the 'shearing' principle applied in the case of *Munro v Commissioners of Stamp Duties of New South Wales, PC [1934] AC 61* will apply.

Introduction of accruers or options

10.14 Where an existing partnership does not contain any automatic accruer or option provision, it would be possible to incorporate one by a supplemental agreement. If this gives rise to an immediate reduction in the value of the father's estate but the son gives full consideration the exemption conferred by IHTA 1984, s 10 should apply. What will amount to full consideration will depend on the precise circumstances and, in particular, the scope of the automatic accruer or option provision itself. If the son does give full consideration, then on the death or retirement of his father full account will be taken of the automatic accruer or option provision and IHTA 1984, s 163 will not be applicable. If, on the other hand, the son does not give full consideration, then any transfer of value by the father will be a potentially exempt transfer for inheritance tax purposes. However, IHTA 1984, s 163 may apply on the subsequent death or retirement of the father to bring the full value of the father's partnership interest into the charge to inheritance tax, subject to the availability of business property relief. It is unlikely there would be a gift with reservation for inheritance tax purposes, since the property given is a right to all or a part of the donor's partnership interest only on his death or retirement and there is therefore no question of the donor ever benefiting from the subject matter of the gift, unless, possibly, the donor becomes entitled to, or receives, an annuity on retirement.

If such a variation in the terms of the partnership is made as part of a bargain of such a kind as would have been reached between parties dealing at arm's length, it is the practice of the Inland Revenue not to impose a charge to capital gains tax (see Statement of Practice D12 paragraph 7). Otherwise, the hold-over relief provisions of TCGA 1992, s 165 should be applicable. Alternatively, capital gains tax taper relief and retirement relief may be available to mitigate any chargeable gain arising.

Gift of capital profits

10.15 Instead of incorporating an automatic accruer or option provision the father could make an immediate gift of any future growth in the capital assets of the partnership by inserting the type of provision which confers the benefit of any capital profits on his son. Provided this does not involve any immediate reduction in the value of the father's estate, there will be no

The Family Business **10.17**

immediate inheritance tax consequences although it could amount to a gift with reservation unless it can be argued either that there is no disposition of any property within FA 1986, s 102 or that if there is, the father's right to benefit from the property given away (by reason of his continuing to draw the same level of profits) is not referable to the subject matter of the gift but to his pre-existing contractual rights under the partnership. The capital gains tax position is the same as above.

Gift of partnership interest

10.16 Alternatively, the father may simply decide to increase his son's share in the capital assets of the partnership with immediate effect by transferring capital between their capital accounts and by altering their respective surplus asset sharing ratios. This may be done without reducing his share of the trading profits at the same time. The advantage of this over the former course is that it avoids completely any question of the application of IHTA 1984, s 163 on the death or retirement of the father. If full consideration is not given by the son, then the variation will constitute a potentially exempt transfer for inheritance tax purposes. For the same reasons as given above in relation to gifts between capital accounts, it is considered that a gift by way of increase in the son's share in the assets of the partnership, without a corresponding increase in his profit share, will not amount to a gift with reservation, although the Inland Revenue may well not share this view.

So far as capital gains tax is concerned, either the disposal is treated as taking place on a 'no gain/no loss' basis (Statement of Practice SP D12) or hold-over relief under TCGA 1992, s 165 should be available.

Trustee partners

10.17 Where there are minor children involved, it would be possible to bring into an existing partnership (or into a new partnership) the trustees of an accumulation and maintenance settlement established for their benefit. The trustees will of course have to have the necessary powers in the trust instrument to enable them to become partners and to contribute capital. As the trustees will pay tax at 34% on their share of the profits of the partnership, the saving in income tax terms may not be that significant, but the arrangement will enable the settlor to pass on some benefit to his children without any inheritance tax consequences. The trustees should ideally pay full consideration for their partnership interest (e.g. by contributing the appropriate amount of capital, etc.), to avoid any argument that the partnership agreement itself amounts to a 'settlement' within ICTA 1988, Part XV and that the settlor could remain taxable on the trustees' share of the trading profits. Further, the trustees should withdraw their share of the profits each year, to avoid any argument that they have made a loan to the settlor or his spouse (by leaving their share in the partnership) and thus fall within ICTA 1988, s 677. Section 677 applies where trustees of a settlement make a loan to the settlor and allows the Inland Revenue to tax the settlor on any undistributed income of the settlement.

10.18 The Family Business

Retirement

10.18 If on the retirement of a partner, his share automatically accrues to the continuing partners or is subject to an option to acquire at nominal value, this should not result in any chargeable transfer if his share has been subject to this provision at all times. This is because the reduction in the value of his share by reason of his retirement will always have been inherent in it and consequently any reduction in the value at the date of his retirement should be minimal. However, the Inland Revenue may not accept this view. The position would undoubtedly be different if the provisions had been introduced as a result of a later agreement (as in the case, for example, of *Attorney-General v Ralli, KB (1936) 15 ATC 523*) since IHTA 1984, s 163 will be applicable and the automatic accruer or option provision will only be taken into account if it was granted for full consideration. This may or may not have been the case. If not, then any reduction in value on retirement should amount to a potentially exempt transfer for inheritance tax purposes, and in any event 100% business property relief is likely to be available provided all the relevant conditions are fulfilled.

The capital gains tax position is more complicated. Either paragraph 4 of the Statement of Practice SP D12 will apply to deem the disposal to take place on a 'no gain/no loss' basis or capital gains tax retirement relief under TCGA 1992, ss 163, 164 and TCGA 1992, Sch 6 or hold-over relief under TCGA 1992, s 165 may be available.

If on retirement the continuing partners are obliged to pay to the outgoing partner an annuity, the payments by them will not give rise to any inheritance tax charge if the annuities form part of an arm's length transaction between them. Otherwise, the payment of the annuities should fall within the normal expenditure out of income exemption.

Death

10.19 The position on death is similar to retirement, except for the fact that no capital gains tax will be payable; and any chargeable transfer arising by reason of the death cannot constitute a potentially exempt transfer and will therefore give rise to an immediate tax charge, subject to the availability of 100% business property relief and the interest-free instalment option (if necessary). There will be no question of any subsequent loss of the business property relief.

Insurance

10.20 The death or retirement of a partner is likely to necessitate the continuing partners (if the partnership continues) finding the cash either to repay to the partner (or his personal representatives) the sums due on his capital account or to purchase his interest in the partnership. To provide for this eventuality, and in particular where the partnership includes members from different generations, the elder partners should take out whole life policies on their lives and hold them on trust for the other partners subject to an overriding power of appointment exercisable in favour of a class consisting of the life assured's spouse and his issue and his parents. Ideally,

The Family Business **10.22**

there should also be power to add other persons (other than the settlor) to the members of this class. Many life offices have standard 'flexible trust' wordings along these lines.

On the death of the life assured, the policy will provide the continuing partners with cash which they can use to fund any payments due to the deceased's personal representatives. In the event that the life assured retires from the partnership the policy may be surrendered and the proceeds similarly used. If the partnership is dissolved the policy can be appointed away from the continuing partners to members of the life assured's family.

If new partners enter the partnership, they may be included in the class of objects of the overriding power and this power may then be exercised in their favour so as to allow them to benefit from the policy along with the existing partners.

The settlor is usually excluded from the trusts to ensure that the inheritance tax gifts with reservation provisions cannot apply. However, the provisions may still apply where all the partners make similar reciprocal arrangements since the settlor, by reason of his being a beneficiary under the other trusts, could be said to have reserved a benefit by associated operations (FA 1986, s 102(1)(b) and FA 1986, Sch 20 para 6(1)(c)). Where such reciprocal arrangements are entered into as part of a commercial agreement between the partners, they may lack the element of gift necessary to bring section 102 into play at all; but the Inland Revenue are known to take the view that if beneficiaries other than just the other partners are capable of benefiting under the trusts then the arrangements will not be regarded as 'commercial'.

Assets held outside the partnership

10.21 It is necessary to consider carefully whether assets should be held within or outside the partnership. Assets, such as the premises from which the business is run, held within the partnership as part of the partnership assets qualify for 100% business property relief, whilst those held outside but used for the partnership business qualify for 50% relief only.

From a taxation viewpoint therefore there is considerable merit in transferring the asset, whether by way of gift or sale, into the partnership. However, other factors must be taken into consideration, and the tax consequences of the transfer into the partnership must not be forgotten. The simplest transaction would involve the creation of a new class of partnership capital to which the transferor is entitled. Any transfer which benefits other members of the partnership will need careful consideration where the partners are other than an individual and his spouse.

Liabilities

10.22 One other important factor to consider is the nature of the assets upon which any debt is secured.

If an asset is eligible for 100% business property relief, securing a debt upon it has the effect that the debt reduces the value of an asset which would, in any event, be wholly exempt from inheritance tax. The benefit of deducting the liability would, therefore, be wasted.

Accordingly, care should be taken to secure the debt against assets which are not otherwise eligible for relief. A partner should therefore borrow against personal assets in order to contribute additional partnership capital. Such borrowings should be a loan rather than an overdraft and should not be secured on any partnership asset or on the partner's interest in the partnership. It will not therefore be an incumbrance on his interest or a partnership asset and will not be deducted from the value of his interest under IHTA 1984, s 162(4).

Such a transaction should not prejudice relief against income tax which will be available under ICTA 1988, s 353 and ICTA 1988, s 362, provided ICTA 1988, s 787 is not invoked.

Limited liability partnerships

10.23 The Limited Liability Partnership Act 2000 ('LLPA 2000') permits the creation of partnerships where members may participate in the management of the business of the LLP whilst having limited liability.

For tax purposes, a LLP is generally transparent, that is to say that the tax is levied on its members rather than on the corporate body itself. Apart from tax, there are other factors which affect the choice of a LLP as an appropriate business structure, the chief one being the protection of limited liability which is offered to its members. This advantage is also afforded by incorporation as a company, but that may also produce for its members liability to pay-as-you-earn tax and Class 1 and 1A National Insurance contributions.

LLPA 2000, s 1(2) provides that such a partnership is a body corporate with a legal personality separate from that of its members.

A LLP is formed by being incorporated under LLPA 2000. Its members are those persons who subscribe their names to the incorporation document and any other persons becoming members by and in accordance with an agreement with the existing members. A person may cease to be a member by death or by dissolution of the LLP, by agreement with the other members or by giving reasonable notice to the other members. The mutual rights and duties of members are governed by agreement between the members or between the LLP and its members.

ICTA 1988 s 118ZA provides that where a LLP carries on a trade, profession or other business with a view to profit, all its activities are treated as carried on in the LLP by its members and not by the LLP itself. Anything done by, to, or in relation to the LLP for the purposes of, or in connection with, any of its activities is treated as done by, to, or in relation to the members as partners. The property of the LLP is treated as held by the members as partnership property.

A LLP carrying on a trade, profession or other business with a view to profit is treated as a partnership for the purposes of capital gains tax. The partnership assets are treated as belonging to the members who are directly taxable on

The Family Business **10.24**

their share of any chargeable gains arising on disposal of those assets. If there is a temporary cessation of trade, the tax status of the partnership continues. This is also the case in a winding up, provided that the process is not unnecessarily prolonged and that the purpose of the winding up is not the avoidance of tax.

On the liquidation of a LLP, however, the LLP ceases to be treated as such from the earlier of the appointment of a liquidator or a court order for winding up. The normal capital gains rules then cease to apply and the LLP is taxed through the liquidator as a company on any chargeable gains arising on disposals of its assets. The only asset then held by the members is their capital interest in the partnership; there will be a disposal of the whole or part when capital distributions are made by the liquidator. The acquisition dates and costs of these capital interests will depend on their actual acquisition by the member concerned.

The commencement and cessation of a partnership's status as a LLP does not of itself give rise to a charge to capital gains tax on its members. TCGA 1992, s 169A, however, provides that any gain held over under TCGA 1992, s 165 when the LLP status no longer applies does not fall out of charge. Where a member holds an asset acquired from a disposal to him, any gain which has been held over under TCGA 1992, s 165 or s 260, immediately becomes chargeable.

As a LLP will have the same tax transparency as a normal partnership, similar considerations in relation to estate planning will apply, as discussed above.

The family company

Gifts of shares

10.24 The majority shareholder in a company may find himself in something of a dilemma. His shareholding, by virtue of its ability to control the company, will carry most of the company's value. Under present legislation, business property relief at 100% is available provided its various conditions are fulfilled (see 10.2 above).

There may be some merit in his giving away some or all of his shares now to take advantage of this relief, which may not still be available at the time of his death. On the other hand, subject to the amount of taper relief and the availability of retirement relief under TCGA 1992, ss 163, 164 and TCGA 1992, Sch 6, a lifetime gift will mean the loss of the tax free uplift on death for capital gains tax purposes under TCGA 1992, s 62 since hold-over relief under TCGA 1992, s 165 merely postpones the liability to tax. In addition, there may be claw-back of the business property relief if the donor dies within seven years (see above).

In addition, for the donor to reduce his holding below 50% may deprive him of control over a business on which his livelihood depends, and a gift of all his shares would have an even more dramatic effect.

10.24 *The Family Business*

Before making any gift of shares, the prospective donor and his advisers should consider the following questions.

(a) Does the donor rely on his director's fees or other emoluments for his livelihood? If so, should any steps be taken to secure these prior to the gift?

(b) Does the donor rely on any dividend income from the shares? Again, can any steps be taken to compensate him for this loss if he gives away his shares?

(c) Is there likely to be a sale or a stock exchange quotation of the shares of the company in the foreseeable future? If so, this may have an impact on any decision whether or not, and if so, to whom, the shares should be given.

(d) Are there any pension arrangements in place for the donor and his wife which may be prejudiced by the gift?

(e) Are there any surplus profits in the company which the donor would like to extract prior to the gift (although any distribution of these by way of dividend will result in an income tax charge)?

(f) Will the intended donees of the shares be involved in running the company or merely passive shareholders? Is there likely to be any friction between them if more than one person is involved?

In many cases where 100% relief is available lifetime gifts may now be positively disadvantageous because the capital gains tax uplift on death will be lost. However, there are a number of circumstances where lifetime gifts may still be worthwhile or necessary. In particular:

(i) where it is likely that the company will be sold prior to the death of the shareholder but probably not in the next seven years;

(ii) where 'excepted assets' within IHTA 1984, s 112 are held in the company and business property relief will therefore be severely restricted; and

(iii) where family circumstances require the next generation, who may be heavily involved in the company, to be given an interest.

In these circumstances it may be sensible for the majority shareholder to consider reducing his holding to the minimum 51% by making regular use of his annual inheritance tax exemption or by making a potentially exempt transfer and insuring against the risk of his death within the seven-year period.

Where 100% business property relief is not available it is sensible for any shareholder who wishes to divest himself of control simply to make the gift (which will be a potentially exempt transfer) and insure his life.

What can be done to protect the shareholder from his loss of control? Any attempt by him to entrench his right to remuneration as, for example, an executive director, by giving himself a long-term service contract, or even a contract for any length which allows him remuneration beyond that commensurate with his duties, may be treated as a gift with reservation within FA 1986, s 102, as would any attempt to secure favourable pre-emption rights over the shares given away. On the other hand, there should be no difficulty in his continuing to draw a reasonable commercial remuneration under a pre-existing service contract or renewing that contract on similar terms (provided they are still appropriate and reasonable) when it expires (CTO Advanced Instruction Manual D.48). Similarly, it is considered that he may still benefit from any pre-emption rights contained in the Articles of Association of the company prior to the gift.

One way of providing a degree of control for the donor would be for him to give the shares to a trust of which he is the first named trustee. Such a trust could be an accumulation and maintenance settlement, where he has children or grandchildren under 25, or an interest in possession settlement where his children or grandchildren are over 25. The case of *Commissioners of Stamp Duties of New South Wales v Way*, *PC [1952] AC 95; [1952] 1 All ER 198* provides authority for the proposition that powers exercisable by a person in a fiduciary capacity do not amount to a reservation of benefit for estate duty purposes and the Inland Revenue appear to take a similar view for inheritance tax purposes (CTO Advanced Instruction Manual D.75). However, the settlor must exercise his votes in the best interests of the beneficiaries under the trust and not in his own interests. Failure to do so may make him susceptible to an action for breach of trust by an aggrieved beneficiary; it may also allow the Inland Revenue to claim that there has in fact been a gift with reservation. The settlor should also bear in mind that although as first named shareholder he is the one who is able, so far as the company is concerned, to exercise the votes (the company having no notice of the trust), he should only exercise them as all the trustees agree, as trustees have to be unanimous in exercising their powers unless the settlement itself says otherwise. Any provision in the settlement attempting to give the settlor sole control over the votes must cast doubt on his exercising them in a fiduciary capacity and hence the gift with reservation provisions may apply.

Where the settlor-trustee is also a director of the company, if the settlement contains any provisions relieving him of his duty to account to the trust for any profits made through using, or failing to use, the trust votes to secure his position, the gift may amount to a gift with reservation. The Inland Revenue, however, have indicated that such relieving provisions will not in their view prejudice a gift where they permit the retention of reasonable commercial remuneration (CTO Advanced Instruction Manual D.76).

When structuring the capital of a company, it is important to consider the precise wording of the definition of 'relevant business property'. For example, if a shareholder has sufficient shares to give him control of the company and also owns non-voting securities, the shares will be relevant business property but the securities will not. This is because the securities do not give the shareholder control of the company together with the unquoted shares. The shares give control in their own right. It should be remembered that for inheritance tax purposes there is a distinction between shares and securities.

Minority holdings

10.25 All sizes of minority shareholdings in unquoted trading companies may be eligible for business property relief at 100%. As for controlling

10.26 *The Family Business*

holdings, it may be sensible to retain the shares until death and obtain the capital gains tax uplift. However, it may be, for the same reasons as are set out above in respect of controlling holdings, that lifetime gifts are appropriate.

The minority shareholder may, however, have fewer non-tax-related problems in deciding whether to make a lifetime gift. If he considers his interest in the company purely as an investment and does not rely on it to help secure any remunerated office, his only loss in giving away the shares will be any dividend income (which in the case of many unquoted companies may be negligible if not non-existent) and any loss in capital appreciation.

To enable shareholders to reduce their taxable estate, but at the same time to retain their dividend rights, the company's Articles of Association could be altered to allow any shareholder to convert each of his shares into two separate shares. One share would carry the right to any dividends declared by the company, the right only to repayment at par on a winding-up of a company but no voting rights; the other share would carry the right to vote and the right to the remaining equity of the company on a winding-up, but no dividend rights. The former share would then be retained and the latter given away. It is not considered that a gift of the voting shares would amount to a gift with reservation for inheritance tax purposes, since no benefit accrues to the donor which is referable to the gift. Although, on the conversion, value will pass out of the original shares, this will not result in a capital gains tax charge under the value shifting provisions contained in TCGA 1992, s 29. For section 29 to apply it is a requirement that the party or parties making the deemed disposal could have obtained consideration for the disposal and, since the new shares are issued to the same shareholder, it is impossible to see how any consideration could have been obtained.

A similar device involves the issue of fixed dividend preference shares by way of bonus to existing shareholders. The preference shares are non-voting and on the winding-up of the company carry the right only to repayment at par. The idea is that the bonus issue frees the ordinary shares (which, depending on the income and net asset value of the company, may well carry the bulk of the value of the company), for gifts, whilst allowing the donor to retain the benefit of the income from the preference shares. This type of scheme may be attractive both to minority shareholders who rely on regular dividends to secure their standard of living and to controlling shareholders nearing the age of retirement who wish to pass control of the family company on to the next generation but at the same time need the security of an income flow to support them in their retirement.

Quoted shares

10.26 If shares become listed on the Stock Exchange they will cease to qualify for any inheritance tax business property relief unless they are part of a controlling holding owned by the transferor (IHTA 1984, s 105(1)(b)). The loss of relief can be a significant disadvantage especially where there are a number of elderly shareholders. Where minority shareholdings are concerned, the effect may be to move the holding from a non-tax paying position (because 100% business property relief was available whilst

The Family Business **10.27**

unquoted) to a position where it is fully taxable at 40%. Additionally, its value may considerably increase.

If the flotation is considered necessary in order to give the company access to the public as a new source of funds, rather than simply to unlock the value inherent in the shares, a solution would be for the company to create and issue a new class of shares for the purposes of the public sale leaving the existing shareholders with their original shares which would continue to be unquoted and therefore capable of qualifying for business property relief. The new class of shares issued should rank *pari passu* with the existing shares in all material respects. To enable the existing shareholders to realise their shares, they could be made convertible into the quoted class at the option of the holder.

A similar problem exists where unquoted shares have been the subject matter of a potentially exempt transfer but have become quoted before the seven-year period has expired. In such a case, the shares would not attract business property relief if the transferor dies within the period (IHTA 1984, s 113A(3)). Again, a new class of shares could be created specially for the purposes of the flotation.

Where there are two or more shareholders who between them control a quoted company, by transferring their shares to a newly formed 'holding' company which they own jointly they can in effect convert shares which will not qualify for inheritance tax business property relief (i.e. the quoted shares) into shares which do (i.e. the unquoted shares in the holding company). Although the only business of the new company is the holding of investments, this does not necessarily prevent shares of the company from being relevant business property (IHTA 1984, s 105(4)(b)).

Once shares or securities have become quoted they cease to be assets capable of qualifying for hold-over relief under TCGA 1992, s 165 unless in the case of an individual the company concerned is the transferor's personal company (as defined in TCGA 1992, Sch 6 para 1(2)) or in the case of trustees, they are able to exercise 25% of the voting rights exercisable by the company's shareholders in general meeting. However, in the appropriate circumstances, hold-over relief under TCGA 1992, s 260 may still be available.

Other devices

10.27 Two other strategies involving companies must be mentioned: the 'deferred share' proposal and the 'value freezing' proposal. Both are designed to pass the value inherent in a company to other members of a family, the first by creating a new class of shares to which deferred rights are attached but which automatically convert into ordinary shares after a specified period of time; the second by creating a new class of shares which from the outset carry any increase in the value of the company over its value at the date of issue. The extent to which schemes of this nature are still relevant in the current climate of 100% business property relief and the consequent merits of retaining assets until death to take advantage of the tax free capital gains tax uplift must be debatable, but it is considered that it is still worthwhile including them in this chapter as they will become relevant if the relief is reduced or abolished.

10.28 *The Family Business*

The deferred share strategy

10.28 A bonus issue of deferred shares is made to the existing ordinary shareholder or shareholders of the company. For a fixed period these deferred shares carry minimal (or no) voting rights, dividend rights or rights to receive distributions on a winding-up. At the end of the period the deferred shares automatically rank *pari passu* with the existing ordinary shares, or assume all the rights previously attached to the ordinary shares, with the ordinary shares correspondingly losing their rights (and becoming valueless).

The idea is to create a new class of shares which are initially of low value (and an important factor in determining this value is the length of the fixed period) and can therefore be given at little or no inheritance tax cost, but which then grow in value over a period of time and at the end of the period assume virtually the full value of the company if at that time the rights attaching to the ordinary shares cease.

It is debatable whether the expiry of the fixed period will result in a disposition by the ordinary shareholders in the company (assuming of course that the company is 'close' for tax purposes) under IHTA 1984, s 98. However, it is understood that the Inland Revenue are of the view that an alteration of rights within the meaning of IHTA 1984, s 98(1)(b) occurs when deferred shares come to rank equally with another class of shares. Even if this is the case it is difficult to see how an inheritance tax charge can arise because the reduction in value (if any) of the shareholders' estates due to the disposition is minimal. This is because the value of the ordinary shares will discount the coming to an end of the fixed period when the deferred shares will rank *pari passu* in all respects with the other shares, and will therefore gradually decrease in value over the years as the value of the deferred shares increases, so that immediately before the disposition the ordinary shares are likely to have virtually the same value as after the disposition.

To counter the argument that prior to the end of the fixed period the failure of the ordinary shareholders to cancel the deferred shares or to liquidate the company results in a transfer of value under IHTA 1984, s 3(3), it is important that the rights of the deferred shareholders are entrenched by giving them the ability to block any resolution to alter the rights attaching to their shares or to wind up the company or to create any new share capital. For the same reason it is also important that the ordinary shareholders ensure that as much of the profits of the company as are not required commercially for its operations are paid out by way of dividend. This is to ensure that value is not left in the company which the ordinary shareholders fail to extract. This 'enforced' payment of dividends may make the scheme unattractive to some shareholders.

To allow as much time as possible for the relevant period to expire (and therefore for the ordinary shares to lose their value) before an event which gives rise to an inheritance tax charge occurs, the ordinary shareholders should leave their ordinary shares to their respective spouses on their deaths.

So far as capital gains tax is concerned, the value shifting provisions contained in TCGA 1992, ss 29 and 30 should not be in point. Section 29 does not apply because the deferred shares are initially issued to the ordinary shareholders and consequently there is no transaction for which any consideration could have been obtained. Section 30 also does not apply because although the gift of the deferred shares would be a disposal for the purposes of the section, there has been no scheme or arrangement whereby the value of the deferred shares has been materially reduced.

Now that gifts of unlimited amounts may be made without inheritance tax implications, provided the donor survives for the necessary seven-year period, and with business property relief at 100% being available, the use of the deferred share scheme has diminished. A straightforward gift of shares must be far less provocative to the Inland Revenue than what is undeniably a very artificial arrangement involving a number of complicated — and potentially contentious — tax points. The scheme also involves the creation of a complex share structure for the company which of necessity must last for a number of years. Having said that, however, the scheme still has its place in estate planning. An owner of a company who expects to retire in ten years in favour of his sons, may find it attractive to enter into a scheme now which can secure the passing of control on his retirement without the need to make an immediate outright gift of his shares and without the worry as to whether the present favourable inheritance tax regime will still remain in a decade's time.

The deferred share strategy is less apposite for investment companies. This is because shares in investment companies tend to be valued on a net asset basis and in this regard the most crucial right attaching to the shares is the ability to wind up the company. As mentioned above, the deferred shares must carry the same voting rights on a winding up as the ordinary shares and although for the duration of the fixed period the ordinary shares carry the right to the bulk of the distributions on a winding up, the ordinary shares will not carry the ability to wind up the company. This may therefore limit the discount attaching to the value of the deferred shares over the ordinary shares (to take account of the other deferred rights).

The value freezing strategy

10.29 Alternatively, investment companies, for reasons which will be discussed, are more suitable vehicles for the value freezing strategy. This proposal involves a new class of shares being issued to the existing shareholders, again by way of bonus, which carry the right to participate in the winding up of the company only insofar as the net asset value of the company then exceeds its value at the date of issue of the new shares. In this event, the new shares carry the right to participate in all the excess. The new shares may carry dividend and voting rights ranking *pari passu* with the ordinary shares. It is important, for the same reasons as was the case with the deferred share strategy, that the new shares are able to block any resolution to wind up the company or to alter the rights attaching to the shares. These additional voting rights will not prevent the ordinary shares from qualifying for business property relief (assuming it to be otherwise available, which in the case of an investment company will often *not* be the case), provided they give control on all other matters (IHTA 1984, s 267).

10.30   The Family Business

The ordinary shares are retained and the new shares, which will initially be of little value, are given away. It should be remembered that shares in an investment company are not capable of qualifying for hold-over relief under TCGA 1992, s 165, although relief under TCGA 1992, s 260 may be available.

This strategy is best confined to investment companies because the basis of calculating value in respect of their shares is more certain — the net value of the company's assets is taken and then discounted by a percentage depending upon the size of the holding. The valuation of shares in a trading company is usually calculated on an earnings basis whereby an appropriate multiplier is applied to the earnings per share. This method of valuation is more difficult to apply and determining the initial value of the company is more problematic. This in turn will make it difficult to 'freeze' the value of the company.

As with the deferred share strategy, the existence of the potentially exempt transfer has lessened the importance of this type of arrangement in estate planning. However, its advantages over a straightforward gift of shares is that it enables the donor to retain an interest in both the capital and income of the company, and also in its management (by reason of the votes attaching to the shares) whilst at the same time enabling the future benefit of the company to flow through to the next generation. Clearly, a value freezing exercise such as this is long-term in its operation and effects.

It is considered that under both strategies the gifts of the new shares will not contravene the gifts with reservation provisions because the donor does not benefit in any way from the property which is the subject matter of the gift, nor does he receive any collateral benefit referable to the gift. Any benefits he continues to receive are from the company and flow from pre-existing property retained in his estate, namely the original shares.

Dividend waivers

10.30   A shareholder paying higher rate income tax might consider waiving his rights to dividends in order to divert the income to taxpayers paying lesser rates of tax, e.g. the trustees of an accumulation and maintenance settlement, or a lower rate taxpayer. With the top rate of income tax on dividends at 32.5%, the saving is modest. Lower and basic rate taxpayers are liable to pay tax at 10% on their dividend income with a tax credit of $\frac{1}{9}$ of the dividend so that the tax credit will entirely cover the income tax liability. Trusts currently pay 34% on their general income and 25% on dividend income also with a tax credit of $\frac{1}{9}$ of the dividend.

Provided the waiver is made within twelve months before any right to the dividend accrues, it will not be a transfer of value for inheritance tax purposes (IHTA 1984, s 15).

In the case of a close investment-holding company, where as a result of a dividend waiver a shareholder receives a greater dividend from the company and is in a position to reclaim all or part of the tax credit attaching to it, the company's Inspector of Taxes may restrict the repayment of the tax credit to such extent as is just and reasonable (ICTA 1988, s 231(3A)).

A close investment-holding company is defined in ICTA 1988, s 13A broadly as a close company which exists to make or hold investments.

Subject to the Articles of Association of the company, in the case of an interim dividend, the right accrues from the date of payment; and in the case of a final dividend, it accrues from the date it is declared unless the dividend is expressed to be payable at a future date, when the right accrues at that date (see *Potel v CIR, [1971] 2 All ER 504; 46 TC 658* at pp 511, 512).

A dividend waiver should be by deed. For the purposes of ICTA 1988, Part XV a dividend waiver is treated as a 'settlement'. Accordingly, any waiver which results in a greater dividend being paid to minor unmarried children of the settlor will result in the dividends continuing to be taxed as part of the total income of the settlor under ICTA 1988, s 660B. In addition, the Inland Revenue may argue that the waiver does not prevent ICTA 1988, s 660A from applying with the result that the increased dividend will continue to be taxed in the hands of the settlor. Although this will clearly destroy any income tax benefit of the waiver, the inheritance tax advantage of reducing the settlor's estate by the after-tax amount of the dividend still remains.

Assets held outside the company

10.31 As with partnerships, there is a significant inheritance tax disadvantage in holding assets outside a company. This is because such assets can only qualify for 50% business property relief where the owner of the asset is the controlling shareholder of the company. Where he is only a minority shareholder there will be no relief at all, even though the asset may be used exclusively for the company's purposes.

For instance, if two or more individuals (not being husband and wife) own an unquoted company equally, their shareholdings in the company will qualify for business property relief at 100%. On the other hand, a property also owned by them equally and let to the company for the purposes of its trade will not qualify for business property relief.

The solution as with a partnership (see above) is to transfer the asset into the company with the owner(s) either giving the asset to the company or selling it for its capital gains tax base cost. In either case to avoid an actual capital gains tax liability a hold-over election under TCGA 1992, s 165 would be required although, of course, the effect of making a hold-over election is that taper relief accrued up to the date of the transfer will be lost.

A gift to a company is not a potentially exempt transfer for inheritance tax purposes (IHTA 1984, s 3A) so care needs to be taken where the company is owned other than by the individual transferor or that individual and his spouse. Even where the property and the shares in the company are owned in the same proportions, there may be an element of loss to the transferor's estate because of the discount applied to minority holdings and a careful valuation will have to be carried out.

It may be possible to issue shares to the transferor(s) in exchange for the asset so as to avoid any element of gift for inheritance tax purposes. As this will prevent an election for hold-over relief for capital gains tax purposes under

10.32   The Family Business

TCGA 1992, s 165, any unrealised gain on the asset will be brought into charge. Where land is being transferred to a connected company a stamp duty charge based on market value will arise.

Where an individual owns assets which are used for the purposes of a business carried on by a personal company, retirement relief will only be available if there is a disposal of the company shares which qualifies for retirement relief and the asset is disposed of as part of the said individual's withdrawal from the business (TCGA 1992, s 164(7)). In the case of *Plumbly & Others (Harbour's Personal Representatives) v Spencer*, CA *[1999] STC 677* land had been used for the purposes of the business of a company of which the taxpayer was a full-time working director and shareholder and rent was paid by the company. At the time of the disposal, the land was used for the purposes of the business and, at the time of the sale, the company ceased to carry on the business. The taxpayer claimed relief not under section 164 but section 163. The court held that section 163 applied not only to assets which were used in a business of the disponer but also to assets of the disponer used in his personal company, and therefore relief was available.

Each case will need to be carefully considered depending on all the circumstances.

Liabilities

10.32   As discussed more fully in the coverage on partnerships at 10.22 above, it is important to ensure that debts are secured on assets which do not qualify for business property relief. In the case of holdings in companies, therefore, it is important to ensure that borrowings are secured on the shareholder's other assets rather than on the shares themselves.

Death

10.33   Historically, unquoted shares have always caused problems on death. These problems, however, are much alleviated by the availability of business property relief at 100%. The main problem, namely of an inheritance tax charge arising on an asset which is not readily realisable, will now only apply:

(*a*)   where there are 'excepted assets';

(*b*)   where the company is not a trading company; or

(*c*)   where the shares are ineligible for relief for some other reason.

Where an actual liability to tax is likely to arise, whole of life insurance should always be considered as a means of funding the tax. This can either be on a single life basis, if a charge is likely to arise on the death of the shareholder, or on a joint life last survivor basis if the shareholder proposes to leave the shares to the surviving spouse, when the inheritance tax charge will arise on the second death. However, particularly where business property relief is available at 100%, leaving shares to the surviving spouse should be avoided unless done for purely practical reasons. It is now preferable to leave assets qualifying for 100% business property relief to children or grandchildren (or in trust for them) compensating the spouse with other assets not qualifying for relief.

Another way of funding the inheritance tax on the death of a shareholder is for the company, assuming it has power to do so in its Articles of Association, to buy some or all of the deceased's shares. The payment made by the company will not amount to a distribution of income or corporation tax purposes provided the company is an unquoted trading company or the unquoted holding company of a trading group and the whole or substantially the whole of the payment is used (apart from paying any capital gains tax) to discharge an inheritance tax liability within two years of the death (ICTA 1988, s 219). This relieving provision does not apply where the tax could be paid in some other way without under hardship.

Where the company has surplus funds sufficient to discharge the inheritance tax liability on the death of a controlling shareholder, the Inland Revenue take the view that there is no hardship since the liability can be met by dividend payments (Hansard 17-3-88).

Enterprise investment scheme (EIS)

10.34 EIS relief is a multi-faceted relief which essentially comprises a capital gains tax deferral, an income tax relief and a capital gains tax exemption. A detailed analysis of the rules surrounding the relief is outside the scope of this book but the following describes the relief in broad terms and goes on to consider how the relief might usefully be employed in an estate planning context.

Capital gains tax deferral

10.35 The relief allows the deferral of capital gains tax arising on the disposal of any assets if the gain is reinvested in newly issued ordinary shares of a qualifying unquoted trading company within certain time limits. The effect is to defer the tax liability until the EIS shares are sold and even then the charge may be further deferred by reinvesting the gain in different qualifying EIS shares.

The asset disposed of can be virtually any asset except that, on the disposal of shares or securities, the investment cannot be in the same company or group of companies (TCGA 1992, Sch 5B para 10).

For this element of the relief there is no connected persons rule beyond substitution of market value in certain cases. It is possible for an individual to invest in a company which he already owns or controls.

The qualifying investment must be made within a period commencing one year before and ending three years after the disposal of the original asset (TCGA 1992, Sch 5B para 1(3)(a)). This period can be extended at the Revenue's discretion. (TCGA 1992, Sch 5B para 1(3)).

10.36 *The Family Business*

A qualifying investment is an acquisition for cash of newly issued eligible shares in a qualifying company. Eligible shares are defined as ordinary shares which for a period of three years, do not carry present or future preferential rights to dividends or assets (TCGA 1992, Sch 5B para 19). Most trades are qualifying trades but amongst those which do not qualify are dealing in land, commodities, futures, shares, other financial instruments, leasing, providing legal or accountancy services, property development, farming, woodlands or market gardening, operating hotels, nursing homes or residential care homes. An investment in the parent company of a trading group will qualify for relief provided that at least 80% of the group's activities as a whole qualify.

The gross assets of the investee company must not exceed £15,000,000 immediately before the investment or £16,000,000 immediately after.

The investment must be by subscribing in cash for 'eligible shares'. The amount of EIS relief is limited to the amount claimed by the taxpayer, which allows him to first make use of capital losses, annual exemptions, retirement relief and hold-over relief. There is no minimum holding period for the shares in which the gain is reinvested. However, relief will be clawed back should the conditions on which the relief was granted cease to be fully met at any time within three years after the investment.

Relief can also be denied or clawed back under complex anti-avoidance provisions. These counteract any return of value within three years after reinvestment. This concept is widely defined, catching, for example, instances where there are advance arrangements for a return of value at any time (e.g. guaranteed exit route).

Any clawback charge can itself be deferred by further investment, subject to satisfying the normal conditions.

Income tax relief and capital gains tax exemption

10.36 To obtain income tax relief of up to 20% on qualifying investments up to £150,000 the following additional conditions must be satisfied:

(a) the taxpayer must be liable to UK tax;

(b) the taxpayer must make a minimum investment of £500;

(c) the taxpayer must not be connected with the company either at the time of investment nor at any time in the 'relevant period'. The 'relevant period' begins two years prior to the issue of the shares or, if later, the date of incorporation and ends three years after the share issue in question;

(d) the taxpayer must not receive value from the company (or have breached any of the other anti-avoidance provisions) during his relevant period.

The taxpayer will be connected with the company where he, and his associates, own (as widely defined) more than 30% of the company.

The Family Business **10.37**

Provided that the EIS shares are held for at least three years and EIS income tax relief has not been withdrawn, any capital gains arising on the disposal of the shares (excluding the held-over gains) will be exempt from capital gains tax.

Relief in estate planning context

10.37 Whilst the relief affords considerable scope for deferring capital gains tax, there are significant commercial risks involved in making any qualifying investment. This point is reinforced by the fact that specific anti-avoidance legislation ensures that relief is denied where there is a guaranteed exit route at the outset. The financial services industry is becoming more successful at developing products which minimise the risks whilst still qualifying for the relief but EIS investments are not low risk investments. The main role of the relief in an estate planning context is in the sphere of the private company proprietor. He will understand the risks involved and, in the case of many disposals, will have a ready made vehicle in which he may invest.

If the investor and his associates own more than 30% of the investee company they will receive capital gains tax deferral relief but not income tax relief or capital gains tax exemption on the later sale of the shares.

Take, for example, a private company proprietor, Mr A, who makes a substantial gain on a disposal of quoted investments when aged 55. The gain will be charged to capital gains tax at 40% (assuming a reasonable level of income). To defer this liability he might, however, subscribe for new shares in his existing private company. Providing he subscribes for 'eligible shares' and the company is a 'qualifying company', EIS capital gains tax deferral relief will, in principle, be available. It will be necessary for the company to retain its qualifying status for the next three years but there is no reason why this should not be achieved providing the cash is wholly employed for permissible purposes. Care must be taken to ensure that there is no return of value (as widely defined) which would result in a clawback of relief but this does not preclude the payment of reasonable remuneration and dividends.

It might be possible to achieve an absolute saving rather than a mere deferral. For example, Mr A might be able to claim retirement relief on the ultimate disposal of the shares providing this is before 6 April 2003. As there is no requirement for additional shares to be held for any particular period, retirement relief should *prima facie* be available providing Mr A's existing shareholding would so qualify. Alternatively, if Mr A were to retain the additional shares until death, the gain deferred will fall out of charge altogether and the base cost of the shares will automatically benefit from a tax-free uplift on death. In view of the likely availability of 100% business property relief for inheritance tax purposes (after the two-year qualifying period), this is likely to be a viable option if no sale of the company is contemplated. Finally, there is also the possibility of Mr A becoming resident outside the UK once the three-year clawback period has expired, although the problems of selling a private company whilst non-resident may make this difficult to achieve in practice.

10.38 *The Family Business*

If, instead of being a company proprietor, Mr A was in business as a sole trader or in partnership with his wife, he might still be able to take advantage of EIS relief. For example, he could form a company and give to it the assets of the existing business, any gain arising being held-over under TCGA 1992, s 165 (although it is likely that a stamp duty charge would arise on the transfer of land to the company under FA 2000, s 119). He could then subscribe for capital in the newly-formed company to the extent of the gain made on his investment disposal. EIS relief should be available provided the necessary criteria are met as regards the new company. It would, of course, be necessary to consider all the other tax and non-tax implications of incorporation if this route were to be pursued.

Venture capital trusts (VCT)

10.38 As with EIS investments, investments in VCTs qualify for a special form of capital gains tax deferral. VCTs are quoted investment trusts which invest in certain qualifying unquoted trading companies. Restrictive rules govern the types of investment which may be acquired, the activities of the investee companies and the size and diversity of the VCTs investments. Gains of up to £100,000 per tax year can qualify for capital gains tax deferral when reinvested in VCTs. However, the reinvestment period is shorter, commencing one year before but ending only one year after the date on which the gain arose. This two-year period may straddle three tax years so that it may be possible to shelter a gain of up to £300,000. When both income tax and capital gains tax deferral applies to a subscription for shares, the individual may qualify for total tax relief of up to 60%. Capital gains tax exemption on gains made on the VCT shares themselves (excluding the rolled-over gains) will also be available.

11 The Family Farm

Introduction

11.1 The farmer has very special, and probably unique, problems when it comes to estate planning as he owns a valuable capital asset which is absolutely vital to his business. In the past, the death of a landowner has often imposed a massive capital taxation burden on those heirs who wished to continue to farm the land for whom the capital value of the land is irrelevant. However, this problem was greatly alleviated by the introduction of agricultural property relief for inheritance tax purposes at a rate of 100% on untenanted land and on let land where the tenancy began (and in some cases where there is a succession) after 31 August 1995. However, it is still necessary to ensure that the criteria for qualification are met and that the best possible use is made of the relief. Inheritance tax is still payable on tenanted land let prior to 1 September 1995 as only 50% relief is available.

Recent years have seen farmers' businesses crippled by the Common Agricultural Policy and by the massive (and massively subsidised) over-production of other European farmers, notably the French, by the beef and pork crises and the foot and mouth epidemic. Planning is often complicated by the fact that the farmer will often want one of several children to succeed to the farming business.

As the farmer is primarily a man of business much of chapter 10 *The Family Business* will also be relevant to the family farm and reference should be made to it. There will be a number of matters in this chapter which will repeat topics covered in that chapter and accordingly they will not be dealt with in such detail here.

The farmer may be the sole proprietor of the farming business; or there may be a partnership or a family company, each of which will be complicated by the existence of the farmland itself. In the case of a partnership or a family company, the land may either be owned by the partnership or the company, or it may be owned by one of the partners or one of the shareholders of the company. In the latter case, the partnership or company may have an agricultural tenancy of the land or it may simply occupy it under a gratuitous licence. Each one of these possibilities has different estate planning ramifications and they will be considered below. First, however, the inheritance tax and capital gains tax provisions having most impact on farmers will be considered.

11.2 *The Family Farm*

Inheritance tax

11.2 Fortunately, the regime for inheritance tax now recognises the difficulty, often encountered by the heirs, in funding the tax payable on the death of the farmer in respect of his farm when there are no other easily realisable assets in the estate out of which the tax may be funded. As a result, the legislation firstly applies a discount to the value of farmland of either 50% or 100% to reduce the burden of the tax or eliminate it completely. Secondly, where tax is payable there is the option of paying it by ten equal annual interest-free instalments.

Agricultural property relief

11.3 The relief for agricultural property is given by IHTA 1984, ss 115–124B, thus reducing the 'agricultural value' of any 'agricultural property' by a stated percentage.

The 'agricultural value' is the value of the property on the assumption that it is subject to a perpetual covenant prohibiting its use otherwise than as agricultural property (IHTA 1984, s 115(3)). Any development or hope value or value attributable to minerals, therefore, is not relieved.

'Agricultural property' means agricultural land or pasture, including any woodland and any building used in connection with the intensive rearing of livestock or fish, if the woodland or building is occupied with agricultural land or pasture and the occupation is ancillary to that of the land or pasture (IHTA 1984, s 115(2)). It also includes such cottages, farm buildings and farmhouses (together with the land occupied with them) as are of a character appropriate to the property.

Property used for the breeding and rearing of horses on a stud farm and the grazing of horses in connection with those activities also qualifies (IHTA 1984, s 115(4)). A field which was let for the grazing of horses used for leisure was held not to be 'occupied for the purposes of agriculture' (*Wheatley's Executors v CIR, Sp C [1998] SSCD 60 (Sp C 149)*). The decision focused on the nature of the animals grazing rather than on the main purpose of the occupation of the land. This decision highlights the difficulty where landowners or their tenants diversify into horse and paddock activities. Under a farm business tenancy, it is the activities of the tenant that are relevant in determining occupation. It is therefore essential that the tenant covenants that the land will only be occupied for agricultural purposes.

The relief also applies to farmland dedicated to wildlife habitats (FA 1997, s 94).

In the recent case of *Dixon v CIR, Sp C 2001, [2002] SSCD 53 (Sp C 297)* it was held that although fruit growing and the use of land as grazing land could be agriculture, whether or not these activities were agriculture was a matter of fact and degree to be determined in the light of the purposes of the Act.

In a landlord and tenant case *Jewell v McGowan and others, CA [2002] All ER (D) 387* the Court of Appeal held that the 'open farming' activities carried

The Family Farm 11.3

on by the tenant were not agricultural in nature and did not become so by virtue of the fact that they were essential to the profitability of the farm.

Where a farmer gives away the bulk of his farm whilst retaining only the farmhouse and a small amount of land, such retained property will rarely qualify for relief (*Starke & Another (Brown's Executors) v CIR, CA [1995] STC 689; [1996] 1 All ER 622*). This problem may be avoided if the farmer remains a partner with perhaps a relatively small share in the overall farm.

The relief only applies to agricultural property in the UK, the Channel Islands or the Isle of Man (IHTA 1984, s 115(5)).

No relief is given unless either the agricultural property was:

(*a*) occupied by the transferor for the purposes of agriculture throughout the period of two years ending with the date of the transfer; or

(*b*) owned by the transferor throughout the period of seven years ending with that date and was throughout that period occupied (by him or another) for the purposes of agriculture (IHTA 1984, s 117).

The CTO Advanced Instruction Manual at L.246 gives illustrations of what land is accepted as being for the purposes of agriculture. For these purposes, occupation by a company which is controlled by the transferor is treated as occupation by the transferor; and occupation of any property by a Scottish partnership is treated as occupation of it by the partners (IHTA 1984, s 119). 'Control' of a company is defined by IHTA 1984, s 269 and means control of powers of voting on all questions affecting the company as a whole which, if exercised, would yield a majority of the votes capable of being exercised on them. When determining if a person has control, the votes attaching to any shares or securities which are 'related property' within the meaning of IHTA 1984, s 161 (broadly, property comprised in the estate of the transferor's spouse or owned by a charity established by the transferor or his spouse) are taken into account. The votes attaching to any shares or securities owned by the trustees of a settlement in which the transferor has a beneficial interest in possession will also be taken into account (IHTA 1984, s 269(2)(3)).

In addition to agricultural property, relief is also given in respect of shares of a company the assets of which include agricultural property where the value of the company's shares can be attributed to the agricultural value of that property (IHTA 1984, s 122(1)). However, the relief only applies if the transferor has control of the company immediately before the relevant transfer (IHTA 1984, s 122(2)). In order for the shares to qualify for the relief, the company must also fulfil the same ownership and occupation requirements of the land as an individual and in addition the transferor must have owned the shares for whichever of the two or seven-year minimum periods is appropriate (IHTA 1984, s 123(1)).

For the purposes of agricultural property relief it is possible for a person to inherit the periods of occupation or ownership of a deceased spouse. If, for example, farmland passes to a farmer's widow, she can add to her period of occupation or ownership that of her husband's (IHTA 1984, s 120(1)(b)). In addition, where farmland is sold and replaced by other farmland, the successive periods of occupation or ownership of the two areas of land may,

11.3 The Family Farm

in certain circumstances, be treated as one to ascertain whether the minimum periods of occupation or ownership are satisfied (IHTA 1984, s 118).

Where there are two successive transfers of agricultural property, and the first transfer was eligible for the relief, or would have been so eligible if the relief had been available at the time, then the relief will be available in respect of the second transfer even if the transferor has not at the time satisfied the minimum ownership or occupation requirements provided:

(i) the transferor in relation to the second transfer (or his spouse) acquired the property as a result of the first transfer,

(ii) at the time of the second transfer the property is occupied for the purposes of agriculture either by the second transferor (or his spouse) or by the personal representatives of the transferor in relation to the earlier transfer, and

(iii) either the first transfer or the second transfer was made on the death of the transferor (IHTA 1984, s 121).

Agricultural property relief operates to reduce the whole or part of the value transferred by a transfer of value which is attributable to the agricultural value of agricultural property. The reduction is either 100% or 50%. Relief at 100% is available where

(a) the interest of the transferor in the property immediately before the transfer carried the right to vacant possession or the right to obtain it within the next twelve months;

(b) the interest does not carry such a right because the property is let on a tenancy which began after 31 August 1995. Where a transfer of value occurs following the death of a tenant after 31 August 1995 but before a new tenancy has been formally granted to a successor who takes under a statutory provision, relief will be available. In addition, where a tenant has, prior to the transferor's death, given notice of his intention to retire in favour of a new tenant and the actual retirement takes place after the death but within 30 months after the notice was given, relief will also be available.

Relief at 100% (50% for deaths and transfers before 10 March 1992) is available for farm cottages where the agricultural worker's occupation of the cottage was protected and the benefit of the 'transitional provisions' contained in IHTA 1984, s 116(2)(b) and IHTA 1984, s 116(3) is available to the transferor; or the agricultural worker occupied the cottage under an unprotected service tenancy; or the worker's occupation arose under a tenancy which began after 31 August 1995. In all other cases, the Inland Revenue take the view that the rate of relief will only be 50%. This view is based upon the fact that under the Rent (Agriculture) Act 1976, the farmer does not have the right to actual unimpeded physical enjoyment of the farm worker's cottage (see Private Client Business 1998, page 171).

Where land is owned by one or more joint tenants or tenants in common, if the interests of all of them together carry that right each interest is taken to carry a right to vacant possession (IHTA 1984, s 116(6)). Accordingly, where land is owned by a farming partnership, the relief will apply to the value

The Family Farm 11.3

transferred by any transfer of a partnership interest so far as its value is attributable to the agricultural property. Where land is owned outside the farming partnership but occupied by the partnership on licence but with no partnership agreement or other documentation detailing the terms of occupation, it is understood that the CTO take the view that 100% relief may not be available to the landowner. This partnership structure is known as the Harrison-Broadley structure. As such a partnership can usually only be terminated on the next accounting date following notice being given, this may take in excess of the twelve month period. The CTO argue that, until the partnership can be determined, the landowner does not have vacant possession. A counter argument to this is that, subject to any agreement to the contrary among the parties, under the Partnership Act 1890, s 26 retirement can be effected simply by notice. The partnership will be dissolved as soon as the notice is communicated to all the parties or, if later, on the date specified in the notice. In such cases, therefore, a document should be entered into confirming that the partnership can be dissolved and the landowner can recover his land within a period of less than twelve months. It is advisable in any event that the partnership agreement contains a clause entitling the owner partner to vacant possession within the twelve month period.

Where the relief is to be applied to the value of shares in a farming company which owns agricultural property, then the rate of relief will depend on the interest of the company itself (IHTA 1984, s 122(3)).

There is one further case where the 100% relief is available. This is where the transferor has been beneficially entitled to his interest since before 10 March 1981 and:

1. if the transferor had disposed of his interest by a transfer of value immediately before that date and had duly made a claim under the earlier agricultural property relief provisions contained in FA 1975, Sch 8, the value transferred would have been relieved in accordance with those provisions and would not have been limited by the restrictions then applying on transfers exceeding £250,000 in value or 1,000 acres; and

2. the transferor's interest did not at any time during the period beginning with 10 March 1981 and ending with the date of the transfer carry a right to vacant possession or the right to obtain it within the next twelve months and it did not fail to carry this right by reason of any act or deliberate omission of the transferor during that period (IHTA 1984, s 116(2)(b)(3)).

Broadly, the old relief applied where the transferor was in at least five of the seven tax years preceding the year of the transfer wholly or mainly engaged in the UK in farming (either as a sole trader, a partner, an employee, a director of a farming company or a person undergoing full-time education) and the property was occupied by him for agricultural purposes and was so occupied throughout the two years immediately preceding the transfer (FA 1975, Sch 8 para 3).

The effect of these provisions, known historically as the 'transitional relief' or the 'double discount', enables tenanted farmland where the transferor would

283

11.4 *The Family Farm*

have qualified for the old relief in respect of a transfer made immediately before 10 March 1981, to qualify for 100% relief. Strangely, the transitional relief is not lost if the transfer would not have qualified for the old relief at any time after 9 March 1981. If, for example, an individual subsequently ceased to be a director of the family farming company the crucial time is the position immediately before 10 March 1981 and later events (apart from the requirement that the land remains tenanted) are irrelevant.

There are three important points to make about the continuing availability of transitional relief. The first is that it is vital to ensure that any tenancies in existence at 10 March 1981 are continued, to ensure that there is no question of the transferor's interest ever carrying the right to vacant possession, or the right to obtain it within twelve months. Secondly, apart from the case where the land passes on death to a surviving spouse when the survivor may step into the deceased's shoes and preserve the relief (IHTA 1984, s 120(2)), the transitional relief will apply only to the first transfer of the relevant land after 9 March 1981. It is important, therefore, not to waste the relief by, for example, an inter vivos transfer of the land to a spouse, when the transfer would be exempt in any event. Thirdly, the relief no longer applies once the cumulative transfers of agricultural property qualifying for the old relief, or in relation to post-9 March 1981 transfers qualifying for the transitional relief, exceed £250,000 in value or 1,000 acres.

Agricultural property relief will be lost if the transferor has entered into a binding contract for its sale prior to the transfer (IHTA 1984, s 124).

Agricultural property relief will also be available on agricultural property owned by trustees, whether or not an interest in possession exists in the settled property. Where the trust has an interest in possession, then the beneficiary with that interest will be regarded as the 'transferor' of the property and also as the 'owner' of the property and the 'owner' of an interest carrying the right to vacant possession. In the case of a trust without an interest in possession, the trustees are the 'transferor', the 'owner' of the property, and the 'owner' of an interest carrying the right to vacant possession.

Farmhouses

11.4 A farmhouse will only qualify as 'agricultural property' under IHTA 1984 s 115(2) if it is 'of a character appropriate' to the bare land or pasture owned and occupied by the householder. There is essentially a dual purpose test. First, the property must be a farmhouse and, secondly, it must be of a character appropriate to the property.

There is no statutory definition of a farmhouse in the inheritance tax legislation. In *Lindsay v CIR, CS 1953, 34 TC 289* it was described as 'a building used by the person running the farm'. In the later case of *CIR v John M Whiteford & Sons, CS 1962, 40 TC 379* the Court of Session accepted the Revenue's contention that *Lindsay* defined a farmhouse as a building used by the person running the farm. In *Korner & Others v CIR, HL 1969, 45 TC 287* Lord UpJohn stated *obiter* that the question should be judged in accordance with 'ordinary ideas of what is appropriate in size, content and layout, taken in conjunction with the farm buildings and the particular area of farmland being

The Family Farm **11.4**

farmed and not part of a rich man's considerable residence'. This appears to be in direct contradiction of the *Lindsay* principle. Despite the Revenue's arguments in the *Korner* case, they seem to accept the *Lindsay* principle (CTO Advanced Instruction Manual L.231.1).

When applying the appropriateness test, the property to which the farmhouse must be appropriate is the farmland and will not, for example, include land subject to fishing rights, industrial units or a farm shop selling bought-in produce (*Starke & Another (Brown's Executors) v CIR, CA [1995] STC 689*).

The criteria which are to be applied in determining whether or not a farmhouse is of a character appropriate to the property is to be found in the decision of Mr Justice Blackburn in *Starke* and the Special Commissioners decision in *Dixon v CIR, Sp C 2001, [2002] SSCD 53 (Sp C 297)*.

It was stated in *Starke* that the building would be of a character appropriate to the property if it is 'proportionate in size and nature to the requirement of the farming activities conducted on the agricultural land or pasture in question'. In the *Dixon* case, the Special Commissioner quoted with approval the ninth supplement of McCutcheon on Inheritance Tax, para 14.72 as follows:

> 'The present position is that the "character test" is considered against three main tests:
>
> 1. the elephant test:
>
>   although you cannot describe a farmhouse which satisfies the character test you will know it when you see it!
>
> 2. man on the (rural) Clapham Omnibus:
>
>   would the educated rural layman regard the property as a house with land or a farm?
>
> 3. Historical dimension:
>
>   how long has the house in question been associated with the agricultural property and is there a history of agricultural production?'

The Special Commissioner's decision in *Dixon* concerned a cottage standing in 0.6 acres of ground comprised of a garden and orchard. The case turned primarily on the question of whether the orchard and garden were agricultural land or pasture. The Commissioner was able to find clearly on the facts that it was not but went on to consider the question of whether 'if the land was agricultural the cottage was of a character appropriate to it'. The Commissioner did not examine whether the criteria laid down in *McCutcheon* were the correct ones to apply but simply applied them to the facts of the case finding that the cottage was clearly not of an appropriate character. The decision is of little help, therefore, in deciding whether the criteria conventionally used are the correct ones to apply in determining the appropriate character test.

The *McCutcheon* tests differ from those set out in a letter from Mr Twiddy to *Taxation Magazine*. He indicated that, in deciding whether or not a farmhouse is of a character appropriate to the property, the current CTO approach was to ask the District Valuer to 'consider the appropriate test through the eyes of the rural equivalent of the reasonable man on the Clapham Omnibus'. To assist with that test, there are the following criteria.

11.5 The Family Farm

'Primary character — Is the unit primarily a dwelling with some land, or is it an agricultural unit incorporating such a dwelling as is appropriate? This might be considered an instinctive test; it seeks to gain a comprehensive impression of the nature of the property.

Local practice — Is it normal for land of this quality, use and area to have with it a dwelling of this type and size? The comparison should be with local functioning agricultural holdings rather than with primarily residential holdings. The underlying purpose is to establish the pattern of the type, size and quality of holdings that function primarily as agricultural properties in the area.

Financial support — Is the size and character of the dwelling commensurate with the scale of agricultural operations appropriate for the land? We are not considering a strict economic viability test of the holding, but adding information in context.

Having applied those criteria and such other information as is available, e.g. a large reduction in the area farmed from the house, we then stand back and take a balanced view in the round, and that may be described as the elephant test — difficult to describe but you know one when you see one.'

(Letter from P Twiddy (CTO) Taxation 15 June 2000 p 277).

The question of whether or not a farmhouse is of a character appropriate is a difficult one in the absence of a High Court decision.

In the past, small farms of one hundred acres or so were carried on on a commercial basis and proved self-sufficient. Due to the changes in farming over recent years, on such a farm it is possible that the farmhouse will now have a higher value than the farmland. The Inland Revenue state that they will pursue cases where

(*a*) the value of the farmhouse is in excess of £250,000, but no more than 100 acres are farmed; and

(*b*) the value of the farmhouse is less than £250,000, but no more than 20 acres are farmed. (CTO Advanced Instruction Manual L.231.4).

Due to the significant increase in property prices, there is no doubt that a number of farmers who fall within these categories will have assumed that agricultural property relief will be available to them. It is therefore advisable that the availability of relief is considered so that, if it is not available, other steps can be taken to mitigate inheritance tax.

Business property relief

11.5 In cases where both agricultural property relief and business property relief might be available, agricultural property relief takes precedence over business property relief (IHTA 1984, s 114(1)). Thus, for example, where there is a transfer of an interest in a partnership which owns agricultural property, the value of that partnership interest which is attributable to agricultural property will qualify for 100% agricultural property relief assuming the relevant conditions are met. The remaining value of the partnership interest will qualify for business property relief.

The Family Farm **11.7**

In a farming context, there will be some cases where business property relief is available where agricultural property relief is not. For example, where the agricultural land is situated outside the UK, the Channel Islands and the Isle of Man; or where the value of agricultural property exceeds its 'agricultural value' because it has some development or hope value. In such cases, business property relief will be capable of applying to the excess value. Business property relief may also be available in relation to assets of a farming business apart from the land, for example, farm machinery and stock. In *Farmer & Giles (Farmer's Executors) v CIR, Sp C [1999] SSCD 321 (Sp C 216)* a farming partnership had carved out of the farming operations some buildings and land which had been let. In deciding whether or not business property relief was available the Special Commissioners decided that the matter must be looked at in the round. They must have regard not just to the issue of profitability but also the turnover of the respective sides of the business, the market values of the underlying assets used in the trading and investment sides of the business, and the time spent on each side of the business. It was held that there was a single business and the let property was not excluded from relief.

It may be advantageous, therefore, to keep a single set of accounts for the whole business, including the farm, and to exercise unified management over the whole business.

The conditions governing the availability of business property relief are considered in chapter 10 *The Family Business* at paragraph 10.2.

The instalment option

11.6 Where an inheritance tax liability payable by the donee on death or in respect of a lifetime transfer is attributable to property which qualifies for agricultural property relief, the tax can be paid by ten annual equal interest-free instalments (IHTA 1984, s 227 and IHTA 1984, s 234).The interest-free instalment option also applies to controlling shareholdings in a family farming company and in certain circumstances (considered in chapter 10 *The Family Business* at paragraph 10.3) to specific minority shareholdings in unquoted companies.

Lifetime exemptions

11.7 A potentially exempt transfer is a transfer of any amount or value either to an individual or to certain types of settlement. It will escape inheritance tax completely provided the donor survives the gift by a period of seven years (IHTA 1984, s 3A). Although the potentially exempt transfer is now less important than before because of the availability of 100% agricultural property relief, it remains important in understanding the implications of a lifetime transfer, particularly where the transferor dies in the seven-year period and the transferee has sold the property.

If the transferor of a potentially exempt transfer dies within the seven-year period, inheritance tax may be payable. Where the tax is attributable to the value of agricultural property, agricultural property relief may be available to reduce the value transferred, provided certain conditions are met. These are:

11.8 The Family Farm

(*a*) that the agricultural property is owned by the transferee throughout the period beginning with the date of the potentially exempt transfer and ending with the death of the transferor (or if earlier the death of the transferee). The property must not at the date of death be subject to a binding contract for sale;

(*b*) that the property has been occupied (by the transferee or another) for the purposes of agriculture throughout this period; and

(*c*) where the agricultural property consists of shares in or securities of a company, throughout the relevant period the land was owned by the company and occupied (by the company or another) for the purposes of agriculture (IHTA 1984, s 124A).

There are provisions extending the availability of the relief, subject to certain conditions, where the original agricultural property is transferred by the transferee to a company in return for an issue of shares in that company (IHTA 1984, s 124A(6)(b)) although there is some doubt as to whether section 124A(6)(b) actually achieves this alone. Where the transferee sells the property and replaces it with other agricultural property which is occupied for agricultural purposes throughout the relevant period (IHTA 1984, s 124B) the relief will be extended. However, it appears that the replacement property provisions contained in section 124B will only operate where the transferee sells land and buys more land (CTO Advanced Instruction Manual L.287). They will not apply where the transferee either sells land and instead buys shares in a land-owning company; or sells shares in a land-owning company and buys land; or sells shares in a land-owning company and buys further shares (IHTA 1984, s 124A(6)).

An even more extraordinary quirk of sections 124A and 124B is apparent where a transferor transfers farmland into an accumulation and maintenance trust under which his son will become entitled to the settled property absolutely (or to a beneficial interest in possession in it) at 25. If the transferor dies within seven years of the transfer and his son is still under 25, then (assuming all the conditions are met) agricultural property relief can apply to relieve the value transferred providing all the conditions are met. If, however, the son has attained 25, then section 124A cannot apply in any circumstances because, on the son attaining 25, the trustees of the settlement (who will be the 'transferees' for the purposes of the section) will cease to 'own' the original property and therefore the condition contained in (*a*) above cannot be satisfied. This should be borne in mind when considering the amount of any insurance cover on the life of the donor.

Gifts with reservation

11.8 The gifts with reservation provisions contained in FA 1986, ss 102–102C and FA 1986, Sch 20 operate where either the donee does not *bona fide* assume the possession and enjoyment of the property given more than seven years before the donor's death or at any time within the seven years preceding the donor's death the property is not enjoyed to the entire exclusion, or virtually to the entire exclusion, of the donor and of any benefit to him by contract or otherwise. They are designed to nullify the

The Family Farm **11.9**

inheritance tax effects of a gift of property where the donor continues to enjoy or benefit from the donated property or receives any other form of collateral benefit which is in some way referable to the original gift. For example, the provisions would nullify the effect of a gift by a farmer of his farm to his son if the donor continues to occupy the property or enjoy any benefits from it. The gifts with reservation provisions are considered further in chapter 2 *Lifetime Planning* at paragraph 2.15. The provisions also have a considerable impact in relation to farming partnerships and this is considered in some detail in chapter 10 *The Family Business* at paragraph 10.9.

Occupation by the donor of land which he has given away is disregarded for the purposes of the provisions if he provides full consideration in money or money's worth e.g. he pays a rack rent under a tenancy (FA 1986, Sch 20 para 6(1)(a)). This exemption also applies where a donor gives away an undivided share in land which is then occupied jointly by the donor, provided the donor does not receive any benefit, other than a negligible one, which is provided by or at the expense of the donee for some reason connected with the gift (FA 1986, s 102B(4)).

The provisions of FA 1986, ss 102A–102C which are designed to frustrate 'shearing' operations are examined in detail in chapter 9 *The Family Home* at paragraph 9.9.

Because agricultural property relief can be given at 100%, the gifts with reservation provisions are now of less concern than before. A farmer can now make the ultimate reservation of benefit (i.e. retaining the property until death rather than giving it away) and still have the property wholly exempt from tax. Nevertheless, the provisions must still be considered in planning for tenanted land let pre-1 September 1995 and other situations where a gift should be made (e.g. where family circumstances dictate it).

Grant of tenancies of agricultural property

11.9 The grant of a tenancy of agricultural property in the UK, the Channel Islands or the Isle of Man for agricultural purposes is not a transfer of value for inheritance tax purposes by the grantor if he makes the grant for full consideration in money or money's worth (IHTA 1984, s 16). This provision is, however, applied strictly.

To ensure in a family context that any grant of an agricultural tenancy is for full consideration in money or money's worth, the initial rent for the tenancy should be that which would be obtainable on a grant of the tenancy in the open market. To ensure that such a value is achieved between the parties, independent valuers should act both for the grantor and the grantee.

In determining whether there is full consideration, the Inland Revenue will take into account all the surrounding circumstances, such as the terms of the tenancy and the personal circumstances of the tenant, and will expect the rent payable under the tenancy to be the 'open market rent', i.e. the rent which would be expected to be achieved on the grant by a willing grantor to a willing grantee of the tenancy in the open market (on its particular terms) of the land in question (Law Society's Gazette, 5 Sept 1984 pg 2361). In

11.10 *The Family Farm*

determining the open market rent, the Inland Revenue are more likely to be guided by evidence of 'tender rents' in the area (i.e. the rent which would be expected to be achieved by an owner inviting tenders for the grant of a new tenancy) rather than local 'arbitration rents' (i.e. the new rent determined on a three-yearly rent review of an existing tenancy).

Capital gains tax

11.10 Where a farm has been in a family for generations and is likely to remain the only or main source of livelihood for succeeding generations, capital gains tax is likely to have minimal impact because the land is unlikely to be sold.

On the gift of farm land or a farming business, taper relief may be available either at the business rate or non-business rate. Taper relief is designed to reduce the gain chargeable by reference to the number of complete years of ownership from 6 April 1998. Therefore, the longer an asset is held, the lower the gain arising. If the gain arising is held over under TCGA 1992, s 165 or TCGA 1992, s 260 taper relief will be lost because it is the *untapered* gain which is held over (TCGA 1992, Sch 7 para 1). Hold-over relief will defer the chargeable gain until a subsequent disposal by the donee. Alternatively, capital gains tax retirement relief (conferred by TCGA 1992, s 163 and TCGA 1992, Sch 6) may be available. Retirement relief is available in respect of both gifts and sales, and may apply to exempt any gain arising on the disposal of a farming business or shares in a family farming company. For an individual to be eligible he must be at least 50 years of age or forced to retire before that age due to ill-health. If full relief is available, the first £50,000 of gain is wholly exempt and 50% of the gain between £50,001 and £200,000 is exempt. The amount of relief depends upon the period of ownership of the relevant assets. 2002/03 is the last year in which retirement relief will be available. Where an individual wishes to preserve the existing level of retirement relief but does not wish to sell business assets, he might consider triggering a disposal for capital gains tax purposes. This could be done by way of transferring either the business assets or the family company shares into an interest in possession trust for the donor. This will trigger a disposal and any remaining gains can be held over under TCGA 1992, s 165. However, careful consideration should be given to the loss of available taper relief as a result of settling the business assets on trust and whether it is more beneficial to retain the assets and obtain taper relief rather than taking advantage of retirement relief in the current tax year.

The farmer who wishes to raise funds by making some small sales from his holding can elect that the transfer should not be treated as a disposal for capital gains tax purposes (TCGA 1992, s 242). TCGA 1992, s 242 provides that an election can be made where there is a disposal of land forming part only of a holding, and the consideration for the sale does not exceed the lower of £20,000 and one-fifth of the market value of the holding prior to the sale. The consideration received will be taken into account on a subsequent disposal of the holding.

ESC D26 provides relief on exchanges of land by joint owners where the land received does not include a dwellinghouse which is or becomes used as an only or main residence or where joint owners exchange interests in their respective residences (see Inland Revenue Capital Gains Manual CG65170). There is a similar concession (ESC D23) where land used for the purposes of a trade carried on in partnership is partitioned by the partners on the dissolution of the partnership. In this case, the Inland Revenue will treat the land acquired by each partner as a 'new asset' for the purposes of TCGA 1992, ss 152–158, which confer a rollover relief on the replacement of business assets.

Where land has been purchased and subsequently part is resold, the gain arising on the disposal cannot be rolled over into the acquisition cost of the property still retained by the taxpayer (*Watton (Insp of Taxes) v Tippett*, CA *[1997] STC 893*).

In considering possible lifetime gifts of farmland where there is a likelihood that the land will one day be sold (e.g. following the death of the present owner/occupier), the loss of the capital gains tax free base uplift available on death (TCGA 1992, s 62) should not be overlooked and should be weighed against the potential inheritance tax saving on the death. This is of even greater importance as agricultural property relief is available at 50% or 100%. Where the land was acquired before 31 March 1982, the capital gains tax rebasing provisions contained in TCGA 1992, s 35 may result in a large part of any unrealised gain inherent in the value of the land falling out of the charge to tax on a subsequent sale which will reduce the value of the base uplift. In addition, taper relief may be available to reduce the gain chargeable to tax. On the other hand, where the land will qualify for 100% inheritance tax agricultural property relief on the death, any liability to capital gains tax will amount to an additional charge to tax as the property could have been retained until death at no inheritance tax cost and the capital gains tax free base uplift obtained. The impact and interaction of these provisions is considered in more detail in chapter 2 *Lifetime Planning* at paragraph 2.19.

Reference should also be made to chapter 2 *Lifetime Planning* at paragraph 2.17 and chapter 10 *The Family Business* at paragraph 10.4 for a more detailed discussion of the workings of TCGA 1992, s 165.

Structure of the business

11.11 The comparative advantages and disadvantages of an incorporated and an unincorporated business have been considered in chapter 10 *The Family Business* at paragraph 10.5. In the context of a farming business, the corporate advantage of limited liability is less likely to be a significant consideration and, in any event, may now be obtained through a limited liability partnership. One must, however, consider the rate of corporation tax payable by a company and the rate of income tax payable by an individual, either as a sole trader or through a partnership. In the average farming family, the ability to spread the farming assets around the family by transfers of small blocks of shares is probably more a theoretical than a practical benefit. However, the principal disadvantage of a company,

11.12 The Family Farm

namely the potential double liability to a capital gains charge, is less likely to be a significant consideration where the company owns land which is unlikely ever to be sold. As always, it is important when structuring a business to aim for as flexible a structure as possible, which will enable both lifetime gifts to be made, but which will also minimise the tax payable on death.

In relation to companies and partnerships, the most difficult question to resolve is exactly what to do about the land. Should it be owned by the partnership or the company; or should it be retained outside the farming vehicles? If so, should it be tenanted or not? With the sole proprietor of an unincorporated business, these questions do not arise.

Tenanted or untenanted?

11.12 Agricultural property relief is available at 100% in respect of vacant possession land, land let on a tenancy commencing after 31 August 1995 and certain succession tenancies providing all the normal criteria are met. This effectively removes inheritance tax from the decision making process where new structures are being contemplated.

However, a tenancy has other implications which can be disadvantageous. One (which is alleviated to some degree by the Agricultural Tenancies Act 1995) is its lack of flexibility, but the principal one is the fact that it will give rise to rental payments. The payment of a rack rent may cause cash flow problems for the company or partnership paying it. The payment of rent under a tenancy will convert earned income into unearned income. Whilst the distinction between unearned and earned income is no longer that significant (although in some respects unearned income is still treated less favourably than earned income), the distinction is something of a political one, and it is by no means impossible that the Labour Government will choose to reimpose the tax penalty which previously attached to unearned income.

Rental income can always be waived by a deed before its due date for payment (waivers of rent after it has fallen due will only be effective in limited circumstances — see ICTA 1988, s 41). However, to avoid the application of the associated operations rules in IHTA 1984, s 268, the waiver should not be made within three years of the grant of the tenancy. Such waivers can themselves constitute transfers of value, but if done on a regular basis, it is understood that the Revenue will accept that the normal expenditure out of income exemption will apply to avoid any liability to inheritance tax. This is equivalent to the provisions in IHTA 1984, s 15 which provide that waivers of dividends do not by reason of the waiver constitute a transfer of value.

It should be remembered that an agricultural tenancy may have a capital value which is important in valuing an interest in a partnership, or shares in a company, which owns a tenancy. To date, the question has been debated in relation to tenancies protected under the Agricultural Holdings Act 1986 and the following discussion relates specifically to such tenancies. With regard to farm business tenancies under the Agricultural Tenancies Act 1995, the position will depend on the degree of security of tenure given to the tenant

The Family Farm 11.12

under the terms of the lease and its length although it seems likely that, in practice, it will be difficult to ascribe any significant capital value to most tenancies dealt with under the 1995 Act.

At one end of the spectrum it has been suggested that an agricultural tenancy has no value and at the other that a tenancy may have a value somewhere in the region of one half of the difference between the vacant possession value and the tenanted value of the land (on the basis that this is what a landlord might be prepared to pay to obtain vacant possession of his farm). The truth probably lies somewhere between these two extremes. Even if an agricultural tenancy may be expressly non-assignable, this does not prevent a hypothetical sale of the tenancy being assumed for valuation purposes, although in valuing the tenancy account must be taken of the fact that the hypothetical purchaser would be in the same position as the hypothetical vendor and accordingly unable to assign the tenancy (*CIR v Crossman, [1939] AC 26*). This factor may mean that the tenancy in question has a very low value because no tenant is likely to pay much in the way of a capital sum for an asset which he himself cannot realise and which commits him to paying a rack rent.

Two general approaches have developed to the valuation of these tenancies. *Baird's Executors v CIR, Lands Tribunal 1990, SVC 188* puts the emphasis on the vacant possession premium. If land subject to a tenancy is worth less than if it were vacant, that difference in value could be unlocked by the merging of the two interests. The valuation of this purchase would be based on the division of the vacant possession premium reflecting the balance between the two parties which is often assumed to be equal. The *Baird* approach would apply where it is shown that there is a special purchaser for the tenancy.

The other approach in the case of *Walton (Walton's Executor) v CIR, CA [1996] STC 68* has confirmed that a tenancy will not automatically be valued on the basis of a percentage of the freehold value on the assumption that the freeholder will always be a special purchaser. The sale has to take place 'in the real world' and the actual persons in addition to the actual property need to be taken into consideration. This reflects the value of the tenancy compared with other tenancies of its kind. It is based on an appraisal of profit rent which compares the current rent, the rent potentially due at the next review and a rent where the land is newly let. The case of *Greenbank v Pickles (The Times 7.11.2000)* appears to confirm the *Walton* basis unless there is evidence of a special purchaser of the tenancy.

It is therefore essential to determine whether there are or were any special purchasers at the date of valuation. This will usually be the landlord.

Where the current rental under the tenancy is less than the open market rent and the next review date is in a couple of years, this may give some value to the tenancy. Another factor to be taken into account is the event which requires the value of the tenancy to be calculated. Under the 'hypothetical sale' procedure, the hypothetical purchaser is placed in exactly the same position as that occupied by the vendor. If the time of valuation is the death of the vendor, the hypothetical purchaser would pay nothing for the tenancy on the basis that the landlord would be in a position to serve an incontestable notice to quit on the deceased tenant's personal representatives (Agricultural Holdings Act 1986, Sch 3 Part I Case G). On the other hand, where the

11.13 *The Family Farm*

tenancy is not vested solely in the deceased, for example, where it is owned by a partnership, the tenancy could have a value as it could continue until the death of the last of the joint owners.

Farming business carried on by company

11.13 If the farmland is owned by the company, then its shares will qualify for 100% inheritance tax agricultural property relief to the extent that their value is attributable to the land, provided the transferor of the shares controls the company. The remaining value of the shares should qualify for business property relief. A minority holding will qualify for 100% business property relief but not agricultural property relief because the transferor will not control the company. On the valuation of a minority holding a significant discount will, of course, be achievable on the net asset value of the company.

If the farmland is let to the company under a rack rent tenancy, then the freehold reversion will qualify for 50% agricultural property relief if the tenancy was entered into before 1 September 1995 and 100% relief if entered into or succeeded to after 31 August 1995. Where the company is wholly owned by the landowner, or is at least controlled by him, the Inland Revenue argue that the 100% or controlling shareholding together with the freehold reversion to the land will have an aggregate value approaching the land's vacant possession value. An open market purchaser would be prepared to pay such a sum, so the argument goes, because of his ability either to liquidate the company and merge the tenancy with the reversion (this assumes a 100% holding), or to compel the company to surrender the tenancy, thereby securing vacant possession.

The argument has some force, but whether an open market purchaser would be prepared to pay anything like the vacant possession value must be doubtful and will depend upon the particular facts in each case. The purchaser in negotiating the price would undoubtedly take into account the taxation and other costs of a liquidation of the company or a surrender by it of its tenancy (the latter possibly constituting a distribution for income and corporation tax purposes). Where the shareholding was less than 100%, he would take into account the fact that to avoid prejudicing the minority interests he (as landlord) would have to purchase the tenancy from the company at its full surrender value with all the taxation and other costs that that would entail.

Even if the Inland Revenue's argument is correct, where the land was let prior to 1 September 1995 the land will nevertheless still only qualify for the 50% relief because of the existence of the tenancy.

In the case of a company owning a tenancy of agricultural property which it farms, the shares will qualify for business property relief at 100%. As we have seen, the tenancy itself may have some value within the company, and probably the shares themselves, if a majority holding, will have an even greater value than that reflected by the value of the tenancy alone, since the company has perpetual existence and since the tenancy, even if non-assignable, becomes *de facto* assignable through a transfer of the shares which are not so restricted.

The Family Farm **11.15**

It can be seen that the letting of farmland to a company with the owner retaining the freehold reversion will now only give rise to an unnecessary exposure to inheritance tax where the land is let on a tenancy which commenced prior to 1 September 1995 and where no succession has occurred since that date. The question arises as to whether such tenancies should be terminated with a new agreement being entered into which will enable the let land to benefit from the 100% relief.

It would seem that the Agricultural Holdings Act 1986, s 4(1)(f) may allow a new tenancy to be granted after 31 August 1995 which qualifies for 100% agricultural property relief. However, the words of Lord Howe (Report Stage, Col 895, 23 January 1995) suggests that the section is meant to apply only to unintentional variations and not those deliberately effected to bring about a surrender and regrant.

Farming business carried on by partnership

11.14 As in the case of a company, a partnership carrying on the farming business may either own the land on which that business is carried on or occupy it either under a rack rent agricultural tenancy or under a gratuitous licence.

Where the partnership owns the land, the partners' interests in the partnership, to the extent that their value is attributable to the value of the land, will qualify for 100% agricultural property relief, with the balance of the value qualifying for 100% business property relief.

Where the partnership occupies the farmland under a tenancy, 50% agricultural property relief will be available if the tenancy was entered into before 1 September 1995 and 100% relief will be available if entered into or succeeded to after 31 August 1995. Business property relief at 100% will be available in respect of the partnership interests of the partners and depending upon the terms of the partnership the value (if any) of the tenancy may be taken into account. Where the land is let to a partnership and the freeholder is himself a major partner, the freehold reversion and partnership share is treated as a single unit of property for the purposes of valuation (see *Fox's (Lady) Executors v CIR, CA [1994] STC 360*). The effect is to remove the majority of the discount normally applicable to tenanted land. In *Walton (Walton's Executor) v CIR, CA [1996] STC 68* no allowance or discount was made in calculating the deceased partner's interest. This basis appears to have been confirmed in *Greenbank v Pickles (The Times 7.11.2000)* unless there is evidence of a special purchaser.

Where an Agricultural Holdings Act 1986 protected tenancy is already in existence see the comments above in relation to a farming business carried on by a company with regard to the possibilities of terminating the existing arrangements and entering into new ones.

Milk quotas

11.15 Milk quota is the specific quantity of milk which a farmer can produce without creating a liability to pay a levy for over-production. The quota can be a very valuable asset to the farmer.

11.16 *The Family Farm*

Capital gains tax

11.16 The quota is treated as a separate asset (*Cottle v Coldicott, Sp C [1995] SSCD 239 (Sp C 40)*). Although this is a Special Commissioner's case and not therefore a legal authority, the Inland Revenue hoped that it would be sufficiently persuasive to enable other cases to be settled without further litigation (Inland Revenue Bulletin December 1995). On the sale of quota a capital gains tax liability will arise. Where quota which was originally allocated in 1984 is disposed of there will be a nil base cost. No deduction is given for any part of the historic cost or March 1982 value of the land. If the quota was purchased after 1984, an allowable acquisition cost and indexation allowance will be available up to 6 April 1998. Taper relief is available from 6 April 1998. It is considered that taper relief will be more beneficial than indexation allowance for quotas received after March 1982.

Where a farming business is carried on in partnership, milk quota may be registered in the name of the partnership firm and treated as a partnership asset. Any gain arising on the disposal of quota will therefore be allocated amongst the partners in the usual manner.

As mentioned above the disposal proceeds in some cases may represent the capital gain arising and a significant tax liability could arise. Retirement relief may be available on the quota for disposals in 2002/03. However, the timing of a sale is important. It has been held that where milk quota was disposed of nearly one year after the sale of a dairy herd, there was a separate and distinct disposal of an asset which had been used in or was part of a business, the disposal of which had already taken place (*Wase v Bourke, Ch D 1995, [1996] STC 18*). Therefore, no retirement relief was available on the disposal of the quota.

Compensation payments for permanent cuts in milk quotas are capital sums derived from an asset which give rise to a deemed disposal under TCGA 1992, s 22(1)(a)(2). This is taxable in the year of receipt.

Inheritance tax

11.17 In general, milk quota should be treated as an asset distinct from the land. Therefore, agricultural property relief will not be available. However, business property relief will be available providing the relevant conditions are satisfied.

Foot and mouth disease

11.18 The outbreak of foot and mouth disease during 2001 has in every respect had a significant effect on farmers. Where animals have been slaughtered and compensation paid by the Government there are a number of tax issues which have to be addressed by the farmer. The majority of these are beyond the scope of this book. However, one cannot ignore the estate planning issues that arise. Where a farmer has received compensation for his stock, the tax consequences depend upon whether a herd basis election has been made. Where compensation was received for a substantial herd disposal (i.e. more than 20%) special arrangements existed. Essentially where any culled herd basis animals were not replaced, any profit arising was not taxable. Where such animals were replaced then any compensation received must eventually be treated as taxable income.

Having been struck by foot and mouth disease, Some farmers decided to stop farming and to dispose of their assets. If so, capital gains tax may have been an issue.

For those farmers who received compensation and ceased trading, inheritance tax will be chargeable on any cash sums held by them on death. If the sums are substantial they may consider investing those sums in assets which qualify for business property relief. Where, however, the monies are held with the intention of restocking, business property relief may be available (see chapter 10 *The Family Business* at paragraph 10.2).

Some strategies for the farmer

11.19 We examine below a selection of estate planning strategies for the farmer and his family. No single strategy is always the best one. Each case must be considered separately taking into account the circumstances of the family, the nature of the farming business and the personalities involved.

Doing nothing

11.20 Doing nothing is a strategy that has appealed to many farmers over the years because they are often by nature conservative. Due to agricultural property relief being available at 100% for untenanted land and for land let on tenancies commencing after 31 August 1995, the vast majority of working farmers can now retain their land until death and obtain complete exemption from inheritance tax on its value. This may not even cause practical problems in most instances as many farmers never really retire as such. Any chargeable gain inherent in the value of the land will also be washed out on death, thus achieving the optimum result in respect of both taxes.

Whilst a policy of doing nothing will now be the most effective policy for most farmers, that will not be the case for all. For example, practical circumstances may require the property to be passed down to the next generation prior to death or there may be a pre-1 September 1995 family tenancy which currently prevents 100% relief being available. There is also the question of land which is let to a third party on a tenancy which commenced prior to 1 September 1995 and which will be relievable only at 50% although in most cases of this nature the transferor will not be carrying on a farming business and the tenanted land can be regarded in a similar light to any other investment asset.

Where action is required by a working farmer, this breaks down into two categories, action on retirement and action before retirement.

11.21 *The Family Farm*

Action on retirement

11.21 On his retirement, the retiring farmer may be prepared to give away his farming business, including the land, to those of his children who wish to continue the business. They may in fact already be farming in partnership with their father and the land may either be an asset of the partnership or may still be owned by the father, with the partnership occupying under a tenancy or a gratuitous licence. Such a gift of the farming business and the land should be structured as a potentially exempt transfer, with the father's life being insured for the seven-year period to the extent that the gift does not qualify for 100% relief. If the father is over 50, capital gains tax retirement relief may be available to exempt part of the chargeable gains which might otherwise accrue for disposals taking place in 2002/03. The relief will not apply to tenanted land nor to land used for the purposes of a business if the business continues to be carried on after the disposal. Where a farming business is being carried on by a farming company and an asset, for example, land, is owned by an individual but is used by the company, retirement relief under TCGA 1992, s 163(2) may be available provided the land and the company shares are disposed of at the same time.

In the case of *Plumbly & Others (Harbour's Personal Representatives) v Spencer, CA [1999] STC 677,* land had been used for the purposes of the business of a company of which the taxpayer was a full-time working director and shareholder and rent was paid by the company. At the time of disposal the land was used for the purposes of the business and at the time of the sale the company ceased to carry on the business. The taxpayer claimed relief not under section 164 but section 163. The court held that section 163 could apply not only to assets which were used in a business owned by the disponer but also to assets used in the disponer's personal company and therefore the relief was available.

In addition, there must be a material disposal which includes a part disposal of a business. In *Barrett v Powell, Ch D 1998, 70 TC 432; [1998] STC 283* it was held that the surrender of a tenancy did not qualify for relief because it was not a disposal of part of the taxpayer's business. This was because, following the disposal, the taxpayer had continued to farm the land under a temporary licence, and so there had been no change in the character of his business and no abrogation of a separate part of the business.

An election may be made under TCGA 1992, s 165 to hold-over the balance of chargeable gains arising on the gift, although one must take into consideration the loss of taper relief on a hold-over claim. In practice, with the fall in value of farmland generally since the rebasing of capital gains tax acquisition values in 1982, it is more likely that a loss will arise. Where a substantial gain will arise, the gift should be considered very carefully as retention by the donor until death will result in the gain being washed out as described above.

A gift 'on retirement' should ideally be made just before retirement to ensure that the farmer will have occupied the property for the purposes of agriculture for the two years prior to the gift. Otherwise, agricultural property relief may be lost unless the seven-year ownership test can be satisfied.

Whilst the retiring farmer may be prepared to give up the farmland and his share of the business to the next generation, he may be reluctant to move out of the farmhouse in which he may well have lived for almost all his life. If the farmhouse remains in the ownership of the farmer, then on his death the Inland Revenue are likely to refuse agricultural property relief on the farmhouse, on the grounds that it was no longer being occupied for agricultural purposes. (*Starke & Another (Brown's Executors) v CIR, CA [1995] STC 689; [1996] 1 All ER 622*). In the past, it was possible to perform a 'shearing operation' in respect of the farmhouse. This would involve the farmer first granting to (say) his wife and himself a fixed term tenancy of the farmhouse (and any necessary rights of way), for a term equal to their life expectancy, at a nominal rent. The farmhouse could then be given, together with the other agricultural land, to the next generation, subject to the retained lease. This arrangement is now ineffective due to the enactment of FA 1986, ss 102A-102C by the Finance Act 1999.

Where the retiring farmer wishes to exercise sporting rights over the land he should ensure that he pays a full commercial rent for doing so, so as to bring himself within the exemption provided by FA 1986, Sch 20 para 6(1)(a) (see CTO Advanced Instruction Manual D.28).

Action before retirement

11.22 Where a farmer has one or more children who wish to come into the business, then he should consider bringing them into partnership. In addition, he should consider bringing his wife into partnership, in order to be able to pay her some of the partnership profits. Similarly, in the case of a farming company, both spouses could be directors and paid directors' fees commensurate with their duties. The Inland Revenue have recently been applying the Part XV provisions to husband and wife partnerships. These provisions deem the partnership to be a settlement and deem the settlement income to be that of the 'settlor'; the settlor for these purposes being the spouse (normally the husband) who was the original farmer of the land.

At the same time as bringing members of his family into partnership, it will usually be appropriate to consider the land. This could always be kept outside the partnership. For the taxation consequences of so doing, see the previous discussion under paragraph 11.13 above. A better alternative might be for the farmer to bring the land into the partnership by transferring it into the joint names of the partners. The farmer may decide to credit his capital account in the partnership with the full value of the land brought in by him, and in this case he may also wish to perform a 'value freezing' exercise by incorporating automatic accruer provisions in the partnership under which any surplus value in the land will pass to his children on his death or retirement from the partnership or by providing that any realised or unrealised capital profits attributable to the land shall belong only to them. Alternatively, he may decide to share the land immediately with his children either by crediting his and their capital accounts equally with its full value or by specifying in the partnership deed how the land is to be beneficially owned. The gifts with reservation rules will not apply if the profits are shared in the proportions in which the partners own the partnership assets at commencement (CTO

11.23 The Family Farm

Advanced Instruction Manual D.41.1). However, if the donor receives profits from the partnership in excess of his share of the land, the gift with reservation rules will apply (CTO Advanced Instruction Manual D.52).

The Revenue have confirmed that agricultural property relief will apply to farm cottages which are occupied by retired farm employees or their surviving spouses provided either of the following conditions are satisfied:

— the occupier is a statutorily protected tenant; or

— the occupation is under a lease granted to a farm worker for his life and that of any surviving spouse as part of his contract of employment for agricultural purposes (ESC F16).

Even if the untenanted land is brought back into the estate of the donor, it may still qualify for 100% relief on death. However, it is dangerous to rely on this as it is necessary for certain criteria to be met at that stage. To avoid a gift with reservation, the children might enter into the partnership on full commercial terms in order to ensure that there is no element of gift — although, in a family context this is often impractical.

As is considered in more detail in chapter 10 *The Family Business* under paragraph 10.10, the introduction of land into a partnership may give rise to a capital gains tax charge which cannot be held-over under TCGA 1992, s 165 to the extent that the landowner receives a credit for the land in his capital account.

Borrowings

11.23 Any borrowings of a farming business secured on land qualifying for inheritance tax agricultural property relief should be restructured and secured on property which does not qualify for any form of relief. This is because the existence of the borrowings will be taken into account when valuing the relevant property *before* the application of the relief. Thus, the deduction of the borrowing will be wasted because it would reduce a value which would otherwise be reduced by agricultural property relief. In addition, it is essential that the donee does not assume any liability or give any indemnities to the donor as otherwise a reservation of benefit issue may arise. Therefore, the opportunity should be taken to restructure any borrowings in this way before the death of the landowner.

The problem with outstanding debts which reduce the value of property qualifying for agricultural property relief is well illustrated by the case of a tenant farmer buying the freehold reversion from his landlord. If the tenant dies between the date of the contract of sale and its completion, the outstanding purchase price will constitute a lien on the property purchased and accordingly reduce its value before agricultural property relief is applied.

The 'two sons' problem

11.24 This is a problem often encountered in farming families. The farmer has two sons, one of whom wishes to take over the business (and the land) and the other of whom does not, as he wishes to pursue his own career. However, to carry on the business, the farming son will require all the land to do so. In many cases this will mean that the bulk of the inheritance will have to pass to the farming son. How may the other son be compensated?

Sadly, there is no general solution to the problem. Possibly, the two sons could inherit the freehold of the land, with the farming son taking a rack rent tenancy. This would enable the non-farming son to derive an income from the land and would at the same time give him a share in the capital asset. However, the payment of rent may place an intolerable burden on the business of the farming son.

Alternatively, the two sons could inherit the land jointly and farm it together in partnership. The non-farming son could be a sleeping or limited partner with a small profit share, to give him an income from the property. This may be a more satisfactory solution than a tenancy, but does make the farming son vulnerable to an attempt by the non-farming son to use his rights as co-owner to force a sale of the land and, in effect, put an end to the farming business. Under Trusts of Land and Appointment of Trustees Act 1996, s 12, a tenant in common no longer has an automatic right to enforce a sale.

Another possibility would be for the parents to leave the non-farming son a legacy charged on the farmland which is to be paid only on the death of the other son or on a sale of the land, if earlier. In practice, such a legacy may be of limited value to the non-farming son because of its deferred payment, although it does enable him to benefit from the land if it is ever sold. Another disadvantage is the fact that the transfer of the land to the farming son on the death of his parents may, depending upon the value of the legacy, give rise to a charge to *ad valorem* stamp duty under Stamp Act 1891, s 57.

Perhaps, ultimately, farming parents who find themselves in this position should grasp the nettle and ensure that the farming son alone inherits the farming business and the land. At the same time, they should endeavour to compensate the non-farming son on their deaths out of their other property and concentrate on building up funds for the benefit of the non-farming son during their lifetimes. These funds could either be left to him on their death or made over to him from time to time during their lifetimes by the appropriate use of the lifetime exemptions. The taking out of a regular premium with profits or unit-linked whole life policy settled in trust for the non-farming son would be one way of achieving this objective.

Death

11.25 Where a farmer dies leaving to his widow his farming business or land which is occupied at his death by either a farming partnership (which may include his widow and one or more of his children) or by a company (the shareholders of which may include his widow and children), the widow has a number of options. She may:

(*a*) retain the land and business in her estate with a view to it passing on her death to the next generation — in many circumstances agricultural property relief at 100% will be available on her death;

11.25 *The Family Farm*

(b) decide to redirect the property to one or more of her children by way of a deed of variation effected within two years of the death — in this case the property would again pass reduced by agricultural property relief normally at 100%; or

(c) where relief at 100% is not available, decide to give the property to one or more of her children by way of a potentially exempt transfer in the hope that she will survive the seven-year period so that the gift will escape tax completely.

The right option will depend on the precise family circumstances in each case, and, of course, the availability of agricultural property relief.

Where an inheritance tax liability is anticipated on the death of the farmer or his widow, consideration should always be given to funding the tax by a whole life insurance policy written either on a single life or a joint life and survivor basis held in trust for the next generation.

12 Woodlands

Introduction

12.1 Prior to the Finance Act 1988 woodland had its own tax treatment which in most cases afforded substantial tax savings. The changes made by that Act removed the most significant of these advantages. However, those remaining are still sufficient to merit separate consideration; but before considering how an estate planning strategy might make sensible use of this favourable tax treatment, the tax treatment is summarised.

Income tax

12.2 Prior to 6 April 1988, income from commercially managed woodlands was assessed under its own schedule for income tax purposes, namely Schedule B, although the taxpayer could elect to be assessed under Schedule D, Case I. The most conspicuous aspect of the Schedule B charge was that tax was charged on the occupation (rather than the profits) of 'woodlands in the UK managed on a commercial basis and with a view to the realisation of profits'.

The Schedule B tax charge was abolished from 6 April 1988 and the right to elect for assessment under Schedule D, Case I from 15 March 1988. The occupation of commercial woodlands can no longer give rise to a Schedule D profit or loss.

Since trees on commercially managed woodland are outside the scope of capital gains tax (TCGA 1992, s 250(1)), any profit arising from the sale of such trees is completely outside the scope of any charge to tax. As a corollary, the expenses of planting and managing such trees cannot create a deduction for income tax purposes.

The occupier of woodland may, however, still be assessed:

(*a*) under Schedule A in respect of income from the grant of an easement of, for example, shooting rights, and

(*b*) under Schedule D on the profits of a separate trade carried on in conjunction with the occupation of the woodlands (for example, the production of finished timber goods) which goes beyond such basic activities as felling and sawing which are necessary to render raw timber marketable.

12.3 Woodlands

Short rotation coppice has since 29 November 1994 been treated for tax purposes as farming rather than forestry, so that land under such cultivation is farm or agricultural land and not woodlands (FA 1995, s 154). Short rotation coppice is a perennial crop of tree species planted at high density, the stems of which are harvested above ground level at intervals of less than ten years.

Capital gains tax

12.3 TCGA 1992, s 250(1) provides that in the case of woodlands managed by the occupier on a commercial basis and with a view to the realisation of profits, the consideration for the disposal of trees from the woodlands is excluded from the capital gains tax computation on the disposal by the occupier. This exemption applies whether the trees are standing, felled or cut. Similarly, sums derived from an insurance policy effected in respect of the destruction of, or damage or injury to, the trees are also excluded. Section 250(3) provides that in this respect the provisions of section 22(1) dealing with disposals arising on the receipt of a capital sum are overridden. Section 250(4) and (5) stipulates that in computing the cost and the gain on the disposal of woodland, the cost or consideration, as the case may be, which is attributable to trees (which by virtue of section 250(6) includes saleable underwood) growing on the land is to be left out of account (Inland Revenue Capital Gains Tax Manual CG73210).

If the woodland has been commercially managed then any consideration for the disposal of the trees alone (whether felled or standing) is excluded in computing any gain on the disposal provided the person making the disposal is the occupier. In any other case, each felled tree is treated as a single chattel and a chargeable gain will only arise if each tree has a value in excess of £6,000 (TCGA 1992, s 262). The provisions of TCGA 1992, s 262(4) regarding 'sets' do not apply to trees (Inland Revenue Capital Gains Tax Manual CG73220).

Trees growing on woodland may be disposed of by the owner granting to another person the right to enter the woodland and fell the trees. If the trees are growing on a commercial woodland, the exemption in TCGA 1992, s 250(1) will apply. If the trees are not growing on a commercial woodland, the capital gains tax consequences will depend on the precise nature of the right which is granted. If the person to whom the right is granted is not entitled to benefit from the future growth of the trees, that is if he must fell the trees within a short time, the owner of the woodlands is treated as disposing of the trees as individual chattels. If the person to whom the right is granted is entitled to benefit from the future growth of the trees, that is if he is granted the right to fell trees over a longer period, then the owner is treated as having made a part disposal of his land (Inland Revenue Capital Gains Tax Manual CG73221).

Woodland managed on a commercial basis is an asset used for the purposes of a trade within TCGA 1992, s 165 and therefore a gift of woodlands is capable of qualifying for hold-over relief under that section.

Inheritance tax

12.4 Woodlands managed on a commercial basis are eligible for business property relief at 100%. However, where the woodlands do not represent a business or an interest in a business in the hands of the transferor or do not qualify for another reason (e.g. they have been held for less than two years) the treatment for inheritance tax purposes will vary depending on whether the woodlands form part of an estate on death or are the subject matter of a lifetime gift.

Relief on death

12.5 Where part of the value of a person's estate immediately before his death is attributable to the value of land in the UK on which trees or underwood (which do not represent agricultural property) are growing, an election can be made to have the value of such trees or underwood excluded in determining the value of the estate on death for inheritance tax purposes (IHTA 1984, s 125). Short rotation coppice is treated as being agricultural property. However, no relief can be claimed in respect of the land on which the trees or underwood stand.

The election is made by the deceased's personal representatives or any other person who would otherwise be liable to pay the inheritance tax on the deceased's estate. The election must be made within two years of the death or such longer period as the Inland Revenue may allow. Where the woodlands can be divided into clearly distinct geographical areas, the Inland Revenue allow elections to be made in relation to one or more of the areas (CTO Advanced Instruction Manual L.311).

To prevent exploitation of the relief by death-bed purchases of woodlands, there is a condition that the deceased must either have been beneficially entitled (which will include being entitled to an interest in possession under a settlement) to the land throughout the five years immediately preceding his death or have become beneficially entitled to the land otherwise than for a consideration in money or money's worth (i.e. by gift or devise).

The effect of a claim under IHTA 1984, s 125 is to reduce the overall inheritance tax bill on the estate. However, the election acts only to give a deferral of the tax that would otherwise have been charged rather than a total exemption.

The deferred inheritance tax will become chargeable on the first disposal of the trees or underwood in respect of which relief has been claimed (excepting a disposal to the transferor's spouse (IHTA 1984, s 126)), provided the disposal occurs before the land on which the trees or underwood stood again passes on someone's death. Thus, if the recipient of woodlands on another's death makes a gift of the trees or underwood or sells it during his lifetime, the inheritance tax charge deferred from the deceased's death will become chargeable. If, however, the recipient dies with the trees or underwood still forming part of his estate the inheritance tax charge deferred from the first deceased owner's death will fall out of charge, although the trees or underwood will form part of the second deceased owner's estate. Relief may

12.5 Woodlands

again be claimed under section 125 in relation to the inheritance tax chargeable on his estate.

The inheritance tax charge which arises on the subsequent disposal depends on whether the disposal is a sale for full consideration in money or money's worth. If it is, the amount on which tax is calculated is the net proceeds of sale whether the disposal is of the trees and underwood or of an interest therein. If the disposal is not such a sale, the amount on which tax is calculated is the net value at the time of disposal of the trees or underwood (IHTA 1984, s 126) (CTO Advanced Instruction Manual L.330). The amount on which tax is charged is then added to the deceased's cumulative total, which for these purposes includes all the property in respect of which inheritance tax was chargeable on his death, and tax is charged at the highest marginal rate. Where there has been a subsequent reduction in the rates (i.e. a raising of the thresholds for each rate band or a change in the rates themselves) the tax chargeable on the disposal is calculated on the rates in force at the date of disposal (IHTA 1984, Sch 2 para 4).

The inheritance tax charged as a result of the subsequent disposal is payable by the person entitled to the sale proceeds or who would be so entitled if the disposal were a sale (IHTA 1984, s 208). The tax is due six months after the end of the month in which the disposal took place (IHTA 1984, s 226(4)).

This last provision could produce some strange results. Suppose, for example, that the deceased has made a specific devise of the woodlands to a beneficiary and, because of a direction in the will, the tax in respect of this devise is to be borne out of residue. The deceased's personal representative (who is 'the person liable for the whole or part of the tax') elects for relief under section 125. The value of the trees and underwood on the woodlands is then left out of the calculation of the tax due on death (to the benefit of the residuary beneficiary). However, if the timber is sold a few years later it is the specific legatee of the woodlands who has to pay the inheritance tax charge arising. Not only is the amount of tax on the timber (almost certainly) more than it would have been had the election not been made, but also the specific legatee is liable to pay that tax despite the direction that the tax should be borne by residue. It is unclear whether the specific legatee could claim to be indemnified by the residuary legatee and/or the personal representative as the Inheritance Tax Act 1984 does not provide him with a specific right of recovery. Equally unclear is whether the specific legatee could apply, as one of the persons liable for the tax on the timber (under IHTA 1984, s 200), to have the personal representative's election under section 125 disallowed. Where a request is made more than two years after death for the election to be withdrawn, the Inland Revenue will enquire as to whether the timber has been or is about to be sold (CTO Advanced Instruction Manual L.313).

If the woodland is agricultural property, relief is not available under section 125 although agricultural property relief will be available if the woodlands are occupied and the occupation is ancillary to that of the agricultural land or pasture.

Where the woodland constitutes 'relevant business property' for the purposes of business property relief, business property relief is still available to relieve the land on which the trees or underwood stand where a section 125 election

Woodlands **12.7**

is made and will also be available when the deferred inheritance tax charge becomes chargeable on the subsequent disposal of the timber provided that business property relief would have been available on the previous owner's death if a section 125 election had not been made (IHTA 1984, s 127(2)). This is only of academic interest in most cases as 100% relief will be available rendering an election under section 125 unnecessary.

For land on which the timber stands, there is no relief for the tax chargeable in respect of its value, apart from business property relief. However, the tax can be paid in ten equal annual instalments provided a written election is made (IHTA 1984, s 227). The balance outstanding will become payable if the land is subsequently sold and interest at normal rates will run on the balance outstanding after the date when the first instalment is due (i.e. six months after the end of the month in which death occurred). Where the land itself qualifies for business property relief then the instalments are only subject to interest if they are not paid on the due date.

Relief for lifetime gifts

12.6 There is generally no other specific relief for a lifetime gift (chargeable transfer or potentially exempt transfer) of woodlands unless business property relief is available.

However, where the lifetime gift is a disposal which revives an inheritance tax charge deferred from the previous owner's death two forms of relief are available. The first is that the amount of tax charged on the transferor by reference to the deceased previous owner's estate and cumulative total can be deducted from the value transferred by him on his subsequent gift (IHTA 1984, s 129). (This is a relief of tax against taxable amount, not tax against tax.) The second is that the tax charged in respect of the subsequent gift can be paid by ten equal annual, interest-free, instalments if an election is made. It is available regardless of whether the donee or the donor is paying the tax. The first instalment is due when the tax as a whole would have been due but for the election to pay by instalments.

For land on which timber stands there is no relief for the tax chargeable in respect of its value, unless business property relief is available. The instalment option will, however, be available.

Making sensible use of the tax treatment of woodlands

For the person who does not own woodlands

12.7 Clearly, the financial returns to the investor in woodlands must be scrutinised as closely as the tax benefits. Investing in woodlands will require substantial expenditure on the purchase of land and planting of trees. Depending on the rate of growth of the trees chosen, there will be no income generated by the investment for several years (ten or more). In addition, the investment will be difficult to realise and the return uncertain (unless the price of timber can be accurately predicted many years hence).

12.8 Woodlands

The incentive to invest in woodlands has over the years been reduced. Apart from the favourable inheritance tax treatment of 100% business property relief available to woodlands managed on a commercial basis, their tax treatment is akin to more conventional forms of investment, with no tax deduction on investment but the advantage of a tax-free profit. However, it will be a considerable length of time before any profit accrues. A gift of immature woodlands into trust has the attraction that it is a gift of an asset producing no income but considerable capital growth in the longer term.

If an individual considers woodlands attractive as a long-term investment for the benefit of his minor children, he might, for example, buy the woodlands, plant them with trees predicted to mature in 15 to 20 years' time and then transfer the woods into an accumulation and maintenance settlement for his children. The gift would be entirely free of inheritance tax provided 100% business property relief was available. When the timber matures and is sold, the profits arising can be passed to the children free of tax. Any gain attributable to the land arising on the gift may be held-over under TCGA 1992, s 165.

For the person who already owns woodlands

12.8 The person already owning woodlands will obviously need to scrutinise carefully the profit his investment is predicted to produce. Equally, he will have to bear in mind the tax consequences of any action he might take.

If he has inherited the woodland, he should consider whether or not an election under IHTA 1984, s 125 should be made in the two years following the deceased's death. Where business property relief is available at 100%, there will be no reason to make the election. In fact, because of an apparent quirk in the drafting of IHTA 1984, s 127(2), it would seem positively disadvantageous to do so as relief would thus only be available at 50%.

Where 100% business property relief is not available, the decision as to whether or not the section 125 election should be made is not always an easy one. There is a definite cash-flow advantage in making the election. In addition, the tax charged on a subsequent disposal of the timber will be at reduced rates (provided there has been a reduction in the rates since the date of death). However, this must be set against the fact that the tax is charged on the net disposal proceeds or market value of the timber at the date of disposal and not the value at the date of the deceased's death. Also, consideration should be given to who will be bearing the tax if an election is not made.

If the present owner has a life expectancy of less than seven years, he is unlikely to obtain much of a benefit by making a lifetime gift of the woodlands. If a section 125 election is made in respect of the timber and in relation to the deceased previous owner's death, then if he dies with the woodlands still forming part of his estate the deferred inheritance tax charge relating to the previous owner's death will never be revived. In such a situation it may be worthwhile for him to make the election, subject to the comments made earlier.

Woodlands **12.8**

Subject to the above comments, the wisdom of making an election will probably depend on the maturity of the trees. If they are very young and the present owner intends to hold the woodlands as part of his estate for some time, it will probably make sense not to make the election. Alternatively, if he intends to give away the timber or the woodlands quite soon, he might consider making the election (particularly if he would be bearing the tax if no election were to be made) if only because the amount of tax charged as a result of the disposal in relation to the deceased previous owner's death can be deducted from the value transferred by his subsequent lifetime transfer. However, if the subsequent lifetime transfer is to be made at a time when the woodlands have become eligible for 100% business property relief, this deduction will be of no relevance. Where he wishes to transfer the woodland within two years of the previous owner's death, he would be well-advised to consider making the transfer by means of a variation and election under IHTA 1984, s 142.

13 Gifts to Charities, Etc.

Introduction

13.1 No book on estate planning would be complete without some mention of charities and how best to structure gifts to them.

A 'charity' means any body of persons or trust established for charitable purposes only (ICTA 1988, s 506(1); IHTA 1984, s 272). A charity is defined by the Charities Act 1993 as 'any institution, corporate or not, which is established for charitable purposes'. Charitable purposes include:

(a) the advancement of religion;

(b) the advancement of education;

(c) the relief of poverty; and

(d) any other purpose, not falling under the above heads, which is beneficial to the community in a charitable sense (Lord MacNaughten in *Special Commrs v Pemsel, HL 1891, 3 TC 53; [1891] AC 531*).

The inclusion of an institution on the register of charities raises a conclusive presumption that an institution is or was a charity at any time when it is or was on the register (CTO Advanced Instruction Manual M.290). However, not all charities have to be registered under the Charities Act 1992 so a body that is not registered may nevertheless be a charity. To qualify as a charity, a charity must be subject to the jurisdiction of the courts of the UK (*Dreyfus (Camille and Henry) Foundation Inc v CIR, HL 1955, [1956] AC 39; 3 All ER 97*). Therefore, a lifetime gift or legacy to a foreign charity will not qualify for the inheritance tax exemption. If a gift is made to a UK charity whose objects include charitable activities overseas with the stipulation that it is passed on to the foreign charity, that activity does not qualify as charitable. It is therefore important to inform a client of this issue when they are deciding to make a charitable gift. The Finance Act 2002, s 58 and Sch 18 introduces special provisions relating to Community Amateur Sports Clubs which, whilst not charitable, are given various reliefs akin to those given to charities. These are dealt with in 13.21 below

Capital gifts

Inheritance tax

13.2 A charitable donation made by an individual is a transfer of value which is generally exempt from inheritance tax (IHTA 1984, s 23) to the

13.3 Gifts to Charities, Etc.

extent that the value transferred by it is attributable to the donated property. Where the value transferred exceeds the value of the gift in the hands of a charity, the Inland Revenue take the view that the exemption extends to the value transferred (Inland Revenue Statement of Practice SP E13).

Example

A holds 60% of the shares in a company. The shareholding is worth £200,000. A 30% shareholding is worth only £50,000, since it is only a minority shareholding. A gives half of his 60% shareholding to a charitable trust. The loss to his estate (because the property in the trust is 'related property' under IHTA 1984, s 161(2)(b)(i)) is £100,000 (1/2 × £200,000). The value of the gift in the hands of the charity is £50,000.

In the above example, the value transferred by the transfer of value is £100,000, but is it wholly or only partly 'attributable to property' given to the charitable trust? The Inland Revenue have stated that in such a case the transfer would be wholly exempt (Statement of Practice SP E13). (The phrase 'attributable to property' is also used in IHTA 1984, s 3A in the definition of potentially exempt transfer. It is understood that the Inland Revenue apply the same interpretation.)

Section 23(1) refers to 'property which is given to charities'. The terms 'give', 'given', 'gift' are rarely to be found in the inheritance tax legislation, and nowhere are the words 'give' and 'gift' actually defined. However, section 23(6) provides that '. . . property is given to charities if it becomes the property of charities or is held on trust for charitable purposes only. . .'. Therefore, to qualify for exemption a gift (*inter vivos* or by will) need not be to a recognised charitable body provided it is applicable only for charitable purposes. This is an important planning point, for it enables the testator of a will to leave a legacy, or a share of residue, for charitable purposes and at the same time express a wish that the money be applied by his executors to particular named charities or to charities of a certain type or class.

Anti-avoidance provisions

13.3 IHTA 1984, s 23 contains provisions (in subsections (2) to (5)) to prevent the avoidance of tax by use of the general exemption for property given to charities in subsection (1).

Since it is only individuals who can make chargeable transfers, there are no charging provisions dealing with the situation where a charitable company or the trustees of a charitable trust make a transfer of value. It might be thought that by giving a limited interest to a charity a transfer could be made by an individual which would be entirely free from inheritance tax.

Example

A wishes to create a discretionary trust. If he transfers property to trustees on discretionary trusts there would be an immediate charge to inheritance tax on A. However, if A were to make the transfer to a trust in which a charity had an initial interest in possession (say for one year) with the remainder on discretionary trusts, he might hope that the transfer would be exempt and that

Gifts to Charities, Etc. **13.3**

there would be no charge on the termination of the charity's interest in possession.

Quite apart from the scheme's vulnerability to an attack under the associated operations rules (IHTA 1984, s 268) and the doctrine in *Ramsay*, such a scheme will be defeated by the operation of section 23(3)(b) which provides that there is no exemption available where the property transferred to the charity is given to it for a limited period.

If, instead of creating an interest for a limited period, it is decided to create a defeasible interest (i.e. one liable to be terminated on the happening of a specified event), the exemption will also not be available by virtue of section 23(2)(c). For these purposes any disposition which has not been defeated within twelve months of the transfer and is not defeasible after that time is treated as not being defeasible (whether or not it was capable of being defeated before that time).

Similarly, where the property transferred consists of an interest in other property, then if the transferee charity's interest is less than the transferor's interest, no exemption will be available (IHTA 1984, s 23(3)(a)). Thus, where the holder of a freehold estate in land grants a lease of that land to charity (with the probable aim of transferring the freehold estate in reversion at a greatly reduced value) no exemption will be available. Relief from income tax will, however, be available (ICTA 1988, s 587C(2)).

If a postponed interest, or an interest subject to a condition precedent which is not satisfied within the following twelve months, is created, no exemption will be available (IHTA 1984, s 23(2)(a) and (b)).

Section 23(4) contains special 'reservation of benefit' provisions applying to gifts to charities. FA 1986, s 102(5)(d) disapplies the general reservation of benefit provisions in section 102 to transfers where the section 23 exemption is available. Subsection (4)(a) disallows the exemption where the transferor transfers land or a building to a charity subject to the right for him, his spouse or a connected person to possess or occupy the property transferred rent-free or other than on arm's length terms. Subsection (4)(b) applies where the property transferred is other than land or a building. The exemption is disallowed where there is an interest reserved to or created by the transferor other than one for full consideration or which does not substantially affect the enjoyment of the property by the transferee charity.

Finally, subsection (5) provides that where the whole or any part of the property given may be applied for purposes other than charitable purposes no exemption will be available in respect of any part of the gift.

As a result of these anti-avoidance provisions there is no economic advantage to an individual in making a gift to charity. While such gifts may be exempt from inheritance tax and other taxes, an individual cannot usually bestow a greater benefit on himself or someone else (a non-charity) by making a gift of property to charity than if he retained the property or gave it to that other person.

13.4 Gifts to Charities, Etc.

Capital gains tax

13.4 TCGA 1992, s 257 provides that gifts to charities are to be treated as disposals for a consideration producing neither a gain nor a loss.

A strategy for capital gifts

13.5 The would-be benefactor of charities should consider making a Gift Aid donation to charity within FA 1990, s 25, so as to obtain income tax relief on his gift as well as inheritance tax relief.

Lifetime gifts v transfers on death

13.6 Since outright gifts to charity are exempt from inheritance tax, it is usually sensible for an individual to make lifetime gifts to his family (since these are not exempt *ab initio* although they may be potentially exempt) and to make any gifts which he wishes to make to charity in his will (given that he will probably need to retain some capital in his estate during his lifetime).

> *Example*
>
> A widow has an estate of £500,000. Her children have already been well provided for. She decides that she would like £100,000 of her estate to go to charity and £400,000 to her children. She calculates that she can afford to give away £100,000 now. If she makes a potentially exempt transfer of £100,000 in favour of her children and survives for the following seven years, no tax would be payable on the potentially exempt transfer and she would leave a chargeable estate (assuming no change) of £300,000 on which inheritance tax at 2002/03 rates amounts to £20,000. If, on the other hand, she makes a lifetime gift of £100,000 to charity and leaves the whole of her estate to her children, she will leave a chargeable estate (assuming no change) of £400,000 on which inheritance tax at 2002/03 rates amounts to £60,000.

If an individual decides to make a lifetime capital gift to charity, he should consider making a direct gift of assets with large unrealised capital gains rather than a gift of cash, since the disposal of the assets will not result in any charge to capital gains tax (TCGA 1992, s 257) and will not reduce his cash resources. The charity, if it requires cash, can immediately sell the assets and realise a gain free of tax provided the proceeds are applicable and applied for charitable purposes (TCGA 1992, s 256). This is an important planning point, because small charities may sometimes be reluctant to receive donations in any form other than cash. If the would-be benefactor informs the charity that he can give them more in non-cash assets than he could if they would only take cash and reminds them that they can sell the assets free of capital gains tax the charity may be willing to receive a donation in a non-cash form.

However, as explained below, 'Gift Aid' is only available for gifts of cash. An income tax deduction will be available, however, on gifts by persons carrying on a trade, profession or vocation of assets which are manufactured or sold in the course of the activity or which are machinery or plant used in that activity (ICTA 1988, ss 83A and 84). An income tax deduction is also available on gifts to a charity of qualifying investments or qualifying interests in land.

Gifts to Charities, Etc. **13.8**

Qualifying investments for this purpose are listed shares or securities, units in an authorised unit trust, shares in an open-ended investment company and interests in offshore funds. A qualifying interest in land is defined as a freehold interest in land, a leasehold interest in land which is a term of years absolute where the land in question is in the UK (ICTA 1988 s 587B(9A)). Agreements to acquire a freehold interest and agreements for lease are not qualifying interests in land.

Gifts from inherited capital

13.7 An individual may want to make a capital gift to charity because of a change in his personal circumstances. If he has inherited capital (by will or on intestacy) he should consider executing a deed of variation to give capital to the charity and making an election under IHTA 1984, s 142 (if the two-year period has not yet expired).

Example

A (a widow) dies leaving the whole of her estate of £300,000 to her son B (an only child). Inheritance tax on the estate at 2002/03 rates amounts to £20,000. Of the £280,000 which B receives he decides he would like to make a gift to charity of £20,000. If he makes a simple gift of £20,000 the gift will be exempt from inheritance tax and he will be left with £260,000. If, on the other hand, he executes a deed of variation of A's will and makes a statement under section 142 to have the disposition treated as if it had been made by A, he will transfer £20,000 to the charity but will be able to claim a repayment from the Inland Revenue of £8,000 (£20,000 at 40%) by way of overpaid inheritance tax, leaving himself with £268,000 (£280,000 − £20,000 + £8,000). No income tax relief under FA 1990, s 25 would be available on the grounds that a benefit under FA 1990, s 25(2)(e) had been received in that the amount of inheritance tax payable on the estate had been reduced (*St Dunstan's v Major (Insp of Taxes), Sp C [1997] SSCD 212 (Sp C 127)*). In that case, it was held that, because under Gift Aid rules a donor should not receive a benefit in excess of 2.5% of the gift (this has now been changed), relief was not available. However, if it can be arranged for the inheritance tax saving to accrue to a third party or be added to the gift, it may be arguable that income tax relief will be due.

Where a gift of either quoted shares or an interest in land is made to a charity, there is a different rule relating to benefits to the donor. The rules operates in a different way and there is no mention of a defined percentage. It may therefore be sensible to have a deed of variation relating to the shares or land. In the above example, if B were to make a gift of quoted shares equal to £20,000, the inheritance tax saving would be £8,000. As a higher rate taxpayer he could claim income tax relief under ICTA 1988, s 587B on £12,000 (£20,000 − £8,000) giving him a saving of £4,800.

Gifts out of income

Covenants and Gift Aid

13.8 The relief for payments made under a covenant which runs for a period capable of exceeding three years (ICTA 1988, s 347A) was abolished

13.9 *Gifts to Charities, Etc.*

for payments due after 5 April 2000. Relief is now given for payments which are qualifying donations to charity within FA 1990, s 25 ('Gift Aid'). To be a qualifying donation, the payment must take the form of a cash payment.

There is no minimum limit for gifts, instead the relief applies to any gift. A simple form of certification is required under which the donor merely gives to the charity an appropriate declaration. This declaration can be given in writing, orally or by means of electronic communication and must contain the following:—

(*a*) his or her name, address and postcode;

(*b*) the name of the charity;

(*c*) a description of the gift which may be a single gift or a series of gifts;

(*d*) a statement that the gift or gifts to which the declaration relates are to be treated as qualifying donations for FA 1990, s 25; and

(*e*) where the declaration is given in writing, a statement explaining the effect of FA 1990, s 25(8).

Where an oral declaration is made (i.e. a gift aid donation is made by telephone) special rules apply The charity must send a written record to the donor who will then have 30 days to change his mind.

(Donations to Charity by Individuals (Appropriate Declarations) Regulations 2000 (SI 2000 No 2074)).

A declaration may cover gifts since 6 April 2000 and all future gifts.

Whilst the making of a qualifying donation is possibly more an exercise in income tax planning than estate planning, since 1 October 1990 the distinction between gifts out of income and gifts out of capital has to some extent become blurred. A one-off gift of capital cash to a charity (in addition to attracting inheritance tax relief) may also qualify for an income tax deduction to the extent that the donor's income for the tax year in which the gift is made exceeds the amount of the gift grossed up at the basic rate of income tax (see above).

FA 2002, s 98 provides that for gifts made after 5 April 2003 a donor may elect that their qualifying donation be treated as if it were made in the previous year of assessment. Such an election must be made in writing within certain statutory time limits.

Gifts of shares and securities

13.9 As mentioned above, Gift Aid payments must be in cash. If a potential donor has shares pregnant with capital gains, it may be better to give the shares to the chosen charity which will be treated as a no gain no loss transfer, rather than sell the shares, pay capital gains tax and give the net proceeds. This is especially so because income tax relief is available on the value of listed shares and securities, units in authorised unit trusts,

Gifts to Charities, Etc. **13.12**

shares in open-ended investment companies and interests in offshore funds given to charities (ICTA 1988, s 587B).

Gifts of real property

13.10 FA 2002, s 97 has introduced a relief from income tax, similar to that given in relation to gifts of shares and securities, where a qualifying interest in land is given to a charity. Therefore, where a potential donor has a qualifying interest in land on which there is an unrealised gain, it may be more tax effective to give the property to the chosen charity rather than sell the property and give the proceeds to the charity.

In order to claim the relief the taxpayer must have received a certificate from the charity which contains a description of the qualifying interest in land, the date of the disposal and a statement that the charity has acquired the qualifying interest in land.

There will be a clawback of relief on the happening of a disqualifying event within the defined relevant period. A disqualifying event occurs if the donor or a person connected with him becomes entitled to an interest or right in relation to all or part of the land to which the disposal relates or becomes party to an arrangement under which he enjoys some right in relation to all or part of that land otherwise than for full consideration in money or moneys worth. There is no disqualifying event if a person becomes entitled to a right or interest as a result of a disposition of property on death. The relevant period is the period beginning with the date of disposal and ending with the fifth anniversary of 31 January following the end of the year of assessment in which the disposal was made.

Gifts made as a trader

13.11 Under ICTA 1988, s 84 a trader is able to donate used plant and machinery to an approved educational establishment in the UK without bringing its market value into account for tax purposes. The same applies for donated trading stock. FA 1998, s 47 extended this relief for the same period as 'Millenium Gift Aid' (i.e. 31 July 1998 to 31 December 2000) to educational projects in those countries contained in the same list of the world's poorest countries. This relief has been further extended to all charities for an unlimited period for gifts made on or after 27 July 1999.

Payroll deduction scheme

13.12 The payroll deduction scheme provides that an employee wishing to make a gift to charity can authorise his employer to withhold any amount from his wages. The deductions must be made pursuant to a scheme which is approved by the Inland Revenue or is of a kind approved by the Inland Revenue. The employer must pay the sums withheld to an Inland Revenue approved agent under the Charitable Deductions (Approved Schemes) Regulations (SI 1986 No 2211). The agency must distribute the donations within 60 days of their receipt from the employer (Charitable Deductions (Approved Schemes) (Amendment) Regulations (SI 2000 No

13.13 *Gifts to Charities, Etc.*

759). The donor will then obtain tax relief as if the deductions were allowable expenses of his employment.

For deductions made between 6 April 2000 and 5 April 2003 (inclusive) a supplement of 10% is made by the Government.

Charities Aid Foundation

13.13 In many cases people would like to be able to earmark some of their salary for charity before the end of each tax year, but postpone payment until such time as they find charities they want to benefit and then divide the sums earmarked amongst whatever charities and in whatever amounts they care to choose. All these demands can be satisfied by the person involved making a Gift Aid payment to the Charities Aid Foundation ('CAF'). The Foundation receives the sums paid and reclaims the basic rate tax withheld at source by the payer. The sums paid (subject to a small deduction for administration) and the tax reclaimed are then held by the Foundation to be distributed to charities as the original payer directs. Directions are given on payment order forms signed by the payer. They resemble cheques and, indeed, it is not an inapt analogy to think of the Foundation as a charitable bank with whom the donor has an account, sums only being capable of being withdrawn from the account for payment to a charity. More details of the scheme can be obtained from the Charities Aid Foundation ('CAF') , Kingshill, West Malling, Kent, ME19 4TA (Tele: 01732 520000; web: www.cafonline.org).

Payments from discretionary trusts

13.14 A further tax-efficient way to support a charity is for income to be paid from a discretionary trust assuming that the trustees have the power to make such a payment. The charity will be able to reclaim the relevant amount of income tax paid by the trustees on the sum given. This is because ICTA 1988, s 687 enables the charity to reclaim a tax credit equal to the rate applicable to trusts (34% for 2002/03) applied to the payment grossed up by the tax credit. If a capital payment is made by the trustees, IHTA 1984, s 76 should ensure that there will be no inheritance tax charge on the property leaving the trust.

General rules for charitable gifts

13.15 The greatest tax saving from making charitable donations is generally achieved by the payments being made direct from the source from which the donor would derive the money with which to make the donation.

Example

As outlined above the recipient of property by will, or on intestacy, might seek to make a capital donation by means of a deed of variation and an election under IHTA 1984, s 142.

Similarly, a director and controlling shareholder of a company might authorise the company (assuming that it has power to do so under its

Gifts to Charities, Etc. **13.17**

memorandum and articles of association) to make charitable donations rather than give some of his own income to charity or make contributions under the payroll deduction scheme. The national insurance saving both to the employee director and the employer company will normally outweigh the loss of the 10% supplement on payroll deduction scheme payments made between 6 April 2000 and 5 April 2003.

Within a family, the income and inheritance tax savings can be maximised by the family member who pays the highest rate of tax making the donations.

Creating your own charitable trust

13.16 A wealthy individual may wish to create his own charitable trust. If he is anticipating doing this by will, he should be careful to ensure that the trust will be a valid charitable trust, since if it fails it will be too late to take any remedial action once the testator has died. The gift would probably lapse as a result. However, it might be effective to create a valid non-charitable trust if the trust is not invalid for uncertainty of objects or void for perpetuity. Alternatively, he could set up a charitable trust with a small sum during his lifetime which is registered with the Charity Commission so the Inland Revenue similarly regard the trust as being charitable. He could then, following the advice given above, make lifetime gifts to non-exempt beneficiaries and in his will make a substantial donation to that trust. If it is considered to be important, he could make donations on identical terms to that trust, to take advantage of a new accumulation period of 21 years from the date of death rather than 21 years from the date of the creation of the original trust. A further advantage of this is that he may relieve his executors from having to apply to the Charity Commission to register a charitable will trust, which can occasionally require a construction summons where there is doubt concerning the trust's validity.

Drafting gifts to charity

13.17 Care needs to be taken in drafting covenants to charity. (The reader is referred to other works which deal with this in greater depth, such as Tolley's Charities Manual.) Care also needs to be taken in drafting deeds of gift and wills containing charitable gifts.

First, and most importantly of all, the charity's correct name and address should be ascertained. It should be checked that the body or trust in question is in fact a charity. Some bodies which have members, such as the Prayer Book Society, are charities (or, as in the particular case of the National Trust, may be a specifically exempt body under IHTA 1984, s 25 and IHTA 1984, Sch 3); however, many are not.

Secondly, when drafting a will it is advisable to include a 'mergers' clause, specifying that if the charity has been taken over, wound up or simply re-named, the gift shall be construed as a gift to the body which has taken over the charity or received the surpluses applicable for charitable purposes on the winding-up or the newly named body. Where no such clause is included, it may be possible to continue the charitable gift through an application to the

13.18 *Gifts to Charities, Etc.*

Charity Commission for a scheme for the property to be applied cy-près i.e. to some other charitable purpose as nearly as possible resembling the original trusts. This depends on whether there is a general charitable intention.

Thirdly, when drafting a will it is helpful to include a receipt clause specifying that the receipt of the treasurer, or other proper officer for the time being of the charity, shall be a good discharge to the testator's executors who need be under no further obligation to see to the application of the monies or assets given.

Temporary charitable trusts

13.18 Mention should be made of funds which are held on charitable trusts for a specified period, following which the funds are held for non-charitable beneficiaries. This situation may occur unexpectedly, for instance, if a site given for a school or village hall is no longer required and reverts to the descendants of the original donor.

Inheritance tax

13.19 During the 'charitable period', there is an exemption from the ten-yearly charge and the charge on distributions. Instead, a charge arises when the property ceases to be held on the charitable trusts and the rates of tax applicable are set out in IHTA 1984, s 70(6). The longer the charitable period, the greater the charge when that period ends but subject to a maximum rate chargeable of 30% after 50 years.

Capital gains tax

13.20 Under TCGA 1992, s 256, when property ceases to be held on charitable trusts, the trustees are deemed to have disposed of, and immediately reacquired, the property at its market value. Any gain arising is not treated as accruing to the charity and is therefore liable to capital gains tax, subject to a claim for hold-over relief under section 260 of that Act. In addition, to the extent that the property at that time represents, directly or indirectly, the consideration for the disposal of assets by the trustees, any gain accruing on that earlier disposal (and previously exempt) is treated as not having accrued to the charity and capital gains tax is applied as if the exemption had never applied. A cumulative liability may therefore arise and an assessment may be made within three years of the end of the year of assessment in which the property ceases to be held for charitable purposes. Such an assessment seems to be able to be made even where the gain arising on the earlier disposal is outside the normal time limit for assessment.

Community Amateur Sports Clubs

13.21 Finance Act 2002, s 58 and Sch 18 introduced a variety of tax reliefs for Community Amateur Sports Clubs ('CASCs') A sports club now

Gifts to Charities, Etc. 13.21

has the choice between applying to the Charity Commissioners for charitable status or to the Inland Revenue for status as a CASC. A CASC must be formally constituted and meet three criteria. It must be

(*a*) open to the whole community;

(*b*) organised on an amateur basis; and

(*c*) have as its main purpose the provision of facilities for the promotion of participation in one or more eligible sports.

It the club only accepts members who have already reached a certain standard, rather than seeking to promote the attainment of excellence by enhancing access and the development of sporting aptitude, then it does not have an open membership and so would not be a CASC. Similarly a club that only allows participation at an elite level with other members being spectators rather than players will not be acceptable, although a club fielding a number of teams ranging from recreation and novice players up to a reasonably high competitive standard would be acceptable.

The Government estimates that there are approximately 110,000 community sports clubs in the UK with a total membership of 5.6 million people. Of these it is estimated that between 30,000 and 40,000 clubs might be eligible to register as CASCs.

The following chart compares the tax reliefs for sporting charities and for CASCs:

	Charitable status	**Community Amateur Sports Clubs**
Direct taxes	Primary purpose trading income exempt from tax.	Gross income from fund-raising and trading exempt from tax where turnover is less than £15,000. (*All* such income is taxable if the threshold is exceeded.)
	All rental income exempt.	Gross income from property exempt from tax where less than £10,000. (*All* such income is taxable if the threshold is exceeded.)
	80% mandatory relief from uniform business rates.	Under separate legislation to take effect in 2004, mandatory rates relief at 50% for clubs with a rateable value of less than £3,000, reducing to no relief for rateable values more than £8,000.
Incentives to give	Gift Aid on individual and company donations.	Gift Aid on individual donations only.

13.22 *Gifts to Charities, Etc.*

	Payroll giving.	No payroll giving.
	Income tax relief on gifts of shares.	No income tax relief on gifts of shares.
	Inheritance tax relief on gifts.	Inheritance tax relief on gifts.
	Gifts of assets on no-gain, no-loss basis for capital gains.	Gifts of assets on no-gain no-loss basis for capital gains.
Fund-raising	Business: relief on gifts of trading stock.	Business: relief on gifts of trading stock.
	Grants available from other charities, e.g. community foundations, and other bodies supporting charities.	Will not attract charitable sources of funding.
Regulation	Charity Commission regulation and audit.	Inland Revenue regulation and audit.
	Public recognition of and trust in 'charity' and 'Gift Aid' concepts.	Public awareness of CASC's 'brand' to be developed.

Gifts for national purposes

13.22 IHTA 1984, s 25 extends the section 23 exemption for gifts to charities to gifts to bodies named in Schedule 3 to the Act. These bodies include UK national museums, local authorities, government departments and universities or colleges. The anti-avoidance provisions in IHTA 1984, s 23 (see under 13.3 above) also apply to gifts for national purposes. Gifts to these bodies are also treated for capital gains tax purposes as disposals for a consideration producing neither a gain nor a loss (TCGA 1992, s 257).

Gifts for public benefit

13.23 Under IHTA 1984, s 26 gifts of eligible property to bodies not established or conducted for profit were, if the Board of Inland Revenue directed, exempt from inheritance tax. This exemption does not apply in relation to transfers of value made on or after 17 March 1998 (FA 1998, s 143).

Gifts to political parties

13.24 A gift of any amount made either during a person's lifetime or on his death to a qualifying political party is exempt from inheritance tax (IHTA 1984, s 24).

A qualifying political party is defined in section 24(2) as one in respect of which, at the last general election preceding the transfer of value, two

Gifts to Charities, Etc. **13.24**

members of the party were elected to the House of Commons or one member was so elected and the party received not less than 150,000 votes overall.

Gifts to non-qualifying political parties do not qualify for any exemption or relief.

The anti-avoidance provisions in IHTA 1984, s 23 (see under 13.3 above) also apply to gifts to political parties.

14 National Heritage Property

Introduction

14.1 Encouraging the preservation of our national heritage through the giving of tax privileges is not a new concept. The Finance Act 1896 first gave the Treasury discretion to waive estate duty in respect of settled chattels considered to be of national, scientific or historical interest, such as paintings, books and other works of art.

The current reliefs, encompassing inheritance tax, capital gains tax, income tax and stamp duty aim to help in the preservation of our national heritage property. Generally, these reliefs tend to encourage continued private ownership of heritage property including land and buildings of outstanding interest as well as land essential for the protection of the character and amenities of an outstanding building and objects historically associated with such a building. This is illustrated by the availability of relief for 'maintenance funds' which are tax-efficient vehicles for providing funds for the upkeep of heritage property kept in private ownership. However, there are also specific reliefs which facilitate tax-free gifts or sales of heritage property to certain national bodies.

Inheritance tax

14.2 The reliefs available can broadly be split into those which enable the property to be placed in some form of public ownership and those which do not. The two sets of reliefs interact.

Transfers where the property is not retained in private ownership

14.3 Transfers of property to various national and local bodies are exempt from inheritance tax (IHTA 1984, s 25). The bodies to which such gifts may be made are listed in IHTA 1984, Sch 3 and include the National Gallery, the British Museum and other national museums, the National Trust, any museum or art gallery maintained by a local authority or university, any university library, and any local authority or government department.

Gifts to such bodies need not be of heritage property as such but, apart from cash and liquid assets, the property must be of some real value or interest.

14.4 National Heritage Property

Transfers where the property is retained in private ownership

14.4 The provisions allowing heritage property to be retained in private ownership are found in IHTA 1984, ss 30–35A which provide that a transfer of value of heritage property is exempt from inheritance tax provided certain conditions are met.

Prior to 31 July 1998, conditional exemption was generally available for chattels where the Treasury (in the form of the Inland Revenue as from 19 March 1985) designated property under IHTA 1984, s 31 as being of national, scientific, historic or artistic interest, i.e. of museum quality. In addition, undertakings had to be given that certain agreed steps would be taken to maintain and preserve the property, to provide reasonable access to the public and to keep movable property in the UK (unless the Treasury agreed to a temporary absence for a specified purpose, for example, an exhibition).

For claims made after 30 July 1998, assets (other than those historically associated with a qualifying building) qualify only if they are pre-eminent for their national, scientific, historic or artistic interest. For undertakings given after that date, the facility allowing owners to opt for public access by prior appointment only is not available.

Conditional exemption applies to transfers of value occurring as a result of death and to certain chargeable lifetime transfers. For lifetime transfers, either the transferor must have acquired the property by a transfer on death which was itself a conditionally exempt transfer or the transferor (or spouse) must have been beneficially entitled to the property for the six years immediately preceding the transfer (IHTA 1984, s 30(3)). Property held on trust may also qualify for conditional exemption in certain circumstances and these are discussed separately below.

Transfers of value which are already exempt from inheritance tax because they are either gifts to charities or inter-spouse transfers cannot also be conditionally exempt transfers (IHTA 1984, s 30(4)).

Similarly, potentially exempt transfers cannot also be conditionally exempt transfers unless the transfer subsequently becomes chargeable due to the transferor dying within seven years. Conditional exemption can only be claimed after the transferor's death if the property has not been disposed of in the interim unless the disposal is to a body within IHTA 1984, Sch 3 or is in satisfaction of tax under IHTA 1984, s 230 and, in either case, the property has been or could be designated as heritage property under IHTA 1984, s 31 (IHTA 1984, s 26A).

Conditional exemption may also be claimed if the property has been disposed of by the donee provided the disposal was by way of gift and the new owner, is prepared to give the necessary undertakings.

Where relief is given, the transfer is a conditionally exempt transfer (IHTA 1984, s 30(2)). Provided the undertakings are observed the inheritance tax liability can be postponed. The deferred charge will become payable if a 'chargeable event' occurs (IHTA 1984, s 32). There are three occasions on which such an event can arise, namely:

National Heritage Property **14.6**

(*a*) the death of the beneficial owner of the property (with certain exceptions);

(*b*) the disposal, whether by sale or gift, of the property (with certain exceptions); and

(*c*) the failure of the relevant person to observe, in any material respect, an undertaking given to the Treasury or Board of the Inland Revenue.

The exceptions to (*a*) and (*b*) above are, broadly, if the transfer of value on death or disposal by gift is itself a conditionally exempt transfer, the sale or disposal is to a body within IHTA 1984, Sch 3 or is in satisfaction of a tax liability under IHTA 1984, s 230 or the requisite undertaking under IHTA 1984, s 31 is given by such persons as the Inland Revenue considers appropriate in the particular circumstances. It is no longer acceptable for such replacement undertakings to simply correspond with the old undertakings.

The inheritance tax charge is calculated according to the rules contained in IHTA 1984, s 33 and the market value of the relevant property at the time of the chargeable event. In addition, the cumulative total of chargeable transfers for the person who made the last conditionally exempt transfer in respect of that property is adjusted upwards by the amount of the value of the property on which tax is paid (IHTA 1984, s 34). Where this person is dead his estate will be similarly increased and this can affect the rate of tax applicable on the event of a second and subsequent chargeable event.

The rules applicable to maintenance funds are dealt with separately below, as are those applicable to settlements.

Meaning of 'disposal'

14.5 There has been much debate about what constitutes a 'disposal' for the purposes of IHTA 1984, s 32. At one time there was concern that mortgaging the property as security for a loan would be treated as a disposal. However, it is understood that in some circumstances mortgaging a property to raise finance to restore it would not be treated as a disposal. (See the summary of the correspondence between the Inland Revenue and the Historic Houses Association published in Historic House Magazine, Spring 1990 and Summer 1991.)

It is understood that the grant of a lease for no premium will not normally be treated as a disposal, but the grant of a long lease for a substantial premium will be. If in doubt, the Heritage Section of the Capital Taxes Office should be consulted before any plans are made to grant leases or raise capital from the property by way of mortgage.

Interaction with agricultural property relief and business property relief

14.6 In the case of landed estates qualifying as heritage property, much of the land will also qualify for agricultural property relief at either 50% or 100%. The relief is given as a reduction in the value transferred by a

14.7 National Heritage Property

transfer of value. In addition, there may be situations where property qualifies not only as heritage property but also for business property relief.

A chargeable event occurs if conditional exemption is forfeited on one of the three occasions mentioned above. A charge under IHTA 1984, s 32 will arise as explained above and also under the associated property provisions of IHTA 1984, s 32A. Under sections 32 and 33, tax is charged on 'an amount equal to the value of the property at the time of the chargeable event' (IHTA 1984, s 32(1)). There is no transfer of value (deemed or otherwise) and therefore any agricultural property relief or business property relief is not available. It is usually better, therefore, to make a chargeable transfer subject to business or agricultural property relief rather than to claim conditional exemption.

Claiming conditional exemption from inheritance tax

14.7 Conditional exemption from inheritance tax relies upon the property being 'designated' by the Board of Inland Revenue and 'appropriate undertakings' being given by the relevant person. Furthermore, if capital gains tax relief is to be claimed under TCGA 1992, s 258(2) (see below), the property must have been, or must be capable of being, designated for inheritance tax purposes and the appropriate undertakings must be given.

Designation

14.8 There is no definition of 'heritage property' in the legislation. However, IHTA 1984, s 31 states that the Treasury may designate:

(a) a relevant object which is pre-eminent for its national, scientific, historic or artistic interest or a collection or group of relevant objects which, taken as a whole, is pre-eminent for its national, scientific or artistic interest. A relevant object is defined as a picture, print, book, manuscript, work of art or scientific object. The test of pre-eminence has replaced the old test of 'museum quality' for claims made after 31 July 1998. This requires a higher standard to be reached;

(b) land of outstanding scenic, historic or scientific interest;

(c) buildings of outstanding historic or architectural interest;

(d) land essential for the protection of the character and amenities of a building falling within (c) above; and

(e) objects historically associated with a building falling within (c) above.

The booklet, IR 67 *Capital Taxation and the National Heritage* published by the Inland Revenue gives useful guidance as to what is considered to be appropriate property.

When determining if an object or collection is pre-eminent, regard should be had to any significant association of the object or collection with a particular place.

The Board of Inland Revenue are, of course, unable to determine themselves what objects, buildings and land should be designated as national heritage property and the Capital Taxes Office (who are responsible for designating property) uses expert advisers recommended by the Museums and Galleries Commission.

As regards land and buildings, the Capital Taxes Office mainly receives advice from bodies such as The Countryside Commission, English Heritage, the Forestry Commission, English Nature, Cadw: Welsh Historic Monuments and other more specialist advisers such as the Royal Botanic Gardens (for rare trees), etc.

Inland Revenue booklet IR67 states that land is likely to be considered of outstanding scenic interest if it lies within a national park in England or Wales, within a designated area of outstanding natural beauty in England, Wales or Northern Ireland or within a national scenic area in Scotland. However, land falling within one of these areas is not certain to qualify and, conversely, land falling outside these areas may still qualify. To qualify on their own merits buildings will need to be listed. Generally only grade 1 or grade 2* will qualify. The Board of Inland Revenue is prepared to be flexible as regards what they will designate and ancient semi-natural woodlands may qualify as national heritage property. Interestingly, such woodlands might qualify on the basis of being of scientific, scenic or historic interest.

For chattels, advice is received from the Museums and Galleries Commission. The Commission consider an object to be 'pre-eminent' if it would constitute a pre-eminent addition to a national, local authority, university or independent museum, or that it is pre-eminent in association with a particular building. Foreign objects as well as British works may fall within the definition.

Undertakings

14.9 During the process of designation, the relevant expert body negotiate with the owner detailed undertakings, i.e. a management plan. The undertakings may include matters such as the maintenance and preservation of the assets, the management of any land, the conservation plans for buildings and their contents and the proposed public access and how it is to be provided and publicised. More information on the procedure is provided in the Inland Revenue's Guidance Notes entitled 'Capital Taxes — Relief for Heritage Assets'.

The Countryside Commission publishes a booklet 'Heritage Landscapes Management Plans' which gives an overview of the type of undertakings which are necessary together with a detailed example of the features which a typical management plan will contain in respect of property qualifying under the 'scenic' category.

Monitoring undertakings and the provision of public access

14.10 Not surprisingly, these are two of the main areas of controversy regarding heritage property.

The government has said that it was concerned that chattels designated as being heritage property have not been as readily available for public viewing as was originally intended and that in many cases owners were not fulfilling

14.10 *National Heritage Property*

their undertaking to provide public access. As a result the Finance Act 1998 provisions claimed to be designed to give the public improved access to tax exempt assets while maintaining the protection of heritage property. This included the withdrawal of the facility for owners to opt for public access by prior appointment only.

Both existing and future undertakings may be varied by the Inland Revenue. For undertakings given after 6 April 1976 and before 31 July 1998, the Inland Revenue are able to re-open the terms of such undertakings for any claim for conditional exemption. At any time the Inland Revenue may propose a variation of the original undertaking to the owner for agreement. Any changes must be confined to either the securing of public access in a way which does not require the public to make any prior appointment with owners or their agents or the securing of publication of the undertakings and any other information relating to the assets. If an agreement cannot be reached within six months of the Inland Revenue's proposal, the matter can be referred to the Special Commissioners. However, the Inland Revenue have indicated that 'providing there has been no undue delay in negotiation on the owner or their agent's part', reasonable further time will be allowed for negotiation (Revenue Guidance Notes 'Capital Taxes — Relief for Heritage Assets', para 4.10). If, at the end of six months from the making of such a proposal, the owner disagrees, the Inland Revenue may refer the matter to the Special Commissioners for a decision as to whether 'it is just and reasonable, in the circumstances, to require the proposed variation to be made'. It has been confirmed that the personal circumstances of those bound by existing undertakings are relevant in making this decision. If the Commissioner is satisfied that the Board's proposal is 'just and reasonable', he may direct that it shall take effect from a date not less than 60 days from when his direction is made. It is understood that a test case is likely to be taken before the Special Commissioners in 2003 in which the taxpayer will contend that a direction for a variation of an undertaking made prior to 17 March 1998 would fail the 'just and reasonable test' set out in IHTA 1984, s 35A (see Taxline issue 08/02, page 10).

The Inland Revenue are not able to seek adjustments to terms attaching to estate duty exemptions.

The legislation imposes a tax charge if the undertakings are not observed in a material respect (IHTA 1984, s 32(2)). There has been little guidance as to what the phrase 'in a material respect' means in practice although it is understood that provided the breach of undertaking can be corrected, with there having been no permanent detrimental impact on the property, the Inland Revenue will overlook the breach as being immaterial.

Under the monitoring procedures it is understood that owners of outstanding land or buildings will generally be required to make annual reports to the Inland Revenue about the maintenance of the assets and the provision of public access. The Inland Revenue have stated that exempt land and buildings will be inspected usually every five years or when they consider appropriate. Periodically, the Inland Revenue will enquire whether there have been any disposals and seek confirmation that all undertakings have been, and are being,

National Heritage Property 14.10

observed (Inland Revenue Guidance Notes 'Capital Taxes — Relief for Heritage Assets', para 2.12).

'Public access' above means that all owners of exempt assets will have to provide a measure of 'open' access to those assets in accordance with the terms of an undertaking agreed with the Inland Revenue. 'Public access' must be reasonable and this will depend upon the nature and type of asset as well as the preservation and maintenance needs of that asset. For example, access to a large building may not be reasonable in the case of a smaller building or, say, a delicate object. In some cases it may be appropriate to mix 'open' access with 'appointment' access if it is required for the preservation of the object. In certain circumstances it may be appropriate to suspend or exclude public access.

In the case of exempt buildings and their amenity land, the minimum period of 'open' access is 25 to 156 days each year. In the case of land, the access will, in general, be all year round during daylight hours and on defined routes but with agreed closure periods for sporting activities, land management, nature conservation, etc. In most circumstances it will be open to the individual to charge a fee to view the exempt building but this must be reasonable from the point of view of the public at large.

For chattels exempt in their own right, 'open access' may be provided by displaying the objects at

(a) the residence of the individual or at the place the object is kept (and unless the building itself is tax exempt, access may be limited to the area of the building where the chattels are displayed);

(b) a museum or gallery to which the public have access;

(c) any other building open to the public, e.g. a local Record Office;

(d) the appropriate European Heritage Open Days event free of charge (i.e. Heritage Open Days (England), Doors Open Days (Scotland), London Open House, and European Open Days (Wales and Northern Ireland); and

(e) local, regional or touring exhibitions.

Objects may be loaned for display in the public collection of a national institution, local authority, university or independent museum and this period counts as 'open'.

Historically-associated objects will normally be displayed in the building with which they have an historical association.

If a chattel is located in a building which is itself tax exempt, the period of access should be the same as that for the building, i.e. 25 to 156 days each year. In other situations the minimum period will be 5 to 100 days a year and the Museums and Galleries Commission will advise the Inland Revenue where this applies. The Inland Revenue may be prepared to consider a two-year accounting period rather than a one-year period in certain circumstances.

Publicising access and undertakings is a requirement of conditional exemption for heritage assets. The Inland Revenue will expect the individual to make any

14.11 *National Heritage Property*

undertaking available to any member of the public who asks to view it. The undertaking in relation to the building or exempt chattel may be displayed at the premises and the Inland Revenue may also enter the details on their Internet website. The information required for the website is

— a description of each object,

— full address of the building and opening times, and

— name, address and telephone number of the contact person (i.e. owner, agent, etc.).

Owners of buildings open to the public may be required to publicise the public access arrangements by:

— advertising details in the local paper, tourist office and/or town hall;

— advertising details in one of the annual national guides to historic houses, i.e. Hudson's Historic Houses and Gardens and Johansen's Historic Houses, Castles and Gardens;

— placing a sign at the main entrance of the property with details of opening times; or

— informing appropriate local council and education authorities.

For undertakings given before 31 July 1998, the Inland Revenue have issued guidelines on what is considered to be reasonable public access as regards works of art, etc. One option for securing access is for the owner to allow viewing by appointment and, subject to conditions, to lend it for special exhibitions on request to directors or curators of public collections for up to six months in any two-year period.

Making a claim

14.11 A written claim for relief from inheritance tax under IHTA 1984, s 30 must be made to the Capital Taxes Office on Form 700A (IHT) in respect of chattels considered to be pre-eminent. A written claim must be made within two years of the date of death or date of transfer. The Inland Revenue have the discretion to extend this period. The Inland Revenue have indicated that an oversight or mistake on an individual's part or his adviser's part, or the making of a post-death variation will not normally by itself be an acceptable reason to allow a late claim (Inland Revenue Guidance Notes 'Capital Taxes — Relief for Heritage Assets', para 2.3). Before 16 March 1998 there was no such time limit. In the case of both lifetime chargeable transfers and transfers on death (including potentially exempt transfers which became chargeable as a result of death), a claim could not be made until after the event. With lifetime chargeable transfers this was, perhaps, not such a problem but where the relevant transfer was as a result of death the procedural delays could have caused significant problems for the executors as regards administration of the deceased's estate.

Unfortunately, there is no formal advance clearance procedure. However, the Countryside Commission will usually give an informal indication of the likelihood of land qualifying for relief on the basis of it being of outstanding scenic interest. Where a claim is likely to be made, perhaps because of the poor health of the current owner, it is worthwhile seeking in advance informal advice from the Countryside Commission. This will, at least, allow alternative planning steps to be considered if the property is unlikely to meet the required standards.

One situation where a claim for designation will be considered in advance is the intended lifetime creation of a maintenance fund in support of an outstanding building, outstanding or amenity land and historically associated chattels (IHTA 1984, Sch 4 para 1(2)).

Another situation where a claim will be considered in advance is in connection with the ten-year charge arising under IHTA 1984, s 64 in respect of property held on discretionary trusts. It is essential to ensure that a claim is accepted and the property designated under IHTA 1984, s 31 and IHTA 1984, s 79 as heritage property *before* the charge actually arises. It is not sufficient merely to have made the claim before the date on which the charge arises. It is understood that the Capital Taxes Office has no discretion to backdate designation to cover an earlier ten-year charge even though the conditions would have been met had a claim been received. Hence, the claim for relief should be submitted in good time, considering that it can take as long as two years to process a claim.

Capital gains tax

14.12 The heritage property provisions tend to be regarded largely as an inheritance tax relief. However, there are equally generous capital gains tax reliefs which interact with the inheritance tax reliefs. This is most obvious in that the capital gains tax legislation only gives relief in respect of property falling within the relevant inheritance tax provisions (TCGA 1992, s 258).

Disposals to certain national bodies within IHTA 1984, Sch 3 (IHTA 1984, s 25) qualify for capital gains tax relief under TCGA 1992, s 258. Relief is given by exempting the gain in full. As indicated above, neither of these inheritance tax provisions are strictly in respect of heritage property only.

Section 258 also gives capital gains tax relief for the gift of any asset which either has been or could be designated heritage property under IHTA 1984, s 31. This relief includes gifts to a settlement and disposals by trustees of property vesting absolutely. If no inheritance tax designation has actually taken place (for example, because the relevant asset was the subject of a potentially exempt transfer and the gift has not therefore created an immediate inheritance tax liability) then the equivalent undertakings required under IHTA 1984, s 31 must be given in order to claim the capital gains tax relief.

As regards heritage property falling within IHTA 1984, s 31, capital gains tax relief is given by deeming the relevant disposal to be a no gain, no loss disposal. Any relief given can subsequently be clawed back by deeming there to have been a disposal at market value upon one of three occasions.

14.13 *National Heritage Property*

(*a*) Where the property is sold and an inheritance tax charge arises under IHTA 1984, s 32.

(*b*) Where an undertaking has not been observed in a material respect.

(*c*) Where there is a disposal other than by way of sale and no new undertaking is given. This could apply, for example, where the new owner of the property subsequently dies and no new undertaking is given by the transferee. In this instance, the owner of the asset is treated as having immediately reacquired it at market value.

These broadly correspond to the occasions on which a chargeable event occurs for inheritance tax (see paragraph 14.4 above).

Therefore, where there is a clawback and the property has increased significantly in value, there will be a gain arising of not only the clawed back gain but also the gain accruing since the no gain, no loss disposal.

Where a capital gains tax charge arises due to the clawback of relief, the tax payable is allowed as a deduction when determining the transfer of value for inheritance tax purposes (TCGA 1992, s 258(8)).

Maintenance funds

14.13 The beneficial tax treatment afforded by the heritage property provisions outlined above may not alone be sufficient to enable a private individual or family to retain and maintain a substantial heritage property. By their very nature, many heritage properties are not income-producing or are unlikely to create sufficient income to be self-maintaining. Generally, other means of support are required.

Legislation designed to alleviate the problems facing the owners of heritage properties exists to exempt funds set aside to maintain the properties from capital taxes. Maintenance funds are now a useful tool in the preservation of heritage properties. They are not, however, always the best solution.

The statutory conditions

14.14 A qualifying maintenance fund is one which falls within IHTA 1984, Sch 4 Part I. Such funds are tax favoured as they attract inheritance tax reliefs, and to some extent, capital gains tax and income tax reliefs.

To qualify for relief, a fund should be for the benefit of land and/or buildings (and/or historically associated objects) which qualify, or could qualify, for conditional exemption and the fund must be held on the terms of a trust. In the first six years the trust fund must not be capable of being applied for a use other than for the maintenance, repair and preservation of, or making provision for public access to, heritage property, except that income not so applied and not accumulated can be paid to a qualifying charity or to a body included in IHTA 1984, Sch 3 (IHTA 1984, Sch 4 para 3). The property comprising the trust fund must be of an appropriate character and amount. In practice, this means it must produce sufficient income to maintain the relevant heritage property. The trustees of the settlement (or a majority of them) should be UK resident and must include either a trust corporation, a solicitor or an accountant or a member of another acceptable professional body (IHTA 1984, Sch 4 para 2).

Although the provisions are reasonably stringent, there is some scope for flexibility. In particular, funds can be withdrawn from the settlement after the initial six year period (subject to an inheritance tax charge) if it becomes apparent that they are required for other purposes or are excess to requirements. It is also possible to add further funds at a later date, for example, on the death of the settlor if this is found to be necessary.

Inheritance tax

14.15 The maintenance fund is, in effect, a discretionary trust. Without any reliefs there would be an inheritance tax charge on transferring funds into the trust, a ten-yearly periodic charge and an exit charge in the event of trust capital being used to maintain or otherwise benefit the heritage property itself. However, there are inheritance tax reliefs which exempt such transfers of value from inheritance tax (IHTA 1984, s 27 and IHTA 1984, Sch 4).

A maintenance fund can be established not only for national heritage property which has already been subject to a claim for conditional exemption, but also prior to a claim for conditional exemption. The Treasury can designate the relevant heritage property (i.e. confirm they believe it to be of sufficient national importance to qualify) and accept undertakings given by the current owner as if it had been the subject of a chargeable transfer. This allows the maintenance fund to be formed prior to, say, the death of the owner. This course of action is a means of testing whether heritage property is of an acceptable standard to be designated prior to claiming conditional exemption.

Additional property can be added to an existing maintenance fund, free of inheritance tax, by an individual. Under IHTA 1984, Sch 4 para 16, property held by a discretionary trust can be appointed to a maintenance fund without an exit charge arising under IHTA 1984, s 65. The property may pass either straight to the maintenance fund or via a beneficiary of the discretionary trust provided the beneficiary transfers the property to the maintenance fund within 30 days. The trustees of the maintenance fund must not have acquired an interest in the discretionary trust for money or money's worth or, where the property passes via an individual, that individual must not have acquired the property for money or money's worth.

On the death of a life tenant, property already in an interest in possession settlement can be transferred to a maintenance fund free of inheritance tax (IHTA 1984, s 57A). The transfer must be made within two years of the death of the life tenant or within three years if a court order is required to change the terms of the settlement.

For transfers of value made after 16 March 1998, a claim for inheritance tax relief must be made within two years of the date of the transfer concerned or within such longer period as the Inland Revenue may allow. For transfers prior to that date, there were no time limits for claiming relief.

14.16 National Heritage Property

If property leaves a maintenance trust for a purpose other than to repair, preserve or maintain the property and is not given to a qualifying charity or to a body falling within IHTA 1984, Sch 3, an exit charge arises (IHTA 1984, Sch 4 Part II). Although property can be reclaimed from the maintenance fund after six years, there is a penalty for doing so. One notable exception to this charge is where the property is transferred to another qualifying maintenance fund (IHTA 1984, Sch 4 para 9) which again gives some flexibility to the arrangement.

Income tax

14.16 The income of a maintenance fund is taxed under the normal income tax provisions applicable to settlements, subject to the provisions contained in ICTA 1988, ss 690 to 694. Where the settlor has retained an interest in the trust fund, even an indirect interest by virtue of his owning the heritage property which the trust is established to benefit, the income arising is treated as that of the settlor. However, sections 690 to 694 enable the trustees to elect that the trust income, which would otherwise be taxable as the settlor's income, be taxable as if it were the trustees' own income. The election must be made within twelve months after 31 January following the year of assessment to which it relates. If the election is made currently the trust's income will be taxable at 34%. If the settlor pays tax at the higher rate of 40%, this will produce a small benefit. If, however, the settlor does not pay higher rate tax it will be better for the trust income to be taxed as if it were the settlor's. Should the settlor be a Lloyd's underwriter, the possibility that losses may become available may make it preferable for the income to be taxed on the settlor.

Where property of the maintenance fund (either capital or income in nature) is applied for a non-qualifying use, or the fund ceases to qualify and the Board of Inland Revenue's direction is withdrawn, any income which has arisen since the establishment of the settlement and which has not been applied in the upkeep of the heritage property is, with certain exceptions, subject to an additional tax charge under ICTA 1988, s 694. This additional tax charge is at a rate equivalent to the difference between the higher rate of income tax and that applicable to discretionary trusts; currently giving an additional tax charge of 6%. Obviously, this will have an impact where property is withdrawn from the maintenance fund after the initial six year period.

As can be seen, the income tax advantages of a maintenance fund are minimal. Indeed, if an election is made to treat the income as the trustees' own income, it may in fact be trapped in the trust, taxable at 34%, while the settlor is not paying tax at all.

Capital gains tax

14.17 Specific relief for transfers into maintenance funds is provided by TCGA 1992, s 260(2)(b)(iii). The relief is available on the establishment of the maintenance fund, on the addition of further funds at a later date and on transferring funds from an existing maintenance fund to a new maintenance fund.

Where the trustees of a maintenance fund realise gains by selling assets, the gains are *prima facie* subject to tax under the normal provisions applicable to settlements. In normal circumstances, the settlor could be charged to tax on trust gains under TCGA 1992, s 77 (the onshore settlor charge provisions). However, where the trustees have made an election, under ICTA 1988, s 691, for the settlor not to be taxed on trust income all trust gains will be taxed on the trustees at 34% (TCGA 1992, s 79(8)).

Despite the availability of hold-over relief on transferring assets into a maintenance fund, such funds do not benefit from a particularly generous capital gains tax regime.

Settled heritage property

14.18 Historically, owners of heritage property have used trusts to ensure continuity of ownership and management and also to protect the property from improvident heirs.

Broadly speaking, property can be subject to the settled heritage property provisions in three circumstances.

(*a*) Where the property is the subject of a chargeable transfer into trust.

(*b*) Where an individual dies with a life interest in settled heritage property.

(*c*) Where property is held on discretionary trusts and is therefore subject to the inheritance tax regime applicable to discretionary trusts.

These three situations are dealt with in turn below, followed by a brief review of problem areas encountered in practice.

Transfer of property into trust

14.19 The lifetime transfer of property to either an interest in possession or an accumulation and maintenance trust is a potentially exempt transfer. Conditional exemption cannot, therefore, be obtained unless the transfer becomes chargeable on the death of the settlor. On the other hand, a transfer to a discretionary trust is a chargeable lifetime transfer and conditional exemption may be an issue. A claim is made in the normal way and, if conditional exemption is granted, the trustees will have to give the required undertakings.

A lifetime transfer of heritage property to a discretionary trust, where conditional exemption is relied upon to mitigate the potential inheritance tax liability, can be an expensive strategy if conditional exemption is not, subsequently, granted.

Termination of life interest on death

14.20 Property in which a life tenant has an interest at the time of his death can be designated as heritage property under IHTA 1984, s 31. This is because any property to which the deceased is beneficially entitled

14.21 National Heritage Property

immediately before his death is included in his estate for inheritance tax purposes and is, therefore, the subject of a deemed transfer of value on death.

Property held on discretionary trust

14.21 A discretionary trust can be exempt from inheritance tax in respect of heritage property for the purposes of the ten-yearly charge (IHTA 1984, s 79) and also when heritage property leaves the trust subject to certain ownership conditions (IHTA 1984, s 78).

Generally, the trust is exempt from the ten-yearly charge if either the trust property has previously been the subject of a conditionally exempt transfer (and has therefore already been designated) or there has been an exempt disposal for capital gains tax purposes (also requiring designation). Alternatively, the trust property may be specifically designated as heritage property prior to the ten-yearly charge to avoid tax on that event. As explained above, this is the only occasion on which the Capital Taxes Office will give advance designation of a property, and the property *must* actually be designated before the ten-year anniversary.

Gifts with reservation

14.22 Where the property is held on life interest trusts, it will form part of the life tenant's estate for inheritance tax purposes and conditional exemption can be claimed on his death. However, if conditional exemption is to be obtained during the lifetime of the current owner, the heritage property must be settled on the terms of a discretionary trust. This enables the original owner to be an active party in negotiations with the Capital Taxes Office and, as the transfer is a chargeable transfer, establishes the conditional exemption (or otherwise) of the property. It also leaves open the choice of ultimate heir and this may be one of the major attractions of a discretionary trust.

Where the original owner is included as one of the initial beneficiaries, the gifts with reservation provisions need to be considered regardless of whether the settlor actually receives any benefit. FA 1986, s 102(5) provides an exemption from the provisions for exempt transfers of property to maintenance funds but not for transfers of the heritage property itself. Presumably this is because the heritage property is conditionally exempt and should continue to be exempt provided the undertakings are not broken and, therefore, the gift with reservation provisions should not cause any difficulty.

Occupation by the settlor

14.23 There is a potential problem where, as is often the case, the settlor occupies the heritage property after the transfer of the property to a discretionary settlement. If the settlor's occupation is under such terms as to create an interest in possession in the property, i.e. if the settlor has an exclusive or joint right of residence (see Inland Revenue Statement of Practice SP 10/79), an exit charge can arise under IHTA 1984, s 65 as the property will cease to be 'relevant property'. If this event occurs within three months of establishing the settlement there will be no exit charge (IHTA 1984, s 65(4)) and if it occurs after six years the trustees will have owned the property long enough themselves to claim conditional exemption (IHTA 1984, s 78(1)). The danger is that an interest in possession will be created after the initial three month period but before six years have elapsed. There are practical difficulties in ensuring that the settlor does not acquire an interest in possession in the settled property if he does intend to live in the property. The right of occupation should be non-exclusive but there may be great difficulty in avoiding practical exclusive occupation. If the Inland Revenue are successful in arguing that an interest in possession has been given over the property occupied by the settlor, there could be an exit charge. Alternatively, the initial gift to the settlement may be deemed not to have been of relevant property to a discretionary settlement and hence not a chargeable transfer.

Strategy

14.24 When considering the strategy for a particular set of circumstances, there are three main questions to be answered.

(a) Does the family wish to, and indeed is it able to, retain and finance the upkeep of the heritage property in future years?

If the answer is 'yes', then it is necessary to consider whether, and how best, to utilise the various heritage property reliefs. In some circumstances where one qualifies for conditional exemption it may be beneficial not to claim it.

(b) Is a lifetime gift appropriate or should conditional exemption be claimed on death?

In general, lifetime gifts are encouraged by the inheritance tax legislation and heritage property is no exception. A gift to a discretionary trust is a chargeable lifetime transfer and conditional exemption can be claimed. Other gifts will generally be potentially exempt transfers and may, therefore, escape the impact of inheritance tax altogether or, if the donor dies within seven years, conditional exemption can be claimed on death. Furthermore, a lifetime transfer is deemed to be a no gain, no loss disposal for capital gains tax purposes where the property is either designated or could be designated as heritage property.

One potentially significant disadvantage of a lifetime gift is the loss of the tax-free capital gains tax uplift on death. This may be relatively unimportant where the property is to be retained by the family and can continue to be designated as heritage property or where the property is unlikely to appreciate significantly prior to the death of the transferor. However, if the property is ever sold, or conditional exemption lost for other reasons, the cost of losing the capital gains tax uplift on death may be substantial.

14.24 National Heritage Property

A lifetime gift to a discretionary trust may be considered as it enables the choice of eventual heir to be left open and the transferor can oversee such matters as the provision of public access to the newly designated heritage property. However, there are problems as explained above with this strategy.

Waiting until the death of the current owner of potential heritage property before claiming conditional exemption may have its advantages. This enables the capital gains tax uplift on death to be utilised. However, it also means that the deceased's executors and family will have to make an application for conditional exemption.

(c) Should 'supporting property' (i.e. property to provide funds for the upkeep of the heritage property itself) be placed in a maintenance fund or not?

Maintenance funds do have advantages and they are flexible vehicles. In particular, a lifetime gift of property to a maintenance fund has the advantage that it requires the relevant heritage property to be designated even where no chargeable transfer of the actual heritage property has been made. The establishment of a maintenance fund can therefore be used to test whether the relevant property is of sufficiently high standard to be designated as heritage property. However, the use of property held in a maintenance fund is severely restricted for the first six years. This restriction will need to be weighed against the tax advantages of using a maintenance fund.

An alternative to a maintenance fund is to advance supporting property direct to the transferor's heir. Such a gift, during lifetime, would be a potentially exempt transfer and no inheritance tax would be payable if the transferor survives for seven years. However, this is risky as, if it fails, it is not then possible to obtain relief retrospectively by transferring the property to a maintenance fund and asking for the now chargeable potentially exempt transfer to be ignored. It is understood that the Inland Revenue are aware that this can cause a problem but have stated that they do not consider the existing rules to be unfair. The income tax and capital gains tax advantages of maintenance funds are not huge and the motivation for using a maintenance fund will be almost purely inheritance tax driven.

The final decision as to whether to use a maintenance fund may well be determined on practical grounds, such as whether the family is comfortable with the supporting property being almost entirely alienated from their control for six years. The attractiveness of a maintenance fund from an inheritance tax perspective should not, however, be overlooked.

15 Matrimonial Breakdown

Note. The non-fiscal laws, practices and procedures referred to in this chapter relate to England and Wales only and not to Scotland.

Overview

15.1 The Matrimonial Causes Act 1973, as amended, governs in England and Wales the law on divorce and the financial consequences of divorce. On 1 December 2000, relevant provisions of the Welfare Reform and Pensions Act 1999 (WRPA 1999) became effective, giving the Courts jurisdiction to make pension sharing orders. On 26 October 2000, the House of Lords gave judgment in the case of *White v White, [2000] All ER (D) 1546*, which judgment some practitioners claim to be revolutionary. It decided that the objective implicit in the provisions of Part II of the Matrimonial Causes Act 1973 was to achieve a fair outcome in financial arrangements on or after divorce, giving first consideration where relevant to the welfare of the children, and it disapproved of any discriminatory appraisal of the traditional role of the woman as home-maker and the man as breadwinner and artiber of the destination of family assets amongst the next generation. Part II confers on the Courts the power to make various forms of order, ancillary to the divorce itself, against one or both of the parties and bring about a redistribution of the family resources of the parties.

The Child Support, Pensions and Social Security Act 2000 substantially changes the rules for the calculation of child support liability and those provisions should be effective in the Spring/Summer of 2003.

Divorce proceedings are usually heard in the County Court by a District Judge but the District Judge may at any time refer an application or any question thereon to a Judge for decision or, if the District Judge considers some important question of law or fact is likely to arise, he may transfer the proceedings to the High Court. The case of *White* above began in a County Court.

Currently, the payment of maintenance under a court order or an agreement does not confer any benefit on the taxpayer and the receipt of the maintenance does not create any tax liability in the recipient's hands. The income remains throughout that of the payer and is taxed at the payer's highest marginal rate. There are a few exceptions such as when the payer or the recipient was over 65 on 5 April 2000 and the payment in question was a qualifying maintenance payment (see 15.8 below). In such a case the payer is entitled to relief on the first £2,110 at 10% — a relief worth only £210.

15.2 Matrimonial Breakdown

Establishing dates

15.2 When a marriage irretrievably breaks down, it is necessary to determine the date the parties permanently separated. This date will be fixed either by a court order, a deed of separation or by mutual agreement. The date of separation is important for capital gains tax. In the limited circumstances where the husband is still entitled to a married couple's allowance (see 15.3 below), his entitlement will cease from the following tax year even if he voluntarily maintains his wife. By way of contrast, it is the date a divorce becomes final that is important for inheritance tax purposes, as will be seen later in this chapter. It may be in the interests of both spouses to defer the date of formal separation until the former matrimonial property has been transferred between them.

Both parties to the marriage should notify the Inland Revenue that they have separated (IR 93). A Form 41 (SEP) will be issued to each spouse which will allow the Inland Revenue to determine the date of permanent separation. If the spouses give differing separation dates, the Inspector of Taxes will write to each party to try to agree a date. However, in some circumstances the Inland Revenue may allow different dates for each spouse in order to bring matters to a close. Where the separated spouses are still living in the same house, the Inspector will usually seek nothing more than a formal assurance that the separation is indeed permanent.

Personal allowances

15.3 The married couple's allowance has been abolished with effect from 6 April 2000 except where one of the spouses was born before 6 April 1935. Where, in the limited circumstances in which the married couple's allowance is still available, the couple separate, the husband and wife will, in the year of separation, continue to receive the married couple's allowance that they were entitled to at the date of separation. If the couple have elected, prior to the start of the tax year in which the separation takes place, to split the married couple's allowance, this cannot be altered after the date of separation and remains in force until the end of the tax year. No married couple's allowance is due to either party for subsequent years although transitional rules apply where a married couple separated before 6 April 1990. In such a case, provided they are not divorced and the husband continues to maintain his wife by *voluntary* payments, full transitional married couple's allowance can be claimed by the husband for years subsequent to the year of separation.

In years of assessment following the year of separation, only the single personal allowance is due.

From 6 April 2001, a children's tax credit at 10% on income up to £5,290 is given but is rateably reduced for those with higher incomes.

Maintenance

15.4 Maintenance agreements can be voluntary, legally binding or under a court order. Maintenance can be made to a spouse for his or herself, to the spouse for children of the marriage, or directly to the children or, alternatively, a combination of orders can be made. The three most important maintenance orders available to the court are as follows.

(a) *Maintenance pending suit.* On a petition for divorce, nullity of marriage or judicial separation, the court may make an order for maintenance pending suit under Matrimonial Causes Act 1973, s 22. The payments will be made periodically (weekly, monthly etc.) for a term beginning with the date of presentation of the petition and ending on the grant of the decree absolute. This form of maintenance is only available to a spouse to provide for the spouse's immediate needs while the question of divorce, nullity, judicial separation and long-term financial provision is being determined.

(b) *Periodical payments.* This type of order, under Matrimonial Causes Act 1973, s 23(1)(a), is the one most commonly recognised as a 'maintenance' order.

Either party can be ordered to pay to the other or to the children directly or to the other for the benefit of the children of the marriage, although it is overwhelmingly more common for the husband to be ordered to make such payments.

A periodical payment order runs from the date of the decree absolute and continues until the death of the recipient or the payer or, if earlier, the remarriage of the recipient (Matrimonial Causes Act 1973, s 28(1)(a)).

The order can be varied by further application to the court under Matrimonial Causes Act 1973, s 31.

(c) *Secured periodical payments.* Under Matrimonial Causes Act 1973, s 23(1)(b), the court can order the payer of the periodical payments under (b) above to set aside a fund from which such payments are to be made. The court can specify the term of the periodical payments, but if they are to the former spouse this will not extend beyond the remarriage or the death of the recipient (Matrimonial Causes Act 1973, s 28(1)(b)). Essentially, this represents an order for the transfer of income-producing assets to trustees with the income to be used to pay maintenance to the other spouse. Once the obligation to pay maintenance ceases, the trust ends and the property reverts back to the transferor.

The advantage of such an order is that it continues for the duration of the payee's life, and will not cease on the death of the payer. Also, the order secures the source of the payments where the payer's other assets diminish or, in an extreme case, where the payer becomes insolvent (although in the latter case it is always necessary to consider the full implications of the Insolvency Act 1986).

Children

15.5 Under the Matrimonial Causes Act 1973, a court can order that provision be made for children in one of three ways.

15.6 Matrimonial Breakdown

(a) Payments can be ordered to be made by one spouse to the other for the maintenance of the child.

(b) The court can order that a trust be set up for an infant unmarried child.

(c) Payments can be ordered to be made either directly to a child or to a third party (e.g. a school) on behalf of the child.

The court can only make the above orders by consent. If the parties cannot agree the amount payable is fixed by the Child Support Agency and not the court because the Child Support Acts took away that jurisdiction.

The Child Support Acts 1991 and 1995

15.6 The Child Support Act 1995 made a number of changes to the Child Support Act 1991 (CSA 1991) including the provision for a departure direction, the introduction of the child maintenance bonus, the review of maintenance assessments, appeals procedures and other miscellaneous provisions.

The Child Support Agency will take over dealing with most court orders involving the children of a marriage although there will be certain exceptions including school fees and disability payments, property/capital orders to children, and payments to top-up maintenance by wealthy parents where the Child Support Agency's maximum is exceeded (CSA 1991, s 8). In such cases, the court will still have jurisdiction.

CSA 1991, s 1(1) provides that 'each parent of a qualifying child is responsible for maintaining him'. The absent parent meets his or her responsibility by paying child support maintenance according to an assessment made by the child support officer. A 'qualifying child' is a child, one or both of whose parents are absent from him (CSA 1991, s 3(1)). 'Parent' is defined as the natural mother and father and adoptive parents, but *not* step-parents (unless they are, in broad terms, looking after the child).

Parents with care who receive income support, family credit or disability working allowance will be contacted by the Child Support Agency. A parent with care who does not receive any of these state benefits, and who has no existing order or agreement, may apply to the Child Support Agency for a maintenance assessment.

The parent with care must apply if they are receiving the state benefits listed above. An exemption applies where the parent with care can show that they or the children might suffer harm or undue distress if an application proceeded (CSA 1991, s 46(3)). If the parent with care fails to provide information to the Child Support Agency and no exemption is possible, the child support officer can direct that the state benefits of the parent with care be reduced by 20% for 26 weeks and then by 10% for a further 52 weeks.

A parent can apply to the Child Support Agency on a prescribed form. The child support officer then sends an enquiry form to the absent parent who must reply within 14 days to avoid incurring an interim maintenance assessment. If the interim assessment proves excessive, the absent parent cannot recover the overpayment. It is clearly important, therefore, to reply to the Child Support Agency promptly. If the absent parent fails to pay maintenance following an assessment, ultimately, a custodial prison sentence can be imposed.

The Child Support Act 1991, together with the Child Support Regulations 1992, sets out a precise formula for calculating the maintenance assessment. The formula approach has given rise to most criticism due to the calculations failing to take into account the individuals' circumstances, although the legislation does contain provisions to try to ensure that the absent parent's income does not fall below a minimum level after paying maintenance. In very broad terms, the child support maintenance is usually half of the absent parent's net income in excess of either the income support he or she receives or an amount equal to the income support he or she would receive if on income support, less child benefit until the basic maintenance requirement is met.

There are also certain other factors which affect the ability of the Child Support Agency to make an assessment. First, the absent parent, the person with care and the child must all be habitually resident in the UK. Secondly, the child must be under 16 or under 19 in full-time education and unmarried.

The maintenance assessment is reduced where the absent parent shares care of the children for at least 104 nights of the year. This does not affect the status of the parent with care where a child attends boarding school.

The Child Support, Pensions and Social Security Act 2000, predicted to come into effect in the Spring/Summer of 2003, brings a new way of calculating child support. The basic scheme is that a payer will pay 15% of his/her net weekly income (up to a maximum of £2,000 per week) for one child, 20% for two, and 25% for three or more. The Child Support (Maintenance Calculations and Special Cases) Regulations 2000 detail how net weekly income should be calculated. Basically, it is net of tax and national insurance, with pension contributions being deducted in full. Income from savings, investments and benefits are excluded but overtime, bonuses and commissions are included.

School fees

15.7 School fees can be an important element in any financial settlement and the court has power to make an order to pay the school fees of a child. At first sight, it may appear sufficient to calculate a global figure for the maintenance of a child. However, the provision for school fees can be more complex. For example, the level of fees will increase over time and the frequency of payments should be coordinated with the school's terms. An added complication can arise where a maintenance assessment has been made under the Child Support Act 1991.

There is now no tax advantage in having a school fees order.

Income tax effects of maintenance payments

15.8 In the tax year 1999/2000, the first £1,970 of maintenance paid to a divorced or separated spouse, or to such a person for the benefit of a

15.9 *Matrimonial Breakdown*

child, qualified for 10% tax relief in the hands of the payer. The relief for 2000/01 and subsequent years is nil.

In respect of

(a) court orders made before 15 March 1988, or applied for before 16 March 1988 and made before 1 July 1988,

(b) maintenance agreements (written, by deed or oral) made before 15 March 1988 and received by an Inspector of Taxes before 1 July 1988, and

(c) court orders and agreements, including Child Support Agency maintenance assessments, which replace, vary or supplement an order or agreement under (a) or (b) above and where the recipient is unchanged

a relief of £2,070 can be claimed if either the payer or the payee is aged over 65.

The current rationale is that there should be no tax relief on maintenance payments, the payee is not taxed on the maintenance payments he or she receives and save, for the very limited reliefs enumerated above, the payer is no longer entitled to any tax relief on the payments he or she makes.

Inheritance tax implications of paying and receiving maintenance

15.9 For inheritance tax purposes, the date of the decree absolute rather than the date of separation is relevant. Up until that date, transfers between spouses are covered by the spouse exemption provided that the recipient spouse is UK-domiciled for inheritance tax purposes. This also includes maintenance payments. Where maintenance is paid to a spouse under a court order, the exemption of transfers which are not gratuitous should apply (IHTA 1984, s 10). In 1975, the Senior Registrar of the Family Division issued a statement with the agreement of the Inland Revenue. The statement, which applied to capital transfer tax but should hold true for inheritance tax, said:

> 'Transfers of money or property pursuant to an order of the court in consequence of a decree of divorce or nullity will, in general, be regarded as exempt from capital transfer tax as transactions at arm's length which are not intended to confer any gratuitous benefit. If, exceptionally, such a benefit is intended it is the duty of the transferor to deliver a capital transfer tax account to the Capital Taxes Office.' (New Law Journal, 28 August 1975, p 241)

This statement was later reported as SP E12, but IR131 indicates that this statement is now considered to be obsolete. Alternatively, it can be argued that the exemption for dispositions for family maintenance under IHTA 1984, s 11 applies. This exemption covers transfers of value by one spouse to another, or to a former spouse. It will also cover transfers to children of either spouse where the transfer is for the maintenance of the recipient or the maintenance, education or training of the child who must be either under 18 or, if older, in full-time education or training.

Maintenance payments will not be within the scope of inheritance tax where either of the above exemptions or the exemption for normal payments out of income applies. Otherwise they will be potentially exempt transfers which will become chargeable if the payer dies within seven years, subject to the £3,000 annual exemption.

Maintenance payments on a voluntary basis to a former spouse or to a child after the decree absolute will be potentially exempt transfers unless they fall within the exemption for dispositions for family maintenance (probably not applicable to payments to a former spouse), or the exemption for normal expenditure out of income.

The matrimonial home

15.10 Usually in a marriage breakdown the most valuable asset is the family home. There are three important factors to take into account.

(a) Who is to remain in the property?

(b) Who will be responsible for the necessary disbursements in respect of the property?

(c) Who will receive any sale proceeds from the property?

The courts can make a variety of property adjustment orders or an agreement can be reached between the parties but there is no longer any income tax relief available regardless of how the orders or the agreement is structured.

Options available to the court

15.11 The courts can make property adjustment orders under Matrimonial Causes Act 1973, s 24(1)(a). The most common options open to the courts in respect of the family home are as follows.

(a) *Outright transfer.* It is unusual for a court to order an outright transfer of the family home if it is the only family asset.

(b) *Mesher orders.* A court can order that the parties retain shares in the former home, but defer the sale of the house until the earlier of the youngest child reaching 18 or the wife co-habiting for more than six months, remarrying or dying. This is called a *Mesher* order. It can leave the spouse who remains in the property very vulnerable if the house must be sold once the youngest child attains 18. Consequently these orders are now less common.

(c) *Martin orders.* A *Martin* order is often considered by the court to be fairer than a *Mesher* order. The conditions are generally the same with the important distinction that there is no requirement to move once the youngest child attains 18. The order takes the form of a settlement.

15.12 *Matrimonial Breakdown*

(*d*) *Charge back.* A variation on *Mesher* and *Martin* orders involves the outright transfer of the house to the occupying spouse, but the house is charged with a payment in favour of the other spouse, the charge not to be realised until a specified event. This charge-back can be on the basis of:

(i) a charge of a fixed percentage of the market value on sale;

(ii) a charge of a percentage of the net market value at the time of the order plus interest accrued at an appropriate rate; or

(iii) a charge of a percentage of the net market value at the time of the order, index-linked to a property-based index.

There are potential drawbacks to the first two of these bases. The first basis provides no incentive for the occupying spouse to improve the property and, in fact, the occupying spouse could allow the property to deteriorate (unless safeguards are added to the order). The second basis is arbitrary and takes no account of fluctuations in the property market. The third basis appears the fairest.

(*e*) *Order for sale.* The court can be asked to make an order for sale. This is most commonly encountered where the former matrimonial home is large or more luxurious than is justified by the needs of the occupying spouse or the non-occupying spouse has greater need of the capital represented by the house.

Capital gains tax implications

15.12 While a husband and wife are living together, transfers between them are deemed to be made for a consideration which gives rise to a no gain, no loss transfer. This relief applies for the years up to and including the year of separation but does not apply in subsequent years. While the spouses are separated but not divorced, they will be connected persons for capital gains tax. This means that transfers between them will be deemed to be at full market value (i.e. a bargain not at arm's length). Once the couple divorce, they will normally cease to be connected and transfers will be for actual consideration, if any.

The matrimonial home will be exempt from capital gains tax provided it was the only or main residence of the transferring spouse throughout the period of ownership. The last three years of ownership always count as a period of residence, even if a new qualifying residence has been acquired. In certain circumstances (for example, where job-related accommodation is provided) other periods of absence are also ignored. In many cases, the house may not be transferred for a period considerably in excess of three years after the transferring spouse leaves it, in which case a time-apportioned part of the gain will be assessable. Even then, the gain may be covered by the annual exemption which for 2002/03 is £7,700.

The Inland Revenue have also published a concession (ESC D6) which provides that the home is regarded as continuing to be the only or main residence of the transferring spouse from the date that spouse ceased to

Matrimonial Breakdown **15.12**

occupy the house until the date of transfer. However, in order for the concession to apply:

(*a*) the house must be transferred to the former spouse as part of the financial settlement (it does not apply, for example, if the house is sold to a third party),

(*b*) it must have remained the only or main residence of the former spouse, and

(*c*) the transferring spouse must not have elected in the meantime for some other house to be treated as his or her only or main residence.

It may in fact be more advantageous not to claim this concessional relief. If the transferring spouse has another property eligible for relief it is clearly better to make the transfer of the former home to the other spouse within three years of leaving the former matrimonial home. Otherwise, a proportion of the relief on the new house may be lost.

The transferring spouse may retain an interest in the matrimonial home being transferred. This may arise from a mutual agreement or an order of the court (see above). If the transferring spouse is to receive a specified sum (not exceeding his or her current entitlement), but postponed until the earliest of certain events, no capital gains tax liability arises when the sum is paid because of the principal private residence exemption which was due when the interest in the home was transferred to the remaining spouse. This would apply, for example, where the former matrimonial home is transferred to the remaining spouse in return for a cash sum paid from the proceeds of its eventual sale. However, if the non-occupying spouse holds a charge for a percentage of the equity on a future sale, a capital gains tax liability could arise when paid. Arguably, the deferred charge is a new chargeable asset for capital gains tax purposes (following the decision in *Marren v Ingles, HL [1980] STC 500; [1980] 3 All ER 95*) and the realisation of the charge will constitute a disposal. However, there is a contrary argument that such a secured charge is in reality a debt and, as such, no capital gains tax charge arises on its realisation. However, the issues are by no means clear cut and each case will turn on its own circumstances. In the case of a *Martin* order, a capital gains tax liability for both spouses will arise when the property is sold. The gain will be based on the respective interest retained in the home. The transferor will be entitled to the principal private residence exemption for the period of occupation before the marriage breakdown plus three years, whilst the spouse remaining in the property should receive the full principal private residence exemption.

With regard to a *Mesher* order, it is understood that the Inland Revenue considers that such an order creates a settlement for capital gains tax purposes. At the date of the order the spouses would make a disposal to the trustees at market value of the whole of the beneficial interest in the property. Any gain would be exempt provided that no more than three years had passed since the spouse had left the family home permanently. When the *Mesher* order lapses there will be a deemed disposal and reacquisition under TCGA 1992, s 71 on termination of the settlement. However, an exemption may be available as the

15.13 Matrimonial Breakdown

beneficiary will have occupied the property throughout the period of ownership by the trustees (TCGA 1992, s 225).

Inheritance tax implications

15.13 The transfer of the matrimonial home between separated, but not divorced, spouses falls within the spouse exemption. After the decree absolute has been made, transfers will be potentially exempt transfers unless it can be shown, as is generally the case, that either the exemption for transfers which are not gratuitous (IHTA 1984, s 10) or the exemption covering dispositions for family maintenance (IHTA 1984, s 11) apply. These exemptions are considered under 15.9 above.

It would be prudent to ensure that all property transfers are effected prior to the decree absolute to take advantage of the spouse exemption.

Pension rights

15.14 Pension sharing orders can be made if the petition for divorce or nullity was filed on or after 1 December 2000 (WRPA 1999, s 85). Pension sharing orders are a revolutionary concept and override all previous Revenue restrictions on the ability of a third party to have the benefit of another person's pension scheme.

WRPA 1999, Sch 3 inserts new sections into the Matrimonial Causes Act 1973. The courts powers extend to 'one or more' pension sharing orders and the new Matrimonial Causes Act 1973, s 21A, as amended, defines a pension sharing order as

'an order which:

(a) provides that one party's—

    (i) shareable rights under a specified pension arrangement, or

    (ii) shareable state scheme rights,

be subject to pension sharing for the benefit of the other party, and

(b) specifies the percentage value to be transferred.'

Until the WRPA 1999 was passed, advisers focussed on the rights to pension in payment, lump sum and death in service benefits but they will now have to focus on

(*a*) the value of all those rights — the cash equivalent transfer value (CETV) and a percentage of that being transferred from one spouse to the other (WRPA 1999, s 29(2));

(*b*) what rights the recipient spouse can derive from the percentage transferred; and

(*c*) what rights will be left with the other spouse.

CETV is the sole method of valuation under WRPA 1999, even if pension is in payment. (Pensions on Divorce (Provision of Information) Regulations

Matrimonial Breakdown **15.14**

2000, Reg 3). Only benefits at the 'valuation date' can be taken into account by the court. The rules for calculating CETV assumes employees service terminates on the valuation date and does not take into account projected increases to the pension fund for possible future service. The court has to use a specific date for the valuation date. In practice, the valuation date will be a date two or three weeks prior to the court hearing.

Pension sharing orders can be made over

- personal pension plans;

- retirement annuity contracts;

- employer's pension schemes (whether money purchase or final salary schemes);

- small self-administered schemes;

- services pension schemes;

- pension plans which are the product of a pension sharing order from a previous marriage;

- pension schemes without Revenue approval (e.g. employers funded arrangements);

- pension in payment; and

- an annuity or insurance policy which provides pension benefits but not widows/dependants pension in payment.

The court does not have power to make a pension sharing order over a pension scheme which is

- subject to an earmarking order from a previous marriage; or

- subject to an earmarking order from the current marriage.

The court will still have the power to make immediate or deferred lump sum orders and/or periodical payments orders taking effect against any of the following benefits under a pension scheme.

- Members retirement pension.

- Lump sum commutation.

- Death in service lump sum.

- Guaranteed lump sum on death in retirement.

These powers were given to the court by Pensions Act 1995, s 166 and are now Matrimonial Causes Act 1973, ss 25B-D as amended. Orders made under Secs 25B-D do not effect a true pension split — they merely attach the members own benefits. The pension continues to be taxed as the member's income while the earmarked maintenance is tax free in the hands of the

351

15.15 Matrimonial Breakdown

recipient. An earmarking order is one kind of financial provision order and, as in the case of maintenance, it lasts only during the joint lives of the parties or until the remarriage of the receiving party.

A pension provided by a pension sharing order has the same tax treatment as any other pension scheme. The recipient spouse will be entitled to a tax free lump sum on drawing benefits and will be taxed on the pension payable as income. Death in service benefits will pass outside the estate for tax purposes provided the right of nomination has been properly used or they are written in trust.

Transfers of other property

15.15 The court can order property other than the matrimonial home or cash sums to be transferred between the spouses. Alternatively, this may be done by mutual agreement. In either event, the capital gains tax and inheritance tax implications will broadly be the same as those considered above under 15.10 above, except for the absence of relief for a principal private residence.

A transfer of assets between spouses on separation will be a disposal which, because spouses are connected persons, will be deemed not to be a bargain at arm's length (TCGA 1992, s 18(2)). The disposal will therefore be deemed to take place at market value. If the recipient spouse gives no actual consideration for the acquisition of the asset, hold-over relief under TCGA 1992, s 165 may be available (relief under TCGA 1992, s 260 will not be available because the inter-spouse exemption applies to the transfer). However, it may not be in the interests of the recipient spouse to join in a hold-over election because he or she will receive the assets at the transferor's original low base cost.

The Inland Revenue argue that in such circumstances assets are normally transferred in exchange for the surrender by the donee of rights to obtain alternative financial provision (Inland Revenue Capital Gains Manual CG 67192). If that were true, there would be actual consideration given for the disposal which would reduce or even eliminate hold-over relief. That may be the case where a formal agreement is entered into between the parties. It is highly unlikely to be the case where one spouse transfers assets to the other unilaterally, even though such transfers may be taken into account by the court in future proceedings for financial provision or on divorce.

The Inland Revenue similarly argue that transfers between former spouses under a court order are made for consideration. It might be seen as extremely doubtful that the coming to an end of a spouse's right to apply to the court for an application of its discretionary powers in relation to maintenance or the division of property, by the exercise of that discretion, constitutes 'consideration'. A taxpayer wishing to challenge the Inland Revenue's view on this matter, however, must be prepared to do so in the courts.

Use of trusts

15.16 A court order or agreement may require the establishment or variation, of one or more trusts. Alternatively, when considering tax planning, a trust may be the most efficient means of providing for a spouse or children of a former marriage.

Possible application of trusts include:

(a) an accumulation and maintenance settlement for the children of the former marriage;

(b) an interest in possession settlement for the former spouse until he or she remarries;

(c) settlement of the former matrimonial home on trust to enable the former spouse to remain in occupation until some specified event (for example, remarriage); and

(d) high income-yielding assets could be settled to provide a fund for maintenance payments, effectively giving the transferor relief for maintenance by taking the income stream out of his or her hands.

Careful prior consideration of the tax effects is vital before using trusts in tax planning on separation and divorce. The different types of trust and their tax treatment are considered in chapter 4 *Creating Settlements* and chapter 5 *Existing Settlements*.

Overseas aspects

Transfers of property — capital gains tax and inheritance tax implications

15.17 In a tax year subsequent to the year of separation, a spouse who is not resident and not ordinarily resident in the UK who transfers property to his or her former spouse will generally not be liable to capital gains tax. Being not resident and not ordinarily resident in the UK does provide scope for numerous tax planning opportunities which are considered elsewhere in this book.

Where the inheritance tax spouse exemption is in point, it is necessary to bear in mind that a transfer to a non-UK domiciled spouse by a UK-domiciled individual is only exempt up to a limit of £55,000. Again, being non-domiciled in the UK provides scope for numerous tax planning opportunities considered elsewhere in this book.

In some cases, one or both spouses may be beneficiaries of an offshore trust. It should be remembered that, depending on their personal circumstances, capital gains tax may be payable in respect of any capital payments to them from the trust as part of the divorce agreement.

Stamp duty

15.18 Stamp duty on the conveyance or transfer of property from one party to a marriage to the other in connection with divorce will not be payable if a certificate is given under category H of the Stamp Duty (Exempt Instruments) Regulations 1987. Otherwise, a £5 duty is payable on instruments transferring assets in pursuance of a court order made on granting a decree of divorce or judicial separation, or under an agreement between the parties in connection with a divorce or judicial separation.

Council tax

15.19 Where the original council tax demand has been issued in joint names, the departing spouse may be able to negotiate a cessation of joint liability with the local authority at the time he or she leaves the property on a permanent basis. Otherwise joint liability will cease on grant of the decree absolute.

Where a separation has taken place and the remaining spouse can prove himself or herself to be the sole adult occupant, a discount of 25% is available.

The effect of separation and divorce on wills and intestacy

15.20 Until a couple are divorced, property will still pass on death under the terms of any will and, commonly, one spouse will have bequeathed a substantial part of his or her estate to the other. Even where no will has been made, the rules on intestacy will apply and a large part of the intestate's estate will go to the spouse. A separated spouse may therefore inherit most of the deceased's assets unless action is taken at the time of separation to reverse the position by executing a new will or codicil to the existing one.

A review of all assets held should be undertaken to identify, for example, joint bank or building society accounts, land and property held as joint tenants and death in service benefits which would normally go to the spouse. A will can be made or amended in favour of other beneficiaries. However, existing property rights will be subject to the court's right to order transfers of property on divorce.

Under the Law Reform Succession Act 1995, which applies to all deaths after 1 January 1995, a divorced spouse will be treated as if he or she predeceased the deceased person on the date of the divorce for all purposes. Previously there were problems where a will provided, for example, that the estate was to pass to the surviving spouse 'but if he or she predeceased me then to the children'. Divorce would generally revoke the gift to the spouse but, if the will was drafted incorrectly, the gifts to the children would also fail. In *Sinclair (Re), [1984] 3 All ER 362* a gift to a charity failed and passed instead under residue as the ex-wife did not predecease the testator. The Law Reform

Succession Act now prevents this problem occurring. Similarly, the appointment of the former spouse as executor and trustee will be void unless the will provides otherwise. If there is a wish to leave property to a former spouse, it should be borne in mind that the spouse exemption does not apply to divorced spouses and such a gift may be liable to inheritance tax.

Where a former spouse has not remarried, she may have a claim under the Inheritance (Provision for Family and Dependants) Act 1975. Therefore the husband, for example, may consider leaving a written statement accompanying his will as to the reasons for excluding such a former spouse from benefiting under the will. He might record, for example, that he made adequate provision for her on the marriage breakdown.

Following the divorce, either or both former spouses may marry a new partner. This revokes a will unless it was made in contemplation of the new marriage. In contrast to divorce where, in general only the gift to the former spouse lapses, in general, on re-marriage the whole will is revoked. This may possibly disinherit the children of the former marriage. Similarly, the children of a new partner will have no rights under intestacy. However, if the children of a new partner are adopted, they will then rank equally with the children of the former marriage. This may well be in accordance with the wishes of those immediately concerned, but if other people, such as grandparents, have left property to 'the children of X' this will equally also include the adopted children.

Conclusion

15.21 Separation and divorce will always remain causes for acrimonious disputes, especially where children are involved. Changes in the legislation since 1988 have taken away all tax benefits of maintenance payments.

16 Planning for Death

Wills

16.1 A crucial element of estate planning for an individual is the preparation of a will, correctly drawn to ensure that the property remaining at death is distributed among his family and dependants and other beneficiaries in a tax-efficient manner. It is essential to this strategy to ensure that the testator's spouse (and other dependants) are adequately provided for at the minimum tax cost in each case. There is no point in the testator causing hardship, or the worry of hardship, to his spouse by assuming that she can rely for financial support in the future on the generosity of their children who are given the bulk of the estate in the will simply to save inheritance tax by ensuring that there is no 'bunching' of their joint estates on the second death. At worst such planning could result in an application to the court by a spouse or by other dependants for 'reasonable financial provision' under the Inheritance (Provision for Family and Dependants) Act 1975 with all the costs (and tax consequences) which this may entail. Furthermore, other events could overtake any good intentions of the children to look after their mother. What if any of them marry, have children of their own or get divorced? In the latter case the court may order that child to make financial provision for his own divorced spouse and children, thereby dividing the testator's bounty between many more than was first intended.

There is no certain formula for determining what will amount to adequate provision for dependants. It has been suggested that a capital sum equal to ten times the husband's annual salary is required to provide adequately for his widow and family. Certainly, in smaller estates (and these days an estate of less than £500,000 is 'small' if the value of the family home is reflected in this figure) there may be little scope for anything but provision for the surviving spouse unless she has means of her own.

The importance of having a will, correctly drawn and regularly reviewed, is twofold. First, it ensures that the deceased's estate devolves exactly as he desires and in as tax-efficient a manner as possible. If there is no will, then the statutory intestacy provisions will apply which may achieve a devolution in the deceased's estate in a manner which does not fulfil his wishes. These provisions are discussed in more detail below. Secondly, it simplifies the administration of the estate thereby saving time and the expense to which an intestacy invariably gives rise. It also enables the testator to choose suitable competent executors to administer his estate, which may be preferable to relying on the statutory order in the case of an intestacy.

16.2 Planning for Death

Use of exemptions and reliefs

Spouse exemption

16.2 Gifts by a donor to his spouse are exempt from inheritance tax whether made in the lifetime of the donor or on his death (IHTA 1984, s 18). The exemption will apply whether the gift is of a life interest in possession or is absolute. Whichever route is chosen will not in itself have any adverse tax consequences on the subsequent death of the spouse, as a person who has a life interest in possession is treated for inheritance tax purposes as owning the assets in which that life interest subsists (IHTA 1984, s 49). In either case there should be scope for the surviving spouse to make potentially exempt transfers if he or she finds that the benefits conferred are in excess of requirements. An *inter vivos* termination of a life interest, whether in part or as to the whole of a fund, may be a potentially exempt transfer (IHTA 1984, s 3A).

Consequently, the decision as to whether a gift by will should be absolute or limited does not involve any inheritance tax considerations but does often involve other considerations such as:

(*a*) the testator's confidence in whether his spouse will pass that property on to their children either by lifetime gifts or by his will;

(*b*) the testator's concern that his spouse may remarry and leave property to the new spouse or the new spouse's family; or

(*c*) the testator's wish to protect a spendthrift spouse from himself.

There is a limitation of £55,000 to the spouse exemption where the transferor spouse is domiciled in the UK but the transferee spouse is domiciled outside the UK (IHTA 1984, s 18(2)).

For further consideration of the spouse exemption, see under paragraph 16.12 below.

Use of the nil rate band

16.3 The use of the inheritance tax nil rate band (i.e. the amount which may be transferred by a chargeable transfer without incurring a liability to inheritance tax) is the obvious route for tax efficient gifts by will to children or other non-exempt beneficiaries. Gifts made within seven years of the death, whether initially potentially exempt transfers or chargeable transfers, will count towards the nil rate band but a legacy of the whole of the unused balance of the band can be given. A will can provide for a legacy of an amount which reflects any changes in the amount of the nil rate tax band.

Nil rate band discretionary trusts

16.4 An alternative use of the nil rate band, perhaps appropriate in a smaller estate, is to leave a legacy equal to its upper limit (or equal to the unused amount of the band taking into account transfers within seven years of death) on discretionary trusts with the surviving spouse as one of the

Planning for Death **16.5**

objects of the discretion. The trustees (given the appropriate guidance in a letter of wishes) can then exercise their discretion over the income of the fund (and where appropriate, capital) each year in favour of the surviving spouse. If there are minor children of the testator included in the class of beneficiaries, then the discretion over income could instead be exercised in their favour to utilise their income tax personal allowances in each year. The income so appropriated may be paid to the spouse as guardian of the children to be used for their maintenance, education or benefit, thereby relieving the surviving spouse's own income from this burden.

This route enables a surviving spouse to benefit from the income of the testator's property whilst at the same time keeping it outside her estate. If the testator's widow dies before the tenth anniversary of the death, then the capital of the trust may in most cases be distributed to the children without incurring any inheritance tax charge regardless of the then value of the fund. This is because inheritance tax on a capital distribution before the first ten-year anniversary is calculated by reference to the initial value of the trust fund plus any chargeable transfers made by the settlor in the seven years before making the settlement. If that total does not exceed the nil rate band, no tax is payable. However, it will be important to ensure that no 'related settlements' are created by the will (e.g. discretionary or accumulation and maintenance trusts of residue) as the value of property in any related settlement is taken into account in calculating the tax on a distribution. The only exception to this advantageous situation is where the value of the property transferred to the trust fund only fell within the nil rate band by virtue of the availability of business property relief or agricultural property relief. In calculating the inheritance tax on a capital distribution before the first ten-year anniversary the initial value of the trust fund in these circumstances is the unrelieved value and a charge may therefore arise. If the widow is likely to survive the tenth anniversary, then a decision will have to be made as to whether it is better to break the trust before the anniversary or to pay the ten-year charge.

Agricultural and business property

16.5 Property which qualifies for agricultural or business property relief should, where possible, be given to non-exempt beneficiaries since the relief will be lost if given to a surviving spouse who fails to satisfy the necessary conditions to obtain the relief on his or her death. In this way a proportionately larger gift can be made for the same inheritance tax cost.

Example

A gift in the testator's will of a property which is valued at £500,000 on death and which is used by a company he controls is entitled to 50% business property relief. If given to his children or other non-exempt beneficiaries no inheritance tax will be suffered on the testator's death (provided he has made no chargeable transfers or potentially exempt transfers within seven years of his death).

Alternatively, it may be possible to obtain either business or agricultural property relief twice by one spouse, for example, the husband leaving the relevant property to a discretionary trust in favour of his family including his

16.6 Planning for Death

widow. On the husband's death agricultural or business property relief would be available. Under the terms of his will, the husband would leave his investment assets to his wife so no inheritance tax would arise on those assets. The wife could then purchase the agricultural or business assets at arm's length from the trustees of the discretionary trust. Provided the widow survives for two years after the purchase, the assets should also be eligible for agricultural or business property relief. In addition, the capital gains tax uplift on death will be available on both the agricultural and business property and the investment assets.

Agricultural property relief

16.6 Agricultural property is defined in IHTA 1984, s 115(2) as agricultural land or pasture and includes both woodland and any buildings used in connection with intensive rearing of livestock or fish if occupied with agricultural land and the occupation is ancillary to that of the agricultural land. It also includes farmhouses, farm buildings and cottages, and the land occupied with them, which are 'of a character appropriate to the property'. Section 115(4) extends the definition to include stud farms. The relief also extends to controlling shareholdings in agricultural companies (IHTA 1984, s 122).

The relief is given on the agricultural value of agricultural property only, and not in respect of any value attributable to non-agricultural use. Relief of 100% is available if vacant possession of the land is available at the time of, or can be obtained within twelve months of, the transfer. By concession, the CTO extend this period to 24 months (see CTO Advanced Instruction Manual, para L.211.3). Land let after 31 August 1995 will also receive 100% relief. Agricultural property relief at 100% is also available on agricultural tenancies acquired as a result of the death of the previous tenant after 31 August 1995. In these cases, the tenancy will be treated as commencing on the date of death. Otherwise relief is at the rate of 50%. The relief is applied to controlling shareholdings on the agricultural value element inherent in the value of the shares at either 100% or 50% as if the company's occupation was occupation by the transferor of the shares. To the extent that agricultural relief is not available, business property relief at either 100% or 50% may apply.

There are minimum ownership requirements contained in IHTA 1984, s 117 and IHTA 1984, s 123. The property must either be:

(*a*) occupied by the transferor (or the company) for the purposes of agriculture throughout the period of two years prior to the transfer (i.e. in the case of a gift by will, two years prior to the death); or

(*b*) owned by the transferor (or company) throughout the period of seven years (ending with the death) and throughout that period occupied (by him or another) for the purposes of agriculture.

Where a company is involved, the shares must have been owned by the transferor throughout the two or seven-year period, whichever is applicable. There are also provisions which modify the ownership requirements in the case of agricultural property which has replaced other agricultural property (IHTA 1984, s 118).

Planning for Death **16.7**

Agricultural property relief is considered in more detail in chapter 11 *The Family Farm*.

Business property relief

16.7 The relief for 'relevant business property' is contained in IHTA 1984, ss 103–114. Relevant business property is defined as:

(*a*) property consisting of a business or interest in a business;

(*b*) securities of a company which are unquoted and which (either by themselves or together with other such securities owned by the transferor and any unquoted shares so owned) gave the transferor control (as defined by IHTA 1984, s 269) of the company immediately before the transfer;

(*c*) any unquoted shares in a company;

(*d*) shares in or securities of a company which are quoted and which (either by themselves or together with other such shares or securities owned by the transferor) gave the transferor control of the company immediately before the transfer;

(*e*) any land or building, machinery or plant which, immediately before the transfer, was used wholly or mainly for the purposes of a business carried on by a company of which the transferor then had control or by a partnership of which he then was a partner; and

(*f*) any land or building, machinery or plant which, immediately before the transfer, was used wholly or mainly for the purposes of a business carried on by the transferor and was settled property in which he was then beneficially entitled to an interest in possession.

Business property relief may thus be available on shares in unquoted family companies and other shareholdings or securities which fulfil the voting criteria specified in the Act. It also includes, in category (*a*), partnership interests and a business of which the deceased was sole proprietor, which includes the underwriting interests of a member of Lloyd's. Categories (*b*) and (*c*) include shares dealt in on the Alternative Investment Market (AIM). Relief is not available in respect of a business or an interest in a business, or shares or securities of a company carrying on a business, where the business consists wholly or mainly of dealing in securities, stocks or shares, land or buildings or making or holding investments (excluding market makers and discount houses and companies which are the holding companies of a trading group, none of the businesses of which are prescribed under the above criteria) (IHTA 1984, s 105(3)). In *Brown's Executors v CIR, Sp C [1996] SSCD 277 (Sp C 83)* a company held the sale proceeds of an asset in a deposit account until suitable premises were found. The Revenue asserted that the company's business had become one of holding investments. It was found that the business continued to consist of the original trading activity and relief was still available. The business of letting furnished flats on assured shorthold tenancies is considered to be a business of making and holding investments and not eligible for relief (see *Burkinyoung (Burkinyoung's Executor) v CIR, Sp C [1995] SSCD 29 (Sp C 3)*). Traditionally, the Inland Revenue has required a minimum number of

16.8 Planning for Death

holiday cottages to be within the business for relief to be available on furnished holiday lets. This particular requirement seems to have been removed (see CTO Advanced Instruction Manual, para L.99.3). A number of recent cases have examined the boundary between business activities consisting of holding investments and those which do not in relation to caravan parks (see, in particular, *Farmer and another (Farmer's executors) v CIR, Sp C [1999] SSCD 321 (Sp C 216)* and *Weston (Weston's Executors) v CIR, Ch D [2000] STC 1064*).

Property which falls within (*a*), (*b*) or (*c*) above qualifies for relief at 100%; all other categories qualify for relief at 50%. There is a two-year minimum period of ownership in order to qualify for relief but relief can be given on business property which has replaced other business property, provided the necessary conditions are met (IHTA 1984, s 107).

No business property relief will be available if the property is subject to a binding contract for sale (IHTA 1984, s 113). The Inland Revenue consider there is a binding contract of sale where partners or shareholder directors of a company enter into an agreement whereby on the death of a partner/director the surviving partners/shareholders are obliged to purchase the deceased's business interest or shares and the deceased's personal representatives are obliged to sell. Statement of Practice SP 12/80 sets out the Inland Revenue view that section 113 applies where there is an obligation to buy and sell but not merely an option to do so.

A gift in a will of any relevant business property may lapse if the testator retires from the business or sells the property in his lifetime. Such a step should be an occasion for the testator to review the will.

Business property relief is considered in more detail in chapter 10 *The Family Business*.

Attribution of values

16.8 IHTA 1984, s 39A contains rules relating to the attribution of values to gifts in a will when part of the residuary estate is given to an exempt beneficiary and part of the residuary estate also qualifies for agricultural or business property relief. Any agricultural or business property relief is in effect apportioned between any specific gifts and the property in the residuary estate. Specific gifts of agricultural or business property are treated as gifts of the value of that property reduced by the relevant relief and if expressed to be free of tax the gifts will be grossed-up (see 16.23 below).

Charitable and other gifts for public benefit

16.9 Gifts by will to charities are exempt from inheritance tax (IHTA 1984, s 23). However, relief will be precluded where the gift to charity only takes effect on the termination after the death of any other interest, or depends on a condition which is not satisfied within twelve months of the death, or is defeasible (section 23(2)).

Exemption is also available for gifts to

Planning for Death **16.11**

(a) political parties (IHTA 1984, s 24);

(b) certain bodies of national importance specified in IHTA 1984, Sch 3 (IHTA 1984, s 25);

(c) maintenance funds for historic buildings (IHTA 1984, s 27); and

(d) Community Amateur Sports Clubs (FA 2002, Sch 18 para 9(2)).

For further details, see chapter 13 *Gifts to Charities, Etc.*

Limitations on reliefs available on death

16.10 Certain reliefs available in respect of lifetime gifts are not available on death (in some cases, for fairly obvious reasons). These are:

(a) the annual exemption, currently £3,000;

(b) the small gifts exemption, currently £250 per person;

(c) the normal expenditure out of income exemption;

(d) the exemption for gifts in consideration of marriage; and

(e) the exemption for certain dispositions for the maintenance of a family.

One relief available only on death is limited to a person who is not domiciled and neither resident nor ordinarily resident in the UK at his death. IHTA 1984, s 157 provides that the balance on any qualifying foreign currency account of such a person is to be left out of account in determining the value of the estate.

Dividing the estate between the family

Intestacy rules

16.11 In the absence of a will the estate will pass on death under the intestacy rules which may, but much more likely will not, bring about the desired result in the distribution of the estate. Where a spouse and issue survive the intestate, the intestacy rules provide for a statutory legacy (currently £125,000), together with the personal chattels, to go to the surviving spouse, together with a life interest in one-half of the residue of the estate. The other one-half of residue is given to the issue at 18 on the statutory trusts. Hence, on the death of the first spouse, the only charge to inheritance tax on the estate will arise in respect of the one-half of the residue passing to the issue. On the death of the second spouse, however, a charge to inheritance tax will arise on his or her estate (reflecting the benefit of the deceased's personal assets and the statutory legacy to the extent it is not spent in that spouse's lifetime) including, for inheritance tax purposes, the one-half share of residue of the deceased's estate which passes to the children.

The intestacy rules are often criticised as being out of touch with reality, but ironically (because the rules pre-date both the capital transfer tax and

16.12 *Planning for Death*

inheritance tax regimes by many years) they can operate to provide a measure of inheritance tax mitigation by ensuring some property passes to non-exempt beneficiaries on the first death.

Gifts to the spouse

Equalisation of estates

16.12 Where possible, some measure of equalisation with regard to the values of the spouses' respective estates should be considered to ensure that both nil rate bands can be utilised regardless of the order in which a husband and wife die. This can be done by lifetime transfers. Such transfers between spouses will generally not give rise to any inheritance tax, capital gains tax or stamp duty liabilities. This equalisation of estates will also help to ensure that the survivor is provided for adequately.

However, the possible impact of the related property provisions contained in IHTA 1984, s 161 should not be overlooked. Section 161 provides that where the value of any property forming part of the estates of both spouses taken together is greater than the value of the spouses' respective shares or interests in the property when valued individually, then the value to be adopted is the appropriate proportion of the value of the property as a whole. However, the provisions only affect the value of the property for inheritance tax purposes and not the underlying principle behind the equalisation procedure. Where gifts are being made between spouses, it is advisable that a deed of gift is used to record the gift so as to provide evidence that the donor intends beneficial ownership to pass to the donee.

Absolute gifts v life interests

16.13 The question as to whether a surviving spouse should be given property absolutely by the will, or be given a life interest only in the whole or part of the estate, has been mentioned briefly above under the heading *Spouse exemption*. The decision may be made for personal rather than fiscal reasons. The inheritance tax consequences on the death of each spouse will be the same because a person who has a life interest is treated as if he or she owns the underlying assets and tax is charged accordingly on his or her death (IHTA 1984, s 49). Hence, property given, absolutely or in trust for life, by a husband to his wife in his will is exempt from tax on his death but on the subsequent death of the wife will be taxed one way or another in her estate. A testator who has confidence in his or her spouse can give capital instead of a life interest at no extra cost in tax terms. If a testator is concerned that the surviving spouse will fritter away or mismanage the estate, or will remarry to a person who will fritter it away, so that there is nothing left for the children, then clearly the testator should consider only giving the spouse a life interest, with the capital passing automatically on the spouse's death to the children. The survivor's life interest could also expressly be made to come to an end on his or her subsequent marriage.

A combination of a life interest, coupled with a power for the trustees (who may or may not, depending on the circumstances in which the gift is made,

Planning for Death **16.15**

include the testator's spouse) to release capital to the life tenant will produce a more flexible provision for the surviving spouse whilst preserving part of the capital for future generations at no extra inheritance tax cost. The release of capital to the spouse, who already has an interest in possession and is consequently treated for inheritance tax purposes as owning the assets, will not give rise to a charge to tax (IHTA 1984, s 53(2)). However, depending upon the nature and value of the assets released, there may be a charge to capital gains tax on the release.

Providing the surviving spouse with a life interest will not preclude the capital of the trust passing from the spouse to the next generation by way of potentially exempt transfers.

Inheritance tax on the second death

16.14 Although a gift to a surviving spouse is exempt from inheritance tax, it is necessary to look further ahead to determine the effect of that gift on the inheritance tax liability on the death of the spouse. On the second death, the charge to inheritance tax may be increased by the bunching effect of the testator's and his spouse's assets all falling into the charge to tax on the same occasion.

> *Example*
>
> Each spouse has assets of £300,000. The husband dies first leaving the whole of his estate to his wife. No tax will be payable on his death. On the subsequent death of the wife, the taxable estate (assuming that values remain constant) will be £600,000 and tax of £140,000 will be payable at current rates. However, had the husband left (say) one third of his estate to non-exempt beneficiaries such as his children then a tax saving of £40,000 would have been achieved, i.e. no tax will be payable on the husband's death and £100,000 on the wife's death.

As there are only two rates of inheritance tax (namely 0% and 40%), a tax saving can only be made where assets of a value not exceeding the upper limit of the nil rate band are left to non-exempt beneficiaries on the first death. That said, however, it is important not to lose sight of the cash flow implications where there is likely to be a significant gap between the deaths of the spouses. A modest overall saving of inheritance tax by the payment of some tax on the first death may prove of little worth if the surviving spouse lives for another 20 years when weighed against having the use of that money for the 20-year period.

Gifts to children and remoter issue

16.15 A gift may be either vested, that is the right to the gift is certain, or contingent, that is dependent upon an uncertain future event. A vested gift may be either vested in possession, that is of immediate effect, or vested in interest, that is coming into effect on a certain future event such as the expiry of a period of time.

16.16 Planning for Death

Vested gifts

16.16 Where a gift is vested in possession, no particular tax problems are usually encountered. If the vested gift is to a legatee who is a minor, the executors will on the completion of the administration hold as bare trustees until the minor attains 18 and can give them a valid receipt. The income and any capital gains will be taxed as those of the minor. In the absence of any contrary intention in the will the Trustee Act 1925, ss 31 and 32 will apply and the trustees will be able to release the income for the minor's maintenance, education and benefit and up to one half of the capital for his advancement or benefit (though it is usual to extend section 32 to enable the whole of the capital to be released).

Contingent gifts and gifts vested in interest

16.17 The tax consequences of contingent gifts are more complex. In the absence of an express direction in the will, the general rule is that the gift will not carry the intermediate income unless it is a gift of residue or is a specific gift (Law of Property Act 1925, s 175). Therefore, the income of a contingent gift which does not carry the intermediate income (such as a general pecuniary legacy to a child of the testator upon attaining an age exceeding the age of majority) will be payable to the residuary beneficiaries until the contingency is attained. On the occurrence of that event the residuary beneficiaries' interests in possession in the contingent fund will be terminated but that termination will usually be a potentially exempt transfer. A charge to inheritance tax will only arise therefore if the residuary beneficiaries fail to survive for seven years from that date. It is, however, preferable that the will expressly provides that any contingent gifts should carry with them the benefit of the intermediate income.

On the occurrence of the contingency there may be a disposal by the trustees for capital gains tax if the gift is of chargeable assets. However, depending upon the nature of the assets a hold-over election under TCGA 1992, s 165 may be available. Where the gift does carry the intermediate income it may qualify as an accumulation and maintenance trust under IHTA 1984, s 71. In such circumstances hold-over relief under TCGA 1992, s 260 might be available whatever the nature of the asset provided the satisfaction of the contingency results in capital and income vesting contemporaneously.

For income tax purposes income which is accumulated or over which the trustees have a discretion will be subject to income tax at the rate applicable to trusts (currently 34% or 25% on dividend income) unless the minor has a vested interest in the income in which case it will be taxed as his or her income.

One other financial burden of a contingent gift will be the costs of administration of the continuing trust including preparation of accounts and tax returns each year and tax advice to the trustees.

Generation skipping

16.18 If the testator's children are sufficiently well provided for, then consideration should be given to skipping a generation in the will to provide for grandchildren, present and future. Even if the testator's children are not particularly wealthy, the advantages of enabling them to use the grandchildren's income tax personal allowances each year, which might otherwise be lost, may be a significant benefit to a child of the testator by relieving his own income from the burden of maintaining or educating his children.

Skipping a generation will ensure that property reaching the grandchildren will avoid at least one charge to inheritance tax which would otherwise have arisen on the death of the parent. The gift to the grandchildren, if in the form of an accumulation and maintenance settlement within the will, has the advantage both of flexibility (the funds would be available to be used, for example, to meet the costs of education of the testator's grandchildren) and of being a protection, under present legislation, against charges to inheritance tax on the death of any grandchildren before attaining a vested interest (at an age not exceeding 25). The income tax and capital gains tax considerations are as mentioned above in relation to contingent gifts.

Accumulation and maintenance settlements are considered in more detail in chapter 4 *Creating Settlements* at paragraph 4.23.

The family home

16.19 Very often a testator will ask for advice on giving away his matrimonial home or, where this is owned by both the spouses, for advice on giving away his share of it. A gift of a share of the home can only be made by will if the property is beneficially owned by the spouses as tenants in common. In the case of a joint tenancy, the share of the property will automatically pass by survivorship. Although a joint tenancy may be severed *inter vivos* merely by notice in writing, it cannot be severed by will.

If the property is owned by husband and wife as tenants in common, the property will be held by them in trust. They each have an interest in the proceeds of sale of the property and a right to reside there while it remains unsold. These rights will pass to a legatee if a share of the property is given by the will.

Where the testator is proposing a gift in his will of his interest in the property, other than to his wife, he will usually be concerned to preserve the ability for his wife to reside in the property. The Inland Revenue's view is that any right given to the wife for her to continue to reside there will create an interest in possession in favour of the wife in the testator's half of the property (*CIR v Lloyds Private Banking Ltd, Ch D [1998] STC 559; Woodhall (Woodhall's Personal Representative) v CIR, Sp C [2000] SSCD 558 (Sp C 261)* and *Faulkner (trustee of Adams, dec'd) v CIR, Sp C [2001] SSCD 112 (Sp C 278)*). A termination of that interest will occur on the subsequent death of the wife or possibly on an earlier sale.

Similar considerations apply where the matrimonial home is in the sole name of one spouse. Should it be left to the surviving spouse alone, to the surviving spouse and children jointly or to the children alone? The primary concern should be the security of the surviving spouse, although fortunately if the

16.20 *Planning for Death*

home is left solely to the children and they allow their surviving parent to occupy it for the rest of his or her life, the gifts with reservation provisions will not apply. Of course, if the house is likely to be sold on the first death, then different considerations apply.

In an age when more unmarried couples are living together, consideration should be given to the surviving cohabitee's position on the first death. Where the property has been purchased in the sole name of the purchasing cohabitee, he should make provision for the surviving cohabitee on his death. The tax consequences are discussed in detail in chapter 9 *The Family Home*.

Survivorship clauses

16.20 It is common practice to make gifts to individuals in wills contingent on them surviving the testator for a given period, usually three months. Such a survivorship clause can serve various purposes.

(*a*) It can prevent a double charge to tax where the legatee dies shortly after the testator.

(*b*) In the case of a gift to a spouse it can prevent a greater charge to inheritance tax arising than would otherwise have arisen on the death of the spouse by preventing the deceased's property from passing to the surviving spouse and being aggregated with his or her own estate.

(*c*) It ensures that property will devolve, in the event of the second death occurring within the survivorship period, to a substituted legatee of the first testator's choosing and will not pass under the will of the second to die.

(*d*) It avoids the same property having to be administered twice over in two different estates within a relatively short space of time.

IHTA 1984, s 92 provides that a survivorship clause for a period not exceeding six months is back-dated to the date of death for inheritance tax purposes and tax will be charged on the death depending on whether the legatee survives for the period or dies before the period expires.

Where the estate of one spouse is significantly larger than that of the other, it is desirable *not* to include a survivorship clause at least in respect of part of any property left to the poorer spouse. This will ensure, for example, that if a wife dies shortly after her husband, some part of the husband's property will fall into the wife's estate and thereby use up his or her available nil rate band. There is no harm in including a survivorship clause in the will of the poorer spouse if she intends to leave the estate to the survivor. However, in such a case, it may be preferable for inheritance tax purposes simply to leave the estate directly to the next generation if the survivor is adequately provided for.

However, in some instances it may be desirable that if a married couple die simultaneously, for example, in a car accident, that the survivorship period should not apply. In the situation where spouses die together and it is not certain who died first, the elder spouse is deemed to die first (Law of Property Act 1925, s 184). Therefore, if the survivorship period does not apply, the elder spouse's estate will pass to the younger. IHTA 1984, s 4(2) provides that

Planning for Death **16.21**

where it cannot be ascertained which of two people survived the other then it is assumed that both deaths occurred at the same instant. This means that the property of the elder falls outside the charge to inheritance tax on the younger's death. Therefore, from the point of view of inheritance tax, a survivorship clause need not operate in the event of a common accident.

Survivorship clauses can cause severe cashflow problems (and worry) for a dependent spouse. For this reason the will should contain a power for the executors to use either the capital or the income to maintain the spouse during the survivorship period. Alternatively, it should be coupled with a joint bank account or other similar arrangements so that the dependent spouse is not deprived of funds for a lengthy period.

Discretionary wills

16.21 Often, an individual wishing to make a will is, at the time, precluded by financial or family circumstances from making a decision as to how his property should be distributed on his death. In these circumstances the appropriate solution may be to give his estate, or some part of it, to his executors to be held on discretionary trusts. The trustees would be given a wide power of appointment exercisable in favour of a specified class of beneficiaries, leaving them to distribute it or declare trusts of it following his death. If the executors exercise the power within two years of the death, then tax will be chargeable as if the gifts or trusts were made by the testator on his death, and the appointment will not be subject to the usual inheritance tax regime for discretionary trusts (IHTA 1984, s 144). It is not essential that the power of appointment is vested in the executors. It could instead be vested in, for example, the testator's spouse (although consideration would then have to be given to the possibility of the spouse predeceasing the testator).

The essential elements are as follows.

(*a*)　The power of appointment must be exercised within two years of the death. To ensure that this is achieved it may be advisable that the will should provide that the trust will automatically terminate at the end of the two-year period and contain a gift in default of the exercise of the power.

(*b*)　The power must be exercised before an interest in possession subsists in the property. To ensure this careful drafting is required but it can be achieved by inserting a two-year power or trust to accumulate the income arising.

(*c*)　The power must be exercisable notwithstanding that the administration of the estate is not completed. It is understood that the Capital Taxes Office take the view (probably fallaciously) that a power such as this cannot be exercised until the estate has been administered unless the will expressly so provides. As a further caution, the will should also provide that the power may be exercisable whether or not there has been an assent by the executors to themselves as trustees.

16.21 Planning for Death

(*d*) The will must give adequate power to the appointor to enable trusts, discretionary or otherwise, to be declared over the property, and to enable the appointor to confer whatever powers are needed or are appropriate, all within the confines of the testator's overall requirements.

The 'back-dating' operation of section 144 only applies where, on a distribution from the trust, tax would otherwise have been charged. As a result, if the discretion is exercised within three months of the death, section 144 will not apply because tax would not otherwise have been chargeable. See *Frankland v CIR, CA [1997] STC 1450* and *Harding & Leigh (Loveday's Executors) v CIR, Sp C [1997] SSCD 321 (Sp C 140)*. This can be a dangerous trap for the unwary.

Example

T creates a two-year discretionary trust. Two months after T's death, the trustees appoint the property to T's wife. This will not be read back to T's death as no charge is imposed on events occurring within three months of the creation of the trust (IHTA 1984, s 64(4)). Therefore the spouse exemption remains unused and inheritance tax is charged on the entire estate.

The disadvantages of a discretionary will should not be overlooked:

1. the circumstances which led the testator to delegate his testamentary responsibility to his executors may still exist at his death or at the end of the period of two years from his death — nonetheless, even if the uncertainties are not fully resolved, the executors/trustees will at least know the latest situation;

2. the executors may be at a disadvantage insofar as they are not as familiar with the circumstances of the family as the testator himself — but the executors will normally be either family members or long-established family advisers; and

3. the testator must appreciate that he will have to rely on others to make decisions and judgements about his family over which he will have no control — he can guide his executors, however, by means of a letter of wishes and provide 'long stop' provisions within the will in the event that the executors cannot agree amongst themselves.

Despite these supposed disadvantages, it is still preferable to have a discretionary will rather than to rely on a possible variation of the will by the beneficiaries, following the death. The scope for a variation may be limited unless all beneficiaries are *sui juris* and willing to agree. In addition, where a parent beneficiary confers a benefit on his minor unmarried children by a variation he will fall within the provisions of ICTA 1988, s 660B in relation to the income of the property. An appointment under a discretionary will is outside the provisions of that section. It has been argued, surely erroneously, that where the power is vested in the deceased's executors a surviving spouse, who is the sole executor (or even one of the executors) may be regarded as a settlor for the purposes of section 660B in exercising, or concurring in the exercise, of this power.

Financial consequences

16.22 There are other financial consequences to be considered in relation to a discretionary will.

1. Inheritance tax will be payable on the application for a grant of probate on the value of the property subject to the discretionary power unless the power is exercised before the application is made. This is assuming that the property does not qualify for the instalment relief in which case only those instalments which have fallen due at that date will be payable. In such cases, executors often have to fund this tax by bank borrowing which is expensive. If the property is subsequently appointed to an exempt legatee such as a spouse, the inheritance tax would be repayable.

2. Capital gains tax complications may arise. TCGA 1992, s 62, which applies to variations within two years of death, does not apply to discretionary wills. An absolute appointment made under the trust is treated as a disposal under TCGA 1992, s 71. Hold-over relief under TCGA 1992, s 260 will not be available because any disposition of the trust assets within the two year period will not be an occasion of charge to inheritance tax as IHTA 1984, s 144 prevents a charge arising. However, hold-over relief under TCGA 1992, s 165 may be available. If relief is not available, whether or not a chargeable gain results will depend on whether there has been any increase in value of the property appointed since the date of death. If the appointment is not absolute but on continuing trusts it will be necessary to consider whether a new settlement has thereby been created or whether the trusts are a continuation of those established by the will, in accordance with the principles laid down in *Roome and Another v Edwards, HL 1981, 54 TC 359; [1981] STC 96; [1981] 1 All ER 736, Ewart v Taylor, Ch D [1983] STC 721*, and *Bond v Pickford, CA [1983] STC 517*. If a new settlement is created a disposal to the new trustees will have taken place (although hold-over relief may be available). If the trusts are merely a continuation there will be no such disposal. However, other difficulties may arise where a number of different trusts are established under an exercise of the power in that each of the trusts established will be treated for capital gains tax purposes as one fund with the result that only one annual exemption, apportioned between the separate funds, will be available.

3. A further complication will arise where an absolute appointment is made before the estate is fully administered, unless the assets which are the subject of the appointment have first been appropriated by the deceased's personal representatives to the trustees.

There is an argument that the subject matter of the appointment will be a chose in action in accordance with *Marshall v Kerr, HL [1994] STC 638; [1994] 2 All ER 106* which will have a nil base cost and therefore a significant chargeable gain could arise. However, the Inland Revenue take the view that where the trustees exercise their powers of appointment before the assets have vested in them, the assets are still held by the personal representatives at that time. When

16.23 *Planning for Death*

the assets vest, they will be treated as passing direct to the appointee (Inland Revenue Capital Gains Manual CG31432).

There is a disposal of the assets in question by the personal representatives to the person who benefits under the appointment.

The Inland Revenue view is that the exercise of the power of appointment is, however, read back into the original will (Inland Revenue Capital Gains Manual CG31433). Thus, the beneficiary takes the asset as legatee and acquires the assets at probate value (TCGA 1992, s 62(4) and TCGA 1992, s 64(2)).

The result of this is somewhat surprising as the capital gains tax implications of an appointment prior to an assent or ascertainment of residue will be completely different from that of an appointment made after assent or ascertainment of the residue of the estate.

For example, where an asset has increased in value since the date of death, appointment of that asset following assent or ascertainment will result in a capital gains tax charge arising to the trustees on the appointment. Hold-over relief will only be available if the assets are business assets (see 2 above).

However, if that asset were to be appointed to the beneficiary before assent or ascertainment, no chargeable gain will arise as the Inland Revenue will treat the beneficiary as if he received the asset at probate value under the terms of the will (Inland Revenue Capital Gains Manual CG31433). No chargeable gain will arise until the subsequent disposal of the asset by the beneficiary.

Trustees wishing to appoint assets to beneficiaries should consider this as it may be important for capital gains tax purposes to exercise the power of appointment prior to assent or ascertainment of the residue if an unwanted tax charge is to be avoided.

4. For income tax purposes the income arising under the discretionary trusts during the period from death to the exercise of the power will be taxed at the rate applicable to trusts (although beneficiaries receiving income distributions may be able to reclaim all or part of this tax).

In spite of these disadvantages, most of which may be overcome by a little forward planning, the flexibility offered by discretionary wills is such that most clients with estates in excess of one million pounds should consider having wills in a discretionary form.

Types of gifts and legacies

Free-of-tax legacies: grossing-up

16.23 Under IHTA 1984, s 38, where the residue of an estate is exempt from inheritance tax because, for example, it passes either to the testator's spouse or to charity, then any legacies and bequests given in the will

Planning for Death 16.23

'free-of-tax' will be grossed-up to determine the amount of tax chargeable which is in respect of those legacies, and payable out of residue. The gross sum which, after deduction of tax at the rate applicable to the chargeable value of the estate, will provide the amount required to meet the legacies and bequests, and inheritance tax is then charged on this grossed-up value. Where gifts have been made within seven years of death, whether chargeable transfers or potentially exempt transfers, these will be aggregated with the value of the free-of-tax legacies and other chargeable property passing on the death to determine the rate at which tax is payable. Such lifetime transfers will have the benefit of the nil rate band in priority to the estate on death.

Where part of the residue is chargeable, and part is exempt, the grossing-up calculation involves a second stage in which the value of the chargeable residue as well as the value of the free-of-tax legacies (and the value of any transfers within seven years of the death) are included. If the calculated net value of the chargeable estate does not exceed the nil rate band at the death, grossing-up becomes irrelevant, and no tax is payable.

Grossing-up will be avoided if gifts to non-exempt beneficiaries are made subject to inheritance tax instead of free of it. However, this will result in the legatee receiving a lower net sum which may not accord with the testator's wishes in every case. Of course, the testator could always increase the size of the legacy if the gift is to bear its own tax which will have a similar (if not identical) effect to the grossing-up provisions. Alternatively, if instead the legatees are given a share of residue to be divided between them, grossing-up will be avoided and some tax saved. However, such a gift is less precise, in that the sum which the legatee will receive often cannot be calculated accurately when the will is drawn up, but only on the distribution of the estate following the testator's death.

Where a will provides for half of the testator's estate to pass to an exempt beneficiary and the other half to a taxable beneficiary, will the estate be divided equally before inheritance tax or after it? In *Lockhart v Harker & Others (re Benham's Will Trusts), Ch D 1994, [1995] STC 210* the court decided that the division was after tax and therefore that the exempt beneficiary's after tax share was equal to the taxable beneficiary's. In *Holmes and Another v McMullan and Others (re Ratcliffe (deceased)), Ch D [1999] STC 262* on similar facts the court decided that the division was before tax so that the exempt beneficiary received a larger net amount than the non-exempt beneficiary. The decision distinguished *re Benham's Will Trusts* on the basis that no general principle was to be applied but rather the intentions of the particular testator were to be determined from a construction of his Will.

Where a will provides for free-of-tax legacies and at the same time there are one or more separate funds (e.g. settlements in which the deceased had an interest in possession) also chargeable to tax on the deceased's death, then an Inland Revenue practice (reported in the Law Society's Gazette of 9 May 1990 on page 14; see *Butterworths Yellow Tax Handbook*) will operate to reduce the total amount of tax payable on the death. The Inland Revenue accept that, as a result of IHTA 1984, s 40 and subject to the *Ramsay* principle and the associated operations provisions, the rate of tax applicable when

16.24 Planning for Death

grossing up free-of-tax legacies is that applicable to the free estate in isolation and not that applicable to the total value of all property chargeable on the deceased's death. This means that where, for example, a will contains free-of-tax legacies and provides for residue to pass to an exempt beneficiary (e.g. a surviving spouse) and there is separately chargeable settled property, either there will be no grossing up if the legacies are less than the nil rate band or only one round of grossing up will be needed if the legacies are in excess of the nil rate band.

Incidence of tax: residue

16.24 Whilst the tax attributable to any tax-free legacies will be borne by the whole of the testator's residuary estate (even if it includes exempt beneficiaries), the burden of tax on non-exempt residuary gifts cannot be shifted by the will on to exempt residuary gifts (IHTA 1984, s 41). Where residue is divided between exempt and non-exempt beneficiaries the tax payable on the estate and attributable to residue will be borne wholly by the non-exempt slice. However, the gifts contained in the will can reflect this fact: for example, instead of gifts of one half of residue to the spouse (exempt) and one half to the children (non-exempt) the will could contain gifts of one third of residue to the spouse and two thirds to the children.

Incidence of tax: land

16.25 Under the estate duty regime, realty bore its own duty but inheritance tax is an expense of administration (see IHTA 1984, s 211). In the absence of a contrary intention in the will, the burden of tax will fall on residue and not on the property given (*Dougal (Re), CS [1981] STC 54*). Therefore, to ensure that a legacy whether of land or other property bears its own tax, the will must state so expressly.

Gift of tax payable on potentially exempt transfers etc.

16.26 A donor of a potentially exempt transfer who dies within seven years of the gift may leave the donee with a problem of funding the tax, for example, where the gift was of private company shares or other assets which are not easily realisable. To avoid this problem the donor may provide in his will that the tax due is paid out of his estate. This is the equivalent of a legacy to the donee of a sum equal to the amount of the tax. Such a legacy, if given free of tax, will have to be grossed-up as explained above. Personal representatives are under a secondary liability to pay the tax on a potentially exempt transfer under IHTA 1984, s 199. Therefore, where a legacy of the amount of the tax is given, rather than expressing this as a gift to the donee of the original gift, consideration should be given to coupling with it a power for the executors themselves to use the sum given to discharge the inheritance tax liability on the potentially exempt transfer (or even imposing a binding obligation on them to do so). This ensures that the gift is used for its intended purpose.

Similar considerations apply to chargeable lifetime gifts, where additional tax will be payable in the event of the donor's death within seven years, and to

Planning for Death **16.28**

gifts where the deceased has reserved a benefit which are therefore taxable on his death as part of his estate. Legacies of the sum equivalent to the tax or additional tax which is payable need not be limited to one particular gift but could be expressed in general terms to cover all gifts by the testator during his lifetime which become chargeable, or give rise to tax payable, as a result of the death.

Annuities

16.27 As a general rule, gifts by will of annuities are best avoided, because of their disadvantageous tax treatment.

For inheritance tax purposes, the setting aside of the annuity fund will be treated as a settlement and a charge to tax will arise on the death of the annuitant or on the termination of his or her interest in possession (IHTA 1984, s 50).

For income tax purposes, the whole of the annuity given by the will is taxable in the hands of the annuitant. However, by contrast, a qualifying annuity purchased by the annuitant from an insurance company will include in each instalment a capital element paid free of income tax. If the will creates an obligation on the executors to purchase such an annuity, then tax relief will be lost (ICTA 1988, s 657(2)(c)). A gift of a capital sum, calculated by reference to annuity rates, coupled with a non-binding suggestion to a legatee that it should be used to purchase an annuity, will, however, be within the exemption granted by ICTA 1988, s 656. An annuity left to a spouse may be advantageous because the transfer will benefit from the spouse exemption and over time the capital fund will reduce.

Precatory gifts

16.28 It is common to give chattels by the will to a legatee or even to the executors with a non-binding condition that they are distributed in accordance with the testator's last known wishes as expressed in any note or memorandum left by the testator at his death (whether written before or after the date of the will). If the distribution is made within two years of the death it is treated as if it was made by the testator in his will and no additional charge to inheritance tax arises on that distribution (IHTA 1984, s 143).

A charge to capital gains tax could arise but in practice it is unlikely to do so. In the case of chattels, the exemption in TCGA 1992, s 262 will be available where the chattel is worth £6,000 or less, and marginal relief may apply where the value exceeds that sum.

The testator must appreciate that his wishes will not be legally binding on the legatee of the chattels, but assuming he is prepared to accept this risk, a 'memorandum of wishes' clause in a will provides a flexible and tax effective way of dealing with gifts of a large number of chattels to individual legatees. There is nothing in IHTA 1984, s 143 which limits the operation of the provision to chattels, although the use of the word 'bequeathed' may limit the operation of the section to personalty and not realty. It could equally well apply to cash, although generally testators are more prepared to put specific chattels at risk rather than sums of money.

Gifts for anatomical and therapeutic purposes

16.29 Directions for disposal of the body or its organs are best dealt with other than in the will. The spouse or next of kin should know whether the testator would be willing for his body and organs to be used for transplant purposes or for medical research. As very prompt action will be required if he would be willing for such use to be made of them, there will not be time to refer to the will. He should therefore record his wishes in writing and ensure that a copy is held by his doctor and his spouse.

Safe keeping and review of wills: personal assets log

16.30 Once signed, a will should be kept safely where, following the death, it can be obtained easily. Banks will usually agree to release the will, following the death, to allow solicitors acting in the estate to make an application for probate. Those who will need to know of its existence should be informed of its location.

There is sometimes a tendency for a testator having made a will to forget about it. The testator should be encouraged to review it regularly and, in any event, following the introduction of any new tax legislation or a significant change in his personal or family circumstances or in the assets in his estate.

Small changes in a will can simply be made by a codicil. There is no requirement that a new will be entered into. Testators should, however, always bear in mind that after death a will and codicils are public documents and he or she may prefer to consolidate an earlier will as varied by subsequent changes into one document to avoid the testator's changing fortunes and/or whims being subject to public scrutiny.

Executors often face a difficult task in locating a will, or a possible will, and share certificates and other documents of title. The testator should be encouraged to complete and to maintain a personal assets log. This should contain full details of

(*a*)   assets;

(*b*)   all insurance cover on the testator's life and assets;

(*c*)   the names and addresses of his banks, building societies and professional advisers (e.g. solicitors, accountants and stock-brokers);

(*d*)   the location of his will; and

(*e*)   lifetime transfers made.

While it cannot be expected to contain details of every liability of the testator, it should at least record details of contingent liabilities under guarantees or indemnities, for example, knowledge of which may be crucial to the executors but which may otherwise be late in being drawn to their attention.

Variation of the will after death

16.31 Whatever provision the testator may make in his will, his beneficiaries, if they are *sui juris*, may rearrange the distribution of the estate by means of a deed of variation or a disclaimer under IHTA 1984, s 142 or by an application to the court either under the Variation of Trusts Act 1958 or under the Inheritance (Provision for Family and Dependants) Act 1975. Any variation may result in different inheritance tax consequences. This should not prevent a testator making proper provision in his will as none of those routes can be relied upon to produce the result which the testator (and perhaps his beneficiaries) would wish and there is always a risk that those who survive him will be unwilling or unable to enter into a variation. In addition, any application to the court will inevitably deplete the value of the testator's estate. These matters are considered more fully in chapter 17 *Post-Death Estate Planning*.

Death in service benefits and pension schemes

16.32 For persons who are members of an approved death in service benefit scheme or pension scheme, the exercise of any right of nomination or request in the form of a letter of wishes, over the payment of such benefits arising on death is of equal importance as making a will. As Inland Revenue limits allow up to four times salary to be available under such schemes the sum is likely to be of some consequence to the provision which the member can make for his dependants.

If the terms of the scheme permit the moneys to be paid to the estate as of right, the moneys will be within the charge to inheritance tax on his death. It is the Inland Revenue's view that if the scheme member has a general right to nominate or appoint the benefit to anyone he wishes and he fails to exercise that right irrevocably, the death benefits will also be within the charge to inheritance tax on his death. It is doubtful whether the Inland Revenue are correct in this opinion.

Usually, however, a power is conferred on the scheme trustees enabling them to distribute the moneys among the member's dependants, at their absolute discretion, and the member merely has the opportunity to express his views in a letter of wishes. This discretion vested in the scheme trustees will enable property to be given to the children of the member without incurring a liability to inheritance tax (see the Inland Revenue Statement of Practice E3 relating to capital transfer tax which the Inland Revenue have confirmed is extended to inheritance tax). The Inland Revenue have also confirmed that such discretionary schemes are outside the gifts with reservation rules contained in the inheritance tax legislation (Press Release dated 9 July 1986).

Trustees are often reluctant to pay moneys to the children, or to settlements established for the children, unless they are satisfied it is in accordance with the member's wishes. This is because the trustees are concerned that the widow may not be adequately provided for. They may therefore be tempted to pay the benefit to the widow or even to the personal representatives, leaving them to distribute it as part of the residuary estate. Depending on the precise

16.33 *Planning for Death*

terms of the power, it may be possible for the trustees to establish accumulation and maintenance trusts for children or even discretionary trusts for the widow and children or to pay the moneys to an existing trust made inter vivos by the member for his dependants. The trustees of such trusts could use the cash from the scheme to purchase assets from the estate as a means of funding the inheritance tax payable on the deceased's death. The main advantage of using a discretionary trust is the fact that the property will not be comprised in the widow's estate when she dies and no tax liability will arise at that time. She can, however, be a beneficiary of the trust and income and capital, if necessary, can be paid to her. The gift with reservation provisions will not apply as she will not have made the 'gift'. The trust will be subject to the inheritance tax regime for discretionary trusts but it is unlikely that any liability so arising will detract substantially from the tax saving that will result on the death of the widow. The inheritance tax implications of such a trust are discussed in greater detail in chapter 8 *Pensions*.

Usually, the nomination requires a minimum of formality and a signed form or letter of wishes to the trustees is all that is necessary. Completed nominations or letters of wishes should be submitted by the member in accordance with the scheme rules or may otherwise be invalid. This usually requires that the completed form or letter of wishes should be lodged with the scheme trustees.

Death-bed planning

16.33 The scope for transferring assets only once it is clear that a person is dying is severely limited because there will be no mitigation of the inheritance tax payable on any lifetime gifts unless the donor survives for three years, when taper relief will commence (see 16.36 below). In addition, the benefit of the valuable capital gains tax base uplift on death will be lost. There are, however, some exercises which may be carried out.

(a) *The conversion of assets into excluded property*. Where persons are not domiciled in the UK and not deemed to be domiciled here, they can dispose of property situated in the UK in favour of property situated abroad. In the case of a person neither resident nor ordinarily resident in the UK any sterling bank accounts can be converted into foreign currency held in a qualifying bank account so that IHTA 1984, s 157 will apply. Alternatively, the purchase of exempt British government securities by persons non-resident and non-domiciled (any deemed domicile being ignored for this purpose) will be excluded property under IHTA 1984, s 6(2).

For individuals who are domiciled and resident in the UK the excluded property provisions do not offer tax planning opportunities. While, for example, excluded property includes reversionary interests in settlements it will not include a reversion purchased for money or money's worth.

(b) *Using up any unused lifetime exemptions such as the annual exemption and the small gifts exemption.*

Planning for Death **16.33**

(c) *Loans.* Where property which will qualify for business or agricultural property relief on a death is subject to a mortgage or charge to secure borrowings, the security should be transferred to other non-qualifying property to ensure that the full advantage of the reliefs is taken. This is because the reliefs only apply on the value of property after it is reduced by the mortgage or charge. Alternatively, the borrowings could be repaid.

(d) *Assets pregnant with gains.* An individual should not make death-bed gifts of assets pregnant with gains because, as mentioned above, the valuable capital gains tax uplift on death will be lost. Where, however, the individual is married and his spouse owns assets which are pregnant with gains, these assets could be transferred to the individual (free of capital gains tax) and then bequeathed back to the spouse by will. The spouse would then obtain a new base cost for the assets i.e. their market value at the date of death. If these arrangements are entered into with a view to a projected sale by the wife, the court may choose to disregard them under the *Ramsay* principle but if they are carried out with no particular sale in view, the device should be effective (*Craven v White, HL [1988] STC 476; [1988] 3 All ER 495*). A more secure method would be for the will to provide that the wife would only have a life interest in the property. In such circumstances it might be more difficult to argue that the *Ramsay* principle applied.

(e) *Joint bank accounts.* The conversion of bank accounts from sole to joint accounts and the transfer of property into joint names will assist in avoiding the need to obtain probate (see below). This will also assist with the funding of the payment of inheritance tax.

(f) *Charitable gifts.* Where an individual is intending to leave either a cash legacy or an interest in land to one or more charities, he could make the gifts whilst still alive so as to obtain an income tax deduction under FA 1990, s 25 (see chapter 13 *Gifts to Charities, Etc.*).

(g) *Heritage property.* Where a donor has heritage property qualifying for conditional exemption for inheritance tax purposes he could sell the heritage property to his children. The crystallised charge would be conditionally exempt provided the children are willing to give the requisite undertakings (see chapter 14 *National Heritage Property*).

Where there is a possibility that the individual may survive for the requisite two-year minimum ownership period, the acquisition of business or agricultural property will be effective in reducing the amount of inheritance tax payable on the death. With the increase in the rates of relief this form of last minute planning will be considerably more worthwhile. Buying a farm or woodlands would qualify for 100% relief provided the two-year period and the other criteria were satisfied. The acquisition of a balanced portfolio of securities dealt in on the Alternative Investment Market would provide relief at 100% if the individual were willing to accept the risks inherent in such an investment. There are also other strategies that might be followed where an

16.34 *Planning for Death*

existing interest is held eligible for 100% relief. The aim would be to enhance the level of relief available.

Funding the inheritance tax payable on death

The estate

16.34 The personal representatives are accountable for the tax on the free estate passing on the death and must pay that tax on the application for the grant of probate or letters of administration. This is with the exception of instalments of tax which have not fallen due on any land or business property qualifying for the instalment option. This can create a number of difficulties as the personal representatives will often need to borrow from a bank to fund the tax. This problem is sometimes aggravated because the principal asset in the estate is a shareholding in a family company or some other asset which is not easily realisable. Borrowing from the bank to fund this tax, let alone the realisation of the asset to repay the bank loan, will be difficult. This burden of funding can be eased in a number of ways, for example, by the use of insurance policies held in trust or joint bank and building society accounts. Even joint shareholdings in quoted companies, all of which will pass to the survivor, can be realised before probate is granted. The survivor could then lend the proceeds to the personal representatives or purchase assets from the estate.

Funding through insurance

16.35 Policies of insurance held in trust for the life assured's children are a useful vehicle for providing funds to pay the inheritance tax on death. In the case of a married couple where the sole or main inheritance tax charge will fall on the death of the survivor, the policy should be taken out on a joint life last survivor basis. The policy proceeds, will be paid to the trustees (or direct to the children if they are of age) on production of a death certificate only and will be available for loans to the personal representatives or for the purchase of estate assets. Ideally, the beneficial interests under the trusts should correspond to those under the will to avoid any question as to whether a loan by the trustees to the personal representatives will be in breach of trust.

Potentially exempt transfers and chargeable lifetime transfers

16.36 In the event of the death of the donor within seven years of a lifetime chargeable transfer or a potentially exempt transfer, inheritance tax (which in the case of lifetime chargeable transfers will be additional inheritance tax) may be payable on that transfer. To determine the rate of tax payable on the death, the transfer will also be aggregated with the value of the donor's free estate at death and any other gifts made within the seven-year period. The donor's nil rate band will be applied to gifts within the seven-year period in the order in which they are made and any balance then remaining will be available in respect of his estate on death.

In addition to the nil rate band, potentially exempt transfers and chargeable lifetime transfers may have the benefit of taper relief. The relief (ranging from 20% where the death occurs in the fourth year following the gift to 80% where the death occurs in the seventh year following the gift) is given against the tax, and not against the value of the property, so that the full value of the gifts is aggregated with the estate throughout the seven-year period and the taper relief does not reduce the tax payable by the estate.

Tax on the gift

16.37 Funding the tax on lifetime gifts which become taxable or subject to additional tax can cause problems for the donee, and for the personal representatives on whom a secondary liability falls. This is particularly the case if the subject matter of the gift is not easily realisable such as private company shares or land. The tax liability can be covered either by a seven-year decreasing term insurance policy effected by the donee on the life of the donor or by the donor effecting such a policy on his own life and assigning it to, or settling it in trust for, the donee. In the latter case any premium paid by the donor will be a gift but may be covered by the annual exemption or by the normal expenditure out of income exemption. Alternatively, the donor might pass funds to the trustees, which would be a potentially exempt transfer, leaving the trustees to pay the premiums themselves.

The cost of insurance will depend on the age, state of health of the donor and the sum insured. The decreasing sum payable under the policy in the fourth and subsequent years from the date of the gift should reflect the benefit of taper relief on the inheritance tax charge on the gift.

Additional tax on the estate

16.38 Where the donor fails to survive for seven years after the potentially exempt transfer or a chargeable transfer is made, an increased charge to inheritance tax may arise on his estate. This is because the benefit of the nil rate band will be applied first to the chargeable lifetime gifts in the order in which they were made which may result in the estate paying a higher rate than would otherwise be the case. In addition, taper relief is only given against the tax on the gift and not against the value of the property given. Consequently, the risk of the higher amount of tax remains constant for the full seven-year term.

This additional tax can be funded by a seven-year term policy for a level sum rather than a decreasing one. The policy can be effected by the donor in trust for the beneficiaries of his estate or by the beneficiaries themselves. If the premiums are funded by the donor, such payments may again be covered by the annual exemption or normal expenditure out of income exemption, or may be potentially exempt.

If the policy is effected by the donor it should be written in trust for the beneficiaries. Otherwise, it will fall into the donor's estate and will be subject to inheritance tax on the death as part of that estate.

16.39 *Planning for Death*

Methods of avoiding probate

16.39 A grant of probate or letters of administration is necessary to prove the title of the executors or administrators to the assets of a person who has died in order that those assets may be collected in for the benefit of his estate. It is not required in respect of any assets where title automatically passes to someone else on the death. Where property is held in joint names the production of a death certificate will be sufficient. As a result considerable legal and other expenses may be saved.

There are other advantages as well. For example, in the case of a joint bank account, the survivor will have access to funds to meet immediate expenses and perhaps to meet some or all of the inheritance tax liability on the death.

Avoiding probate does not override the duty to submit an inheritance tax account of the property and to pay the relevant tax. Any liability to inheritance tax arising on the death will still have to be paid, even if all assets are in joint names and pass by survivorship. The duty to submit the account falls jointly upon the co-owner and the personal representatives and both are jointly liable for the tax although the incidence of tax falls on the deceased's share of the joint property (IHTA 1984, s 211(3)). Where, as often happens, the tax is borne by the estate in the first instance this can cause cashflow difficulties in the estate and this factor should not be overlooked.

Property held in joint names

16.40 All property may be held in joint names. In the case of land, the maximum number of joint owners permitted by the Law of Property Act 1925, s 34(2) is four, and in practice a similar restriction is often applied to other types of property, for example, shares and bank and building society accounts. It should be remembered that because property is in joint names, and legal title passes to the survivor or survivors, the beneficial interest may not always pass in exactly the same way. The survivors may be holding as trustees. When property is first transferred into joint names some separate statement of the beneficial ownership will be desirable as evidence of the parties' intentions.

Benefits under death in service policies and pension schemes

16.41 Such benefits can very often be paid to beneficiaries following production of a death certificate and without production of probate. This is the case where the trustees have a discretion to pay the proceeds among the dependants and are not required to pay them to the personal representatives. Where the proceeds are payable to personal representatives title must be proved by production of probate or letters of administration. The absence of a letter of wishes from the scheme member may lead to a delay and may tempt the trustees to avoid the issue of dividing the moneys between the dependants and to pay them to the personal representatives. In this case payment will be made when the grant is eventually produced some months later.

Planning for Death **16.44**

Care should be taken to ensure that the letter of wishes is lodged by the member with the scheme's trustees if this is required under the rules of the scheme or, if lodged elsewhere, can be obtained from safe custody and sent to the trustees without first having to obtain probate or letters of administration.

Insurance policies

16.42 Life policies and personal accident policies can all be effected in trust for dependants and the proceeds paid to the named trustees on production of a death certificate and without production of probate. The Married Women's Property Act 1882 provides a relatively simple route for trust policies for the benefit of a spouse and/or children. More elaborate trusts, and trusts for beneficiaries other than spouse and children, will require individual drafting, although most life offices can provide standard trust wordings on request.

Policy documents, if lodged at a bank or elsewhere in safe custody, should be held jointly to the order of the life assured and some other person, preferably the policy trustees or the beneficiary. If they are deposited in safe custody to the order of the assured alone, a grant of representation may be necessary to obtain the release of the policy document and therefore the policy proceeds cannot be used to fund inheritance tax payable before the grant is issued.

Retirement annuity contracts and personal pension arrangements

16.43 Usually, on death before retirement, a death benefit will be payable (related to the value of premiums paid) under retirement annuity contracts within ICTA 1988, ss 620 and 621 and personal pension arrangements within ICTA 1988, Part XIV, Chapter IV. Where this amounts to a substantial sum, consideration should be given to settling the death benefit (by way of an *inter vivos* assignment of the policy to trustees) upon trust for the benefit of the deceased's heirs to prevent the benefit falling within his taxable estate for inheritance tax purposes. Such assignments into trust are dealt with in more detail in chapter 8 *Pensions*.

Assets worth less than £5,000

16.44 Certain assets, if valued at less than £5,000 each, may be collected in by personal representatives, or intending personal representatives, without production of a grant. The Administration of Estates (Small Payments) Act 1965 authorises building societies, industrial and provident societies, trade unions and loan societies to pay over balances, etc. held if less than £5,000 without production of a grant of representation. The Department of National Savings similarly permits balances on accounts, premium savings bonds, national savings certificates and government stock held on the department's register to be released without production of a grant where the total invested is not more than £5,000 per set of regulations.

16.45 *Planning for Death*

National Savings investments

16.45 Where these are required to meet the inheritance tax due on the death in order to obtain a grant of representation, there are procedures available through the Probate Registry and the Capital Taxes Office for most forms of national savings investments to be encashed prior to the grant being obtained.

Foreign assets

16.46 Small holdings of directly owned foreign assets are usually best avoided in the absence of overriding investment (or recreational) criteria. Proving title to these assets on the death of the registered owner will often require the involvement of lawyers both in England and in the foreign country concerned as well as probate formalities (or the equivalent) in both countries because title in foreign countries will usually be established through title granted in the court of the place of domicile. Often the expenses involved do not justify collecting in an asset of modest value. Foreign death duties may be payable and foreign death duty returns will need to be submitted. There will usually be relief given against inheritance tax for foreign tax paid. In the case of land situated abroad, where there is a double tax treaty between the UK and the country where the land is situated, the credit is usually to be given in the overseas country for inheritance tax paid in the UK.

Ownership of foreign assets through offshore settlements or companies or through UK nominees may overcome difficult and expensive foreign probate requirements and may also avoid the payment of local death duties. These possibilities should be considered before a foreign asset is acquired, as should the disposal costs arising on death.

Where a testator is likely to die owning foreign realty consideration should be given to the succession implications of the law of the country in which the land is situated. The law of the jurisdiction may specify how the property is to devolve on the death regardless of any will left by the deceased. It may also be sensible to have a separate will dealing solely with that particular asset drawn up by a local lawyer under the local law.

Ownership of foreign assets is considered in more detail in chapter 18 *Investing Abroad*.

Lloyd's underwriting interests

16.47 As underwriting membership of Lloyd's terminates on death it should be discussed in conjunction with wills. The taxation of Lloyd's underwriters is an extensive topic and is dealt with in *Tolley's Taxation of Lloyd's Underwriters*.

In relation to inheritance tax, property used in connection with such membership attracts significant advantages. Investments and cash held in the Lloyd's deposit and underwriting reserves (the member's personal reserves and his special reserve) and profits on the open years' accounts at death (see

Planning for Death **16.47**

below) will qualify for business property relief at 100%. However, where the underwriting property has a value in excess of £100,000 the Capital Taxes Office limit such relief in cases where they consider that the deposits and reserves are excessive compared to the level of business written. It is understood that in certain cases they have sought to limit the amount of the deposits and reserves eligible for relief to 50% of the Name's premium income limit. Where the Lloyd's deposit or underwriting reserves are funded by a letter of credit or guarantee from a bank, the assets held by the bank as security for those arrangements will qualify for business property relief currently at 100% up to the face value of the letters of credit or guarantee. The Revenue have confirmed that the amount of business property relief will no longer be restricted by reference to the nature of the underlying asset or assets against which the guarantee is secured (Lloyds Market Bulletin dated 23 April 2002). It should be noted, however, that the Revenue will treat the value of underlying assets as reduced by the amount of the guarantee for the purpose of giving any other reliefs or exemptions. Therefore, guarantees should not be secured against assets that would qualify for either business property relief or agricultural property relief.

Names may underwrite either through a MAPA (Members Agents Pooling Arrangement) or through a limited liability company as well as through a traditional bespoke portfolio. Each of the three methods of underwriting carry different requirements for Lloyd's deposits which may affect the amounts qualifying for business property relief.

In addition to business property relief the investments and cash in the deposits and reserves are also discounted to reflect the fact that they are unavailable for up to three years from the year of death. Lloyd's employs a three-year accounting method and as a result the deposit and reserves will not be released until the open years at death (that is the remainder of the three-year accounting period in which the testator's estate will continue to participate after his death) have closed. With business property relief at 100%, this further discount has become less important and is only likely to be relevant where the amount of deposits and reserves eligible for the relief is restricted (see above).

Profits or losses on the open years' accounts at death may be valued:

(a) on the Lloyd's audit basis, which is the strict legal basis and is adopted as the market value at date of death, usually producing a conservative result, or

(b) on the basis of the actual results of the open years. An election by the personal representatives to base the valuation on actual results must be made within twelve months of the grant of representation.

In either event the value will be discounted to reflect the fact that the profits will not have been available to the Name until after the accounts for the year have closed. Consequently, a member can use his underwriting property to make substantially larger gifts by will to children or other non-exempt beneficiaries at minimum tax cost, particularly if all or part of his nil rate band is available.

Very often, the testator will be advised to take advantage of business property relief by giving his Lloyd's underwriting property to his children or other

16.47 *Planning for Death*

non-exempt beneficiary by his will. It should be borne in mind that some part of the underwriting property, including unpaid profits on a closed year of account which are simply debts due to the member, may not qualify for business property relief. If the will refers to underwriting property in general terms, but it is the testator's intention that only property which qualifies for business property relief is to be passed under that gift, it is necessary to use words of limitation to limit the gift and ensure that underwriting property which does not so qualify is excluded.

Where a member funds his Lloyd's deposit or underwriting reserves by a banker's letter of credit, the testator will have to consider whether the property held as security by the bank should be included in the gift. As mentioned above, the property so held by the bank will qualify for business property relief, up to the face value of the letter of credit.

Two other matters also need consideration.

1. In the absence of express words in the will, a gift of Lloyd's underwriting profits will not carry the burden of income tax on those profits. If there are profits accruing to the estate, income tax at the basic rate will have been deducted at source. There may, however, be substantial income tax liabilities at the higher rate (as these are assessable as part of the member's income and not the income of his executors) which could significantly erode the residue of the estate. It is therefore desirable that a gift of underwriting profits or gains should be made subject to payment out of that property of all attributable tax liabilities and similarly the gift should carry with it the benefit of income and capital gains tax repayments resulting from underwriting losses. Any income tax and capital gains tax repayments will not qualify for business property relief.

2. It is desirable that the testator is advised to effect an estate protection plan policy which on his death would protect his estate from underwriting losses and enable the executors to distribute assets without waiting until the open years have closed. Even so, the will should authorise the executors to reinsure the open years' underwriting at death or to effect stop-loss insurance, in case for any reason the estate protection plan policy is not kept in force by the testator.

As membership of Lloyd's terminates on death the opportunity to utilise business property relief is only available on that occasion. There is no carrying on of the business after death so that relief will not be available on the death of a surviving spouse (unless he or she is also a member in his or her own right). It is also possible for the surviving spouse to apply to join Lloyd's and take over the deceased's underwriting capacity. If the Lloyd's underwriting property is not given by the will to a child or other non-exempt beneficiary, consideration should be given to dealing with it in this way, if possible, in a deed of variation of the will.

17 Post-death Estate Planning

Introduction

17.1 Personal representatives do not have an easy task and the administration of an estate is made more complicated by the various options open to them and the beneficiaries of the deceased's estate following the death to mitigate the impact of inheritance tax and to take the estate planning steps which the deceased ought to have taken but failed (for whatever reason) to take during his lifetime. This is the case even where the deceased died intestate.

If the estate is subject to inheritance tax, it will be important to identify any property which may qualify for any of the available reliefs to reduce the amount of inheritance tax payable (such as relevant business property within the meaning of IHTA 1984, s 105 or agricultural property within the meaning of IHTA 1984, s 115) and to ascertain whether or not the relief will apply in the particular circumstances of the estate.

If the estate includes any assets such as works of art or land and buildings which are pre-eminent for national, scientific, historic or artistic interest, then a claim under IHTA 1984, s 31 may be made to the Treasury by the personal representatives to have the assets made exempt from tax. If the claim is allowed, an exemption will be granted, subject to various undertakings being given in relation to the preservation of the asset and the provision of public access to it. Therefore, no tax will be payable at death on the relevant assets but the exemption will be lost if there is a breach of one of the undertakings or if the asset is sold and the tax will become payable at that stage. If an estate includes assets which might qualify for such relief, expert advice should be taken at an early stage to ascertain whether or not a claim should be made for an exemption and as to which assets should be included in the claim. (See chapter 14 *National Heritage Property* for a more detailed explanation of the rules.)

The personal representatives must also consider whether the inheritance tax may be paid by instalments; and must also establish upon whom the burden of the tax falls: for example, whether a legacy is to be paid subject to or free from inheritance tax.

The personal representatives should also consider that if any investments or land forming part of the deceased's estate are to be sold after the death and the values at the date of sale are less than the values at the date of death, then the sale price can be substituted for the value at death, provided that certain conditions are fulfilled. The timing of the sales is all important.

17.2 Post-death Estate Planning

An amended IHTA 1984, s 217 imposes an onerous duty of inquiry in relation not only to the deceased's estate at death but also in relation to lifetime chargeable transfers. These onerous duties are reflected in the new version of form IHT 200 on which personal representatives make a return of the deceased's estate. Anybody, but especially professional advisers, should now consider carefully before accepting an executorship in view of their personal liability for a failure to comply with these duties. That liability was increased by amendments to the penalty and interest charges.

By far the most important estate planning consideration for personal representatives and the beneficiaries of the deceased's estate will be their ability to vary the dispositions effected by the will or by the applicable intestacy rules so as to redirect parts of the estate to different members of the family. Such variations may be solely tax-driven or they may arise from other personal or family considerations. The personal representatives will wish to draw this possibility to the attention of the beneficiaries at as early a stage as possible.

Post-death estate planning must be undertaken within strict time limits in order to be tax effective, which may be during a particularly stressful and difficult period for the beneficiaries. An adviser will need to establish his clients' requirements with sensitivity and care but without delay.

Inheritance tax

Variations

17.2 The provisions of IHTA 1984, s 142 enable the beneficiaries under a will or on an intestacy to alter the dispositions of the deceased's estate effected by the terms of the deceased's will or by the intestacy rules.

The popular notion that one is 'varying' the terms of a will is a misconception, since the terms of a will can never be varied once the testator has died. Section 142 speaks of 'varying' the dispositions of the deceased's estate effected by his will and is directed at cases where the recipient of property from the deceased chooses to redirect it to other persons whether by way of an outright gift or a declaration of trust or a settlement. If the provisions of section 142 are satisfied then the redirection will for inheritance tax purposes be treated as if it had been effected by the deceased on his death and tax will be charged accordingly. There is a similar back-dating provision for capital gains tax which is considered below. It must never be forgotten, however, that this retroactive effect is a fiction imposed for tax purposes — as a matter of strict law any redirection takes effect when the instrument effecting the redirection (be it a deed of gift, a stock transfer form or a declaration of trust) is entered into and not from the date of death. Thus, the redirection does not alter the income tax treatment of any income arising before the redirection is made.

Reasons for a variation

17.3 In most cases the primary purpose of a variation is to reduce the burden of inheritance tax. But there may be a secondary purpose which is

Post-death Estate Planning 17.4

more in keeping with the concept of a family arrangement, namely to effect an equitable distribution of the deceased's assets between the beneficiaries and other members of the deceased's family.

There may be many personal or family reasons which prompt beneficiaries to surrender or redirect the whole or part of their entitlement under a will or on intestacy. It may be that a will does not provide adequately for a particular beneficiary. For example, a widow inheriting the whole of her late husband's estate may wish to make immediate provision for her children. This action may also reduce the ultimate inheritance tax burden on the estate by making use of the deceased's nil rate band. Conversely, children who inherit under their father's will at the expense of their mother might wish to redirect part of their entitlement to her.

Occasionally, the personal representatives receive a claim under the Inheritance (Provision for Family and Dependants) Act 1975. This Act enables a person who was maintained by the deceased to make an application to the court for provision to be made for him out of the estate on the grounds that the deceased's will did not make reasonable financial provision for him. An order in favour of one or more members of the deceased's family and dependants will of necessity require rearrangement of the estate. If such a claim is anticipated, it might be preferable for the beneficiaries to reach an agreement with the potential claimants and to embody such an agreement in a written variation made within two years of the death without an application to the court.

Where the beneficiaries under a will are already wealthy, a generation might be missed out; this is known as 'generation skipping'. For example, a son of a deceased testator might wish to pass on a legacy bequeathed to him under his father's will to his own son. Once again, the desired result can be achieved by the testator's son entering into a written variation.

There are other non-tax motives which can sometimes prompt a variation. For example, if a will is defective in some respect, perhaps because of a typing error or some mistake made by the testator in the description of an asset or beneficiary, it may be possible to avoid applying to the court for a remedy by rewriting that defective part of the will in the form of a variation which would save both time and expense.

Legislation and practice

17.4 IHTA 1984, s 142(1) states that:

'Where within the period of two years after a person's death—

(a) any of the dispositions (whether effected by will, under the law relating to intestacy or otherwise) of the property comprised in his estate immediately before his death are varied, or

(b) the benefit conferred by any of those dispositions is disclaimed,

by an instrument in writing made by the persons or any of the persons who benefit or would benefit under the dispositions, [the Inheritance Tax] Act shall apply as if the variation had been effected by the deceased or, as the case may be, the disclaimed benefit had never been conferred.'

17.4 Post-death Estate Planning

The variation must be made by an instrument in writing within two years of the death. There is no requirement that the variation be by deed as any instrument in writing which effectively transfers property, or an interest in property, will suffice. Although in some cases, a deed may be necessary to transfer the property. The Inland Revenue have published guidelines setting out the requirements that an instrument must satisfy (Law Society's Gazette dated 18.12.91 and CTO Advanced Instruction Manual P.22). The variation may be made not only in relation to the dispositions effected by a will but also in relation to those taking place under the intestacy rules. In addition, the section will apply to a redirection by a joint owner of the interest in property which automatically passes to him by survivorship on the other co-owner's death.

By virtue of IHTA 1984, s 142(5), an instrument of variation will not be effective for property comprised in a settlement in which the deceased had an interest in possession at his death. Thus, if the deceased had a life interest under a settlement and, under the terms of the settlement, his son takes an absolute interest therein on his death, his son cannot use the provisions of section 142 to redirect that interest in remainder elsewhere following the life tenant's death. Estate planning in relation to settlements therefore must be achieved during the life tenant's lifetime. There is nothing to prevent a variation being made in respect of a trust created by the will itself.

The subsection also ensures that property which is treated as forming part of the deceased's estate at the date of death because he has retained a benefit in it within the terms of FA 1986, s 102 (gifts with reservation) cannot be the subject matter of a post-death variation.

For a variation to be effective the person entering into the variation must not receive any extraneous consideration for the variation as the provisions of IHTA 1984, s 142(1) do not apply to a 'variation . . . made for any consideration in money or money's worth other than consideration consisting of the making in respect of another of the dispositions, of a variation . . . to which [section 142(1)] applies' (section 142(3)). An indemnity given by one party to the variation to another in respect of tax liabilities or legal costs could amount to such extraneous consideration if making the variation is conditional upon giving the indemnity as the indemnity is given as part of a single transaction with the variation.

The persons entering into the variation must be of full age and capacity and willing to act. If minor or unborn beneficiaries are involved, it may be possible to apply on their behalf to the court under the Variation of Trusts Act 1958 for the court's consent (embodied in a court order). However, in those circumstances to be effective the court order must be made within the two-year period.

The Inland Revenue state that a variation must be implemented 'in the real world' (CTO Newsletter December 2001). IHTA 1984 s 17 expressly provides that a variation or disclaimer within IHTA 1984, s 142(1) is not a transfer of value. The instrument in writing should be more than an empty piece of paper. An example is given where A leaves a life interest in property to B with remainder to C. On B's death (but within two years of A's death) C makes a deed of variation which purports to vary A's will by redirecting B's interest to

Post-death Estate Planning 17.4

C. The Inland Revenue say that, in the real world, B's interest does not exist at that time and there is nothing for the deed to do, so section 142 cannot apply. There has been much debate about this amongst commentators. Section 142 is artificial, in any event, as it retrospectively rewrites the will of the deceased and treats the retrospectively revised will as if the deceased had made different dispositions on his death to those he actually made. In the example given, the variation would not have been made by C alone. It would be made by B's executors and C. Certainly, there is no dispute that the executors can execute a deed of variation which itself makes the whole matter more artificial. However, that is the purpose of section 142. In the example, C is entitled to the assets both before and after the variation, the difference being the route by which he obtained them. One could argue that this was not an empty piece of paper because it could increase or decrease the amount of inheritance tax payable.

It is suggested that the deed of variation is ineffective under the general law, however, one must question the relevance of general law to this situation as section 142 is a deeming provision upon which a tax charge is based.

In their April/May Newsletter, the Inland Revenue have published their responses to two letters relating to the above.

> *'It would appear that in a situation where A dies leaving his estate outright to his widow B, who dies within two years leaving her estate to her children, your view is now that a deed of variation redirecting the estate to the children would be ineffective. Is this correct?*
>
> The example you give is one where an absolute interest is given to the survivor. On the death of the survivor, the property inherited on the first death still exists in the survivor's estate and it is therefore possible, in the real world, for those inheriting on the second death to redirect the estate of the first to die. Contrast this with the example given in our Newsletter where, on the first death, the survivor is given a life interest in property. That interest is extinguished on the death of the survivor, so that when, in the real world, those inheriting on the second death come to consider a variation, there is nothing for the variation to bite on.
>
> *You say that B's life interest does not exist because "there is nothing for the deed to bite upon". Surely:*
>
> - *The interest exists until the variation, and*
>
> - *It is a type of property which can be disposed of by B (or his personal representatives) at any time up to the deed of variation.*
>
> As the variation was made after the death of the life tenant, there was then no life interest in existence. Whilst such an interest is capable of disposition by the life tenant, the fact that it ceases on his death means that it is not capable of being disposed of after that has occurred."

The Inland Revenue's view has received some confirmation in the Special Commissioner's decision in *Souter's Executry v CIR [2002] SPC 325*. In that case, under the Will of Miss Souter, Miss Greenlees received a life interest in a property which had been the two ladies' residence. Miss Greenlees continued to live in the property after Miss Souter's death but died within two years of the death of Miss Souter. The executors and beneficiaries of Miss Souter's

17.4 Post-death Estate Planning

estate (including the executors of Miss Greenlees' estate) then entered into a deed under which they provided that Miss Souter's Will was to take effect as if Miss Greenlees had not received the life interest. The Commissioners accepted the Inland Revenue's contention that Miss Greenlees' executors could not have continued to enjoy the life interest after Miss Greenlees' death and therefore that they had nothing to vary. In order to satisfy section 142, the deed had to vary a disposition under Miss Souter's Will and there could be no disposition following Miss Greenlees' death.

For instruments executed before 1 August 2002, a written election must be given to the Board of Inland Revenue (in practice the Capital Taxes Office) within six months after the date of the instrument (or such longer time as the Board may allow). For instruments executed after 31 July 2002, provided they contain a statement made by all the relevant persons to the effect that section 142 should apply to the variation, it will automatically apply. There is no need for a further election. Section 142(2) provides that the 'relevant persons' are:

'(a) the person or persons making the instrument, and

(b) where the variation results in additional tax being payable, the personal representatives;

but personal representatives may decline to join in an election only if no, or no sufficient, assets are held by them in that capacity for discharging the additional tax.'

This means that where additional tax is payable as a result of the variation, but the personal representatives are holding sufficient assets to discharge the liability, the personal representatives are necessary parties to the instrument and can be compelled to join in if they initially refuse to do so. However, where, the personal representatives validly decline to join in the instrument, then IHTA 1984, s 142(1) will not apply to the variation, although it will be legally effective for all other purposes.

Where a deed of variation is made which results in additional tax being payable, the relevant persons must submit a copy of the instrument and notify the Inland Revenue of the amount of additional tax payable within six months of the instrument being executed (IHTA 1984 s 218A). It should be noted that the Inland Revenue do not have the discretion to extend that period for instruments executed after 31 July 2002.

There are occasions when it may be desirable for the beneficiaries to enter into more than one variation. Whilst this is clearly permissible with regard to different property in the estate, the Inland Revenue take the view that an instrument would not fall within IHTA 1984, s 142 if it further redirected any property or any part of any property that had already been redirected under an earlier instrument of variation (CTO Advanced Instruction Manual P.43). The case of *Russell and Another v CIR, Ch D [1988] STC 195; [1988] 2 All ER 405* confirmed that this view is correct.

The Inland Revenue's views on instruments of variation are contained in CTO Advanced Instruction Manual P.22. This is helpful in that it sets out the Inland Revenue's practice in relation to variations and clears up a number of earlier uncertainties.

Post-death Estate Planning **17.5**

An instrument of variation is exempt from stamp duty under the Stamp Duty (Exempt Instruments) Regulations 1987 (SI 1987 No 516) provided it contains the required certificate.

Stock transfer forms and other instruments which transfer legal title to property pursuant to an instrument of variation will not fall within this exemption and will require stamping at £5.

Disclaimers

17.5 A person cannot be made to accept a gift (whether lifetime or testamentary) if he does not wish to do so. He always has the right to decline the gift at any time before he expressly or impliedly accepts it but he will be treated as having accepted a gift once he takes any benefit from it or after a reasonable time has elapsed during which he could have disclaimed but failed to do so. A disclaimer is the refusal to accept a gift. It can be withdrawn but only if it has not been acted upon by any party relying upon it. While a legatee can accept one gift and refuse another, if they are separate and distinct, under the same will, he cannot in England and Wales accept only part of a gift and disclaim the remainder. (The law in Scotland is different.)

In the case of *Smith v Smith and others [2001] 1 WLR 1937* the High Court held that a disclaimer in advance of the death of the relevant estate owner was not valid because, since the estate owner was alive at the date of the disclaimer and could vary her will, there was no real interest which could be disclaimed.

The effect of a disclaimer is that the original gift becomes void *ab initio*. Thus, if a legacy or other bequest or devise is disclaimed, it falls into the residue of the testator's estate and, if the residue is not effectively disposed of by will, it will pass under the intestacy rules. If a residuary gift is disclaimed, that part of the residuary estate disclaimed will pass as on intestacy. To be a genuine disclaimer, the person disclaiming must simply refuse to accept the benefit being disclaimed and must not have any ability to decide its ultimate destination. Thus, before contemplating a disclaimer, one should look to see to whom the benefit to be disclaimed will pass under the operative rules of law.

For example, if residue is left to A, B and C in equal shares and A disclaims his share, that share will pass as on the testator's intestacy and will not accrue to B's and C's shares. The disclaimer of a life interest in residue will either accelerate the vesting of subsequent interests or create a partial intestacy of income if the doctrine of acceleration is not applicable. However, if an interest in remainder is disclaimed, this will (unless there are subsequent remainders) result in the trust property passing on the partial intestacy of the testator. Where on an intestacy one of a class of beneficiaries disclaims, his or her share passes to the remaining members of the class.

IHTA 1984, s 142 applies to disclaimers and thus the effect of a disclaimer for inheritance tax purposes is that the ultimate beneficiary is treated as having received the benefit in question from the deceased and not from the person disclaiming. An election is not required to bring a disclaimer within the operation of the section. Thus, in an appropriate case, where a disclaimer will

17.6 *Post-death Estate Planning*

achieve the desired result, it is a simple alternative to a written variation. However, for the disclaimer to be effective for inheritance tax purposes, it must still be made within two years of the deceased's death.

A disclaimer is not liable to stamp duty, as it does not effect the transfer of any property.

Planning points

17.6 The fact that a variation or disclaimer may be made within two years of a person's death should not be used as an excuse for not taking estate planning steps during his lifetime. IHTA 1984, s 142 does provide, however, a two-year breathing space in which oversights may be corrected and account taken of changes in legislation since the will was made. The two-year period is also the appropriate time to review all the family's financial circumstances and in particular the needs of any surviving spouse.

Use of nil rate band

17.7 A widow who has inherited the bulk of her husband's estate on his death may, on finding her foreseeable needs more than adequately met, redirect a part of it to her children or grandchildren in order to use her husband's nil rate band.

Business and agricultural property relief

17.8 Where property qualifying for business or agricultural property relief has been left to the surviving spouse, consideration should be given as to whether it will still qualify as at the date of his or her death. If there is any prospect of the property not so qualifying (for example, if the property is likely to be sold) then the property might be redirected to non-exempt beneficiaries to ensure that the relief is not wasted. Any amount of property qualifying for 100% relief can be redirected at no tax cost. £500,000 of property qualifying for 50% relief may be redirected to children tax-free if the deceased died without having used any of the available nil rate band (see above). Where the surviving spouse requires the income from the property, consideration can be given to redirecting the property to a discretionary trust of which the survivor is a beneficiary (see 17.11 below).

Increase in asset value after death

17.9 Where the deceased's estate has significantly risen in value during the two-year period a deed of variation can be used to pass the gain element on to the next generation free of inheritance tax.

Example

A man leaves his entire estate worth £250,000 to his wife and eighteen months after his death the estate has trebled in value.

If the widow declares in writing that she will hold the estate upon trust as if she had been left a legacy of £250,000 with the residue passing to her children, the inheritance tax provisions will operate so as to attribute the value of the estate at death (i.e. £250,000) wholly to the legacy (which is exempt from tax by virtue of the spouse exemption) with the result that the remaining £500,000 ((3 × £250,000) − £250,000) passes to the children tax-free.

Gifts with reservation

17.10 The interaction of IHTA 1984, s 142 with the gifts with reservation provisions contained in FA 1986, s 102 could provide useful possibilities regarding the matrimonial home. For example, a widow inheriting her late husband's house may decide to redirect the gift so that the house passes to her children. However, her children may allow her as their licensee to continue to occupy the property for the rest of her life. Provided the variation has been entered into within two years and a valid instrument has been delivered where relevant, it will fall within IHTA 1984, s 142(1). IHTA 1984, s 142 overrides FA 1986, s 102 preventing the gifts with reservation provisions applying, which they clearly would have done had the widow simply given the house to her children but continued to live there. The Capital Taxes Office accept this interpretation (CTO Advanced Instruction Manual D.23). A legatee who redirects a legacy has by implication never owned the property comprised in that legacy and cannot therefore have made a gift of it within FA 1986, s 102.

Use of discretionary trusts

17.11 Where the deceased has not made any gifts within seven years of his death and has left the bulk of his estate to his widow, who requires all the income generated to live on, consideration should be given to the widow resettling an amount equal to the deceased's nil rate band (or any unused part thereof if the deceased made lifetime chargeable transfers) on discretionary trusts of which she and her children and grandchildren (if any) are the beneficiaries. The income of the trust fund may then be distributed to the widow but, if she dies before the tenth anniversary of the death, the trust can be broken and the capital distributed to the beneficiaries without, in most cases, any inheritance tax cost regardless of the then value of the trust fund. This is because the rate at which inheritance tax is calculated on a capital distribution is determined by reference to the initial value of the trust fund aggregated with any chargeable transfers made by the deceased within seven years of his death. If these values do not exceed the nil rate band, then the nil rate is applicable.

The inheritance tax charge on the first ten-year anniversary will, however, be calculated by reference to the *then* value of the trust fund and thus a decision must be taken before then as to whether the trust should be broken or continued.

The creation of the discretionary trust by the widow will not fall foul of the gifts with reservation provisions for exactly the same reason which was given above in relation to the matrimonial home (CTO Advanced Instruction Manual D.23).

17.12 *Post-death Estate Planning*

This route might also be considered where property qualifying for 100% business or agricultural property relief has been left to a widow and it is likely that the property will no longer qualify for such relief on her death (see 17.8 above). In these circumstances there may be an exit charge if the trust is broken prior to the tenth anniversary of the death as might be the case where any relievable property is transferred to a discretionary trust (see chapter 16 *Planning for Death* under paragraph 16.4). However, the exit charge at current rates cannot exceed 6% and this must be compared with a possible 40% rate of tax on unqualifying property in the spouse's estate on death. A further factor to bear in mind is that the discretionary trust formed in this way will be caught by the onshore settlor charge (TCGA 1992, s 77). See *Marshall v Kerr, HL [1994] STC 638; [1994] 2 All ER 106* under the heading *Capital gains tax on variations* below and the income tax settlement provisions (ICTA 1988, Part XV) (see comments later).

Potentially exempt transfers

17.12 A gift qualifying as a potentially exempt transfer by a widow or other beneficiary should not be overlooked as an alternative to post-death variations of wills and other rearrangements. A potentially exempt transfer (of any amount or value) will be completely free from inheritance tax provided the transferor survives the transfer by seven years. Inheritance tax taper relief will apply if the transferor survives the gift by three years but not by the full seven. Thus, for example, a surviving spouse inheriting the deceased spouse's estate (free of inheritance tax) may wish to make lifetime gifts by way of potentially exempt transfers rather than become involved in varying the terms of the will especially if her life expectancy is greater than seven years. However, if the deceased spouse had not made gifts *inter vivos* or by will using up his nil rate band, it would be advisable for the widow to enter into a deed of variation to deal with the unused part of the nil rate band. As there is now only one rate of inheritance tax applying after the nil rate band (40%), from a tax planning point of view it is advisable that any further transfers of property in excess of the nil rate band are made by the widow by way of potentially exempt transfers. Then, if she survives for the seven-year period, such transfers will be completely exempt. Even if the spouse does not survive for the entire seven years, but survives for at least three years, the rate of tax will still be lower than if the transfers were taxed at the 40% rate which would have applied if they had been made from the deceased's estate by way of a variation.

The CTO Advanced Instruction Manual P.60 states that a variation should not be accepted as being within IHTA 1984, s 142 until any investigation in accordance with their instructions on abuse has been satisfactorily concluded. Whether this is a prelude to an attack on the making of a potentially exempt transfer by the donee of property under a deed of variation, either under the principles laid down by the House of Lords in *Ramsay (WT) Ltd v CIR, HL [1981] STC 174; [1981] 1 All ER 865*, or by the application of the associated operations provisions contained in IHTA 1984, s 268, remains to be seen, but clearly an arrangement under which it is contemplated by all the parties that the beneficiary under a variation (e.g. a surviving spouse) will return particular property by way of a potentially exempt transfer to the original legatee or

Post-death Estate Planning **17.14**

beneficiary under a will (e.g. a child of the deceased) is vulnerable to an attack on these lines (CTO Advanced Instruction Manual P.62). If the subject matters of the variation and the subsequent gift are different assets, then the transaction will be strengthened but may still be susceptible. One possible way of further strengthening the position would be to ensure that the property should be settled on an interest in possession trust for the benefit of the surviving spouse, with the children having an interest in the remainder. Should the surviving spouse ultimately decide that she no longer requires the income, she could surrender her interest under the trust, thereby accelerating the interests of the children. Such a surrender should be treated as a potentially exempt transfer, and it is difficult to envisage how the Inland Revenue might seek to challenge this under the *Ramsay* principle where it is clear that none of the steps were pre-ordained.

The outlook for variations

17.13 Following the 1989 Budget, the first draft of the 1989 Finance Bill contained a clause which severely restricted the operation of IHTA 1984, s 142 by limiting its application to disclaimers only. It also repealed IHTA 1984, ss 143 and 144 of the Act which apply to precatory trusts and discretionary wills. These clauses were eventually dropped. The Labour Party in their paper 'Tackling tax abuses — tackling unemployment' (November 1994) stated that they will make inheritance tax more effective and less easy to avoid. In that paper it was said one of the inheritance tax loopholes was the treatment of deeds of variation. Since forming the government, however, they have taken no action in this area although it is often rumoured that the Labour government are about to do so.

Capital gains tax on variations

17.14 TCGA 1992, s 62(1) provides that the assets of a deceased person's estate shall be deemed to be acquired on his death by his personal representatives for a consideration equal to their market value at the date of death but shall not be deemed to be disposed of by him on his death. Therefore, no capital gains tax is payable on the death.

The provisions of TCGA 1992, s 62(6)-(9) dealing with variations and disclaimers, correspond to those applicable to inheritance tax. Thus TCGA 1992, s 62(6) provides that:

> 'where within the period of two years after a person's death any of the dispositions (whether effected by will, under the law relating to intestacy or otherwise) of the property of which he was competent to dispose are varied, or the benefit conferred by any of those dispositions is disclaimed, by an instrument in writing made by the persons or any of the persons who benefit or would benefit under the dispositions —
>
> (a) the variation or disclaimer shall not constitute a disposal for the purposes of this Act, and
>
> (b) this section shall apply as if the variation had been effected by the deceased or, as the case may be, the disclaimed benefit had never been conferred.'

17.15 *Post-death Estate Planning*

The above provisions apply only to property of which the deceased person was 'competent to dispose' as defined by TCGA 1992, s 62(10). Such property includes an interest under a joint tenancy but not property subject to a general power of appointment.

For instruments executed after 31 July 2002 TCGA 1992, s 62(6) will apply provided that the instrument contains a statement by the persons making the instrument that they intend that section 62(6) will apply to the variation. There is no longer a specified time period by which the instrument has to be submitted to the Inland Revenue. This is because 'the Government . . . are content that the consequences of a variation should be considered, if necessary, by the Inland Revenue only if and when they become relevant to the capital gains tax liabilities of the beneficiaries'.

In most cases the inclusion of the relevant statement stating the intention of the parties for section 62(6) to apply will in any event be appropriate, regardless of whether the administration of the estate has been completed or not. Where, however, the value of the relevant asset has increased since the date of death and any gain would fall within the donor beneficiary's annual exemption or within the exemption for chattels, then the advantage of not including such a statement is that the donee will acquire the asset at a higher base cost. Where, on the other hand, the asset has fallen in value, not to include a statement for the operation of section 62 will create a capital loss for the donor beneficiary, but if the donee is a 'connected person' within TCGA 1992, s 286 (and he often will be), such a loss can only be set against a gain on another disposal to the same donee (TCGA 1992, s 18), so little will be gained from not including a statement.

Where a statement to the effect that it is intended that section 62 should apply is included, it provides that 'section 62(6) shall apply as if the variation had been effected by the deceased'. Where the person effecting the variation creates a settlement in which he and/or his spouse are interested, the question arises as to who is the settlor for the purposes of TCGA 1992, ss 77–79. Is it the deceased, in which case the settlor charges (TCGA 1992, s 77 and TCGA 1992, s 86) cannot apply or is it the person effecting the variation? This question was considered in relation to TCGA 1992, s 87 in *Marshall v Kerr, HL [1994] STC 638; [1994] 2 All ER 106* where the House of Lords held that the deeming provisions of TCGA 1992, s 62(7) were not powerful enough to deem the testator to be the settlor of a settlement set up under a deed of variation. Accordingly, the person effecting the variation will be regarded as the settlor and TCGA 1992, ss 77–79 will charge that person to tax on gains made by the trustees where the necessary criteria are met. A similar position will arise under TCGA 1992, s 86 where a variation in favour of non-resident trustees is entered into.

Income tax on variations

17.15 The income tax legislation does not provide the reliefs which are available in the case of inheritance tax and capital gains tax following a variation of beneficial interests in a deceased's estate. Income arising between the date of death and the date of the variation is generally taxed as

Post-death Estate Planning 17.15

though it were that of the beneficiary entitled prior to the variation. Disclaimers, because of their legal nature (and because they are not a fiction of fiscal legislation as is the case with variations), are treated differently and relate back to the date of death for income tax purposes.

Subject to the express terms of the will, a general pecuniary legacy will normally bear interest from one year after the date of death if it still remains unpaid. The interest is payable when the legacy is paid. The interest rate is presently 6% p.a. from the first anniversary of the death to the date of payment (The Rules of the Supreme Court (Amendment No 2) Order 1983). Where such a legacy is varied the interest paid on the legacy should only be taxable in the hands of the new beneficiary under the variation, even though it covers a period prior to the variation. This is because the liability to income tax depends on actual receipt of the income and not receivability.

The main exceptions to the above rule are contingent legacies, which do not bear interest until the contingencies are fulfilled unless they are set aside for the benefit of the legatee, and certain legacies to minors, which bear interest from the date of death. In practice, these types of legacies are rarely subject to any variation.

Income from property which is the subject of a specific legacy is taxed in the hands of the legatee from the date of death. Where the property is redirected to another person by way of variation, the original legatee will only be taxable on the income arising up to the date of the variation.

ICTA 1988, s 695 provides for the taxation of income paid to beneficiaries with limited interests in residue during the course of the administration of the estate. Sums paid over to the beneficiary during the course of administration are taxed as the income of the beneficiary for the year of assessment in which they are paid. Any amount that remains payable in respect of the limited interest on the completion of administration of the estate is deemed to have been paid to the beneficiary as income of the year of assessment in which the administration period ended.

Where there is an absolute interest in residue the provisions of ICTA 1988, s 696 apply. The beneficiary is taxed on amounts he receives in any tax year to the extent that they do not exceed the residuary income for that year plus any residuary income of previous years on which he has not already been subject to tax. At the end of the administration period the residuary income for the whole period is aggregated and, where this aggregate exceeds the total amount on which he has already been taxed, the excess is treated as income paid to him immediately before the end of the administration period.

The rules contain specific provisions (ICTA 1988, s 698(1A), (1B) and (2)) dealing with successive interests in residue such as might arise where a residuary gift is varied. The overall effect of these provisions is to ensure that each beneficiary is taxed on the amount to which he is entitled.

An instrument of variation will be a settlement within ICTA 1988, Part XV whereas a disclaimer will not. As a result, any variation by a parent in favour of his unmarried minor children will fall within ICTA 1988, s 660B and any income paid to or for the benefit of the children will be taxed in his hands. In addition, any variation which involves the legatee resettling property upon

17.16 *Post-death Estate Planning*

trusts under which he retains an interest may be caught by ICTA 1988, s 660A and, if so, the income of the trust will remain taxable in his hands.

Instruments of variation should expressly deal with the right to income accrued up to the date of the instrument as between the donor and the donee. It is usually appropriate to provide that the income should belong to the person who would bear the burden of paying income tax on it and this will usually be the donor.

Discretionary wills

17.16 Some testators may have provided the means for a variation of their wills by conferring on their executors an overriding power of appointment drafted in wide terms which is exercisable over their entire estate in favour of a specified class of beneficiaries (relying on IHTA 1984, s 144). Such a will usually contains provisions which the testator wishes to take effect in default of an appointment. Provided the power of appointment is exercised within two years of the testator's death to make outright distributions from the estate or to create interest in possession or accumulation and maintenance trusts, the relief in section 144 will operate to back-date the exercise of the power to the date of death. It is important not to make distributions from a discretionary trust within three months of the death because section 144 only operates when there would otherwise be a charge to inheritance tax (IHTA 1984, s 144(1)). There is no inheritance tax charge on property leaving a discretionary trust within three months of its creation (IHTA 1984, s 68(2)) (see *Frankland v CIR, CA [1997] STC 1450*). To avoid an accidental advancement within the three month period the will should provide that such advancements within three months of death are invalid.

A discretionary will offers considerable opportunities for estate planning, more so than relying on a variation which can usually only be made by adult beneficiaries acting unanimously. When drafting his will a testator cannot be certain what resources he and his survivors will have at his death or indeed who his survivors will be. After his death it will be much clearer to the executors and the family to what extent assets should be divided between the surviving spouse and subsequent generations and also whether there is scope to skip a generation. Unlike a variation, a discretionary will can also avoid the income tax disadvantages under ICTA 1988, s 660B of a parental settlement.

There is no provision in the capital gains tax legislation corresponding to IHTA 1984, s 144. TCGA 1992, s 62(6) has no application to an exercise of the overriding power of appointment, because the variation will not be made 'by the persons or any of the persons who benefit or would benefit under the disposition [made by the will]'. Consequently, if the power is exercised to make outright distributions of property to any beneficiary, a charge to capital gains tax may arise. There will usually only be a chargeable gain if the relevant assets have increased in value since the date of death because of the base cost uplift on the testator's death. Where a chargeable gain arises on business assets, it may be possible to make an election under TCGA 1992, s 165 to hold over the gain. However, where the power is exercised before the

Post-death Estate Planning 17.17

administration of the estate is complete, the Inland Revenue take the view that the beneficiary acquires the asset as a legatee under the will and his base cost will be probate value.

This and other aspects of discretionary wills are considered in more detail in chapter 16 *Planning for Death*.

Precatory trusts

17.17 So-called precatory trusts are not in fact trusts at all. They are outright gifts coupled with an expression of preference by the donor as to how he would like the donee to exercise his ownership which is not enforceable against the donee. They are commonly used to deal with the distribution of chattels within a class of beneficiaries. For example, a testator may give a collection of paintings to one of his sons with the wish that he distribute the individual paintings between all the children of the testator in a fair and agreed manner. However, as a matter of law, the named beneficiary is the owner of the bequest. This might have caused inheritance tax problems if the named beneficiary then distributed the property comprised in the bequest to the intended recipients in accordance with the testator's wishes as this would *prima facie* be a transfer of value by him. However, IHTA 1984, s 143 provides that, if the legatee transfers any of the property bequeathed to him in accordance with the testator's wishes within the period of two years of the testator's death, IHTA 1984, s 143 will apply as if the property transferred had been bequeathed to the transferee by the testator. It is probable that this relief will not apply to real property as the reference in section 143 is to property 'bequeathed' and not 'devised' and a bequest is a disposition by will of personal and not real property.

In *Harding & Leigh (Loveday's Executors) v CIR, Sp C [1997] SSCD 321 (Sp C 140)* the Special Commissioners held that section 143 did not apply to an appointment in exercise of a fiduciary power under a discretionary will trust, that is, one where there was no interest in possession between the deceased's death and the appointment. It is arguable whether section 143 applies to a distribution in exercise of a fiduciary power where there has been an interest in possession between the deceased's death and the exercise of the power, because one of the grounds for the decision in *Harding* was that, because an event within section 143 is expressly declared not to be a transfer of value (IHTA 1984 s 17), section 143 only applies to events which would be transfers of value apart from that provision. An appointment out of a discretionary trust is never a transfer of value, whereas the termination of an interest in possession is deemed to be a transfer of value (IHTA 1984 s 52(1)).

There was no debate in *Harding* as to whether section 143 was confined to gifts of personalty, although land does seem to have been comprised in the residuary estate which was appointed, and it may therefore be that the argument that section 143 only applies to personalty was not a point taken by the Inland Revenue.

Therefore, where is it intended that property disposed of by will should be distributed by the executors in accordance with the testator's wishes, at least

401

17.18 *Post-death Estate Planning*

where the property subject to such a gift will be valuable, it will be safer to provide that there is no interest in possession pending the executors' decision on how to distribute the property, so that section 144 can apply.

No special capital gains tax reliefs apply to precatory trusts, although the property concerned will often fall within the exemption for chattels valued at £6,000 or less (TCGA 1992, s 262).

Intestacy — redemption of surviving spouse's life interest

17.18 On intestacy where the deceased leaves a surviving spouse and issue, the surviving spouse is entitled to the deceased's personal chattels, a statutory legacy of £125,000 (together with interest while unpaid: SI 1983 No 1374) and a life interest in half the residue of the estate (Administration of Estates Act 1925, s 46(1); Family Provision (Intestate Succession) Order 1993).

The surviving spouse under the Administration of Estates Act 1925, s 47A can elect to capitalise her life interest and to receive, instead of the income, part of the capital determined according to tables specified in the Intestate Succession (Interest and Capitalisation) Order 1977 (SI 1977 No 1491). If the surviving spouse does so elect, IHTA 1984, s 17(c) and IHTA 1984, s 145 provide that the election is not a transfer of value and inheritance tax is charged as though the surviving spouse had not been entitled to the life interest but had been entitled to the capital sum.

It should be noted that such an election, despite the advantage of giving the surviving spouse capital, will reduce the property qualifying for the spouse exemption on the death and may thus increase the tax charge on the death. This is because, if the surviving spouse had taken a life interest, the spouse exemption for inheritance tax purposes would have applied to the entire property in which the life interest subsisted.

Changes in value after death

17.19 IHTA 1984, ss 178–198 provide relief for investments or land forming part of a deceased person's estate which are sold shortly after the date of death and have fallen in value. Although this section concentrates on personal representatives, it should always be borne in mind that these provisions will also apply to the trustees of a settlement following the death of a beneficiary entitled to an interest in possession in the settled property.

Where an estate includes qualifying investments, such as quoted shares and securities and units in authorised unit trusts, which are sold within twelve months of the death for a sum less than the value at the date of death by the personal representatives or by the beneficiary if he is liable for the tax, they can apply to have the gross sale proceeds substituted for the value at the date of death for the purposes of inheritance tax. The lower value will be substituted for the probate value and the inheritance tax payable on the death will be recalculated accordingly. This relief has also been extended to situations where qualifying investments:

Post-death Estate Planning 17.19

(a) are cancelled, without being replaced, within twelve months after the date of death. These must be held immediately before cancellation by the personal representatives or by the beneficiary if he is liable for the tax; or

(b) have their quotation on a recognised stock exchange suspended at the end of the twelve month period following death and their value was at that time lower than at death. The investments must be held at the end of the twelve month period by either the personal representatives or by the beneficiary if he is liable for the tax.

These provisions deem qualifying investments within (a) above to have been sold for a nominal consideration of one pound and those within (b) to have been sold at their value at the end of the twelve month period following death.

It is important to note that where a claim is made all the investments sold within twelve months of the death have to be valued. The claim cannot be restricted to the investments which have fallen in value. Where some qualifying investments have risen in value since the date of death, but others have fallen, the personal representative should consider appropriating those that have risen in value to the relevant beneficiaries prior to selling the investments. This will enable a claim to be made only in relation to those investments which have fallen in value.

A similar relief applies to land forming part of the deceased's estate which is sold within three years (or four years in certain circumstances, see below) after the date of death. The relief for land differs from that of qualifying investments in that in respect of sales within three years of death, a claim may be made even where the land has increased in value. In some circumstances this can be advantageous where the capital gains tax saving from making the election is greater than the increase in inheritance tax that results (for example, where the land is eligible for 50% business property relief reducing the effective inheritance tax rate to 20%). The claim must be made by the appropriate person, usually the personal representatives, or by the beneficiary if he is liable for the tax and, if there is more than one sale, the sale values must be substituted for all the sales of land and cannot be confined to one sale only.

In the case of *Stonor & Mills (Dickinson's Executors) v CIR, Sp C [2001] SSCD 199 (Sp C 288)* the residuary estate was left to charities and the executors made a claim under IHTA 1984 s 191 so the higher property values on death could be used as base values for capital gains tax purposes. The legislation defines the 'appropriate person' as being the person liable for inheritance tax. The gifts to the charities were exempt transfers and no tax was chargeable on them. There was only a liability for tax which was actually payable. If there was no tax payable, there was no person liable to pay the tax and the executors claim was dismissed.

The relief for land will not apply if the sale price differs from the value at the date of death by less than £1,000 or 5% of the value on death, whichever is the lower. If the Inland Revenue are of the opinion that the sale was for an under-value, they can substitute the best consideration that could reasonably have been obtained for it at the date of sale.

17.19 Post-death Estate Planning

In certain circumstances, the relief is extended in relation to sales within four years of death. However, claims made in respect of sales in the fourth year following death are only valid where the sale value is less than the value on death unlike claims made in the three year period. Therefore, the extension to the relief cannot be used to obtain an advantageous capital gains tax position as discussed below.

For the purpose of each relief, the date of sale is the date of the contract for sale provided that the contract proceeds to completion, see *Jones & Another (Balls' Administrators) v CIR*, Ch D [1997] STC 358. There are special rules in relation to sales pursuant to the exercise of options and under compulsory purchase powers. Where the sale or purchase results from the exercise of an option, if the option is exercised not more than six months after the grant of the option, the material date is the date of grant (IHTA 1984 s 198(2)). In the event that the sale follows a notice to treat under compulsory acquisition powers, the date of sale is generally the date on which compensation is agreed or otherwise determined or the date when the authority enters the land (if earlier) (IHTA 1984 s 198(3)). Where the sale is an acquisition under a general vesting declaration or a vesting order, the date of sale is then as stated in IHTA 1984, s 198(4).

It should be noted that the relief available for falls in value of qualifying investments and the relief for sales of land are entirely separate and are not aggregated for the purpose of the adjustment. Thus, a large gain on a sale of land will not reduce a loss on a sale of qualifying investments.

The object of the provisions is to grant relief where assets have been sold to meet tax and other liabilities. For this reason there are anti-avoidance provisions which deny relief where investments or land are purchased within two or four months respectively of the last of the sales. Sales of land made in the fourth year after death are ignored for this purpose. However, a sale by the personal representatives followed by a cash distribution to the relevant beneficiary will enable that beneficiary to repurchase the investments sold without falling foul of these provisions.

If it is anticipated that qualifying investments or land which the personal representatives intend to sell in the course of administration, will have changed in value within the relevant period from the date of death, then it is essential that the sale of such assets is correctly timed to ensure that they receive the benefit of the relief provided for in these sections.

Under TCGA 1992, s 274, the value of an asset as determined for inheritance tax purposes in charging a deceased person's estate is deemed to be the market value on death for capital gains tax purposes. Thus, where the value of land is amended under the above provisions, it is the amended value that applies for capital gains tax purposes. This is why an advantageous capital gains tax position can be obtained on sales within three years of death at an increased value. If, however, the assets will not bear inheritance tax (because, for example, the estate is less than the nil rate band) the Inland Revenue's view is that no election can be made (Capital Gains Tax Manual CG 32462). (*Stonor & Mills (Dickinson's Executors) v CIR*, Sp C [2001] SSCD 199 (Sp C 288)).

Post-death Estate Planning **17.21**

As regards qualifying investments, IHTA 1984, s 187 contains provisions for ascertaining the values for capital gains tax purposes of specific investments sold after death, which will usually be their respective sale values.

Where assets are sold after the death at a value lower than probate value and a claim for the relief is made, the result will be to reduce a capital loss for capital gains tax purposes. (There will still be a capital loss attributable to the difference (if any) between the gross sale proceeds and the net sale proceeds.) Where the person making the claim is a personal representative, the advantage of reducing an inheritance tax liability at 40% will outweigh the disadvantage of losing a capital loss which could at most save capital gains tax at a rate of 34%. Where, however, the person making the claim is, for example, the specific legatee of land who also bears the burden of the inheritance tax payable in respect of that land, the inheritance tax saving (at 40%) may have no intrinsic advantage if the claim deprives the legatee of a capital loss which would have saved him capital gains tax payable also at a rate of 40%. With the introduction of taper relief, however, capital losses will usually only save capital gains tax at an effective rate of less than 40%.

Payment by instalments

17.20 Tax chargeable on certain property passing on death may, while the property remains unsold, be paid in ten equal annual instalments (IHTA 1984, ss 227–229). The relief applies to:

(*a*)   land wherever situated,

(*b*)   unfelled timber (where exempt on death but later disposed of),

(*c*)   a business or an interest in a business,

(*d*)   controlling shareholdings, and

(*e*)   unquoted shareholdings where either:

  (i)   the Board of Inland Revenue are satisfied that the tax attributable to their value cannot be paid in one sum without undue hardship; or

  (ii) the tax payable on the shares represents not less than 20% of the tax payable by that person on the estate; or

  (iii) the value of the shares is over £20,000 and they form not less than 10% of the capital of the company.

The first instalment of tax will fall due for payment six months from the end of the month in which the death occurs.

Interest on unpaid tax

17.21 Interest accrues on unpaid tax from six months from the end of the month in which the death occurs. The current rate of interest is 3%, applicable from 6 November 2001 (previously 4% from 6 May 2001 to 5 November 2001). However, tax payable by instalments, other than where

17.22 *Post-death Estate Planning*

attributable to certain securities or to land (which is neither a business asset nor attracts agricultural property relief), is not chargeable to interest provided each instalment is paid on the due date (IHTA 1984, s 234). Therefore, if paid on time, tax on each instalment is interest-free.

Repayments of overpaid tax carry with them the benefit of interest supplement at the same rate (IHTA 1984, s 235(1)). Interest paid on unpaid tax is not deductible from the income of the estate for income tax purposes so that the beneficiaries receive no income tax relief in respect of it. However, the interest supplement is not taxable in the hands of the personal representatives or the beneficiaries (IHTA 1984, s 235(2)).

Capital gains tax exemption and rates of tax

17.22 Personal representatives have the same annual capital gains tax exemption as an individual (£7,700 for 2002/03) for the tax year in which the death occurs and for the following two tax years (TCGA 1992, s 3(7)). When deciding whether to sell an investment and distribute the proceeds to a beneficiary or whether to distribute the investment in specie allowing the beneficiary to use his own annual exemption on the sale the annual exemption should be considered. Another factor to be taken into account is the marginal tax saving as personal representatives pay capital gains tax at the rate of 34% whereas the beneficiary in question may be taxable at the rate of 40% on any gains he realises.

Where the beneficiary is neither resident nor ordinarily resident in the UK, consideration should be given to distributing assets in specie rather than selling and distributing the proceeds as the beneficiary will not be chargeable to UK capital gains tax. Advice on the beneficiary's liability to tax in the jurisdiction where he is resident must be taken, however, to ensure that his overall position is not worsened.

Death benefits under insurance policies and pension schemes

17.23 Death benefits under death-in-service benefit schemes and pension schemes often provide for the trustees of the scheme with a discretion as to the person to whom the payment is to be made. If the deceased has, by letter of wishes, nominated someone to receive the moneys then the trustees will normally follow those instructions. If no such nomination has been made then the trustees will usually either make payment to the next-of-kin or to the deceased's personal representatives, having first consulted the family. The opportunity should be taken to arrange for the payments to be made to specific members of the deceased's family with a view to satisfying immediate financial needs and to minimising the inheritance tax burden on subsequent deaths. On intestacy it will usually be preferable to arrange for the payment to be made direct to the widow or to the children rather than to the personal representatives to avoid the statutory trusts. The discretionary trusts usually have to be exercised within two years of death,

Post-death Estate Planning 17.23

so the personal representatives should be sure to encourage the trustees not to miss the deadline.

Death benefits payable under retirement annuity contracts within ICTA 1988, Part XIV, Chapter III or personal pension arrangements within ICTA 1988, Part XIV, Chapter IV may similarly be payable under discretionary trusts exercisable within two years of the death (if the contract or policy has been assigned to trustees) and if this is the case the same considerations apply.

Planning in relation to death benefits should always be dovetailed with any planning in relation to the deceased's own estate.

Some types of insurance policies are sometimes written under trusts which include a power for the trustees to appoint the proceeds to the life assured's widow. It is important that the trustees make any such appointment (if appropriate) within the two years following the date of death to take advantage of the exemption available under IHTA 1984, s 53(4) from the charge which would otherwise arise on the termination of the default beneficiaries' interests in possession. As with pension death benefits, the deceased's personal representatives and family should discuss with the trustees the most appropriate recipient of the policy proceeds in the light of family circumstances after the death.

18 Investing Abroad

Introduction

18.1 Increasing numbers of individuals cross national barriers in business or in the employment of multi-national companies and so may acquire assets situated outside the UK. Improved worldwide communications and the varying fortunes of national economies and governments encourage individuals even if firmly domiciled and resident in the UK to spread assets and risks by investing internationally.

The network of double taxation treaties has developed largely to encourage the international operations of business but may equally facilitate multi-national investment by an individual. The private international laws of national legal systems have also grown up in recognition of the increasing involvement of individuals (and their assets) in various legal jurisdictions. The development of the law of the European Union is increasingly effecting the direct taxation of member countries.

Foreign investments may be made and retained by an individual in his own name. However, direct ownership of those foreign assets can present disadvantages such as the obligation to comply with local administrative procedures and succession laws on death and the payment of gift or death duties imposed by the country in which the assets are situated. In these circumstances consideration may be given to other means of ownership of foreign assets.

By investing overseas an individual may also wish to secure some measure of protection against the now remote chance of a reintroduction of exchange controls in the UK, although that seems as unlikely as a return to the gold standard.

The planning steps that may be taken by the individual who is immigrating to or emigrating from the UK and the steps a foreign domiciled and resident individual may take in relation to the ownership of assets both in the UK and abroad are examined in chapter 19 *Immigration and Emigration* and chapter 20 *The Foreign Client*. This chapter primarily considers the advantages and disadvantages of direct ownership of foreign assets by an individual domiciled and resident in the UK and the indirect ownership of those same assets through a nominee, a company or a trust.

18.2 Investing Abroad

Direct ownership

18.2 An individual may hold assets in a foreign country in his own name. As a UK resident and domiciled individual he will be liable to income tax on income arising from those assets, capital gains tax on gains realised on the disposal of those assets and inheritance tax on any gift (whether made during his lifetime or on his death) of those assets. In addition, similar taxes may be imposed in the country in which those assets are located. The existence of a double taxation treaty may alleviate the position in one of two ways. Either the profit or gift which the tax system of the country in which the asset is situated and the UK tax system both seek to tax may be exempted from tax in one of those jurisdictions (or the liability may be reduced); or credit may be given in one country for any tax suffered in the other. Even where no double tax treaty exists between the UK and the country in which the asset is situated relief may be given unilaterally by the UK. Relief may be given for tax suffered in the foreign jurisdiction against income tax or capital gains tax suffered on the same profits or for gift or death duties suffered in a foreign jurisdiction against inheritance tax chargeable in respect of the same assets.

Ownership of assets in a foreign jurisdiction will not only cause the UK individual to fall within that foreign country's tax net on his death but local administration procedures will apply. Title to the assets will have to be established by his personal representatives or beneficiaries. In some circumstances a UK grant of representation may be re-sealed by local authorities (as in, for example, most Commonwealth countries). In other jurisdictions (principally those governed by a civil code such as France and Spain) the concept of a personal representative is alien and it may be necessary to arrange for title to pass directly to the beneficiaries of the property.

In addition to the conflicting formalities in foreign jurisdictions relating to the transfer of property to an individual's heirs on his death, succession to that property may also be governed by the law of the foreign country.

Under the English doctrine of the conflict of laws, succession to immovable property (i.e. land) is governed by the law of the country in which that land is situated. Where a foreign country has particular rules relating to the devolution of a fixed portion of an individual's estate on death to his surviving spouse and/or children, any attempt to displace these rules by provision in his will, will be unsuccessful.

Even though succession to movable property (such as shares) situated abroad is usually governed (under the conflict rules of most foreign countries) by the law of the individual's country of domicile (or nationality) taxation difficulties may arise if the property is given by his will to his personal representatives to be held for others. These difficulties stem from the fact that many civil law jurisdictions do not recognise the role and duties of a personal representative in relation to the deceased's assets and those beneficiaries for whose benefit he holds and administers the deceased's property. Therefore, if a UK domiciled individual were to leave all his movable assets to his executors to be held by them for his widow, some foreign jurisdictions would attempt to impose death duties on his movable property situated there as though the deceased's gift had been an outright gift to the executors.

In many countries, death duties are imposed at rates determined according to the proximity of the relationship between the deceased and those who take his property on his death, the lowest rates being charged on gifts to widows, higher rates on gifts to children and grandchildren and the most punitive rates on gifts to unrelated individuals. Unless the foreign jurisdiction will accept that the 'gift' to the UK individual's executors is not a beneficial gift but, rather, an administrative measure, death duties may be imposed at the highest rates unless the deceased's executors are his close relations. The provisions of an applicable double tax treaty may alter this position but these problems require investigation at the outset. An individual owning assets abroad (in particular, land) should consider if there is any significant value in making a will (in the local language) in accordance with the applicable laws of each of those countries where his assets are situated to ensure that he achieves the transfer of those assets to his chosen heirs at the lowest possible cost.

When dealing with more than one jurisdiction a timing issue may arise where there is a delay in concluding the tax liabilities in one country. In *Whittaker v CIR, Sp C [2001] SSCD 61 (Sp C 272)* the Commissioners held that an executor could not validly appeal against an inheritance tax determination in respect of foreign property on the grounds that the Italian tax liabilities had not yet been concluded.

Obviously, where an individual wishes to invest in stocks and shares of companies in various foreign jurisdictions and intends that these investments will be bought and sold over a period of time, it is likely to be impractical, expensive and burdensome administratively for him to investigate the taxation and succession laws of each country and to make a will under the laws of those countries. In these circumstances, the individual may wish to simplify his affairs by making his investment through another medium situated in the UK, such as a unit trust or investment trust or a unit-linked life policy, which in turn invests in foreign companies. This will avoid any problems with foreign succession laws or taxes on his death.

Similarly, the enjoyment of foreign land may be achieved by participation in a 'time share' arrangement rather than by owning foreign property direct. The procedural and succession rules applying to the transfer of the individual's rights of occupation to his heirs will depend upon the nature of the time share structure and the terms of the individual's rights. However, if the occupation rights are conferred by a trustee holding land for the benefit of members of a time share club and permitting those members occupation of the property on specified terms the individual's asset may be his chose in action against the trustee (i.e. his entitlement to enforce his rights against the trustee). If this is so, the chose in action is likely to be situate in the jurisdiction of residence of the trustee to which the individual would have to go to enforce his rights. Frequently, the trustee of a time share arrangement will be resident in a jurisdiction other than that in which the property is held (and often in a tax haven such as Jersey or the Isle of Man) where procedural and succession rules on the death of the individual may be more akin to those of the UK than those of the countries in which the land is situate.

Ownership by a nominee and other possibilities

18.3 It may be possible for the individual to avoid local succession procedures and laws by holding assets in the joint names of himself and

18.3 Investing Abroad

another if the local law permits beneficial ownership to pass automatically to the survivor of joint owners. Land in Ireland, for example, held by an individual and his son as joint tenants would pass automatically to the sole survivor of them on the death of one, thus avoiding the need to obtain a grant of probate on the first death. A problem may still arise, however, on the death of the surviving co-owner.

Alternatively, assets may be held in the names of corporate nominees which will never die. An individual investing abroad could set up his own nominee company in the UK specifically for this purpose. On the death of the beneficial owner of the assets, his personal representatives need only direct the nominee to hold to the order of the beneficiary to whom the asset devolves under the will. There is no requirement for the legal ownership of the foreign assets to change.

This will avoid any local administrative procedures on death but may also, if the local law does not recognise the concept of a trust (which is what the nominee relationship is), avoid both local succession laws and local death duties. This is because the local law will treat the nominee as the absolute owner of the assets and will not recognise any changes in the underlying beneficial ownership.

If the local laws do not recognise beneficial ownership then it is necessary to ensure that any foreign assets are purchased in the name of the nominee since to transfer foreign assets into the name of the nominee may result in a charge to local gift taxes. A liability to gift tax might also arise on a transfer of the assets by the nominee company to any new beneficial owner or owners and if the rates of tax depend upon the proximity of relationship between the transferor and the transferee, the highest rates would be likely to apply.

Another potential problem is that if the nominee were to transfer assets into the names of the deceased's heirs shortly after the death it might constitute itself an 'executor de son tort' if the local law recognised such a concept, with a resulting exposure to death duties on the assets in the jurisdiction. The case of *CIR v Stype Investments (Jersey) Ltd, [1982] 3 All ER 419; [1982] 3 WLR 228* is a reverse illustration of this potential risk, where a foreign nominee owned UK situs assets.

In relation to the purchase of foreign stocks and shares many stockbroking firms have in-house nominee companies, called 'marking names', in the name of which the investments are registered or which, in the case of bearer securities, hold the bearer certificate on behalf of the investors thereby saving the expense of registering each purchaser with the security or providing him with a separate bearer certificate.

In some countries (e.g. Switzerland) it may be possible to give another person a power of attorney, valid under local law, to deal with the individual's assets in the event of his death. In such a situation, normally the attorney will acquire no beneficial interest in the assets but only the right to administer them. This may assist in relation to procedural matters but will not prevent any application of local succession laws or the imposition of local death duties.

Investing Abroad **18.4**

Ownership by a company

18.4 Ownership of foreign investments by a company, the shares of which are owned by the individual investor, may avoid local succession procedures and laws and duties on the death of the individual if that company is incorporated and resident outside the jurisdictions in which its investments are made. However, it will be necessary to arrange the transfer of the shares of the company itself to the heirs of the deceased who will inherit the company's shares. The ownership of the underlying investments will remain unchanged.

The cost-effectiveness of this arrangement as a means of holding foreign assets will depend upon the value of the investments to be acquired (in view of the costs of setting up and administering the company), the tax liability of that company in its country of residence and in the countries in which its investments are made and the UK tax liability of the shareholder. Overall, some simplification of the administration of the deceased's estate may be achieved.

An individual resident and domiciled in the UK would not, by holding his assets through a foreign resident company, save any UK income, capital gains or inheritance tax. If he held foreign assets directly he would be charged to income tax on his foreign income under Schedule D, Case IV or V. Dividends received from a foreign resident company interposed between the individual and his investments would be charged under Schedule D, Case IV. However, unless it was successfully claimed that the transfer of assets abroad was not to avoid any liability to UK tax (ICTA 1988, s 741(a)), where the income from the foreign assets was rolled-up in the offshore company and not distributed by way of dividend, such undistributed income would be deemed to be the individual investor's for all purposes (ICTA 1988, s 739). This charge is under Schedule D, Case VI on a current year basis. The individual would, however, receive the benefit of any rebates or reliefs under any double taxation treaties between the UK and the country in which any investment is situated (ICTA 1988, s 743(2)).

Whilst domiciled and resident in the UK the individual will suffer capital gains tax on all gains realised on his worldwide assets. Even if assets are held beneficially by a non-resident company, gains realised by that company may be deemed to be his by virtue of TCGA 1992, s 13. Where the provision applies, its effect can be unduly harsh. Whilst gains can be apportioned, losses attributed to shareholders can only be offset against other gains attributed during the same year of assessment. Unless gains are distributed within two years of having arisen, there can be a partial doubling-up effect. Unlike ICTA 1988, ss 739 and 740, there is no 'commercial' defence available to mitigate the charge to tax.

Any transfer *inter vivos* or on death of foreign assets or the shares of a foreign company through which foreign assets are held will be chargeable to inheritance tax provided the individual is domiciled in the UK (IHTA 1984, s 6).

One possibility is that the company could be initially funded by way of a cash loan. This will enable capital to be subsequently extracted from the company

18.5 *Investing Abroad*

tax-free by way of repaying the loan. Alternatively, a special type of redeemable share capital could be considered. However, the provisions of ICTA 1988, s 703 (cancellation of tax advantages from certain transactions in securities) might be used. Any income received by the company may be extracted by payment of a dividend. In practice, this may not give rise to an additional income tax charge for the investor if he had already been taxed on the income under ICTA 1988, s 739 (ICTA 1988, s 743(4)). However, strictly speaking, the payment of the dividend represents an additional source of income. In such circumstances, ICTA 1988, s 744(1) (no duplication of charge) may not help as like is not being compared to like. In practice, the Inland Revenue do not appear to take the point, albeit that the risk of them so doing would increase where an offshore investment company retains income for a substantial period of time before paying a dividend.

Because of the UK tax consequences both for the company and for the individual, the holding of foreign investments through a UK resident company is unlikely to be attractive. In practice, the company will be incorporated and resident in an offshore tax haven.

The complexity of the interaction of the taxation laws of the several jurisdictions in which the individual, the company and the investments are located should be closely examined. For example, some countries may impose an annual tax charge on any land held by a foreign company which makes the use of a company as a land holding vehicle unattractive.

Exchange control

18.5 The avoidance of exchange controls used to be as important in estate planning as the avoidance of taxation. The Exchange Control Act 1947 was suspended in 1979 and finally repealed in 1987. Economic life moves on and its reintroduction is now about as likely as Her Majesty repeating the experiment of her predecessor Canute, in attempting to hold back the tide.

Offshore settlements

18.6 If one is concerned about the reintroduction of exchange control one might hold one's foreign investments through an offshore settlement. By transferring assets to trustees all of whom are resident outside the UK the settlor removes them from his control. The terms of the settlement should be such that neither he nor any other beneficiary can require the trustees to return assets to them. Nor should the settlor or any UK resident person have the power to appoint or remove the trustees or to direct how the trust fund should be invested.

Although no individual resident in the UK should be able, under the terms of the settlement, to enforce the distribution of assets from the settlement, whether to himself or others, it may be possible for the cautious settlor to retain some say in the running of the settlement if its terms provide that any distribution of assets from the settlement can only be made by the trustees with his consent. To reverse the balance and repose a power of appointment in the settlor but provide that it is exerciseable only with the trustees' consent, is more dangerous.

Protector

18.7 It is not unusual, before certain trustee powers can be exercised, for the consent to be required of someone upon whom the settlor feels he can rely who is resident outside the UK. That person is often called the protector. In practice, the status of 'protectors' has yet to be firmly established. Essentially, his role is to act as a 'watchdog' over the trust's affairs, sometimes on behalf of the settlor, and sometimes in order to provide comfort for the beneficiaries. Sometimes this function is delegated to an Advisory Committee or Board.

It is comparatively rare to find any statutory mention or reference in case law which deals with protectors. An exception to this is in Jersey law which seeks to distinguish the role fulfilled in such cases from that of a trustee. There are similar statutory provisions in the law of the Cook Islands as well as in the case of the Turks and Caicos Islands.

It is not clear whether the powers held by protectors, are fiduciary in nature. In other words, whether protectors are subject to the same obligations and constraints as those faced by trustees. Whilst this does not seem to be an issue where they simply act as a 'sounding board', it is more relevant where they possess directional powers, including the ability to replace trustees. Where protectors in effect possess a power of veto over the exercise of certain trustees powers, there may be reasonable grounds for arguing that the powers are not of a fiduciary nature. However, where more active powers are involved, there is a higher possibility that they are of a fiduciary nature.

The risk in all of this goes to the status of a protector for both UK income tax and capital gains tax. Although the position is not clear, there must be a real risk that protectors possessing fiduciary powers may be held to be a type of trustee, and their residence in the UK may affect the residence of the trust for tax purposes. It is prudent to ensure that where protectors are appointed, they are both resident and ordinarily resident outside the UK. Naturally, it will be important to confirm that there are no local tax difficulties for the person accepting the position. Alternatively, if the settlor insists in opposition to the donee on the appointment of a UK protector it will be prudent to ensure that the powers held only fall into the power of veto category.

Generally, the role of a protector is to provide an extra degree of comfort for clients, often faced with offshore trusts for the first time. In practice, the solution to the concerns felt in such circumstances might be relatively straightforward. It might be better to identify one of the many reputable and professional offshore trustees right from the start, rather than rely on an arrangement which remains untested in the courts.

'Flee clauses'

18.8 The possibility of the introduction of exchange controls in third world countries or expropriatory measures in the country of residence of the

18.9 Investing Abroad

trustees should not be overlooked. To provide some protection against this, it is usual to include a 'flee clause' in the settlement document which provides that in the happening of certain events the trustees will automatically be removed from office and other trustees resident in another jurisdiction appointed. The success of such clauses (which are largely untested) may depend on whether they are triggered before or after the happening of the event the effect of which they are seeking to avoid. If a particular event occurs before the new trustees are automatically appointed it may be impossible to transfer assets out of the names of the old trustees and into those of the new trustees. Even if the automatic appointment of new trustees is triggered before the measures sought to be avoided are introduced there may still be difficulty in transferring assets out of the names of the old trustees. The flee clause may provide that assets will, from the date of the automatic appointment, be held by the old trustees merely as nominees for the new trustees but the success of this provision will depend upon the nature of the measures introduced.

Another solution to this problem would be for the trustees to hold all their investments through an investment company wholly owned by them and incorporated in a different jurisdiction to that in which the trustees are resident. The terms of the settlement — or the governing instrument of the company — would then provide for the automatic vesting of the shares in the company in the new trustees if the flee clause is triggered.

The costs of appointing trustees resident outside the UK and of their administering the trust property on a continuing basis should be considered as it will usually be necessary to use a professional person or trust company as a trustee rather than a lay associate of the settlor.

Also, it is important to establish the basis on which fees are to be charged. *Ad valorem* based charges, although they offer a measure of certainty as compared to a time-based system of charging, can be onerous. It is also important to establish if the trustees will expect to receive any *ad valorem* based payment on distributions of the trust assets, or on being removed from office. 'Parting payments' are not as common as they used to be, and given the increasing competition in this area amongst professional offshore trustees, it is usually possible to ensure that such conditions do not apply.

Forms of settlement

18.9 Historically, the most common form of settlement has been a (revocable) life interest upon the settlor (and his spouse) under which the trustees have power to pay capital to the settlor at their discretion. Such settlements secure the division of ownership between settlor and trustees whilst leaving the settlor almost in the same position as if he owned the assets directly. For inheritance tax purposes, provided the settlement confers an interest in possession on the settlor, no inheritance tax charge will arise on the transfer of assets to the trustees since he will be treated as remaining the beneficial owner of all the settled property in which his interest subsists (IHTA 1984, s 49).

Investing Abroad **18.10**

It is no longer attractive for a UK domiciled settlor to create a discretionary offshore settlement of which he remains a beneficiary even if he were prepared to suffer an inheritance tax charge on creation. This is because he will be treated as remaining beneficially entitled to the property settled and under the gifts with reservation provisions a further charge may arise if he is not excluded from benefit before his death or if he dies within seven years of being excluded at which time he will be deemed to make a potentially exempt transfer (FA 1986, s 102(4)).

On creation of the settlement, the settlor will make a disposal for capital gains tax purposes of any chargeable assets transferred to the trustees and a charge to tax will arise on any gains arising on this occasion. Similarly, such a settlor will be assessed on gains realised by the trustees whilst he continues to be either resident or ordinarily resident, and domiciled.

Tax position of trustees and beneficiaries

18.10 Prior to creating the settlement, the income and capital taxes position of the trustees in their country of residence should be considered together with the applicability of double tax treaties between the country of residence of the trustees and those countries where their assets are situate. Treaties with those countries without a local law of trusts may not cover trusts and trustees.

It is usual to create a settlement in a tax haven which does not impose taxes on income or capital gains in the hands of the trustees or on a change of interests under the settlement or upon beneficiaries becoming absolutely entitled to the settled property. However, since there are also unlikely to be full double taxation treaties between those countries and the countries in which assets are invested or those where the beneficiaries are resident, it may be difficult to secure relief for any foreign taxes paid.

Trustees will be regarded as non-resident for UK income tax purposes if all the trustees are resident outside the UK (FA 1989, s 110(1)(a)). To the extent that non-resident trustees invest outside the UK they will suffer no UK income tax and income arising from UK assets will be paid gross.

The UK resident settlor who is entitled to the income from foreign situate trust property will suffer UK income tax on that income under Schedule D, Case IV or V. The correct case will depend upon whether, under the proper law of the settlement, he is treated as entitled to the income of the underlying assets or merely to the income after the trustees have deducted administration expenses and other costs incurred by them (*Garland v Archer-Shee, HL 1930, 15 TC 693; [1931] AC 212*).

If all or a majority of the trustees are resident outside the UK and provided that the administration of the settlement is carried on outside this country, they will be outside the charge to capital gains tax (TCGA 1992, s 2(1) and TCGA 1992, s 69) except in relation to assets which are held in a UK trade carried on through a branch or agency (TCGA 1992, s 10). The settlor, because of his interest in the settlement, will be subject to capital gains tax on gains realised by the trustees in the same tax year as they are realised (TCGA 1992, s 86 and TCGA 1992, Sch 5).

18.11 Investing Abroad

Where a settlement confers a life interest on the settlor (or another individual) his death or the earlier termination of his interest will give rise to a potential inheritance tax charge under IHTA 1984, s 52. Earlier terminations of his interest may, depending upon the nature of the trusts upon which the trust fund then becomes held, constitute potentially exempt transfers. His interest may be followed by absolute interests for his beneficiaries or by interests in possession, accumulation and maintenance trusts or discretionary trusts. It should be remembered that any trusts following his interest which are within IHTA 1984, Part III Chapter III will be treated as being created at the time that the settlor's (or his spouse's) life interest terminates (IHTA 1984, s 80). Thus, inheritance tax charges on any discretionary trusts will be calculated by reference to the settlor's (or his spouse's) cumulative total at the time of the termination of his interest. If the termination arises on death, charges on the tenth anniversaries of the settlement will take account of any other property which became comprised in trusts at the settlor's death by virtue of his will or the statutory trusts on his intestacy since these trusts will be 'related' (IHTA 1984, s 62). The date of each ten-year anniversary will be calculated by reference to this occasion and not to the date of creation of the settlement.

'International wills'

18.11   An offshore settlement may be used by an individual settlor as an 'international will' and are often marketed as such by professional trustee companies. The settlement may either provide a life interest for the settlor, flexibility being maintained by the incorporation of a wide-ranging power of appointment in favour of a broad class of beneficiaries, or may be discretionary. Although, as discussed above, the inheritance tax consequences for a UK domiciled settlor of creating a discretionary settlement will make the latter alternative unattractive.

The holding of assets situate in a number of foreign jurisdictions in one settlement may centralise administration and may avoid the need to comply with local succession procedures, laws and taxes on the death of the settlor. This will especially be the case if the trustee is a corporate trustee and if the assets held are situate in a civil law jurisdiction which recognises only the trustee's title to the trust assets and not the beneficial ownership of those assets or any change in it arising on the settlor's death.

If the intention behind creating a settlement is to ensure that the death of an individual does not give rise to charges to local death duties in the countries in which foreign assets are situated it may be advisable to ensure that the settlement is either discretionary or that, if the settlement is a life interest settlement, successive life interests are created so the property will continue to be held in the settlement for as long as possible. This is subject to the perpetuity restrictions upon the length of time for which assets may continue to be held in a settlement which may be imposed by the law governing the settlement. At the time when the settlement terminates and one or more individuals become absolutely entitled to the trust assets it will be necessary to comply with the formal requirements for transfer of the foreign assets laid down by the laws of the countries in which those assets are situated (unless the trustee continues to hold, as their nominee, the assets to which the individuals have become absolutely entitled or those individuals re-settle those assets).

Care should be taken where assets situated in a civil law country are to be held in a settlement. The ability of an individual to dispose of immovable property may be governed by the law of the country in which that property is situated. A transfer of that property to a settlement may contravene succession laws which reserve fixed portions of the individual's estate for his widow and children. Since succession to movable property will (in most cases) be governed by the law of the individual's domicile (i.e. that of the UK) such property may be transferred to a settlement. However, the transfer into the settlement may have extreme tax consequences of the nature described above in relation to gifts to personal representatives in those countries where the concept of a trust and the division of ownership of property between the legal owner and the equitable owners is not recognised or understood. The transfer of property to trustees may suffer gift duties at the highest rates in jurisdictions where such duties are charged at rates determined by the degree of relationship between donor and donee since the transferor and the trustee are likely to be unrelated. Similar consequences may arise when beneficiaries become absolutely entitled to the assets held in a settlement.

A number of civil law jurisdictions already recognise trusts established by foreigners to a varying degree, although it is fair to say that the vast majority still do not fully do so. Examples of countries which recognise trusts include Switzerland to a degree, and to a lesser extent France. Other jurisdictions still experience great difficulty in both recognising the concept, and taxing it in a satisfactory manner. This lack of uniform treatment was the driving force behind the adoption in draft by The Hague Conference on Private International Law on 20 October 1984 of the Convention on the law applicable to trusts and on their recognition. It is important to stress that is not a purely Western European based initiative, but involves amongst others, Egypt, Japan and Turkey.

The Convention does not introduce the trust concept into the legal system of civil law states, but rather sets out the ground rules under which individual states will give legal recognition to trusts, in accordance with a system of common conflict of laws rules.

The Convention has been signed and implemented by only seven countries (Italy, the Netherlands, Malta, Australia, Hong Kong, Canada and the UK). It has been signed but not yet implemented by France, Luxembourg and the United States.

If the Convention is fully ratified and embodied into the national laws of the signatory states, the overall position will to some extent improve but the change is likely to be slow. This simply highlights the need to take appropriate legal advice in the areas where trusts are established and where their assets are held, to ensure that, irrespective of the tax consequences, no legal or other difficulties will ensue. Civil law jurisdictions will seldom recognise or enforce a trust but will instead treat the trustee who is resident there as the absolute owner of the assets. If the trustee becomes bankrupt the trust assets may go to satisfy his creditors and if he breaches his trust few remedies will be available

18.11 *Investing Abroad*

to the aggrieved beneficiaries. Even in those jurisdictions such as Switzerland, where trusts will, in certain circumstances, be recognised, it will be difficult to recover from a third party any trust property which has wrongly passed to him.

19 Immigration and Emigration

Introduction

19.1 Although 'immigration' and 'emigration' normally indicate moving to and from the UK with long-term plans in mind, the position of individuals coming to or leaving the UK for limited periods, usually but not necessarily connected with their work, will also be considered in this chapter.

By far the greater part of this chapter deals with the position of the immigrant.

The chapter does not address the non-tax immigration rules applied by the Home Office to individuals resident abroad wishing to come to the UK to live or to work or European Union law on the free movement of nationals of Member States. These aspects should be reviewed well in advance of the anticipated date of entry into the UK.

Domicile, residence and ordinary residence

19.2 This chapter provides a brief summary of the concepts of domicile, residence and ordinary residence. For a guide to the Inland Revenue's practice in relation to these topics and their relevance for the purposes of UK taxation, reference should be made to the Inland Revenue explanatory pamphlet 'Residents and Non-residents — Liability to Tax in the UK' (IR20).

Domicile

19.3 Domicile is of fundamental importance in estate planning. There are two types of domicile; domicile under the general English law and an artificial deemed domicile which applies specifically for inheritance tax purposes.

Actual domicile

19.4 Under English law every individual must at any time have a domicile in one specific country. An individual is born with a *domicile of origin*, usually that of his father. While under the age of 16 his domicile of origin will remain but if his parent's domicile changes (while he is under that age) his domicile will follow that of his parent, and will be a *domicile of dependence*. Once he is 16, he has the legal capacity to acquire an

19.4 Immigration and Emigration

independent domicile in a different country — a *domicile of choice* (Domicile and Matrimonial Proceedings Act 1973, s 3). This is acquired by both actual physical presence in another country and forming a definite intention (evidenced by all the circumstances surrounding the individual and his way of life) to make his home in that country permanently or indefinitely. If he does not acquire a domicile of choice in this way, he will retain his domicile of dependence, and if he loses that without acquiring a domicile of choice, his domicile of origin will revive.

The fact that an individual makes an application for naturalisation in another country does not of itself indicate a change of domicile (*Wahl v Attorney-General, HL 1932, 147 LT 382* and *Mrs F and S2 (Personal Representatives of F deceased) v CIR, Sp C 1999, [2000] SSCD 1 (Sp C 219)*.

It is difficult to lose a domicile of origin. There must be clear and positive evidence that a change has been made. Going abroad for a period of years is unlikely to result in the acquisition of a domicile of choice, unless when taking up residence in another country or subsequently, there is a genuine intention to remain there permanently or indefinitely. That intention has to be formed free of all external constraining factors. For example, in *Mrs F and S2 (Personal Representatives of F deceased)* above the deceased moved to the UK for various reasons including religious persecution. He had maintained a settled intention to return but was unable to do so because of an exit bar which would have prevented him leaving again. It was held that he did not acquire a domicile of choice. An individual may be taken to have acquired a new domicile of choice for a period even if he later changes his mind and returns to the UK. In practice, however, the evidence of the necessary intention at the outset will have to be very strong to convince the Inland Revenue of this. It has not been uncommon for Englishmen to spend many years in a foreign country (for example, in government service in India, or working in the Far East), with the intention of leaving that country eventually, either to retire to England or some other country. In those circumstances, the individual will not acquire a domicile of choice in the foreign country regardless of the length of the period he resides there. This approach was confirmed in *Civil Engineer v CIR, Sp C 2001, [2002] SSCD 72 (Sp C 299)*.

An individual loses a domicile of choice (and a domicile of dependency) by leaving the country in question with the intention (supported by clear evidence) of ceasing to regard it as his permanent home. An individual may thereupon acquire a new domicile of choice, if the requirements mentioned above are met. If they are not, his domicile of origin will be reinstated.

It used to be the case that a woman on her marriage automatically took her husband's domicile as a domicile of dependence. Her domicile is now determined in the normal way (Domicile and Matrimonial Proceedings Act 1973, s 1). Where a woman already married on 1 January 1974 had acquired her husband's domicile as a domicile of dependence, that domicile is her domicile of choice until such time as she acquires a new domicile. A married woman can, therefore, have a different domicile to that of her husband. If an Englishwoman marries a man with a domicile of origin in New York and after the marriage the couple live in Europe for the time being (e.g. due to the husband's employment) she will not acquire a domicile of choice in New

York. She will retain her English domicile. By way of further example, suppose a man with an English domicile of origin works for most of his life in Hong Kong. At the time of his retirement he marries a woman domiciled in California, and they decide to live in California for a while, but not necessarily permanently. His wife, having never lived in England and having no intention of doing so, remains domiciled in California, but the husband, at any rate initially, does not become domiciled in California. So they have different domiciles. The case of *CIR v Bullock, CA [1976] STC 409; [1976] 3 All ER 353* is authority for the proposition that a married couple (only one of whom already has an English domicile) may set up home in England on a permanent basis without the spouse with the foreign domicile necessarily thereby acquiring an English domicile of choice. If one spouse maintains links with his or her original country and demonstrates a clear intention (rather than 'a vague hope or aspiration') of returning there should he or she survive the other or in the event that the other were to agree to go and live in that original country, then that spouse will retain his or her domicile in that original country.

Reform of domicile

19.5 In the past proposals have been announced to reform the law of domicile. Prior to the 1992 general election, proposals were announced to introduce a new Domicile Act based on the joint report of the Law Commission and the Scottish Law Commission made in 1987. This report, entitled 'Private International Law: the law of Domicile' proposed a number of changes in this area as they relate to individuals. In outline the proposals were that

(*a*) the general standard of proof in domicile disputes would be the balance of probabilities;

(*b*) in the case of adults, a future domicile of choice would be acquired by an intention to 'settle indefinitely' in a new country;

(*c*) the doctrine of revival of domicile of origin should be abandoned so that the domicile of an adult person should continue until such time as that person acquired a new domicile of choice;

(*d*) the general rule relating to children is that their domicile would be determined as being the country with which they are most closely connected;

(*e*) in the case of married women, the Law Commissions recommended the abolition of certain provisions of the Domicile and Matrimonial Proceedings Act 1973. Under these a married woman's domicile of dependency which she acquired on marriage prior to the implementation of the 1973 rules (1 January 1974), continued after that date as a notional domicile of choice.

Under the proposals a person's domicile position was to be determined as if the new law had always been in force. As a result a number of individuals would have found that their domicile changed had the new rules come into effect as originally envisaged.

19.6 Immigration and Emigration

Due to this the Lord Chancellor's Department received a significant number of representations from the legal and accountancy professions, and their representative bodies. In November 1992, there was a meeting between the Institute of Taxation, the Inland Revenue and the Lord Chancellor's Department to address differences over the proposed content of the Domicile Bill. The text of that meeting was agreed by the Inland Revenue, and was published in the April 1993 edition of *Taxation Practitioner* (pp 27–29). This made interesting reading, and most importantly seemed to reflect acceptance by government ministers that any new rules should contain transitional provisions, similar to those in the Domicile and Matrimonial Proceedings Act 1973, in order to safeguard the domicile position of a number of individuals who might otherwise have been prejudiced.

In view of the number of representations received, the then Prime Minister, John Major, confirmed in reply to a written question that the government had no immediate plans to introduce legislation on this subject (Hansard, 26 May 1992). This reply was not free from ambiguity but the Conservative Government decided not to proceed with the proposals. The Labour Party tried to introduce these proposals in the Finance Bill at that time and whilst in Opposition indicated that similar measures would be introduced by them when they were elected ('Tackling tax abuses — tackling unemployment', November 1994). Since the Labour Party came into power there have been widespread rumours of proposed changes to domicile and numerous newspaper articles detailing how high profile non-domicilliaries are taking advantage of their status to avoid paying taxes in the United Kingdom. In his 2002 Budget Speech the Chancellor announced that he was 'reviewing the complex rules of residence and domicile'. No consultation document has been issued. Instead, professional bodies have been asked to submit their comments to the Inland Revenue. Due to a lack of detail about the review, it is extremely difficult to advise a client about the implementation of structures to take advantage of a non-domicile status.

Deemed domicile

19.6 For inheritance tax purposes a person who is not domiciled in the UK under the general law will be deemed to be domiciled here when a transfer of value is made if:

(*a*)   he was domiciled in the UK under general English law within the period of three calendar years immediately preceding that time; or

(*b*)   he was resident in the UK for income tax purposes in 17 of the 20 years of assessment ending with the year in which the relevant time falls (IHTA 1984, s 267).

In determining whether the individual is resident in any year for purposes of the rule, residence is determined as for income tax purposes (see 19.7 below).

It is often the case that an individual is, under general principles, not domiciled in the UK but is deemed domiciled in the UK. The deemed domicile rules may in certain situations be overridden (IHTA 1984, s 267(2)). If an individual is domiciled in a country which has a suitable double tax treaty with the UK, then assets held outside the UK will not be subject to UK

Immigration and Emigration **19.8**

inheritance tax provided they do not pass under a disposition governed by law of any part of Great Britain. Such countries include France, India and Pakistan.

Residence

19.7 The term 'residence' is not defined by legislation, although the term has been interpreted by the UK courts many times. To be regarded as resident in the UK for tax purposes, an individual must be physically present in the UK for at least part of the tax year (ending 5 April). Strictly speaking, an individual is either resident or non-resident for the whole tax year. However, by concession, the tax year can be split into separate periods of residence and non-residence for income tax purposes (ESC A11). The year can only be split for capital gains tax purposes where the taxpayer has not been, broadly, a long-term resident of the UK (ESC D2). In practice, the Inland Revenue will normally regard an individual as resident in the UK for tax purposes where

(*a*) he has been in the UK for 183 days or more (TCGA 1992, s 9); or

(*b*) he visits the UK regularly and after four years the visits during those years average 91 days or more. The individual is treated as resident from the fifth year (IR 20 para 3.3);

(*c*) he has 'left the UK for the purpose only of occasional residence abroad', provided that he is a citizen of the Commonwealth or Ireland (ICTA 1988, s 334). The meaning of occasional residence abroad was considered in *Reed v Clark, Ch D 1985, 58 TC 528; [1985] STC 323*.

Although the consideration in deciding residence status of whether an individual had available accommodation in the UK has been abolished, it does not mean that the existence of UK accommodation can be ignored.

The Inland Revenue will continue to operate their practice of regarding a visitor to the UK as being resident on his arrival if he comes to the UK for a purpose (for example, employment) that will mean he will remain in the UK for at least two years (IR 20 para 3.7). If an individual already owns UK property or purchases freehold or leasehold property or a lease of more than three years duration, he will be treated as being ordinarily resident. However, if he is treated as ordinarily resident solely because of the accommodation and leaves the UK within three years of his arrival, an individual may be treated as not ordinarily resident for the duration of his stay if this is to his advantage. (IR 20 paras 3.11, 3.12).

Ordinary residence

19.8 Ordinary residence is also not defined by legislation, but is taken to mean habitual residence. The Inland Revenue's practice is to treat an individual as being ordinary resident in the following circumstances.

(*a*) Where it is clear that a visitor intends to remain in the UK for at least three years, he will be ordinarily resident from the date of his arrival. In the absence of any such clear intention, he will be treated as

19.9 Immigration and Emigration

ordinarily resident from the beginning of the tax year in which the third anniversary of his arrival falls.

(b) Where visits for four consecutive tax years have averaged 91 days or more per tax year.

(c) Where accommodation is acquired which suggests that he will stay in the UK from three years or more.

By concession, it may be possible for a tax year to be split for income tax purposes (ESC A11). For capital gains tax purposes the split year concession is not relevant in determining ordinary residence in the year of arrival. In the year of departure the split year concession is not available to taxpayers who, broadly, have been long-term residents in the UK. However, in the absence of such treatment, the individual will be ordinarily resident for the entire tax year in question. Conversely, an individual who leaves the UK will not normally be treated as ceasing to be ordinarily resident unless he intends to, and does in fact, leave the UK for at least three years to work full-time under a contract of employment provided his absence from the UK and the employment abroad both last for at least a whole tax year and any visits made to the UK total less than 183 days in any tax year and average less than 91 days a tax year (IR 20 para 2.2). In such a case he will normally be regarded as neither resident nor ordinarily resident for the period of his absence.

For a more detailed summary of the Inland Revenue practice on residence and its implications, reference may be made to the Inland Revenue explanatory pamphlet (IR 20) mentioned above. It should always be remembered that IR 20 is not necessarily an accurate statement of the law. However, all professional advice will take account of the Inland Revenue's views which are set out in this booklet.

Overseas law

19.9 It must be emphasised how important it is for a would-be immigrant to understand the application of the general and tax laws of his previous country to the UK, and for a would-be emigrant from the UK to understand the effect of the laws of his new country. This applies to both long-term and short-term residents. The individual, depending on his circumstances, should consider these matters and take any necessary advice in the appropriate country before taking any irrevocable steps. Timing may be all-important, and the time to consider these matters is before departure, rather than en route to the country or on arrival.

The long-term immigrant

19.10 It is essential that the individual plans well in advance of his arrival. He should consider his position well before the UK tax year in which he plans to arrive, so that appropriate action may be taken before the start of that tax year.

Immigration and Emigration 19.10

In advising such an individual, the following factors should be taken into consideration:

(a) his age and the period for which he is coming to the UK;

(b) his domicile of origin and general background;

(c) his family circumstances;

(d) his employment or professional situation;

(e) the composition of his estate and his sources of income;

(f) his likely financial needs in the UK;

(g) the existence of any funds not required for actual expenditure in the UK;

(h) whether he has any intention of making gifts of capital assets to family members and others, the nature of those assets and the residence and circumstances of the donees;

(j) his intentions for his estate in the event of his death.

A long-term immigrant should always consider that there is a risk that the UK Inland Revenue authorities may argue that he has acquired, or reacquired, a domicile within the UK upon his arrival if he intends to reside in the UK permanently. As discussed earlier, it may however, be that (following *CIR v Bullock, CA [1976] STC 409; [1976] 3 All ER 353*), one spouse of a married couple may be able to retain a domicile in his or her home country. There may be circumstances where an individual will not acquire a UK domicile until he has been here for a few years. It may be possible to take advantage of his foreign domicile whilst resident in the UK by making gifts which will not be within the charge to inheritance tax. However, it is sensible that any such gifts are made, or structuring is completed, before his arrival in the UK.

An individual who arrives in this country will be required to complete a residence questionnaire by the Inland Revenue (Form P86) which includes questions as to his intentions for his stay in the UK. A person who intends to reside permanently will be treated as being resident and ordinarily resident in the UK from the date of his arrival. Where the immigrant does not intend to settle in the UK permanently, it is possible that the issue of domicile will not be raised with or by the Inland Revenue for a number of years after the individual's arrival, and in that event it may be that, depending on the evidence, he will not be treated as domiciled in the UK until some later date. It would, however, be unwise to assume before arrival that this will happen, and in the normal case it will be sensible for the immigrant, soon after his arrival, to raise the matter with the Inland Revenue so that his domicile and residence status for UK tax purposes are confirmed.

If a UK domicile is acquired upon or soon after arrival, it is impossible to avoid UK income tax on the individual's income, wherever it arises, including income received from trusts of which he is a beneficiary (whether he is entitled to income or dependent on the trustee's discretion for income). If a UK domicile is not obtained, income tax and capital gains tax may be avoidable for such a period (by not remitting foreign source income or assets

19.11 *Immigration and Emigration*

representing capital gains). In particular, the use of non-resident trusts can achieve valuable tax savings, and not simply deferment, as will be seen later. Gifts of foreign assets will be possible during such a period without liability to inheritance tax. As indicated above, however, it is dangerous to rely on the ability to do this, if the individual's intention is to remain here permanently or indefinitely (e.g. after retirement).

Limited spouse exemption

19.11 There is a limited spouse exemption of £55,000 if the surviving spouse is not domiciled in the United Kingdom but the deceased spouse was. Any sum in excess of that amount can run the risk of being within the gift with reservation rules. It should be noted that other exemptions may be appropriate, such as the exemption in relation to a disposition between spouses for the maintenance of the other party (IHTA 1984 s 11(1)). This would be appropriate where a domiciled spouse gives a half share in the family home to the non-domiciled spouse.

Purchase of property

19.12 One of the main considerations of the long-term immigrant will be where he is going to live in the UK. This will normally be settled (at least in principle) before he arrives, even though the purchase of an actual property may not be completed until after his arrival. It is unlikely that an immigrant and his family will want to live with relatives or friends or in rented accommodation or a hotel for any appreciable period of time.

The straightforward solution will be for the individual to purchase a property in his own name or in the joint names of his wife and himself. This means that the property will on his death (regardless of domicile because it is a UK situs asset) be wholly within the scope of inheritance tax. If he leaves the property under his will (or his share in it as a tenant in common) to his wife, or if he and his wife are joint tenants, there will be no inheritance tax liability on the property until the death of the survivor of them. However, there will be a limited spouse exemption of £55,000 if the surviving spouse is not domiciled in the UK but the deceased spouse was (IHTA 1984, s 18(2)). In such circumstances the property will be subject to inheritance tax on the first spouse's death, subject to the exemption. In such a case it may be preferable for the property to be bought in the name of the non-domiciled spouse and left by will to the domiciled spouse.

Alternatively, for the more wealthy individual, in the past it has been advised that the UK property could be acquired by a non-resident company, the shares in which are owned by a trust established by the individual before he acquires a UK domicile. The trust should be created and funded before arriving in the UK. The property can be purchased afterwards. This arrangement is designed to convert the property into 'excluded property' for inheritance tax purposes under IHTA 1984, s 48(3) and therefore avoid inheritance tax. Section 48(3) excludes from charge non-UK property (i.e. the shares in the non-resident company) in a settlement made by an individual who was not domiciled in the

UK at the date of settlement. There are, however, a number of difficulties and uncertainties in such an arrangement.

Care must be taken to avoid (as far as is possible) incurring a tax liability on the individual under ICTA 1988, ss 145 and 146. These provisions treat the value of any living accommodation provided for an employee (including a director of a company) or his family by his employer as a taxable emolument.

For some years the Inland Revenue have held that, where an individual has a controlling shareholding in a non-resident company which holds a UK property in which the individual lives, a Schedule E charge can arise. The argument runs as follows. ICTA 1988, s 168(8) defines a director as including any person 'in accordance with whose directions or instructions the directors of the company are accustomed to act'. The Inland Revenue argued that in many circumstances the individual would be a director under this definition. ICTA 1988, s 167(1)(a) states that Chapter II of Part V of ICTA 1988 (which imposes Schedule E charges on benefits given to directors and higher-paid employees) applies both to employments as a director and other employments with emoluments of £8,500 per annum or more. Thus, a 'director' is treated as having an employment. ICTA 1988, s 168(2) defines employment as 'an office or employment, the emoluments of which fall to be assessed under Schedule E'. Thus, the shadow director's employment is an employment for the purposes of the Schedule E charge. ICTA 1988, s 154 then imposes a charge where accommodation is provided to an employee by reason of the employment.

It was frequently considered that there were many things wrong with this argument. However, the decision by the House of Lords in *R v Allen, HL [2001] STC 1537* has supported the Revenue's view. In the case it was argued that because a shadow director has no 'actual emoluments' and no 'actual duties', it is not possible to determine whether there is an employment which falls within Schedule E, unless it could be said that the benefits of every shadow director anywhere in the world are taxable without any territorial limits. This argument was dismissed. It was held that a deemed director is taxable on the benefit of living accommodation under Cases I, II and III in the same way that actual emoluments would have been. It is now clear that all three cases of para 1 of Schedule E apply to shadow directors.

Does that mean that using offshore companies to hold UK property for non-UK domiciled but resident individuals will result in a Schedule E charge? Not at all. *Dimsey* concerned a situation in which it had been found as a fact by the High Court that the defendants had centrally managed and controlled the offshore company in the UK. The defendants were, therefore, clearly shadow directors. This argument does not get off the ground unless it can be said of an individual resident in the UK that he is a person in accordance with whose instructions or directions the directors of the company are accustomed to act. Any reputable offshore company management business will ensure that they do not simply instruct or accept instructions from shareholders.

The taxpayer will have added protection on this point if the offshore company is in turn owned by an offshore trust in which he has only a limited interest. Even so, the Inland Revenue may still argue that the company's board acts in

19.12　Immigration and Emigration

accordance with his instructions (see the Inland Revenue's letter of 25 January 1989 to the Chartered Institute of Taxation).

For some clients the risks may be felt to be too high. Instead, the property could be owned directly by the trust and any resulting tax charges simply accepted. Where the settlement consists of an interest in possession, a charge to inheritance tax is only likely to arise on the death of the life tenant and this liability can be insured against. Alternatively, the property could be purchased by an individual in his own name, financed by way of a 100% loan charged on the property, which will effectively reduce the initial value of the property to nil for inheritance tax purposes, although any increase in value in the property will be within the scope of an inheritance tax charge.

For a non-domiciled individual who occupies a UK property owned by an offshore company which in turn is owned by an offshore trust, it is suggested that the directors of the offshore company sell the property to a new offshore trust for a promissory note in the form of a deed governed by an appropriate law. If the 'specialty' debt is kept outside the United Kingdom, it will have the effect of stripping out the value of the UK property and retaining it in the form of a foreign situs security. There are a number of difficulties with such an arrangement.

If the offshore company sells the property to the new trust, it will realise a gain on the sale and there will be a double-tiered gain in respect of the company shares in the trust. It is possible that these double gains will ultimately be distributed to UK-domiciled children of the settlor and taxable under TCGA 1992 s 87. They may also incur a supplementary charge. Consideration should therefore be given to transferring the property back to the trust or the settlor before the sale. The transfer of the property back to the trust before being sold to a new trust will mean that they will only be subject potentially to one tier of gain under TCGA 1992 s 87. Where the property is transferred back to the settlor, the gain will be free of tax. However, if the reservation of benefit rules relating to non-domiciliary trusts were to change in the near future this may not achieve favourable results. It would seem that it may be more efficient for the property to be transferred back to the settlor and for the settlor to settle the specialty debt on new offshore trusts.

There have been rumours that the reservation of benefit rules will be applied to trusts created by non-UK domiciliaries. In that event, the rules would apply to new trusts set up by non-domiciliaries after a certain date as and when the settlor becomes deemed domiciled.

The sale of the property to an offshore trust will result in a stamp duty charge at 4% for values exceeding £500,000. Provided the consideration is less than £10 million this can be avoided by resting on contract.

Where a non-domiciled individual owns a UK property and wishes to change the situs of that asset by transferring the property to a non-UK company, this was usually done by way of gift which would be exempt from stamp duty provided that the gift was certified under Category L of the 1987 Exempt Instruments Regulations. However, FA 2000, s 119 makes it no longer possible to certify the gift under category L. Section 119 applies where land is transferred to a company in exchange for an issue of shares or the company

Immigration and Emigration **19.13**

and the transferor are connected within the terms of ICTA 1988, s 839. For stamp duty purposes, the transfer document is deemed to be a transfer on sale for the market value of the land at the date of transfer. Therefore, where an individual transfers the property to a company to which he is connected, stamp duty at rates of up to 4% will be payable on the market value. There are some exceptions to this rule detailed in FA 2000 s 120 including where there is a transfer to an independent corporate trustee. If the tax savings are significant, it may be possible to avoid a stamp duty charge by resting on contract, provided the market value of the property is less than £10 million.

Where a UK property is purchased by a family discretionary trust, a ten-year charge may be triggered under the inheritance tax rules under IHTA 1984, Chapter III. This used to be avoided by converting the UK property into 'excluded property' before that date. This was achieved by transferring the property to an underlying offshore registered company. However, this strategy now creates a potential stamp duty charge of up to 4% if there is a transfer to a connected company (see above). It is therefore necessary to compare the cost of the stamp duty charge against the possible IHT charge if the property remains directly owned by the trust.

Example

A non-domiciled individual set up an offshore discretionary trust on 30 September 1990 and immediately transferred a UK property to it. The property is now worth £1,000,000 and the individual has not used his inheritance tax nil rate band of £250,000.

Because the property is situated in the UK, there is an IHT ten-year charge of £45,000 ((£1,000,000 − £250,000) × 6%). If the property is transferred to an offshore company on 29 September 2002, there will be a stamp duty charge of £40,000 (£1,000,000 × 4%).

In addition, there was a concern that the extension to the transfer pricing rules in ICTA 1988, Sch 28AA could apply to such a structure. These rules apply where any provision in a transaction made between two different persons differs from what it would have been had it been at arms' length, and this results in a potential UK tax advantage to one of those persons. For the legislation to apply at the time of making the provision, one of the two persons must directly or indirectly control the other. One might consider that this condition would not be satisfied if a company is owned by overseas trustees. However, ICTA 1988, Sch 28AA para 4 provides that the rights and powers of connected persons can be taken into account and it is specifically stated that the trustees of the settlement are a connected person with the settlor. There is a potential UK tax advantage to the offshore company as if the company charged rent for the property, it would have a UK source of income and therefore be liable to UK income tax. Fortunately, the Inland Revenue have stated that they will not take this point (Taxation, 1 April 1999, p 5).

Use of excluded property trusts for other assets

19.13 An individual not domiciled in the UK who wishes to avoid inheritance tax applying to his worldwide estate on transfers should

19.14 *Immigration and Emigration*

establish a non-UK resident trust-based structure to hold a substantial proportion of his personal wealth. Although the rules are complex, provided a suitable trust is established with non-situs UK assets by an individual who is not domiciled in the UK for inheritance tax purposes, no inheritance tax will be chargeable on the assets held in the trust (IHTA 1984, s 48(3)).

Reservation of benefit

19.14 It can be inadvisable for individuals who are not domiciled in the UK for inheritance tax purposes to establish discretionary trusts under which they retain a benefit. This would occur where the settlor is either a beneficiary or is capable of being subsequently added as one (*Gartside v CIR*, HL 1967, [1968] 2 WLR 277; [1968] 1 All ER 121).

How does the rule in IHTA 1984, s 48(3) that non-UK situs settled property is excluded property if the settlor is not domiciled in the UK at the time the settlement was made relate to the reservation of benefit rules? The Inland Revenue's position seems to be a confused one. In correspondence published in the Law Society Gazette on 10 December 1986, the Inland Revenue accepted that if a settlor settled property in which he reserved a benefit when he was not domiciled in the UK, and then died while domiciled in the UK, the settled property would be excluded from charge under IHTA 1984, s 48. Recently, it has become evident that the Inland Revenue are changing their view. Although there has not been any formal announcement made, the example given in CTO Advanced Instruction Manual at para D.8 has been altered to read:

> 'The donor, who is domiciled in Australia, puts foreign property into a discretionary trust under which he is a potential beneficiary. He dies five years later domiciled in England without having released the reservation. The property is property subject to a reservation and is therefore deemed to be part of the donor's death estate.'

It is understood that despite this change the Revenue have said that their position has not formally changed.

One has to be careful where an initial life interest of either the settlor or his spouse is followed by a discretionary trust. To ensure excluded property status, the individual must be both non-domiciled when the trust is created and on the termination of the initial life interest or the spouse's successive life interest.

Situs of assets

19.15 When establishing an offshore structure, the inheritance tax rules as to *situs* should be considered subject to contrary provisions in double taxation treaties. Below is a brief outline of the rules.

(*a*) *Land*. Immovable property is situated where it is actually located.

(*b*) *Registered shares and securities*. The general rule is that these are situated where they are registered or, if transferable upon more than one register, where they would normally be dealt with in the ordinary course of business.

(c) *Bearer shares and securities.* Such assets are transferable by delivery and are situated where the certificate or other document of title is kept (*Attorney-General v Bouwens*, [1838] 4 M & W 171).

(d) *Government securities.* Here the *situs* is determined by the place of registration or inscription or, if bearer securities, where the certificate is kept.

(e) *Specialty debts.* These are debts under a deed. The *situs* is determined by the place where the deed is kept and not, if different, by reference to the country in which the debtor resides.

Where a trust, established by a settlor who was not domiciled in the UK, holds UK *situs* assets, that property will be within the UK inheritance tax regime. However, the use of a non-UK incorporated holding company can change the *situs* of the underlying assets for inheritance tax purposes, even if that holding company is itself resident in the UK (although corporation tax, capital gains tax and income tax issues would, of course, have to be addressed). In addition, where an individual is not domiciled in the UK for inheritance tax purposes and owns shares in a UK private company it may be possible to arrange matters so that the *situs* of the asset is itself changed prior to inclusion in an offshore structure. Such steps require careful planning.

Location of the trust

19.16 For inheritance tax purposes it is not necessary for the trust to be located outside the UK. A trust with trustees resident in the UK which contains trust property not situated in the UK will be as effective for inheritance tax purposes as a trust with trustees resident outside the UK. However, it is usual, to establish the trust outside the UK (i.e. with the trustees or a majority of them being non-resident and the general administration of the trust carried on outside the UK, TCGA 1992, s 69). This is to avoid capital gains tax being payable by the trustees in respect of their gains. It is important, however, to remember that, even though the foreign trustees may not be liable for capital gains tax, if the settlor later becomes domiciled and resident in the UK he will become taxable on all gains realised by the trustees if (broadly) either he or his spouse or their children or their grandchildren or their spouses are beneficially entitled under the trust (TCGA 1992, s 86 and TCGA 1992, Sch 5).

The objective of ensuring that the trustees will not be made liable to capital gains tax will also be achieved by a settlor who is neither domiciled, resident nor ordinarily resident in the UK at the time the settlement is made if the trustee is a resident in the UK provided the trustee carries on a business which consists of, or includes, the management of trusts (TCGA 1992, s 69(2)). The provisions in TCGA 1992, s 86 and TCGA 1992, Sch 5 will become applicable if the settlor later becomes domiciled and resident in the UK. The capital payments charge imposed by TCGA 1992, s 87 will apply to all settlements regardless of the domicile of the settlor.

Normally, however, an individual will want to keep his trust completely offshore in the hope of avoiding future UK taxes and also perhaps, because of an anxiety, probably unnecessary, about the unlikely reintroduction of

19.17 *Immigration and Emigration*

exchange control. He will also be able to obtain the benefit of the remittance basis for income tax on foreign source income and gains for as long as he can defer the acquisition of an actual domicile of choice in the UK.

Clients often ask if one of the trustees may be resident in the UK. This is generally inadvisable although:

(*a*) for capital gains tax purposes the trustees of a trust will be regarded as non-resident if a majority of the trustees are non-resident and the general administration of the trust is carried on abroad (TCGA 1992, s 69), and

(*b*) for income tax purposes the trustees will be regarded as non-resident if there is at least one trustee resident outside the UK and the settlor was neither resident, ordinarily resident nor domiciled in the UK when the settlement was created (FA 1989, s 110).

If a minority trustee is resident in the UK, the trust could accidentally become resident by the removal or death of a non-resident majority trustee. Having a UK resident trustee means there is someone from whom the Inland Revenue may demand and obtain information and against whom assessments may be made.

Where a UK resident is undertaking a trusteeship as part of a business which consists of or includes the management of trusts, or as acting as trustee, there are special capital gains tax rules which apply. This includes such persons as solicitors, or a bank trustee company. In these circumstances, the rules provide that the residence of the trust is to be determined without taking into account the actual residence of the UK professional trustee, provided that the assets were settled by a person who was not UK resident, ordinarily resident or domiciled at that time. The mere fact that the actual administration of the trust is undertaken in the UK is ignored if the majority of the trustees would be deemed resident and ordinarily resident outside the UK.

Trustees and protectors

19.17 For both UK tax and possible exchange control reasons, neither the settlor nor his spouse should be a trustee. This can sometimes cause difficulty for the proposed settlor in the selection of the trustees of his settlement. He may not have any non-resident individual friends or relations whom it would be appropriate or fair to ask to act, and so usually professional trustees or a trustee organisation are appointed. The settlor has to decide on trustees whom he can trust and whose charges he finds acceptable. He may want to appoint a 'protector' to oversee in some respects the actions of the trustees. A protector is usually an individual or company, whose duty is to give or withhold consent to the exercise of certain powers by the trustees. A protector is appointed under the terms of the trust. Generally, the protector should take care that his appointment does not have any tax or other repercussions for him in his country of residence. Although the protector may give some comfort to the settlor over the running of the trust, care must be taken not to make his involvement too complicated, in order to avoid confusion and an unsatisfactory administration of the settlement in practice. For a more detailed outline, see chapter 18 *Investing Abroad*.

Form of the trust

19.18 If an individual wishes to benefit his children and grandchildren to the exclusion of himself and his wife, he should establish either a discretionary trust or an accumulation and maintenance trust. Under current legislation there is little reason to prefer one against the other, since the general UK tax considerations are similar for both. However, a cautious settlor whose beneficiaries will be living in the UK may choose an accumulation and maintenance trust taking the view that future legislation is likely to be kinder to such trusts than wide discretionary trusts and bearing in mind that an accumulation and maintenance trust can be drawn in very wide and flexible terms with discretionary powers to vary the shares of beneficiaries. Given that the trust will be outside the scope of inheritance tax forever, the trust (of whichever type) should be as long-lasting as possible and not vest automatically at an early age or necessarily in the first generation.

Settlor and spouse as beneficiaries

19.19 If an individual and his spouse are to be beneficiaries the type of trust should be considered. The trust could be discretionary with the individual and his wife amongst the class of beneficiaries or the settlor and his wife could have successive life interests under the trust (with the trustees having a discretionary power to distribute capital to them).

If it is desired to continue the settlement on discretionary trusts after the deaths of both the settlor and his spouse for inheritance tax purposes, a life interest trust may not be appropriate. This is because the trust property will not remain excluded property after the death of the survivor of the settlor and his spouse if either of them is domiciled in the UK when his or her interest terminates (IHTA 1984, s 80 and IHTA 1984, s 82). It should be emphasised, however, that the settled property will be excluded property at the survivor's death, provided it is then wholly situated out of the UK.

A trust with successive life interests for the settlor and his spouse will therefore preserve the property (not situated in the UK) as excluded property during their joint lifetimes and up to and including the death of the survivor. However, where the trust continues thereafter as settled property without an interest in possession, it will not remain excluded property if the survivor of the settlor and his spouse is domiciled in the UK when his or her life interest terminates. Where accumulation and maintenance trusts within IHTA 1984, s 71 come into effect at that stage there will still be no liability on the vesting of interests under the trust. If the beneficiaries then become entitled to interests in possession rather than to the capital outright (so that the property remains settled), arguably no inheritance tax charges will arise on the beneficiaries' deaths as the property will be excluded property again (because IHTA 1984, s 82 has no application to settlements with interests in possession).

19.20 Immigration and Emigration

By incorporating a wide overriding power of appointment exercisable by the trustees over the entire trust fund, a life interest trust can be made almost as flexible as a discretionary trust. This would enable the trustees to completely reorganise the beneficial interests under the trust. In addition, a power to accumulate the income of the trust can also be included. This has the advantage of enabling the trustees to roll-up income within the trust, rather than being under an obligation to distribute it to the life tenant. It also prevents the trust having an interest in possession for inheritance tax purposes. Should it be considered important to ensure that the trust does satisfy the inheritance tax interest in possession criteria, consideration should be given to the use of an underlying investment holding company resident outside the UK to act as a 'money trap' thereby enabling *de facto* accumulation of income.

A discretionary trust should constitute excluded property during its life but it is not completely certain that the 'reserved benefit' rules will not apply resulting in the trust property being treated as part of the settlor's estate on death. If he is domiciled in the UK at that time the property would not be excluded property and therefore subject to inheritance tax. As stated above, the Inland Revenue have confirmed this view (CTO Advanced Instruction Manual D.8). However, as noted earlier, difficulties may arise in such circumstances where a reservation ceases otherwise than on death. By way of contrast, a life interest trust should not give rise to any problems under the 'reserved benefit rules', because the settlor's life interest is not a benefit reserved in any property given away but is an interest retained by the settlor, the remainder to which is the subject matter of the gift.

Since the income tax and capital gains tax treatments of both types of trust are very similar in certain respects, the decision will often be determined by the personality of the settlor. Many individuals seem happier with the life interest settlement, under which they will have a more substantial interest than simple membership of a class of potential beneficiaries as is the case under a discretionary trust. On the other hand, an individual who wants maximum flexibility may well opt for the discretionary trust.

Capital gains tax

19.20 The taxation of non-UK resident trusts established by a settlor who later becomes resident in the UK and finally domiciled here is subject to a complex set of rules.

Gains realised by offshore trustees cannot be attributed to a settlor until the settlor becomes both resident or ordinarily resident *and* domiciled in the UK (TCGA 1992, s 86). However, a beneficiary will be subject to the capital payments charge under TCGA 1992, s 87 regardless of the residence or domicile status of the settlor. A beneficiary will not make a chargeable gain under section 87 if he is not domiciled in the UK at some time in the year in which he receives the capital payment.

These rules are highly advantageous for non-UK domiciled individuals resident in the UK. By using the appropriate offshore trust structure it is possible for gains to be made and the proceeds ultimately enjoyed in the UK without incurring an immediate charge to capital gains tax, as would have been the case had the assets been retained by the individual concerned.

For a settlor resident but not yet domiciled in the UK it is essential that the trust assets are periodically rebased for capital gains tax purposes so that the base cost of the assets held are as high as possible prior to the settlor becoming domiciled in the UK. This is because, if he has an interest in the settlement when be becomes domiciled in the UK, future gains will become immediately chargeable under the offshore settlor charge (TCGA 1992, s 86) rather than being chargeable when capital payments are made under the capital payments charge (TCGA 1992, s 87).

It is important to appreciate that the capital gains tax status of a trust can fluctuate over the course of the years. Whilst the settlor is non-UK domiciled the trust is outside the offshore settlor charge. Once the settlor becomes both resident and domiciled in the UK the trust will be brought within that charge. After the settlor's death the trust will revert to being within the capital payments charge alone. Indeed, if the beneficiaries who receive capital payments are either not resident or not domiciled in the UK, the trust gains may escape capital gains tax entirely. Yet it is still important to bear in mind that, irrespective of the trustees residence status, they will be subject to UK capital gains tax where they hold assets used in a UK trade undertaken on their behalf through a branch or agency there. This situation would arise where the trustees own farmland which is run on their behalf by their manager. In practice, there are a number of ways round this, including ensuring that the land is held by one legal entity, whilst being farmed by another. Alternatively, the entire farming business could be incorporated.

Income tax

19.21 The UK has a complex régime of anti-avoidance provisions aimed at nullifying any income tax advantages which might be obtained through a resident establishing a trust for his own benefit, or for his spouse, or for his unmarried children under the age of 18. These are contained in ICTA 1988, Part XV. Under ICTA 1988, s 660A, if a settlor or his spouse can benefit as a result of the exercise of any discretion under a trust, all the settlement's income will be treated as his regardless of whether or not the trustees distribute that income. Where the settlor is UK resident but non-domiciled, foreign source income within this provision will only be taxed if remitted to the UK. However, all UK source income will be assessed upon an arising basis.

In addition to this provision the UK has a number of anti-avoidance provisions which seek to nullify the income tax advantages to be derived from offshore trusts.

ICTA 1988, s 739 is an extremely widely drawn anti-avoidance provision which seeks to prevent the avoidance of income tax by individuals who are ordinarily resident in the UK and who establish offshore structures to shelter income. The aim of the legislation is to prevent such individuals transferring funds offshore, leading to tax-free accumulation of income. These rules only apply where a settlor or his spouse is capable of benefiting under the terms of

19.21 *Immigration and Emigration*

the trust. In general terms, the net effect of the provisions is to 'look through' any offshore arrangement, deeming the income received to be that of the settlor/beneficiary. The *quantum* of the assessable income is, in general, the gross income received by the trustees.

The scope of section 739 came under detailed scrutiny by the House of Lords in the case of *CIR v Willoughby & Another, HL [1997] STC 995; [1997] 4 All ER 65*. Although the case was more concerned with the tax treatment of offshore personal portfolio bonds (see chapter 7 *Insurance* under paragraph 7.20), it was confirmed that in order for section 739 to apply, it was essential that the transfer of assets should be made by an individual who was UK ordinarily resident at that time. Such a finding was consistent with the House of Lord's decision in *Vestey v CIR, HL 1979, [1980] STC 10; [1979] 3 All ER 976*, but at variance with the earlier decisions of *Congreve and Congreve v CIR, HL 1948, 30 TC 163; [1948] 1 All ER 948*, and *Herdman v CIR, HL 1969, 45 TC 394* which the Court declined to follow. However, for income arising after 25 November 1996, section 739 applies regardless of the ordinary residence status of the individual when the transfer is made. In addition, section 739 will apply where the purpose of a transfer is to avoid any form of direct taxation (rather than just income tax) (ICTA 1988, s 739(1A)).

In *R v Allen; R v Dimsey, HL [2001] STC 1537* it was argued unsuccessfully that because the income of the transferee offshore companies was deemed to be the individual transferor's income, it was therefore also deemed not to be the company's income. The House of Lords held that on the true construction of ICTA 1988, s 739(2) a foreign transferee of assets was not relieved of liability to tax on income. The effect of section 739 is confined to be confined to the transferor.

In calculating the income which is chargeable under section 739, the transferor is only entitled to such deductions and reliefs as he would have been allowed had he actually received the income (ICTA 1988, s 743(2)). Trust management expenses are generally not deductible. Relief for foreign taxes is allowable only to the extent that such taxes would have been paid if the income had been received by the individual himself. No relief is given if the foreign tax arose because the income was diverted abroad rather than having arisen there itself. Where a foreign investment holding company, owned by an offshore trust, itself owns UK shares and securities, the transferor will be assessed under ICTA 1988, s 739 on dividends paid by the UK company and will receive the applicable tax credit to set against his UK taxation liability on the dividends.

There are two defences to these anti-avoidance provisions which are contained in ICTA 1988, s 741. Essentially, an individual has to establish that either:

(a) there was no UK tax avoidance motive involved; or

(b) it is a *bona fide* commercial arrangement not designed for the purposes of avoiding taxation.

The *Willoughby* decision provided further insight into the operation of the defence available under ICTA 1988, s 741(a). The House of Lords held that as the offshore policies or bonds held by Professor Willoughby were themselves subject to a separate statutory charging regime it would not be possible to

Immigration and Emigration 19.21

allege that the transfers to them had been effected with a view to avoiding income tax. Accordingly, it was also held that Professor Willoughby could avail himself of the defence set out in ICTA 1988, s 741(a), as the transaction itself was entirely commercial.

Where ICTA 1988, s 739 does apply, it is important to bear in mind that the remittance basis of taxation will apply for non-UK domiciled individuals in respect of non-UK source income. UK source income will be taxed on the arising basis.

ICTA 1988, s 740 applies where, as a result of a transfer of assets, income becomes payable to a person resident or domiciled outside the UK, and an ordinarily resident individual receives a benefit provided out of those assets. The provisions apply regardless of the tax status of the settlor, but are only relevant where the UK beneficiary is not otherwise liable to income tax under ICTA 1988, s 739. As is the case under ICTA 1988, s 739, the rule will only apply where there is a UK tax avoidance motive which leads to the creation of the structure, and taxpayers can therefore rely upon the same defences outlined above for ICTA 1988, s 739.

The rationale behind the legislation is to negate any tax advantage in permitting gross funds to accumulate offshore. In essence, the rules apply a remittance basis with UK beneficiaries paying tax when the benefit is received. If the trustees confer a benefit on a beneficiary at a time when they have undistributed income which could be used to benefit him, he is liable to income tax on the value of that benefit to the extent of the undistributed income. Where there is insufficient relevant income to match the value of a benefit, future receipts of relevant income can be set against the unmatched element of any benefit and will result in a liability to income tax arising at that time. Tax credits on UK dividend income cannot be utilised.

The definition of benefits is particularly wide and includes benefits in kind, such as the interest foregone on an interest-free loan, as well as straightforward distributions of capital. The Inland Revenue consider that the free use of property is a 'benefit'. There has been much comment about whether or not an interest-free loan repayable on demand conferred a benefit on the recipient under TCGA 1992, s 97. Interestingly, in *Billingham (Inspector of Taxes) v Cooper; Edwards (Inspector of Taxes) v Fisher, CA [2001] STC 1177* the Court of Appeal held that an interest-free loan to the life tenant repayable on demand was a benefit and by conferring such a benefit, a capital payment had been made under TCGA 1992, s 97. (The Special Commissioners had held that the benefit of such a loan was nil.) The appointment of a life interest is not a benefit within the meaning of the section because it is not 'provided out of assets' as required by the provisions (Law Society: agreed note of meeting with the Board of Inland Revenue 1981). The remittance basis of taxation can apply to non-domiciled individuals where benefits are received outside the UK.

FA 1997, s 81 effectively reversed the *Willoughby* decision for UK resident but non-domiciled beneficiaries. Generally, there is now a transparency under ICTA 1988, s 660A and ICTA 1988, s 739 so that if income is segregated and kept offshore, the capital can then be remitted to the UK tax free. It is therefore essential that income and capital are kept separate at all times. It is

19.22 *Immigration and Emigration*

generally safer to pay the income by way of dividend or an appointment to a non-resident beneficiary before any benefit is made available to a beneficiary resident in the UK. If this is not done, beneficiaries other than the settlor or his spouse may be subject to income tax under ICTA 1988, s 740 if they receive a benefit.

Capital v income

19.22 Where ICTA 1988, s 739 or the income tax settlement rules apply, as distinct from cases where ICTA 1988, s 740 is in point, it is usually beneficial for offshore trusts established by non-domiciled individuals to realise capital rather than income related profits. Whilst the settlor retains his non-UK domicile, capital profits will not constitute 'trust gains' and any application of these will not result in an immediately assessable remittance. By way of contrast, non-UK source income is taxed on a remittance basis and does not enjoy this advantage. Care has to be taken by appropriately segregating resources to avoid any inadvertent remittance of income.

There are two noteworthy instances where an apparent capital profit has an income nature for UK tax purposes.

The first is under the accrued income scheme where the capital profit taken on bond washing is recharacterised as income and is therefore subject to the income tax settlement provisions and ICTA 1988, ss 739 and 740 considered above (ICTA 1988, s 720).

The second instance arises under the offshore funds rules. A charge to tax under Schedule D, Case VI arises following the disposal of a material interest in an offshore fund which is or has been at any relevant time (and not necessarily throughout the time it was held) a non-qualifying offshore fund (ICTA 1988, s 761). ICTA 1988, s 759 makes it clear that an offshore fund is to be equated with a 'collective investment scheme' as defined by the Financial Services and Markets Act 2000. An offshore insurance policy is not an offshore fund. Therefore, an individual resident in the UK but non-domiciled will have a UK tax liability on a chargeable event in relation to an offshore life policy even if he does not remit the money to the UK. Material interests exist where it could be reasonably expected that the value of the interest in the offshore fund could be realised within seven years from acquisition (ICTA 1988, s 759(2)). The owner must be able to realise an amount reasonably approximate in value to the proportion that his interest bears to the market value of the offshore fund as a whole.

Wealth tax and exchange control

19.23 The main reason for putting assets into a foreign trust at a time when the settlor is not domiciled in the UK is usually to keep those assets outside the scope of inheritance tax and to establish a favoured vehicle for capital gains tax purposes. Other reasons may well be to avoid a future UK wealth tax or future UK exchange controls. The chances of the re-introduction of exchange control or the introduction of a wealth tax may appear remote and in any event it is uncertain whether, if such tax or exchange controls were introduced, a trust would circumvent them. Often, however, nothing is lost by putting assets into a trust (except the costs of formation and administration) and it may provide some insurance against future developments.

General points

19.24 The following general points should be remembered.

1. If a UK domicile is not acquired immediately upon, or within a short time after, arrival in the UK, any funds held abroad in the immigrant's personal ownership representing foreign source income or the realised gains of foreign assets, may be used outside the UK for expenditure as appropriate (e.g. for travel, holidays or maintenance of a property abroad), without involving a liability to UK income tax or capital gains tax because neither income nor capital will have been remitted to the UK.

2. Wherever possible, an immigrant should, before arrival (and preferably in the tax year before arrival), sell and repurchase personally held capital assets to ensure new base costs for future UK capital gains tax purposes. The same applies to any trust property previously settled by him. This is to achieve a higher base cost for the trust assets before the trust comes within the scope of the capital payments charge (TCGA 1992, s 87) or the offshore settlor charge (TCGA 1992, s 86 and TCGA 1992, Sch 5). Such sales and purchases will also ensure the cessation of old sources of income and the creation of new sources, so that income arising from the original assets before the immigrant becomes resident in the UK can be remitted to the UK without incurring an income tax charge. He should also close foreign deposit accounts and open new accounts at different banks located outside the UK for the same reason.

   Any income arising from new sources should of course be kept outside the UK.

3. An immigrant should make a new will. Probably, if he is going to be domiciled in the UK, this will should be written under English law. If, however, he retains real property abroad it may (subject to local advice) be appropriate for him to make a will under the local law to deal specifically with that property, leaving his new English will to deal with his remaining assets.

The short-term visitor

19.25 This section deals with the short-term visitor who becomes resident in the UK but does not acquire a UK domicile.

(*a*) He should ensure that his behaviour does not suggest that he is acquiring a domicile in the UK, since if he did he would be within the charge to inheritance tax not only on his UK assets but also on all his worldwide assets.

(b) He should keep his assets in the UK to a minimum (ideally below the threshold for the actual payment of inheritance tax). For instance, his main bank account should be held abroad rather than in the UK.

(c) He may need to purchase accommodation in the UK. This can be arranged either through a non-UK resident trust structure, or through a direct purchase in his own name or in the joint names of himself and his wife by means of a non-UK loan charged on the property. The loan (plus any accrued interest) should be repaid after he leaves the UK. He should not repay any part of the loan while he is resident in the UK. This is to avoid income arising abroad being treated as having been received by him in the UK under the provisions relating to constructive remittances in ICTA 1988, s 65(6). He may, however, pay interest on the loan without giving rise to a constructive remittance. He may consider purchasing a property, in his own name or in joint names, and effect life assurance (outside the UK) to provide funds to meet any inheritance tax liability in respect of the property either on his death or if the property is in joint names on the death of the survivor of him and his wife. The holding of UK situs assets through the medium of a non-resident company owned by the individual will be enough on its own to take the assets outside the scope of inheritance tax, but where the property is the individual's residence, the fact that no trust is interposed between the individual and the company may make it more difficult for him to counter an attack under ICTA 1988, ss 145 and 146 — see under 19.12 above. This is because the individual will have a much greater connection with the company and its directors by reason of his ownership of the company's shares.

(d) Funds required in the UK should be obtained by remitting capital from abroad. Care should be taken, through separate capital and income bank accounts, to demonstrate that remittances have clearly been made from a capital source unless income can be remitted free of UK tax under a double tax treaty. It is important not to remit capital which includes overseas capital gains realised after the individual becomes resident in the UK. The Inland Revenue take the view that any capital gain element cannot be separated from the original capital. They will assess capital gains tax on a remittance of capital, even though prior to remittance an amount equal to the realised capital gain may have been separated (Inland Revenue Capital Gains Manual CG 25410, 25411).

The short-term visitor is not within the inheritance tax regime except in relation to UK assets. Even then he may be protected under a double tax treaty. However, he will probably still be subject to the tax and succession laws of his home country in which case his scope for estate planning may well be governed by those laws. He should, therefore, take advice in that country, as well as in the UK, before taking any steps whilst in the UK.

The long-term emigrant

19.26 An individual leaving the UK is not in a position to make disposals of assets which are outside the scope of inheritance tax until he has lost his UK domicile and his deemed UK domicile. Even if he loses his domicile under the general law (i.e. he acquires an overseas domicile of choice) soon after leaving the UK, under IHTA 1984, s 267 he will have to wait for at least three calendar years (and possibly three complete tax years) before his property will be excluded property. See under 19.6 above.

Even the transfer of non-UK situs assets will not avoid inheritance tax until the donor has ceased to be domiciled in the UK and three years have elapsed. However, the transfer of certain British Government securities ('exempt gilts') may be made free of inheritance tax by a person not domiciled under the general law even if he is deemed to be domiciled under IHTA 1984, s 267(1). A way of reducing the value of assets after an individual has emigrated may be to borrow on the security of such assets and to invest the borrowed funds in exempt gilts. Alternatively, a possibly more cost effective solution would be to cover the inheritance tax liability which would arise if the emigrant died within the relevant period by entering into a term insurance policy written in trust for the benefit of his heirs.

A potentially exempt transfer made when the donor was domiciled in the UK will still be chargeable even if he is no longer domiciled in the UK at his death.

A relevant question in planning for the emigrant is where the individual's heirs live. If they live in the UK estate planning will still be substantially affected by inheritance tax and other UK taxes, but generally it will be possible for a non-domiciled individual (i.e. an individual who has shed his UK domicile under the general law for at least three years) to give or bequeath non-UK property to his heirs who are resident in the UK, or to set up an offshore trust for them, without liability to inheritance tax.

It is very important for the emigrant to have a clear understanding of the tax regime of his new country before he leaves the UK. There may well be timing considerations in that action might need to be taken before residence is taken up in the new country (for example, the creation of a discretionary trust to avoid taxes in that country). On the other hand, if such action is taken too soon it will involve an inheritance tax liability since the emigrant will not have shed his UK domicile. A temporary period in a 'third' country will probably not be helpful in that a domicile of choice will not be acquired there. It is often possible to devise an arrangement which has advantages in both the UK and the new country, but each case must be considered carefully on its precise facts.

If the emigrant is a beneficiary under a foreign trust, there could be timing problems in obtaining distributions of income or capital from the trust. Generally, from the UK tax viewpoint, distributions should be delayed until he becomes non-resident, but by then he may be resident in another country and distributions affected by tax in that country. Again, every case has to be examined on its own particular facts.

Where a person is considering emigrating, it is often advisable to defer the setting up of any settlements until the UK domicile is lost to retain complete flexibility and to avoid potentially locking the trust assets into the UK tax net.

19.27 *Immigration and Emigration*

The short-term emigrant

19.27 The short-term emigrant is not really an emigrant at all. He is usually someone who ceases to be resident or ordinarily resident in the UK for a period, for example, through full-time employment abroad which lasts for a period including a full tax year.

He is likely to remain domiciled in the UK and therefore subject to the inheritance tax regime in the same way as any UK domiciliary. Therefore, opportunities for estate planning generally do not exist. It may be possible, however, for an individual working abroad earning a large salary, subject only to low local income tax, to make substantial regular gifts out of his net income which would be exempt from inheritance tax under the 'normal expenditure' exemption (IHTA 1984, s 21). To take advantage of this exemption, it is advisable for the individual not simply to make regular voluntary gifts but to create a commitment to do so (for example, by effecting life policies in trust involving regular premium payments or by entering into a deed of covenant to make regular payments). However, consideration should be given to the position of the payments when the individual returns to the UK and has a much lower net surplus income.

20 The Foreign Client

Introduction

20.1 This chapter deals with a foreign individual who does not himself become resident or domiciled in the UK, but becomes involved with UK laws and with actual or potential liabilities to UK taxation through:

(*a*) the ownership of assets in the UK; or

(*b*) the wish to benefit persons resident in the UK.

It is assumed that the individual is and remains domiciled, resident and ordinarily resident outside the UK. For a consideration of the meaning of these terms, and the concept of 'deemed domicile' which applies for inheritance tax purposes only, see chapter 19 *Immigration and Emigration*.

Tax considerations

20.2 First, the UK tax situation of a foreign individual who directly owns an asset in the UK should be considered. Subject to the provisions of any applicable double tax treaty (see below), the asset will be within the scope of inheritance tax either on a lifetime transfer by the owner or in the event of his death. It may, however, be a transfer eligible for exemption under IHTA 1984, Part II which include:

(*a*) transfers between spouses;

(*b*) annual exemption;

(*c*) small gifts;

(*d*) normal expenditure out of income;

(*e*) gifts in consideration of marriage; and

(*f*) gifts to charities or political parties or for national purposes or public benefit.

An asset may also be eligible for business relief, agricultural property relief or relief on woodlands under IHTA 1984, Part V.

For example, if a foreign individual gives or bequeaths an asset to his spouse (wherever she is domiciled) or to a body recognised as a charity under English law, the transfer will be exempt, and if he invests in agricultural or business property he may be eligible for the appropriate relief. For further details see

20.3 The Foreign Client

chapter 2 *Lifetime Planning* (for exemptions), chapter 10 *The Family Business*, chapter 11 *The Family Farm* and chapter 12 *Woodlands*. However, from a capital gains tax perspective, a capital gains tax charge can be levied on disposals made by non-UK residents of UK sited trading-related assets (TCGA 1992, s 10) (see later).

A foreign individual may make a lifetime transfer of a UK asset by accident (for example, a sale at an undervalue) or without his realising the implications of a particular transfer. It will be more usual for him to die owning a UK asset. Very often he will have acquired the asset without much thought of the possibility of UK inheritance tax being payable in the event of his death. Not all countries levy a charge to tax on death or, where they do, at rates as high as in the UK. Alternatively, the tax may operate as a true form of inheritance tax, so it is the recipient of the property bequeathed who has to pay the tax, rather than the estate.

Excluded property

20.3 Certain property situated in the UK is excluded from the scope of inheritance tax.

(a) Under IHTA 1984, s 6(2), certain British Government securities (known as 'exempt gilts') are excluded property for inheritance tax purposes if they are in the beneficial ownership of a person domiciled and ordinarily resident outside the UK. 'Domicile' for this purpose is not extended by the deemed domicile provisions of IHTA 1984, s 267 and so exempt gilts are also held by emigrants who do not want to suffer inheritance tax on their assets if they should die within the period of three years after their departure from the UK (IHTA 1984, s 267(1)(2)).

(b) Under IHTA 1984, s 6(3) certain property owned by a person who is domiciled in the Channel Islands or the Isle of Man is exempt, such as war savings certificates, national savings certificates, premium bonds, deposits with the National Savings Bank or a trustee savings bank and any certified contractual savings scheme within ICTA 1988, s 326.

(c) Exemption from inheritance tax on death is given by IHTA 1984, s 157 to a qualifying foreign currency bank account, at a bank or post office in the UK, which is owned by a person who immediately before his death was not domiciled, resident or ordinarily resident in the UK.

Capital gains tax

20.4 The disposal of an asset situated in the UK by a foreign individual will not generally give rise to a capital gains tax liability. This is because a person is chargeable to capital gains tax in respect of chargeable gains accruing to him in a year of assessment during any part of which he is resident in the UK or during which he is ordinarily resident in the UK (TCGA 1992, s 2(1)).

However, TCGA 1992, s 10 provides that a person who is neither resident nor ordinarily resident in the UK *will* be chargeable to capital gains tax on gains accruing to him on a disposal, at a time when he is carrying on a trade, profession or vocation in the UK through a branch or agency, of:

(a) assets in the UK used in or for the purposes of the trade, profession or vocation at or before that time,

(b) assets in the UK used or held for the purposes of the branch or agency, and

(c) assets acquired for use by or for the purposes of the branch or agency. It would seem that on a strict reading of the legislation this charge applies whether or not the asset is situated in the UK. The Inland Revenue's view, however, appears to be that the charge applies only to UK-situated assets (Inland Revenue Capital Gains Manual CG25531).

A chargeable gain can arise in respect of such assets where the non-resident person ceases to carry on the trade, profession or vocation through the branch or agency or the assets become situated outside the UK (TCGA 1992, s 25). In practice, it is possible to side-step these rules. Generally speaking, the trading entity should be kept apart from the vehicle used to hold the valuable asset likely to generate the gain. Farming activities would represent a typical example where land could be held by a vehicle other than the one which was going to farm it.

TCGA 1992, s 10A provides that individuals who have acquired assets before they leave the UK for a period of residence abroad of less than five complete tax years will remain chargeable to capital gains tax on gains made on those assets while abroad. Gains made after the year of departure will be chargeable in the year of return. These provisions will apply if the following conditions are satisfied.

(i) The individual must be a previous resident in the UK who is resuming tax residence in the UK.

(ii) The individual has been resident outside the UK for less than five complete tax years between the year of departure and the year of return.

(iii) The individual was resident or ordinarily resident in the UK for some part of at least four of the seven years preceding the year of departure.

Income tax

20.5 A foreign individual will be liable to UK income tax on income arising from a source in the UK. This is not considered in depth as it is beyond the scope of this chapter.

Double tax agreements

20.6 The liability of the foreign individual, or his estate, to inheritance tax, capital gains tax and income tax may be relieved or modified under a

20.7 The Foreign Client

double tax agreement between the UK and his country of residence. For example, the provisions of TCGA 1992, s 10 (see above) do not apply to a person who under any relevant double tax agreement is exempt from income tax for the particular year of assessment in respect of his profits from the branch or agency. The charge on temporary non-residents under TCGA 1992, s 10A is specifically stated to be without prejudice to any right to claim relief in accordance with any double taxation relief arrangements (TCGA 1992, s 10A(10)).

Generally, the double tax agreements deal with the interaction of inheritance tax with similar taxes in other jurisdictions by detailing rules for determining the domicile of an individual for the purposes of the agreement, and allowing primary taxing rights to the country in which the individual is so domiciled. Charges on the basis of situs are usually restricted to land and business property. There are currently double tax agreements applying to, or capable of applying to, inheritance tax between the UK and Ireland, France, India, Italy, the Netherlands, Pakistan, South Africa, Sweden, Switzerland and the United States of America.

In the absence of a relevant double tax agreement, the Inland Revenue will allow unilateral relief by way of credit for a foreign tax similar in character to inheritance tax which has been imposed on property upon a disposition or event on which inheritance tax is chargeable in respect of the same property (IHTA 1984, s 159).

Planning points

20.7 It is now appropriate to consider whether it is possible to avoid any of the liabilities to UK taxation discussed above for a foreign individual who wishes, for whatever reason, to own assets in this country.

It is possible for inheritance tax to be avoided on a UK asset if it is owned by a company incorporated outside the UK rather than by a foreign individual directly. This arrangement 'converts' the UK asset into a non-UK asset since the property will be 'excluded property' (by virtue of IHTA 1984, s 6(1)). This will generally be sufficient protection against inheritance tax for the foreign individual who is never likely to become domiciled in the UK. Care should be taken when UK land is being transferred to a connected company as a stamp duty charge based on market value can arise under FA 2000, s 119. This is discussed in more detail in Chapter 19 *Immigration and Emigration*.

Such a company structure runs the risk of the Inland Revenue attempting to impose an income tax charge under ICTA 1988, ss 145 and 146 where living accommodation owned by the company is provided to an individual. The possible impact of these provisions is discussed in detail in chapter 19 *Immigration and Emigration* under paragraphs 19.12 and 19.25. There can be no charge under these sections where the individual is neither resident nor ordinarily resident in the UK, unless he performs any of his duties as a director or 'deemed director' in the UK (Schedule E, Case II). In the case of a 'deemed director' it is hard to see what duties he could owe to the company which could be performed in the UK and there would therefore seem to be no scope for the charge to bite. Alternatively, some relief against the charge

The Foreign Client **20.8**

(whether by way of credit or exemption) may be available under the terms of any applicable double tax treaty. There was initially a concern that the extension to the transfer pricing rules introduced by the Finance Act 1998 could apply to such a structure. The Inland Revenue have, however, stated that they will not take this point. This is discussed in more detail in chapter 19 *Immigration and Emigration*.

A method of reducing exposure to inheritance tax on death in respect of a UK asset would be to borrow in the UK for the purposes of the investment so that on death the value of the loan could be deducted from the value of the UK assets (IHTA 1984, s 5 and IHTA 1984, s 162). A loan could also be taken out abroad, to reduce the net estate chargeable to inheritance tax but would need to be secured by a charge on property situated in the UK (IHTA 1984, s 162(5)).

If funding has already been used to purchase a UK asset, a loan secured by a charge on the asset could still be taken out and then the funds invested in excluded property, for example, exempt gilts (see above).

Inheritance tax will not be payable on an asset owned by an individual in the UK if it passes to his spouse on his death, either under his will or under the relevant succession laws or through the right of survivorship under a joint tenancy.

A foreign individual may consider it worthwhile to take out life assurance to provide funds to meet an inheritance tax liability in respect of UK assets in the event of his death. Any such policy should either be effected outside the UK or written in trust to avoid the proceeds being treated as part of his taxable estate in the UK. If the policy is effected outside the UK, the proceeds would be remitted to the UK after his death to assist in paying the tax.

Other considerations

Probate

20.8 If an individual dies owning assets in the UK, it will usually be necessary for a grant of probate or letters of administration to be obtained in this country. This will normally be an ancillary grant to the administration of the deceased's estate in his home country, issued to the person(s) entitled to administer the deceased's estate under the law of his home country. The procedure involves submitting an account of the UK assets to the Inland Revenue, together with a statement giving the reason why it is considered that the deceased died domiciled in a foreign country. No grant will be issued until all the tax due is paid. All this can involve time and expense, often in order to administer a small estate in the UK. For example, the proceeds of a UK bank account will not be released by the bank without production of a UK grant of probate. It is also unwise for any UK assets to be disposed of or transferred abroad without production of a UK grant and without the tax position having been settled, since the person so disposing of or transferring the asset may be treated as an executor *de son*

20.9 The Foreign Client

tort and accountable for any inheritance tax payable (*New York Breweries Co Ltd v Attorney-General, [1899] AC 62*).

A will in respect of which a grant of probate has been issued is a public document which can be inspected by anyone. Double tax agreements often permit the exchange of information between two Revenue authorities. The administration of the UK estate of a foreign individual can result in the exchange of information between the relevant authorities. Therefore, where UK assets are owned, consideration should be given to making a will governed by UK law dealing solely with these assets.

Exchange control

20.9 If a foreign individual personally owns assets in the UK, he takes a chance that they may be restricted under some future UK exchange controls or other currency rules. Exchange control regulations in the UK were suspended in 1979, and subsequently repealed. Their reintroduction is extremely unlikely.

Wealth tax

20.10 Individuals may also be concerned that a left wing government may impose an annual wealth tax on assets located in the UK owned by individuals who are not resident or domiciled in the UK. There is nothing to indicate that the present Government intends to do so.

Planning

20.11 There are generally no ways of avoiding these considerations for a foreign individual who wishes to own UK assets beneficially himself. The use of a UK nominee to hold the assets on his behalf will not avoid the need to obtain a grant of probate (or letters of administration) nor the payment of UK taxes. The use of a foreign nominee may avoid the need for a grant of probate although the nominee may itself constitute an executor *de son tort* if it deals with the assets following the death (see *CIR v Stype Investments (Jersey) Ltd, [1982] 3 All ER 419; [1982] 3 WLR 228*). This structure does not avoid the obligation to submit an account of the assets for inheritance tax purposes, and to pay the tax due.

Where the only UK asset is a joint bank account, on the death of one of the owners its ownership will automatically pass to the survivor. The bank will normally only want to see the death certificate and not a UK grant of probate. If, however, the survivor is not the deceased's spouse there will be a duty to submit an inheritance tax account and pay any liability due (unless the account is a qualifying foreign currency bank account which is exempt from inheritance tax, see under 20.3 above).

The safest way to avoid the need to obtain a UK grant of probate is for the foreign individual to incorporate a company outside the UK to own the property as discussed earlier in the chapter. In the event of the death of the owner of the company a grant of probate is not applicable or necessary for UK assets owned in that way.

For foreign investors wishing to invest in shares in UK companies, there are various types of offshore collective investment schemes which avoid the problems of directly owning assets located in the UK.

Benefitting persons resident in the UK

Outright gifts

20.12 The simplest way in which a foreign individual can benefit a person resident in the UK is to make a gift to such a person of non-UK assets, e.g. foreign currency or foreign investments, which are subsequently remitted to the UK by the donee as desired. A gift made in this way will not involve any inheritance tax liability. For capital gains tax purposes, the donee will have acquired the asset given to him on the date of the gift at its market value on that date.

It is important to ensure that any gift of cash is made in a way which avoids the gift being of a UK asset and therefore liable to inheritance tax. A gift of cash in any currency at a bank in the UK will be liable to tax. The delivery of a sterling cheque cleared through a London bank will render the amount liable. A gift of a foreign bank account or the opening of another account at the same foreign bank as that of the donor and the transfer of sterling from one account to the other are ways of implementing gifts of sterling without inheritance tax problems.

Offshore settlements

20.13 If the foreign donor does not wish to make outright gifts to his beneficiaries in the UK, or his objective is to benefit his beneficiaries in the most tax efficient way, he may consider establishing a trust outside the UK. Assuming that he settles non-UK assets, the creation of the trust will not involve any UK tax liability. During its life the trust will not usually attract any liability to inheritance tax, assuming that its funds continue not to include UK assets. This applies regardless of whether the settlement is a life interest trust for a UK based life tenant, an accumulation and maintenance trust for a class consisting of or including UK based beneficiaries or a discretionary trust for a similar class. Disposals by the trustees resident outside the UK will not be liable to UK capital gains tax. However, the capital payments charge will apply where capital payments are made to beneficiaries who are both resident and domiciled in the UK when the gain is deemed to accrue to them. (TCGA 1992, s 87).

If income is distributed to UK resident beneficiaries, they will be liable to income tax in the normal way, unless they are non-UK domiciled and the distributions are not remitted here. If benefits, which are not otherwise liable to income tax, are given by the trustees to a beneficiary ordinarily resident in the UK, he will be liable to income tax to the extent that the value of the benefit falls within the 'relevant income' of the trust, but only if UK tax avoidance is the motive for the transfer (ICTA 1988, s 740). This is subject to relief being given for a non-domiciled beneficiary where there has been no

20.14 The Foreign Client

remittance of the relevant income to, and the benefit was not received in, the UK. This will catch, for example, capital payments to a beneficiary ordinarily resident in the UK, if income has been accumulated in the trust (or in any underlying foreign company) rather than distributed.

With regard to the trustees, provided at least one trustee is resident outside the UK, *all* of them will be treated as resident outside the UK for income tax purposes (FA 1989, s 110) and therefore they will only be liable to tax on UK source income.

UK settlements

20.14 It may also be worth considering a trust with UK resident trustees. Inheritance tax may be avoided if non-UK assets are settled and retained throughout the life of the trust. In addition, the trustees will not be liable to capital gains tax if they carry on their trusteeship as part of their trust management business (TCGA 1992, s 69(2)). This is because such persons carrying on the business of managing settlements are treated as not resident in relation to the settlement if the property was settled by an individual not domiciled, resident or ordinarily resident in the UK at that time.

ICTA 1988, s 740 has no application to a trust with UK resident trustees. However, the trustees will be liable to UK income tax on all trust income in the normal way. Income of a UK resident discretionary or accumulation and maintenance trust will be liable to tax at 34% year by year, subject to the special Schedule F rate of 25% on dividends. An offshore trust will not normally be so liable (assuming it does not have UK source income) but income tax liabilities may arise under ICTA 1988, s 740. Care is required in particular where an offshore trust subject to ICTA 1988, s 740 is imported into the UK. Whilst in general terms the trust will not normally generate 'fresh' relevant income, importation does not cause any previously retained income to cease to be 'relevant income'.

It can be seen that there are advantages for a foreign individual, wishing to create a trust for beneficiaries who are likely to remain based in the UK, to create a trust governed by UK law and having a 'professional' UK trustee. To avoid inheritance tax the trust assets must remain located outside the UK. If, however, the settlor establishes a simple accumulation and maintenance trust, it is not necessary for the trust fund to consist always of foreign assets, since no inheritance tax liabilities arise during the life of the trust. This is assuming the capital vests absolutely when the beneficiaries reach the vesting age, which must not be greater than 25. If the trust is to continue after the age of 25 (i.e. the beneficiaries become entitled to life interests in possession at 25 rather than to the capital outright), to avoid inheritance tax when a beneficiary's life interest comes to an end, the trust fund must not be invested in UK investments. There is a capital gains tax advantage in an offshore trust continuing after the beneficiary reaches 25. Disposals by the trustees will not usually be liable to capital gains tax. No capital gains tax liability will arise on a UK resident beneficiary unless he receives a capital payment (wherever the funds are invested). A beneficiary resident in the UK who receives the assets outright at the age of 25, will be liable to capital gains tax on disposals made by him. In addition, if the beneficiary is also domiciled in the UK, the assets, wherever situated, will form part of the beneficiary's estate for inheritance tax purposes.

Conclusions

20.15 For the wealthy foreign individual it may be appropriate to have both a trust in the UK and a trust abroad, both of which might include UK residents as beneficiaries. The former would be regarded as a 'spending' fund (i.e. the capital and income would be paid out to the beneficiaries as necessary), and the latter would be a 'roll-up' fund with neither capital nor income being remitted to the UK except in emergency situations.

The foreign individual who wishes to benefit beneficiaries resident in the UK should take advice in his home country regardless of the proposed structure to ensure that he is aware of the tax and other implications of his proposed action in that country as well as the UK.

The foreign individual who on his death wishes to benefit persons resident in the UK should also be advised to consider setting up, by his will, a continuing trust (probably outside the UK) along the lines suggested above rather than making outright bequests which would bring the property bequeathed into the UK tax net. The trust could either be contained in the will itself or be established by the individual during his lifetime, with his will simply directing the relevant assets into the trust.

21 Lifetime Planning — A Case Study

A person will generally plan his estate with the primary intention of benefiting his family. The individual's family will, therefore, normally be the people who primarily benefit from his estate planning.

Where the individual has grown-up children, and particularly where these children have children of their own, it will usually be appropriate for the other members of the individual's family to consider planning their own estates in conjunction with the individual's plans for his own estate.

The purpose of this chapter is to illustrate how such an estate planning strategy can be developed and the need for it to be continually reviewed. This is done by using the example of a single man ('Henry Clerestory') and considering some of the factors to be taken into account when, for example, he comes of age, gets married, becomes a parent and subsequently a grandparent, and eventually enters his final years.

Planning when single

It is never too soon to consider planning one's estate. In some cases, the question should be addressed as soon as a person reaches the age of 18.

> Henry Clerestory is the eldest son of David and Eleanor Clerestory. He has just reached 18 and will shortly be going to university. He has no substantial assets of his own and very little income. He has two younger brothers, Richard aged 12 and Charles aged 10. His parents have independent means.

In the circumstances, the planning of Henry's estate can be postponed until it is larger.

> Henry leaves university at 21 and takes up a full-time job. At this stage, he has a regular income but still a small estate.

Again, the planning of his estate can be postponed.

> A year later, his grandmother dies and leaves him £50,000 which he puts towards the purchase of a flat worth £200,000. He takes out a mortgage to finance the purchase and calculates that on his death his estate should be worth almost £245,000.

At this stage it would be appropriate to make a simple will. Since his parents are not dependent upon him for support, Henry could leave the whole of his estate to his two brothers, Richard and Charles, who are both still unmarried minors. He could appoint his parents, David and Eleanor, as his executors.

Lifetime Planning — A Case Study

There is a potential inheritance tax saving to the Clerestory family in Henry leaving his estate directly to his two brothers. If he were to leave his estate to his parents, there would be no charge to inheritance tax because it is less than the nil rate band. However, his parents would probably want to pass this and other property on to Henry's two brothers (either by lifetime transfers or by will). Unless a deed of variation altering the effects of the will is entered into within the two years following Henry's death, inheritance tax could be charged a second time on the transfers by David and Eleanor. Therefore, generally it is inadvisable, for inheritance tax reasons, to bequeath or transfer property up the family tree, since it may well be taxed both on the way up and on the way back down. Henry can avoid this potential double taxation charge by leaving his estate directly to his brothers.

In the event of Henry's premature death, there may also be a small income tax advantage to the Clerestory family from Henry leaving his estate directly to his two brothers rather than to his parents. If he were to draw up his will in favour of his parents (or, for that matter, if he were to die intestate) on his death his parents would receive the whole of his estate. The property would then belong to David and Eleanor and the income arising from it would be taxed as part of their respective incomes, probably in the hands of at least one of them at the higher rate. On the other hand, if Henry were to leave his estate directly to Richard and Charles, on his death they would receive the whole of his property and the income arising from it would be taxed as their income. Each of them would be able to set their personal allowance against their share of the income and would have the advantage of being taxed at the lower rates. Moreover, if David and Eleanor were subsequently to make a gift of the property to Richard and Charles (or were to execute a deed of variation varying Henry's will in favour of Richard and Charles) the income from the property would continue to be taxed as their unearned income whilst Richard and Charles were unmarried minors (ICTA 1988, s 660B).

When making his will, Henry could also consider whether he would like to benefit someone outside his immediate family, such as a charity, friend or distant relative.

On getting married

> Henry marries Fiona. She has a brother and sister. They buy a new flat, worth £300,000, which they hold as beneficial joint tenants so that if either of them dies it will pass automatically to the survivor. The purchase is financed by a repayment mortgage. They have also taken out a policy of life assurance, the proceeds of which will be used to repay the mortgage on the death of the first of Henry and Fiona. Henry's employer has a pension scheme which provides for a lump sum to be paid to Henry's wife and family in the event of his death in service. The scheme also provides for a small widow's pension. In addition, Henry has a few small investments.

For the first time Henry has someone he wishes to provide for and he should calculate the size of his estate. Having done so he may come to the conclusion that he has not yet made adequate provision for Fiona, who might not be working at the time of his death.

Lifetime Planning — A Case Study

Life assurance

Henry has a number of options open to him.

(*a*) He could take out a level term policy to cover the next few years, after which he could review the position. The policy probably ought to be written in trust for Fiona and any children they might have. The advantage of this option is that term assurance is comparatively cheap.

(*b*) He could take out an endowment policy maturing in ten years (or possibly longer). This would have the advantage of giving him an investment on which he should have some return in his lifetime, while also insuring his life. If the policy were not written in trust, the proceeds on his death would form part of his estate in the normal way.

(*c*) He could take out a convertible term policy which he could convert later into an endowment or whole life policy. This ability to convert would guard against the risk that Henry might through injury or illness become uninsurable at normal rates before, at some later date, needing to effect an endowment policy if he wants, for example, to take on a larger mortgage.

Making a will

Henry should also make a new will as his old one will have been automatically revoked on his marriage to Fiona. Unfortunately, the rules on intestacy do not automatically provide for a surviving spouse in the manner that the deceased might wish. As Henry and Fiona have no children, under the intestacy rules on Henry's death Fiona would be entitled to:

(*a*) his personal chattels; plus

(*b*) a statutory legacy of £200,000; plus

(*c*) half the residue absolutely.

The other half of residue would pass to Henry's parents, David and Eleanor (or, if they had died, to Richard and Charles). For these purposes, Henry's half share in the flat would not be included in his estate since it would pass automatically to Fiona as the surviving joint tenant. It is likely, therefore, that if Henry were to die intestate the whole of his estate would pass to Fiona.

When drawing up a will Henry should consider the following.

1. What would happen if he were to die and Fiona were to die shortly thereafter? Under the intestacy rules, his estate would probably pass in whole to Fiona. As she is, as yet, childless, on her death their combined estate would pass to her parents, failing whom to her brother and sister. Henry might prefer his estate to pass to Richard and Charles in these circumstances.

2. What would happen if he and Fiona had had a child by the time he died? Under the intestacy rules, on Henry's death Fiona would be entitled to his personal chattels plus a statutory legacy of only

Lifetime Planning — A Case Study

£125,000 plus a life interest in half the residue. The remaining residue would pass to their child or children 'on the statutory trusts', i.e. at 18. Fiona would have the right to redeem the life interest for a capital sum out of residue but, apart from this, if the children were minors, there would be no scope for rearranging the estate without an application to the court. The expense and delay of making such an application to the court can easily be avoided by Henry making a new will.

Henry makes a new will leaving two small legacies and the whole of the residue to Fiona. He appoints her as sole executrix, with the proviso that should Fiona have died before him then David and Eleanor are to be his executors and the whole of residue is to pass to any children of him and Fiona in equal shares, failing whom to his brothers, Richard and Charles, in equal shares.

There are no tax pitfalls which he needs to avoid. There will be no charge to inheritance tax on assets passing to Fiona (assuming that she is domiciled in the UK for inheritance tax purposes). She will also have the benefit of the capital gains tax free uplift in the value of Henry's estate on death.

For the same reasons it is sensible for Fiona to also make a will. Subject to any legacies, she should leave the whole of residue to Henry and appoint him as sole executor, with a similar proviso that, if he should predecease her, then her parents are to be executors and the whole of the residue is to pass to their children in equal shares, failing whom to her brother and sister.

Other provisions in the wills

Both wills should also stipulate that, should the testator not be survived by the other spouse by a certain period of time, typically three months ('the survivorship period'), then the other spouse must be treated for the purposes of the will as having died before the testator. A special clause allowing the executors to make payments to the other spouse for his or her maintenance during the survivorship period should also be included.

Adequate powers of investment for their executors and trustees must be included since there is the possibility of a continuing will trust until any children come of age.

Commorientes

If Henry and Fiona were to die simultaneously, or in circumstances where no-one could ascertain which of them had died before the other, and there was no survivorship period specified in their wills, their estates would devolve according to the 'commorientes' rule. This rule means that for succession purposes the elder of the two spouses is deemed to have died first (Law of Property Act 1925, s 184). Where the elder of the spouses dies intestate, when administering the estate of the elder spouse only the younger spouse is presumed to have predeceased. However, for inheritance tax purposes their estates would be charged to tax as if they had died at the same instant (IHTA 1984, s 4(2)).

Becoming a parent

> Henry and Fiona have just had their first child, Simon. They hope to send him to an independent school.

Henry should consider taking out a unit-linked endowment policy to mature in ten years' time and write it in trust for Simon. Next year, he can take out a similar policy, maturing ten years thereafter, and so on. Alternatively, Henry could take out a series of policies maturing in years 11, 12, etc. The proceeds on maturity of each policy will provide for Simon's school fees from the age of ten onwards. As other children are born, Henry can take out additional policies.

Alternatively, he might like to consider taking out an individual savings account ('ISA'). In 2002/03 he can invest up to £7,000 in an ISA. All income arising is tax-free and there is no capital gains tax liability on the sale of any shares in the ISA.

Since Henry and Fiona have both made wills, each leaving the bulk of his or her estate to the other, the potential snags under the intestacy rules have been avoided. However, they should also consider what would happen if they were to die in rapid succession but outside the survivorship period of three months.

> Henry and Fiona calculate that together their estates on death would be worth £355,000.

Under their present wills, the residue of the estate of the first to die would pass to the survivor, whose estate would devolve according to the survivor's will and thereby pass to their son, Simon. There would be no inheritance tax charge on the property passing to the surviving spouse on the first death, but inheritance tax would be charged on the property passing to Simon on the second death. While inheritance tax on £355,000 would be only £42,000 at present rates, they must bear in mind that their estates are likely to increase in value and that the rates of tax might be changed.

> Twelve years later, Henry and Fiona have three children, Simon, Hilary and Rupert. Henry has a good salary and Fiona has started paid work again. Fiona has recently received legacies from her grandmother and godmother and they calculate that Henry's estate is worth £200,000 and Fiona's £380,000. They reckon that they now have some disposable capital.

For inheritance tax purposes they should try to transfer property between each other so they are each able to make full use of the nil rate tax band. Also, with surplus cash, some sort of gift to the children is sensible.

Inter-spouse transfers

A lifetime gift by Fiona to Henry will:

(a) be completely exempt from inheritance tax (IHTA 1984, s 18);

(b) transfer Fiona's base cost in the property to Henry for capital gains tax purposes (TCGA 1992, s 58); and

(c) be exempt from stamp duty if the appropriate certificate is given under the Stamp Duty (Exempt Instruments) Regulations 1987.

Lifetime Planning — A Case Study

Thus, assets can be passed between Fiona and Henry free of tax.

As estates are separately charged to inheritance tax, the manner in which assets are held by Henry and Fiona could affect their children. Under their present wills, if they were to die within three months of each other, both their estates would pass directly to Simon, Hilary and Rupert. It is therefore sensible for Henry and Fiona to ensure that full use of Henry's nil rate band is made on his death. Since the nil rate tax band is currently £0–£250,000, if Fiona were to transfer property worth £50,000 to Henry to make their estates less unequal, this would potentially reduce their overall tax liability by £20,000.

Gifts to children

Two types of gift in favour of children are leniently treated for inheritance tax purposes. These are:

(*a*) an outright gift (or gift on bare trust); and

(*b*) a gift into an accumulation and maintenance settlement or a settlement in which another individual has a beneficial interest in possession.

Such gifts are potentially exempt transfers and will be exempt from inheritance tax provided the relevant transferor survives for a period of seven years after making the gift and no benefit is reserved.

Outright gifts

An outright gift direct into a child's name has administrative disadvantages. The property will become the child's and only he will have the power to invest it, spend it or realise it for cash. Whilst he is a minor, these powers will be more limited than the corresponding powers of an adult. Moreover, since the child cannot appoint his mother or father as a trustee for him, his parents will have no legal right, or even power, to handle the property on his behalf. In addition, the settlor would continue to be taxed on the income of the assets given (ICTA 1988, s 660B).

Bare trusts

A bare trust can be created in favour of a child by transferring property to an adult (the bare trustee) and instructing him to hold the property for the benefit of the child. The child must be absolutely entitled as against the bare trustee, who must not have any discretion to withhold income or capital from the child. When the child reaches 18, he will be able to call for the property to be vested in him by the trustee and to give the trustee a valid receipt for the property, thereby discharging the trustee from the trust.

For capital gains tax purposes, the bare trustee is ignored and the child is treated as owning the property. As with an outright gift, there is a disposal of the property by the settlor. Since the child is treated as owning the property in the trust, the trustee will be able to utilise the child's annual exemption (£7,700 for the current year) on capital gains realised by the trust.

For income tax purposes, if the settlor is the child's parent, any income of the trust arising before he reaches the age of 18 will be deemed to be the settlor's unearned income.

Parents can be bare trustees for their children. Once they hold the property as bare trustees, however, they will not be able to treat the property as their own thereafter. Any money or property of the trust will have to be paid to or for the benefit of the children no later than the children's eighteenth birthdays. Otherwise bare trusts are simple, require the minimum of administration and, where the parent settlors are trustees, do not require the continuing involvement of anyone outside the family.

Accumulation and maintenance settlements

IHTA 1984, s 71 sets out the conditions which a settlement must satisfy to be an accumulation and maintenance settlement for inheritance tax purposes.

(*a*)   One or more of the beneficiaries must become entitled to the property, or to the income from the property, on or before reaching a specified age of no more than 25.

(*b*)   There must be no-one who is entitled to an interest in possession in the property, and the trustees must be directed to accumulate the income (i.e. invest it and treat it as an accretion to capital) insofar as it is not applied by them towards the maintenance, education or benefit of the beneficiaries.

(*c*)   There must be a living beneficiary when the trust is created.

(*d*)   There is a time limit of 25 years from the commencement of the trust after which it will automatically cease to be an accumulation and maintenance settlement (if it has not done so already) unless all those who are or have been beneficiaries are:

   (i)   the grandchildren of a common grandparent; or

   (ii)   the children, widows or widowers of such grandchildren who were themselves beneficiaries but who died before attaining a vested interest in the property or its income.

An advantage of using an accumulation and maintenance settlement as compared to a bare trust is that provision can be made for beneficiaries as yet unborn. In addition, the amount held under a bare trust for each child must be fixed at the time of the gift and, on attaining the age of 18, each child will become entitled to call for his property. That is a considerable drawback because few children are mature enough to handle considerable sums at the age of 18. Under an accumulation and maintenance settlement, it is possible to postpone indefinitely the time when the child receives the capital of his share by making any advance subject to the trustees' discretion. In many cases the time when the beneficiary becomes entitled to the income from his share may also be postponed, although the extent to which this is possible will depend on the rules concerning accumulation of income in the Law of Property Act 1925, s 164 and the Perpetuities and Accumulation Act 1964, s 13. By selecting an appropriate accumulation period it may often be possible to accumulate income to the age of 21 or 25.

Under an accumulation and maintenance settlement it is also possible to vary the size of each child's share, for example, to provide more for a child whose needs are greater. Such a settlement is, therefore, more flexible than a bare trust although it will require more administration, such as separate tax returns by the trustees as opposed to simpler returns for the beneficiary.

For inheritance tax purposes, the creation of the settlement and any subsequent transfer of property to it will, as with a bare trust, be potentially exempt transfers. During the life of the settlement, the share of a child can be reduced (and another child's share increased) without any inheritance tax charge provided the child whose share is reduced has not yet acquired the right to be paid any income from the settlement and the child whose share is increased is still under 25. There will be no tax charge should another child be born, or one of the children die under the age of 25, again provided that the child whose share ceases, or is reduced, has not yet acquired the right to be paid any income from the settlement.

For income tax purposes, if the settlor is a parent, any income (or capital to the extent of the trust income) of the trust paid to or for the benefit of his children whilst they are under 18 and unmarried will be taxed as part of the settlor's unearned income. Where income is accumulated by the trustees and added to the capital of the trust, the income will be taxed at the rate applicable to trusts (34% for the current year subject to the reduced 25% rate on UK dividend (Schedule F) income). Trustees are not entitled to any annual personal allowance for income tax purposes (ICTA 1988, s 256).

For capital gains tax purposes there is a disposal by the settlor to the trustees. Unlike a bare trust, however, the beneficiaries are not treated as owning the property. The trustees are charged to capital gains tax as a single and continuing body (TCGA 1992, s 69(1)). They are charged to tax on the capital gains of the trust at a rate of 34% (TCGA 1992, s 5), but have an annual exemption of only one half that of an individual i.e. £3,850 for 2002/03, and possibly even less if the settlor has made more than one settlement (TCGA 1992, Sch 1).

Interest in possession settlements

Under the terms of such trusts one or more beneficiaries are entitled to the income from the trust fund although the vesting of capital can be postponed or held back for another generation.

For inheritance tax purposes, the settlor's transfer of property to the settlement will generally be a potentially exempt transfer (IHTA 1984, s 3A(1)(2)) as will any termination of the beneficiary's interest by surrender or assignment (IHTA 1984, ss 3A(6), 51, 52). The inheritance tax consequences of an interest in possession settlement need, therefore, be no worse than those arising on an outright gift.

For capital gains tax purposes, there is a disposal of the property by the settlor to the trustees. While the interest in possession continues, the trustees are

Lifetime Planning — A Case Study

charged to capital gains tax as a single and continuing body (TCGA 1992, s 69(1)) on the capital gains of the trust at a rate of 34% (TCGA 1992, s 4). They have an annual exemption of one half that for an individual i.e. £3,850 for 2002/03 (or less if the settlor has made more than one settlement (TCGA 1992, Sch 1)).

For income tax purposes, a beneficiary entitled to the income from the settlement will be charged to tax on that income by aggregation with his other income. Where, however, the settlor is a parent of the beneficiary, all the income of the settlement to which the beneficiary is entitled before he reaches the age of 18 will be deemed to be the settlor's unearned income.

> Henry and Fiona wish to give their children £35,000 made up of £31,000 in quoted shares and £4,000 currently on deposit. However, some of the income or capital will need to be spent on the children before the age of 18 as school fees have increased more than they anticipated. They would also like to use some of the money in trust to send the children on holidays on their own, when they are older, or, possibly, to buy them a boat.

Under the circumstances it might be prudent to reduce the amount of the gift to £25,000 and retain the balance to meet the expenditure. Shares worth £15,000 could be put into bare trust for the children Simon, Hilary and Rupert in equal shares absolutely. As capital gains tax hold-over relief will not be available on the gift, Henry and Fiona should select investments which (taking into account both gains and losses) have unrealised gains of less than £7,700 (their individual annual capital gains tax exemption). If they can do this, no capital gains tax liability will arise on the transfer into the trust. It should be possible for the trustees to subsequently sell the shares free of capital gains tax since each of the children could set their annual exemption against their share of any gains realised. If the trust fund is then invested in assets with good capital growth but producing little or no income, capital from the bare trust could be built up for the children, in all probability with no capital gains tax. The income arising in the trusts until the beneficiary concerned reaches the age of 18 will be deemed to be that of the settlors (i.e. Fiona and Henry).

With the remaining £15,000 Henry and Fiona could create an accumulation and maintenance settlement in favour of their children, as a class, (to provide for the possibility that they might have further children) in equal shares, with power to vary the shares. They should try to avoid any capital gains tax liability on the creation of the settlement in the same way as for the bare trust.

They can add to both of the trusts at a later date if they find they have more disposable capital.

Additionally, Henry and Fiona each have an annual inheritance tax exemption of £3,000 which they can use to make totally exempt gifts to, or in trust for, their children.

> Just under six years later, the eldest son Simon has reached 18 and is about to go to university. The assets of the bare trust are worth £24,000. Henry has no definite plans as to how he intends to maintain Simon at university but he does have sufficient disposable income to do so.

Since Simon is now an adult he can call for his one third share under the bare trust to be transferred to him by Henry and Fiona (the bare trustees). If he prefers his parents to look after the investments on his behalf he can leave them vested in them. Simon should make a simple will leaving the whole of his estate to his brother and sister absolutely in equal shares.

Gaining a daughter-in-law

Simon has now left university. He is 22 and has just started work. He has recently become engaged to Caroline and would like to buy a flat.

Henry and Fiona can each give £5,000 to Simon as a gift in consideration of marriage which will be completely exempt from inheritance tax under IHTA 1984, s 22.

Simon is still a beneficiary under the accumulation and maintenance settlement. Provided the trustees have a power to advance a beneficiary's share to him before attaining the specified vesting age, Henry and Fiona as trustees can advance one third of the capital of the trust fund to Simon. The advance may give rise to a capital gains tax charge unless Simon has not yet become entitled to an interest in possession under the settlement. If not, then hold-over relief under TCGA 1992, s 260 will be available.

It would also be an appropriate time for Henry and Fiona to review their wills. With the passage of time they may well want to change some of the legacies and they ought to start thinking about the possibility of their becoming grandparents. As Henry and Fiona are now better off and their children will soon be financially independent, it is possible that the survivor may not need to inherit everything if one of them should die. They cannot, of course, be sure of this. However, by providing for some property to be left otherwise than to the surviving spouse on the first death, a husband and wife can make an overall tax saving. For example, if both had assets of £300,000 and only £50,000 were given directly to the survivor, this would reduce the aggregate tax paid on both their deaths from £140,000 to £40,000. A possible solution is a discretionary will for each of them, including as beneficiaries each other and their children and issue.

Under the discretionary trust, the trustees would be able (within the two years of the testator's death) to distribute the residuary estate among the testator's surviving spouse and issue in such amounts and on such trusts as they consider appropriate. An appointment within two years will not give rise to an inheritance tax charge as it will be read back into the will for inheritance tax purposes (IHTA 1984, s 144). The advantage of this is that only the amount which the surviving spouse actually requires needs to be given to the survivor. There is flexibility as to the division of the balance between children and grandchildren, with some perhaps being appointed on accumulation and maintenance trusts for the grandchildren. This could be done even if there were no grandchildren at the date of his death, provided a grandchild was born within the following two years. This is preferable to leaving property to the children and relying on them to vary the will. Although this has the same consequences for inheritance tax purposes, the children would be regarded as the settlors of any accumulation and maintenance trusts created for the grandchildren which would result in distributions of income or capital to the grandchildren being taxed as the income of the children (ICTA 1988, s 660B).

Since the income from the property left to the grandchildren under a discretionary will will be taxed as their income, this might even be more beneficial to the children than if they had been left the property themselves. Discretionary wills do not appeal to everybody as they leave the devolution of the estate in the hands of the executors, who have to be relied upon to carry out the wishes of the testator.

Alternatively, each spouse could leave their residuary estates to the other, relying on them to vary the will so as to pass property on to the children and/or grandchildren.

Losing a parent

Henry's father David, has just died, leaving the whole of his estate, worth £300,000, to his wife, Eleanor. The major asset of the estate is the family home worth £200,000 and Eleanor cannot afford to give up the income from the other investments.

To reduce the inheritance tax liability on Eleanor's death, she could give some of the property to her children, Henry and his brothers Richard and Charles. Ideally, full use should be made of David's nil rate band, by executing a deed of variation of his will within the two years following his death. For inheritance tax purposes, under IHTA 1984, s 142, such a variation will take effect as if it were part of the original will. Eleanor could vary the will so that the house is held on trust for her, Henry, Richard and Charles as tenants in common in equal shares. David will then have left £150,000 of property to Henry, Richard and Charles, without an inheritance tax liability. There should not be any reserved benefit in her continuing to occupy the house because IHTA 1984, s 142 provides that 'this Act shall apply as if the variation had been effected by the deceased or, as the case may be, the disclaimed benefit had never been conferred', and FA 1986, s 114(5) provides that the gifts with reservation of benefit provisions (FA 1986, s 102) are to be 'construed as one with the [Inheritance Tax] Act 1984'. As her occupation of the house will depend entirely upon her interest as a tenant in common and the property will not be held in a settlement for inheritance tax purposes, she will not be treated as having an interest in possession in the whole house (distinguishing *IRC v Lloyds Private Banking Ltd, Ch D [1998] STC 559*).

Becoming a grandparent

Eleanor has now died, leaving Henry one third of the residue of her estate amounting to £60,000. Caroline is pregnant with Henry and Fiona's first grandchild. Henry also has free disposable capital of his own amounting to £55,000.

When the baby is born, Henry could vary Eleanor's will so that the £60,000 is held on accumulation and maintenance trusts for his grandchildren. This will have the same tax benefits as the accumulation and maintenance settlement which Henry and Fiona have already made in favour of Simon, Hilary and Rupert, with the added benefit that, because Henry will not be the parent of any of the beneficiaries, ICTA 1988, s 660B will not apply to income or capital of the trust paid to or for the benefit of a beneficiary. Where an election under TCGA 1992, s 62(7) is made, the variation will not result in any disposal and for these purposes the variation will be read back into the will.

Once the baby is born, Henry might also put his free disposable capital of £55,000 into an accumulation and maintenance trust for his grandchildren (not just Caroline's baby but future grandchildren as well). The gift will be a potentially exempt transfer for inheritance tax purposes. To avoid a capital gains tax charge, Henry should select investments which do not have unrealised gains in excess of his annual exemption. Alternatively, he might consider establishing a discretionary trust, making a hold-over election under TCGA 1992, s 260 and then converting the trust into an accumulation and maintenance trust before its first ten-year anniversary. A gift to a discretionary trust will not be a potentially exempt transfer for inheritance tax purposes, but it will not give rise to an immediate tax charge as the value transferred falls within Henry's nil rate band. If Henry survives the gift for seven years, it will drop out of cumulation, giving Henry a full nil rate band again.

Entering the final years

Henry is now 70 and he and Fiona have retired. Henry's estate is now worth £365,000 and Fiona's £385,000. Their house, which they own as beneficial joint tenants, is worth £300,000. The remainder of their estates consists of a cottage, which is owned by Fiona and which she and Henry still use, worth £60,000, and £390,000 in investments. There are no life insurance policies under which moneys would become payable in the event of either of them dying; the term policies have expired and all the endowment policies have matured. Henry and Fiona have very substantial pension incomes and have decided they can give away £500,000. They intend to sell the family home and retire to a smaller house which they believe will cost about £100,000. They therefore decide to give away £300,000 immediately, and a further £200,000 when they sell the house. They do not want to make outright gifts of the money to the children and they feel that their grandchildren are already well provided for by the accumulation and maintenance settlement.

Provided neither of them has used his or her annual exemption for the current and previous tax years they could each put up to £256,000 (the £250,000 nil rate band plus the current and preceding year's annual exemptions of £3,000 each) into a discretionary settlement as joint settlors free of inheritance tax and, provided they both survived for seven years, the transfers would fall out of their cumulative totals.

The terms of the discretionary settlement must ensure that Henry and Fiona are not beneficiaries to avoid the application of the reservation of benefit rules in FA 1986, s 102. They could transfer £390,000 to the settlement straightaway in shares. However, to avoid a capital gains tax charge, a hold-over election under TCGA 1992, s 260 would have to be made. This would put unrealised capital gains into the settlement. However, if Henry and Fiona wait until the house is sold, the proceeds of sale will be exempt from capital gains tax and can therefore be passed to the settlement without any hold-over election being necessary. It is usually advisable for an older donor to retain assets pregnant with capital gains, since there would be a tax-free uplift in their base cost on

Lifetime Planning — A Case Study

his death, and transfer, during his lifetime, assets which have little unrealised capital gain. Given that they will need £100,000 from the sale proceeds of this present house to buy the new house (since no hold-over relief will be available for any investments), Henry and Fiona settle £300,000 (i.e. £500,000 − (£300,000 − £100,000)) in investments and make a hold-over election in respect of these assets. That is an amount calculated to enable them to make the maximum possible transfer of cash when the house is sold.

> A year later, Henry and Fiona sell their house and move to the country. They have realised the £200,000 and transferred £194,000 of it to the discretionary trust. The strain of moving house has caused Henry to have a heart attack. His doctors warn him and Fiona that he has only an even chance of surviving the next three years.

Since they have moved into a new tax year, they can each make transfers of up to a further £3,000 within the annual exemption. This is clearly the first priority.

In view of his health, Henry should consider executing an enduring power of attorney in the statutory form under the Enduring Powers of Attorney Act 1985, appointing Fiona as his attorney. Unlike an ordinary power of attorney, this will enable Fiona to act on Henry's behalf even if he loses mental capacity.

> Eighteen months later, Henry is very ill and has not long to live. He and Fiona no longer use the cottage and she decides she would like to give it to the children.

However, since Henry has probably only a few months to live, Fiona could transfer the cottage (and any other investments pregnant with capital gains) to Henry. When he dies, the cottage can pass to her under his will and she can then give it to the children by way of potentially exempt transfers. The advantage gained is a capital gains tax free uplift in the base cost of the cottage.

> This they do. Six months later Henry dies.

Summary — when to consider estate planning

Every family should have an estate planning strategy. In an ideal world, this would be subject to continuous review. In the real world, someone may, for example, make a will and at the same time draw up a plan for his estate. Some of the plan will be put into effect, but after a while the whole process will lose momentum and be left in an incomplete form. Years later some major event will occur within the family and once again the question of estate planning will be addressed.

The following milestones in a family's history are sensible occasions on which to carry out a review of the family's estate planning strategy.

(*a*)   On buying a house.

(*b*)   On becoming engaged.

(*c*)   On the births of children or grandchildren.

Lifetime Planning — A Case Study

(*d*) On each member of the family reaching 18.

(*e*) Before each member of the family reaches 25.

(*f*) On the sale of a family business.

(*g*) On separation or divorce.

(*h*) On retirement.

(*i*) On a member of the family becoming frail or terminally ill.

(*j*) On, and within the two years following, the death of any member of the family.

Table of Cases

A

Abacus Trust Company (Isle of Man) Ltd v NSPCC,
[2001] STC 1344   3.16
Attorney-General v Boden,
KB [1912] 1 KB 539   10.8, 10.11
Attorney-General v Bouwens,
[1838] 4 M & W 171   19.15
Attorney-General v Ralli,
KB (1936) 15 ATC 523   10.18
Attorney-General v Seccombe,
KB [1911] 2 KB 688   2.15
Attorney-General v Worrall,
QB [1895] 1 QB 99   2.15

B

Baird's Executors v CIR,
Lands Tribunal 1990, SVC 188   11.12
Barclays Bank Trust Co Ltd v CIR,
Sp C [1998] SSCD 125 (Sp C 158)   10.2
Barrett v Powell,
Ch D 1998, 70 TC 432; [1998] STC 283   11.21
Beatty's Will Trusts (No 2)(Re),
(unreported)   6.8
Beckman v CIR,
Sp C [2000] STCD 59 (Sp C 226)   10.13
Bennett and Others v CIR,
Ch D 1994, [1995] STC 54   2.7
Bernstein, CIR v
CA 1960, 39 TC 391; [1960]1 All ER 320   3.28
Billingham (Inspector of Taxes) v Cooper,
CA [2001] STC 1177   19.21
Bond v Pickford,
CA [1983] STC 517   5.11, 5.14, 5.15, 6.4, 16.22
Breadner v Granville-Grossman
[2001] Ch 523   3.16
Brockbank (Re),
Ch D [1948] 1 All ER 287   3.20, 5.7
Brown's Executors v CIR,
Sp C [1996] SSCD 277 (Sp C 83)   16.7
Browne v Browne,
(Times Law Reports, 25 November 1988)   3.8

Table of Cases

Buckinghamshire (Earl of) Settlement Trusts, Cole and Another v
Hope-Morley and Another (In re),
TLR 29 March 1977   5.19
Bullock, CIR v,
CA [1976] STC 409; [1976] 3 All ER 353   19.4, 19.10
Burdett-Coutts v CIR,
[1960] 1 WLR 1027; [1960] 3 All ER 153   10.11
Burkinyoung (Burkinyoung's Executor) v CIR,
Sp C [1995] SSCD 29 (Sp C 3)   16.7

C

Chapman v Chapman,
[1954] AC 429; [1954] 1 All ER 978   5.7
Chick & Chick v Commissioners of Stamp Duties of New South Wales,
PC [1958] AC 435; [1958] All ER 623   2.15
Civil Engineer v CIR,
Sp C 2001, [2002] SSCD 72 (Sp C 299)   19.4
Clore's Settlement Trust (Re),
[1966] 1 WLR 955; [1966] 2 All ER 272   3.27
Commissioners of Stamp Duties of New South Wales v
Perpetual Trustee Co Ltd,
PC [1943] AC 425   2.15
Commissioners of Stamp Duties of New South Wales v Way,
PC [1952] AC 95; [1952] 1 All ER 198   10.24
Congreve and Congreve v CIR,
HL 1948, 30 TC 163; [1948] 1 All ER 948   19.21
Cooper v Billingham,
CA 2001 [2001] STC 1177   6.4
Cottle v Coldicott,
Sp C [1995] SSCD 239 (Sp C 40)   11.16
Cowan v Scargill,
[1984] 2 All ER 750   3.11
Craven v White,
HL [1988] STC 476; [1988] 3 All ER 495   16.33
Crossman, CIR v,
[1939] AC 26   11.12

D

Dalby v London Life Assurance Co,
(1854) 15 CB 365   7.23
Delamere's Settlement Trusts (Re),
CA 1983, [1984] 1 WLR 813; [1984] 1 All ER 584   3.23
Dennis's Settlement Trusts (Re)
[1942] 1 All ER 520   3.31
Dixon v CIR,
Sp C 2001, [2002] SSCD 53 (Sp C 297)   11.3, 11.4
Dougal (Re),
CS [1981] STC 54   16.25

Table of Cases

Dreyfus (Camille and Henry) Foundation Inc v CIR,
HL 1955, [1956] AC 39; 3 All ER 97   13.1

E

Edwards (Inspector of Taxes) v Fisher,
CA [2001] STC 1177   19.21
Evan's Settlement (Re),
[1967] 1 WLR 1294; [1967] 3 All ER 343   3.28
Eversden and another (executors of Greenstock deceased), CIR v,
Ch D 2002 EWHC 1360(Ch)   2.15, 4.47, 9.4, 9.11, 9.14
Ewart v Taylor,
Ch D [1983] STC 721   5.11, 16.22

F

Farmer & Giles (Farmer's Executors) v CIR,
Sp C [1999] SSCD 321 (Sp C 216)   11.5, 16.7
Faulkner (trustee of Adams, dec'd) v CIR,
Sp C [2001] SSCD 112 (Sp C 278)   9.4, 16.19
Fisher v Edwards,
CA 2001 [2001] STC 1177   6.4
Forster's Settlement (Re),
[1942] 1 All ER 180   3.29
Fox's (Lady) Executors v CIR,
CA [1994] STC 360   11.14
Frankland v CIR,
CA [1997] STC 1450   2.17, 4.21, 16.21, 17.16
Fry (Re),
[1946] 2 All ER 106   2.25

G

Garland v Archer-Shee,
HL 1930, 15 TC 693; [1931] AC 212   18.10
Gartside v CIR,
HL 1967, [1968] 2 WLR 277; [1968] 1 All ER 121   19.14
Green and others v Cobham and others,
Ch D 2000, [2002] STC 820   3.16
Greenbank v Pickles
(The Times 7.11.2000)   11.12, 11.14
Grey (Earl) v Attorney-General,
KB [1900] AC 124; [1900-1903] All ER 268   2.15
Grindal v Hooper
(The Times 8 February 2000)   9.2

H

Harding & Leigh (Loveday's Executors) v CIR,
Sp C [1997] SSCD 321 (Sp C 140)   2.17, 16.21, 17.17
Hashmi & Hashmi,
CA 3 May 2002 unreported   3.7

Table of Cases

Hastings-Bass (deceased),
   [1975] CH 25   3.16
Herdman v CIR,
   HL 1969, 45 TC 394   19.21
Holmes and Another v McMullan and Others (re Ratcliffe (deceased)),
   Ch D [1999] STC 262   16.23

I

Ingram & Palmer-Tomkinson (Lady Ingram's Executors) v CIR,
   HL 1998, [1999] STC 37   2.15, 9.9

J

J v J,
   [1989] 1 All ER 1121   3.8
Jewell v McGowan and others,
   CA [2002] All ER (D) 387   11.3
John M Whiteford & Sons, CIR v,
   CS 1962, 40 TC 379   11.4
Jones & Another (Balls' Administrators) v CIR,
   Ch D [1997] STC 358   17.19

K

Keckskemeti v Rubens Rabin & Co,
   TLR 31.12.1992   9.2
Keeler's Settlement Trust (Re),
   [1981] 1 Ch 156; [1981] 1 All ER 888   2.15
Kershaw's Trust (Re),
   1868 LR 6 Eq 322   3.26
Knight v Knight,
   [1840] 3 Beav. 148   3.6
Korner & Others v CIR,
   HL 1969, 45 TC 287   11.4

L

Landau (a bankrupt) (Re),
   [1997] 3 All ER 322   8.16
Levy, CIR v,
   Ch D 1982, 56 TC 68; [1982] STC 442   2.30
Lindsay v CIR,
   CS 1953, 34 TC 289   11.4
Lloyds Private Banking Ltd, CIR v,
   Ch D [1998] STC 559   9.4, 16.19
Lockhart v Harker & Others (re Benham's Will Trusts),
   Ch D 1994, [1995] STC 210   16.23

M

MacGregor v Adcock,
   Ch D [1977] STC 206; [1977] 3 All ER 65   10.6

Table of Cases

MacNiven v Westmoreland Investments Ltd,
   HL [2001] STC 237   2.17
Marren v Ingles,
   HL [1980] STC 500; [1980] 3 All ER 95   15.12
Marshall v Kerr,
   HL [1994] STC 638; [1994] 2 All ER 106   16.22, 17.11, 17.14
Melville and Others v CIR,
   Ch D [2000] STC 628   2.15
   CA [2001] STC 1271   5.39
Miller & Others v CIR,
   CS 1986 [1987] STC 108   5.23
Moxon's Will Trust (Re),
   [1958] 1 All ER 386; [1958] 1 WLR 165   3.27
Mrs F and S2 (Personal Representatives of F deceased) v CIR,
   Sp C 1999, [2000] SSCD 1 (Sp C 219)   19.4
Muir and Williams v Muir,
   (1943) AC 468   3.19
Munro v Commissioners of Stamp Duties of New South Wales,
   PC [1934] AC 61   2.15, 9.9, 10.13

N

Nadin v CIR,
   Sp C [1997] SSCD 107 (Sp C 112)   2.7
New York Breweries Co Ltd v Attorney-General,
   [1899] AC 62   20.8
Nichols v CIR,
   CA [1975] STC 278   2.15

O

Oakes v Commissioners of Stamp Duties of New South Wales,
   PC [1954] AC 57   2.15
Owen Dec'd (Re),
   Ch D, [1949] 1 All ER 901   2.25

P

Pearson & Others v CIR,
   HL [1980] STC 318; 2 All ER 479   4.6, 5.23
Pemsel, Special Commrs v,
   HL 1891, 3 TC 53; [1891] AC 531   13.1
Pennington v Crompton
   (The Times, 1 April 2002)   3.6
Pettitt v Pettitt,
   [1970] AC 824   9.1
Pilkington's Will Trust (Re),
   41 ATC 285; [1962] 3 All ER 622   3.26, 3.27, 3.30
Plumbly & Others (Harbour's Personal Representatives) v Spencer,
   CA [1999] STC 677   10.31, 11.21
Potel v CIR,
   [1971] 2 All ER 504; 46 TC 658   10.30

Table of Cases

R

R v Allen, HL [2001] STC 1537	19.12, 19.21
R v Dimsey, HL [2001] STC 1537	19.21
Ramsay (WT) Ltd v CIR, HL [1981] STC 174; [1981] 1 All ER 865	17.12
Re Mettoy, [1990] 1 WLR 1587	3.16
Re Power, Public Trustee v Hastings, [1947] Ch 572	3.11
Re Wragg, Wragg v Palmer, [1919] 2 Ch 58	3.11
Reed v Clark, Ch D 1985, 58 TC 528; [1985] STC 323	19.7
Rennington v Crompton (The Times, 1 April 2002)	2.25
Richard v Mackay (1990) 1 OTPR 1	6.8
Roome and Another v Edwards, HL 1981, 54 TC 359; [1981] STC 96; [1981] 1 All ER 736	5.11, 6.4, 16.22
Rose (Re), [1952] Ch 499	2.25, 3.6
Russell and Another v CIR, Ch D [1988] STC 195; [1988] 2 All ER 405	17.4
Rysaffe Trustee Co (Channel Islands) Ltd v CIR, Ch D [2002] STC 872	4.40, 4.41, 4.44

S

St Aubyn v Attorney-General (No 2), HL 1951, [1952] AC 15; [1951] 2 All ER 473	2.15
St Dunstan's v Major (Insp of Taxes), Sp C [1997] SSCD 212 (Sp C 127)	13.7
Saunders v Vautier, (1841) 4 Beav 115	5.7
Seale's Marriage Settlement (Re), [1961] Ch 574; [1961] 3 All ER 136	6.8
Sinclair (Re), [1984] 3 All ER 362	15.20
Smith v Smith and others [2001] 1 WLR 1937	17.5
Souter's Executry v CIR [2002] SPC 325	17.4
Starke & Another (Brown's Executors) v CIR, CA [1995] STC 689	11.3, 11.4, 11.21
Stevenson v Wishart and Others (Levy's Trustees), CA [1987] STC 266; [1987] 2 All ER 428	3.21, 4.31

Table of Cases

Stoneham (Re),
  [1919] 1 Ch 149 — 2.25
Stonor & Mills (Dickinson's Executors) v CIR,
  Sp C [2001] SSCD 199 (Sp C 288) — 17.19
Stype Investments (Jersey) Ltd, CIR v,
  [1982] 3 All ER 419; [1982] 3 WLR 228 — 18.3, 20.11
Swires v Renton,
  Ch D 1991, 64 TC 315; [1991] STC 490 — 5.11, 5.12

T

Turner v Turner,
  [1983] 2 All ER 745 — 3.15
Turner's Will Trust (Re),
  [1937] Ch 15; [1936] 2 All ER 1435 — 3.23

V

Vestey v CIR,
  HL 1979, [1980] STC 10; [1979] 3 All ER 976 — 19.21

W

Wahl v Attorney-General,
  HL 1932, 147 LT 382 — 19.4
Walton (Walton's Executor) v CIR,
  CA [1996] STC 68 — 11.12, 11.14
Wase v Bourke,
  Ch D 1995, [1996] STC 18 — 11.16
Watton (Insp of Taxes) v Tippett,
  CA [1997] STC 893 — 11.10
Wensleydale's Settlement Trustees v CIR,
  Sp C, [1996] SSCD 241 (Sp C 73) — 6.8
Weston (Weston's Executor) v CIR,
  Ch D [2000] STC 1064 — 10.2, 16.7
Weston's Settlements (Re),
  [1969] 1 Ch 223; [1968] 1 All ER 720, 3 All ER 388 — 6.8
Wheatley's Executors v CIR,
  Sp C [1998] SSCD 60 (Sp C 149) — 11.3
White v White,
  [2000] All ER (D) 1546 — 15.1
Whitehead's Will Trusts (Re),
  [1971] 1 WLR 833; [1971] 2 All ER 1334 — 6.8
Whiteley (Re),
  [1910] 1 Ch 600 — 3.11
Whittaker v CIR,
  Sp C [2001] SSCD 61 (Sp C 272) — 18.2
Whittingham v Whittingham,
  [1978] 3 All ER 805 — 3.8
Willoughby & Another, CIR v,
  HL [1997] STC 995; [1997] 4 All ER 65 — 7.21, 19.21

Table of Cases

Windeatt's Will Trusts (Re),
[1969] 1 WLR 692; [1969[2 All ER 324   6.8
Woodhall (Woodhall's Personal Representative) v CIR,
Sp C [2000] SSCD 558 (Sp C 261)   9.4, 16.19

Table of Statutes

1774 Life Assurance Act
s 1 — 7.23

1867 Policies of Assurance Act — 7.41

1882 Married Women's Property Act — 16.42
s 11 — 7.39

1890 Partnership Act
s 26 — 11.3
s 31 — 10.5
s 44 — 10.8

1891 Stamp Act
s 57 — 11.24
Sch 1 — 7.39

1906 Public Trustee Act
s 4 — 6.8

1925 Administration of Estates Act
s 35 — 9.2
s 46 — 2.13, 9.2, 9.3, 17.18
s 47A — 17.18

1925 Law of Property Act — 4.25
s 27 — 9.7
s 34 — 9.2, 16.40
s 35 — 9.2
s 36 — 9.2
s 53 — 5.28, 6.8
s 149 — 9.9
s 175 — 16.17
s 184 — 2.35, 9.2, 16.20

1925 Settled Land Act — 3.28, 5.7

1925 Trustee Act — 3.10
s 22 — 3.12
s 31 — 3.18, 3.21-3.23, 4.25, 4.26, 4.30, 4.31, 5.10, 5.17, 16.16
s 32 — 3.25, 3.28, 3.29, 4.38, 5.7, 5.13, 5.17, 5.22, 16.16
s 33 — 3.31, 4.9, 5.7
s 34 — 9.7
s 36 — 6.8
s 37 — 6.8
s 40 — 3.10, 6.8

Table of Statutes

s 41	6.8
s 61	3.13
s 68	6.8
1952 Intestates' Estates Act	
s 5, Sch 20	9.3
1958 Variation of Trusts Act	5.7, 5.17, 16.31, 17.4
s 1	6.8
1961 Trustee Investments Act	3.10, 3.11
1964 Perpetuities and Accumulations Act	3.7, 3.30, 4.25
s 9	2.32
1965 Administration of Estates (Small Payments) Act	16.44
1967 Leasehold Reform Act	9.8
1970 Income and Corporation Taxes Act	
s 226	8.13
s 448	7.47
1970 Taxes Management Act	
s 76	5.36
1973 Domicile and Matrimonial Proceedings Act	
s 1	19.4
s 3	19.4
1973 Matrimonial Causes Act	3.8, 15.5
s 21A	15.14
s 22	15.4
s 23	15.4
s 24	15.11
ss 25B-25D	15.14
s 28	15.4
s 31	15.4
1975 Finance Act	11.3
1975 Inheritance (Provision for Family and Dependants) Act 1975	3.9, 9.3, 15.20, 16.1, 16.31, 17.3
1980 Finance Act	
s 79	2.17, 4.35, 5.25, 6.4
1984 Inheritance Tax Act	
s 3	2.4, 2.13, 2.32, 4.32, 5.23, 5.39, 5.43, 8.9, 10.28
s 3A	2.5, 2.32, 4.2, 4.23, 4.32, 5.4, 5.23, 7.45, 10.6, 10.31, 11.7, 13.2, 16.2
s 4	7.36, 8.15, 16.20
s 5	2.26, 4.32, 7.36, 8.9, 8.15, 20.7
s 6	7.21, 16.33, 18.4, 20.3, 20.7
s 7	2.3
s 10	5.23, 5.34, 5.39, 5.43, 10.5, 10.8, 10.14, 15.9, 15.13
s 11	2.11, 5.23, 7.30, 15.9, 15.13, 19.11
s 12	5.23, 8.5, 8.9

Table of Statutes

s 15	10.30, 11.12
s 16	11.9
s 17	17.4, 17.17, 17.18
s 18	2.10, 4.32, 4.35, 4.47, 9.11, 10.10, 16.2, 19.12
s 19	2.6, 2.17, 5.23
s 20	2.8, 5.23
s 21	2.7, 5.23, 7.45, 19.27
s 22	2.9, 4.19, 5.23
s 23	2.14, 2.15, 4.35, 13.2, 13.3, 13.22, 13.24, 16.9
s 24	2.17, 13.24, 16.9
s 25	13.17, 13.22, 14.3, 14.12, 16.9
s 26	2.17, 13.23
s 26A	14.4
s 27	2.17, 14.15, 16.9
s 30	2.17, 14.4, 14.11
s 31	14.4, 14.8, 14.11, 14.12, 14.20, 17.1
s 32	14.4-14.6, 14.10, 14.12
s 32A	14.6
s 33	14.4
s 34	14.4
s 35A	14.10
s 38	2.26, 16.23
s 39A	16.8
s 40	16.23
s 41	16.24
s 43	4.3, 4.44
s 47	2.13, 5.8, 5.18
s 48	2.13, 5.3, 5.18, 5.30, 5.39, 5.43, 19.12-19.14
s 49	4.6, 4.20, 4.32, 5.2, 5.23, 5.34, 9.10, 16.2, 16.13, 18.9
s 50	16.27
s 51	4.32, 5.23
s 52	4.32, 5.23, 5.24, 5.34, 5.43, 17.17, 18.10
s 53	4.32, 4.38, 5.17, 5.23, 5.34, 5.47, 16.13, 17.23
s 54	9.4
s 54A	4.32, 4.46
s 54B	4.32, 4.46
s 55	5.39
s 55A	5.39
s 57	4.32, 5.23
s 57A	14.15
s 58	4.6, 5.3
s 60	4.44
s 62	2.25, 4.40, 4.45, 18.10
s 64	4.44, 7.44, 14.11, 16.21
s 64	4.44
s 65	4.42, 4.45, 4.50, 5.3, 7.43, 14.15, 14.23
s 66	4.44, 7.44
s 67	4.43, 4.44, 4.45, 7.43
s 68	4.48, 17.16
s 69	4.42

479

Table of Statutes

s 70	13.19
s 71	2.5, 3.22, 4.24-4.26, 4.28, 4.29, 5.10, 5.17-5.19, 5.23, 7.43, 9.5, 16.17, 19.19
s 76	13.14
s 78	14.21, 14.23
s 79	14.11, 14.21
s 80	4.47, 18.10, 19.19
s 81	8.6, 5.18, 5.19
s 82	19.19
s 88	4.9
s 89	2.5, 4.8, 4.38, 5.23, 9.5
s 92	16.20
s 98	5.4, 10.28
s 102A	2.22
s 105	2.28, 10.2, 10.26, 16.7, 17.1
s 106	10.2
s 107	10.2, 10.5, 16.7
s 108	10.2
s 110	10.6
s 112	10.2, 10.24
s 113	10.2, 16.7
s 113A	4.20, 7.11, 10.2, 10.8, 10.26
s 113B	7.11, 10.2
s 114	11.5
s 115	11.3, 11.4, 16.6, 17.1
s 116	11.3
s 117	11.3, 16.6
s 118	11.3, 16.6
s 119	11.3
s 120	11.3
s 121	11.3
s 122	11.3, 16.6
s 123	11.3, 16.6
s 124	11.3
s 124A	4.20, 11.7
s 124B	11.7
s 125	12.5, 12.8
s 126	12.5
s 127	12.5, 12.8
s 129	12.6
s 131	2.3
s 132	2.3
s 142	9.4, 12.8, 13.7, 13.15, 16.31, 17.2, 17.4-17.6, 17.10, 17.12, 17.13
s 143	16.28, 17.13, 17.17
s 144	16.21, 16.22, 17.13, 17.16
s 145	17.18
s 151	8.15, 8.7, 8.9
s 157	16.10, 16.33, 20.3
s 159	20.6

Table of Statutes

s 161	11.3, 16.12
s 162	10.6, 10.22, 20.7
s 163	2.32, 10.11, 10.14, 10.16, 10.18
s 165	2.17, 2.27
s 167	7.42
ss 178–198	17.19
s 191	17.19
s 198	17.19
s 199	7.11, 16.26
s 200	12.5
s 204	7.11
s 208	12.5
s 211	9.4, 16.25, 16.39
s 217	17.1
s 218	4.52
s 218A	17.4
s 226	12.5
s 227	10.3, 11.6, 12.5
ss 228, 229	10.3, 17.20
s 230	14.4
s 234	10.3, 11.6, 17.21
s 235	17.21
s 263	7.49
s 266	2.25
s 267	6.5, 7.11, 10.29, 19.6, 19.26, 20.3
s 268	2.10, 2.15, 2.23, 2.30, 4.44, 5.4, 7.49, 11.12, 13.3
s 269	10.2, 10.3, 11.3, 16.7
s 272	4.44, 5.39
s 270	10.8
s 272	13.1
s 273	5.5
Sch 2	2.3, 7.11, 12.5
Sch 3	13.17, 14.3, 14.4, 14.12, 14.14, 14.15, 16.9
Sch 4	14.11, 14.14, 14.15
Sch 6	2.13, 5.5, 5.8
Sch 20	9.8

1986 Agricultural Holdings Act   11.12, 11.14

1986 Finance Act

s 102	2.15, 2.17, 2.27, 2.30, 4.12, 4.47, 5.2, 5.8, 5.18, 5.29, 5.52, 7.46, 8.7, 8.15, 9.4-9.6, 9.9-9.11, 10.6, 11.8, 10.9, 10.15, 10.20, 10.24, 13.3, 14.22, 17.4, 17.10, 18.9
s 102A	2.15, 9.8, 9.9, 10.9, 11.8, 11.21
s 102B	2.15, 9.7, 9.9, 10.9, 11.8, 11.21
s 102C	2.15, 9.9, 10.9, 11.8, 11.21
Sch 20	2.15, 4.12, 7.46, 7.47, 9.4-9.6, 9.8, 9.9, 10.20, 11.8, 11.21

1986 Financial Services Act   7.2
    s 3   7.3

Table of Statutes

1986 Insolvency Act
s 341	3.7
s 423	3.7
s 435	3.7

1986 Social Security Act
s 7	8.4

1988 Income and Corporation Taxes Act
s 13A	10.30
s 41	11.12
s 65	19.25
s 74	8.7
s 83A	13.6
s 84	13.6, 13.11
s 118ZA	10.23
ss 145, 146	19.12, 19.25, 20.7
s 154	19.12
s 167	19.12
s 168	19.12
s 189	8.7
s 219	10.33
s 231	10.30
s 266	7.18
s 326	20.3
s 334	19.7
s 347A	13.8
s 353	7.49, 10.22
s 362	10.22
s 365	7.49
s 445	7.21
s 506	13.1
s 540	7.18, 7.20
s 541	7.18, 7.20
s 542	7.18
s 543	7.18
s 546	7.20
s 547	7.18, 7.19, 7.22
s 550	7.18, 7.19
s 553	7.21
s 553C	7.21
s 587B	13.6, 13.7, 13.9, 2.14
s 587C	13.3
s 590	8.5, 8.6
s 590C	8.5
s 591	8.5, 8.6
s 592	8.4, 8.5
s 593	8.5
s 595	8.7
s 596	8.7
s 596A	8.7

Table of Statutes

s 612	8.7
ss 619, 620	8.13, 16.43
s 621	16.43
s 624	8.7
s 626	8.13
s 632	8.9
s 634	8.9
s 638	8.9
s 639	8.9
s 640	8.9, 8.13
s 640A	8.9
s 641	8.9
s 642	8.9
s 643	8.9
s 644	8.9
s 646	8.9
s 656	7.49, 16.27
s 657	7.49, 16.27
s 660A	2.10, 4.13, 10.30, 17.15, 19.21
s 660B	2.24, 4.2, 4.31, 5.4, 5.20, 5.29, 5.36, 5.41, 5.45, 6.6, 7.26, 7.47, 10.30, 16.21, 17.15, 17.16,
s 674	7.47
s 677	2.30, 10.17
s 686	4.11, 4.31, 5.26, 5.36, 6.6, 8.7
s 687	4.31, 5.36, 6.61, 3.14
s 691	14.17
s 694	14.16
s 695	17.15
s 696	17.15
s 698	17.15
s 703	18.4
s 720	19.22
s 739	6.6, 6.20, 7.21, 18.4, 19.21, 19.22
s 740	6.6, 6.20, 18.4, 19.21, 19.22, 20.13, 20.14
s 741	18.4, 19.21
s 743	18.4, 19.21
s 744	18.4
s 759	19.22
s 761	19.22
s 787	10.22
s 839	19.12
Sch 15	7.16, 7.21
Sch 28AA	19.12

1989 Finance Act

s 76	8.7
s 110	6.6, 18.10, 19.16, 20.13

1989 Local Government and Housing Act

Sch 10	9.8

Table of Statutes

1990 Finance Act
s 25   13.5, 13.7, 13.8, 16.33

1991 Child Support Act   15.6
ss 1, 3, 8, 46   15.6

1991 Finance Act
s 110   7.41

1992 Taxation of Chargeable Gains Act
s 2   10.4, 18.10, 20.4
s 2A   10.4
s 3   17.22
s 4   2.24, 4.10
s 5   4.10
s 6   8.7
s 7   2.17, 9.13
s 9   19.7
s 10   5.3, 18.10, 20.2, 20.4, 20.6
s 10A   6.4, 6.9, 20.4, 20.6
s 13   6.14, 18.4
s 17   9.10
s 18   2.32, 15.15, 17.14
s 22   11.16
s 25   5.3, 20.4
s 29   10.25, 10.28
s 30   10.28
s 35   2.17, 11.10
s 37   7.18
s 39   7.18
s 44   5.35
s 46   5.35
ss 53–55   2.17
s 59   10.7
s 60   4.3, 4.34
s 62   2.21, 4.20, 4.35, 4.48, 10.4, 10.24, 11.10, 16.22, 17.14, 17.16
s 64   16.22
s 68   4.3
s 69   6.4, 18.10, 19.16, 20.14
s 71   2.17, 4.34, 4.35, 5.10-5.12, 5.14, 5.17-5.19, 5.25, 5.30, 5.35, 5.40, 5.44, 5.48, 15.12, 16.22
s 72   4.10, 4.35, 4.36, 5.25
s 73   4.10, 4.35, 4.36
s 74   4.35, 5.8, 5.25
s 76   5.40, 5.44
s 76A   5.40
s 77   2.24, 5.8, 5.10, 5.29, 5.38, 6.3, 6.4, 14.17, 17.11, 17.14
s 78   2.24, 5.29, 5.38, 5.8, 17.14
ss 77–79   2.24, 5.29, 5.38, 5.8, 14.17, 17.14
s 80   6.2, 6.3
s 83   6.3

Table of Statutes

s 85	5.40
s 86	5.3, 6.2, 6.4, 6.9, 17.14, 18.10, 19.16, 19.20, 19.24
s 86A	6.9, 6.10
s 87	4.52, 6.2, 6.4,, 6.16, 6.19, 17.14, 19.16, 19.20, 19.24, 20.13
s 89	6.4
ss 91–96	6.2, 6.19
s 97	6.2, 6.4, 6.18, 6.19, 19.21
s 87	19.12
s 144	2.32
ss 152–158	11.10
s 162	10.5
s 163	10.4, 10.6, 10.18, 10.24, 11.10, 11.21
s 164	10.6, 10.18, 10.24, 10.31
s 165	2.17, 2.23, 4.2, 4.20, 4.21, 4.30, 4.32, 4.34, 4.35, 4.38, 5.8, 5.10, 5.17, 5.18, 5.25, 5.26, 5.35, 5.40, 5.44, 5.48, 6.4, 10.4-10.6, 10.10-10.12, 10.14, 10.16, 10.18, 10.23, 10.24, 10.26, 10.29, 10.31, 10.37, 11.10, 11.21, 12.3, 12.7, 15.15, 16.17, 16.22, 17.16
s 166	2.17, 4.52
s 168	2.17
s 169A	10.23
s 210	7.42
s 222	9.13, 9.14
s 225	15.12
s 242	11.10
s 250	12.2, 12.3
s 251	9.10, 10.4
s 256	2.14, 13.6, 13.20
s 257	2.14, 13.4, 13.6, 13.22
s 258	14.7, 14.12
s 260	2.12, 2.17, 2.23, 4.2, 4.21, 4.30, 4.32, 4.35, 4.38, 4.49, 5.8, 5.10, 5.17, 5.53, 6.4, 9.13, 10.4, 10.26, 10.29, 11.10, 14.17, 15.15, 16.17, 16.22
s 261	2.17, 4.52
s 262	12.3, 16.28, 17.17
s 274	17.19
s 281	2.17, 2.27, 4.30, 5.26, 9.13
s 282	2.27
s 286	17.14
Sch 1	4.38
Sch 4	5.25
Sch 4A	5.7, 5.26, 5.40
Sch 5	5.3, 6.2, 6.4, 6.10, 6.12, 6.15, 18.10, 19.16, 19.24
Sch 5B	10.35
Sch 6	2.17, 10.6, 10.18, 10.24, 10.26, 11.10
Sch 7	10.4, 11.10

1993 Pension Schemes Act

s 9	8.4
s 43	8.9
s 45	8.4, 8.9

Table of Statutes

1994 Finance Act
s 108   8.7

1995 Agricultural Tenancies Act   11.12

1995 Child Support Act   15.6

1995 Finance Act
s 128   6.6
s 154   12.2

1995 Pensions Act   8.1, 8.3, 8.14

1996 Trusts of Land and Appointment of Trustees Act   3.10, 3.11, 9.2
s 5   9.2
s 9   3.15
s 11   3.15, 9.2
s 12   11.24
s 14   3.20, 9.2, 9.4
s 15   9.2
s 19   3.20

1997 Finance Act
s 81   19.21
s 94   11.3

1998 Finance Act
s 143   13.23

1999 Finance Act
s 64   2.24
Sch 13 para 17   2.18

1999 Welfare Reform and Pensions Act
s 29   15.14
s 85   15.14
Sch 3   15.14

2000 Finance Act
s 119   10.37, 19.12, 20.7
s 120   19.12

2000 Limited Liability Partnership Act   10.23
s 1   10.23

2000 Trustee Act   3.10, 3.11, 3.15
ss 3-5   3.11
s 8   3.11
ss 28, 29   3.14

2002 Finance Act
s 58   13.21
s 98   13.8
Sch 18   13.21, 16.9

Index

A

Accumulation and maintenance settlements, 2.24, 4.7, 4.17, 4.23–4.31, 5.17–5.20
  accumulated income, 4.27
  accumulation period, 4.25
  advanced fund, 5.18
  borrowed beneficiaries, 4.28
  capital gains tax, 4.30
  income tax, 4.31
  inheritance tax, 4.17, 4.23–4.29
  qualifying conditions, 4.24
  resettlement before interest in possession, 5.18–5.20
  varying shares of beneficiaries, 4.29
Accumulations, 3.7
Advance fund, 5.18
Advancement, power of, 3.19, 3.25, 5.13
Agricultural property, 4.20, 11.1–11.25
see also Family Farm,
  discretionary settlements, 4.45
  grant of tenancies, 11.9
  post-death planning, 17.8
  relief, 5.9, 11.3, 14.6, 16.5
Allocation, power of, 5.14
Annual exemption,
  inheritance tax, 2.6
Annuities, 2.7, 7.32, 7.49, 16.27
Appointment, power of, 3.18, 3.19, 5.12
Assets,
  capital
  —conversion of, 2.34
  change in value, 2.21
  conversion of, 2.28, 5.3
  creating surplus assets, 2.22, 5.5
  fall in value after death, 17.19
  foreign, 2.35, 16.46
  freezing of, 2.29–2.33, 5.4
  low-income-producing, 2.20
  reduction of, 2.3–2.27
  sale of, 2.31
  situs, 19.15

B

Bankruptcy, 3.7
  pensions and, 8.16
Bare trustees, 2.24, 4.4
Beneficiaries, 3.5
  borrowed, 4.28
  dealing with interests of, 5.6–5.16
  excluded property trusts, 19.13–19.24
  rights, 3.20
  varying shares of, 4.29
Borrowed beneficiaries, 4.28
Business property, 4.20, 11.5, 16.5
see also Family business,
  discretionary settlements, 4.45
  post-death planning, 17.8
  relief, 5.9, 10.2, 11.5, 14.6, 16.5

C

Capital assets,
  conversion of, 2.34
Capital gains tax,
  accumulation settlements, 4.30
  discretionary settlements, 4.49, 5.53
  enterprise investment scheme, 10.34–10.37
  excluded property trusts, 19.20
  export of settlements, 6.3, 6.4
  family business, 10.4
  family home, 9.13
  farms, 11.10
  interests in possession, 4.33–4.36
  life interests, 5.25, 5.35, 5.44
  lifetime gifts, 2.17
  maintenance funds for historic buildings, 14.17
  milk quotas, 11.15
  national heritage property, 14.12
  overseas persons, 20.4
  partnership formation, 10.10
  payment of, 2.27
  personal representatives, 17.22
  reorganising trusts, 5.10–5.16
  settlements, general, 4.10, 4.14, 4.21
  taper relief, 10.4
  variations of wills, 17.14
  woodlands, 12.3

Index

Charities, 2.14, 13.1–13.20
  capital gains tax, 13.4
  capital gifts, 13.2–13.7
  Charities Aid Foundation, 13.13
  creating charitable trusts, 13.16
  income gifts, 13.8–13.14
  inheritance tax, 13.2, 13.3
  payroll deduction scheme, 13.12
  temporary charitable trusts, 13.18–13.20
Chattels, transfer of, 2.25
Children,
  gifts on death, 16.15–16.17
  insurance policies for, 7.25
  lifetime gifts to, 2.24
Community Amateur Sports Clubs, 13.21
Council tax,
  marriage breakdown, 15.19
Covenants, 2.7
  to charities, 13.8
Creating settlements, 4.1–4.52
  accumulation and maintenance, 4.17, 4.23–4.31
  agricultural property relief, 4.20, 4.45
  anti-avoidance, 4.46
  business property relief, 4.20, 4.45
  capital gains tax, *see* Capital gains tax,
  discretionary, 4.19, 4.39–4.50
  general principles, 4.3–4.11
  income tax, *see* Income tax,
  insurance policies, 7.37–7.44
  interests in possession, 4.18, 4.32–4.37
  offshore settlements, 4.51, 4.52
  preliminary considerations, 4.12–4.22
  related settlements, 4.40
  reservation of benefit, 4.12
  stamp duty, 4.22
  trusts for disabled, 4.8, 4.38

D

Death, *see* Planning for death, Post-death estate planning,
Death benefits, 2.35, 16.32, 16.41, 17.23
Death-bed planning, 16.33
Deeds of covenant, 2.7
  to charities, 13.8

Deferred annuities, 7.49
Deferred share strategy, 10.28
Disabled persons,
  trusts for, 4.8, 4.38
Disclaimers, 17.5
Discretionary settlements, 4.19, 4.39–4.50, 5.51–5.54, 13.14, 16.4
  additional property, 4.43
  agricultural property relief, 4.45
  alteration of beneficiaries' interests, 5.7
  anti-avoidance provisions, 4.46
  business property relief, 4.45
  capital gains tax, 4.49, 5.53
  charities, payments to, 13.14
  creation of several, 4.44
  distributions, 4.42
  income tax, 4.50, 5.45
  inheritance tax, 4.19, 4.39–4.50, 5.52
  national heritage property, 14.21
  post-death estate planning, use in, 17.11
  related settlements, 4.40
  ten-yearly charge, 4.41
  transfers between spouses, 4.47
Discretionary wills, 16.21, 17.16
Dividend waivers, 10.30
Divorce *see* Matrimonial breakdown,
Domicile, 19.3–19.6
Donee of lifetime gifts, 2.24
Double tax agreements, 20.6

E

Educational trusts, 7.31
Emigration, 19.27
Endowment policies, 2.7, 7.12, 7.28
Enterprise investment scheme, 10.34–10.37
Equalisation of estates, 2.12, 16.12
Exchange control, 18.5–18.8, 19.23
Excluded property, 2.13, 20.3
  trusts, 19.13–19.24
Existing settlements, 5.1–5.54
  accumulation and maintenance, 5.17–5.20
  agricultural property relief, 5.9
  asset conversion, 5.3
  beneficiaries, interests of, 5.6–5.16
  business property relief, 5.9
  discretionary, 5.51–5.54
  export of, 6.3–6.8
  life interests, 5.21–5.50
  reorganising, capital gains tax effect, 5.10–5.16

Index

surplus assets, 5.5
value freezing, 5.4
Export of settlements, 6.3–6.8
  capital gains tax, 6.3, 6.4, 6.9–6.20
  cost of export, 6.7
  income tax, 6.6
  inheritance tax, 6.5
  legal issues, 6.8
  taxing the settlor, 6.9–6.20

F

Family *see also* Family business, Family home, Family farm,
  gifts for maintenance of, 2.11
Family business, 10.1–10.38
  assets held outside business, 10.21, 10.31
  business property relief, 10.2
  capital gains tax, 10.4
  death, 10.19, 10.33
  deferred share strategy, 10.28
  dividend waiver, 10.30
  family company, 10.24–10.33
  gifts of shares, 10.24, 10.25
  incorporation, 10.5
  interest-free instalment option, 10.3
  liabilities, 10.22, 10.32
  limited liability partnerships, 10.23
  minority holdings, 10.25
  partnerships, 10.7–10.22
  quoted shares, 10.26
  reservation of benefit, 10.9
  sole proprietor, 10.6
  value freezing strategy, 10.29
Family farm, 11.1–11.25
  agricultural property relief, 11.3
  borrowings, 11.23
  business property relief, 11.5
  capital gains tax, 11.10
  company, 11.3, 11.13
  death, 11.25
  double discount, 11.3
  farm business tenancy, 11.3
  farmhouses, 11.4
  foot and mouth disease, 11.18
  gifts with reservation, 11.8
  inheritance tax, 11.3–11.9
  instalment option, 11.6
  lifetime exemptions, 11.7
  milk quotas, 11.15–11.17
  partnerships, 11.14
  retirement, 11.21
  shearing, 11.8
  structure of business, 11.11–11.17
  tenancies, grant of, 11.9
  two sons' problem, 11.24
Family home, 9.1–9.14, 16.19
  capital gains tax, 9.13
  co-ownership, 9.7
  full consideration exemption, 9.8
  gifts with reservation, 9.6
  joint tenancy, 9.2
  lifetime planning, 9.5–9.14
  marriage breakdown, 15.10–15.13
  purchase of, 9.3
  shearing, 9.9
  tenancy in common, 9.2
  wills, 9.4
Farming *see* Family farm
Flee clauses, 18.8
Foot and mouth disease, 11.18
Foreign clients, 20.1–20.15
  benefiting UK residents, 20.12–20.14
  double taxation agreements, 20.6
  exchange control, 20.9
  excluded property, 20.3
  gifts by, 20.12–20.14
  off-shore settlements, 20.13
  probate, 20.8
  tax considerations, 20.2–20.7
  UK settlements, 20.14

G

Generation skipping, 16.18
Gifts,
  anatomical purposes, 16.29
  annual exemption, 2.6
  capital gains tax, 2.17
  cash, 2.23
  charities, *see* Charities,
  children, 2.24
  donee, 2.24
  excluded property, 2.13
  family company shares, 10.24, 10.25
  maintenance of family, 2.11
  marriage, 2.9
  national purposes, 14.3
  nil rate band, 2.12
  normal expenditure out of income, 2.7
  outright v trust, 4.2
  political parties, 13.24
  potentially exempt transfers, 2.5
  precatory, 16.28
  public benefit, 13.23
  small, 2.8
  spouses, 2.10
  stamp duty, 2.18
  timing of, 2.25

Index

Gifts with reservation, *see* Reservation of benefit,
Grandchildren, 2.24, 16.18

H

Holdover relief, 2.17, 4.21, 10.4
Home *see* Family home

I

Immigration, 1911–19.25
  domicile, 19.3–19.6
  long-term, 19.10–19.24
  ordinary residence, 19.8
  purchase of property, 19.12
  residence, 19.7
  short-term visitor, 19.25
Income tax,
  accumulation and maintenance settlements, 4.31
  discretionary settlements, 4.50, 5.54
  enterprise investment scheme, 10.36
  excluded property trusts, 19.21
  export of settlements, 6.6
  gifts to charities, 13.8–13.15
  interest in possession settlements, 4.37
  life interests, 5.36, 5.41
  maintenance funds for historic buildings, 14.16
  personal pensions plans, 8.10
  settlements generally, 4.11
  variations, 17.15
  woodlands, 12.3
Incorporating a business, 10.5
Inheritance laws, 3.9
Inheritance tax,
  accumulation and maintenance settlements, 4.16, 4.23–4.29, 5.17–5.20
  agricultural property relief, 4.20, 5.9, 11.3, 16.5
  annual exemption, 2.6
  business property relief, 4.20, 5.9, 10.2, 11.5, 16.5
  creating settlements, 4.6, 4.16–4.20
  discretionary trusts, 4.19, 4.39–4.48, 5.52
  excluded property, 2.13
  existing settlements, 5.34, 5.39
  export of settlements, 6.5
  family business, 10.2, 10.3
  family farm, 11.3–11.9
  family home, 9.5–9.14
  funding of, 16.34–16.38
  gifts in consideration of marriage, 2.9
  gifts to charities, 2.14, 13.2, 13.3
  gifts with reservation, *see* Reservation of benefit
  interest in possession trusts, 4.32, 5.23, 5.24, 5.39
  maintenance funds for historic buildings, 14.15
  maintenance of family, gifts for, 2.11
  milk quotas, 11.16
  mitigation of, 2.2
  national heritage property, 14.2–14.11
  nil rate tax band, 2.12, 16.3, 17.7
  normal expenditure out of income, 2.7
  payment of, 2.26, 17.20
  post-death estate planning, 17.2–17.12
  potentially exempt transfers, 2.5
  rates of, 2.3
  related settlements, 4.40
  small gifts, 2.8
  spouses, gifts between, 2.10, 16.2, 16.12–16.14
  ten-yearly charge, 4.41
  variations and disclaimers, 17.2–17.13
  woodlands, 12.4–12.6
Inheritance trusts, 7.47
Instalments,
  interest free, 10.3, 11.6
  payment of IHT by, 17.20
Insurance, 7.1–7.49
  annuities, 7.49
  assignment of policies to trustees, 7.41
  avoiding probate, 16.42
  child's policy, 17.25
  creation of trusts, 7.37–7.44
  death in service policies, 17.23
  deferred annuities, 7.32
  educational trusts, 7.31
  endowment, 7.12, 7.28
  funding of inheritance tax, 7.8
  home ownership, 7.7
  inheritance trusts, 7.47
  insurable interest, 7.23
  life policy taxation, 7.16–7.23
  long-term nursing care, 7.14
  nature of, 7.4–7.15
  non-qualifying policies, 7.19, 7.20
  normal expenditure, 2.7

Index

offshore policies, 7.21
onshore policies, 7.21
partial surrenders, 7.20
partnerships, 10.20
payment of premiums, 7.45
personal portfolio bonds, 7.2, 7.21
planning in early years, 7.24–7.34
planning in later years, 7.48, 7.49
planning in middle years, 7.35–7.47
policies, organisation of, 2.35
protection, 7.6
qualifying policies, 7.16–7.18
reservation of benefit, 7.46
school fees, 7.27–7.34
single premium bonds, 7.26
taxation, 7.16–7.23
term policies, 7.11, 7.17
traded endowment policies, 7.12, 7.18
trusts, 7.31, 7.37–7.44
types of, 7.4–7.15
uses of, 7.6–7.9
whole life, 7.13
with/without profits, 7.15
Interest in possession, 4.6
Interest in possession settlements, 4.18, 4.32–4.37, 5.21–5.50
alteration of beneficiary's interests, 5.7
capital gains tax, 4.33–4.36
income tax, 4.37
inheritance tax, 4.32, 5.23, 5.24, 5.34, 5.39
termination of life interest, 4.34, 5.23
Interest-free instalments, 10.3, 11.6
Intestacy, 9.3, 16.11, 17.18
marriage breakdown, 15.20
Investing abroad, 18.1–18.11
direct ownership, 18.2
exchange control, 18.5–18.8
nominees, 18.3
offshore settlements, 18.6–18.11
—beneficiaries, 18.1
—flee clauses, 18.8
—international wills, 18.11
—protectors, 18.7
—trustees, 18.10
ownership by companies, 18.4

J
Joint names, 2.35, 16.40
Joint tenancy, 9.2, 11.3

L
Land,
agricultural property relief, 11.3
business property relief, 10.2, 10.3
Legacies,
free of tax, 16.23
precatory gifts, 16.28
Life insurance, *see* Insurance
Life interest,
assignment of, 5.28
definition of, 5.22
surrender of, 5.29
Life interest settlements, 5.21–5.50
assignment of interest in remainder, 5.30, 5.39
assignment of life interest, 5.28
—capital gains tax on, 5.35
—income tax on, 5.36
—inheritance tax on, 5.34
—stamp duty on, 5.37
interest in possession, 5.23
meaning of, 5.22
motive for breaking, 5.26
national heritage property trusts, 14.19, 14.20
partition of fund, 5.32
—capital gains tax on, 5.44
—income tax on, 5.45
—inheritance tax on, 5.43
—stamp duty on, 5.46
sale of interest under, 5.31
— capital gains tax on, 5.35
—income tax on, 5.36
—inheritance tax on, 5.34
surrender of life interest, 5.29
—capital gains tax on, 5.35
—income tax on, 5.36
—inheritance tax on, 5.34
—stamp duty on, 5.37
termination of interest in possession,
—inheritance tax on, 5.23, 5.24
—capital gains tax on, 5.25
Lifetime planning, 2.1–2.35
agricultural property, 11.7
annual exemption, 2.6
annuities, 2.7, 7.32, 7.49, 16.27
asset conversion, 2.28
asset freezing, 2.29–2.33
asset reduction, 2.3–2.27
case study, 21

Index

cash gifts, 2.23
charities, gifts to, 2.14
choice of donee, 2.24
creating surplus assets, 2.22
estate organisation, 2.35
excluded property, 2.13
family farm, 11.7
family home, 9.5–9.14
gifts in consideration of marriage, 2.9
gifts with reservation, *see* Reservation of benefit,
insurance, 7.24–7.49
loans, 2.30
maintenance of family, 2.11
nil rate tax band, 2.12
normal expenditure out of income, 2.7
organisation of estate, 2.35
payment of inheritance tax, 2.26
potentially exempt transfers, 2.5
small gifts, 2.8
spouses, gifts between, 2.10
timing of gifts, 2.25
woodlands, 12.6
Limited liability partnerships, 10.23
Lloyd's underwriters, 2.28, 16.47
Loans, 2.30
Lump sum death benefits, 2.35, 8.6, 8.15

M

Maintenance funds for historic buildings, 14.13–14.17
Maintenance of family, gifts for, 2.11
Maintenance payments, *see* Matrimonial breakdown,
Maintenance, powers of, 3.18, 3.21
Marriage, gifts in consideration of, 2.9
Married persons, *see* Spouses,
Matrimonial breakdown, 15.1–15.21
council tax, 15.19
date of, 15.2
intestacy, 15.20
maintenance, 15.4–15.9
—children, 15.5
—income tax effects, 15.8
—inheritance tax, 15.9
—overseas aspects, 15.17
—school fees, 15.7
matrimonial home, 15.10–15.13
—capital gains tax, 15.12
—inheritance tax, 15.13

pension rights, 8.14, 15.14
personal allowances, 15.3
property transfers, 15.15
—overseas aspects, 15.17
stamp duty, 15.18
trusts, use of, 3.8, 15.16
wills, 15.20
Milk quotas, 11.15–11.17
Minors, *see* Children

N

National heritage property, 14.1–14.24
agricultural property, 14.6
business property relief, 14.6
capital gains tax, 14.12
claiming conditional exemption, 14.7–14.11
discretionary trusts, 14.11
gifts for national purposes, 14.3
inheritance tax, 14.2–14.11
maintenance funds, 14.13–14.17
monitoring undertakings, 14.10
public access, 14.10
reservation of benefit, 14.22
settled property, 14.18–14.23
settlor, occupation by, 14.23
strategies, 14.24
undertakings, 14.9
National purposes, gifts for, 13.22, 14.3
Nil rate tax band, 2.12, 16.3, 17.8
Nominees, 18.3
Non-qualifying policies, 7.19, 7.20
Normal expenditure out of income, inheritance tax exemption, 2.7

O

Occupational pension schemes, 8.4–8.6
Offshore policies, 7.21
Offshore trusts, 4.51, 4.52, 6.1–6.19, 18.6–18.10, 20.13
capital gains tax, 6.3, 6.4, 6.9–6.19
cost of export, 6.7
creating, 4.51, 4.52
export charge, 6.3–6.8
flee clauses, 18.8
income tax, 6.6
inheritance tax, 6.5
protectors, 18.7
supplementary charges, 6.18–6.20
taxing the settlor, 6.9–6.17

Index

Option, grant of, 2.32
Ordinary residence, 19.8
Overseas persons, 20.1–20.15
  benefiting UK residents, 20.12–20.14
  capital gains tax, 20.4
  exchange control, 20.9
  excluded property, 20.3
  gifts by, 20.12
  offshore settlements, 20.13
  probate, 20.8
  tax considerations, 20.2–20.7
  UK settlements, 20.14

P

Partnerships, 10.7–10.22
  accruers and options, 10.11, 10.14
  assets outside partnership, 10.21
  death, 10.19
  farming, 11.14
  formation of, 10.8–10.11
  —inheritance tax, 10.8
  —options and accruers, 10.11
  —capital gains tax, 10.10
  —reservation of benefit, 10.9
  gifts of capital profit, 10.15
  gifts of partnership interest, 10.16
  insurance, 10.20
  liabilities, 10.22
  retirement, 10.18
  sleeping partners, 2.28
  transfer of capital, 10.13
  trustee partners, 10.17
Payroll deduction scheme, 13.11
Pensions, 8.1–8.16
  additional voluntary contributions, 8.5
  avoiding probate, 16.39
  bankruptcy, 8.16
  death benefits, 2.35, 8.15, 16.32, 16.41, 17.23
  divorce, 8.14
  lump sum death benefits, 2.35, 8.6, 8.15, 16.32, 16.41
  marriage breakdown, 15.14
  non-pensionable employment, 8.13
  occupational schemes, 8.4–8.6
  pensionable employment, 8.2–8.12
  personal pensions, 8.9–8.11
  retirement annuity contracts, 8.15
  self-administered schemes, 8.8
  self-employment, 8.13
  stakeholder pensions, 8.12
  unapproved schemes, 8.7

Perpetuities, 3.7
Personal pensions, 8.9–8.11, 16.43
Personal portfolio bonds, 7.2, 7.21
Personal representatives, 17.1–17.23
Planning for death, 16.1–16.47
  agricultural property, 16.5
  annuities, 16.27
  avoiding probate, 16.39–16.46
  business property, 16.5
  charitable gifts, 16.9
  children, gifts to, 16.15–16.17
  death bed planning, 16.33
  death in service benefits, 16.32
  discretionary trusts, 16.4
  dividing the estate, 16.11–16.22
  equalisation of estates, 16.12
  exemptions, 16.2–16.10
  family home, 16.19
  funding the inheritance tax, 16.34–16.38
  generation skipping, 16.18
  gifts to spouse, 16.12–16.14
  gifts, types of, 16.23–16.29
  inheritance tax, 16.14, 16.34–16.38
  intestacy, 16.11
  legacies, types of, 16.23–16.29
  Lloyd's underwriting interests, 16.47
  nil rate tax band, use of, 16.3
  potentially exempt transfers, 16.26, 16.36
  precatory gifts, 16.28
  probate, avoidance of, 16.39–16.46
  reliefs, 16.2–16.10
  spouse exemption, 16.2
  survivorship clauses, 16.20
  wills, 16.1, 16.21, 16.30
Political parties,
  gifts to, 13.24
Post-death estate planning, 17.1–17.23
  capital gains tax, 17.14, 17.22
  death benefits, 17.23
  disclaimers, 17.5
  discretionary trusts, 17.11
  discretionary wills, 17.16
  income tax, 17.15
  inheritance tax by instalments, 17.20
  intestacy, 17.18
  nil rate tax band, 17.7
  precatory trusts, 17.17
  redemption of surviving spouse life interest, 17.18
  unpaid tax, interest on, 17.21
  value, falls in, 17.19
  variations, 17.2–17.15

Index

Potentially exempt transfers, 2.5
  funding the inheritance tax, 16.36
  gifts of tax on, 16.26
  tax on, 2.26
  variations and disclaimers, 17.12
Power of appointment, 3.18, 3.19, 5.12
Precatory gifts, 16.28
Precatory trusts, 17.17
Private residence, see Family home
Probate,
  methods of avoiding, 16.39–16.46
  overseas persons, 20.8
Protective trusts, 3.31, 4.9
Public benefit,
  gifts for, 13.23

Q

Qualifying policies, 7.16

R

Rates of tax,
  inheritance tax, 2.3
Reservation of benefit,
  disclaimers and variations, 17.10
  excluded property trusts, 19.14
  family business, 10.9
  family farm, 11.8
  family home, 9.6
  insurance, 7.46
  lifetime planning, 2.15
  loans, 2.30
  national heritage trusts, 14.22
  partnerships, 10.9
  settlements, 4.12
  settlors, 4.12
Residence, 19.7
  ordinary, 19.8
Retirement annuity contracts, 8.15
  avoiding probate, 16.43

S

School fees, 7.27–7.34
Self-administered pension schemes, 8.8
Separation, see Matrimonial breakdown,
Settlements,
  see also Creating settlements, Existing settlements, Offshore trusts, Trust
  definition, 4.3
  general principles, 4.3–4.11

  interest in possession, 4.18, 4.32–4.37, 5.21–5.50
  terms of, 4.15
Settlor,
  exclusion from benefit, 4.10
  national heritage trusts, 14.23
  offshore trusts, 6.9–6.17
Shares,
  business property relief, 10.2
  death, 10.33
  deferred share strategy, 10.28
  dividend waivers, 10.30
  fall in value after death, 17.19
  family company, 10.24–10.33
  gifts of, 10.24, 10.25
  minority holding, 10.25
  quoted, 10.26
  value freezing strategy, 10.29
Shearing,
  family farm, 11.8
  family home, 9.9
Single premium bonds, 7.26
Situs of assets, 19.15
Small gifts,
  inheritance tax, 2.8
Sole proprietors, 10.6
Spouses,
  see also Matrimonial breakdown,
  beneficiaries of excluded property trusts, 19.19
  discretionary trusts, 4.47
  gifts between, 2.10, 16.2
  —on death, 16.12–16.14
  redemption of surviving spouse life interest, 17.18
Stamp duty, 2.18
  assignment of insurance policy, 7.41
  assignment of life interest, 5.37
  assignment of remainder, 5.42
  marriage breakdown, 15.18
Survivorship clauses, 16.20

T

Taper relief, 10.4
Temporary charitable trusts, 13.18–13.20
Tenancy in common, 9.2, 11.3
Tenanted land, 11.12
Ten-yearly charge, 4.41
Term policies, 7.11, 7.17
Timing of gifts, 2.25
Traded endowment policies, 7.12, 7.18
Trust law, 3.1–3.31
Trustees, 3.4
  powers and duties, 3.10–3.19

Index

—accounts, 3.12
—advancement, 3.19, 5.13
—allocation, 5.14
—appointment, 5.12
—decisions, 3.15, 3.16
—distributing assets, 3.13
—investments, 3.11
—not to profit, 3.14
—power of advancement, 3.26
—power of appointment, 3.18, 3.19
—power of maintenance, 3.18, 3.21
—power over capital, 3.19
—power over income, 3.18
unanimity, 3.17
Trusts,
see also Accumulation and maintenance settlements, Creating settlements, Discretionary trusts, Existing settlements, Offshore trusts, Settlements
accumulations, 3.7
bankruptcy, 3.7
bare, 4.4
beneficiaries, 3.5
—rights, 3.20
charitable, 13.16, 13.18
definition, 3.2
disabled persons, 4.8, 4.38
educational, 7.31
excluded property, 19.13–19.24
fixed interest, 4.5, 4.32–4.37
law, 3.1–3.31
life interest, 5.21–5.50
marriage breakdown, 15.16
national heritage property, 14.18–14.23
perpetuities, 3.7
precatory, 17.17
protective, 3.31, 4.9

settlors, 3.3
trustees, 3.4
—powers and duties, 3.10–3.19

U

Unpaid tax, interest on, 17.21
Untenanted land, 11.12

V

Value freezing, 2.29–2.34, 5.4
shares, 10.29
Venture capital trusts, 10.38

W

Wealth tax, 19.23, 20.10
Whole life policies, 7.13
Wills, 2.35, 16.1
see also Planning for death,
discretionary, 16.21, 17.16
family home, 9.4
marriage breakdown, 15.20
personal assets log, 16.30
review of, 16.30
safe keeping, 16.30
survivorship clauses, 16.20
variations after death, 16.31, 17.2–17.15
Woodlands, 2.28, 12.1–12.8
capital gains tax, 12.3
death, 12.5
income tax, 12.2
inheritance tax, 12.4–12.6
—relief on death, 12.5
lifetime gifts, 12.6
short rotation coppice, 12.29

Tolley
LexisNexis™

NEW TITLE

Corporate Fraud: Prevention and Detection

By **Julia Penny**, Chantrey Vellacott

Tolley's Corporate Fraud: Prevention and Detection is a new and unique title which identifies, step-by-step, the risk of fraud and sets out the most effective counter-measures you can take. Aimed at increasing awareness of the issues surrounding fraud, this innovative new title from Tolley is a useful tool for advisers, accountants and consultants who are involved in advising private sector organisations. It is also essential reading for all managers of those organisations.

Tolley's Corporate Fraud:
- clearly identifies the common types of fraud which can affect any type of organisation
- suggests how fraud might effectively be prevented in the business environment
- gives practical advice on the steps that need to be taken when a fraud is suspected
- sets out directors' responsibilities, including the role of non-executive directors
- discusses specialist areas including charity fraud, internet and computer fraud, public sector fraud and money laundering.

With the aid of **Tolley's Corporate Fraud** you will appreciate that fraud is a threat, assess the internal controls which are needed to tackle it and start to establish your role in fraud prevention.

Price: £39.95   **ISBN:** 0754512983   **Product Code:** CFDP   **Publishing:** August 2002

How To Order

To order, please contact LexisNexis Butterworths Tolley
Customer Service Dept: LexisNexis Butterworths Tolley,
FREEPOST SEA 4177, Croydon, Surrey CR9 5WZ
Telephone: 020 8662 2000   Fax: 020 8662 2012

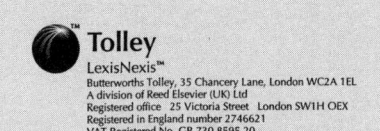

Tolley
LexisNexis™
Butterworths Tolley, 35 Chancery Lane, London WC2A 1EL
A division of Reed Elsevier (UK) Ltd
Registered office 25 Victoria Street   London SW1H OEX
Registered in England number 2746621
VAT Registered No. GB 730 8595 20

Tax Direct is the ultimate online service that provides you with instant access to the most authoritative information ... all via the internet.
For more information on all of our products, please visit our website at www.lexisnexis.co.uk

Tolley
LexisNexis™

Tax Adviser's Diary

The **Tax Adviser's Diary 2002-03** is both a useful organiser and an invaluable source of UK tax information for busy tax practitioners, accountants and solicitors. This attractively bound, pocket-sized diary contains a wealth of essential information conveniently arranged to save you valuable time.

- Provides a diary for appointments
- Diary runs from September 2002 to December 2003 to allow you to plan ahead
- Provides basic information about tax in the UK with lots of facts and figures and useful addresses
- Contains addresses of all Inland Revenue and Customs & Excise offices
- Includes vital information on tax rates, allowances and reliefs, exemptions, exchange rates and taxable benefits

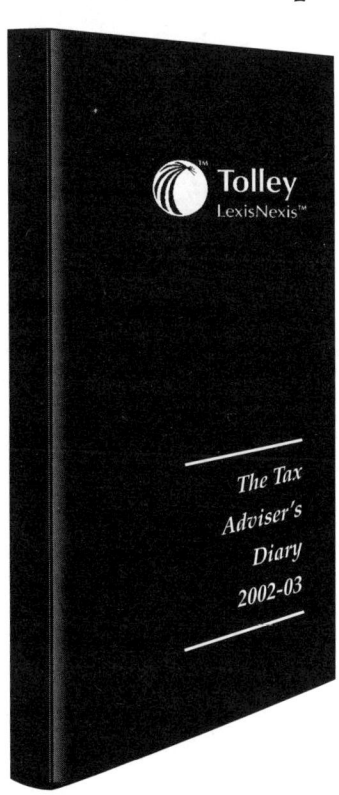

Price: £21.95   **ISBN:** 0 406 95030 X   **Product Code:** TPD2   **Publishing:** August 2002

How To Order

To order, please contact LexisNexis Butterworths Tolley Customer Service Dept: LexisNexis Butterworths Tolley, FREEPOST SEA 4177, Croydon, Surrey CR9 5WZ
Telephone: 020 8662 2000   Fax: 020 8662 2012

Tolley
LexisNexis™
Butterworths Tolley, 35 Chancery Lane, London WC2A 1EL
A division of Reed Elsevier (UK) Ltd
Registered office 25 Victoria Street London SW1H OEX
Registered in England number 2746621
VAT Registered No. GB 730 8595 20

Tax Direct is the ultimate online service that provides you with instant access to the most authoritative information ... all via the internet.
For more information on all of our products, please visit our website at www.lexisnexis.co.uk

Tolley
LexisNexis™

Available in both looseleaf and online formats

Sergeant & Sims on Stamp Duties

Michael Quinlan, LLM, Barrister, Head of Stamp Tax, Deloitte & Touche

Sergeant and Sims on Stamp Duties is the leading and most widely used information source on stamp duties. With detailed explanatory commentary and an innovative electronic format to facilitate rapid searching and dissemination of information, **Sergeant & Sims** continues to be the number one text in its field and remains an ideal publication for barristers, solicitors, accountants, stockbrokers, investment managers, clearance service operators, company secretaries, central and local governments, banks and financial institutions.

The text has been completely revised to include enhanced commentary on:

- Transaction types
- SDRT for investment managers and capital markets
- Loan capital
- Stamp duty group relief
- Anti-avoidance provisions for land and shares

Product code: SSSDMW / SSSOMW (CD or Online version)
ISBN: 0 406 91759 0 / 0 406 93491 6
Price: £425.00 Looseleaf service, Looseleaf and CD or Looseleaf and Online service

How To Order
To order, please contact LexisNexis Butterworths Tolley Customer Service Dept: LexisNexis Butterworths Tolley, FREEPOST SEA 4177, Croydon, Surrey CR9 5WZ
Telephone: 020 8662 2000 Fax: 020 8662 2012

Tolley
LexisNexis™
Butterworths Tolley, 35 Chancery Lane, London WC2A 1EL
A division of Reed Elsevier (UK) Ltd
Registered office 25 Victoria Street London SW1H OEX
Registered in England number 2746621
VAT Registered No. GB 730 8595 20

Indirect Tax Online is the ultimate online service that provides you with instant access to the most authoritative information ... all via the internet.
For more information on all of our products, please visit our website at www.lexisnexis.co.uk

Tolley's
Tax Annuals
2002-03

Tolley LexisNexis™

Tolley's Tax Annuals 2002-03 are the 'must have' reference works for all taxation professionals who want to make the tax advice they provide on behalf of clients more effective. They have served accounting professionals and taxation practitioners for decades and are the most reliable, authoritative, comprehensive and user-friendly tax guides ever published. The latest developments to **Tolley's Tax Annuals 2002-03** include:

- Full expert coverage of FA 2002
- Updated case studies
- Fully updated computational examples

Available with or without Budget supplements for as little as £59.95.

Title	Pub.date	Price	Code	ISBN
Tolley's Income Tax 2002-03				
With post Budget supplement	May/Sept	£74.95	IT2	0 7545 1726 8
Without supplement	Sept	£59.95	IT2AO	0 7545 1710 1
Tolley's Corporation Tax 2002-03				
With post Budget supplement	May/Sept	£74.95	CT2	0 7545 1728 4
Without supplement	Sept	£59.95	CT2AO	0 7545 1711 X
Tolley's Capital Gains Tax 2002-03				
With post Budget supplement	May/Sept	£74.95	CGT2	0 7545 1727 6
Without supplement	Sept	£59.95	CGT2AO	0 7545 1709 8
Tolley's NI Contributions 2002-03				
With post 'Green' Budget supplement	Dec	£74.95	NIC2	0 7545 1858 2
Without supplement	July	£59.95	NIC2AO	0 7545 1708 X
Tolley's Value Added Tax 2002-03	March/Sept	£99.00*	VAT2	0 7545 1705 5

* Price includes two complete volumes. The first edition will be dispatched with an invoice and the second edition will be sent out without charge in September 2002

Tolley's Inheritance Tax 2002-03	Sept	£59.95	IHT2	0 7545 1712 8

How To Order

To order, please contact LexisNexis Butterworths Tolley
Customer Service Dept: **LexisNexis Butterworths Tolley,**
FREEPOST SEA 4177, Croydon, Surrey CR9 5WZ
Telephone: **020 8662 2000** Fax: **020 8662 2012**

Tolley
LexisNexis™
Butterworths Tolley, 35 Chancery Lane, London WC2A 1EL
A division of Reed Elsevier (UK) Ltd
Registered office 25 Victoria Street London SW1H OEX
Registered in England number 2746621
VAT Registered No. GB 730 8595 20

Tax Direct is the ultimate on-line service that provides you with instant access to the most authoritative tax information ... all via the internet.
For more information on all of our products, please visit our website at www.butterworths.com